Lecture Notes in Compu

Edited by G. Goos, J. Hartmanis and J. van Leeuwen

52

Springer
Berlin
Heidelberg
New York
Barcelona
Hong Kong
London
Milan
Paris
Tokyo

Çetin K. Koç   David Naccache
Christof Paar (Eds.)

Cryptographic Hardware and Embedded Systems – CHES 2001

Third International Workshop
Paris, France, May 14-16, 2001
Proceedings

 Springer

Series Editors

Gerhard Goos, Karlsruhe University, Germany
Juris Hartmanis, Cornell University, NY, USA
Jan van Leeuwen, Utrecht University, The Netherlands

Volume Editors

Çetin K. Koç
Oregon State University, ECE Department
Corvallis, Oregon 97331, USA
E-mail: Koc@ece.orst.edu

David Naccache
Gemplus Card International
34 rue Guynemer, 92447 Issy les Moulineaux Cedex, France
E-mail: David.Naccache@gemplus.com

Christof Paar
Worcester Polytechnic Institute, ECE Department
Worcester, MA 01609, USA
E-mail: christof@ece.wpi.edu

Cataloging-in-Publication Data applied for

Die Deutsche Bibliothek - CIP-Einheitsaufnahme

Cryptographic hardware and embedded systems : third international workshop ;
proceedings / CHES 2001, Paris, France, May 14 - 16, 2001. Çetin K. Koç ...
(ed.). - Berlin ; Heidelberg ; New York ; Barcelona ; Hong Kong ; London ;
Milan ; Paris ; Tokyo : Springer, 2001
  (Lecture notes in computer science ; Vol. 2162)
  ISBN 3-540-42521-7

CR Subject Classification (1998): E.3, C.2, C.3, B.7.2, G.2.1, D.4.6, K.6.5, F.2.1, J.2

ISSN 0302-9743
ISBN 3-540-42521-7 Springer-Verlag Berlin Heidelberg New York

Springer-Verlag Berlin Heidelberg New York
a member of BertelsmannSpringer Science+Business Media GmbH

http://www.springer.de

© Springer-Verlag Berlin Heidelberg 2001
Printed in Germany

Typesetting: Camera-ready by author, data conversion by Steingräber Satztechnik GmbH
Printed on acid-free paper   SPIN 10840313   06/3142   5 4 3 2 1 0

Preface

These are the proceedings of CHES 2001, the third Workshop on Cryptographic Hardware and Embedded Systems. The first two CHES Workshops were held in Massachusetts, and this was the first Workshop to be held in Europe. There was a large number of submissions this year, and in response the technical program was extended to 2 1/2 days.

As is evident by the papers in these proceedings, many excellent submissions were made. Selecting the papers for this year's CHES was not an easy task, and we regret that we had to reject several very intersting papers due to the lack of time. There were 66 submitted contributions this year, of which 31, or 47%, were selected for presentation. If we look at the number of submitted papers at CHES '99 (42 papers) and CHES 2001 (51 papers), we observe a steady increase. We interpret this as a continuing need for a workshop series which combines theory and practice for integrating strong security features into modern communications and computer applications. In addition to the submitted contributions, Ross Anderson from Cambridge University, UK, and Adi Shamir from The Weizmann Institute, Israel, gave invited talks.

As in previous years, the focus of the workshop is on all aspects of cryptographic hardware and embedded system design. Of special interest were contributions that describe new methods for efficient hardware implementations and high-speed software for embedded systems, e.g., smart cards, microprocessors, DSPs, etc. CHES also continues to be an important forum for new theoretical and practical findings in the important and growing field of side-channel attacks.

We hope to continue to make the CHES workshop series a forum of intellectual exchange in creating secure, reliable, and robust security solutions of tomorrow. CHES Workshops will continue to deal with hardware and software implementations of security functions and systems, including security for embedded wireless ad-hoc networks.

We thank everyone whose involvement made the CHES Workshop such a successful event, in particular we would like to thank André Weimerskirch from WPI, and Delphine Abecassis and Cécile Osta from Novamedia for their efforts.

May 2001

Çetin K. Koç
David Naccache
Christof Paar

Acknowledgements

The program chairs express their thanks to the program committee, the referees for their help in selecting the best quality papers, and also the companies which provided support to the workshop.

The program committee members of CHES 2001:

- Ross Anderson (`Ross.Anderson@cl.cam.ac.uk`)
  University of Cambridge, U.K.
- Jean-Sebastien Coron (`Jean-Sebastien.CORON@gemplus.com`)
  Gemplus, France
- Kris Gaj (`kgaj@gmu.edu`)
  George Mason University, USA
- Jim Goodman `JGoodman@chrysalis-its.com>`
  Chrysalis-ITS, Canada
- Anwar Hasan (`ahasan@arith1.vlsi.uwaterloo.ca`)
  University of Waterloo, Canada
- Peter Kornerup (`kornerup@imada.sdu.dk`)
  Odense University, Denmark
- Bart Preneel (`Bart.Preneel@esat.kuleuven.ac.be`)
  Université Catholique de Louvain, Belgium
- Jean-Jacques Quisquater (`jjq@dice.ucl.ac.be`)
  Université Catholique de Louvain, Belgium
- Patrice L. Roussel (`proussel@ichips.intel.com`)
  Intel Corporation, USA
- Christoph Ruland (`RULAND@nue.et-inf.uni-siegen.de`)
  Universität Siegen, Germany
- Erkay Savaş (`erkay@rTrust.com`)
  rTrust, USA
- Joseph Silverman (`jhs@ntru.com`)
  Brown University and NTRU Cryptosystems, Inc., USA
- Jacques Stern (`Jacques.Stern@ens.fr`)
  Ecole Normale Superieure, France
- Colin Walter (`C.Walter@sna.co.umist.ac.uk`)
  Computation Department - UMIST, U.K.
- Michael Wiener (`michael.wiener@entrust.com`)
  Entrust Technologies, Canada

The referees of CHES 2001:

- Tolga Acar (`tacar@novell.com`)
- Andre Adelsbach (`anadel@cs.uni-sb.de`)
- Ross Anderson (`Ross.Anderson@cl.cam.ac.uk`)
- Philippe Anguita (`Philippe.Anguita@gemplus.com`)
- Eric Brier (`Eric.Brier@gemplus.com`)
- Marco Bucci (`Marco.Bucci@gemplus.com`)

- Denis Carabin (`Denis.Carabin@gemplus.com`)
- Mahieu Ciet (`ciet@dice.ucl.ac.be`)
- Christophe Clavier (`Christophe.Clavier@gemplus.com`)
- Jean-Sebastien Coron (`coron@clipper.ens.fr`)
- Nora Dabbous (`nora.dabbous@gemplus.com`)
- Jean-Francois Dhem (`Jean-Francois.Dhem@gemplus.com`)
- Adam Elbirt (`aelbirt@nac.net`)
- Nathalie Feyt (`Nathalie.Feyt@gemplus.com`)
- Kris Gaj (`kgaj@gmu.edu`)
- Jovan Golic (`Jovan.Golic@gemplus.com`)
- Guang Gong (`ggong@cacr.math.uwaterloo.ca`)
- Jim Goodman (`jimg@mtl.mit.edu`)
- Jorge Guajardo (`guajardo@ece.wpi.edu`)
- Frank Gurkaynak (`kgf@WPI.EDU`)
- Helena Handschuh (`Helena.Handschuh@gemplus.com`)
- Anwar Hasan (`ahasan@claude.uwaterloo.ca`)
- Marc Joye (`Marc.Joye@gemplus.com`)
- Cetin Koc (`koc@ece.orst.edu`)
- Francois Koeune (`koeune@dice.ucl.ac.be`)
- Peter Kornerup (`kornerup@imada.sdu.dk`)
- Spyros Magliveras (`spyros@cse.unl.edu`)
- Bill Martin (`martin@WPI.EDU`)
- Renato Menicocci (`Renato.Menicocci@gemplus.com`)
- Tom Messerges (`Tom_Messerges-ADTL01@email.mot.com`)
- Pascal Moitrel (`Pascal.Moitrel@gemplus.com`)
- Guglielmo Morgari (`Guglielmo.MORGARI@gemplus.com`)
- Christophe Mourtel (`Christophe.Mourtel@gemplus.com`)
- David Mraihi (`David.Mraihi@gemplus.com`)
- Gerardo Orlando (`Gerardo.Orlando@GSC.GTE.Com`)
- Christof Paar (`christof@ece.wpi.edu`)
- Marco Paggio (`Marco.Paggio@gemplus.com`)
- Pascal Paillier (`Pascal.Paillier@gemplus.com`)
- Bart Preneel (`bart.preneel@esat.kuleuven.ac.be`)
- Florence Ques (`Florence.Ques@gemplus.com`)
- Jean-Jacques Quisquater (`jjq@dice.ucl.ac.be`)
- Jean-Marc Robert (`jean-marc.robert@gemplus.com`)
- Francisco Rodriguez (`rodrigfr@ece.orst.edu`)
- Ludovic Rousseau (`Ludovic.Rousseau@gemplus.com`)
- Patrice Roussel (`proussel@ichips.intel.com`)
- Christoph Ruland (`RULAND@nue.et-inf.uni-siegen.de`)
- Erkay Savas (`savas@ece.orst.edu`)
- Tom Schmidt (`toms@math.orst.edu`)
- Joseph Silverman (`jhs@ntru.com`)
- Nigel Smart (`nigel@cs.bris.ac.uk`)
- Jacques Stern (`jacques.stern@ens.fr`)
- Berk Sunar (`sunar@ece.wpi.edu`)

- Alex Tenca (tenca@ece.orst.edu)
- van Trung Tran (trung@exp-math.uni-essen.de)
- Michael Tunstall (Michael.Tunstall@gemplus.com)
- Christophe Tymen (Christophe.Tymen@gemplus.com)
- Colin Walter (C.Walter@co.umist.ac.uk)
- Andre Weimerskirch (weika@ece.wpi.edu)
- Michael Wiener (michael.wiener@entrust.com)
- Ed Witzke (elwitzk@sandia.gov)
- Huapeng Wu (h3wu@cacr.math.uwaterloo.ca)

The companies which provided support to CHES 2001:

- Gemplus - http://www.gemplus.com
- NTRU Cryptosystems, Inc. - http://www.ntru.com
- rTrust - http://www.rtrust.com
- Secusys - http://www.secusys.com

Table of Contents

Embedded Implementations and New Ciphers

Side Channel Attacks II

Hardware Implementations of Ciphers

Side Channel Attacks on Elliptic Curve Cryptosystems

Protecting Embedded Systems –
The Next Ten Years

Ross Anderson

Computer Laboratory,
Pembroke Street, Cambridge, England
Ross.Anderson@cl.cam.ac.uk

Abstract. In this talk, I will speculate about the likely near-term and medium-term scientific developments in the protection of embedded systems.

A common view of the Internet divides its history into three waves, the first being centered around mainframes and terminals, and the second (from about 1992 until now) on PCs, browsers, and a GUI. The third wave, starting now, will see the connection of all sorts of devices that are currently in proprietary networks, standalone, or even non-computerized. By the end of 2003, there might well be more mobile phones connected to the Internet than computers. Within a few years we will see many of the world's fridges, heart monitors, bus ticket dispensers, burglar alarms, and electricity meters talking IP. By 2010, 'ubiquitous computing' will be part of our lives.

Some of the likely effects of ubiquitous computing are already apparent. For example, applications with intermittent connectivity will have to maintain much of their security state locally rather than globally. This will create new markets for processors with appropriate levels of tamper-resistance. But what will this mean?

I will discuss protection requirements at four levels.

Invasive attacks on hardware are likely to remain possible for capable motivated opponents, at least for devices that cannot be furnished with effective tamper responding barriers. That said, even commodity smartcards are much harder to probe than was the case five years ago. Decreasing feature sizes, 32-bit processors, and layout that makes bus lines harder to find and to probe, all combine to push up the entry cost. Attacks that could be done in a few weeks with ten thousand dollars' worth of equipment now take months and require access to equipment costing several hundred thousand dollars. However, this field rides on the coat-tails of the semiconductor test industry, and will remain unpredictable. Every so often, bright ideas lead to powerful new low-cost testing tools, that may be used in attacks. The scanning capacitance microscope may be one such.

Non-invasive attacks on hardware – such as power and glitch attacks – might become infeasible against even the smallest processors. However, this is not as easy as it seemed three or four years ago. Current techniques, such as randomised clocking, can only do so much. New ideas are needed, and I will discuss an EU-funded

Ç.K. Koç, D. Naccache, and C. Paar (Eds.): CHES 2001, LNCS 2162, pp. 1–2, 2001.

research project (G3Card) to develop these. Its goal is produce a prototype smartcard CPU that is inherently resistant to noninvasive attacks. The prototypes currently being designed at Cambridge under G3Card use asynchronous (self-timed) dual-rail logic, which holds out the prospect of power consumption that is independent of the data being processed. This technology holds out the prospect of important side benefits as well, such as reduced RFI/EMI and lower power consumption.

Protocol-level attacks continue to be a terrible problem. The design of ordinary authentication protocols is well known to be hard; yet a typical cryptographic processor performs much more than one protocol. Its API may have to support somewhere between a few dozen and a few hundred different cryptographic transactions. The paper in these proceedings by Mike Bond shows that attacks can be found on even the most mature and thoroughly-studied cryptographic APIs. Developing the tools and concepts to design robust cryptographic APIs looks set to be a major research challenge for some years to come, and may be the next big topic for the protocol research community.

Business process failures are coming to be recognised as perhaps the main cause of attacks on real systems. Once the principal providing the protection is no longer the same as the principal who will suffer loss if it fails, things become messy. While a traditional monolithic pay-TV operator might have owned the smartcard designer, the satellite transponder, the set-top boxes and indeed the entire customer base, things are now becoming much more fragmented. Design, evaluation, implementation and operations are being ever more widely distributed, and this is starting to introduce serious evaluation and assurance issues. There are also economic issues such as network externalities, asymmetric information, moral hazard, adverse selection, liability dumping and the tragedy of the commons.

The above themes interact in unexpected ways. For example, even a completely tamper-proof chip can have its design read out by a litigation attack; the attacker buys a vaguely relevant patent, brings a lawsuit against the device designer for infringement, and obtains full design details as part of the legal discovery process. This may be a further argument in favour of Kerckhoffs' principle. On the other hand, a highly obscure design can greatly complicate matters for an attacker whose tools allow him to observe only partial information about the computations being undertaken.

Ultimately, though, information security is about power. While at the technical level it is about controlling who may use which resource and how, while at the level of business strategy it is increasingly about raising barriers to trade, segmenting markets and differentiating products. A final point is that sometimes insecurity is welcome. For example, it may foster economic growth by making monopolies harder to defend.

A Sound Method for Switching between Boolean and Arithmetic Masking

Louis Goubin

Schlumberger – CP8
68 route de Versailles, F-78431 Louveciennes, France
Louis.Goubin@louveciennes.tt.slb.com

Abstract. Since the announcement of the Differential Power Analysis (DPA) by Paul Kocher and al., several countermeasures were proposed in order to protect software implementations of cryptographic algorithms. In an attempt to reduce the resulting memory and execution time overhead, a general method was recently proposed, consisting in "masking" all the intermediate data.

This masking strategy is possible if all the fundamental operations used in a given algorithm can be rewritten with masked input data, giving masked output data. This is easily seen to be the case in classical algorithms such as DES or RSA.

However, for algorithms that combine boolean and arithmetic functions, such as IDEA or several of the AES candidates, two different kinds of masking have to be used. There is thus a need for a method to convert back and forth between boolean masking and arithmetic masking.

A first solution to this problem was proposed by Thomas Messerges in [15], but was unfortunately shown (see [6]) insufficient to prevent DPA. In the present paper, we present two new practical algorithms for the conversion, that are proven secure against DPA.

The first one ("BooleanToArithmetic") uses a constant number of elementary operations, namely 7, on the registers of the processor. The number of elementary operations for the second one ("ArithmeticToBoolean"), namely $5K + 5$, is proportional to the size K (in bits) of the processor registers.

Key words: Physical attacks, Differential Power Analysis, Electric consumption, AES, IDEA, Smartcards, Masking Techniques.

1 Introduction

Paul Kocher and al. introduced in 1998 ([12]) and published in 1999 ([13]) the concept of *Differential Power Analysis* attack, also known as DPA. The initial focus was on symmetrical cryptosystems such as DES (see [12,16]) and the AES candidates (see [1,3,7]), but public key cryptosystems have since been shown to be also vulnerable to the DPA attacks (see [17,5,11]).

In [10,11], Goubin and Patarin proposed a generic countermeasure consisting in splitting all the intermediate variables. A similar "duplication" method

Ç.K. Koç, D. Naccache, and C. Paar (Eds.): CHES 2001, LNCS 2162, pp. 3–15, 2001.

was suggested shortly after by Chari and al. in [3] and [4]. Although the authors of [3] state that these general methods generally increase dramatically the amount of memory needed, or the computation time, Goubin and Patarin proved that realistic implementations could be reached with the "duplication" method. However, it has been shown in [9] that even inner rounds can be aimed by "Power-Analysis"-type attacks, so that the splitting should be performed on all rounds of the algorithm. This makes the issue of the memory and time computation overhead even more crucial, especially for embedded systems such as smartcards.

In [15], Thomas Messerges investigated on DPA attacks applied on the AES candidates. He developped a general countermeasure, consisting in masking all the inputs and outputs of each elementary operation used by the microprocessor. This generic technique allowed him to evaluate the impact of these countermeasures on the five AES algorithms.

However, for algorithms that combine boolean and arithmetic functions, two different kinds of masking have to be used. There is thus a need for a method to convert back and forth between boolean masking and arithmetic masking. This is typically the case for IDEA [14] and for three AES candidates: MARS [2], RC6 [18] and Twofish [19].

T. Messerges proposed in [15] an algorithm in order to perform this conversion between a "$\oplus$ mask" and a "$+$ mask". Unfortunately, Coron and Goubin described in [6] a specific attack, showing that the "BooleanToArithmetic" algorithm proposed by T. Messerges is not sufficient to prevent Differential Power Analysis. In a similar way, his "ArithmeticToBoolean" algorithm is not secure either.

In the present paper, we present two new "BooleanToArithmetic" and "ArithmeticToBoolean" algorithms, proven secure against DPA attacks. Each of these algorithms uses only very simple operations: "XOR", "AND", subtractions and "logical shift left". Our "BooleanToArithmetic" algorithm uses a constant number (namely 7) of such elementary operations, whereas the number of elementary operations involved in our "ArithmeticToBoolean" algorithm is proportional (namely equal to $5K + 5$) to the size (*i.e.* the number K of bits) of the processor registers.

2   Background

2.1   The "Differential Power Analysis" Attack

The "Differential Power Analysis" (DPA) is an attack that allows to obtain information about the secret key (contained in a smartcard for example), by performing a statistical analysis of the electric consumption records measured for a large number of computations with the same key.

This attack does not require any knowledge about the individual electric consumption of each instruction, nor about the position in time of each of these instructions. It applies exactly the same way as soon as the attacker knows the outputs of the algorithm and the corresponding consumption curves. It only relies on the following fundamental hypothesis:

Fundamental hypothesis: *There exists an intermediate variable, that appears during the computation of the algorithm, such that knowing a few key bits (in practice less than 32 bits) allows us to decide whether two inputs (respectively two outputs) give or not the same value for this variable.*

2.2   The Masking Method

In the present paper, we focus on the "masking method", initially suggested by Goubin and Patarin in [10], and studied further in [11].

The basic principle consists in programming the algorithm so that the fundamental hypothesis above is not true any longer (*i.e.* an intermediate variable never depends on the knowledge of an easily accessible subset of the secret key). More precisely, using a secret sharing scheme, each intermediate variable that appears in the cryptographic algorithm is splitted. Therefore, an attacker has to analyze multiple point distributions, which makes his task grow exponentially in the number of elements in the splitting.

2.3   The Conversion Problem

For algorithms that combine boolean and arithmetic functions, two different kinds of masking have to be used:

$$\text{Boolean masking}: \quad x' = x \oplus r$$
$$\text{Arithmetic masking}: A = x - r \bmod 2^K$$

Here the variable x is masked with random r to give the masked value x' (or A). Our goal is to find an efficient algorithm for converting from boolean masking to arithmetic masking and conversely, in which all intermediate variables are decorrelated from the data to be masked, so that it is secure against DPA.

In all the present paper, we suppose that the processor has K-bit registers (in practice, K is most of the time equal to 8, 16, 32 or 64). All the arithmetic operations (such as the addition "+", the subtraction "−", or the doubling "$z \mapsto 2z$") are considered modulo 2^K. For simplicity, the "$\bmod 2^K$" will often be omitted in the sequel.

3   From Boolean to Arithmetic Masking

3.1   A Useful Algebraic Property

Let $I = \{0, 1, 2, \ldots, 2^K - 1\}$, with $K \geq 1$ being an integer. Let $x' \in I$. We consider the function $\Phi_{x'} : I \to I$, defined by:

$$\Phi_{x'}(r) \equiv (x' \oplus r) - r \bmod 2^K.$$

We identify each element of I with the sequence of coefficients in its binary representation, so that I can be viewed as a vector space of dimension K over GF(2), isomorphic to GF(2)^K.

Theorem 1

$$\Phi_{x'}(r) = x' \oplus \bigoplus_{i=1}^{K-1} \left[\left(\bigwedge_{j=1}^{i-1} (2^j \overline{x'}) \right) \wedge (2^i x') \wedge (2^i r) \right],$$

where $\overline{x'}$ stands for the ones complement of x', and $\wedge$ stands for the boolean "AND" operator.

See Appendix 1 for a proof of Theorem 1.

Corollary 1.1 *The function $\Phi_{x'}$ is affine over GF(2).*

This result is an easy consequence of Theorem 1.

3.2 The "BooleanToArithmetic" Algorithm

Since $\Phi_{x'}$ is affine over GF(2), the function $\Psi_{x'} = \Phi_{x'} \oplus \Phi_{x'}(0)$ is *linear* over GF(2). Therefore, for any value γ,

$$\Psi_{x'}(r) = \Psi_{x'}(\gamma \oplus (r \oplus \gamma)) = \Psi_{x'}(\gamma) \oplus \Psi_{x'}(r \oplus \gamma).$$

Corollary 1.2 *For any value γ, if we denote $A = (x' \oplus r) - r$, we also have*

$$A = [(x' \oplus \gamma) - \gamma] \oplus x' \oplus [(x' \oplus (r \oplus \gamma)) - (r \oplus \gamma)].$$

$A = (x' \oplus r) - r$ can thus be obtained from the following algorithm:

Algorithm 1. BooleanToArithmetic

Require: (x', r) such that $x = x' \oplus r$
Ensure: (A, r) such that $x = A + r$
  Initialize Γ to a random value γ
  $T \Leftarrow x' \oplus \Gamma$
  $T \Leftarrow T - \Gamma$
  $T \Leftarrow T \oplus x'$
  $\Gamma \Leftarrow \Gamma \oplus r$
  $A \Leftarrow x' \oplus \Gamma$
  $A \Leftarrow A - \Gamma$
  $A \Leftarrow A \oplus T$

The "BooleanToArithmetic" algorithm uses 2 auxiliary variables (T and Γ), 1 random generation and 7 elementary operations (more precisely: 5 "XOR" and 2 subtractions).

3.3   Proof of Security against DPA

From the description of the "BooleanToArithmetic" algorithm, we easily obtain the list of all the intermediate values V_0, ..., V_6 that appear during the computation of $A = (x' \oplus r) - r$:

$$\begin{cases} V_0 = \gamma \\ V_1 = \gamma \oplus r \\ V_2 = x' \oplus \gamma \\ V_3 = (x' \oplus \gamma) - \gamma \\ V_4 = [(x' \oplus \gamma) - \gamma] \oplus x' \\ V_5 = x' \oplus \gamma \oplus r \\ V_6 = (x' \oplus \gamma \oplus r) - (\gamma \oplus r) \end{cases}$$

If we suppose that γ is randomly chosen with a uniform distribution on $I = \{0,1\}^K$, it is easy to see that:

– the values V_0, V_1, V_2 and V_5 are uniformly distributed on I.
– the distributions of V_3, V_4 and V_6 depend on x' but not on r.

4   From Arithmetic to Boolean Masking

4.1   A Useful Recursion Formula

Theorem 2 *If we denote $x' = (A + r) \oplus r$, we also have $x' = A \oplus u_{K-1}$, where u_{K-1} is obtained from the following recursion formula:*

$$\begin{cases} u_0 = 0 \\ \forall k \geq 0, \ u_{k+1} = 2[u_k \wedge (A \oplus r) \oplus (A \wedge r)]. \end{cases}$$

See Appendix 2 for a proof of Theorem 2.

4.2   The "ArithmeticToBoolean" Algorithm

Let γ be any value. The change of variable $t_k = 2\gamma \oplus u_k$ leads to the following consequence of Theorem 2.

Corollary 2.1 *For any value γ, if we denote $x' = (A + r) \oplus r$, we also have $x' = A \oplus 2\gamma \oplus t_{K-1}$, where t_{K-1} is obtained from the following recursion formula:*

$$\begin{cases} t_0 = 2\gamma \\ \forall k \geq 0, \ t_{k+1} = 2[t_k \wedge (A \oplus r) \oplus \omega], \end{cases}$$

in which $\omega = \gamma \oplus (2\gamma) \wedge (A \oplus r) \oplus A \wedge r$.

As a consequence, $x' = (A + r) \oplus r$ can be obtained from the "Arithmetic-ToBoolean" algorithm below.

This method requires 3 auxiliary variables (T, Ω and Γ), 1 random generation and $(5K + 5)$ elementary operations (more precisely: $(2K + 4)$ "XOR", $(2K + 1)$ "AND" and K "logical shift left").

Algorithm 2. ArithmeticToBoolean

Require: (A, r) such that $x = A + r$
Ensure: (x', r) such that $x = x' \oplus r$

  Initialize Γ to a random value γ
  $T \Leftarrow 2\Gamma$
  $x' \Leftarrow \Gamma \oplus r$
  $\Omega \Leftarrow \Gamma \wedge x'$
  $x' \Leftarrow T \oplus A$
  $\Gamma \Leftarrow \Gamma \oplus x'$
  $\Gamma \Leftarrow \Gamma \wedge r$
  $\Omega \Leftarrow \Omega \oplus \Gamma$
  $\Gamma \Leftarrow T \wedge A$
  $\Omega \Leftarrow \Omega \oplus \Gamma$
  for $k = 1$ to $K - 1$ **do**
    $\Gamma \Leftarrow T \wedge r$
    $\Gamma \Leftarrow \Gamma \oplus \Omega$
    $T \Leftarrow T \wedge A$
    $\Gamma \Leftarrow \Gamma \oplus T$
    $T \Leftarrow 2\Gamma$
  end for
  $x' \Leftarrow x' \oplus T$

4.3   Proof of Security against DPA

From the description of the "BooleanToArithmetic" algorithm, we easily obtain the list of all the intermediate values W_0, ..., W_{5K+4} that appear during the computation of $x' = (A + r) \oplus r$:

$$
\begin{cases}
W_0 = \gamma \\
W_1 = 2\gamma \\
W_2 = \gamma \oplus r \\
W_3 = \gamma \oplus \gamma \wedge r \\
W_4 = 2\gamma \oplus A \\
W_5 = \gamma \oplus 2\gamma \oplus A \\
W_6 = (\gamma \oplus 2\gamma \oplus A) \wedge r \\
W_7 = \gamma \oplus (2\gamma) \wedge r \oplus A \wedge r \\
W_8 = (2\gamma) \wedge A \\
W_9 = \gamma \oplus (2\gamma) \wedge (A \oplus r) \oplus A \wedge r = \omega \\
\quad\text{for } k = 1 \text{ to } K - 1 :
\begin{cases}
W_{5k+5} = (2\gamma \oplus u_{k-1}) \wedge r \\
W_{5k+6} = \gamma \oplus (2\gamma) \wedge A \oplus u_{k-1} \wedge r \oplus A \wedge r \\
W_{5k+7} = (2\gamma \oplus u_{k-1}) \wedge A \\
W_{5k+8} = \gamma \oplus u_{k-1} \wedge (A \oplus r) \oplus A \wedge r \\
W_{5k+9} = 2\gamma \oplus u_k
\end{cases}
\end{cases}
$$

If we suppose that γ is randomly chosen with a uniform distribution on $I = \{0, 1\}^K$, it is easy to see that:

- the values W_0, W_2 and W_{5k+8} $(1 \leq k \leq K-1)$ are uniformly distributed on I.
- the values W_1 and W_{5k+9} are uniformly distributed on the subset $\{0,1\}^{K-1} \times \{0\}$ of I.
- the distributions of W_3 and W_{5k+5} $(1 \leq k \leq K-1)$ depend on r but not on A.
- the distributions of W_4, W_8 and W_{5k+7} $(1 \leq k \leq K-1)$ depend on A but not on r.

To study the distribution of the remaining values (W_5, W_6, W_7, W_9 and W_{5k+6}), we will make use of the following result:

Theorem 3 *For any $\delta \in I$, the following function is bijective:*

$$\Theta_\delta : \begin{cases} I \to I \\ \gamma \mapsto \gamma \oplus (2\gamma) \wedge \delta. \end{cases}$$

See Appendix 3 for a proof of Theorem 3. As a result:

- the values $W_5 = \Theta_{-1}(\gamma) \oplus A$, $W_7 = \Theta_r(\gamma) \oplus A \wedge r$, $W_9 = \Theta_{A \oplus r}(\gamma) \oplus A \wedge r$ and $W_{5k+6} = \Theta_r(\gamma) \oplus u_{k-1} \wedge r \oplus A \wedge r$ $(1 \leq k \leq K-1)$ are uniformly distributed on I.
- the distribution of $W_6 = (\Theta_{-1}(\gamma) \oplus A) \wedge r$ depends on r but not on A.

5   Conclusion

In this paper, we solved the following open problem (stated in [6]): "find an efficient algorithm for converting from boolean masking to arithmetic masking and conversely, in which all intermediate variables are decorrelated from the data to be masked, so that it is secure against DPA".

The construction of our "BooleanToArithmetic" and "ArithmeticToBoolean" algorithms also led us to prove some results of independent interest. In particular we proved that $r \mapsto (a \oplus r) - r \bmod 2^K$ is an affine function, which seems to be a new result.

Finally, a direction for further research would be to find an improved version of the "ArithmeticToBoolean" algorithm, in which the number of elementary operations is less than $5K + 5$, or (even better) a constant independent of the size K of the registers.

Acknowledgement

I would like to thank Jean-Sébastien Coron for interesting discussions and suggestions.

References

1. Eli Biham and Adi Shamir, "Power Analysis of the Key Scheduling of the AES Candidates", in *Proceedings of the Second Advanced Encryption Standard (AES) Candidate Conference*,
   http://csrc.nist.gov/encryption/aes/round1/Conf2/aes2conf.htm, March 1999.
2. Carolynn Burwick, Don Coppersmith, Edward D'Avignon, Rosario Gennaro, Shai Halevi, Charanjit Jutla, Stephen M. Matyas, Luke O'Connor, Mohammad Peyravian, David Safford and Nevenko Zunic, "MARS - A Candidate Cipher for AES", NIST AES Proposal, June 1998. Available at:
   http://www.research.ibm.com/security/mars.pdf
3. Suresh Chari, Charantjit S. Jutla, Josyula R. Rao and Pankaj Rohatgi, "A Cautionary Note Regarding Evaluation of AES Candidates on Smart-Cards", in *Proceedings of the Second Advanced Encryption Standard (AES) Candidate Conference*,
   http://csrc.nist.gov/encryption/aes/round1/Conf2/aes2conf.htm, March 1999.
4. Suresh Chari, Charantjit S. Jutla, Josyula R. Rao and Pankaj Rohatgi, "Towards Sound Approaches to Counteract Power-Analysis Attacks", in *Proceedings of Advances in Cryptology – CRYPTO'99*, Springer-Verlag, 1999, pp. 398-412.
5. Jean-Sébastien Coron, "Resistance Against Differential Power Analysis for Elliptic Curve Cryptosystems", in *Proceedings of Workshop on Cryptographic Hardware and Embedded Systems*, Springer-Verlag, August 1999, pp. 292-302.
6. Jean-Sébastien Coron and Louis Goubin, "On Boolean and Arithmetic Masking against Differential Power Analysis", in *Proceedings of Workshop on Cryptographic Hardware and Embedded Systems*, Springer-Verlag, August 2000.
7. John Daemen and Vincent Rijmen, "Resistance Against Implementation Attacks: A Comparative Study of the AES Proposals", in *Proceedings of the Second Advanced Encryption Standard (AES) Candidate Conference*,
   http://csrc.nist.gov/encryption/aes/round1/Conf2/aes2conf.htm, March 1999.
8. John Daemen, Michael Peters and Gilles Van Assche, "Bitslice Ciphers and Power Analysis Attacks", in *Proceedings of Fast Software Encryption Workshop 2000*, Springer-Verlag, April 2000.
9. Paul N. Fahn and Peter K. Pearson, "IPA: A New Class of Power Attacks", in *Proceedings of Workshop on Cryptographic Hardware and Embedded Systems*, Springer-Verlag, August 1999, pp. 173-186.
10. Louis Goubin and J. Patarin, "Procédé de sécurisation d'un ensemble électronique de cryptographie à clé secrète contre les attaques par analyse physique", European Patent, Schlumberger, February 4th, 1999, Publication Number: 2789535.
11. Louis Goubin and Jacques Patarin, "DES and Differential Power Analysis – The Duplication Method", in *Proceedings of Workshop on Cryptographic Hardware and Embedded Systems*, Springer-Verlag, August 1999, pp. 158-172.
12. Paul Kocher, Joshua Jaffe and Benjamin Jun, "Introduction to Differential Power Analysis and Related Attacks", http://www.cryptography.com/dpa/technical, 1998.
13. Paul Kocher, Joshua Jaffe and Benjamin Jun, "Differential Power Analysis", in *Proceedings of Advances in Cryptology – CRYPTO'99*, Springer-Verlag, 1999, pp. 388-397.
14. Xuejia Lai and James Massey, "A Proposal for a New Block Encryption Standard", in *Advances in Cryptology - EUROCRYPT '90 Proceedings*, Springer-Verlag, 1991, pp. 389-404.

15. Thomas S. Messerges, "Securing the AES Finalists Against Power Analysis Attacks", in *Proceedings of Fast Software Encryption Workshop 2000*, Springer-Verlag, April 2000.
16. Thomas S. Messerges, Ezzy A. Dabbish and Robert H. Sloan, "Investigations of Power Analysis Attacks on Smartcards", in *Proceedings of USENIX Workshop on Smartcard Technology*, May 1999, pp. 151-161.
17. Thomas S. Messerges, Ezzy A. Dabbish and Robert H. Sloan, "Power Analysis Attacks of Modular Exponentiation in Smartcards", in *Proceedings of Workshop on Cryptographic Hardware and Embedded Systems*, Springer-Verlag, August 1999, pp. 144-157.
18. Ronald L. Rivest, Matthew J.B. Robshaw, Ray Sidney and Yiqun L. Yin, "The RC6 Block Cipher", v1.1, August 20, 1998. Available at: ftp://ftp.rsasecurity.com/pub/rsalabs/aes/rc6v11.pdf
19. Bruce Schneier, John Kelsey, Doug Whiting, David Wagner, Chris Hall and Niels Ferguson, "Twofish: A 128-Bit Block Cipher", June 15, 1998, AES submission available at: http://www.counterpane.com/twofish.pdf

Annex 1: Proof of Theorem 1

To prove theorem 1, we prove the following more precise result:

Lemma 1 *For any integer $k \geq 1$:*

$$\Phi_a(r) \equiv \left\{ a \oplus \bigoplus_{i=1}^{k-1} \left[\left(\bigwedge_{j=1}^{i-1} (2^j \bar{a}) \right) \wedge (2^i a) \wedge (2^i r) \right] \right\}$$

$$- \left[\left(\bigwedge_{j=1}^{k-1} (2^j \bar{a}) \right) \wedge (2^k a) \wedge (2^k r) \right] \bmod 2^K,$$

where $\bar{a}$ stands for the ones complement of a, and $\wedge$ stands for the boolean "AND" operator.

Theorem 1 easily follows from Lemma 1, by considering the particular value $k = K$ (and taking $a = x'$).

To prove Lemma 1, we will use the following elementary result.

Lemma 2 *For any integers u and v:*

$$u - v \equiv (u \oplus v) - 2(\bar{u} \wedge v) \bmod 2^K.$$

Proof of Lemma 2 (sketch): $u \oplus v$ gives almost the same result as $u - v$, except that carries have been forgotten. For a given index, a carry appears if and only if a '1' bit (from v) is subtracted from a '0' bit (from u), which corresponds to a '1' bit in $\bar{u} \wedge v = 1$. Since the carry is then subtracted in the *next* index, $\bar{u} \wedge v$ has to be shifted left, which is the same as to be doubled, before being subtracted from $u \oplus v$.

Proof of Lemma 1: We proceed by induction on k.

- We first apply Lemma 2 with $u = a \oplus r$ and $v = r$:

$$\Phi_a(r) \equiv (a \oplus r) - r \equiv a - 2(\overline{a \oplus r} \wedge r) \bmod 2^K.$$

Since $\overline{a \oplus r} = a \oplus \bar{r}$, we have:

$$\Phi_a(r) \equiv a - 2((a \oplus \bar{r}) \wedge r) \equiv a - 2(a \wedge r) \bmod 2^K,$$

which proves the case $k = 1$ of Lemma 1 (conventionally, the empty product $\bigwedge_{j=1}^{0}$ equals the identity element of the $\wedge$ operator).

- Let us suppose that the result of Lemma 1 is true for k:

$$\Phi_a(r) \equiv \left\{ a \oplus \bigoplus_{i=1}^{k-1} \left[\left(\bigwedge_{j=1}^{i-1} (2^j \bar{a}) \right) \wedge (2^i a) \wedge (2^i r) \right] \right\}$$

$$- \left[\left(\bigwedge_{j=1}^{k-1} (2^j \bar{a}) \right) \wedge (2^k a) \wedge (2^k r) \right] \bmod 2^K$$

and let us show that it is also true for $k + 1$.

Let

$$u = a \oplus \bigoplus_{i=1}^{k-1} \left[\left(\bigwedge_{j=1}^{i-1} (2^j \bar{a}) \right) \wedge (2^i a) \wedge (2^i r) \right]$$

and

$$v = \left(\bigwedge_{j=1}^{k-1} (2^j \bar{a}) \right) \wedge (2^k a) \wedge (2^k r).$$

We first obtain:

$$u \oplus v = a \oplus \bigoplus_{i=1}^{k} \left[\left(\bigwedge_{j=1}^{i-1} (2^j \bar{a}) \right) \wedge (2^i a) \wedge (2^i r) \right].$$

Moreover,

$$\bar{u} = \overline{a \oplus \bigoplus_{i=1}^{k-1} \left[\left(\bigwedge_{j=1}^{i-1} (2^j \bar{a}) \right) \wedge (2^i a) \wedge (2^i r) \right]}$$

$$= \bar{a} \oplus \bigoplus_{i=1}^{k-1} \left[\left(\bigwedge_{j=1}^{i-1} (2^j \bar{a}) \right) \wedge (2^i a) \wedge (2^i r) \right],$$

so that:

$$\bar{u} \wedge v = \left\{ \bar{a} \oplus \bigoplus_{i=1}^{k-1} \left[\left(\bigwedge_{j=1}^{i-1} (2^j \bar{a}) \right) \wedge (2^i a) \wedge (2^i r) \right] \right\}$$

$$\wedge \left(\bigwedge_{j=1}^{k-1} \left(2^j \bar{a}\right) \right) \wedge \left(2^k a\right) \wedge \left(2^k r\right).$$

Therefore

$$\bar{u} \wedge v = \left(\bigwedge_{j=0}^{k-1} \left(2^j \bar{a}\right) \right) \wedge \left(2^k a\right) \wedge \left(2^k r\right)$$

because to each index i, $1 \le i \le k-1$ in u corresponds an index j, $1 \le j \le k-1$ in v (namely $j = i$), such that:

$$\left(2^i a\right) \wedge \left(2^j \bar{a}\right) = 0.$$

Therefore, applying Lemma 2:

$$\Phi_a(r) \equiv \left\{ a \oplus \bigoplus_{i=1}^{k} \left[\left(\bigwedge_{j=1}^{i-1} \left(2^j \bar{a}\right) \right) \wedge \left(2^i a\right) \wedge \left(2^i r\right) \right] \right\}$$

$$- \left[\left(\bigwedge_{j=1}^{k} \left(2^j \bar{a}\right) \right) \wedge \left(2^{k+1} a\right) \wedge \left(2^{k+1} r\right) \right] \bmod 2^K.$$

Annex 2: Proof of Theorem 2

We begin by the following elementary result:

Lemma 3 *For any z and δ, the following identity holds:*

$$z + \delta \equiv \overline{\bar{z} - \delta} \bmod 2^K.$$

Proof of Lemma 3: It is easy to see that, for any λ,

$$\lambda + \bar{\lambda} + 1 \equiv 0 \bmod 2^K.$$

Applying this identity successively with $\lambda = \bar{z} - \delta$ and $\lambda = z$, we obtain:

$$\overline{\bar{z} - \delta} \equiv -(\bar{z} - \delta) - 1 \equiv -((-z - 1) - \delta) - 1 = z + \delta \bmod 2^K.$$

Proof of Theorem 2: We first apply Lemma 3 with $z = A$ and $\delta = r$:

$$A + r = \overline{\bar{A} - r}$$

Moreover,

$$\bar{A} = A \oplus (-1) = ((A \oplus r) \oplus (-1)) \oplus r = \overline{A \oplus r} \oplus r.$$

Hence

$$A + r = \overline{(\overline{A \oplus r} \oplus r) - r} = \overline{\Phi_{A \oplus r}(r)}.$$

From Theorem 1 (with $\overline{A \oplus r}$ instead of x'), we know that:

$$\Phi_{\overline{A \oplus r}}(r) = \overline{A \oplus r} \oplus \bigoplus_{i=1}^{K-1} \left[\left(\bigwedge_{j=1}^{i-1} \left(2^j(A \oplus r)\right) \right) \wedge \left(2^i(\overline{A \oplus r})\right) \wedge \left(2^i r\right) \right],$$

so that

$$A + r = A \oplus r \oplus \bigoplus_{i=1}^{K-1} \left[\left(\bigwedge_{j=1}^{i-1} \left(2^j(A \oplus r)\right) \right) \wedge \left(2^i A\right) \wedge \left(2^i r\right) \right].$$

Let us denote, for any integer $k \geq 0$,

$$u_k = \bigoplus_{i=1}^{k} \left[\left(\bigwedge_{j=1}^{i-1} \left(2^j(A \oplus r)\right) \right) \wedge \left(2^i A\right) \wedge \left(2^i r\right) \right].$$

From the definition of u_k, we have $u_0 = 0$ and $A + r = A \oplus r \oplus u_{K-1}$. Moreover for all $k \geq 0$,

$$u_{k+1} = \bigoplus_{i=1}^{k+1} \left[\left(\bigwedge_{j=1}^{i-1} \left(2^j(A \oplus r)\right) \right) \wedge \left(2^i A\right) \wedge \left(2^i r\right) \right]$$

$$= 2(A \wedge r) \oplus \bigoplus_{i=2}^{k+1} \left[\left(\bigwedge_{j=1}^{i-1} \left(2^j(A \oplus r)\right) \right) \wedge \left(2^i A\right) \wedge \left(2^i r\right) \right],$$

so that, if we denote $i' = i - 1$ and $j' = j - 1$:

$$u_{k+1} = 2(A \wedge r) \oplus \bigoplus_{i'=1}^{k} \left[\left(\bigwedge_{j'=0}^{i'-1} \left(2^{j'+1}(A \oplus r)\right) \right) \wedge \left(2^{i'+1} A\right) \wedge \left(2^{i'+1} r\right) \right]$$

$$= 2\left\{ (A \wedge r) \oplus \bigoplus_{i'=1}^{k} \left[\left(\bigwedge_{j'=0}^{i'-1} \left(2^{j'}(A \oplus r)\right) \right) \wedge \left(2^{i'} A\right) \wedge \left(2^{i'} r\right) \right] \right\}$$

$$= 2\left\{ (A \wedge r) \oplus (A \oplus r) \wedge \bigoplus_{i'=1}^{k} \left[\left(\bigwedge_{j'=1}^{i'-1} \left(2^{j'}(A \oplus r)\right) \right) \wedge \left(2^{i'} A\right) \wedge \left(2^{i'} r\right) \right] \right\}$$

$$= 2[(A \wedge r) \oplus (A \oplus r) \wedge u_k].$$

Annex 3: Proof of Theorem 3

Let δ be any value in I. We begin by proving that Θ_δ is surjective.
    Let $y \in I$. If we denote:

$$\gamma = \bigoplus_{i=0}^{K-1} \left[\left(\bigwedge_{j=1}^{i} \left(2^{j-1}\delta\right) \right) \wedge \left(2^i y\right) \right]$$

(conventionally, the empty product $\bigwedge\limits_{j=1}^{0}$ equals the identity element of the $\wedge$ operator), we have:

$$\gamma \oplus (2\gamma) \wedge \delta = \gamma \oplus \bigoplus_{i=0}^{K-1} \left[\left(\bigwedge_{j=0}^{i} (2^j \delta) \right) \wedge (2^{i+1} y) \right],$$

so that, if we denote $i' = i + 1$ and $j' = j + 1$:

$$\gamma \oplus (2\gamma) \wedge \delta = \gamma \oplus \bigoplus_{i'=1}^{K} \left[\left(\bigwedge_{j'=1}^{i'} (2^{j'-1} \delta) \right) \wedge (2^{i'} y) \right].$$

From the definition of γ, it is easy to see that:

$$\bigoplus_{i'=1}^{K} \left[\left(\bigwedge_{j'=1}^{i'} (2^{j'-1} \delta) \right) \wedge (2^{i'} y) \right] = \gamma \oplus y$$

Therefore:

$$\gamma \oplus (2\gamma) \wedge \delta = y.$$

We have proven that, for any $y \in I$, a value $\gamma \in I$ exists such that $\Theta_\delta(\gamma) = y$. As a consequence, Θ_δ is surjective. Since it maps I onto itself, we deduce that Θ_δ is bijective.

Fast Primitives for Internal Data Scrambling in Tamper Resistant Hardware

Eric Brier[1], Helena Handschuh[2], and Christophe Tymen[3]

[1] Gemplus Card International, Card Security Group
Parc d'Activités de Gémenos, B.P. 100, 13881 Gémenos, France
eric.brier@gemplus.com
[2] Gemplus Card International
34 rue Guynemer, 92447 Issy-les-Moulineaux, France
helena.handschuh@gemplus.com
[3] École Normale Supérieure
45 rue d'Ulm, 75230 Paris, France
christophe.tymen@gemplus.com

Abstract. Although tamper-resistant devices are specifically designed to thwart invasive attacks, they remain vulnerable to micro-probing. Among several possibilities to provide data obfuscations, keyed hardware permutations can provide compact design and easy diversification. We discuss the efficiency of such primitives, and we give several examples of implementations, along with proofs of effectively large key-space.

Keywords. Tamper-resistance, Probing attacks, Data scrambling, Keyed permutations, Smart-cards.

1 Introduction

Microprobing techniques are invasive attacks consisting in introducing a conductor point into certain parts of a tamper-resistant chip to monitor the electrical signal at this spot[3,1], in order to extract some secret information. A natural means to thwart these attacks consists in encrypting the data stored or exchanged inside the chip. Using classical block-ciphers like DES provides a natural solution, but this method becomes quickly illusory when the concerned data transit through highly time critical processes, like for example the communication between the microprocessor and the RAM. In this case, more hasty techniques must be used to provide very fast processing at the expense of a lower, but acceptable security level. This category of techniques is usually and informally called scrambling, or obfuscation, as opposed to encryption[4].

A popular primitive for scrambling in highly constrained environments consists simply in bit permutations, these permutations being parameterized by a key. As it appears in what follows, such functions result in very compact designs, where only one cycle is needed to process the data. Furthermore, a large number of permutations can be generated, with a one-to-one correspondence with the key space. Ultimately, keyed permutations can be easily used in more complex functions which require some keyed linear components.

Ç.K. Koç, D. Naccache, and C. Paar (Eds.): CHES 2001, LNCS 2162, pp. 16–27, 2001.

More precisely, this paper addresses the problem of designing keyed permutations of compact shape, that generate a large set of permutations when the key runs over the key space, and that offer good properties against chosen plaintext attacks in the context of physical probing. This combinatorial issue is tractable for a small number of bits, but becomes more intricate for realistic values like 16 or 32, which brings intrinsic interest to the results of Section 3. The rest of this paper is organized as follows. Section 2 defines a security model for scrambling functions, and proposes a criterion for the design of keyed permutations. Section 3 is the main part of our paper. Three different constructions for keyed permutations are proposed, along with proofs of some of their properties. Hardware engineers interested in quickly evaluating the practical contribution of this paper can directly jump to Section 4, which contains some numerical data about our new keyed permutations. Some possible applications are also listed. An example of a very fast on-chip data scrambler which integrates keyed permutations is proposed.

2   Scrambling Functions and Probing Attacks

2.1   Security Model

We consider the context of a smart-card microprocessor, which communicates with the RAM. The memory, and the channel which links it to the microprocessor, are subject to probing attempts. Consequently, to prevent information disclosure, a data word $(b_0, \ldots, b_{n-1})$ is encrypted with a key K using a scrambling function C_K before being sent to the memory. The key K may be refreshed each time the card is reset, but might also be regenerated more often, using multiple keys encryption techniques. We assume that the attacker is allowed to play with the microprocessor, which implies that he can send any data he wants to the memory. His goal is to decipher a secret data present in the card, read from the RAM at some time. The difference with a classical chosen plaintext attack on a block-cipher is that the attacker has only a partial knowledge of the ciphertext. Indeed, probing attacks are usually not easy to mount, and in particular, the attacker might rarely probe wherever he wants[3]. Consequently, we restrict the capabilities of the attacker to recovering only *some* of the bits $(b'_0, \ldots, b'_{n-1}) = C_K(b_0, \ldots, b_{n-1})$.

2.2   A Security Criterion for Linear Functions

For efficiency reasons, it is practical to choose for C_K a linear function. This choice does not provide any security against full chosen plaintext attacks, but might be sufficient if we assume that the attacker knows very few bits b'_i. One of the possible strategies of the attacker to decrypt a secret data might be to recover completely K during a preliminary phase when several plaintext messages are sent to the scrambling function. In this context, we can quantify the security provided by C_K by determining the number of wires that the attacker has to be able to probe simultaneously to recover the key. In particular, when C_K is a permutation σ_K of the group S_n of the permutations of $\{0, \ldots, n-1\}$, this question boils down to: what is the minimal number of pairs $(i, \sigma_K(i))$ the attacker needs to know to recover K entirely ? To formalize this condition, we introduce some definitions and notations. If μ and σ are two elements of S_n, we denote by $\mu\sigma$ the permutation defined by $i \mapsto \mu(\sigma(i))$. We also denote by ι the permutation such that $\iota(i) = i$ for all $i \in \{0, \ldots, n-1\}$.

An (n, k)−*keyed permutation* is a map from the set $\{0, 1\}^k$ to S_n :

$$\sigma : \{0, 1\}^k \longrightarrow S_n$$
$$K \longmapsto \sigma_K \ .$$

The *degree of freedom* of an (n, k)−keyed permutation is the smallest integer $m \geq 1$ such that there exists an $(m+1)$−tuple $(i_1, \ldots, i_{m+1})$ of pairwise distinct elements of $\{0, \ldots, n-1\}$, such that the map

$$\{\sigma_K / K \in \{0, 1\}^k\} \longrightarrow \{0, \ldots, n-1\}^{m+1}$$
$$\sigma_K \longmapsto (\sigma_K(i_1), \ldots, \sigma_K(i_{m+1}))$$

is injective. Informally, the degree of freedom is equal to the minimum number of pairs $(i, \sigma_K(i))$ we have to fix to determine uniquely σ_K. Note that this does not mean that this suffices to determine K, as the map from $\{0, 1\}^k$ to S_n might not be injective, but in our context, the secret key is completely recovered as soon as σ_K is known. From a practical standpoint, this definition implies also that we should look for keyed permutations with a degree of freedom as high as possible.

For example, in the strongest case, if σ is surjective in S_n, then σ has degree of freedom $n-1$: we need exactly $n-1$ distinct pairs $(i, \sigma_K(i))$ to determine completely σ_K (the missing value is infered from the $n-1$ others, since σ_K is a bijection). For the weakest case, let $\mu \neq \iota$ be in S_n, and consider the keyed permutation σ_b from $\{0, 1\}$ to S_n such that $\sigma_0 = \iota$ and $\sigma_1 = \mu$. Then σ as degree of freedom one: as $\mu \neq \iota$, there exist i_1 such that $\sigma_b(i_1) \neq i_1$ iff $b = 1$.

3   A Recursive Construction

3.1   Outline of the Result

This section explains the construction of three different (n, k)−keyed permutations when n is a power of two. These three constructions can be realized using combinatorial logic, and the corresponding circuits are of depth $\log_2 n$. Consequently, they achieve a very compact shape, and very short propagation delay features.

The construction of Section 3.3 generates 2^{n-1} permutations, which are in one-to-one correspondance with the key space. This construction is improved in Section 3.4, where we generate $n^{n/2}$ permutations. Section 3.5 still improves this result by generating at least $n^{\alpha n} 2^{-\beta n}$ permutations, with $\alpha = (\log_2 6)/4 \approx 0.65$ and $\beta = (\log_2 6)/4 - 1/2 \approx 0.15$. Furthermore, we prove that the last two constructions have degree of freedom at least $n/2 - 1$.

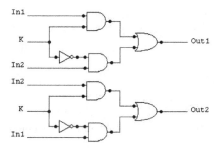

Fig. 1. Hardware realization of a switch

3.2   Hardware Representation of Keyed Permutations

The most natural approach to design hardware permutations is to use the set of
the transpositions of S_n. We recall that a transposition is an element (i, j) of S_n
which exchanges the symbol i with the symbol j. A well-known fact is that every
permutation on can be expressed as a product of transpositions. If t is a transposition, a keyed permutation $b \mapsto t^b$ with one bit of key can be realized using two
parallel multiplexers. We call such a block a *switch*. A hardware realization of
a switch is given in figure 1. Oriented graphs provide a compact representation
of switch based circuits. For example, figure 2 represents the keyed permutation
$(b_0, b_1) \mapsto (1, 3)^{b_0} (0, 1)^{b_1} \in S_4$. The grey nodes correspond to the switches, and
are commanded by additional key wires, which do not appear on the figure. In
the following, the *depth* of a circuit will refer to the number of stages composing
the circuit, this number being related to a switch-based design. Note that the
switch-depth is less than or equal to the multiplexer-depth.

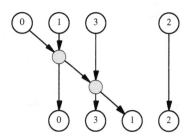

Fig. 2. Graphical representation of the keyed permutation $(1, 3)^{b_0} (0, 1)^{b_1}$

3.3   A Group Theoretic Construction

We denote by $\mathcal{H}_2^n$ a greatest subgroup of S_n which order is a power of two. $\mathcal{H}_2^n$
is called a *Sylow 2−subgroup* of S_n. In all the following, we will suppose that n
is a power of two. In this case, $\mathcal{H}_2^n$ has order 2^{n-1}[5]. A set of generators of $\mathcal{H}_2^n$
can be constructed recursively as follows. Consider the set $\{0, \ldots, n-1\}$, and

the permutation $g \in \mathcal{H}_2^n$ which exchanges $\{0, \ldots, n/2 - 1\}$ with $\{n/2, \ldots, n-1\}$ by $i \leftrightarrow i + n/2$. Now, we can repeat inductively this procedure by considering the sets $\{0, \ldots, n/2 - 1\}$ and $\{n/2, \ldots, n-1\}$. We get finally $n - 1$ elements of S_n which generate $\mathcal{H}_2^n$.

These generators are very easy to implement in hardware, since permuting two sets of k bits can be done using k switches parameterized by the same bit of key. This yields to a $(n, \log_2 n - 1)$–keyed permutation, that can be realized using $(n \log_2 n)/2$ switches. Figure 3 summarizes schematically this recursive construction.

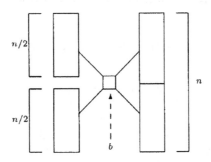

Fig. 3. Recursive contruction based on Sylow 2–subgroups

An interesting property of this design is that the set of generated permutations forms a group. We can take advantage of this fact to increase the number of generated permutations: In our previous construction, we built a hardware design which realized the keyed permutation g_K, where g_K takes all the values of $\mathcal{H}_2^n$ when K runs over the key space. Denote by ρ a well-chosen permutation, which we implement in hardware, that is, by permuting physically the wires. Then, by reusing the previous construction, we can realize the keyed permutation

$$s_{(K_1, K_2)} = g_{K_1} \circ \rho \circ g_{K_2} \; ,$$

which should generate more permutations. The question is to determine how many permutations are effectively generated by this method. It is easy to see that no collisions appear (i.e. the number of generated permutations is equal to $|\mathcal{H}_2^n|^2$) iff the following algebraic condition is verified:

$$\rho \mathcal{H}_2^n \rho^{-1} \cap \mathcal{H}_2^n = \{\iota\} \; . \tag{1}$$

The naive complexity of checking if a given permutation ρ verifies (1) is equal to $|\mathcal{H}_2^n| = 2^{n-1}$. Consequently, our approach fails as soon as say $n \geq 32$, since this last verification has to be made $32!/2$ times on average before finding a solution. Nevertheless, for $n = 32$, we may still get a result using the following trick: we define H, the subgroup of $\mathcal{H}_2^{32}$ which preserves $\{0, \ldots, 15\}$ and $\{16, \ldots, 31\}$. H is isomorphic to $\mathcal{H}_2^{16} \times \mathcal{H}_2^{16}$, and has cardinality 2^{30}. Consider the keyed permutation $(K_1, K_2) \mapsto h_{K_1} \beta g_{K_2}$, where h_{K_1} runs over H, g_{K_2} runs over $\mathcal{H}_2^{32}$, and where β is a fixed permutation. This map is injective iff

$$\beta H \beta^{-1} \cap \mathcal{H}_2^{32} = \{\iota\} \ . \tag{2}$$

A simple method to find such a β is first to solve (1) for $n = 16$, and then to set $\beta = (\rho(\cdot), \rho(\cdot - 16) + 16)$. This search terminates on average after $(|S_{16}/\mathcal{H}_2^{16}| \cdot |\mathcal{H}_2^{16}|)^{1/2} \approx 2^{22}$ trials. For instance, the following permutation is a solution of (1) for $n = 16$:

$$\rho = (0, 15, 9, 10, 11, 12, 13, 14)(1, 2, 3)(4, 5, 6, 7, 8) \ .$$

The resulting number of generated permutations is equal to $2^{30} \cdot 2^{31} = 2^{61}$.

3.4 Generalization of the Group-Based Design

Unfortunately, this improvement works only for $n \leq 32$. Furthermore, we generate only 2^{61} permutations, among the $32! \approx 2^{118}$ elements of S_{32}. Nevertheless, as we will see, a slight modification of the set of generators leads to generating a much larger subset of S_n. The price to pay for this improvement is to lose the group property, but this has no impact for our application. As before, the solution is built recursively by induction on $\log_2 n$, so that at each step of the induction, we add a new stage to the corresponding circuit.

Theorem 1. *If n is a power of two, then there exists a circuit of depth $\log_2 n$ involving $(n \log_2 n)/2$ switches, which realizes a $(n, (n \log_2 n)/2)$−keyed permutation δ. Furthermore, the number of distinct generated permutations is equal to the number of keys, that is $n^{n/2}$.*

Proof. We proceed by induction. Let σ be a $(n/2, ((n/2) \log_2(n/2))/2)$−keyed permutation with the properties stated in the theorem. For convenience, we set $k = ((n/2) \log_2(n/2))/2$. First, we defined the $(n, 2k)$−keyed permutation μ as

$$\mu_{(K_1, K_2)}(i) = \begin{cases} \sigma_{K_1}(i) & \text{if } 0 \leq i < n/2 \\ \sigma_{K_2}(i - n/2) + n/2 & \text{if } n/2 \leq i < n \ , \end{cases} \tag{3}$$

where $K_1, K_2 \in \{0, 1\}^k$. Let set $k' = 2k + n/2$, and define the (n, k')−keyed permutation δ by

$$\delta_{(K_1, K_2, E)} = \nu_E \circ \mu_{(K_1, K_2)} \ ,$$

where

$$\nu_E = \prod_{j=0}^{n/2-1} (j, j + n/2)^{e_j} \ ,$$

and $E = (e_0, \ldots, e_{n/2-1}) \in \{0, 1\}^{n/2}$. First, $k' = 2k + n/2 = n(\log_2 n - 1)/2 + n/2 = (n \log_2 n)/2$, which corresponds to what we expect. Furthermore, the number of switches used for realizing δ is equal to $2k + n/2 = k'$. It remains to prove that δ is injective. This comes from the fact that for all $0 \leq i < n/2$,

$\delta_{(K_1,K_2,E)}^{-1}(i) < n/2$ iff $e_i = 0$. Consequently, we can uniquely recover E from $\delta_{(K_1,K_2,E)}$. As μ is injective, we can also recover uniquely K_1 and K_2 from $\mu_{(K_1,K_2)} = \nu_E^{-1} \circ \delta_{(K_1,K_2,E)}$, which concludes the proof.   □

Figure 4 represents an example of this construction for the case $n = 8$.

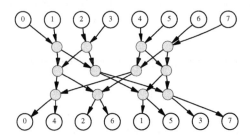

Fig. 4. Representation of δ for $n = 8$

As motivated in section 2.2, we want to check that δ has high enough degree of freedom. This is guaranteed by the following result :

Theorem 2. *The degree of freedom d_δ of the keyed permutation δ of theorem 1 verifies*

$$d_\delta \geq n/2 - 1 .$$

Proof. We proceed by induction on n. When $n = 2$, the theorem is true, as in order to guess the state of the switch, we have to know at least one pair $(i, \delta_K(j))$. Suppose that the theorem is true at step $n/2$. Recall that with the notations of theorem 1, δ is given by the recursion formula

$$\delta_{K=(K_1,K_2,E)} = \nu_E \circ \mu_{(K_1,K_2)} ,$$

where μ is defined from the $(n/2, k)-$keyed permutation σ following (3). The induction formula implies that σ has degree of freedom $n/4 - 1$. We set $r = n/2 - 1$, and we choose an $r-$tuple $(i_1, \ldots, i_r)$ of pairwise distinct elements of $\{0, \ldots, n-1\}$, a key $K = (K_1, K_2, E)$, and we set $j_l = \delta_K(i_l)$. Consider the set $I_1 = \{l/\nu_E^{-1}(j_l) < n/2\}$, and $I_2 = \{l/\nu_E^{-1}(j_l) \geq n/2\}$. As $|I_1| + |I_2| = n/2 - 1$, one of the two sets (for example I_1) has strictly less than $n/4$ elements: $|I_1| \leq n/4 - 1$. Furthermore, as μ preserves $\{0, \ldots, n/2 - 1\}$ and $\{n/2, \ldots, n - 1\}$, for all $l \in I_1$, $i_l < n/2$. Consequently, there exists $K_1' \neq K_1$ such that

$$\forall l \in I_1, \quad \sigma_{K_1}(i_l) = \sigma_{K_1'}(i_l) .$$

This implies that

$$\delta_{(K_1,K_2,E)}(i_1, \ldots, i_r) = \delta_{(K_1',K_2,E)}(i_1, \ldots, i_r) .$$

This proves that δ has degree of freedom greater than $n/2 - 1$.   □

3.5   Further Improvements

We may still try to improve the previous construction by modifying it so that we could generate a larger set of permutations. We always consider the keyed permutation δ as defined above, with the recursion formula

$$\delta_{K=(K_1,K_2,E)} = \nu_E \circ \mu_{(K_1,K_2)} \; .$$

Define the vector $\epsilon = (\epsilon_0, \ldots, \epsilon_{n-1})$ as $\epsilon_i = 1\{\delta_K^{-1}(i) < n/2\}$, where $1\{P\}$ is equal to one when the predicate P is true, and to zero otherwise. As underlined in the proof of theorem 1, there is a one-to-one correspondence between the set of all the keys E and the set of all the $n/2$−tuples $(\epsilon_0, \ldots, \epsilon_{n/2-1})$. This is because μ preserves the segments $i < n/2$ and $i \geq n/2$. This means that ϵ contains twice too much information. Consequently, our idea is to group the transpositions $(j, j + n/2)$ of μ two by two, and to compose them with a cycle of the four concerned elements, so that we could still invert our map thanks to the associated 4-tuple of bits ϵ_i.

Consider first the set $\{0, 1, 2, 3\}$, and the map

$$g : (b_0, b_1, b_2) \in \{0,1\}^3 \longmapsto (0,2,1,3)^{b_0}(0,2)^{b_1}(1,3)^{b_2} \; .$$

We consider also the map defined by

$$h(b_0, b_1, b_2) = \left(1\{g(b_0, b_1, b_2)^{-1}(i) < 2\}\right)_{0 \leq i \leq 3} \; .$$

The truth table of h is given below:

(b_0, b_1, b_2)	$h(b_0, b_1, b_2)$
$(0,0,0)$	(1,1,0,0)
$(0,0,1)$	(1,0,0,1)
$(0,1,0)$	(0,1,1,0)
$(0,1,1)$	(0,0,1,1)
$(1,0,0)$	(0,0,1,1)
$(1,0,1)$	(1,0,1,0)
$(1,1,0)$	(0,1,0,1)
$(1,1,1)$	(1,1,0,0)

As it can be seen, $h(\{0,1\}^3)$ has cardinality six.

Now, group the points of $\{0, \ldots, n-1\}$ four by four (when $n \geq 4$):

$$A_0 = (0, 1, n/2, n/2 + 1),$$
$$A_1 = (2, 3, n/2 + 2, n/2 + 3),$$
$$\vdots$$
$$A_{n/4-1} = (n/2 - 2, n/2 - 1, n - 2, n - 1) \; .$$

Finally, form the cycles $c_0, \ldots, c_{n/4-1}$, with support respectively equal to the A_i, obtained from the cycle $(0, 2, 1, 3)$ by applying for each $0 \leq i < n/4$ the substitutions

$$0 \mapsto i, 1 \mapsto i + 1, 2 \mapsto n/2 + i, 3 \mapsto n/2 + i + 1 \; .$$

We are now ready to build recursively a keyed permutation χ, with the same method as in the proof of theorem 1. Following analogous notations, we define $\chi_{(K_1,K_2,E,F)}$ inductively as

$$\chi_{(K_1,K_2,E,F)} = \xi_F \circ \nu_E \circ \mu_{(K_1,K_2)} \ , \tag{4}$$

where

$$\xi_F = \prod_{j=0}^{n/4-1} c_j^{f_j} \ ,$$

with $F = (f_0, \ldots, f_{n/4-1}) \in \{0,1\}^{n/4}$.

Theorem 3. χ is a $(n,k)-$keyed permutation, where $k = \frac{3}{4}n \log_2 n$. χ can be realized using k switches, and has degree of freedom at least $n/2-1$. Furthermore, χ generates at least a_n distinct permutations, where a_n verifies the recursion formula

$$\begin{cases} a_n = 6^{n/4} a_{n/2}^2 & \text{if } n \geq 4 \\ a_2 = 2 \ . \end{cases}$$

Proof. We prove the recursion formula, the verification of the other points being straightforward. Suppose that we have constructed an $(n/2,k)-$keyed permutation σ that verifies our statements. We denoted by $\mathcal{E}$ the largest set of the keys such that σ restricted to $\mathcal{E}$ is injective. Referring to the recursive construction of χ of equation (4), it is clear that μ restricted to $\mathcal{E} \times \mathcal{E}$ is injective: this is a direct consequence of definition (3) of μ. Consider for each $0 \leq i < n/4$ the 3-tuples $U_i = (e_{2i}, e_{2i+1}, f_i)$, and the set

$$\mathcal{A} = \big\{(0,0,0),(0,0,1),(0,1,0),(0,1,1),(1,0,1),(1,1,0)\big\} \ .$$

Using the truth table of h, we see that h restricted to $\mathcal{A}$ is injective. Consider the set $\mathcal{F}$ of the keys defined by $\mathcal{F} = \big\{(E,F)/\forall i \ U_i \in \mathcal{A}\big\}$. It is clear that

$$|\mathcal{F}| = |\mathcal{A}|^{n/4} = 6^{n/4} \ . \tag{5}$$

Now, since $\mu_{(K_1,K_2)}$ preserves the sets $\{0, \ldots, n/2-1\}$ and $\{n/2, \ldots, n-1\}$, we have that

$$\chi_K^{-1}(i) < n/2 \iff (\xi_F \circ \nu_E)^{-1}(i) < n/2 \ .$$

This implies that χ restricted to $\mathcal{E} \times \mathcal{E} \times \mathcal{F}$ is injective. Using equality (5) and the fact that $|\mathcal{E}| \geq a_{n/2}$, this proves the theorem. □

It is easy to check by induction that $\log_2 a_n > (n \log_2 n)/2$, which means that χ generates effectively more permutations than δ. The explicit expression of a_n announced in section 3.1 results from the fact that the sequence $(\log_2 a_n)/n$ is in arithmetic progression.

Contrary to δ, the distribution of the permutations generated by χ_K, when K is chosen uniformly, is not uniform. We leave open the question of determining exactly this distribution. Anyway, it is easy to reduce the key space so that the restriction of χ becomes injective. For that, it suffices to restrict the keys (E, F) to the set $\mathcal{F}$ defined in the proof above, and to proceed by induction. We leave open the question of the exact distribution of the generated permutations.

The practical realization of χ implies to design in hardware a keyed permutation with a cycle of length four, like $(0, 1, 2, 3)^b, b \in \{0, 1\}$. This can be easily done in one stage using four multiplexers

Figure 5 shows a realization of χ for the case $n = 8$. The nodes with 8 edges represent the cycle $(0, 2, 1, 3)$ involved in the construction of χ.

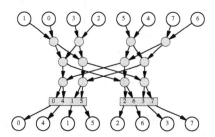

Fig. 5. Representation of χ for $n = 8$

4 Practical Examples and Applications

4.1 Numerical Examples

Table 1 shows the characteristics of the two keyed permutations δ and χ for various values of $n = 8, 16, 32, 64$. The number of multiplexers needed for their construction is denoted by N_{mux}, and the number of distinct generated permutations is denoted by N_{perm}.

Table 1. Characteristics of δ and χ for various values of n

	δ	χ	δ	χ	δ	χ	δ	χ
n	8		16		32		64	
N_{mux}	32	40	88	112	224	288	544	704
Depth	3	6	4	8	5	10	6	12
Key size	12	16	32	44	80	112	192	272
$\lceil \log_2 N_{\text{perm}} \rceil$	12	14	32	39	80	99	192	239
$\lceil \log_2 n! \rceil$	15		44		118		296	

An important fact is the very small number of stages needed to implement δ and χ. For example, for $n = 32$, the design has only five levels of gates. This property makes these functions particularly suitable for data scrambling in critical pathes. Non exhaustive applications are: scrambling of the bus between the microprocessor and the memory, scrambling of the RAM, or scrambling of the bus between the CPU and the cryptoprocessor.

4.2   Protecting the Secrecy of the Design

These functions can also easily be diversified, and thus provide a customizable design, so that the final scrambling function can remain secret. Recall that δ is built recursively from the equation

$$\delta_{(K_1,K_2,E)} = \nu_E \circ \mu_{(K_1,K_2)} \ .$$

This definition would correspond to the "normal form" of our construction. Derivated forms can be obtained as follows: at each step of the induction, we choose two permutations α_1, α_2, acting respectively on $\{0, \dots, n/2 - 1\}$ and on $\{n/2, \dots, n-1\}$, and we implement these permutations in hardware, that is, we permute physically the wires of the circuit. Here, α_1 and α_2 are supposed to be kept secret. With the same material, we can now build δ using the modified equation

$$\delta_{(K_1,K_2,E)} = \nu_E \circ \alpha_1 \circ \alpha_2 \circ \mu_{(K_1,K_2)} \ .$$

It is not difficult to see that we generate *mutatis mutandis* the same number of permutations as before, and that the resulting keyed permutation has the same degree of freedom. It suffices for this to rewrite the proofs of theorems 1 and 2. The same construction can be applied to χ, with the same consequences.

4.3   Non-linear Data Scrambling Using Keyed Permutations

The primitives that we have just described can easily be incorporated into more complex non-linear data scrambling functions. One major advantage of the proposed constructions is the large size of the key-space and of the resulting function space. Besides, the very compact shape of the resulting circuits allows to use them several times in more complex functions.

Following Shannon's basic confusion-diffusion paradigm, these keyed permutations can be used in alternating layers with small, say 4 bit to 4 bit substitution boxes (S-boxes). Clearly, such constructions cannot achieve the same security level as classical block ciphers do : following Shamir's security analysis [6], a five layer SASAS construction using alternating layers of S-boxes and affine functions (of which permutations are a special case) can be broken using approximately 2^{16} chosen plaintexts for 128 bit blocks and 8-bit to 8-bit Sboxes.

However, this kind of construction still yields a sub-exponential security bound instead of a linear security bound in terms of chosen plaintext attacks. As the attacker has quite limited resources in the probing setting anyhow, bearing in mind that she is not able to probe more than a handful of wires simultaneously using the same session scrambling key, a limited number of layers of additional key-dependent S-boxes will sufficiently increase the difficulty of unscrambling the memory and bus contents in the context of tamper-resistant objects such as smart-cards.

In terms of circuit complexity, a 4 bit to 4 bit S-box can be efficiently implemented using an average of 32 gates with a circuit depth three (in a completely optimized architecture this depth may become as low as one). Thus for the example SASAS structure for a 32 bit input size, each substitution layer adds approximately 256 gates to the 224 gates of the proposed keyed permutation. With five layers altogether, the circuit has around 1200 gates for a depth of 19. It is then left to the designer to select whatever circuit complexity is acceptable in the concerned architecture compared to the obfuscation level fit for purpose.

5 Conclusion

We proposed three implementations of keyed permutations, which achieve very short depth, and effectively large key space. We indicated also a criterion to identify keyed permutations with good properties against chosen plaintext attacks realized by probing. These functions are particularly well suited for data obfuscation in very constrained environments like smart-cards.

Acknowledgments

We thank Guglielmo Morgari and Vittorio Bagini for careful reading, and David Naccache for fruitful discussions. We are also grateful to the anonymous referee for helpful comments.

References

1. Ross Anderson and Markus Kuhn. Tamper resistance – a Cautionary Note. In *The second USENIX Workshop on Electronic Commerce Proceeding*, pages 1–11, Oakland, California, November 1996.
2. Tamás Horváth. Arithmetic Design for Permutation Groups. In Ç.K. Koç and C. Paar, editors, *Cryptographic Hardware and Embedded Systems (CHES '99)*, number 1717 in Lecture Notes in Computer Science, pages 109–121. Springer Verlag, 1999.
3. Olivier Kömmerling and Markus Kuhn. Design principles for Tamper-Resistant Smartcard Processors. In *USENIX Workshop on Smartcard Technology*, Chicago, Illinois, USA, May 1999.
4. S. Rankl and W. Effing. *Smart Card Handbook*. John Wiley & Sons, 1999.
5. Derek Robinson. *A Course in the Theory of Groups*. Number 80 in GTM. Springer Verlag, 1991.
6. Adi Shamir. Assassinating SASAS. Rump session of Crypto'2000.

Random Register Renaming to Foil DPA

D. May, H.L. Muller, and N.P. Smart

Department of Computer Science,
Woodland Road, University of Bristol, BS8 1UB, UK
{dave,henkm,nigel}@cs.bris.ac.uk

Abstract. Techniques such as DPA and SPA can be used to find the secret keys stored in smart-cards. These techniques have caused concern for they can allow people to recharge their stored value smartcards (in effect printing money), or illegally use phone or digital TV services. We propose an addition to current processors which will counteract these techniques. By randomising register usage, we can hide the secret key stored in a smartcard. The extension we propose can be added to existing processors, and is transparent to the algorithm.

1 Background

Modern cryptography is about ensuring the integrity, confidentiality and authenticity of digital communications. As such it has a large number of applications from e-commerce on the Internet through to charging mechanisms for pay–per–view-TV. As more and more devices become network aware they also become potential weak links in the chain. Hence cryptographic techniques are now being embedded into devices such as smart cards, mobile phones and PDA's. This poses a number of problems since the cryptographic modules are no longer maintained in secure vaults inside large corporations. For a cryptographic system to remain secure it is imperative that the secret keys used to perform the required security services are not revealed in any way.

The fact that secret keys are now embedded into a number of devices means that the hardware becomes an attractive target for hackers. For example if one could determine the keys which encrypt the digital television transmissions, then one could create decoders and sell them on the black market. On a more serious front if one could determine the keys which protect a number of stored value smart cards, which hold an electronic representation of cash, then one could essentially print money.

Since cryptographic algorithms themselves have been studied for a long time by a large number of experts, hackers are more likely to try to attack the hardware and system within which the cryptographic unit is housed. A particularly worrying attack has been developed in the last few years by P. Kocher and colleagues at *Cryptography Research Inc.*, see [6] and [7]. In these attacks a number of physical measurements of the cryptographic unit are made which include power consumption, computing time or EMF radiations. These measurements are made over a large number of encryption or signature operations and then,

Ç.K. Koç, D. Naccache, and C. Paar (Eds.): CHES 2001, LNCS 2162, pp. 28–38, 2001.

using statistical techniques, the secret key embedded inside the cryptographic unit is uncovered.

These attacks work because there is a correlation between the physical measurements taken at different points during the computation and the internal state of the processing device, which is itself related to the secret key. For example, when data is loaded from memory, the memory bus will have to carry the value of the data, which will take a certain amount of power depending on the data value. Since the load instruction always happens at the same time one can produce correlations between various runs of the application, eventually giving away the secret of the smart card. The three main techniques developed by Kocher et. al. are timing attacks, simple power analysis (SPA) and differential power analysis (DPA). It is DPA which provides the most powerful method of attack, which can be mounted using very cheap resources.

Following Kocher's papers a number of people have started to examine this problem and propose solutions, see [1], [2], [3] and [8]. Goubin and Patarin [3] give three possible general strategies to combat DPA type attacks:

1. Introduce random timing shifts so as to decorrelate the output traces on individual runs.
2. Replace critical assembler instructions with ones whose signature is hard to analyse, or reengineer the crucial circuitry which performs the arithmetic operations or memory transfers.
3. Make algorithmic changes to the cryptographic primitives under consideration.

In [9] May, Muller and Smart propose a method for introducing highly aggressive randomised execution into a conventional processor. They argue that this produces a great deal of temporal misalignment of traces, which can help defeat DPA. The methodology is to take standard techniques from the design of super-scalar architectures and replace parallel execution with random execution. They call this new processor architecture NDISC for *Non-Deterministic Instruction Stream Computer.*

This defence essentially combines all three of the above defences in that it adds considerable timing shifts to the instructions, it introduces circuitry which is hard to analyse and essentially makes algorithmic changes to the program "on the fly".

In this paper we expand on this philosophy by proposing a technique which allows the non-deterministic altering of the register to register or memory to register transfers. As such this produces a defence more akin to the second of the proposed defences above. This new defence can be implemented using a very small number of changes to the underlying processor and is completely transparent to the algorithm.

In super-scalar architectures, see [4], [5] or [10], it is standard practice to implement a form of register renaming. This allows the processor to schedule more instructions in parallel. If such a system was implemented in the NDISC processor then the instruction stream could be executed in an even greater randomised order. However, if the register renaming was performed in a randomised, rather than the standard deterministic manner, then one would obtain the extra effect of the power consumed by each register write operation would be different from one run to the next.

The concept of randomised register renaming can be implemented in a conventional processor to obtain some defence against DPA, but when implemented in an NDISC processor we expect the overall defence against DPA to be greatly enhanced. Hence, we first present an introduction to what an NDISC processor is.

2   NDISC Processors

In order to prevent attacks based on correlating data, we have designed a simple addition to standard processors that randomises instruction issuing [9]. Crucially, an attack works because two runs of the same program give comparable results; everything compares bar the data. By changing the data even slightly the attacker will get a knowingly different trace, and by correlating the traces, one builds a picture of what is happening inside the processor.

An NDISC processor removes correlation between runs, thereby making the attack much harder. A conventional processor executes a sequence of instructions deterministically; it may execute instructions *out-of-order*, but it will always execute instructions out-of-order in the same way. If the same program is run twice in a smart card, then the same instruction trace will be executed. By allowing the processor to at run time choose a random instruction ordering, we get multiple possible traces that are executed.

2.1   Random Issuing

In single pipeline processors a sequence of instructions is executed in the order in which they are fetched by the processor. There is a little out-of-order execution to help with branch prediction but this all occurs on a very small scale. On multiple pipeline processors there are a number of *execution units* through which independent instructions can be passed in parallel. For example, if a processor has a logic pipeline and an integer-arithmetic pipeline, then the following two instructions

```
ADD R0, R1, R1
XOR R4, R5, R5
```

may be executed in parallel in the two pipelines. One pipeline will execute the ADD, the other will execute the XOR.

Our idea is the following: like a superscalar we identify instructions that can be issued independently, but instead of using this information to issue instructions in parallel, we use this information to execute instructions out-of-order, where the processor makes a random choice as to issue order. We call this process *Instruction Descheduling*. This creates a level of non-determinism in the internal workings of the processor. This is illustrated in Figure 1.

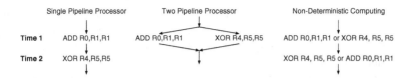

Fig. 1. Simple comparison of how a Non-deterministic processor executes two instructions as opposed to other processors

The reduction in the effectiveness of DPA results from the fact that the power trace from one run will be almost completely uncorrelated with the power trace from a second run, since on the two runs different execution sequences are used to produce the same result.

Instruction descheduling means that at run time the processor will select, at random, an instruction to execute, thereby randomising the instruction stream, and randomising the access pattern to memory caused by both data and instruction streams.

A full description of how an NDISC machine can be implemented is discussed in [9], we outline the NDISC architecture here. The set of instructions waiting to be executed is held in a block called an issue window. The random instruction selection unit randomly selects instructions from the issue window that are executable. An instruction is considered executable if it does not depend on any result that is not yet available, and the instruction does not overwrite any data that is still to be used by other instructions that are not yet executed, or instructions that are in execution in the pipeline.

The implementation of this closely follows the implementation of multi-issue processors. There is a block of logic that determines conflicts between instructions, resulting in a set of instructions that is executable. From this set we select an instruction at random. Given a random number generator, which will normally be constructed from a pseudo random number generator that is reseeded regularly with some entropy, we select one of the executable instructions and schedule it for execution.

3   Random Register Renaming

3.1   Basic Register Renaming

Register renaming is a common technique used to improve the performance of processors. Renaming works by defining a set of virtual register identifiers (which are used in the instruction set of the processors) and a set of physical registers (which are used in the execution unit). At any moment in time, each virtual register identifier is associated uniquely with a physical register identifier.

This binding is unique at any time, but the strength of renaming is that it changes with time. Any time that a virtual register is overwritten, the binding between the virtual and physical register can be severed, and a fresh physical register can be assigned to the virtual register. The reason that this increases performance in a standard processor is that this physical register can be used immediately for storing new values, whereas the old physical register can still hold values that are used by instructions which are still in execution. This allows out of order parallel execution.

As an example, consider the following bit of code which implements the two assignments A=B ; C=D ;:

```
LOAD     B, R0
STORE    R0, A
LOAD     D, R0      ; R0 is overwritten
STORE    R0, C
```

Upon execution of the code the third instruction will overwrite the value of register R0 with the value of D. This instruction can only be executed if the previous store instruction has been completed. If the registers are renamed so that we use R1 instead of R0, we would get the following code:

```
LOAD     B, R0
STORE    R0, A
LOAD     D, R1      ; R1 is overwritten
STORE    R1, C
```

In this code segment the third line of code can be executed in parallel with the first two, speeding up the processor. Static register allocation (by the compiler) does not achieve the same effect as register renaming for two reasons. First with register renaming one needs less bits in the instruction set to encode registers. Second, register renaming works at run time; register assignments are based on which instructions are in progress, and which are waiting for execution.

3.2   Random Register Renaming

We employ *Random Register Renaming* in order to weaken a DPA attack. Our observation is that a large fraction of power trace is produced by overwriting register values. Each time a value of a register is overwritten, the power consumption is related to the number of bits that are flipped. We are going to rename registers non deterministically; that way, any time that a register is overwritten, it overwrites a non predetermined value, randomising the power trace.

As an example, consider the following code:

```
LOAD   B,R0
STORE  R0,A
LOAD   D,R0
STORE  R0,C
```

Where we suppose that we have just one virtual register identifier (R0) and we have two physical registers (Reg0, Reg1). When this piece of code is executed there will be four different ways to execute it:

```
LOAD  B,Reg0      LOAD  B,Reg0      LOAD  B,Reg1      LOAD  B,Reg1
```

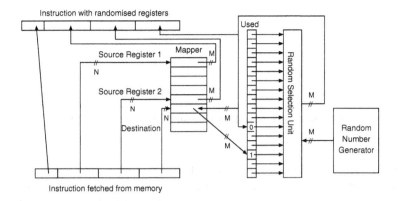

Fig. 2. Random register renaming for simple processor

```
STORE Reg0,A      STORE Reg0,A      STORE Reg1,A      STORE Reg1,A
LOAD  D,Reg0      LOAD  D,Reg1      LOAD  D,Reg0      LOAD  D,Reg1
STORE Reg0,C      STORE Reg1,C      STORE Reg0,C      STORE Reg1,C
```

Each of these execution traces has its own individual power-trace. Indeed, for longer instruction sequences the number of possible traces grows exponentially, and combined with NDISC execution [9], we can attain high levels of protection.

4   Implementation

4.1   Basic Implementation

In order to implement random register renaming we distinguish between virtual register identifiers (these are the registers as specified by the instruction set), and physical registers (which are the ones used by the processor). We assume that the number of physical registers is greater or equal to the number of virtual register identifiers. In particular we assume that there are 2^V virtual register identifiers and 2^P physical registers, where P is larger than V.

An instruction is fetched into the processor and preprocessed to rename its registers. The registers are renamed using a Virtual to Physical mapping table. This process is illustrated in Figure 2. The register mapper maintains a mapping from virtual identifiers to physical registers, this can be seen as an array of register values. A series of bits called **used** maintains whether a physical register is at present in use.

Each instruction has a number source and destination operands. In most instructions these operands are virtual register identifiers. On an instruction prefetch, the virtual register identifiers of the source operands are mapped onto physical registers using the virtual-to-physical mapper. This is done by using the virtual register number as an index in the mapping table, and thus locating a physical register number.

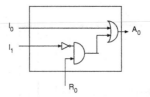

Fig. 3. Selecting a random register from a set of 2 (R-box^0)

The physical register for the destination operand is selected from the set of available free physical registers using a run time calculated random value as shown in the next section. The virtual register identifier of the destination operand was mapped onto another physical register. This physical register is now marked as free. The physical register that has been selected as the destination operand is marked as used and the the mapping table is updated associating the randomly selected physical register with the virtual identifier of the destination operand. Note that in a pipelined processor the register will only be marked free later; this is common practice in register renaming hardware. When source and destination registers have been mapped, the remapped instruction can be passed to the issue mechanism.

4.2   Selecting a Random Register from a Set

It is essential that in a single clock cycle we extract a free register. Generating a random number in a clock cycle is not difficult, but we must only pick from the set of *free* registers. For this purpose, we have devised a random selection unit. The random selection unit is a tree structure. Its simplest form consists of a single "R-box^0" selecting one random element from a set of 2, shown in Figure 3.

This box has two inputs I_0 and I_1 which denote whether register 0 and register 1 are currently in use, a random input bit R_0, and an output-bit A_0 pointing to the randomly selected free register. If I_0 and I_1 are both zero (i.e., both registers are free), then the random bit determines whether the output is zero or one. If one of the registers is not free, then the output is fixed to point to the other register.

We now construct a tree of AND-gates, AND-ing the used-bits of each register as shown in Figure 4. The output of each of the AND gates is '0' if there is at least one free register in the set of registers covered by that AND gate, and '1' if there are no free registers in that set. So, the output of the left-hand top-level AND gate is '0' if there is at least one free register in the lower half of the registers. The output of the right-hand top-level AND gate is '0' if there is at least one free register in the higher half of the registers. We use R-box^0 to determine which of those two halves of the register set we are going to pick a register from.

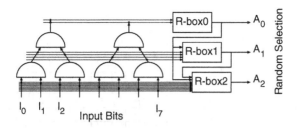

Fig. 4. Tree to reduce free set

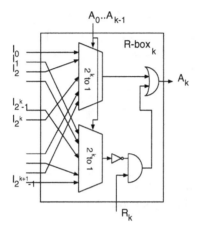

Fig. 5. General R-box

At the next level down in the tree we have outputs of four AND gates, which outputs state whether there are free registers in each of the four quarters of the register bank. R-box^0 has determined whether the free register is picked from the top or the bottom half, and R-box^1 is going to decide which of the two quarters to use.

We generalise R-box^1, and R-box^k from R-box^0 to have 2^{k+1} inputs $I_0, \ldots,$ $I_{2^{k+1}}$, k input-address bits $A_0, \ldots, A_{k-1}$ and one output bit A_k, as shown in Figure 5. This R-box selects a value for A_k so that bit $I_{A_0,\ldots,A_k}$ is zero. The selection is based on the assumption that all the higher address bits ($A_0 \ldots A_k$, the inputs provided by previous R-boxes) have been selected before in such a way that there is an empty register available. The selection process works by selecting two bits from the set $I_0, \ldots, I_{2^{k+1}}$ using $A_0 \ldots A_{k-1}$, and subsequently uses the random bit to decide which of those two bits to select. This gives us one more address bit, which results in the picking of a single input $I_{A_0,\ldots,A_k}$.

This architecture works since we can guarantee to have at least one physical register free at any point in the program. This solution selects a random bit which is set to zero in a constant time; at the cost of the random selection being skewed. In particular, if all but one of the bits in one half of the set are one,

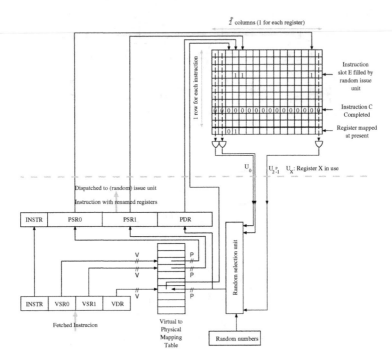

Fig. 6. Register renaming in conjunction with (non deterministic) out of order execution

than this solution will favour that solution with a 50% probability. This can be improved by performing a random rotation on the input bits prior to selecting a random bit.

4.3   Random Register Renaming in a Non Deterministic Processor

Random register renaming can be applied to any processor. For a standard microprocessor we have shown that random register renaming requires very little alteration to the standard renaming unit found in modern super-scalars. When attaching this unit to a NDISC processor [9], one needs to be more careful. For NDISC processors we determine the set of free registers as shown in Figure 6. A matrix of size $I \times 2^P$ (where I is the issue window size) maintains for each instruction in the issue window which registers that instruction uses. A one in element (i, p) in the matrix indicates that register p will be used by instruction i. A zero in element (i, p) indicates that register p will not be used by instruction i. When an instruction is stored in location E of the issue buffer, the bits in row E associated with its source and destination registers are set to one. An extra row at the bottom of the matrix keeps track of which registers are currently mapped and could, therefore, be used by future instructions.

When an instruction C has been dispatched and completed, the bits for row C are reset to zero (an optimisation would be to reset the source registers when the source registers have been read by the execution unit, and to reset the destination register when the results value has been written). The logical OR of all bits in a column r determines whether a register r is in use, a one value indicating that the register is used. These values are used by the renaming unit in order to determine which register to use in order to remap a destination register, as in the previous example of a standard processor.

5   Conclusion and Future Work

We have shown how one can use ideas from super-scalar architectures to produce a randomised *non-deterministic* processor. This idea essentially allows a single instruction stream to correspond to one of an exponential number of possibly executed programs, all of which produce the same output.

In the case of random register renaming used on its own the actual executed program is in the same program sequence but with the source and destination registers randomly altered. In the case of using both random register renaming and the ideas in [9] we obtain not only a program whose registers have been randomly reassigned, but the program sequence is now randomised as well. Since attacks such as differential power analysis rely on the correlation of data across many execution runs of the same program, the idea of random register renaming can help to defeat such attacks.

Further research still needs to be carried out, yet we feel that the proposed solution to differential power analysis gives a number of advantages; such as the fact that program code does not need to be modified and neither speed nor power consumption are compromised. In the near future we aim to produce a demonstration version of an the NDISC processor with the random register renaming included in the main execution unit. This demonstration will then be tested for resistance to DPA on a number of cryptographic algorithms.

References

1. S. Chari, C.S. Jutla, J.R. Rao and P. Rohatgi. Towards sound approaches to counteract power-analysis attacks. *Advances in Cryptology, CRYPTO '99*, Springer LNCS 1666, 398–412, 1999.
2. S. Chari, C.S. Jutla, J.R. Rao and P. Rohatgi. A cautionary note regarding evaluation of AES candidates on Smart-Cards. *Second Advanced Encryption Standard Candidate Conference*, Rome March 1999.
3. L. Goubin and J. Patarin. DES and differential power analysis. The "duplication method". *Cryptographic Hardware and Embedded Systems*, Springer LNCS 1717, 158–172, 1999.
4. J.L. Hennessy and D.A. Patterson. *Computer architecture: a quantitative approach.* Morgan Kaufmann Publishers, Palo Alto, California, 1990.
5. N. P. Jouppi and D. W. Wall. *Available instruction-level parallelism for super-scalar and super-pipelined machines.* ASPLOS-III, 272–282, 1989.

6. P. Kocher. Timing attacks on implementations of Diffie-Hellman, RSA, DSS and other systems. *Advances in Cryptology, CRYPTO '96*, Springer LNCS 1109, 104–113, 1996.

7. P. Kocher, J. Jaffe and B. Jun. Differential Power Analysis. *Advances in Cryptology, CRYPTO '99*, Springer LNCS 1666, 388–397, 1999.

8. O. Kömmerling and M. Kuhn. Design Principles for Tamper-Resistant Smartcard Processors. *USENIX Workshop on Smartcard Technology*, Chicago, Illinois, USA, May 10-11, 1999.

9. D. May, H. Muller and N.P. Smart Non-Deterministic Processors To appear *ACISP 2001*, Springer Verlag, LNCS, July 2001.

10. D Sima, T Foutain and P Kacsuk. *Advanced Computer Architectures*. Addison Wesley, 1997.

Randomized Addition-Subtraction Chains as a Countermeasure against Power Attacks

Elisabeth Oswald and Manfred Aigner

Institute for Applied Information Processing and Communications
Graz University of Technology, Inffeldgasse 16a, A-8010 Graz, Austria
{Elisabeth.Oswald,Manfred.Aigner}@iaik.at

Abstract. Power Analysis attacks on elliptic curve cryptosystems and various countermeasures against them, have been first discussed by Coron ([6]). All proposed countermeasures are based on the randomization or blinding of the inputparameters of the binary algorithm. We propose a countermeasure that randomizes the binary algorithm itself. Our algorithm needs approximately 9% more additions than the ordinary binary algorithm, but makes power analysis attacks really difficult.

Keywords: Power Analysis, Elliptic Curve Cryptosystems

1   Introduction

Elliptic curve cryptosystems (ECC) have attracted much attention since they were first proposed in 1985 by Miller [24] and Koblitz [15]. The underlying discrete logarithm problem seems to be much harder than in other groups. Today, no subexponential-time algorithm is known for this problem in the case of non-supersingular curves. This results in much shorter keylengths for ECC, which makes those cryptosystems especially attractive for hardware implementations for instance on smartcards. One must consider therefore not only mathematical attacks on ECC, but also attacks that exploit weaknesses in the implementation.

In the last years, attacks have been published that use leaked side-channel-information such as the power consumption or timing measurement. These methods are all passive, this means that an attacker just needs to monitor the cryptographic device. The most popular method today, the *differential power analysis* (DPA) was introduced 1998 by Cryptography Research. DPA exploits the information drawn from the leakage of power consumption. First, mostly applied to symmetric cryptosystems, DPA was then applied successfully on public key cryptosystems, see [6], [12] and [20]. Power analysis is a very strong attack. For a successful attack on a straightforward DES implementation only a few hundred measurements are needed. Also the technical effort is comparatively small. One just needs a digital sampling oscilloscope with an appropriate sampling rate for the power measurements, and a standard PC to process the obtained measurement data. The processing of the data itself is also very easy and it is not necessary to understand the concept of the attack to perform it successfully.

Ç.K. Koç, D. Naccache, and C. Paar (Eds.): CHES 2001, LNCS 2162, pp. 39–50, 2001.
© Springer-Verlag Berlin Heidelberg 2001

To make a long story short, this attack can be mounted by not only experienced cryptanalysts, but by everyone! This fact makes it even more necessary to counteract this attack for both private and public key cryptosystems.

In this paper we deal exclusively with elliptic curve cryptosystems. The countermeasures that were proposed in the before mentioned articles, rely on randomizing or blinding the parameters (the elliptic curve point P and the secret key k) of the binary algorithm. In our article we present a countermeasure based on randomizing the binary algorithm itself. Our method does not only provide security against power attacks, but also does not slow down the encryption algorithm, or require the storage of additional elliptic curve parameters (for instance the number of points on the curve) as other methods do.

The paper is organized as follows. Considering the binary algorithm, we review the concept of power analysis in section 2. In section 3 we explain the method of addition-subtraction chains as a speedup for the standard binary algorithm. Finally we present our randomization method on the grounds of these addition-subtraction chains.

2   Elliptic Curve Cryptosystems, the Binary Algorithm and Power Attacks

Some public key cryptosystems require the computation of a modular exponentiation ($P = M^k \mod p$) or a scalar multiplication ($P = kM$). This is usually done by the binary algorithm $binalg(P, M, k)$ which is sketched (in its bottom-up version) in the following figure:

binalg(P,M,k)
$Q = M$
if $k_0 = 1$ then $P = M$ else $P = 0$
for $i = 1$ to $n - 1$
$\quad Q = Q * Q$
$\quad$ if ($k_i == 1$) then
$\qquad P = P * Q$
return P

For validity and explanation see [14]. The $*$ denotes hereby an appropriate operation, which can be the multiplication for instance, but also the addition.

2.1   ECC Basics

Elliptic curve cryptosystems make use of the binary algorithm for the computation of the scalar point multiplication. An elliptic curve over a field K, short $E(K)$, is defined as a nonsingular homogeneous cubic polynomial $F(x_0, x_1, x_2) \in K[x_0, x_1, x_2]$, provided there is at least one rational point on $E(K)$ [13]. The set of rational points can be made into an abelian group in a natural way. If $P_1, P_2 \in E(K)$, then the line connecting both points intersects the elliptic curve in a third point P_3. Further, one calls the third point of intersection of the line connecting 0 (for example) and P_3 with $E(K)$, the sum of P_1 and P_2. For char $K \neq 2, 3$ every elliptic curve can be written as

$$x_0 x_2^2 = x_1^3 - A x_0^2 x_1 - B x_0^3, \qquad A, B, \in K. \tag{1}$$

This curve has only one point at infinity, which is the identity element of the group. With the transformation $x = x_1/x_0$ and $y = x_2/x_0$, $x_0 \neq 0$, one gets the equation for an elliptic curve in affine coordinates :

$$y^2 = x^3 - Ax - B. \tag{2}$$

The point at infinity is lying infinitely far off in the direction of the y axis. Thus the inverse of a point $P = (x, y) \neq \mathcal{O}$ is $-P = (x, -y)$. Formulas for the point addition and point duplication on an elliptic curve defined over a finite field can be found for example in [5]. The following tables give a brief overview of the different costs of the two operations. I denotes the inversion, M the multiplication and S the squaring in K. Conversion from projective to affine coordinates is not taken into account. Also more efficient projective representations are not included in the tables, see therefore again [5].

Characteristic $K > 3$		
Operation	Coordinates	
	affine	projective
Point addition	1I+3M	16M
Point doubling	1I+4M	10M

Characteristic $K = 2$		
Operation	Coordinates	
	affine	projective
Point addition	1I+2M+1S	15M+5S
Point doubling	1I+2M+1S	5M+5S

Remark 1. In a finite field of characteristic 2, the inverse of an elliptic curve point $P = (x, y)$ is given as $-P = (x, x + y)$. Having that an addition of two elements is calculated by bit by bit Xor, we get the inverse of an elliptic curve point for free again.

2.2   Power Analysis

Power analysis attacks use the fact that the instantaneous power consumption of a hardware device is related to the instantaneous computed instructions and the manipulated data. An unskilled implementation of an elliptic curve point duplication and an elliptic curve point addition, can therefore easily be used to mount a simple power attack (or *simple power analysis*, short SPA). An adversary just needs to monitor the devices power consumption and identify the parts of the power trace that correspond to the additions and duplications. This gives trivially the secret key. It is clear that in order to be SPA resistant, one must try to prevent data depending branches, as sketched in algorithm $binalg'(P, M, k)$. Note, that the computational effort is much higher than in the standard binary algorithm.

binalg'(P,M,k)
$P = 1, Q = M$
for $i = 0$ to $n - 1$
$\quad P[0] = P$
$\quad P[1] = P * Q$
$\quad Q = Q * Q$
$\quad P = P[k_i]$
return P

Differential power analysis uses more sophisticated, statistical techniques to attack the secret key. One power analysis variant is to partition the measurements in two (or more) different sets by some oracle (for instance the guess of a secret key bit) and then look if these two sets are statistically different. This will only be the case if the oracle was correct and thus reveal some parts of the key. Since statistical difference is usually computed by the *distance−of−mean−test*, which basically compares the means of two distributions, we will refer to this method as the *mean method* in subsequent sections. The second method computes the covariance between the measurements and the oracle. Also, only a correct oracle can correlate to the measurements (we will refer to this as the *correlation method*). We give some examples to clarify this description.

Example 1 (Single-Exponent, Multiple-Data Attack). The SEMD attack [20] compares the power signal of an encryption operation using a known parameter (public key) to a power signal using an unknown parameter (secret key). The attacker can learn where the two signals differ and thus learn the unknown (secret) parameter. Due to noise components, direct comparisons of power signals are unreliable, thus DPA techniques are applied. One computes n random values with the secret and the known parameter. The average signals are calculated and subtracted as in the *mean method* . The portions of the DPA signal that depend on the (random) data will be wiped out by the averaging and subtraction. The portion of the DPA signal that is dependent on the parameter will average out to two different values depending on the performed operation. The portions in the DPA signal that are ≈ 0 are data dependent or the operations in the binary algorithm agree. The other portions indicate that the operations in the binary algorithm differ.

This attack also can be seen as an extension of a SPA attack, and therefore be prevented by the modification sketched in $binalg'(P, M, k)$. Note that this variant does not make much assumptions on the cryptographic device. More sophisticated versions, that make more assumptions can be found in [20].

Example 2 (Correlation Attack). When using algorithm *binalg'* the *mean method* will be not successful because there is no difference in the sequence of instructions. But if one knows the representation of the computed points one can again mount a successful attack (which has been shown in [6]). At step i, the processed point depends only on the first bits $k_0 \ldots k_{i-1}$ of the secret parameter k. When $P[i]$ is processed, power consumption is correlated to the bits of $P[i]$.

No correlation will be observed if the point is not computed. The value of the least significant bit of k can be learned by calculating the correlation between the power consumption and any specific bit of $2M$. As one can see in algorithm binalg' the only key dependent operation in the for-loop is whether the value of $P[1]$ or $P[0]$ is copied to P. If $k_0 = 0$, the value of $P[0]$ (which is 1 in this case) remains in P and therefore a correlation between $2M$ and the power consumption in the subsequent path of the for-loop must be observed, otherwise if $k_0 = 1$, the value of $P[1]$ (which is M in this case) will be copied to P and no correlation between $2M$ and the power consumption of the computation of $P[1]$ in the subsequent path in the for-loop will be observed. The other bits can be recursively recovered in the same way.

Coron also shows in [6] how to extend the *correlation method* to any scalar multiplication algorithm executed in constant time with a constant addition-subtraction chain.

2.3   Countermeasures

Basically all proposed countermeasures suggest blinding or randomizing the secret parameters. When computing $P = kM$ one has the possibility to

- **randomize (blind) k:** One needs to know the number of points $\#E(K)$ on the elliptic curve. Then one chooses a random number r and calculates $k' = k + r * \#E(K)$. Obviously $P = kM = k'M$, because of $\#E(K) * M = \mathcal{O}$. For this approach one has to store an additional parameter of the elliptic curve, on the cryptographic device, which is often not desirable. The second disadvantage is that depending on the bitlength of $r * \#E(K)$, the effective keylength may increase.
- **blind M :** A point is blinded by adding a secret random point R for which one knows $S = kR$. Scalar multiplication is done by calculating $k(R + M)$ and subtracting S to get $P = kM$. The points R and S can be stored inside the cryptographic device and updated for each new execution as follows: $R = (-1)^b 2R$ and $S = (-1)^b 2S$, where b is a random bit. Note that there must be stored two additional points inside the device, which is also often not desirable.
- **randomize M:** Projective coordinates can be used to avoid the inversions as well as for randomization. Because of the fact that

$$(X, Y, Z) = (\lambda X, \lambda Y, \lambda Z), \quad \forall \lambda \neq 0$$

one can choose for each new execution another random λ. As one can see, this variant relies on the usage of projective coordinates instead of affine coordinates.

All these countermeasures require to store additional parameters or to make additional operations.

3 Speeding Up the Binary Algorithm

As pointed out in section 2, an elliptic curve cryptosystem needs to efficiently compute the scalar multiplicative of an elliptic curve point. The simplest efficient method, the binary algorithm, is also the oldest. A good survey on (more recent) methods is [10]. Most of these methods try to give an answer to the question, how to find the shortest addition chain. An *addition chain* for an integer k is a list of positive integers $a_1 = 1, a_2, \ldots, a_l = k$, such that for each $i > 1$, there is some j and m, with $1 \leq j \leq m < i$ and $a_i = a_j + a_m$. Thus, if one has an addition chain with length l, one can compute $k * P$ with l additions. Finding the best addition chain is impractical, but there are several methods for finding near-optimal ones. With elliptic curves one has the possibility to use addition-subtraction chains, because the computation of the inverse of a point has no cost. Morain and Olivos discuss in [23] two algorithms that use addition-subtraction chains. We describe their approach in the two subsequent sections.

3.1 First Algorithm

The idea comes from the observation that long chains of 1's in the binary representation of k are better treated by a subtraction. For instance if one calculates $15 * P$ like
$$15 * P = 16 * P - P = 2(2(2(2P))) - P,$$
one has to perform less operations than in the standard binary algorithm. So the enhancement is to replace a block of at least two 1's in the binary representation of k, by a block of 0's and a $-1 : 1^a \mapsto 10^{a-1} - 1$. Automaton 1 in Figure 1 represents this idea. Morain and Olivos state that the expected gain of this version is about 8.33%.

3.2 Second Algorithm

The idea is to treat isolated 0's inside a block of 1's. Using the map of the first algorithm it is
$$1^a 01^b \mapsto 10^{a-1} - 110^{b-1} - 1.$$
Since $-2 + 1 = -1$ we can write -11 as $0 - 1$ and therefore
$$1^a 01^b \mapsto 10^a - 10^{b-1} - 1.$$

In automaton 2, the state 110 takes this modification into account. In both figures the input path is marked by a distinct arrow, and the output paths are marked by an additional bar. Intermediate states are drawn as circles, and transitions between these intermediate states are represented as arrows. The initial conditions for the automatons are $P = 0$ and $Q = M$. An iterative version of this algorithm can be found in [23]. The expected gain for this variant is about 11.11%.

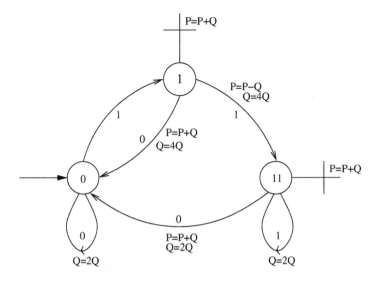

Fig. 1. Automaton 1

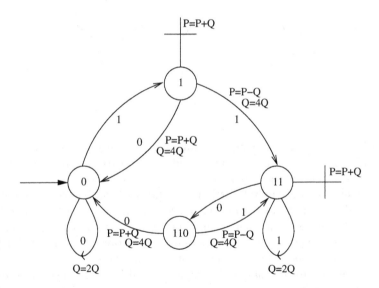

Fig. 2. Automaton 2

4   The New Countermeasure

In contrary to the previously described countermeasures which were introduced by Coron in [6], we intend to randomize the binary algorithm itself. This can be easily done by inserting a random decision in the two algorithms in section

3.1 and 3.2. For example, if we are in state 1 we draw a random variable e. If $e = 0$ we take the path of algorithm 1, else we proceed as in the standard binary algorithm. The finite automaton in figure 3 shows the randomized algorithm according to this idea.

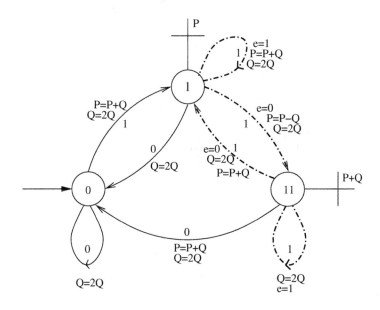

Fig. 3. Randomized Automaton 1

In order to make SPA attacks more difficult, we changed all multipliers so that always only one double or one double and one add (or subtract) is necessary. Note, that the bits of the binary representation don't correspond directly to doubles (resp. adds) anymore! For both, 1 and 0 in the binary representation, there is one path in the algorithm where, for instance, the double operation is performed. In the same manner we modified finite automaton 2 (see figure 4). In both figures, the paths that are randomized are drawn dash-dotted for better visibility. Again, in both figures the input path is marked by a distinct arrow, and the output paths are marked by an additional bar. Intermediate states are represented by circles, and transitions are represented as arrows between them. The initial conditions are again $P = 0$ and $Q = M$. For the sake of completeness we give an iterative algorithm implementing figure 4.

4.1   Analysis of the Randomized Algorithms

As noted before, the binary representation does not correspond directly to the performed operations anymore. A second observation is that due to the fact,

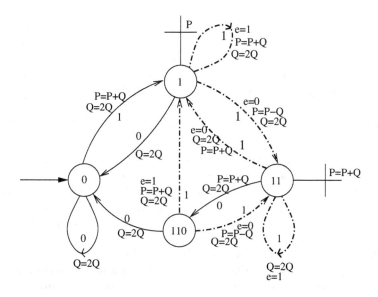

Fig. 4. Randomized Automaton 2

```
randomized_version_automaton2(k,M) {
      state=0;P=0;Q=M;
      while (k>0) {
        if ((k&1) == 0) {
          if (state == 11) P = P+Q;
          state=0;Q = 2*Q;
        }
        if ((k&1) == 1) {
          switch (state) {
              case 1: e=rand();
                      if (e==1) P= P+Q;
                          else P = P-Q and state=3;
                      Q = 2*Q;
              case 11: e = rand();Q = 2*Q;
                          if (e==0) P = P+Q and state=1;
              case 0: P = P+Q;Q=2*Q;state=1;
          }
        }k >>=1;
      }
      if (state==11) {P = P+Q;}
      return P;
}
```

Fig. 5. Iterative Version of the Randomized Automaton 2

that $-P(x, y) = P(x, -y)$ e.g. $-P(x, y) = P(x, x + y)$(the add and subtract operations are basically the same), they aren't distinguishable in the power trace. The difference of add (subtract) and double depends on the underlying number field, and the used coordinates. For instance, as listed in the table in section 2.1, in $GF(2^m)$ with affine coordinates, for both add and double operation, 1 inversion, 2 multiplications and 1 squaring is needed. We consider now some possible scenarios for a power attack :

- **SPA case :** Suppose one has an implementation were the distinction between double and add (subtract) is possible with a single measurement (this could be the case when working with projective coordinates). It would be possible to identify a block of 0's at the beginning of the algorithm. Also, blocks of 0's result more likely in consecutive doubles than blocks of 1's. Basically there are more likely binary representation than others, and this could be used to identify the correct key. But that this is not as easy as mounting an SPA attack on the standard binary algorithm.
- **DPA case :** Let us assume now, that we don't have such a dumb implementation, and therefore the difference between a double and an add (or a subtract) operation is not visible with only one power measurement. Every time the algorithm is performed, it takes due to the randomization a different path. Therefore the sequence of doubles, adds, and subtracts is slightly different. If the random numbers are close to uniform, this makes an attack like the mean method infeasible. But also the correlation method does not work anymore. Because of the randomization, the intermediate values that are attacked, are computed at different times, or are sometimes not even calculated. This washes out the DPA bias signal.

The performance of the randomized algorithms is close to the standard binary algorithm. The following table shows the percentage of additional operations (additions and subtractions) in comparison with the ordinary binary algorithm for various key lengths (which were chosen according to the commonly suggested field sizes). For this table we counted the number of additions and subtractions (the number of doublings is for both variants approximately the same) for several thousands of executions (for several values of k) of the algorithm given in figure 5. The table shows that the additional number of operations is almost independent of the keylength and is approximately 9%.

What can we say about the storage of additional parameters? The speedup in the article of Morain and Olivos uses the bottom-up variant of the binary algorithm, which requires the additional storage of one elliptic curve point. This is obviously a disadvantage. On the other hand, the proposed standard IEEE P1363a, includes this version of the binary algorithm. The other additional parameter which we have to store, is the random bit e.

5   Conclusion

We described an alternative approach for the development of countermeasures against power attacks. Our countermeasure does not depend on any input pa-

Table 1. Performance comparison

Bitlength	Additional operations (mean value)	Variance
112	9%	3%
128	10%	5%
160	9%	3%
192	8%	3%
224	8%	3%
236	7%	3%
384	9%	2%
521	9%	2%

rameters of the binary algorithm, but on the algorithm itself. We've analyzed its efficiency in preventing the mean and the correlation method, and its efficiency in performance. Fact is, that our method prevents recent power analysis attacks largely without the necessity to store large additional parameters or do any precomputations. One can also combine this countermeasure with the other suggested countermeasures to achieve a higher security level.

References

1. E. Biham, A. Shamir, *Power Analysis of the Key Scheduling of the AES Candidates* Second AES Candidate Conference, Rome, March 1999, pp 115-121.
2. S. Chari, Ch. Jutla, J. Rao, P. Rohatgi.*A Cautionary Note Regarding Evaluation of AES Candidates on Smart-Cards.* Second AES Candidate Conference, Rome, March 22-23,1999, pp 133-147.
3. S. Chari, Ch. Jutla, J. Rao, P. Rohatgi.*Towards Sound Approaches to Counteract Power-Analysis Attacks*, Proceedings of Advances in Cryptology-CRYPTO'99, Lecture Notes in Computer Science, vol. 1666, Springer, 1999, pp.398-412
4. C. Clavier, J.-S. Coron, N. Dabbous, *Differential Power Analysis in the presence of Hardware Countermeasures*, Proceedings of Workshop on Cryptographic Hardware and Embedded Systems (CHES 2000), Lecture Notes in Computer Science, vol. 1965, Springer, 2000, pp. 252-263
5. I. Blake, G. Seroussi, N. Smart, *Elliptic Curves in Cryptography*, London Mathematical Society, Lecture Notes Series 265, Cambridge Universtiy Press
6. J.-S. Coron, *Resistance against differential power analysis for elliptic curve cryptosystems*, Proceedings of Workshop on Cryptographic Hardware and Embedded Systems (CHES 1999), Lecture Notes in Computer Science, vol. 1717, Springer,1999, pp.292-302
7. J.-S. Coron, L. Goubin, *On Boolean and Arithmetic Masking against Differential Power Analysis*, Proceedings of Workshop on Cryptographic Hardware and Embedded Systems (CHES 2000), Lecture Notes in Computer Science, vol. 1965, Springer, 2000, pp. 231-237
8. J.-S. Coron, P. Kocher, D. Naccache, *Statistics and Secret Leackage*, to appear in Proceedings of Financial Cryptography, Springer-Verlag, February 2000
9. P. Fahn, P. Pearson. *IPA: A New Class of Power Attacks*, Proceedings of Workshop on Cryptographic Hardware and Embedded Systems (CHES 199), Lecture Notes in Computer Science, vol. 1717, Springer 1999

10. D. M. Gordon, *A survey of fast exponentiation methods.*, J. Algorithms, 27, pp. 129-146, 1998

11. L. Goubin, J. Patarin.*DES and Differential Power Analysis*. Proceedings of Workshop on Cryptographic Hardware and Embedded Systems (CHES 199), Lecture Notes in Computer Science, vol. 1717, Springer 1999, pp 158-172.

12. M. A. Hasan, *Power Analysis Attacks and Algorithmic Approaches to Their Countermeasures for Koblitz Cryptosystems*, Proceedings of Workshop on Cryptographic Hardware and Embedded Systems (CHES 2000), Lecture Notes in Computer Science, vol. 1965, Springer 2000, pp. 93-108

13. K.F. Ireland, M. Rosen, *A Classical Introduction to Modern Number Theory*, Graduate Texts in Mathematics, vol. 84, Springer-Verlag, Fifth printing, 1998

14. D. E. Knuth. *Seminumerical algorithms*. The Art of Computer Programming. T. II, Addison-Wesley.

15. N. Koblitz. *Elliptic Curve Cryptosystems*, Mathematics of Computation, vol. 48, 1987, pp.203-209

16. P. Kocher, J. Jaffe and B. Jun, *Differential Power Analysis*, Proceedings of Advances in Cryptology-CRYPTO'99, Springer 1999, pp. 388-397

17. R. Mayer-Sommer, *Smartly Analyzing the Simplicity and the Power of Simple Power Analysis on Smartcards*, Proceedings of Workshop on Cryptographic Hardware and Embedded Systems (CHES 2000), Lecture Notes in Computer Science, vol. 1965, Springer 2000, pp. 78-92

18. A. J. Menezes, *Elliptic Curve Public Key Cryptosystems*, Kluwer Academic Publishers, 1993

19. T.S. Messerges, E. A. Dabbish and R. H. Sloan, *Investigations of Power Analysis Attacks on Smartcards*, Proceedings of USENIX Workshop on Smartcard Technology, May 1999, pp. 151-61.

20. T.S. Messerges, E. A. Dabbish and R. H. Sloan, *Power Analysis Attacks of Modular Exponentiation in Smartcards*, Workshop on Cryptographic Hardware and Embedded Systems, Lecture Notes in Computer Science, vol. 1717, Springer 1999.

21. T. S. Messerges, *Using Second-Order Power Analysis to Attack DPA Resistant Software*, Proceedings of Workshop on Cryptographic Hardware and Embedded Systems (CHES 2000), Lecture Notes in Computer Science, vol. 1965, Springer 2000, pp. 238-251

22. A. Shamir,*Protecting Smart Cards from Passive Power Analysis with Detached Power Supplies*, Proceedings of Workshop on Cryptographic Hardware and Embedded Systems (CHES 2000), Lecture Notes in Computer Science, vol. 1965, Springer 2000, pp. 71-77

23. F. Morain, J. Olivos. *Speeding up the computation on an elliptic curve using addition-subtraction chains*, Inform. Theory Appl. 24 (1990), 531-543.

24. V. S. Miller. *Use of Elliptic Curves in Cryptography*, Proceedings of Crypto 85, Lecture Notes in Computer Science 218, Springer, 1986, pp. 417-426

25. N. Weste and K. Eshraghian, *Principles of CMOS VLSI Design*, Addison-Wesley Publishing Company, 1993.

Architectural Optimization for a 1.82Gbits/sec VLSI Implementation of the AES Rijndael Algorithm

Henry Kuo, Ingrid Verbauwhede

Electrical Engineering Department, University of California Los Angeles.
henrykuo@ee.ucla.edu ingrid@ee.ucla.edu

Abstract. This paper discusses the architectural optimizations for a special purpose ASIC processor that implements the AES Rijndael Algorithm. In October 2000 the NIST chose Rijndael as the new Advanced Encryption Standard (AES). The algorithm has variable key length and block length between 128, 192, or 256 bits. VLSI architectural optimizations such as parallelism and distributed memory are discussed, and several hardware design techniques are employed to increase performance and reduce area consumption. The hardware architecture is described using Verilog XL and synthesized by Synopsys with a 0.18μm standard cell library. Results show that with a design of 173,000 gates, data encryption can be done at a rate of 1.82 Gbits/sec.

1 Introduction

Although many encryption algorithms can be relatively efficiently implemented in software on general-purpose or embedded processors, there is still a need for special purpose cryptographic processors.

First of all, high throughput applications, such as the encryption of the physical layer of Internet traffic, require an ASIC that does not affect the data throughput. For example, software implementation of the Rijndael algorithm on a Pentium 200 Pro yields a throughput of around 100 Mbits/sec [1], which is too slow for high-end Internet routers.

Moreover, in terms of mobile application like cellular phones, PDA's, etc., software implementation on general-purpose processors consumes much more power than special purpose ASIC's do. Last of all, it is often the case that applications require the encryption logic be physically isolated from the rest of the system, so that the encryption can be secured more easily. In this case a hardware accelerator is a more suitable solution as well.

The AES Rijndael algorithm was chosen in October 2000 and is expected to replace the DES and Triple DES because of its enhanced security levels [2]. In this paper, VLSI optimizations of the Rijndael algorithm are discussed and several hardware design modifications and techniques are used, such as memory sharing and parallelism. The circuits are synthesized using a 0.18μm CMOS standard cell library, and estimations are done on timing and gate counts.

Ç.K. Koç, D. Naccache, and C. Paar (Eds.): CHES 2001, LNCS 2162, pp. 51–64, 2001.

In the following sections, we will briefly discuss the algorithm flow, followed by detailed hardware implementations and techniques. After that we will present the simulation results, followed by future developments and conclusions.

2 Rijndael: Algorithm Flows

The main flow of the algorithm, as shown in Fig. 1, uses many lookup tables and XOR operations. The algorithm accepts blocks of size 128, 192, or 256 bits. Independently, the key length can be 128, 192, or 256 bits as well. All encryptions are done in a certain number of rounds, which varies between 10, 12, and 14, and it depends on the size of the block length and the key length chosen. An encryption module is used to generate all the intermediate encryption data, and a separate key-scheduling module is used to generate all the sub-round keys from the initial key.

For encryption, it can be divided into four blocks: Key Addition, Shift Row, Mix Column, and Substitution. The Key Addition module is byte XOR between the round key and the encryption data. The Shift Row and the Substitution modules involve mainly table lookups. Last of all, the Mix Column module composes of XOR operations. The algorithm flow is shown in Fig. 1. The Key Scheduling module is totally independent of the encryption module, and it also involves table lookups and XOR operations.

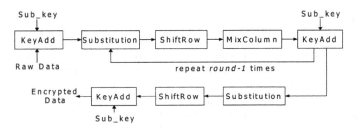

Fig. 1. Algorithm Flows.

There are a total of three sets of tables used by key scheduling and encryption. One of them is 256 bytes; one of them contains 30 bytes; the remaining one has 24 bytes of entries.

3 Architecture Optimizations

The initial specification of the Rijndael algorithm was implemented mainly in software. Although the algorithm is designed with hardware implementation in mind, the transition from software to hardware involves modifications. The main challenge in the hardware implementation is to maximize the encryption throughput while minimizing the area consumption at the same time. Maximizing the throughput will minimize the critical paths and solve the memory access conflicts. As shown in Fig. 2

[3], there are a lot of regularities in the design of Rijndael algorithm. Therefore, with careful VLSI design, the critical path as well as the overall area can be minimized.

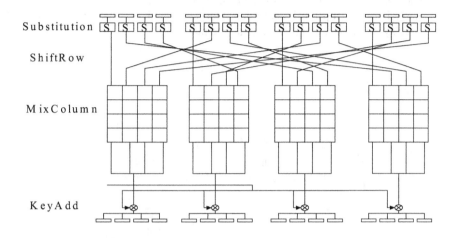

Fig. 2. 2D diagram illustrating data flow, adapted from [3].

3.1 Basic Architecture Decisions

In our implementation of the algorithm, there is only hardware for one encryption round and we re-use the same piece of hardware to complete the whole encryption process. While this implementation can help conserve most area, the main reason for this design is to incorporate different kinds of feedback modes that are currently available in the industry. Although NIST is currently initiating another new counter mode of operation, the common mode of operations used today do not allow pipelining of encryption modules. Therefore having two or more encryption modules in the processor is not the most flexible design.

Besides having hardware for one encryption round, we also designed the processor to complete one encryption round in one clock cycle. This design is very important, for example, in high throughput systems, because it ensures that the design is run at the lowest clock frequency possible with the same throughput. The drawback of this design is that we have to duplicate some of the modules, especially lookup tables, in order to finish all the required operations in one clock cycle for one encryption round.

The third basic architecture decision we made was the key scheduling. There are two ways for generating the round keys for encryption, either by generating all the sub-keys beforehand and storing them in a buffer, or generating all the sub-keys on the fly in parallel with the encryption module.

Since buffer storage could take up substantial amount of space, we decided to generate the sub-keys on the fly during encryption. Therefore we implemented the hardware required to generate one set of sub-key and re-use it for calculating all the sub-keys, and at the same time also use one clock cycle for one sub-key generation.

3.2 System Setup

The general block diagram is shown in Fig. 3. Besides the Encryption and Key Scheduling modules, there are one controller for the input channel, one controller for the output channel, and a top-level controller interfacing with the user modules. There is only one system clock, and it is fed to all the modules.

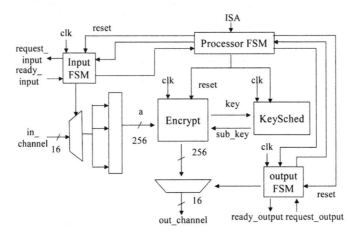

Fig. 3. Overall block diagram.

Both the input and output channels are 16 bits wide. Therefore, in order to read in the whole cipher or key, a handshaking protocol is used. The top-level controller takes in a 4-bit instruction and returns a ready signal when it is idle. In order to allow both 128, 192, and 256 bits for Encryption and Key Scheduling, the internal data path are all 256 bits. The user has the ability to set the block length and the key length using specific instructions, and the input and output controller will automatically adjust the input and output sequences.

Specifically, pipelining and unrolling are not implemented in the system. As a result, there is only one module for Encryption and one module for Key Scheduling, and these modules are reused to generate all the intermediate data and key. This design should be the most area efficient with the best module utilization.

As shown in table 1, the instructions are four bits long. Feedback modes (1110 and 0110) take in the raw data and encrypt the data for one thousand times using OFB feedback mode, and this is used for calculating the maximum operating frequency of the core during tests. Decryption is not implemented in the current design since it requires a separate datapath. Nonetheless, in order to implement decryption, either the generation of the entire sub round-keys has to be done beforehand, or there needs to be another datapath generating the inverse process of Key Scheduling. The first case requires an additional 3584 register storage while the second method requires more routing, both result in much larger area.

Table 1. Instruction sets used for this processor.

Reset		0000
Set Block Length	128 bits	1010
	192 bits	1011
	256 bits	1100
Set Key Length	128 bits	0010
	192 bits	0011
	256 bits	0100
Input Data		1001
Input Key		0001
Encrypt		1101
Encryption – Feedback Mode (for testing)		1110
Decryption		0101
Decryption – Feedback Mode (for testing)		0110
Output Data		0111

3.3 Memory Architecture Optimization

Since the design is based on one clock cycle for each encryption round, we have to duplicate memory modules several times. Consequently, the choice of memory architecture is very critical. Since all the table entries are fixed and defined in the standard, Random Access Memory (RAM) is not needed, but in fact Read Only Memory (ROM) is enough. Specifically, the algorithm will require a lot of small ROM modules instead of one large memory modules, since each lookup will only be based on a maximum of 8-bit address, which translates to 256 entries. However, the ROM has to be asynchronous; otherwise several clock cycles would be required for all the memory reads. In our design, combinational logic is used to implement the table lookups.

There are three types of tables we used in our design. The first one, which is the most used, is the S-box. It is a 256-entry table with each entry 8-bit. Using combinational network we were able to use around 2200 gates to translate the table, which converts to around 51000μm^2. The access time for the table is around 1.89ns. We have a total of 48 copies of the table in our design; 32 of them in the Encryption module and 16 in the Key Scheduling module.

The second table lookup is for deciding the shift amount in the shift row module, which has 24 entries. We implemented four copies of the tables in our design, and we were able to achieve that using 55 gates with an area of 1000μm^2. The last type of table lookup has 30 entries, and it is used to generate the round constant in the key-scheduling module. It is only accessed once in each round, so we have only one copy of the table, with 70 gates occupying 1300μm^2.

3.4 Simplification of Modulus Operation

There are several modulus operations in the algorithm: modulo 4, 6, and 8. Since the modulus values are known already, generic modulo operations are unnecessary since they require a lot of area. Therefore, it is beneficial to look into the data set and break down the modulus operations into more efficient combinational logic, which consumes less area.

For the modulus 4 and 8 operations, they are relatively easy to implement using simple shifting. Result of modulus 4 is the last 2 bits in the operand, and result of modulus 8 is the last 3 bits of the operand. In simplifying modulus 6, it is necessary to look at the set of values the operands take since there is no simple method for reducing them. In the algorithm, modulus 6 takes on values from 0 to 13, therefore a Karnaugh Map was used to implement the operation efficiently using gates.

3.5 Encryption Datapath

As discussed before, the encryption module can be broken down into four different sub-modules, and the same case applies on the hardware implementation of the algorithm. We implemented the four modules (Substitution, Shift Row, Mix Column, and Key Addition) using mainly lookup tables, XOR's, and pure combinational logic. Moreover, the datapath is 256 bits wide despite of the actual block length.

3.5.1   Substitution
The 256 bit data is broken down into 32 chunks, 8 bit each, and each of them is used as the address for S-box table lookup. The S-box contains 256 entries, and each entry is 8 bits wide. The S-box is implemented using combinational logic with an access time of around 1.89ns. In order to achieve parallelism and finish one round of encryption in one clock cycle, the same S-box is duplicated 32 times. Fig. 4 shows the block diagram for this module.

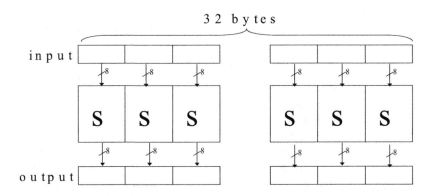

Fig. 4. Block diagrams for Substitution.

3.5.2   Shift Row
Inside Shift Row, the 256 bit data is broken down into four chunks. Each of the 64-bit chinks is called a roll and it contains eight bytes. Byte-wise cyclic shifts will be performed on each "row" (Fig. 5), and the amount of shifts is determined by the block

length through a simple table lookup (24 entries). Modulus 4, 6, and 8 operations determine the boundaries on which wrap around happens.

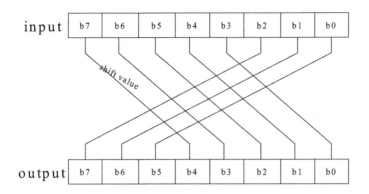

Fig. 5. Block diagram for Shift Row (only one of the four 8-byte "rows" is shown).

3.5.3   Mix Column

In Mix Column, four bytes in the corresponding position in the four "rows" are used for matrix multiplication in $GF(2^8)$, which involves byte-wise multiplication and addition. Byte-wise additions are easily done by XOR, and several tricks are used for multiplications.

Byte-wise multiplications include multiplying the data by 1, 2, and 3. Multiplying by 1 the data remains the same. For multiplication by 2, the 8 bit data is left shifted by 1 bit, and the LSB is replaced by 0. Then the MSB of the original data is used for comparison. If it is 0, then the left shifted data is the result; if it is 1, then the left shifted value is XORed with the reduction polynomial, in this case 00011011, to generate the result. For multiplication by 3 we simply XOR the original byte with the result of multiplication by 2.

Using the above method, the multiplications by 1, 2, and 3 of each of the bytes in the data are determined. Then the correct combinations of values are XORed with each other to produce a new byte. The same process goes on until all the 32 bytes in the data are replaced.

Fig. 6 shows the block diagram for generating the first byte of each row.

3.5.4   Key Addition

In Key Addition, the 256 bit data is XORed with the 256 bit keys to generate the result, as shown in Fig. 7.

3.6 Key Scheduling Datapath

The datapath for Key Scheduling is also 256 bits wide to accommodate different key lengths. Moreover, the sub-keys are all generated on the fly, meaning that there is no buffer storage for keys generation.

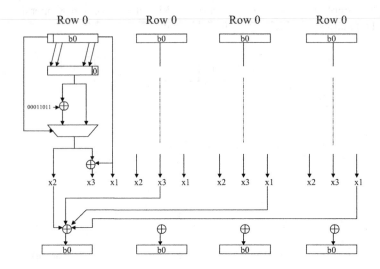

Fig. 6. Block diagram for Mix Column (only byte 0 calculation is shown).

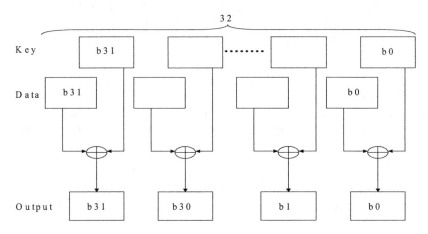

Fig. 7. Block diagram for Key Addition.

3.6.1   Datapath breakdown

The datapath can be broken down into three parts. In the first part, the 256-bit key is separated into four 64-bit "rows," and the lowest byte of each "row" is used as the address to access the S-box. The returned 8-bit result is XOR with the original byte to produce the new byte. For parallel access the S-box is duplicated four times.

The second part involves XOR between the zeroth byte with the round constant. A pointer, which increments every clock cycle, is used as an address to access the 30-entry round constant table for the round constant.

In the third part, the 256-bit data is again broken down into four "rows" of 64 bits each. Each "row" contains eight bytes, and each byte is XORed with the previous byte in a sequential manner.   The block diagram is shown in Fig. 8.   Since the datapath is slightly different for Key Length of 256 bits, a MUX is used for the selection of the fourth byte and is controlled by the key length.

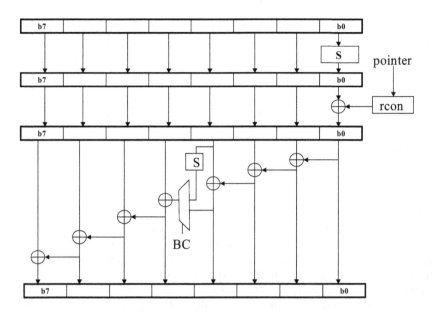

Fig. 8. Block diagram for Key Scheduling (only one of the four 8-byte "rows" is shown).

3.6.2   Key Alignment

Since the Rijndael algorithm allows different key lengths and block lengths, each sub-key is carefully set to have the same length as the data do. From the specification of the algorithm, the original key is used to generate a sequence of the entire sub-key stream, and chunks of sub-keys are selected for the encryption module according to the block length. This algorithm works if we have a buffer storage in our design to store the whole sub-key sequence, but is not applicable to our implementation.

In the case of 128-128 (block-key), 192-192, and 256-256 the generated sub-keys could be fed into the encryption module directly with any reorganization (Fig. 9a). However, in the case of 256-128, since both the encryption and key-scheduling modules are sharing the same clock, it means that the key-scheduling module has to create two set of 128-bit sub-keys to combined for the 256-bit sub-key for the encryption module (Fig. 9b).

On the other hand, in the case of 192-128, the original 128-bit keys are used for the lower 128 bits of the sub-key fed to the encryption module. Then the 128-bit key goes through the key-scheduling module to generate the next set of 128-bit sub-key. The lower half of this key is used as the upper 64 bits of the first sub-key fed into the encryption module, and the upper half is used for the next sub-key (Fig. 9c). In this case we will sometimes need to access the next sub-key and sometimes the previous sub-keys.

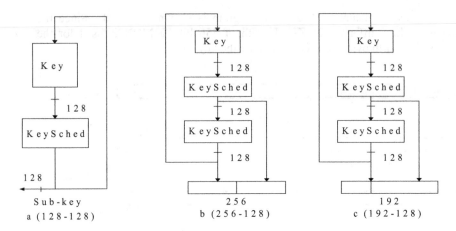

Fig. 9. Illustration of alignments of sub-keys.

3.6.3   Key Scheduling Architecture

By careful analysis of all the nine combinations between the Block Length and Key Length, we noticed that in the worst case the Key Scheduling module will need to maintain the previous, current, and also the next sub-keys in order to generate the appropriate set of keys that are fed into the encryption module.

Therefore, we decided to implement two sets of the encryption modules to achieve this. Fig. 10 shows the block diagram of our design. An extra selection module is used to select from the three sub-keys, based on the key length, block length, and the round count, the correct combination of keys that should be fed to the encryption module.

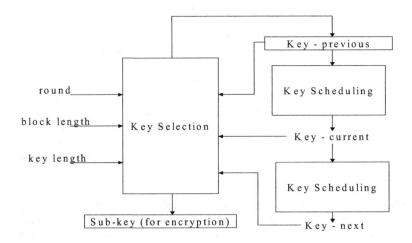

Fig. 10. Architecture of Key Scheduling used.

4   Results

The hardware design is done using the Cadence Verilog-XL, and synthesis was done using Synopsys DesignCompiler and National Semiconductor's 0.18μm standard cell library. The synthesis was done using two libraries: the worst-case library, which uses 1.2V at 120F and worst case processing, and the typical-case library, which uses 1.8V at 60F with best processing parameters. Results are in table 2.

Table 2. Synthesis Results.

	Worst-case library	Typical-case Library
Critical Path	21ns	10ns
Frequency	48MHz	100MHz
Chip Area	4.23mm^2	3.96mm^2
Gate Count	184,000	173,000
Max. Throughput (256 bits data / 128 bits key)	870 Mbits/sec	1.82 Gbits/sec
Min. Throughput (128 bits data / 256 bits key)	435 Mbits/sec	910 Mbits/sec

The critical path lies in the Key-Scheduling module, and it is shown in Fig. 11. It involves going through a S-box lookup XOR, and then the round constant lookup and XOR, followed by a sequence of XOR and one more S-box lookup. This path is duplicated one more time since we have two key-scheduling modules, and since one path is around 4.5ns, going through the two modules would take a total of 9ns. Together with the sub-key selection module, which is around 3ns, the whole critical becomes 10ns.

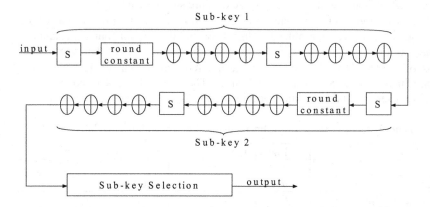

Fig. 11. Critical path for Key Scheduling.

The critical path in the Encryption module is illustrated in Fig. 12. It involves a S-box lookup, then the shift row module, which includes table lookup and XOR, four sets of XOR in Mix Column, and a final XOR operation in key addition. The overall path is around 6ns.

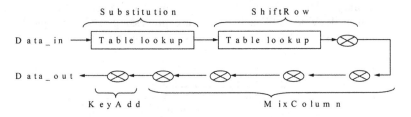

Fig.12. Critical path breakup on Encryption module.

Since the critical path is as long as 10ns, the system could operate under a clock of 100MHz in typical environment. When calculating the throughput, we measure the critical path of the processor core (Encryption and Key Scheduling modules), calculate the time to finish one encryption, and determine the throughput.

In the worst case, where the cipher is 128 bits, the key is 256 bits, and the encryption requires 14 rounds, the throughput is 910 Mbits/sec. In the best case, where the cipher is 256 bits and the encryption takes 14 rounds, the throughput is 1.82 Gbits/sec. For comparison, in software implementation, on a Pentium Pro 200MHz Pro system running Linux, the best-case throughput is about 100 Mbits/sec. Compared to the hardware implementation, the hardware implementation is about 18 times faster.

The whole chip has a size of around $3.96mm^2$, with a gate count of around 173,000 gates. The input and output controller each takes 1.6% of the overall area, and the top-level controller takes around 3.9% of the overall area. The Key Scheduling module consumes about 35% of the area, and the remaining Encryption module occupies 57.5% of the overall area. All these data are summarized in table 3.

On the other hand, each 256 bytes table consumes about $5100\mu m^2$. In the whole system, together with the four tables for Shift Row and the one for round constant are very small, all the lookup tables combine to $2.5mm^2$, around 63% of the overall area. In terms of register storage, the current design requires a total of $13200\mu m^2$ for registers, which is about 8% of the overall area. Therefore, all memory components, including registers and table lookups, occupy around 71% of the area of the chip.

Table 3. Comparison between Encryption and Key Scheduling modules.

	Encryption	Key Scheduling
Area	$2.28mm^2$	$1.39mm^2$
Gate Count	99,300	60,100
Percentage of Chip Size	57.5%	35%
Critical Path	6ns	10ns

Table 4 compares the design described in this paper with the design by National Security Agency (NSA) [6]. The research conducted by NSA was primary used as a reference for NIST, therefore it did not include special architecture techniques in order to create fair results between all AES candidates. Also, notice the library used was a 0.5μm library.

Table 4. Comparison with results from NSA.

	Design from NSA (0.5μm)	Design in this paper (0.18μm)
Chip Area	46mm^2	3.96mm^2
Gate Count	1.000,000	173,000
Max. Throughput	447 Mbits/sec	1.82 Gbits/sec
Min. Throughput	320 Mbits/sec	910 Mbits/sec

From our results, we noticed that the generation of sub-keys on the fly creates a serious bottleneck for the system. Since the encryption module has a critical path of around 6ns and the key scheduling module has a critical path of 10ns, the encryption module is idle for almost 4ns. If we could reduce path inside the key scheduling module to around 10ns the throughput would be maximized.

This implementation is entirely possible. As we have discussed, one key-scheduling module has a critical path of around 4.5ns, therefore if we implement some buffer storage for sub-key generation, where we only need to maintain one key-scheduling module, the critical path inside key-scheduling drop substantially from 10ns to at most 5ns, which matches precisely with the encryption module.

The tradeoffs with this implementation would be the excessive area for buffer storage and also the time required to generate all the sub-keys before encryption can start. By analyzing the current Key Scheduling module, each of the two sub-key generation parts consumes 0.53mm^2 and the sub-key selection module consumes 0.33mm^2, whereas 3584 bits of register storage takes up around 0.5mm^2. Therefore if we generate all sub-keys ahead of time, we can save the sub-key selection module and one sub-key generation module, replace that by 3584 bits of register storage and actually save around 0.35mm^2 of chip size.

On the other hand, although the critical path could be reduced from 10ns to 6ns, the new design would require time to initialize all the keys. In the worst case, where block size is 256 bits and key size is 128 bits, it would require 28 cycles to generate all the required sub-keys for encryption. Compared to the 14 cycles required for actual encryption, the overhead could be as much as 200%.

5   Conclusion

In this paper, a hardware implementation of the AES Rijndael algorithm is described. In order to better fit the algorithm for hardware implementation, several modifications are introduced, including memory access, modulo reduction, and key scheduling on the fly. Synthesized using a 0.18μm library, the gate count is estimated to be around 173,000. It can sustain a maximum throughput of around 1.82 Gbits/sec at a clock frequency of 100MHz, which is substantially faster than the software implementation.

Moreover, area tradeoff for memory sharing and addition of decryption is also discussed.

For future development, estimation on the real time required for key initialization and time for a whole encryption should be done on the real chip. Moreover, more detailed estimation should be done on the actual area increment for the addition of decryption. Power consumption analysis is essential as well for mobile application, and research on the actual resistance towards timing and power attack will be investigated [7]. Last of all, analysis on using buffer and sub-key pre-calculation should be implemented should be done as well.

Acknowledgements: UC Micro #00-097, Atmel Corporation, Panasonic, and National Semiconductor Corporation sponsored this work.

References

1. J. Daemen and V. Rijimen, "AES Proposal: Rijndael." Available at http://csrc.nist.gov/encryption/aes/rijndael/Rijndael.pdf
2. E. Barker, L. Bassham, W. Burr, M. Dworkin, J. Foti, J. Nechvatal, and E. Roback, "Report on the Development of the Advanced Encryption Standard (AES)." Available at http://csrc.nist.gov/encryption/aes/round2/r2report.pdf
3. J. Savard, "The Advanced Encryption Standard (Rijndael)." Available at http://home.ecn.ab.ca/~jsavard/crypto/co040801.htm
4. W. Diffic and M. Hellman, "Privacy and Authentication: An Introduction to Cryptography." Proceedings of IEEE, 67 (1979), pp. 397-427.
5. I. Verbauwhede, F. Hoornaert, H. De Man, and J. Vandewalle, "ASIC Cryptographical Processor Based on DES." Proceedings of EURO-ASIC-91, Paris, May 1991.
6. M. Bean, C. Ficke, T. Rozylowicz, and B. Weeks, "Hardware Performance Simulations of Round 2 Advanced Encryption Standard Algorithms." Available at http://csrc.nist.gov/encryption/aes/round2/NSA-AESfinalreport.pdf
7. J. Jaffe, B. Jun, and P. Kocher. "Introduction to Differential Power Analysis and Related Attacks." Available at http://www.cryptography.com/dpa/technical/index.html

High Performance Single-Chip FPGA Rijndael Algorithm Implementations

Máire McLoone and J.V McCanny

DSiP™ Laboratories, School of Electrical and Electronic Engineering,
The Queen's University of Belfast, Belfast BT9 5AH, Northern Ireland
Maire.McLoone@ee.qub.ac.uk, J.McCanny@ee.qub.ac.uk

Abstract. This paper describes high performance single-chip FPGA implementations of the new Advanced Encryption Standard (AES) algorithm, Rijndael. The designs are implemented on the Virtex-E FPGA family of devices. FPGAs have proven to be very effective in implementing encryption algorithms. They provide more flexibility than ASIC implementations and produce higher data-rates than equivalent software implementations. A novel, generic, parameterisable Rijndael encryptor core capable of supporting varying key sizes is presented. The 192-bit key and 256-bit key designs run at data rates of 5.8 Gbits/sec and 5.1 Gbits/sec respectively. The 128-bit key encryptor core has a throughput of 7 Gbits/sec which is 3.5 times faster than similar existing hardware designs and 21 times faster than known software implementations, making it the fastest single-chip FPGA Rijndael encryptor core reported to date. A fully pipelined single-chip 128-bit key Rijndael encryptor/decryptor core is also presented. This design runs at a data rate of 3.2 Gbits/sec on a Xilinx Virtex-E XCV3200E-8-CG1156 FPGA device. There are no known single-chip FPGA implementations of an encryptor/decryptor Rijndael design.

Keywords: FPGA Implementation, AES, Rijndael, Encryption

1 Introduction

In September 1997 the National Institute of Standards and Technology (NIST) issued a request for possible candidates for a new Advanced Encryption Standard (AES) to replace the Data Encryption Standard (DES). In August 1998, 15 candidate algorithms were selected and a year later, in August 1999 five finalists were announced: MARS, RC6, Rijndael, Serpent and Twofish. On 02 October 2000, the Rijndael algorithm [1], developed by Joan Daemen and Vincent Rijmen was selected as the winner of the AES development race. In performance comparison studies carried out on all five finalists [2,3,4,7], Rijndael proved to be one of the fastest and most efficient algorithms. It is also easily implemented on a wide range of platforms and is extendable to other key and block lengths.

In this paper two fully pipelined Rijndael algorithm designs are presented. The designs are implemented using Xilinx Foundation Series 3.1i software on the Virtex-E FPGA family of devices [5]. A fully pipelined Rijndael design requires considerable memory, hence, its implementation is ideally suited to the Virtex-E and

Ç.K. Koç, D. Naccache, and C. Paar (Eds.): CHES 2001, LNCS 2162, pp. 65–76, 2001.

Virtex-E Extended Memory range of FPGAs, which contain devices with up to 280 RAM Blocks (BRAMs). The first design presented is an encryption-only design capable of supporting 128-bit, 192-bit and 256-bit keys. The 128-bit key design is implemented on the XCV812E-8-BG560 device. The 192-bit and 256-bits are implemented on XCV3200E-8-CG1156 devices, as they are too large to place on the XCV812E device. The authors are not aware of any other Rijndael hardware design capable of supporting varying key sizes. However, software designs do exist. The fastest known software implementations of Rijndael are by Brian Gladman [6]. On a 933 MHz Pentium III processor, his 128-bit key design achieves a throughput of 325 Mbits/sec, the 192-bit key design runs at 275 Mbits/sec and the 256-bit key design at 236 Mbit/sec. Hardware implementations of a 128-bit key design do exist. An implementation on a Virtex XCV1000 FPGA device by Gaj and Chodowiec [4] achieved a data-rate of 331.5 Mbits/sec. Dandalis, Prasanna and Rolim [2] carried out an implementation on a Xilinx Virtex device and achieved an encryption rate of 353 Mbits/sec. A partially unrolled design by Elbirt, Yip, Chetwynd and Paar [7] on the Virtex XCV1000-BG560 FPGA performed at a data-rate of 1937.9 Mbits. The second design [8] presented is capable of both encryption and decryption operations and is implemented on an XCV3200E-8-CG1156 device. There are no known single-chip FPGA implementations of the Rijndael algorithm, which perform both encryption and decryption. However, Ichikawa, Kasuya and Matsui's [3] implementation on a CMOS ASIC achieves 1950 Mbits/sec. The encryptor/decryptor implementation by Weeks, Bean, Rozylowicz and Ficke [9] performs at a rate of 5163 Mbits/sec on a CMOS ASIC.

Section 2 of the paper provides a description of the Rijndael Algorithm. Section 3 outlines the design of the fully pipelined Rijndael implementations. Performance results are given in section 4. Finally, concluding remarks are made in section 5.

2   Rijndael Algorithm

The Rijndael algorithm is an iterated block cipher. The block and key lengths can be 128, 192 or 256 bits. The NIST requested that the AES must implement a symmetric block cipher with a block size of 128 bits, hence the variations of Rijndael which can operate on larger block sizes will not be included in the actual standard. Rijndael also has a variable number of iterations or '*rounds*': 10, 12 and 14 when the key lengths are 128, 192 and 256 respectively. The transformations in Rijndael consider the data block as a 4 column rectangular array of 4-byte vectors or *State*, as shown in Fig. 1. A 128-bit plaintext consists of 16 bytes, B_0, B_1, B_2, B_3, B_4... B_{14}, B_{15}. Hence, B_0 becomes $P_{0,0}$, B_1 becomes $P_{1,0}$, B_2 becomes $P_{2,0}$ ... B_4 becomes $P_{0,1}$ and so on. The key is also considered to be a rectangular array of 4-byte vectors, the number of columns, N_k, of which is dependent on the key length. This is illustrated in Fig. 2. The algorithm design consists of an initial data/key addition, nine, eleven or thirteen rounds when the key length is 128-bits, 192-bits or 256-bits respectively and a final round, which is a variation of the typical round. The Rijndael key schedule expands the key entering the cipher so that a different sub-key or *round key* is created for each algorithm iteration. An outline of Rijndael is shown in Fig. 3.

$P_{0,0}$	$P_{0,1}$	$P_{0,2}$	$P_{0,3}$
$P_{1,0}$	$P_{1,1}$	$P_{1,2}$	$P_{1,3}$
$P_{2,0}$	$P_{2,1}$	$P_{2,2}$	$P_{2,3}$
$P_{3,0}$	$P_{3,1}$	$P_{3,2}$	$P_{3,3}$

			$N_k = 4$			$N_k = 6$		$N_k = 8$	
$K_{0,0}$	$K_{0,1}$	$K_{0,2}$	$K_{0,3}$	$K_{0,4}$	$K_{0,5}$	$K_{0,6}$	$K_{0,7}$
$K_{1,0}$	$K_{1,1}$	$K_{1,2}$	$K_{1,3}$	$K_{1,4}$	$K_{1,5}$	$K_{1,6}$	$K_{1,7}$
$K_{2,0}$	$K_{2,1}$	$K_{2,2}$	$K_{2,3}$	$K_{2,4}$	$K_{2,5}$	$K_{2,6}$	$K_{2,7}$
$K_{3,0}$	$K_{3,1}$	$K_{3,2}$	$K_{3,3}$	$K_{3,4}$	$K_{3,5}$	$K_{3,6}$	$K_{3,7}$

Fig. 1. State Rectangular Array   **Fig. 2.** Key Rectangular Array

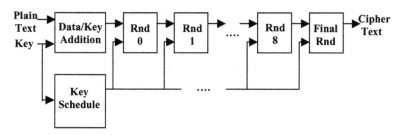

Fig. 3. Outline of 128-bit Key Rijndael Encryption Algorithm

2.1 Rijndael Round

The Rijndael round comprises a ByteSub Transformation, a ShiftRow Transformation, a MixColumn Transformation and a Round Key Addition. The ByteSub transformation is the *s-box* of the Rijndael algorithm and operates on each of the State bytes independently. The s-box is constructed by finding the multiplicative inverse of each byte in $GF(2^8)$. An affine transformation is then applied, which involves multiplying the result by a matrix and adding to the hexadecimal number '63'. In the ShiftRow transformation, the rows of the State are cyclically shifted to the left. Row 0 is not shifted, row 1 is shifted 1 place, row 2 by 2 places and row 3 by 3 places. The MixColumn transformation operates on the columns of the State. Each column is considered a polynomial over $GF(2^8)$ and multiplied modulo x^4+1 with a fixed polynomial $c(x)$, where,

$$c(x) = '03'x^3 + '01'x^2 + '01'x + '02' \qquad (1)$$

Finally the State bytes and round-key bytes are XORed in Round Key Addition. A typical Rijndael round is illustrated in Fig. 4. In the final round the MixColumn transformation is excluded.

2.2 Key Schedule

The Rijndael key schedule consists of two parts: Key Expansion and Round Key Selection. Key Expansion involves expanding the cipher key into a linear array of 4-byte words, the length of which is determined by the data block length, N_b, multiplied

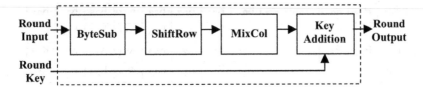

Fig. 4. Rijndael Round

by the number of rounds, N_r plus 1, i.e. $N_b * (N_r + 1)$. The data block length, $N_b = 4$. When the key block length, $N_k = 4$, 6 and 8, the number of rounds is 10, 12 and 14 respectively. Hence the lengths of the expanded key are as shown in Table 1.

Table 1. Length of Expanded Key for Varying Key Sizes

Data Block Length, N_b	4	4	4
Key Block Length, N_k	4	6	8
Number of Rounds, N_r	10	12	14
Expanded Key Length	*44*	*52*	*60*

The first N_k words of the expanded key contain the cipher key. When $N_k = 4$ or 6, each remaining word, W[i], is found by XORing the previous word, W[i-1] with the word N_k positions earlier, W[i-N_k]. For words in positions, which are a multiple of N_k, a transformation is applied to W[i-1] before it is XORed. This transformation involves a cyclic shift of the bytes in the word. Each byte is passed through the Rijndael s-box and the resulting word is XORed with a round constant. However, when $N_k = 8$, an additional transformation is applied. For words in positions, which are a multiple of ($N_k.i + 4$), each byte of the word, W[i-1], is passed through the Rijndael s-box. The round keys are selected from the expanded key. In a design with N_r rounds, N_r +1 round keys are required. For example a 10-round design requires 11 round keys. Round key 0 is W[0] to W[3] and is utilized in the initial data/key addition, round key 1 is W[4] to W[7] and is used in round 0, round key 2 is W[8] to W[11] and used in round 1 and so on. Finally, round key 10 is used in the final round.

2.3 Decryption

The decryption process in Rijndael is effectively the inverse of its encryption process. It comprises an inverse of the final round, inverses of the rounds, followed by the initial data/key addition. The data/key addition remains the same as it involves an XOR operation, which is its own inverse. The inverse of the round is found by inverting each of the transformations in the round. The inverse of ByteSub is obtained by applying the inverse of the affine transformation and taking the multiplicative inverse in $GF(2^8)$ of the result. In the inverse of the ShiftRow transformation, row 0 is not shifted, row 1 is now shifted 3 places, row 2 by 2 places and row 3 by 1 place. The polynomial, $c(x)$, used to transform the State columns in the inverse of MixColumn is given by,

$$c(x) = \text{'0B'}x^3 + \text{'0D'}x^2 + \text{'09'}x + \text{'0E'} \tag{2}$$

Similarly to the data/key addition, Round Key addition is its own inverse. During decryption, the key schedule does not change, however the round keys constructed are now used in reverse order. For example, in a 10-round design, round key 0 is still utilized in the initial data/key addition and round key 10 in the final round. However, round key 1 is now used in round 8, round key 2 in round 7 and so on.

3   Design of Pipelined Rijndael Implementations

The Rijndael algorithm implementations presented in this paper are based on the Electronic Codebook (ECB) mode. Although ECB mode is less secure than other modes of operation, it is commonly used and its operation can be pipelined [10]. The fully pipelined Rijndael implementation will also operate in Counter mode. Counter mode is a simplification of Output Feedback (OFB) mode and it involves updating the input plaintext block, P, as a counter, $P_{j+1} = P_j+1$, rather than using feedback. Hence, the ciphertext block, C, is not required in order to encrypt plaintext block, $P+1$ [11]. Counter mode provides more security than ECB mode and operation in either mode will achieve high throughputs.

A number of different architectures can be considered when designing encryption algorithms [7]. These are described as follows. Iterative Looping (IL) is where only one round is designed, hence for an n-round algorithm, n iterations of that round are carried out to perform an encryption. Loop Unrolling (LU) involves the unrolling of multiple rounds. Pipelining (P) is achieved by replicating the round and placing registers between each round to control the flow of data. A pipelined architecture generally provides the highest throughput. Sub-Pipelining (SP) is carried out on a partially pipelined design when the round is complex. It decreases the pipeline's delay between stages but increases the number of clock cycles required to perform an encryption.

The Rijndael designs described in this paper are coded using VHDL and are fully pipelined: the encryption design having ten, twelve or fourteen pipeline stages and the encryption/decryption design having ten pipeline stages.

3.1 Design of Generic Rijndael Encryptor Core

The main consideration in both designs is the memory requirement. The Rijndael s-box in the ByteSub transformation can be implemented as a look-up table (LUT) or ROM. This proves a faster and more cost-effective method than implementing the multiplicative inverse operation and affine transformation. Since the State bytes are operated on individually, each Rijndael round requires sixteen 8-bit to 8-bit LUTs. In the key schedule, LUTs can also be used, as words are passed through the s-box. The

Virtex-E and Virtex-E Extended Memory range of FPGAs are utilized for implementation as they contain devices with up to 280 Block SelectRAM (BRAM) memories. A single BRAM can be configured into two single port 256 x 8-bit RAMs, hence, eight BRAMs are used in each round. When the write enable of the RAM is low ('0'), transitions on the write clock are ignored and data stored in the RAM is not affected. Hence, if the RAM is initialized and both the input data and write enable pins are held low then the RAM can be utilized as a ROM or LUT.

The ShiftRow transformation is simply hardwired as no logic is involved. The MixColumn transformation can be written as a matrix multiplication as given in Equation 3, with a 4-byte input, a_0, a_1, a_2, a_3 and output, b_0, b_1, b_2, b_3.

$$\begin{bmatrix} b_0 \\ b_1 \\ b_2 \\ b_3 \end{bmatrix} = \begin{bmatrix} 02 & 03 & 01 & 01 \\ 01 & 02 & 03 & 01 \\ 01 & 01 & 02 & 03 \\ 03 & 01 & 01 & 02 \end{bmatrix} \begin{bmatrix} a_0 \\ a_1 \\ a_2 \\ a_3 \end{bmatrix} \tag{3}$$

The transformation is implemented by XORing the results of the multiplications in $GF(2^8)$ in accordance with Equation (3), as illustrated in Fig. 5.

The flowchart in Fig. 6 outlines the various stages involved in the Rijndael key schedule for key lengths of 128, 192 and 256-bits in length. N_k, N_b and N_r represent the key block length, the data block length and the number of rounds respectively. The input to the key schedule is the cipher key and key block length and the outputs are the Round keys. The Round keys are created as required, hence, Round key [0] is available immediately, Round key [1] is created one clock cycle later and so on. The various functions utilized in the key schedule are as follows:

Rem Function	: Returns the remainder value in a division
SubByte Function	: Operates on a 4-byte word and each byte is passed through the Rijndael s-box
RotByte Function	: Involves a cyclic shift to the left of the bytes in a 4-byte word. For example, an input of x_0, x_1, x_2, x_3, will produce the output x_1, x_2, x_3, x_0.
Rcon Function	: Returns a 4-byte vector, $Rcon[i] = RC[i]$, '00', '00', '00') where the values of $RC[i]$ are outlined in Table 2.

Table 2. Rijndael Key Schedule Round Constants

RC[1]	=	RC[2]	=	RC[3]	=	RC[4]	=	RC[5]	=
'01'		'02'		'04'		'08'		'10'	
RC[6]	=	RC[7]	=	RC[8]	=	RC[9]	=	RC[10]	=
'20'		'40'		'80'		'1B'		'36'	

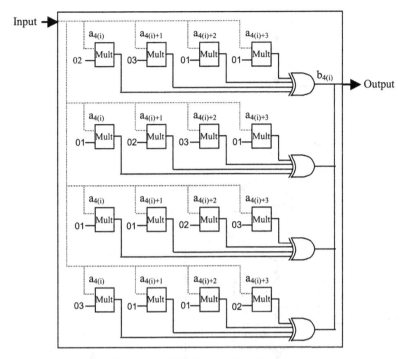

Fig. 5. Design of MixColumn Transformation

When utilizing a 128-bit key, 40 words are created during expansion of the key and every fourth word is passed through the s-box with each byte in the word being transformed. Forty 8-bit to 8-bit LUTs and hence 20 BRAMs are required in its implementation. Similarly, for a 192-bit key 16 BRAMs are required. With a 256-bit key, 26 BRAMs are needed – 14 are utilized for words in positions which are a multiple of 8 and a further 12 are used for words in positions which are a multiple of $(8.i + 4)$ for $8 < i < 60$.

Thus, in the overall 128-bit key design, a total of 100 ROMs are required, 80 ROMs are required for the 10 rounds and a further 20 for the key schedule. Similarly, 112 ROMS are required for the 192-bit design (96 for the 12 rounds and 16 for the key schedule) and 138 for the 256-bit design (112 for the 14 rounds and 26 for the key schedule).

3.2 Design of 128-bit Key Rijndael Encryptor/Decryptor Core

In the decryption operation, the inverse of the ByteSub transformation can also be implemented as a LUT. However the values in this LUT are different to those required for encryption. Therefore, it is necessary to accommodate for both encryption and decryption. One method would involve doubling the number of BRAMs utilized, however, this would prove costly on area. In the Rijndael

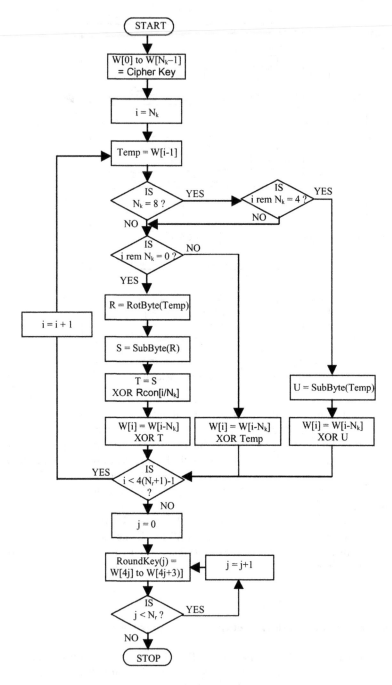

Fig. 6. Rijndael Key Schedule

encryption/decryption design, this was overcome by the addition of two BRAMs, which were utilized as ROMs, one containing the initialization values for the LUTs required during encryption, the other containing the values for the LUTs required during decryption. Therefore, instead of initializing each individual BRAM as a ROM, when the design is set to encrypt, all the BRAMs are initialized with data read from the ROM containing the values required for encryption. When the design is set to decrypt, the BRAMs are initialized with data from the ROM containing the values required for the decryption operation. This initialization procedure is outlined in Fig. 7.

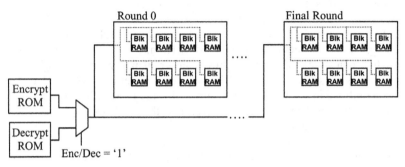

Fig. 7. Initialization of Block RAMs in Rijndael Design

The Inverse ShiftRow transformation is also hardwired. Multiplexors (MUXs) select between the ShiftRow and Inverse ShiftRow wiring. Similarly to Fig. 5, the Inverse MixColumn transformation can be implemented by XORing results of the multiplications in $GF(2^8)$ and again, MUXs are used to select between the values required for encryption and those required during decryption.

Since the encryptor/decryptor core design assumes a key length of 128 bits, the design of the key schedule is a simplification of that shown in the flowchart illustrated in Fig. 6. During decryption, the values of the LUTs utilized in the key schedule do not change, hence, the LUTs can simply be implemented as ROMs. However, the round keys are used in reverse order. The initialization process for either encryption or decryption takes 256 clock cycles as the 256 values contained in each ROM are read. Since the system clock for the encryption/decryption design is 25.3 MHz, this corresponds to an initialization time of only 10 μs. When encrypting data, the keys are produced as each round requires them, therefore, the encryption will take 10 clock cycles corresponding to the 10 rounds when using a 128-bit key. The design assumes that the same key is utilized during a session of data transfer. If decrypting data, the initialization process will be as described above. However, initial decryption will take 20 clock cycles, 10 clock cycles for the required round keys to be constructed and a further 10 corresponding to the 10 rounds. The overall 128-bit key encryptor/decryptor design, therefore, requires 102 BRAMs.

4 Performance Results

The Rijndael designs are implemented using Xilinx Foundation Series 3.1i software and Synplify Pro V6.0 on Xilinx Virtex-E FPGA devices. Data blocks can be accepted every clock cycle and after an initial delay the respective encrypted/decrypted data blocks appear on consecutive clock cycles. The first design implemented is the generic encryptor core, which supports 128-bit, 192-bit and 256-bit keys. The performance results obtained for this implementation will be similar to those of a design with only decryption capabilities. The main difference in the two implementations would be the initial delay time as mentioned in section 3. The 128-bit key encryption design implemented on the Virtex-E XCV812e-8bg560 device, utilizes 2222 CLB slices (23%) and 100 BRAMs (35%). Of IOBs 384 of 404 are used. The design uses a system clock of 54.35 MHz and runs at a data-rate of 7 Gbits/sec (870 Mbytes/sec). This result proves faster than similar existing FPGA implementations, as illustrated in Table 3 below. The implementations included in the table are as outlined in section 1. The design is also the most efficient in terms of CLB utilization although it must be remembered that the previous implementations were limited in their use of device.

Table 3. Specifications of 128-bit Key Rijndael Encryption FPGA Implementations

	Type	Device	Area (CLB Slices)	Through put (Mbits/s)	Throughput /Area (Mbits/s*Slices)
Gaj et al[4]	IL	XCV1 000	290 2	331.5	0.11
Dandalis et al[2]	IL	XCV1 000	567 3	353	0.06
Elbirt et al[7]	S P	XCV1 000	900 4	1940	0.22
McLoone et al	P	XCV81 2E	2222	6956	3.1

Both the 192-bit and 256-bit key encryption designs are implemented on Virtex-E XCV3200e-8-cg1156 devices, as they require a higher number of IOBs than that available on the XCV812E device. The 192-bit key encryption design utilizes 2577 CLB slices (7%) and 112 BRAMs (53%). Of IOBs 448 of 804 are used. The design uses a system clock of 45.44 MHz and runs at a data-rate of 5.8 Gbits/sec (727 Mbytes/sec). The 256-bit key encryption utilizes 2995 CLB slices (9%) and 138 BRAMs (66%). Of IOBs 512 of 804 are used. The design uses a system clock of

39.88 MHz and runs at a data-rate of 5 Gbits/sec (638 Mbytes/sec). There have been no FPGA implementations of Rijndael designs capable of supporting 128-bit, 192-bit and 256-bit keys published to date.

The second design implemented is the Rijndael encryptor/decryptor design. On the Virtex-E XCV3200e-8-cg1156 device, this design utilizes 7576 CLB slices (23%) and 102 BRAMs (49%). Of IOBs 385 of 804 are used. The design uses a system clock of 25.3 MHz and runs at a data-rate of 3239 Mbits/sec (405 Mbytes/sec). There are no known similar single-chip FPGA encryptor/decryptor implementations. Also, the results obtained compare very well with existing ASIC implementations, as illustrated in Table 4 below.

Table 4. Specifications of Rijndael ASIC Implementations

	Device	**Throughput (Mbits/sec)**
Ichikawa, Kasuya ,Matsui [3]	CMOS	1950
Weeks, Bean, Rozylowicz, Ficke [8]	CMOS	5163
McLoone, McCanny	XCV3200E	3239

It is possible to enhance the performance figures of the two designs presented by further optimization of the algorithm specific to the requirements of the FPGA device on which the design is to be implemented. However, this would result in the design being less easy to migrate to other devices and technologies.

5   Conclusions

To conclude, this paper describes high performance single-chip FPGA implementations of the Rijndael algorithm. The generic, parameterisable encryption design is the only hardware Rijndael encryption design that supports varying key sizes, reported to date. When implemented, the 128-bit key encryption design performs at a data-rate of 7 Gbits/sec, which is 3.5 times faster than similar existing FPGA implementations and 21 times faster than software implementations. Previous Rijndael encryption-only designs are implemented on Virtex XCV1000 devices, which consist of only 32 BRAMs and therefore, cannot support a fully pipelined Rijndael design. The Virtex-E and Virtex-E Extended Memory family of FPGAs, however, contains up to 280 BRAMs and can easily accommodate large unrolled designs. The encryptor/decryptor core runs at 3.2 Gbits/sec. This implementation not only compares favorably with similar ASIC designs but is also the only known single-chip FPGA Rijndael design capable of both encryption and decryption. Future work will include parameterising the Rijndael encryption/decryption design so as it may also accept varying key sizes. Rijndael is set to be approved by NIST and replace DES as the Federal Information Processing Encryption Standard (FIPS) in the summer of 2001. It will replace DES in applications such as IPSec protocols, the Secure Socket Layer (SSL) protocol and in ATM cell encryption. In general, hardware implementations of encryption algorithms and their associated key schedules are physically secure, as they cannot easily be modified by an outside attacker. Also, the high speed Rijndael encryptor core and Rijndael encryptor/decryptor core presented, should prove beneficial in applications where speed is vital as with real-time communications such as satellite communications and electronic financial transactions.

Acknowledgements

This research has been supported by Amphion Semiconductor Ltd. and by a University Research Studentship, which incorporates funding by the European Social Fund.

References

1. J. Daemen, V.Rijmen: The Rijndael Block Cipher: AES Proposal : First AES Candidate Conference (AES1) : August 20-22, 1998
2. A. Dandalis, V.K. Prasanna, J.D.P. Rolim: A Comparative Study of Performance of AES Candidates Using FPGAs: The Third Advanced Encryption Standard (AES3) Candidate Conference, 13-14 April 2000, New York, USA.
3. T. Ichikawa, T. Kasuya, M. Matsui: Hardware Evaluation of the AES Finalists: The Third Advanced Encryption Standard (AES3) Candidate Conference, 13-14 April 2000, New York, USA.
4. K. Gaj, P. Chodowiec: Comparison of the Hardware Performance of the AES Candidates using Reconfigurable Hardware: The Third Advanced Encryption Standard (AES3) Candidate Conference, 13-14 April 2000, New York, USA.
5. Xilinx Virtex^{TM}-E 1.8V Field Programmable Gate Arrays: URL: http://www.xilinx.com: November 2000.
6. Brian Gladman: The AES Algorithm (Rijndael) in C and C++: URL: http://fp.gladman.plus.com/cryptography_technology/rijndael/index.htm: April 2001.
7. A.J. Elbirt, W. Yip, B. Chetwynd, C. Paar: An FPGA Implementation and Performance Evaluation of the AES Block Cipher Candidate Algorithm Finalists: The Third Advanced Encryption Standard (AES3) Candidate Conference, 13-14 April 2000, New York, USA.
8. M.McLoone, J.V. McCanny: Apparatus for Selectably Encrypting and Decrypting Data: UK Patent Application No. 0107592.8: Filed March 2001.
9. B. Weeks, M. Bean, T. Rozylowicz, C. Ficke: Hardware Performance Simulations of Round 2 Advanced Encryption Standard Algorithms: The Third Advanced Encryption Standard (AES3) Candidate Conference, 13-14 April 2000, New York, USA.
10. J.C.A Van Der Lubbe: Basic Methods of Cryptography: Cambridge University Press, 1998
11. A.Menezes, P. Oorschot, S. Vanstone: Handbook of Applied Cryptography: CRC Press, 1997

Two Methods of Rijndael Implementation in Reconfigurable Hardware

Viktor Fischer[1] and Miloš Drutarovský[2]

[1] Laboratoire Traitement du Signal et Instrumentation,
Unité Mixte de Recherche CNRS 5516, Université Jean Monnet,
Saint-Etienne, France
`fischer@univ-st-etienne.fr`
[2] Department of Electronics and Multimedial Communications,
Technical University of Košice,
Park Komenského 13, 041 20 Košice, Slovak Republic
`Milos.Drutarovsky@tuke.sk`

Abstract. This paper presents an evaluation of the Rijndael cipher, the Advanced Encryption Standard winner, from the viewpoint of its implementation in a Field Programmable Devices (FPD). Starting with an analysis of algorithm's general characteristics a general cipher structure is described. Two different methods of Rijndael algorithm mapping to FPD are analyzed and suitability of available FPD families is evaluated. Finally, results of proposed mapping implemented in Altera FLEX, ACEX and APEX FPD are presented and compared with the fastest known Xilinx FPGA implementation. Results obtained are significantly faster than that of other implementations known up to now.

1 Introduction

Since 1997 the National Institute of Standards and Technology (NIST) has been working with the international cryptographic community to develop an Advanced Encryption Standard (AES). One of requirements given by the NIST on AES candidates [1] was the possibility of their efficient hardware implementation [2]. Compared with software-based solution, hardware implementation offers superior performance and significantly higher system security. Implementation in Field Programmable Devices (FPD)[1] adds to these two parameters a possibility to modify the algorithm in the field. Several papers dealing with implementation of AES candidates in reconfigurable hardware have been published so far. Some of them give only estimation of these parameters [3], while others present results based on implementation in FPGA [4], [5], [6]. Although some authors (e.g. [4], [5]) analyze the possibility to increase the speed using pipeline structures, the use of these structures in current cryptography is limited, because they are not

---

[1] There are several vendors of FPD. These vendors use different names for their FPD – e.g. Field Programmable Gate Arrays (FPGA) by Xilinx and Complex Programmable Logic Devices (CPLD) by Altera. FPD abbreviation is used as common name for all of them.

Ç.K. Koç, D. Naccache, and C. Paar (Eds.): CHES 2001, LNCS 2162, pp. 77–92, 2001.

suitable for encryption/decryption in the most common feedback modes such as Cipher Block Chaining mode, Cipher Feedback Mode, and Output Feedback Mode. All of above mentioned papers present results of implementation in Xilinx FPGA (mostly in a high performance Virtex family [7]) and the final AES NIST report [2] is based on these results. Some research groups [8], [9], [10], [11] presented also results of the implementation of AES candidates in Altera FLEX logic devices [12]. In October 2, 2000 NIST has decided to propose Rijndael cipher [13] as the Advanced Encryption Standard and it is expected that Rijndael will be used by U.S. Government and, on voluntary basis, by the private sector. Based on this decision our further optimization effort was concentrated to the Rijndael algorithm and performance results presented in [9], [14] have been significantly improved in our new implementations. This improvement is based on different method of algorithm mapping, better VHDL encoding and usage of Altera low-cost ACEX[2] [15] and high-performance APEX [16] FPD families. This paper evaluates two different methods of the Rijndael cipher implementation from the viewpoint of its hardware mapping into high performance Altera FPD and it is organized as follows. A brief overview of Rijndael cipher algorithm and its basic building blocks is given in Section 2. In Section 3 aspects of proposed methods are discussed and different solutions from the viewpoint of the FPD embedded memory occupation and speed are presented. The limitations and implementation results of VHDL design for advanced Altera FPD are described in Section 4. In Section 5, the results obtained for both methods are compared and some comparisons with the fastest known implementations are made. Finally, in Section 6, possible future work is described and concluding remarks are made.

2   Rijndael Cipher Overview

2.1   Basic Algorithm Characteristics

Rijndael is a block cipher using 128, 192 and 256-bit input/output blocks and keys [13]. The sizes of data blocks and keys can be chosen independently. Number of rounds depends on both of these parameters and it is given in [13]. In the next analysis 128 bits for both I/O block and user key are assumed. Therefore, the cipher in all presented configurations operates in $N_r = 10$ rounds.

Encryption and Decryption Algorithms. Encryption and decryption (in the following text referred as *standard decryption*) algorithms for 128-bit input/output block and 128-bit user key are depicted in Fig. 1a and Fig. 1b, respectively. Round keys K_0 to K_{10} are obtained by the expansion of the user key, following the algorithm, described bellow.

As it can be seen, the cipher core is composed mostly of operations that are easy to implement in a reconfigurable hardware: byte rotation (permutation), byte substitution and bit-wise addition modulo 2 (XOR). The only exception is the *MixColumn* function and its inverse (*InvMixColumn* function), that involve

---

[2] Low-cost FPD are optimal for many practical cost-sensitive cryptographic applications.

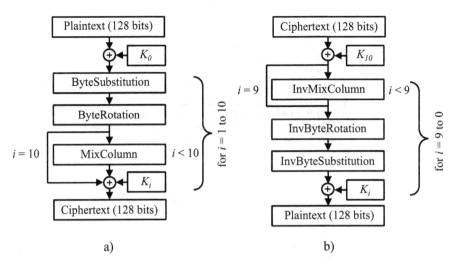

Fig. 1. Structure of Rijndael cipher a) encryption algorithm b) standard decryption algorithm

matrix multiplication on 32-bit blocks in Galois field $GF(2^8)$. Byte substitution operation uses 8×8-bit S-boxes (*byte substitution boxes*). There is one type of S-boxes for encryption and another one for decryption. Both of them are applied byte-wise on the whole 128-bit block.

Key Scheduling. Round keys K_i are derived from the user key by means of the key schedule. It consists of two components: key expansion and round key selection. Total number of round keys is equal to $N_r + 1$. The key expansion algorithm (see Fig. 2) uses bit-wise additions modulo 2 of 32-bit values obtained from user key combined with byte substitution, the byte rotation and round constants (*RCons*) addition. The order of round key calculation is the same for both encryption and decryption, although decryption uses round keys in reverse order.

Difference between Encryption and Decryption. Standard encryption and decryption algorithms use different ordering of basic operations. Moreover, basic operations for decryption are different (they implement inverse versions of basic encryption operations). As a consequence of this fact resource sharing between encryption and decryption logic is very limited.

Modification of the Order of Operations. In the table-lookup implementation it is essential that the only nonlinear step (inverse byte substitution) is the first transformation in a round and that the rows are shifted before MixColumn is applied. In the standard decryption algorithm inverse byte substitution is the last operation in the round. It is shown in [13] that order of inverse byte substitution and inverse byte rotation can be changed (both operation are byte oriented).

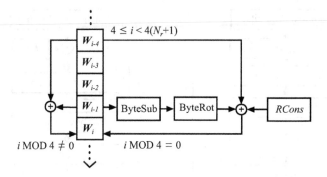

Fig. 2. Key expansion algorithm

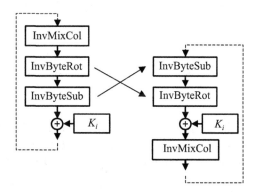

Fig. 3. Round modification for decryption

This feature is depicted in Fig. 3. Since InvMixCol is a linear transformation, the following equation is valid

$$InvMixColumn(d \oplus K) = InvMixColumn(d) \oplus InvMixColumn(K) . \quad (1)$$

Using properties described above, the standard Rijndael decryption algorithm can be transformed into its *modified form* described in Fig. 4. Comparing Fig. 3 and Fig. 1a it can be found that order of operation of encryption and modified decryption algorithms is the same (although significance of each operation is different). Moreover, round keys have to be inverted by InvMixColumn function with the exception of the first and last round keys.

2.2 Classification of Basic Cipher Operations and Choice of Technology

Rijndael has a relatively simple structure, while most of operations can be easily implemented in FPD. Efficient implementation of Rijndael algorithm requires ability to implement the following basic cipher operations:

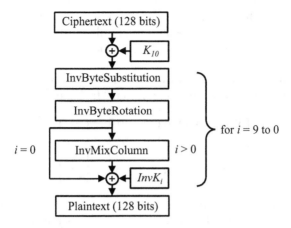

Fig. 4. Modified decryption algorithm

Bit-wise Addition Modulo-2 (XOR). This operation is easily realisable in FPD using input lookup table of *Logic Element* (LE) of Altera FPD or Configurable Logic Block (CLB) of Xilinx FPD. XOR operation with two to four inputs can be implemented in each LE or CLB slice (1/2 of CLB).

Fixed Rotation (Byte Permutation). Also this operation can be easily implemented but in this case routing resources are used. Cell interconnections can be reordered in a very simple way to implement rotations in both directions. Byte permutation order is different for encryption and for decryption.

8 × 8-bit S-boxes. Rijndael cipher uses 2 types of fixed 8×8-bit S-boxes: S-box $S[x]$ for encryption and inverse S-box $S^{-1}[x]$ for decryption. For memory limited implementations both S-boxes can be efficiently computed using the algorithm described in [13]. Actual design choice depends on features of FPD family. 8×8-bit S-boxes should preferably be realised using large embedded memories, because combinatorial function would occupy many resources (input LUTs of LE or CLB). Dedicated embedded memory blocks are ideal for implementing S-boxes. We have used them in implementations based on Altera devices.

In general, S-boxes can be implemented as lookup tables using dedicated embedded memories or within a set of small memories of LEs or CLBs configured as memory elements. Actual design choice depends on features of FPD family. 8×8-bit S-boxes should preferably be realised using large embedded memories, because combinatorial function would occupy many resources (input LUTs of LE or CLB). Dedicated embedded memory blocks are ideal for implementing S-boxes and they were used in implementations based on Altera devices.

The size of required memory depends on number of bytes that should be substituted in one clock period. If the whole 128-bit word should be processed in one period, 16 identical 8×8-bit S-boxes have to be used for encryption and for decryption. This requires the total memory capacity of 65536^3. Since all operations of the round can be executed in parallel during one clock period, the algorithm can be executed in at least $N_r + 1$ clock periods.

MixColumn and InvMixColumn Functions. There is a quite important difference between encryption and decryption. MixColumn function

$$
\begin{bmatrix} Y_0 \\ Y_1 \\ Y_2 \\ Y_3 \end{bmatrix} = \begin{bmatrix} 02 & 03 & 01 & 01 \\ 01 & 02 & 03 & 01 \\ 01 & 01 & 02 & 03 \\ 03 & 01 & 01 & 02 \end{bmatrix} \bullet \begin{bmatrix} X_0 \\ X_1 \\ X_2 \\ X_3 \end{bmatrix}, \tag{2}
$$

where $\bullet$ represents the multiplication in $GF(2^8)$ using the primitive polynomial $m(x) = x^8 + x^4 + x^3 + x^1 + 1$ and $X_i, Y_i \in GF(2^8)$, is replaced by its inverse – InvMixColumn

$$
\begin{bmatrix} Y_0 \\ Y_1 \\ Y_2 \\ Y_3 \end{bmatrix} = \begin{bmatrix} 0E & 0B & 0D & 09 \\ 09 & 0E & 0B & 0D \\ 0D & 09 & 0E & 0B \\ 0B & 0D & 09 & 0E \end{bmatrix} \bullet \begin{bmatrix} X_0 \\ X_1 \\ X_2 \\ X_3 \end{bmatrix}. \tag{3}
$$

Matrix Multiplications in $GF(2^8)$. These operations constitute the main obstacle in efficient implementation of this cipher in programmable devices. Authors of Rijndael propose a method using so called *XTime* function [13] to solve this problem. This 8-bit function can be easily implemented also in FPD and the matrix multiplication represents XOR operations applied on the outputs of this function. There is also another possibility to realise matrix multiplication. Since square matrices in MixColumn (2) and InvMixColumn functions (3) contain constant elements (polynomials in $GF(2^8)$), it can be shown [17], that this multiplication can be replaced by several XOR ($\oplus$) operations that are simple to implement in FPD. For example, operation

$$
Y = 03 \bullet X, \quad \text{for } X, Y \in GF(2^8) \tag{4}
$$

represents multiplication in $GF(2^8)$ using primitive polynomial $m(x)$. It can be implemented using following bit-wise XOR operations

$$
\begin{aligned}
y_7 &= x_7 \oplus x_6 & y_6 &= x_6 \oplus x_5 \\
y_5 &= x_5 \oplus x_4 & y_4 &= x_7 \oplus x_4 \oplus x_3 \\
y_3 &= x_7 \oplus x_3 \oplus x_2 & y_2 &= x_2 \oplus x_1 \\
y_1 &= x_7 \oplus x_1 \oplus x_0 & y_0 &= x_7 \oplus x_7 \oplus x_0
\end{aligned} \tag{5}
$$

This way matrix multiplication can be replaced by several XOR operations.

---

[3] In some FPD families that include large dedicated embedded memory blocks (e.g. 4 kbit blocks in Altera FLEX 10KE and ACEX 1K) it make no sense to use compact S-box and inverse S-box representation based on the affine transform [13].

Key Scheduling. The key scheduling is different for both encryption and decryption. Encryption round keys are used in normal order and can be computed on-the-fly. During standard decryption encryption round keys are used in reverse order and so they cannot be computed on-the-fly. For modified decryption depicted in Fig. 4, additional InvMixColumn function have to be applied on encryption round keys [13]. Round keys can be calculated easily from the user key using operations as XOR and rotation on 32-bit data. So the key schedule computation is very fast. Since round key preparation for modified decryption algorithm is more complex (application of InvMixColumn function on encryption round keys), *decryption latency* (cipher preparation time) could be higher than that of encryption. Encryption and decryption use $(N_r + 1)$ 128-bit keys, so the RAM capacity should be at least 1408 bits.

Choice of FPD Technology. From the above analysis it follows that critical operations from the point of view of their implementation in FPD are byte substitution and matrix multiplication. While fast byte substitution necessitates the presence of huge and fast memory blocks, matrix multiplication needs high fan-in combinatorial parts and significant count of global interconnections. Altera FLEX, ACEX and APEX families seem to fulfil better the first condition. On the contrary, Xilinx VIRTEX family offers more interconnection flexibility and more convenient combinatorial part of CLB (two LUTs per CLB). Since the speed of byte substitution operation seemed to be dominant in overall cipher speed, we have selected Altera FPD to implement the algorithm.

3   Methods of Rijndael Mapping to FPD

The speed and FPD resource requirements of Rijndael cipher mapping depends on the method used for actual mapping into available FPD resources. This section analyzes two mapping methods optimized for FPD with large embedded memory blocks (EMB), e.g. *Embedded Array Block* (EAB) in FLEX and ACEX devices or *Embedded System Block* (ESB) in APEX devices. Two types of cipher core configurations in feedback mode based on basic iterative architecture without loop unrolling are assumed: a *fast configuration* and an *economic configuration*. For both configurations it is assumed that encryption and/or decryption round keys are precomputed and stored in the EMBs.

The cipher architecture in the fast configuration is shown in Fig. 5. One round of the cipher is implemented as a mixture of combinational logic and access to EMBs, supplemented with a single register and a multiplexer. In the first clock cycle, complete input block of data (128 bits) is fed through a multiplexer, and stored in the register. In each subsequent clock cycle, one round of the cipher is evaluated, the result is fed back to the circuit through the multiplexer, and stored in the register. Therefore encryption and decryption can be made in 11 clock cycles.

The cipher architecture in the economic configuration is very similar to that in the fast configuration. The only difference is that it uses cipher core with

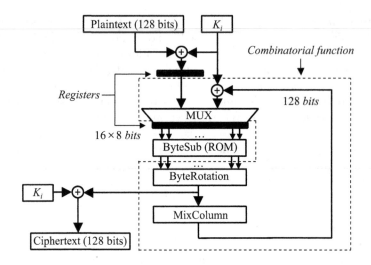

Fig. 5. Cipher architecture in the fast configuration

resource (especially EMBs) sharing. Internal data block, the 128-bit cipher state, is processed in 64 (32) bit sub-blocks in 2 (4) subsequent clock cycles. One round of cipher is executed in 2 (4) clock cycles and complete encryption/decryption can be made in 22 (44) clock cycles. The economic configuration needs 2 (4) times less S-boxes than the fast configuration.

3.1 Mapping Based on 8×8-Bit S-boxes

This approach was used in all known FPD implementations of Rijndael algorithm since it has minimal memory requirements. For the fast configuration (see Fig. 5) it uses 16 identical 8×8-bit S-boxes. Algorithm mapping for encryption is based on block diagram described in Fig. 1a and for decryption on that in Fig. 1b. It is clear that the logic for encryption and decryption is different and cannot be shared. Encryption and decryption S-boxes are also different. Since EAB in FLEX 10KE and ACEX 1K families contains 4096 bits RAM/ROM bits, two S-boxes, one for encryption and one for decryption, occupy exactly one EAB. Derivation of the cipher structure in economic configuration is straightforward and contains only some additional multiplexers and counters.

We shall now discuss some aspects of MixColumn and InvMixColumn transformations implementation. The complexity of these transformations is very different from the point of view of their implementation in FPD. Each of 32 output bits of the MixColumn block is a function of 5 or 7 input bits. On the contrary, InvMixColumn's output bits depend on 11 to 19 (!) input bits. Since LE is optimized for implementation of 4-input logic functions, these large combinatorial functions have to be implemented in several levels, e.g. 5 or 7-input functions in two levels and 17 or 19-input functions in 3 levels. This multilevel logic slows down significantly the final cipher speed, especially in the decryption logic. We have studied the possibilities to adapt function implementation to the structure of available logic cells. While APEX family offers the possibility to use high fan-in product term logic, this possibility could not be exploited, because product term logic is not suitable for XOR function mapping. Therefore we have tried to take advantage of another feature of Altera FPD families - the fast carry chain interconnections of neighboring logic cells. Although these interconnections are designed to implement fast arithmetic functions, they can also be used for wide logic functions implementations. Advantage of this method is that signal transitions via carry chain are several times (up to four times) faster than the transitions through complete logic cell. Disadvantage of the method lies in the fact that only neighboring cells can be interconnected. Unfortunately, matrix multiplication in MixColumn, but especially in InvMixColumn transformations represents a huge logic function with a lot of interconnections. For this reason, the use of carry chain for multiplication implementation has brought some speed improvement (up to 20 %), but it did not attained our expectations. Other negative aspect of the use of carry chains is their vendor specific character. Nevertheless, we can conclude that the utilization of carry chains in Altera FPD stays useful and we use them as often as possible in our cipher implementations.

3.2 Mapping Based on 8 × 32-Bit T-boxes

This approach was originally proposed for 32-bit processors [13]. From the point of view of memory requirements, it is less attractive than method based on 8 × 8-bit S-boxes, since in the worst case it uses 4-times more embedded memory. This is clear disadvantage of this approach. On the other hand, in FPD with 4-kbit EABs it uses just 2-times more EABs. Since the high performance FPD (e.g. APEX devices) include relatively large embedded memories, these FPD can be used for mapping fast cipher configuration based on larger 8 × 32-bit T-boxes. Features and advantages of FPD implementation based on T-boxes are described in this section.

T-boxes approach combines S-boxes and the MixColumn operation for the encryption process into four 8 × 32-bit tables [13]

$$T_0[a] = \begin{bmatrix} S[a] \bullet 02 \\ S[a] \\ S[a] \\ S[a] \bullet 03 \end{bmatrix} \qquad T_1[a] = \begin{bmatrix} S[a] \bullet 03 \\ S[a] \bullet 02 \\ S[a] \\ S[a] \end{bmatrix}$$

$$T_2[a] = \begin{bmatrix} S[a] \\ S[a] \bullet 03 \\ S[a] \bullet 02 \\ S[a] \end{bmatrix} \qquad T_3[a] = \begin{bmatrix} S[a] \\ S[a] \\ S[a] \bullet 03 \\ S[a] \bullet 02 \end{bmatrix} \tag{6}$$

These tables with 256 4-byte word entries make up 4 Kbytes of total space. Using these tables, the complete round transformation for a 32-bit block can be expressed as [13]

$$e_j = T_0[a_{0,j}] \oplus T_1[a_{1,j-1}] \oplus T_2[a_{2,j-2}] \oplus T_3[a_{3,j-3}] \oplus K_j \tag{7}$$

where K_j is the round key in round j. Since MixColumn operation is not performed in the last round of encryption algorithm, the last round have to be specially handled: S-boxes have to be used instead of T-boxes. Fortunately, S-boxes can be easily extracted from T-boxes: since all $T_i[a]$, $i = 0, 1, 2, 3$ boxes contain in some rows direct $S[a]$ values, we can get substitution result by combining T-boxes outputs of selected bytes (where S-box output value has not been multiplied by the constants 02 or 03).

In order to use T-boxes approach for decryption, the cipher structure described in Fig. 1b have to be modified. This implementation aspect has been anticipated in the design of Rijndael cipher [13]. The modified structure of decryption algorithm (see Fig. 4) is the same, as the structure of encryption algorithm, therefore T-box approach shown in Fig. 6 can be directly used also for decryption with the exception that new set of inverse T^{-1}-boxes must be used:

$$T_0^{-1}[a] = \begin{bmatrix} S^{-1}[a] \bullet 0E \\ S^{-1}[a] \bullet 09 \\ S^{-1}[a] \bullet 0D \\ S^{-1}[a] \bullet 0B \end{bmatrix} \qquad T_1^{-1}[a] = \begin{bmatrix} S^{-1}[a] \bullet 0B \\ S^{-1}[a] \bullet 0E \\ S^{-1}[a] \bullet 09 \\ S^{-1}[a] \bullet 0D \end{bmatrix}$$

$$T_2^{-1}[a] = \begin{bmatrix} S^{-1}[a] \bullet 0D \\ S^{-1}[a] \bullet 0B \\ S^{-1}[a] \bullet 0E \\ S^{-1}[a] \bullet 09 \end{bmatrix} \qquad T_3^{-1}[a] = \begin{bmatrix} S^{-1}[a] \bullet 09 \\ S^{-1}[a] \bullet 0D \\ S^{-1}[a] \bullet 0B \\ S^{-1}[a] \bullet 0E \end{bmatrix} \qquad (8)$$

Since none row of T_j^{-1}, $j = 0, 1, 2, 3$ contains unmodified $S^{-1}[a]$ values, extraction of $S^{-1}[a]$ values from T^{-1}-boxes must be done by multiplication of selected row by the multiplicative inverse in $GF(2^8)$ of the corresponding constant $(0E^{-1} = E5, 09^{-1} = 4F, 0D^{-1} = E1, 0B^{-1} = C0$) according to equations

$$S^{-1}[a] = 09^{-1} \bullet [S^{-1}[a] \bullet 09] = 4F \bullet [S^{-1}[a] \bullet 09] \qquad (9)$$

similarly

$$S^{-1}[a] = E5 \bullet [S^{-1}[a] \bullet 0E] = S^{-1}[a] = C0 \bullet [S^{-1}[a] \bullet 0B] \qquad (10)$$

Multiplication by these constants in $GF(2^8)$ can be represented using following bit-wise XOR operations

$$S^{-1}[x] = E5 \bullet X \rightarrow \begin{array}{l} s_7^{-1} = x_7 \oplus x_5 \oplus x_4 \oplus x_2 \oplus x_1 \oplus x_0 \\ s_6^{-1} = x_7 \oplus x_6 \oplus x_4 \oplus x_3 \oplus x_1 \oplus x_0 \\ s_5^{-1} = x_6 \oplus x_5 \oplus x_3 \oplus x_2 \oplus x_0 \\ s_4^{-1} = x_5 \oplus x_4 \oplus x_2 \oplus x_1 \\ s_3^{-1} = x_7 \oplus x_5 \oplus x_3 \oplus x_2 \\ \mathbf{s_2^{-1} = x_6 \oplus x_5 \oplus x_0} \\ \mathbf{s_1^{-1} = x_7 \oplus x_5 \oplus x_4} \\ s_0^{-1} = x_6 \oplus x_5 \oplus x_3 \oplus x_2 \oplus x_1 \oplus x_0 \end{array} \qquad (11)$$

$$S^{-1}[x] = 4F \bullet X \rightarrow \begin{array}{l} s_7^{-1} = \mathbf{x_7} \oplus \mathbf{x_4} \oplus \mathbf{x_1} \\ s_6^{-1} = \mathbf{x_6} \oplus \mathbf{x_3} \oplus \mathbf{x_0} \\ s_5^{-1} = \mathbf{x_5} \oplus \mathbf{x_2} \\ s_4^{-1} = \mathbf{x_4} \oplus \mathbf{x_1} \\ s_3^{-1} = x_7 \oplus x_4 \oplus x_3 \oplus x_1 \oplus x_0 \\ s_2^{-1} = x_7 \oplus x_6 \oplus x_4 \oplus x_3 \oplus x_2 \oplus x_1 \oplus x_0 \\ s_1^{-1} = x_6 \oplus x_5 \oplus x_3 \oplus x_2 \oplus x_1 \oplus x_0 \\ s_0^{-1} = \mathbf{x_5} \oplus \mathbf{x_2} \oplus \mathbf{x_0} \end{array} \quad (12)$$

$$S^{-1}[x] = C0 \bullet X \rightarrow \begin{array}{l} s_7^{-1} = x_7 \oplus x_6 \oplus x_4 \oplus x_1 \oplus x_0 \\ s_6^{-1} = x_7 \oplus x_6 \oplus x_5 \oplus x_3 \oplus x_0 \\ s_5^{-1} = x_6 \oplus x_5 \oplus x_4 \oplus x_2 \\ s_4^{-1} = x_7 \oplus x_5 \oplus x_4 \oplus x_3 \oplus x_1 \\ s_3^{-1} = \mathbf{x_3} \oplus \mathbf{x_2} \oplus \mathbf{x_1} \\ s_2^{-1} = x_7 \oplus x_6 \oplus x_4 \oplus x_2 \\ s_1^{-1} = x_7 \oplus x_6 \oplus x_5 \oplus x_3 \oplus x_1 \\ s_0^{-1} = x_7 \oplus x_5 \oplus x_2 \oplus x_1 \end{array} \quad (13)$$

Since equations (11)-(13) enable to get the same $S^{-1}[x]$ value, all output bit values s_i^{-1}, $i = 0, 1, \ldots, 7$ of $S^{-1}[x]$ can be computed as combinatorial logic function with maximally 3 logical inputs (chosen from equations (11)-(13) and typed in bold face) implemented within one LE. This function is implemented in a "Multiplication elimination" block depicted in Fig. 6.

4   Results of Implementation in Altera FPD

To map Rijndael algorithm into Altera FPD, the VHDL-based design methodology has been used. It should be stressed, that all presented results have been obtained using timing analysis and implementation reports generated by Altera MAX+PLUS II v.9.6 and QUARTUS v.2000.5 development tools. The results of mapping based on 8×8-bit S-boxes are summarized in Tables 1-3 and results for 8×32-bit T-boxes in Tables 4-5.

Table 1. Fast configuration with 16 S-boxes and 128-bit data blocks in APEX 20KE200-1 (using 50 ESBs = 98% of total ESB count)

Logic Elements Used						Speed (Mbits/s)		
Encrypt		Decrypt		Both		Enc	Dec	Both
LE	%	LE	%	LE	%			
1257	15	1738	21	2493	30	964	694	612

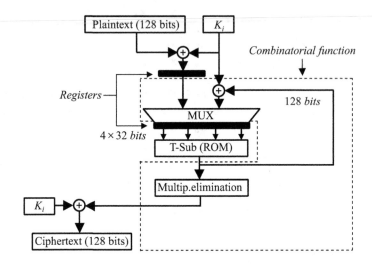

Fig. 6. Cipher architecture based on T-boxes approach

Table 2. Fast configuration with 16 S-boxes and 128-bit data blocks in FLEX 10KE200-1 (using 24 EABs = 100% of total EAB count)

Logic Elements Used						Speed (Mbits/s)		
Encrypt		Decrypt		Both		Enc	Dec	Both
LE	%	LE	%	LE	%			
1265	12	1801	18	2530	25	570	505	451

Table 3. Economic configuration with 8 S-boxes and 64-bit data blocks in ACEX 1K100-1 (using 12 EABs = 100% of total EAB count)

Logic Elements Used						Speed (Mbits/s)		
Encrypt		Decrypt		Both		Enc	Dec	Both
LE	%	LE	%	LE	%			
1461	29	2006	40	2923	59	282	238	212

Table 4. Fast configuration with 16 T-boxes and 128-bit data blocks in APEX 1K400-1 (using 86 ESBs = 82% of total ESB count)

Logic Elements Used						Speed (Mbits/s)		
Encrypt		Decrypt		Both		Enc	Dec	Both
LE	%	LE	%	LE	%			
529	3	529	3	845	5	750	750	750

Table 5. Economic configuration with 4 T-boxes and 32-bit data blocks in ACEX 1K50-1 (using 10 EABs = 100% of total EAB count)

Logic Elements Used						Speed (Mbits/s)		
Encrypt		Decrypt		Both		Enc	Dec	Both
LE	%	LE	%	LE	%			
824	29	824	29	1213	42	115	115	115

5   Discussion

5.1   Comparison of Two Methods of Rijndael Implementation

Analyzing results given in previous section we can present next advantages of the method using S-boxes approach:

- lower memory requirements for S-boxes implementation,
- no latency during encryption/decryption changing,
- very fast encryption, but significantly slower decryption.

As disadvantages of this method we can name:

- low-level of resources sharing,
- high count of logic elements used.

The second method based on T-boxes brings following advantages:

- faster overall cipher speed (for both encryption and decryption),
- high level of resources sharing, due to the symmetry of encryption/decryption
- very few logic elements used, because matrix multiplication is realized using look-up tables.

The disadvantages of the second method are:

- relatively high latency when changing encryption to decryption and vice versa – T-boxes have to be generated from S-boxes stored in one EMB (this latency can be reduced to zero, if double amount of EMBs is used),
- double (or quadruple) memory needs for T-boxes implementations (one T-box has 8 kbits, while one S-box has 2 kbits).

We can conclude that the first method could be better for applications, where only encryption algorithm is used. On the contrary, the second method should give better results if both encryption and decryption have to be fast. In the economic version (where commutation latency is acceptable) T-boxes can be computed from S-boxes stored in one EMB after each direction commutation. In the fast version separate T-boxes can be used for both encryption and decryption. This will reduce commutation latency to zero.

5.2   Comparison with Known FPD Implementations

Several Rijndael cipher implementations have been published up to now. Table 6 gives the FPD implementation results of encryption/decryption speed in the feedback cipher mode published in [4] - ELB, [6] - DAN, [8] - GAJ and [10] - MUT. For comparison NSA implementation in 0.5 μm ASIC [8] is included as well. Figure 7 compares known implementations in low-cost Altera FPD. It can be seen, that our 16 S-boxes implementation is the fastest implementation of Rijndael cipher in low-cost Altera FPD. T-boxes approach permits to implement the Rijndael cipher in as small circuit as ACEX 1K50,leaving almost 60 % of resources free! As it can be seen in Fig. 8, the encryption/decryption in our fast configuration based on T-boxes implementation is more than 80 % faster than the fastest FPD implementation known to us. It can also be seen that S-boxes approach for comparable Altera FLEX and Xilinx VIRTEX families gives similar results.

Table 6. Results of Rijndael implementations

Logic Elements Used	Speed Mbits/s
Fast (T-boxes, 128 bit blocks)	**750**
Fast (S-boxes, 128 bit blocks)	**612**
NSA	606
GAJ	414
DAN	353
ELB	300
MUT	248
Economic (S-boxes, 64 bit blocks)	212
Economic (T-boxes, 32 bit blocks)	115

6   Conclusions

In this paper we have evaluated the Rijndael cipher from the point of view of its implementation in reconfigurable hardware. The implementation results given in the previous sections depend significantly on the used FPD family. The Altera ACEX FPD have been found to be an excellent solution for very fast Rijndael cipher implementation in the reconfigurable hardware. Presented new solution based on T-boxes allows implement Rijndael cipher with the same high speed of encryption and decryption. On the other side, low-cost ACEX FPD family is suitable for cost-sensitive encryption applications. Future development will include integration of circuits for key exchange based on public-key schemes. Although current implementation uses only 128-bit keys, extension to larger keys (192 and 256 bits) requires just minor algorithm modifications and allows reach higher security with only minimal additional development effort.

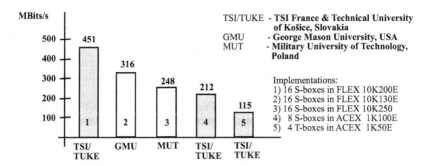

Fig. 7. Comparison of known Rijndael cipher implementations in Altera FLEX 10K and ACEX 1K FPD

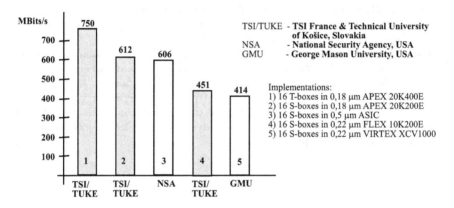

Fig. 8. Comparison of fastest known Rijndael cipher implementations in feedback mode for different FPD and ASIC

References

1. Advanced Encryption Standard. http://www.nist.gov/aes/
2. Nechavatal, J. at al.: Report on the development of the Advanced Encryption Standard (AES). NIST [1], October (2000) 1–116
3. Weaver, N., Wawrzynek, J.: A Comparison of the AES Candidates Amenability to FPGA Implementation. Proc. of The Third Advanced Encryption Standard Candidate Conference, NIST, Gaithersburg, MD, April 13-14, (2000) 28–39
4. Elbirt, A. at al.: An FPGA Implementation and Performance Evaluation of the AES Block Cipher Candidate Algorithm Finalists. Proc. of The Third Advanced Encryption Standard Candidate Conference, NIST, Gaithersburg, MD, April 13-14, (2000) 13–27
5. Gaj, K., Chodowiec, P.: Comparison of the hardware performance of the AES candidates using reconfigurable hardware. Proc. of The Third Advanced Encryption Standard Candidate Conference, NIST, Gaithersburg, MD, April 13-14, (2000) 40–56.

6. Danalis, A., Prasanna, V., Rolim, J.: A Comparative Study of Performance of AES Final Candidates Using FPGAs. Submission for The Third AES Candidate Conference, New York, March 21, 2000 available at [1]
7. Virtex series FPGAs. http://www.xilinx.com/products/virtex.com
8. Gaj, K., Chodowiec, P.: Hardware performance of the AES finalists-survey and analysis of results. Available at http://ece.gmu.edu/crypto/
9. Fischer, V.: Realization of the Round 2 Candidates using Altera FPGA. Submitted for The Third Advanced Encryption Standard Candidate Conference, New York, March 21, (2000), available at [1]
10. Bora, P., Czajka, T.: Implementation of the Serpent Algorithm Using Altera FPGA Devices. Public Comments on AES Candidate Algorithms-Round 2, available at [1]
11. Mroczowski, P.: Implementation of the block cipher Rijndael using Altera FPGA. Public Comments on AES Candidate Algorithms-Round 2, available at [1]
12. FLEX 10KE Embedded Programmable Logic Family. http://www.altera.com
13. Daemen, J., Rijmen, V.: AES Proposal: The Rijndael Block Cipher. Version 2, September (1999) 1–45, available at [1]
14. Fischer, V. Realisation of the RIJNDAEL Cipher in Field Programmable Devices. Proceedings of DCIS 2000, Montpellier, November (2000) 312–317
15. ACEX 1K Programmable Logic Family. http://www.altera.com
16. APEX 20K Programmable Logic Family. http://www.altera.com
17. Chodowiec, P., Gaj, K. Implementation of the Twofish Cipher Using FPGA Devices. Technical Report, George Mason University, July (1999) 1–24, available at http://ece.gmu.edu/crypto/

Pseudo-random Number Generation on the IBM 4758 Secure Crypto Coprocessor

Nick Howgrave-Graham, Joan Dyer, and Rosario Gennaro

IBM T.J.Watson Research Center
P.O. Box 704, Yorktown Heights, NY 10598.
nahg,joandy,rosario@watson.ibm.com

Abstract. In this paper we explore pseudo-random number generation on the IBM 4758 Secure Crypto Coprocessor. In particular we compare several variants of Gennaro's provably secure generator, proposed at Crypto 2000, with more standard techniques based on the SHA-1 compression function. Our results show how the presence of hardware support for modular multiplication and exponentiation affects these algorithms.

1 Introduction

The use of cryptographic techniques is a key element of modern e-business applications. Such applications use cryptography in a variety of ways to protect the privacy and confidentiality of data, to ensure the integrity of data, and to provide user accountability through digital signature techniques.

The security of cryptographic algorithms in real life applications, however relies mostly on two main assumptions:

1. that the secret keys used in the algorithms have not been compromised,
2. that the code executing the algorithms is really performing the tasks that it is supposed to.

Thus, in real life there is a concrete need to address these issues: the physical security of the keys and the code used in cryptographic algorithms. This is why most of the time, the keys are stored in a secure, protected memory device which is not easily tampered with. Similarly the code must be run in a protected environment. One answer to these issues is to use a *secure coprocessor*.

A secure coprocessor is a device that offloads computationally intensive cryptographic processes from the hosting server, and performs sensitive tasks unsuitable for less secure general purpose computers. Depending on the applications, it may be a special-purpose computational engine (say a hardware RSA chip), or it may be more useful to have a general-purpose computing environment. Such a device must withstand physical and logical attacks; it must run the programs that it is supposed to, unmolested. The host server should be able to (remotely) distinguish between the real device and a possible impersonation. The coprocessor must remain secure even if adversaries carry out destructive analysis of one or more devices.

Ç.K. Koç, D. Naccache, and C. Paar (Eds.): CHES 2001, LNCS 2162, pp. 93–102, 2001.
© Springer-Verlag Berlin Heidelberg 2001

An important class of secure coprocessors are the so-called *field programmable* ones, which allow the user to write custom software for the device, which then loads it under some controlled condition and subsequently runs it.

In this paper we consider the IBM 4758 PCI Secure Crypto Coprocessor, which is an example of such a field programmable device [12]. The IBM 4758 is the only programmable device on the market which has been certified at FIPS 140-1 Level 4, the highest security classification for a commercial cryptographic device [8]. We elaborate more on the technical specifications of the IBM 4758 in Section 2.

We report the implementation results, on the IBM 4758, of a random number generator recently proposed at CRYPTO'2000 [5].

1.1   The Problem of Pseudo-random Bit Generation

Many, if not all, cryptographic algorithms rely on the availability of truly random bits. However perfect randomness is a scarce resource. Fortunately for almost all cryptographic applications, it is sufficient to use pseudo-random bits, i.e. sources of randomness that "look" sufficiently random to the adversary.

This notion can be made more formal. The concept of cryptographically strong pseudo-random bit generators (PRBG) was introduced in papers by Blum and Micali [3] and Yao [14]. Informally a PRBG is cryptographically strong if it passes all polynomial-time statistical tests or, in other words, if the distribution of sequences output by the generator cannot be distinguished from truly random sequences by any polynomial-time judge.

A PRBG is called *provably secure*, if its security can be reduced to a well-established conjectured hard problem (like factoring or computing discrete logarithms.)

[5] assumes a variation of the Discrete Log Assumption. More specifically it assumes that if solving the discrete log problem modulo an n-bit prime p is hard even when the exponent is small (say only c bits long with $c < n$), then the function $f : \{0,1\}^c \longrightarrow Z_p^*$ defined as $f(x) = g^x \bmod p$ has strong pseudo-randomness properties over Z_p^*. In particular it is possible to think of it as a pseudo-random generator itself. By iterating the above function and outputting the appropriate bits, an efficient pseudo-random bit generator is obtained. The generator outputs $n - c - 1$ bits per iteration, which consists of a single exponentiation with a c-bit exponent.

An attractive feature of this generator is that all the exponentiations are computed over a fixed basis, and thus precomputation tables can be used to speed them up.

Using typical parameters $n = 1024$ and $c = 160$ we obtain roughly 860 pseudo-random bits per 160-bit exponent exponentiations. Using the precomputation scheme proposed in [7] one can show that such exponentiation will cost on average roughly 40 multiplications, using a table of only 12 Kbytes. Thus we obtain a rate of more than 21 pseudo-random bits per modular multiplication. Different tradeoffs between memory and efficiency can be obtained.

1.2   Interesting Questions and Our Results

When we started this implementation project we had the following questions which we thought were worth investigating:

- The IBM 4758, as many other crypto coprocessors, provides hardware support for modular math operations (modular multiplications and exponentiations). How effective are precomputation techniques like [7] in the presence of hardware support? Is the extra storage worth the potential gain in speed?
- The generator proposed in [5] is the fastest provably secure PRBG in the literature, based on established number theoretic conjectures. It would be interesting to know how it compares to other PRBGs whose security is assumed "from scratch" since they are related to block ciphers and hash functions. In particular it is interesting to see the results of this comparison in a constrained computing environment like a secure coprocessor.

For the first question, we ran the algorithm with various settings of the [7] precomputation scheme, as well as with no precomputation at all. In the latter case, modular exponentiations were computed completely in hardware, while in the former case the dedicated hardware was invoked only for modular multiplications. Quite surprisingly we obtained timing results that showed no increase in speed with the use of precomputation tables. Actually the algorithm was substantially slowed down. This seems to indicate that hardware support for modular exponentiations totally eliminates the need for precomputation schemes.

For the second question, we ran the [5] generator against an implementation of a pseudo-random generator consistent with the ANSI X9.17 Key Management standard[1]. This generator is based on repeated application of the hash function SHA-1. The timing results show that it is still considerably more efficient than our number theoretic construction (but, as mentioned above, this is at the cost of not being able to be proven to be reducible to any (supposed) hard mathematical problem).

2   The IBM 4758 Architecture

The IBM 4758 Secure Crypto Coprocessor is a hardware card, that plugs into industry-standard PCI slots in personal computers and other systems that support the PCI bus. The Coprocessor secure processing environment contains a 486-compatible microcoprocessor, custom hardware to perform DES and public key cryptographic algorithms, a secure clock/calendar, and a hardware random number generator. See Figure 1 for a complete list of specifications.

It also has protective shields, sensors, and control circuitry to protect against a wide variety of attacks against the system. More specifically the 4758 is protected against attacks involving probe penetration, power sequencing, radiation

---

[1] In fact it is the implementation that is used by the card itself for pseudo-random number generation.

Features:	Card type:	PCI 32-bit Bus Master
	Internal Processor:	486 99MHz
	RAM:	4 Mbytes
	ROM/FLASH:	4 Mbytes
	Battery-backed RAM:	32 Kbytes
Crypto:	DES:	Hardware support
	RSA, DSS:	Software with hardware support
		for 1024-bit modular math
	Hashing:	SHA-1 in hardware
	Random numbers:	Noise-based hardware RNG

Fig. 1. Features of the IBM 4758

and temperature manipulation, consistent with the FIPS 140-1 Level 4 Certification. The basic element of the protective layer is a grid of conductors which is monitored by circuitry that can detect changes in the properties of the conductors. The conductors themselves are non-metallic and closely resemble the material they are embedded in. This makes discovery, isolation and manipulation all the more difficult. These grids are arranged in several layers and the sensing circuitry can detect accidental connections between layers as well as changes in an individual layer. The sensing grids are made of flexible material and are wrapped around and attached to the secure processor package as if it were being gift-wrapped. After the package is wrapped, it is embedded in a potting material (which as mentioned closely resembles the conductors). Finally the entire package is enclosed in a grounded shield to reduce susceptibility to electromagnetic interference and to reduce detectable electromagnetic emanations.

During the final manufacturing step, the Coprocessor generates a unique public key pair, which is stored in the device. The tamper detection circuitry is activated at this time and remains active throughout the useful life of the Coprocessor, protecting this private key, as well as all other keys and sensitive data. The Coprocessor public key is certified at the factory by a global IBM private key and the certificate is retained in the Coprocessor. Subsequently, the Coprocessor private key is used to sign the Coprocessor status responses which in conjunction with the public key certificate, demonstrate that the Coprocessor remains intact and is genuine.

From the time of manufacture, if the tamper sensors are ever triggered, the Coprocessor zeroizes its critical keys, destroys its certification, and is rendered inoperable.

2.1 Developing Applications for the 4758

The Coprocessor contains firmware to manage its specialized hardware and to control loading of additional software. The card runs the IBM CP/Q embedded operating system, which has been extended with device drivers and other features specific to the Coprocessor. The resulting control program, CP/Q^{++}, provides the platform for application development. A complete custom application (like our pseudorandom generator) can be built on the CP/Q^{++} environment.

During development, the security features of the 4758 and the public key signatures used to validate download requests are irrelevant, but enabling symbolic debugging capability by adding a debug probe to CP/Q^{++} is essential. Preparing the 4758 for development is a one-time process. This step allows an external party to identify a 4758 by means of the identification of the officer assigned to the operating system layer. It is important in the overall picture of security provided by a 4758, in that a card with debug capability cannot masquerade as a secure card to the external world.

Application code is written in C, with one portion destined for the 4758 and the other its partner on the host machine. The 4758-based software is cross-compiled using supplied headers. After the normal link step, there are a few additional steps:

1. translation from host-native executable format to the format accepted by the CP/Q^{++} loader, as well as translating debug symbols to a format understood by the symbolic debugger supplied with the Toolkit
2. packing the translated executable into a disk image for the read-only file system within the 4758, used by CP/Q^{++}
3. downloading the disk image

The last, download, step is a bit lengthy in that the 4758 must be rebooted in order to open the hardware locks that protect flash to enable writing of code, and the hardware is tested each time the 4758 is reset (essential parts of the security architecture).

After development has completed, software can be deployed using any of the host platforms for which a device driver is available (includes AIX, OS/2, Linux, others). The development Toolkit is available for NT, with a version hosted in Linux to appear shortly.

3   The New Pseudorandom Generator

In this section we briefly recall the [5] generator.

NUMBER-THEORETIC PRELIMINARIES. Let p be a prime. We denote with n the binary length of p. It is well known that $Z_p^* = \{x : 1 \leq x \leq p - 1\}$ is a cyclic group under multiplication $\bmod\, p$. Let g be a generator of Z_p^*. Thus the function

$$f : Z_{p-1} \longrightarrow Z_p^*$$

$$f(x) = g^x \bmod p$$

is a permutation. The inverse of f (called the *discrete logarithm* function) is conjectured to be a function hard to compute (the cryptographic relevance of this conjecture first appears in the seminal paper by Diffie and Hellman [4] on public-key cryptography). The best known algorithm to compute discrete logarithms is the so-called *index calculus* method [1] which however runs in time sub-exponential in n.

In some applications (like the one we are going to describe in this paper) it is important to speed up the computation of the function $f(x) = g^x$. One possible way to do this is to restrict its input to small values of x. Let c be a integer which we can think as depending on n ($c = c(n)$). Assume now that we are given $y = g^x \bmod p$ with $x \le 2^c$. It appears to be reasonable to assume that computing the discrete logarithm of y is still hard even if we know that $x \le 2^c$. Indeed the running time of the index-calculus method depends only on the size n of the whole group. Depending on the size of c, different methods may actually be more efficient. Indeed the so-called *baby-step giant-step* algorithm by Shanks [6] or the *rho* and *lambda* algorithms by Pollard [10] can compute the discrete log of y in $O(2^{c/2})$ time. If one restricts the field to *generic* algorithms (i.e. algorithms that can only perform group operations and cannot take advantage of specific properties of the encoding of group elements) then Schnorr in [11] proves that this is the best that can be done.

If the complete factorization of $p-1$ is known, then the running time of these algorithms can be improved by using the Pohlig-Hellman decomposition [9]. This is done by reducing the original discrete log problem, into several "smaller" problems (one for each distinct prime factor in $p - 1$).

Van Oorschot and Wiener in [13] present a new method of combining the Pollard *lambda* method with a partial Pohlig-Hellman decomposition. Their end result is that for *random* primes, using short exponents is *not* secure. However their attack can be avoided by restricting the moduli to be *safe* primes p (i.e. such that $\frac{p-1}{2}$ is also a prime) since in this case the Polhig-Hellman decomposition is useless.

Thus if we set $c = \omega(\log n)$, there are no known polynomial time algorithms that can compute the discrete log of $y = g^x \bmod p$ when $x \le 2^c$ and p is a safe prime. One can explicitly assumed that *no* such efficient algorithm can exist. This is called the *Discrete Logarithm with Short c-Bit Exponents (c-DLSE)* Assumption and we will adopt it as the basis of our results as well.

Assumption 1 (c-DLSE) *Let $SPRIMES(n)$ be the set of n-bit safe primes and let c be a quantity that grows faster than $\log n$ (i.e. $c = \omega(\log n)$). For every probabilistic polynomial time Turing machine $\mathcal{I}$, for every polynomial $P(\cdot)$ and for sufficiently large n we have that*

$$\Pr \left[\begin{array}{l} p \leftarrow SPRIMES(n); \\ x \leftarrow R_c; \\ \mathcal{I}(p, g, g^x, c) = x \end{array} \right] \le \frac{1}{P(n)}$$

In practice, given today's computing power and discrete-log computing algorithms, it seems to be sufficient to set $n = 1024$ and $c = 160$. This implies a "security level" of 2^{80} (intended as work needed in order to "break" 160-DLSE).

3.1 The Algorithm

Consider the following function:

$$\dot{RG}_{n,c} : Z_{p-1} \longrightarrow Z_p^* \qquad RG_{n,c}(s) = \hat{g}^{(s \text{ div } 2^{n-c})} g^{s_1} \bmod p$$

That is we consider modular exponentiation in Z_p^* with base g, but only after zeroing the bits in positions $2, \ldots, n - c$ of the input s (these bits are basically ignored).

The function RG induces a distribution over Z_p^* in the usual way. We denote it with $RG_{n,c}$ the following probability distribution over Z_p^*

$$Prob_{RG_{n,c}}[y] = Prob[y = \mathsf{RG}_{n,c}(s) \; ; \; s \leftarrow Z_{p-1}]$$

It is possible to prove (see [5]) that the distribution $RG_{n,c}$ is computationally indistinguishable from the uniform distribution over Z_p^* if the c-DLSE assumption holds.

It is now straightforward to construct the new generator. The algorithm receives as a seed a random element s in Z_{p-1} and then it iterates the function RG on it. The pseudo-random bits outputted by the generator are the bits ignored by the function RG. The output of the function RG will serve as the new input for the next iteration.

In more detail, the algorithm $\mathsf{IRG}_{n,c}$ (for Iterated-RG generator) works as follows. Start with $x^{(0)} \in_R Z_{p-1}$. Set $x^{(i)} = \mathsf{RG}_{n,c}(x^{(i-1)})$. Set also $r^{(i)} = x_2^{(i)}, x_3^{(i)}, \ldots, x_{n-c}^{(i)}$. The output of the generator will be $r^{(0)}, r^{(1)}, \ldots, r^{(k)}$ where k is the number of iterations (chosen such that $k = poly(n)$ and $k(n-c-1) > n$).

Notice that this generator outputs $n - c - 1$ pseudo-random bits at the cost of a modular exponentiation with a random c-bit exponent (i.e. the cost of the computation of the function RG).

3.2   Efficiency Analysis

Let's fix $n = 1024$ and $c = 160$. With these parameters we can safely assume that the complexity of the best known algorithms to break c-DLSE is beyond the reach of today's computing capabilities.

We obtain 863 bits at the cost of roughly 240 multiplications, which yields a rate of about 3.5 bits per modular multiplication. The most expensive part of the computation of our generator is to compute $\hat{g}^s \bmod p$ where s is a c-bit value.

We can take advantage of the fact that the modular exponentiations are all computed over the same basis $\hat{g}$. This feature allows us to precompute powers of $\hat{g}$ and store them in a table, and then use this values to compute fastly $\hat{g}^s$ for any s.

Lim and Lee [7] present flexible trade-offs between memory and computation time to compute exponentiations over a fixed basis. Their approach is applicable to our scheme as well. In short, the [7] precomputation scheme is governed by two parameters h, v. The storage requirement is $(2^h - 1)v$ elements of the field. The number of multiplications required to exponentiate to a c-bit exponent is $\lceil \frac{c}{h} \rceil + \lceil \frac{c}{hv} \rceil - 2$ in the worst case.

Using the choice of parameters for 160-bit exponents suggested in [7] we can get roughly 40 multiplications with a table of only 12 Kbytes. This yields a rate of more than 21 pseudo-random bits per multiplication. A large memory implementation (300 Kbytes) will yield a rate of roughly 43 pseudo-random bits per multiplication.

4   Implementation Timing Results

We ran a C implementation of the above generator on the IBM 4758 card using the implementation procedures described in Section 2.1. In particular this means that we used the 4758 native hardware support for modular exponentiations and modular multiplications.

We first ran 1024 iterations of the generator (i.e. an output of 863 Kbits) without using precomputation tables. The task took approximately 4.75 seconds, which implies a rate of 22.7 Kbytes/sec. Thus, for example, this is the rate at which two secure coprocessors can securely encrypt data (via symmetric encryption) under a strong mathematical guarantee of security.

We then ran the algorithm using the [7] precomputation scheme with various settings of the parameters h, v described above. The experimental results confirmed the theoretical speed-ups between different choices of the parameters, however they also demonstrated a major slowdown of the algorithm compared to the case in which we computed the whole exponentiation in hardware.

The explanation is that the overhead of invoking in software the hardware chip for modular multiplication several times, offset whatever gain we could obtain in decreasing the number of multiplications by use of precomputation tables.

The results are summarized in Figure 2.

(h, v)	Storage (Kbytes)	Time (sec)
–	0	4.75
(5,8)	32	79.33
(8,2)	64	68.4
(8,4)	128	57.21
(8,5)	160	55.10
(8,10)	320	50.82
(10,4)	512	46.41
(10,8)	1 Mbyte	42.57

Fig. 2. Timing Results

These can be compared to the SHA-1 based implementation, which took 1.22 seconds to produce a similar 863 Kbit block of pseudo-random data. This implementation is written in highly optimised C code; in fact this is the code that the CP/Q operating system itself uses to generate pseudo-random data. However we do note that we ran the code as a standard "loaded-in" application, just as the number theoretic generator was, to enable a fair comparison.

Another useful comparison is to the BBS generator (see [2]), where one obtains at least 1 bit (and at most[2]) about 4 bits) of pesudorandom data from

---

[2] This has to do with assumptions on the hardness of factoring; see [5] for more details.

each modular squaring. Theoretically this should be similar to our exponentiation method (see [5] for a more rigorous comparison), however the overhead of calling the modular math hardware adversely affects this generator. In fact it takes 2.3 seconds to generate just a 1Kbit block of data using this approach (assuming one bit per exponentiation).

5 Conclusions

The results show that the SHA-1 based pseudorandom number generation is still considerably faster than the one based on discrete logarithms. However the difference, a factor of less than 4 on this hardware, may be considered not too high a price to pay by some who wish to have a "provably secure", rather than a "seemingly secure" (i.e. one that has withstood cryptographic attack thus far) system for pseudorandom number generation.

It should be stressed however that this result is strongly reliant on the fact that the algorithms were tested on the IBM 4758 secure coprocessor, which has support for hardware modular exponentiation. All of the software-based exponentiation variants of [5] that we tried were considerably slower (another factor of 10 to 20), even though they made use of hardware support for modular multiplication, and used precomputed tables.

The discrepancy was even more significant with the BBS generator due to the low output rate of the generator for each call to the modular math hardware; it turned out to be between 100 and 400 times slower than the "pure exponentiation" generator on this hardware.

References

1. L. Adleman. *A Subexponential Algorithm for the Discrete Logarithm Problem with Applications to Cryptography.* IEEE FOCS, pp.55-60, 1979.
2. L. Blum and M. Blum and M. Shub *A Simple Unpredictable Pseudo-Random Number Generator.* SIAM J.Computing, 15(2):364–383, May 1986.
3. M. Blum and S. Micali. *How to Generate Cryptographically Strong Sequences of Pseudo-Random Bits.* SIAM J.Computing, 13(4):850–864, November 1984.
4. W. Diffie and M. Hellman. *New Directions in Cryptography.* IEEE Trans. Inf. Theory, IT-22:644–654, November 1976.
5. R. Gennaro. *An Improved Pseudo-random Generator Based on Discrete Log.* CRYPTO'2000, LNCS 1880, pp.469–481, 2000. Updated version available at http://www.research.ibm.com/people/r/rosario/prng.ps
6. D. Knuth. *The Art of Computer Programming (vol.3): Sorting and Searching.* Addison-Wesley, 1973.
7. C.H. Lim and P.J. Lee. *More Flexible Exponentiation with Precomputation.* CRYPTO'94, LNCS 839, pp.95–107.
8. National Institute of Standards and Technology. FIPS 140-1, *Security Requirements for Cryptographic Modules.* Available at http://csrc.nist.gov/cryptval/140-1.htm
9. S.C. Pohlig and M.E. Hellman. *An Improved Algorithm for Computing Logarithms over GF(p) and its Cryptographic Significance.* IEEE Trans. Inf. Theory, vol.IT-24, no.1, p..106–110, January 1978

10. J. Pollard. *Monte-Carlo Methods for Index Computation (mod p)*. Mathematics of Computation, 32(143):918–924, 1978.
11. C. Schnorr   *Security of Allmost ALL Discrete Log Bits.*   Electronic Colloquium on Computational Complexity. Report TR98-033. Available at `http://www.eccc.uni-trier.de/eccc/`.
12. S. Smith and S. Weingart. *Building a High-Performance, Programmable Secure Coprocessor*. Special Issue on Computer Network Security, Elsevier, 1990, v.31, pp 831-860. Also, IBM Research Report RC21102, February 1998.
13. P.C. van Oorschot and M. Wiener. *On Diffie-Hellman Key Agreement with Short Exponents*. EUROCRYPT'96, LNCS 1070, pp.332–343, 1996.
14. A. Yao. *Theory and Applications of Trapdoor Functions*. IEEE FOCS, 1982.

Efficient Online Tests
for True Random Number Generators

Werner Schindler

Bundesamt für Sicherheit in der Informationstechnik (BSI)
Godesberger Allee 183, 53175 Bonn, Germany
Werner.Schindler@bsi.bund.de

Abstract. General problems and difficulties are discussed which have
to be considered when testing true random numbers. Requirements are
formulated which appropriate online tests should fulfill. Then we propose
an online test procedure which meets these requirements.

Keywords: True random number generator, statistical test, online test.

1 Introduction

Random numbers play an important role in many cryptographic applications.
Random numbers are used, for instance, to generate random session keys, signature parameters and challenges for challenge-response protocols and zero knowledge proofs. Roughly speaking, the class of random number generators can be
divided in three subclasses. First, there are true (physical) random number generators. Usually, an analog signal generated by a physical noise source is digitalized
after uniform time intervals, e.g. by a comparator. Many true random number
generators use a mathematical follow-up-treatment, i.e. an algorithm applied on
the digitalized analog signals. The goal of a mathematical follow-up treatment
is to reduce or at least to mask weaknesses of the digitalized analog signals.
In contrast, pseudorandom number generators derive (pseudo-)random numbers
deterministically from a randomly chosen seed. Pseudorandom number generators are very cheap as they merely require some additional lines of code. Their
drawback is that the whole entropy is "contained" in the seed. Finally, there
are "mixed" generators which derive random numbers from user's interaction
(mouse movement or key strokes) or register values of the used PC.

In the following we restrict our attention to true random number generators
(TRNGs). We denote the digitalized analog signals as *das-random numbers* and
the values after the mathematical follow-up treatment has been applied on as
internal random numbers. Upon an external call the TRNG outputs internal
random numbers.

Obviously, non-appropriate random numbers can weaken strong cryptographic
mechanisms considerably. To assess a TRNG a mathematical model of the physical noise source should be evaluated and analyzed, and suitable (that is, suitable
with respect to the mathematical model) statistical tests should be applied on

Ç.K. Koç, D. Naccache, and C. Paar (Eds.): CHES 2001, LNCS 2162, pp. 103–117, 2001.

the das-random numbers generated by some TRNGs prototypes. A lot of research work has been devoted to the generation of good physical noise sources and the determination of suitable statistical tests ([2], [10], [12] etc.).

Tolerances of the components of the random noise sources may cause that a particular TRNG produces worse das-random numbers than the carefully investigated prototypes. Further, ageing of these components may also affect the statistical quality of the generated das-random numbers. As a consequence statistical tests ("online tests") have to be executed while the TRNG is in operation to ensure that the generated random numbers are appropriate. Especially, if the TRNG is integrated in a smart card online tests should run fast, require only few lines of additional code and little memory.

Section 2 considers the question whether the das-random numbers or the internal random numbers should be tested and in Sect. 3 general demands are formulated which online tests should fulfill. In Sect. 4 we briefly discuss the drawbacks of a widely used online test. In Sects. 5 – 9 a new online test procedure is described, analyzed and illustrated at two examples. The paper ends with final remarks.

2   Which Random Numbers Should Be Tested?

If there is no mathematical follow-up treatment the das-random numbers coincide with the internal random numbers. Otherwise, the online tests can be applied on the das-random numbers or, alternatively, to the internal random numbers.

For many cryptographic applications it is inevitable that random numbers cannot be determined or guessed with a reasonable probability, even if predecessors or successors are known. Pseudorandom number generators rely on the complexity of their algorithms which shall ensure *practical security* (see, e.g. [1]). For TRNGs the situation is much more comfortable as the total entropy of a das-random number sequence increases per generated das-random number. If the increase of entropy is sufficiently large, this ensures *theoretical security*. (Clearly, a lucky attacker could guess a randomly chosen session key, for instance, but if the key length is sufficiently large his success probability is negligible.)

Hence it is desirable to control the increase of entropy. Unfortunately, entropy is not a function of random numbers but of random variables. In the following we will interpret das-random numbers as values assumed by random variables whose distribution usually is at least not exactly known. We use statistical tests to compare das-random number sequences with sequences generated by ideal random number generators.

Remark 1. In [3] a variant of Maurer's "universal" statistical test (cf. [11], [4]) is introduced. Its test value is closely related to the entropy per bit block *provided that the bits were generated by a stationary binary random source with finite memory.* If this is not the case, however, as for Maurer's test the test value need not yield a reliable estimate of the entropy. For pseudorandom bits generated by a linear feedback shift register, for example, the increase of entropy per bit equals zero whereas the test value "suggests" a considerable amount of entropy per bit block. Moreover, as Maurer's test it requires a lot of memory and gigantic sample sizes. Hence both tests are not suitable as online tests but may be used for the investigation of TRNG prototypes.

Example 1. Let the TRNG produce binary das-random numbers and let a linear feedback shift register of length 63 with primitive feedback polynomial be synchronized with the digitalization of the analog noise signal. In each time step the feedback shift register delivers an internal random number (a single bit). The actually generated das-random number is XOR-ed to the feedback value and the sum is fed back into the shift register.

For each initial value of the feedback shift register this mathematical follow-up treatment is a one-to-one mapping and thus cannot increase the average entropy per bit. Statistical weaknesses of the das-random numbers are not reduced but only transferred into others. If, for example, the das-random numbers are independent but not equidistributed (i.e., if the probability for "0" is not 0.5) the internal random numbers are essentially equidistributed but dependent. Unless its linear complexity profile is tested applying statistical tests on the internal random number sequence will presumably even not detect the worst case, i.e. if the physical noise source has totally broken down. In fact, after this moment the das-random numbers are constant and the internal random numbers are generated deterministically.

This brief analysis of Example 1 has revealed an important fact: The internal random numbers may pass certain statistical tests which the das-random numbers do not. However, this does not necessarily imply that the mathematical follow-up treatment reduces statistical weaknesses of the das-random numbers. Maybe they are merely masked and transformed into others. An increase of the entropy per bit can only achieved by a data compression which in turn lowers the bit rate. (In the simplest case non-overlapping bits are XORed.) Of course, the das-random numbers may not be equidistributed and there may exist dependencies on preceding das-random numbers but in contrast to the internal random numbers there will not exist complicated algebraic dependencies. Consequently, the das-random numbers but not the internal random numbers should be tested, especially if the TRNG is used for sensitive applications.

3 Which Requirements Should Online Tests Fulfill?

As motivated in the previous section online tests should be applied on das-random numbers which usually (but not necessarily) are single bits.

Definition 1. A *realization* of a random variable X is a value assumed by X. The term *iid* abbreviates "independent and identically distributed". We call a random variable *binary* if it only assumes the values 0 and 1. A random variable X is called *equidistributed* on a finite set $\Omega := \{\omega_1, \ldots, \omega_k\}$ if $\mathrm{Prob}(X = \omega_j) = 1/k$ holds for all $j \leq k$. Applying a statistical test on a sample delivers a numerical value called *test value* or *test statistic*.

Mathematical Model and Definitions. Das-random numbers assume values in Ω_{das} (usually, but not necessarily, $\Omega_{das} = \{0,1\}$). We assume that the das-random numbers are realizations of random variables $B_1, B_2, \ldots$ so that the test value $\widetilde{T}$ itself may be interpreted as a realization of a random variable T, the so-called *test variable*. The distribution of $B_1, B_2, \ldots$ and that of T clearly depend on the particular TRNG. For an *ideal random number generator* (a fiction!), of course, the random variables $B_1, B_2, \ldots$ are iid and equidistributed on Ω_{das}. To avoid clumsy formulations we call bit sequences generated by an ideal random number generator *ideal sequences*. A χ^2-distribution with k degrees of freedom is denoted with χ_k^2.

We will use statistical tests to compare das-random numbers with ideal sequences. To a certain degree statistical deviations of the das-bits from ideal sequences, however, are tolerable. (Assume, for example, that the das-bits were realizations of iid random variables $B_1, B_2, \ldots$ with $\text{Prob}(B_j = 1) = 0.49$. Then the average entropy per das-bit was about 0.9997.) Clearly, "tolerable" essentially depends on the intended applications for which the random numbers shall used and, to a certain degree, on the mathematical follow-up treatment which may increase the entropy per random number (cf. Sect. 2). If the statistical properties of the das-random number sequence deviate too much from that of ideal sequences the online test should generate a noise alarm. The preceding considerations suggest various requirements which online tests should fulfill. Recall that due to tolerances of components or ageing effects a TRNG may produce worse das-random number sequences than the carefully investigated TRNG prototypes. Clearly, also ideal sequences would occasionally fail statistical tests.

Requirements for online tests.
(R1) An online test has to detect a total breakdown of the noise source very soon.
(R2) An online test should detect non-tolerable statistical weaknesses of the das-random numbers.
(R3) The probability for a noise alarm should be small if the deviation of the statistical properties of the das-random numbers from that of ideal sequences is tolerable.
(R4) An online test should run fast and require only a few lines of code and little memory.

4   Drawbacks of a Widely Used Online Test and General Difficulties

In this section we discuss briefly problems of a near-at-hand online test procedure which is widely used in practice.

Example 2. Let the TRNG generate binary das-random numbers. A FIFO stores internal random numbers. If the FIFO is full the generated internal random numbers are neither used nor stored. Upon external request, the FIFO outputs internal random numbers. Periodically every minute and whenever the FIFO has to be refilled $n = 320$ consecutive das-bits are segmented into 80 non-overlapping four-bit blocks $\widetilde{W}_1 := (\widetilde{B}_1, \ldots, \widetilde{B}_4), \ldots, \widetilde{W}_{80} := (\widetilde{B}_{317}, \ldots, \widetilde{B}_{320})$. On each sample a χ^2-test (or more precisely, a χ^2-test for goodness of fit ([7], 69)) is applied. For this, the $\widetilde{W}_j$ are interpreted as binary representations of four-digit numbers. For $i = 0, \ldots, 15$ the frequencies $fr(i) := |\{j \leq 80 \mid \widetilde{W}_j = i\}|$ are determined and finally

$$\widetilde{T} := \sum_{i=0}^{15} \frac{(fr(i) - 5)^2}{5} \ . \tag{1}$$

The null hypothesis, i.e. that the tested sample was generated by an ideal noise source, is rejected if the test value $\widetilde{T}$ exceeds 65.0. A rejection of the null hypothesis causes a noise alarm which puts the TRNG out of service. The TRNG has to pass extensive investigations before it can manually be restarted by an authorized person.

The system administrator has laid down that there should not occur more than 0.027 noise alarms per TRNG and year in average if the TRNG produces tolerable das-random numbers. (The numerical value 0.027 clearly depends on the concrete application. For other applications, however, smaller values may be appropriate.) To reach this goal the designer of this online test has chosen the rejection area $(65.0, \infty)$. His considerations were the following: It is reasonable to assume that each TRNG executes about 530000 χ^2-tests per year. If the das-random numbers were generated by an ideal random number generator the test variable T was approximately χ^2_{15}-distributed ([7], 69) and thus $\text{Prob}(T > 65.0) \approx 3.4 \cdot 10^{-8}$. This yields an expected number of 0.018 noise alarms per year. As the das-random numbers generated by the investigated TRNG prototypes did not reveal serious statistical weaknesses the online test designer expects that the average number of noise alarms per TRNG and year will not exceed the given upper bound $0.027 = 1.5 \cdot 0.018$.

However, this argumentation is not quite correct. Even for ideal sequences the test variable T is not exactly but merely *approximately* χ^2_{15}-distributed. In fact, the 4-tuples are multinomially distributed and the exact probability $\text{Prob}(T > 65.0)$ is about $3.8 \cdot 10^{-7}$. If X denotes a χ^2_{15}-distributed random variable the *absolute error* $|\text{Prob}(T > 65.0) - \text{Prob}(X > 65.0)|$ is surely small but not the *relative error*

$$\frac{|\text{Prob}(T > 65.0) - \text{Prob}(X > 65.0)|}{\text{Prob}(X > 65.0)} \approx 10.1 \ . \tag{2}$$

(Note that we use $\text{Prob}(X > 65.0)$ as denominator but not $\text{Prob}(T > 65.0)$ because the predictions of the test designer are based on the approximate probability.) For the scenario described in Example 2 this means that even ideal random number generators would cause about $11 \cdot 0.018 \approx 0.2$ noise alarms per year in average; the TRNGs maybe even more. Anyway, this exceeds the upper bound 0.027 considerably. To avoid this, of course, the test parameter 65.0 could be increased (e.g. to 75.0). However, as the amount of increase is not based on a solid computational basis but more or less arbitrary it may happen that even serious statistical weaknesses will not be detected. In particular, a strong (data-compressing and hence throughput-reducing) mathematical follow-up treatment is absolutely inevitable.

The χ^2_{15}-approximation may seem to be terribly bad. However, this is not the case: Note that $\text{Prob}(T > 30.6) = 0.01025$ and $\text{Prob}(X > 30.6) = 0.00993$, for example, with an relative error of about 0.03. The relative error is maximal at the tail of the χ^2_{15}-distribution, i.e. for large rejection boundaries z. Increasing the sample size (here: 320 bits) reduces the relative error for each fixed value z (here: for $z = 65.0$) since the exact distributions converge to the χ^2_{15}-distribution as the sample sizes tend to infinity.

However, these considerations point to a serious general problem. In partic-ular, especially if the sample size of a statistical test is small, one has to be very careful when using an approximate distribution of the respective test variable at its tail. To obtain the exact rejection probability for ideal sequences in Example 2 we just had to count the tuples in $(\{0,1\}^4)^{80}$ for which the χ^2-test value is ≤ 65.0. However, although symmetries were exploited the computational effort was considerable. For non-ideal sequences it was *not practically feasible* to decide whether demand (R2) or (R3), resp., is fulfilled. However, online tests with such unpleasant properties are widely used in practice. In many cases even for ideal sequences the exact distribution of the test variable cannot be determined.

5   A New Online Test Procedure

In Sect. 5 we describe a new online test procedure. We will show later that it meets all requirements formulated in Sect. 3. In Sect. 8 it will be illustrated at two examples.

Step 1: First, the statistician has to choose a statistical test, the so-called "basis test", and to fix its sample size n. This may be a χ^2-test or any tests from [7], for example, provided that the needed memory, the lines of code and the execution time are acceptable for the used device and the intended applications. Ideally, the basis test should be chosen with respect to the mathematical model of the TRNG, or more precisely, of the random variables $B_1, B_2, \ldots$. (Of course, this mathematical model should have been confirmed by extensive statistical investi-gations of some TRNG prototypes. As the choice of the basis test does not affect the general principle of our online test procedure we will not pursue this topic in the remainder.) In the following $E_0(T)$ denotes the mean of the test variable T under the null hypothesis, that is, if the random variables $B_1, B_2, \ldots$ were iid and equidistributed on Ω_{das}.

Step 2: With respect to the intended applications minimal requirements on the distribution of the random variables $B_1, B_2, \ldots$ have to be specified. (Exam-ple: Based on the mathematical model of the noise source and the evaluation of TRNG prototypes the test designer concludes that the binary random vari-ables $B_1, B_2, \ldots$ are Markovian. For the intended applications $\text{Prob}(B_j = 1) \in$

$[0.48, 0.52]$ and $|\text{Prob}(B_{j+1} = 1 \mid B_j = 0) + \text{Prob}(B_{j+1} = 0 \mid B_j = 1) - 1| \leq 0.01$ are viewed as sufficient. In particular, it may be reasonable to choose a basis test which considers the one-step transition frequencies.) Time intervals or events have to be specified after those a basis test has to be executed, e.g.: always, one basis test per second, one basis test after an external call for random numbers, basis tests within the idle time of the device (if the TRNG is part of a larger cryptographic system) etc. With regard to the intended applications a reasonable upper bound for the average number of noise alarms within a time interval (year, month etc.) has to be specified. This upper bound should not be exceeded for any distribution of the random variables $B_1, B_2, \ldots$ which meets the minimal requirements specified before. Moreover, the consequences of a noise alarm have to be laid down, e.g.: The TRNG is put out of service, no further random numbers are produced till a check of the noise source and / or a manual restart of the TRNG, or something like that.

<u>Step 3:</u> A *test suite* consists of at most N basis tests. The basis test values are denoted with $\widetilde{T}_1, \widetilde{T}_2, \ldots$ while $\widetilde{H}_0 := E_0(T)$. In step $j \geq 1$ a basis test is performed, and the basis test value $\widetilde{T}_j$ is determined. Then $\widetilde{H}_j := (1 - \beta)\widetilde{H}_{j-1} + \beta\widetilde{T}_j$ is computed ($\beta \ll 1$) and rounded to a multiple of 2^{-c} where c is a fixed integer. Moreover, the following decision rules have to be considered:

$$\text{(A): if } \widetilde{T}_j \notin [r, s] \quad \Rightarrow \quad \text{noise alarm} \tag{3}$$

$$\text{(B): if } \widetilde{T}_{j-k+1}, \ldots, \widetilde{T}_j \notin [t, u] \quad \Rightarrow \quad \text{stop the test suite} \tag{4}$$

$$\text{(C): if } \widetilde{H}_j \notin [v, w] \quad \Rightarrow \quad \text{stop the test suite} \tag{5}$$

The parameter r and s should be chosen that a violation of decision criterion (A) is absolutely unlikely unless the random noise source has totally broken down. Consequently, a violation of decision rule (A) causes a noise alarm. Alternatively, if x consecutive test suites have been stopped due to (B) or (C) this also causes a noise alarm. Otherwise, after a test suite has been finished (due to a stop or because N basis tests have been executed) the next test suite begins.

The choice of the parameters $n, N, \beta, c, r, s, t, u, v, w$ and x should consider the goals formulated in Step 2. Without loss of generality we may assume that the parameters v and w are multiples of 2^{-c}. We point out that storing and updating the "history value" $\widetilde{H}_j$ needs no more than integer arithmetic. For this, we set $\beta := 2^{-b}$ for a suitable integer b. Before the test suite begins $\widetilde{H}_0 := E_0(T)$ is rounded to a multiple of 2^{-c}. To update the history value $\widetilde{H}_{j-1}$ the actual basis test value $\widetilde{T}_j$ is rounded to a multiple of 2^{-c} and then

$$\widetilde{H}_j := ((2^b - 1)\widetilde{H}_{j-1} + \widetilde{T}_j + 2^{b-1}) >> b \tag{6}$$

is calculated. (As usually, "$>> b$" denotes a right shift of b bits.) We point out that if $\widetilde{H}_j$ is calculated with a floating point arithmetic the basis test value $\widetilde{T}_j$ need not to be rounded before (cf. Remark 2 in Sect. 7).

6   Rationale and Advantages of the New Online Test Procedure

Roughly speaking, statistical results get more reliable the more tests are performed. The value $\widetilde{H}_j$ "contains" the history of the actual test suite up to step j without storing the test values $\widetilde{T}_1, \widetilde{T}_2, \ldots, \widetilde{T}_j$ explicitly. Decision rules (A) and (B) shall detect a total breakdown of the noise source or if the statistical quality of the das-random numbers has rapidly become worse, resp. The main task of decision rule (C), however, is to detect weaknesses in the long-term behaviour.

If the basis test values can be calculated with integer arithmetic (which should exist anyway) then the whole online test procedure needs no more than integer arithmetic (cf. Sect. 5). As the evaluation of the decision rules (A), (B) and (C) requires only little running time, a few extra lines of code and little extra memory our online test procedure perfectly meets demand (R4). In the worst case decision rule (A) requires only a few das-random numbers more than the sample size n of one basis test to detect a total breakdown of the noise source. Hence requirement (R1) is also fulfilled. In Example 2 we described an online test which is widely used in practice. Even for ideal random number generators it required enormous computational power to determine the expected number of noise alarms within a particular time interval. For (non-ideal) TRNGs however, the system designer had almost no control what is going on. For the online test procedure described in Sect. 5, however, for each parameter set *and for each assumed distribution* of the $B_1, B_2, \ldots$ we can at least approximately determine the expected number of noise alarms within a time interval. That is, we also have control on the effects of the test procedure if it is applied on non-ideal das-random number sequences. A suitably chosen parameter set n, N, b $(\beta := 2^{-b}), c, r, s, k, t, u, v, w$ and x supports the goals formulated in Step 2 of Sect. 5. Especially, it meets the requirements (R2) and (R3).

7   Mathematical Background

In this section we determine the average number of test suites until a noise alarm occurs. As each basis test requires a large number of das-random numbers we may assume that the test variables

$$T_1, T_2, \ldots \qquad \text{are iid,} \qquad (7)$$

regardless of the distribution of the random variables $B_1, B_2, \ldots$ (which may be dependent!) and the test strategy, i.e whether all das-random numbers are tested or not (see Sect. 5, Step 2). The *distribution* of the test variables $T_1, T_2, \ldots$, of course, depends essentially on that of $B_1, B_2, \ldots, B_n$.

The only task of decision rule (A) is to detect an eventual total breakdown of the noise source. The probability that (A) causes a noise alarm is absolutely negligible unless the random noise source has indeed totally broken down. We hence restrict our attention to decision rules (B) and (C). First, we first derive a formula to calculate the probability p_{st} for a stop of a test suite. Recall that the history values $\widetilde{H}_1, \widetilde{H}_2, \ldots$ and the parameters v and w are multiples of 2^{-c}.

Let $\widetilde{Y}_j$ denote the largest integer for which $\widetilde{T}_{j-\widetilde{Y}_j+1}, \widetilde{T}_{j-\widetilde{Y}_j+2}, \ldots, \widetilde{T}_j \notin [t, u]$. (Especially, $\widetilde{Y}_j := 0$ if $T_j \in [t, u]$.) We interpret the numbers $\widetilde{Y}_1, \widetilde{Y}_2, \ldots$ as realizations of random variables $Y_1, Y_2, \ldots$. Due to (7) the random vectors $(H_0, Y_0 := 0), (H_1, Y_1), \ldots$ form a homogeneous Markov chain on the infinite state space $\{\ldots, -2^{-c}, 0, 2^{-c}, 2 \cdot 2^{-c} \ldots\} \times \{0, 1, \ldots\}$. Therefrom we derive a homogeneous Markov chain $Z_0, Z_1, \ldots$ on the *finite* state space

$$\Omega = \{(h, y) \mid h \in [v, w], h \text{ is a multiple of } 2^{-c}, 0 \le y < k\} \cup \{\infty\}. \qquad (8)$$

In particular, Z_j attains the state ∞ if $(1 - \beta)H_{m-1} + \beta T_m \notin [v, w]$ or $Y_m = k$ for any $m \le j$ whereas $Z_j := (H_j, Y_j)$ else. That is, Z_j attains the state ∞ if the test suite has been stopped till time step j. Especially, ∞ is an absorbing state. (For the mathematical background of finite Markov chains the interested reader is referred to [8].)

Next, we determine the transition matrix $Q = (q_{\omega_1, \omega_2})_{\omega_1, \omega_2 \in \Omega}$. We point out that $(\widetilde{H}_{j-1}, \widetilde{H}_j) = (h, h')$ for $h, h' \in [v, w]$ iff $(1 - \beta)h + \beta \widetilde{T}_j \in [h' - 2^{-c-1}, h' + 2^{-c-1})$, or equivalently, iff $\widetilde{T}_j \in \beta^{-1}[h' - 2^{-c-1} - (1 - \beta)h, h' + 2^{-c-1} - (1 - \beta)h)$. Elementary but careful considerations yield the transition matrix

$$Q = (q_{\omega_1, \omega_2})_{\omega_1, \omega_2 \in \Omega} \qquad \text{with transition probabilities} \qquad q_{\omega_1, \omega_2} =$$

$$
\begin{cases}
\text{Prob}\,(T_j \in A_{h,h'} \cap (\mathbb{R} \setminus C)) & \text{if } \omega_1 = (h, y), \omega_2 = (h', y+1) \text{ and } y < k-1 \\
\text{Prob}\,(T_j \in A_{h,h'} \cap C) & \text{if } \omega_1 = (h, y), \omega_2 = (h', 0) \\
\text{Prob}\,(T_j \in \mathbb{R} \setminus D_h) & \text{if } \omega_1 = (h, y), \omega_2 = \infty \text{ and } y < k-1 \\
\text{Prob}\,(T_j \in (\mathbb{R} \setminus D_h) \cup (\mathbb{R} \setminus C)) & \text{if } \omega_1 = (h, k-1), \omega_2 = \infty \\
1 & \text{if } \omega_1 = \omega_2 = \infty \\
0 & \text{else}
\end{cases}
\qquad (9)
$$

where we used the abbreviations

$$A_{h,h'} := \beta^{-1}[h' - 2^{-c-1} - (1 - \beta)h, h' + 2^{-c-1} - (1 - \beta)h) \,,$$
$$C := [t - 2^{-c-1}, u + 2^{-c-1}) \quad \text{and}$$
$$D_h := \beta^{-1}[v - 2^{-c-1} - (1 - \beta)h, w + 2^{-c-1} - (1 - \beta)h) \,.$$

Remark 2. If the basis test value $\widetilde{T}_j$ is rounded to a multiple of 2^{-c} before it is "mixed" with $\widetilde{H}_{j-1}$ (cf. end of Sect. 5) in (9) the terms "Prob($T_j \in \ldots$)" should read "Prob($round(T_j) \in \ldots$)" where $round(\cdot)$ temporarily denotes the round-off function.

Now let $\boldsymbol{v}_{(\omega)}$ denote the column vector with $|\Omega|$ components which are all zero except the component indexed by ω which equals 1. As $Z_0 = (H_0, Y_0) = (E_0(T), 0)$ we obtain

$$p_{\text{st}} := \text{Prob}(\text{test suite is stopped}) = \text{Prob}(Z_N = \infty) = \boldsymbol{v}_{(E_0(T),0)}^{\text{t}} Q^N \boldsymbol{v}_{(\infty)}. \qquad (10)$$

The probability that x particular test suites are stopped is
$1 - \sum_{i=1}^{x}(1 - p_{st})p_{st}^{i-1} = 1 - (1 - p_{st}^{x}) = p_{st}^{x}$. Wald's equation ([5], 50) hence implies

$$E(\#test\ suites\ per\ noise\ alarm) = \frac{\sum_{i=1}^{x} i(1 - p_{st})p_{st}^{i-1} + xp_{st}^{x}}{p_{st}^{x}} \quad (11)$$

In the following we denote the distribution of $B_1, B_2, \ldots, B_n$ with $\nu[n]$ while $F_{\nu[n]}(\cdot)$ denotes the cumulative distribution function of the test variable T_i if the basis test is applied on $B_1, \ldots, B_n$. Especially, $\mu[n]$ means that the B_j are iid and equidistributed on Ω_{das} (null hypothesis).

To initialize the transition matrix Q we have to know the cumulative distribution function of T_i. What's the difference to the situation in Example 2? Also there the knowledge of $F_{\nu[n]}(65.0)$ would have solved the main problems. In particular, one could check whether (R2) and (R3) are fulfilled. As already mentioned in Sect. 4 even for $\mu[n]$ the relative error between the exact cumulative distribution $F_{\mu[n]}(\cdot)$ of T_i and that of the χ_{15}^2-distribution is very large at the (extreme) tails of both distributions. In the online test procedure described in Sect. 5, however, the factor β is small and thus even an extremely large single basis test value $\widetilde{T}_j$ will not influence the history variable $\widetilde{H}_j$ considerably unless a total breakdown of the noise source has just occurred. For decision rule (C) the totality of all basis test values up to this moment is essential while the probability that decision rule (B) stops the actual test suite depends essentially on $1 - (F_{\nu[n]}(u) - F_{\nu[n]}(t))$ and, of course, on k. We recommend to choose t and u that for the tolerable distributions $\nu[n]$ this probability is $\geq 10^{-3}$. In particular, unlike as in Example 2, for $\nu[n] = \mu[n]$ the deviation the approximate cumulative distribution function of T_i from $F_{\mu[n]}$ will not influence p_{st} considerably.

For general $\nu[n]$ we may approximate $F_{\nu[n]}$ by an empirical cumulative distribution function $F_{\nu[n]emp}$ which we derive with a stochastic simulation (see, e.g. [9], [5]). For this, we need a fast pseudorandom number generator with good statistical properties. (Unpredictability of the pseudorandom numbers is irrelevant in this context.) A sound candidate is, for example, the recursive algorithm

$$x_{n+1} \equiv ax_n + 1 \pmod{2^{64}}, \quad \text{with} \quad a \equiv 1 \pmod{4}, \quad a > 2^{48}, \quad (12)$$

a so-called *linear congruential generator*. Setting $v_j := x_j 2^{-64}$ yields a sequence of standard random numbers. The standard random numbers behave similarly as realizations of iid random variables $V_1, V_2, \ldots$ which are equidistributed on the unit interval $[0, 1)$. From the standard random numbers one derives a sequence $\widetilde{B}_1', \widetilde{B}_2', \ldots$ which is viewed as a realization of $B_1, B_2, \ldots$. (Example: Let the B_j be iid binary random variables with $\text{Prob}(B_j = 1) = 0.48$. Then we set $\widetilde{B}_j' := 1$ if $v_j \leq 0.48$ and $\widetilde{B}_j' := 0$ else.) We apply the basis test to $\widetilde{B}_1', \ldots, \widetilde{B}_n'$ and compute the respective basis test value $\widetilde{T}_1'$. Repeating this process K times ($K \geq 10^5$) we obtain an empirical cumulative distribution function $F_{\nu[n]emp}$ which we use for the initialization of the transition matrix Q. Due to Glivenko-Cantelli's theorem ([6], 145) the absolute value $\sup_{x \in \mathbb{R}} |F_{\nu[n]}(x) - F_{\nu[n]emp}(x)|$ should be small which is essential for decision criterion (C). Concerning decision rule (B), the relative error $|(1 - F_{\nu[n]}(u) + F_{\nu[n]}(t)) - (1 - F_{\nu[n]emp}(u) + F_{\nu[n]emp}(t))|/(1 - F_{\nu[n]emp}(u) + F_{\nu[n]emp}(t))$ should be small as $1 - F_{\mu[n]}(u) - F_{\mu[n]}(t) \geq 10^{-3}$ for typical choices of t and u. To obtain a reliable approximation of $1 - F_{\nu[n]}(65.0)$ for the χ^2-square test in Example 2, however, the parameter K had to be gigantic.

Remark 3. (i) Of course, $F_{\nu[n]emp}$ is not exact. In principle, this could cause a bad approximation of the exact probability p_{st}. We gave reasons why this should not be the case. Moreover, stochastic simulations support this opinion. If the empirical distribution was derived twice ($K = 10^6$) for the same distribution $\nu[n]$ the respective p_{st}-values usually differed less than 1 per cent from their arithmetical mean. This shows that the derived results are stable. In (ii) we give a formal argumentation that decision rule (B) amplifies small relative errors no more than by factor k.

(ii) The probability that at least k consecutive test values $\widetilde{T}_1, \widetilde{T}_2, \ldots, \widetilde{T}_N$ lie outside $[t, u]$ is about $1 - (1 - p^k)^{N(1-p)}$ where p temporarily stands for the probability $\text{Prob}(T_i \notin [t, u])$ (or $\text{Prob}(round(T_i) \notin [t, u])$, resp.; cf. Remark 2) If p' denotes an approximation of p the relative error equals $|(1 - (1 - p^k)^{N(1-p)}) - (1 - (1 - p'^k)^{N(1-p')})|/(1 - (1 - p'^k)^{N(1-p')})$. If $(Np^k)^2, (Np'^k)^2 \ll 1$ the relative error is about $|(1 - p)p^k - (1 - p')p'^k|/(1 - p')p'^k$. If additionally $p \approx p'$ (which is likely, for example, if $p \geq 10^{-3}$ and $K \geq 10^5$) this term further simplifies to $k|p - p'|/p'$.

8   Examples

In Sect. 8 we discuss two examples. Especially, Example 3 provides an appropriate solution for Example 2. The effect of the particular parameters is explained in Sect. 9.

Example 3. We consider the same situation as in Example 2 (cf. Sect. 3). Due to the construction of the noise source it may be assumed that the random variables $B_1, B_2, \ldots$ are iid but not necessarily equidistributed (cf. Remark 4(iii)). Extensive statistical investigations of TRNG prototypes have confirmed this hypothesis. For the intended applications it is absolutely acceptable ("tolerable") if $\text{Prob}(B_j = 1) \in [0.49, 0.51]$. Otherwise, a noise alarm should occur sooner or later, depending on the "degree" of the statistical weaknesses of the das-random numbers. If $\text{Prob}(B_j = 1) < 0.475$ or $\text{Prob}(B_j = 1) > 0.525$, however, a noise alarm should occur soon. Recall that per TRNG about 530000 basis tests are performed per year (cf. Example 2).

<u>Proposed solution:</u> Basis test: χ^2-test on 128 four-bit blocks (i.e. $n = 512$). Further, we use the parameter set $N = 512$, $\beta = 1/64$ (i.e. $b = 6$), $c = 5$, $r = 0.0$, $s = 200.0$, $k = 3$, $t = 0.0$, $u = 26.75$, $v = 13.0$, $w = 17.0$, $x = 3$.

The values in Table 1 were derived on basis of empirical distribution functions as described in Sect. 7 ($K = 10^6$). The right-hand column of Table 1 gives the expected number of noise alarms per year. In particular, if $\text{Prob}(B_j = 1) \notin [0.475, 0.525]$ a noise alarm will occur after a few test suites.

Table 1. Example 3: Expected number of noise alarms per year

$\mathrm{Prob}(B_j = 1)$	p_{st}	$E\left(\dfrac{\text{\# noise alarms}}{\text{year}}\right)$
0.500	0.0162	0.004
0.495	0.0184	0.006
0.490	0.0289	0.024
0.485	0.0745	0.396
0.480	0.2790	16.6
0.475	0.7470	

Table 2. Example 4: Expected number of noise alarms per year

$\mathrm{Prob}(B_j = 1)$	p_{st}	$E\left(\dfrac{\text{\# noise alarms}}{\text{year}}\right)$
0.500	0.0151	0.00005
0.495	0.0180	0.00011
0.490	0.0349	0.0015
0.485	0.1096	0.1332
0.480	0.3866	14.5
0.475	0.8501	

Remark 4. (i) The calculation of the basis test values requires no more than integer multiplication and addition and, finally, a division by $8 = 2^3$.
(ii) For $c = 6$ instead of $c = 5$ the p_{st}-values are some percent larger as the Markov process $Z_0, Z_1, \ldots$ is less "inert" (cf. Sect. 9).
(iii) For simplicity, in Examples 3 and 4 we assume that the random variables $B_1, B_2, \ldots$ are iid. This, however, need not be the case for all types of random noise sources. We point out that dependent random variables B_j can be handled in the same way as iid ones. (Numerical example: Let the random variables $B_1, B_2, \ldots$ be Markovian with $\mathrm{Prob}(B_{j+1} = 1 \mid B_j = 0) = 0.490$ and $\mathrm{Prob}(B_{j+1} = 0 \mid B_j = 1) = 0.490$. Using the same parameters as in Example 3 yields $p_{st} \approx 0.0243$, and hence about 0.014 noise alarms are expected per year.) Of course, if we drop the assumption that the B_j are iid we usually have to consider much more distributions than listed in Table 1.

Example 4. We consider the same situation as in Example 3. However, due to the intended application the expected number of noise alarms per year must not larger than 0.0015 if the TRNG produces appropriate das random numbers. (For example, the noise source could be part of a smart card which is used by customers to execute e-commerce applications. If the TRNG causes a noise alarm the smart card denies further service and has to be replaced by a new one.)

Proposed solution: Basis test: χ^2-test on 128 four-bit blocks (i.e. $n = 512$). Further, we use the parameter set $N = 512$, $\beta = 1/64$ (i.e. $b = 6$), $c = 5$, $r = 0.0$, $s = 200.0$, $k = 4$, $t = 0.0$, $u = 24.0$, $v = 13.125$, $w = 16.875$, $x = 4$.

Remark 5. Our online test procedure enables "controlled" testing. If "sound" TRNGs generate das random numbers which themselves are appropriate for the intended applications and if the mathematical model of the physical noise source and thus that of the das random numbers is reliable (i.e., if we can be sure that the (eventually TRNG-specific) distribution of the das random numbers is contained in the assumed class of distributions) this usually makes a strong, data-compressing (throughput-reducing!) mathematical follow-up treatment dispensable. If also the reduced data-rate is sufficiently large for the intended applications, however, a data-compressing follow-up treatment may be used as an additional security mechanism, even if this may not actually be necessary.

9   Fine-Tuning of the Parameter Set

If the basis test and the parameter set have been chosen suitably the online test procedure should perfectly meet the particular requirements of the intended applications. In Sect. 7 we described how to compute p_{st} and the expected number of test suites until a noise alarm occurs. However, as the computation of p_{st} is time-consuming we cannot try thousands of randomly chosen parameter sets. Below, we briefly describe the effect of particular parameters.

n: Unless it is too small the sample size n usually does not influence the distribution of the basis test variables T_j if $\nu[n] = \mu[n]$. If $\nu[n] \neq \mu[n]$, however, increasing n often implies higher rejection rates. Example: Let $\widetilde{T} := 2(\widetilde{B}_1 + \cdots + \widetilde{B}_n - 0.5n)/\sqrt{n}$ which merely considers the number of ones within the sample. If the B_j are iid with $\mathrm{Prob}(B_j = 1) = p$ the central limit theorem implies $\mathrm{Prob}(|T| > \alpha) = 1 - \Phi\left(\alpha/\sqrt{4p(1-p)} - \sqrt{n}(p-0.5)/\sqrt{p(1-p)}\right) + \Phi\left(-\alpha/\sqrt{4p(1-p)} - \sqrt{n}(p-0.5)/\sqrt{p(1-p)}\right)$ where $\Phi(\cdot)$ denotes the cumulative distribution function of the standard normal distribution. If $\alpha = 2.575$ and $p = 0.48$, for example, for $n = 128$ (resp., for $n = 512$) we obtain the probability 0.018 (resp., 0.048). If $p = 0.5$, however, this probability equals 0.01 for both, $n = 128$ and $n = 512$.

N: Due to (10) it is reasonable to choose a power of 2 as this minimizes the number of matrix multiplications and thus the computation time. Furthe, it avoids unnecessary round-off errors when computing the probability p_{st}.

x: For small p_{st} equation (11) is essentially determined by the term p_{st}^{-x}. Thus, for different p_{st}-values increasing the parameter x amplifies the ratio of the expected number of test suites till the first noise alarm occurs. (Example: If $p_{st;1} = 2p_{st;2}$ it is $p_{st;1}^{-3} = p_{st;2}^{-3}/8$ but $p_{st;1}^{-4} = p_{st;2}^{-4}/16$.) This effect can be used to "separate" the tolerable from the non-tolerable distributions.

β: The smaller $\beta := 2^{-b}$ the smaller is the influence of single basis test values on the history values $\widetilde{H}_1, \widetilde{H}_2, \ldots$.

c: The history variables $H_0, H_1, \ldots$ may be interpreted as a "weighted" random walk on $[v,w] \cap \{\ldots, -2^{-c}, 0, 2^{-c}, 2 \cdot 2^{-c}, \ldots\}$ with absorbing state ∞. The smaller c the more "inert" is this random walk and hence the smaller is p_{st}. In particular, $\widetilde{H}_j \neq \widetilde{H}_{j-1}$ iff $(1 - \beta)\widetilde{H}_{j-1} + \beta\widetilde{T}_j \notin \widetilde{H}_{j-1} + [-2^{-c-1}, 2^{-c-1})$ iff $\widetilde{T}_j \notin \widetilde{H}_{j-1} + \beta^{-1}[-2^{-c-1}, 2^{-c-1})$. We recommend to choose $b, c \in \{5, 6\}$. (Recall, however, that the transition matrix Q has $|\Omega|^2 = [k(2^c(v-w)+1)+1]^2$ entries.).

10   Conclusions and Final Remarks

In this paper we proposed a new online test, or more precisely, a new online test procedure for which it is *practically feasible* to determine the expected number of noise alarms within a time interval, even if the tested random numbers are not independent and equidistributed. The system designer can vary a whole parameter set and hence can fit the test to the very special requirements of the intended applications. In particular, this makes data-compressing (i.e. throughput-reducing) mathematical follow-up treatments in many cases dispensable. Compared with "ordinary" online tests the proposed online test procedure does only need a little more memory, some additional lines of code and slightly more running time.

References

1. AIS 20: Functionality Classes and Evaluation Methodology for Deterministic Random Number Generators. (English Translation, mandatory if a German security certificate is applied for). (December 1999). www.bsi.bund.de/aufgaben/ii/zert/jil_ais/ais20e.pdf
2. V. Bagini and M. Bucci: A Design of Reliable True Number Generators for Cryptographic Applications. In: Ç.K. Koç and C. Paar (eds.): Cryptographic Hardware and Embedded Systems. First International Workshop, CHES '99. Springer, Lecture Notes in Computer Science, Vol. **1717**, Berlin (1999), 204–218.
3. J.-S. Coron: On the Security of Random Sources. In: H. Imai and Y. Zheng (eds.): Public Key Cryptography. Second International Workshop on Practice and Theory in Public Key Cryptography, PKC '99. Springer, Lecture Notes in Computer Science, Vol. **1560**, Berlin (1999), 29–42.
4. J.-C. Coron, D. Naccache: An Accurate Evaluation of Maurer's Universal Test. In: S. Tavares and H. Meijer (eds.): Selected Areas in Cryptography '98, SAC '98. Springer, Lecture Notes in Computer Science, Vol. **1556**, Berlin (1999), 57–71.
5. L. Devroye: Non-Uniform Random Variate Generation. Springer, New York (1986).
6. P. Gänssler und W. Stute: Wahrscheinlichkeitstheorie. Springer, Berlin (1977).
7. G.K. Kanji: 100 Statistical Tests. Sage Publications, London (1995).
8. J.G. Kemeny and J.L. Snell: Finite Markov Chains. D. Van Nostrand, New York (1960).
9. D.E. Knuth: The Art of Computer Programming. Vol. 2, Addison-Wesley, London (1981).

10. D.P. Maher and R.J. Rance: Random Number Generators founded on Signal and Information Theory. In: Ç.K. Koç and C. Paar (eds.): Cryptographic Hardware and Embedded Systems. First International Workshop, CHES '99. Springer, Lecture Notes in Computer Science, Vol. **1717**, Berlin (1999), 219–230.
11. U. Maurer: A Universal Statistical Test for Random Bit Generators. J. Crypt. **5** (1992), 89–105.
12. NIST Special Publication 800–22: A Statistical Test Suite for Random and Pseudorandom Numbers. (December 2000).

The Hessian Form of an Elliptic Curve

N.P. Smart

Dept. Computer Science, University of Bristol,
Merchant Venturers Building, Woodland Road, Bristol, BS8 1UB
nigel@cs.bris.ac.uk

Abstract. In this paper we use the Hessian form of an elliptic curve
and show that it offers some performance advantages over the standard
representation. In particular when a processor allows the evaluation of a
number of field multiplications in parallel (either via separate ALU's, a
SIMD type operation or a pipelined multiplication unit) one can obtain
a performance advantage of around forty percent.

1 Introduction

Much research has been conducted on implementing cryptographic operations
on various types of computer architectures. For example standard superscalar
RISC and CISC processors [3] [6], smart cards [9] and FPGAs [8] . In this paper
we are interested in producing highly efficient implementations of operations
needed in elliptic curve cryptography by exploiting parallelism.

In [3] the instruction level parallelism (ILP) in the various AES candidates
was examined. This is an important area of research for any cryptographic algorithm as most algorithms will be implemented on superscalar processors which
make use of ILP to increase performance. In most cryptographic algorithms the
basic blocks are dependent, hence the only natural level of parallelism is at the
instruction level. We shall show in this paper that this is not true for elliptic
curve cryptosystems. We shall show that for elliptic curve systems one can make
use of parallelism at the basic block, or function, level. We shall then go on to
show that a special class of elliptic curves, namely those with a point of order
three, have addition laws which are highly parallel. In addition the curves will
be able to be used in both even and large characteristic. We shall give a comparison of a standard elliptic curve representation against the Hessian form on
an FPGA.

We see significant advantages for using the ideas in this paper when we
consider the use of custom processors for cryptographic operations. These are
common at both the high and low end of the markets: Smart cards require specialized cryptographic coprocessors to be able to perform a single cryptographic
operation in a reasonable amount of time, whilst high end servers often require
cryptographic accelerator boards to as to increase the throughput of the overall
traffic.

We envisage a processor which has the ability to conduct a number of multi-
precision arithmetic operations in parallel. We assume that the field is either

Ç.K. Koç, D. Naccache, and C. Paar (Eds.): CHES 2001, LNCS 2162, pp. 118–125, 2001.
© Springer-Verlag Berlin Heidelberg 2001

$\mathbb{F}_p$ or $\mathbb{F}_{2^n}$, as is common in elliptic curve systems. This can be implemented in a number of ways, either as a SIMD operation, via a number of standard coprocessors operating in parallel, by having a number of Arithmetic Logic Units (ALUs) operating in parallel or by having a single pipelined multiplication unit. To aid the discussion later we shall assume up to three field operations can be applied in parallel in a SIMD fashion, i.e. at most three multiplications or three additions. It will turn out that performing additions in parallel is not as important, and in any case can be done virtually for free in characteristic two.

2   Cryptographic Algorithms

It is clear that standard implementations of RSA and discrete logarithm type systems cannot make use of the architecture proposed in the previous section. Of course they could perform a number of RSA exponentiations in parallel, but we would not obtain a performance advantage for a single modular exponentiation. The reason for this lack of improvement is that each modular multiplication required in a group exponentiation algorithm is dependent on the previous operations.

For elliptic curve cryptography (ECC) systems the situation is very different. In ECC one trades smaller sizes for the field elements against a more complicated group operation. We have already remarked that the group exponentiation techniques do not offer any opportunity for parallelism. However, the group operation itself does offer such opportunities.

To see this consider the following description of the doubling formulae for a point $P = (X, Y)$ on a curve over a field of characteristic $p > 3$ given by

$$Y^2 = X^3 - 3X + b.$$

We assume the point is given in Jacobian projective coordinates $P = (x/z^2, y/z^3)$ and the output is given by (x', y', z');

$$
\begin{aligned}
&\lambda_1 = x^2 && \lambda_2 = z^2 && \lambda_3 = y^2 \\
&\lambda_4 = yz && \lambda_5 = x\lambda_3 && \lambda_6 = \lambda_3^2 \\
&\lambda_7 = \lambda_2^2 && z' = 2\lambda_4 && \lambda_8 = 4\lambda_5 \\
&\lambda_9 = \lambda_1 - \lambda_7 \\
&\lambda_{10} = 8\lambda_6 && \lambda_{11} = 3\lambda_9 \;\; \lambda_{12} = 2\lambda_8 \\
&\lambda_{13} = \lambda_{11}^2 \\
&x' = \lambda_{13} - \lambda_{12} \\
&\lambda_{14} = \lambda_8 - x' \\
&\lambda_{15} = \lambda_{11}\lambda_{14} \\
&y' = \lambda_{15} - \lambda_{10}
\end{aligned}
$$

Each row corresponds to the (at most) three operations which can be carried out in parallel. As one can see one can obtain a limited improvement in performance by exploiting the parallel nature of the computation. However, this is rather restricted due to our SIMD based constraint of not allowing the mixing of field additions and multiplications. Even if we dropped this constraint the above algorithm would not improve performance that much. If we assume each row in the above table can be executed in the same time on a SIMD/pipelined style processor as a single operation could on a standard processor, we would obtain roughly a 50 percent performance improvement.

Similar considerations apply to all the other standard algorithms for addition and doubling on elliptic curves in even and large prime characteristic. There is generally a set of operations at the beginning of each operation which lend themselves to parallel execution followed by a sequence of operations which are highly dependent. Overall one can obtain roughly a 50–60 percent improvement in performance.

In the next section we present a special type of elliptic curve which allows one to obtain a five fold increase in performance over the standard sequential point addition algorithm and a three fold increase over the standard sequential point doubling algorithm.

3   The Hessian Form of an Elliptic Curve

Let $k = \mathbb{F}_q$ denote a finite field with q a prime power such that $q \equiv 2 \pmod{3}$, we include the case of characteristic two fields. Let E denote an elliptic curve over k which has a k-rational point of order 3. The restriction on the choice of k is for two reasons; Firstly it implies that although we have a point of order 3 we only have two of them rather than a full set of eight. Secondly it implies that the construction below is guaranteed to apply.

Note that this constraint on the field and curve means that the recommended curves specified in the ANSI and FIPS standards cannot be made into Hessian form. However, these constraints are consistent with the recommendations for curve parameters specified in the IEEE, ANSI and SECG standards. So the Hessian form is still able to be used in standard compliant implementations, one just cannot use the recommended curves contained in some standards.

By moving a point of order three to the origin, we can assume our elliptic curve has the form
$$E : Y^2 + a_1 XY + a_3 Y = X^3.$$
This curve has discriminant
$$\Delta = a_3^3(a_1^3 - 27a_3) = a_3^3 \delta.$$
The points of order three on E are given by $(0, 0)$ and $(0, -a_3)$.

We wish to find a more convenient model for our elliptic curve E. To do this we perform the following transformations: We let μ denote a root of the polynomial
$$T^3 - \delta T^2 + \delta^2 T/3 + a_3 \delta^2 = 0.$$
Since $q \equiv 2 \pmod{3}$ every element in k has a unique cube root and we can determine μ from the formula
$$\mu = \frac{1}{3}\left(\left(-27a_3\delta^2 - \delta^3\right)^{1/3} + \delta\right).$$

Now define

$$D = 3\frac{\mu - \delta}{\mu}.$$

The curve E is then birationally equivalent to the curve

$$C : x^3 + y^3 + z^3 = Dxyz,$$

which is called the cubic Hessian form [2]. The change of variable to pass from E to C is given by

$$x = \frac{a_1(2\mu - \delta)}{3\mu - \delta}X + Y + a_3,$$

$$y = \frac{-a_1\mu}{3\mu - \delta}X - Y,$$

$$z = \frac{-a_1\mu}{3\mu - \delta}X - a_3.$$

3.1 Example Curve

Our example curve will be in characteristic two, defined over the field of 2^{191} elements. We shall represent the field by a polynomial basis in t over $\mathbb{F}_2$, where

$$t^{191} + t^9 + 1 = 0.$$

Elements of k we will represent by hexadecimal numbers, prefixed by the string 0x, which correspond to the associated polynomial being thought of as a polynomial over the integers and then evaluated at 2. For example 0x11 corresponds to the polynomial $x^4 + 1$.

Consider the elliptic curve given by

$$E' : y^2 + xy = x^3 + x^2 + b$$

where

$$b = \text{0x4DE3965E00F2A1C6C9750156A6FEFBE5EEF780BF3EF20E48}.$$

This curve has group order

$$6 \cdot q = 3138550867693340381917894711648254768837315541933943803842,$$

where q is a prime. A point of order 3 on E' is given by the point (x_3, y_3), where

$$x_3 = \text{0x4763CFBC4340674B749E57887850E92C9B6BEDF58EEDC3BF},$$
$$y_3 = \text{0x14A96A1E53DCC3E73CFB22B80E8658CE0D6D8E82ED2AEC7D}.$$

If we perform the following change of variable

$$X = x + x_3, \quad Y = y + sx + x_3^2,$$

where

$$s = \frac{x_3^2 + y_3}{x_3},$$

then we obtain an elliptic curve E in the form

$$E : Y^2 + XY + x_3 Y = X^3.$$

We can now use the above transformation to determine that the Hessian form C is given by

$$x^3 + y^3 + z^3 = Dxyz,$$

where

$$D = \text{0x16A4C7C2030FAD1380ABF8C2D47DC3E0C20AF62F6EDD06A7}.$$

A point of order q on C is given by (x, y, z), where

$$x = \text{0x52FD0CE78D0651B4F66D2F4E12E170CA3E429F6A06433B22},$$
$$y = \text{0x1BECA50368403F3D13173968082B035397C77830A9D90E5D},$$
$$z = \text{0x2B08F7C0CCAC86151AA6FECABDD2D052BD60924F28A6A78E}.$$

4   The Hessian Group Law

The group law on curves in Hessian form has been known to be particularly simple for a long time, see [1, Formulary], [2] and [5]. The zero of the group law on C is given by $(1, -1, 0)$. The two points of order three are given by $(0, 1, -1)$ and $(1, 0, -1)$. If $P = (x_1, y_1, z_1)$ and $Q = (x_2, y_2, z_2)$, we define

$$-P = (y_1, x_1, z_1),$$
$$P + Q = (x_3, y_3, z_3),$$

where

$$x_3 = y_1^2 x_2 z_2 - y_2^2 x_1 z_1,$$
$$y_3 = x_1^2 y_2 z_2 - x_2^2 y_1 z_1,$$
$$z_3 = z_1^2 y_2 x_2 - z_2^2 y_1 x_1.$$

The formulae for point doubling are given by $[2]P = (x_2, y_2, z_2)$ where

$$x_2 = y_1(z_1^3 - x_1^3),$$
$$y_2 = x_1(y_1^3 - z_1^3),$$
$$z_3 = z_1(x_1^3 - y_1^3).$$

These formulae apply both in even and large prime characteristic. The addition formulae requires 12 field multiplications, whilst the doubling formulae requires 6 field multiplications and three squarings.

We first compare the sequential operation of the above group law with the usual formulae.

For curves over fields of large prime characteristic, given by the usual model, it is best to use a mixed coordinate representation of points, see [4]. In the most common case of using Jacobian projective coordinates for doubling and mixed Jacobian/affine coordinates for addition we can perform an addition in 8 multiplications and 3 squarings. A doubling will take 4 multiplications and 4 squarings.

In fields of characteristic two, again in the standard model, we can again use a mixed coordinate system, but this time using the projective coordinates proposed in [7]. One can now perform an addition using 9 multiplications and 4 squarings. A doubling can be performed in 4 multiplications and 5 squarings.

So for sequential execution of the multiplication operations the standard representation appears to be more efficient. However, the group operations for the Hessian form can be performed in a highly parallel way. As before we assume that at most three multiprecision multiplications can be performed in parallel.

The addition of two points, $P = (x_1, y_1, z_1)$ and $Q = (x_2, y_2, z_2)$, in the Hessian form can be carried out as follows

$$
\begin{array}{lll}
\lambda_1 = y_1 x_2 & \lambda_2 = x_1 y_2 & \lambda_3 = x_1 z_2 \\
\lambda_4 = z_1 x_2 & \lambda_5 = z_1 y_2 & \lambda_6 = z_2 y_1 \\
s_1 = \lambda_1 \lambda_6 & s_2 = \lambda_2 \lambda_3 & s_3 = \lambda_5 \lambda_4 \\
t_1 = \lambda_2 \lambda_5 & t_2 = \lambda_1 \lambda_4 & t_3 = \lambda_6 \lambda_3 \\
x_3 = s_1 - t_1 & y_3 = s_2 - t_2 & z_3 = s_3 - t_3
\end{array}
$$

The case of the two projective points being equivalent, and the doubling operation needing to be called, can be detected from the condition

$$\lambda_1 = \lambda_2 \text{ and } \lambda_3 = \lambda_4.$$

The point doubling operation on the Hessian can also be expressed in a similar highly parallel way

$$
\begin{array}{lll}
\lambda_1 = x_1^2 & \lambda_2 = y_1^2 & \lambda_3 = z_1^2 \\
\lambda_4 = x_1 \lambda_1 & \lambda_5 = y_1 \lambda_2 & \lambda_6 = z_1 \lambda_3 \\
\lambda_7 = \lambda_5 - \lambda_6 & \lambda_8 = \lambda_6 - \lambda_4 & \lambda_9 = \lambda_4 - \lambda_5 \\
x_2 = y_1 \lambda_8 & y_2 = x_1 \lambda_7 & z_2 = z_1 \lambda_9.
\end{array}
$$

5   FPGA Implementation

We implemented the example curve above both using the standard representation and the Hessian form on a Xilinx4000XL FPGA. The code was written using the HandelC language and compiler produced by Embedded Solutions Ltd. This converts a C like language into a netlist which is then passed through Xilinx tools to produce the final FPGA bitmap.

The implementation was made to test the relative performance of the two models and not to maximize the speed. The FPGA implemented a simple point multiplication algorithm; taking as input a 191 bit integer m and returning the projective point corresponding to $[m]P$, where P is the point of order q on the appropriate models given earlier.

The point multiplication used was the simple right-to-left binary method. The code for both representations made as much use of the parallel nature of the double and add routines as could be accommodated.

The following timings were obtained as an average over a number of calls to the FPGA;

Form of Curve	Point Multiplication Time
Standard (Sequential)	77.238 ms
Standard(Parallel)	17.711 ms
Hessian	11.821 ms

So we see that the Hessian form gives around a 40 percent performance improvement over the standard form, even when we exploit all the inherent parallelism in the standard formulae.

6   Conclusion

We have shown that using the Hessian form of an elliptic curve allows us to implement the point addition and point doubling operation in a highly parallel way. This can be exploited by a number of processor architectures such as those which have a SIMD style instruction set, those which have multiple ALU's or those which have a pipelined finite field multiplier.

We have shown, by implementing a demonstration example on an FPGA in characteristic two, that the Hessian form does in fact give a significant performance improvement in real life.

References

1. J.W.S. Cassels. *Lectures on Elliptic Curves*. LMS Student Texts, Cambridge University Press, 1991.
2. D.V. Chudnovsky and G.V. Chudnovsky. Sequences of numbers generated by addition in formal groups and new primality and factorisation tests. *Adv. in Appl. Math.*, **7**, 385–434, 1987.
3. C. Clapp. Instruction level parallelism in AES Candidates. *Second Advanced Encryption Standard Candidate Conference*, Rome March 1999.
4. H. Cohen, A. Miyaji and T. Ono. Efficient elliptic curve exponentiation using mixed coordinates. In *Advances in Cryptology, ASIACRYPT 98*. Springer-Verlag, LNCS 1514, 51–65, 1998.
5. M. Desboves. Résolution en nombres entiers et sous sa forme la plus générale, de l'équation cubique, homogène, à trois inconnues. *Nouvelles Ann. de Math.*, **45**, 545–579, 1886.
6. C.K. Koc, T. Acer and B.S. Kaliski Jnr. Analyzing and comparing Montgomery multiplication algorithm. *IEEE Micro*, **16**, 26–33, June 1996.

7. J. López and R. Dahab. Improved algorithms for elliptic curve arithmetic in $GF(2^n)$ In *Selected Areas in Cryptography - SAC '98*, Springer-Verlag, LNCS 1556, 201–212, 1999.
8. G. Orlando and C. Paar. A high-performance reconfigurable elliptic curve processor for $GF(2^m)$. In *Cryptographic Hardware and Embedded Systems (CHES) 2000*, Springer-Verlag, LNCS 1965, 41–56, 2000.
9. A.D. Woodbury, D.V. Bailey and C. Paar. Elliptic curve cryptography on smart cards without coprocessors. In *Smart Card and Advanced Applications, CARDIS 2000*, 71–92, Kluwer, 2000.

Efficient Elliptic Curve Cryptosystems from a Scalar Multiplication Algorithm with Recovery of the y-Coordinate on a Montgomery-Form Elliptic Curve

Katsuyuki Okeya[1] and Kouichi Sakurai[2]

[1] Hitachi, Ltd., Software Division,
5030, Totsuka-cho, Totsuka-ku, Yokohama, 244-8555, Japan
okeya_k@itg.hitachi.co.jp
[2] Kyushu University,
Department of Computer Science and Communication Engineering
6-10-1, Hakozaki, Higashi-ku, Fukuoka, 812-8581, Japan
sakurai@csce.kyushu-u.ac.jp

Abstract. We present a scalar multiplication algorithm with recovery of the y-coordinate on a Montgomery form elliptic curve over any non-binary field.

The previous algorithms for scalar multiplication on a Montgomery form do not consider how to recover the y-coordinate. So although they can be applicable to certain restricted schemes (e.g. ECDH and ECDSA-S), some schemes (e.g. ECDSA-V and MQV) require scalar multiplication with recovery of the y-coordinate.

We compare our proposed scalar multiplication algorithm with the traditional scalar multiplication algorithms (including Window-methods in Weierstrass form), and discuss the Montgomery form versus the Weierstrass form in the performance of implementations with several techniques of elliptic curve cryptosystems (including ECES, ECDSA, and ECMQV). Our results clarify the advantage of the cryptographic usage of Montgomery-form elliptic curves in constrained environments such as mobile devices and smart cards.

Keywords: *Elliptic Curve Cryptosystem, Montgomery form, Fast Scalar Multiplication, y-coordinate recovery*

1   Introduction

Lim and Hwang give the following problem [LH00, page 409]: "Montgomery's method is not a general algorithm for elliptic scalar multiplication in $GF(p^n)$, since it can't compute the y-coordinate of kP." This paper completely solves this problem, and shows that Montgomery's method is indeed a general algorithm.

Ç.K. Koç, D. Naccache, and C. Paar (Eds.): CHES 2001, LNCS 2162, pp. 126–141, 2001.
© Springer-Verlag Berlin Heidelberg 2001

1.1 Montgomery-Form Elliptic Curves

Montgomery introduced the non-standard form $E^M : BY^2 = X^3 + AX^2 + X$ for elliptic curves in [Mon87], while the most standard form of elliptic curves is $E : y^2 = x^3 + ax + b$, which is called the (short) Weierstrass form. While investigating efficient scalar multiplication algorithms on elliptic curves, some researchers [LD99,LH00,Kur98,OKS00] have independently observed that Montgomery's method [Mon87] has an advantage in preventing timing attacks [Koc, Koc96].[1]

1.2 Elliptic Curve Cryptosystems without the y-Coordinate

The scalar multiplication algorithm on a Montgomery-form elliptic curve is fast, because it requires information on the x-coordinate only. Recall that previous proposed algorithms on a Montgomery form consider only the x-coordinate of kP, the k-time scalar multiplication of the point P over the elliptic curve. This is enough for application to some elliptic curve cryptosystems including the key-establishment scheme ECDH, and signature generation ECDSA-S [IEEEp1363].

However, we should note that the ECDSA verifying algorithm cannot be executed without referencing the y-coordinate of kP. Also ECSVDP-MQV, ECSVDP-MQVC, ECVP-NR, and ECVP-DSA, which are described in the draft standard IEEE P1363 [IEEEp1363], need a scalar multiplication with recovery of the y-coordinate.

1.3 Montgomery Form with Recovery of the y-Coordinate

Recently, López and Dahab [LD99] extended the idea of Montgomery's method [Mon87] to binary fields (i.e. $\mathbf{F}_{2^m}$), and developed an algorithm for a scalar multiplication with recovery of the y-coordinate.

However, their algorithm is valid only over binary fields, and designing an efficient algorithm for recovering a y-coordinate in the Montgomery form with non-binary fields has remained open.

1.4 Our Contributions

We present a scalar multiplication algorithm with recovery of the y-coordinate on a Montgomery-form elliptic curve over non-binary fields.

We further compare our proposed scalar multiplication algorithm with the traditional scalar multiplication algorithms (including Window-methods on the Weierstrass form), and discuss the cryptographic advantage of using the Montgomery-form elliptic curve.

Our analysis shows that the scalar multiplication on a Montgomery-form elliptic curve, which requires no precomputation, is faster than that of the window-method on a Weierstrass-form elliptic curve, if the size of the definition field is smaller than 391 bits in a reasonable implementation with $(S/M) = 0.8$ and

---

[1] It was shown that a Montgomery-form elliptic curve is effective for preventing differential power analysis [OS00].

$(I/M) = 30$ [LH00]. Recall that elliptic curve cryptosystems over prime fields whose sizes are larger than 272 bits are believed to be secure until the year 2050 even if some cryptanalytic developments occur [LV00].

We further consider the Montgomery form versus the Weierstrass form in the performance of implementations with several techniques of elliptic curve cryptosystems (including ECES, ECDSA, and ECMQV). We compare the amounts of computation and storage of our Montgomery method with recovery of the y-coordinate to those of the Weierstrass window methods (with simultaneous techniques) for point multiplication kP (resp. for $kP + Q$ and for $kP + lQ$). Our results suggest new advantages of the Montgomery form over the Weierstrass form in the implementation of elliptic curve cryptosystems

2   Elliptic Curve Schemes Using the y-Coordinate

The elliptic curve signature scheme ECDSA cannot be executed without referencing the y-coordinate of the point kP, the k-time scalar multiplication of the point P. This is in contrast to some elliptic curve schemes (e.g. ECDH), which can be executed without the y-coordinate. The verifying algorithm of ECDSA requires the operation $kP + k'Q$. To put it simply, computation requires the addition of a scalar-multiplied point and another point. Addition of points, without using their differences, on a Montgomery-form elliptic curve requires the y-coordinates of the points. That is the reason why ECDSA requires the y-coordinate of kP.

The same applies to ECSVDP-MQV, ECSVDP-MQVC, ECVP-NR, and ECVP-DSA, which are described in the draft standard IEEE P1363 [IEEEp1363]. These schemes also require the operation $kP+Q$, which is an addition of a scalar-multiplied point and another point.

We would like to emphasize that recovering the y-coordinate completely solves these problems. Therefore, Montgomery's method of scalar multiplication becomes a general algorithm.

3   Recovering the y-Coordinate

Research has studied recovery of the y-coordinate on a Montgomery-like scalar multiplication method in the case of an elliptic curve defined over a finite field with characteristic 2 [LD99]. However, no similar algorithm is known in the case of a Montgomery-form elliptic curve [Mon87] defined over a prime field (nor over an OEF [BP98]). First, we will take up the case of characteristic 2, and then we will focus our attention on the case of a Montgomery-form elliptic curve.

3.1   Recovering the y-Coordinate $(p = 2)$[LD99]

Let $\mathbf{F}_{2^m}$ be a finite field with characteristic 2. A non-supersingular elliptic curve over $\mathbf{F}_{2^m}$ is defined as follows.

$$y^2 + xy = x^3 + ax^2 + b,$$

where $a, b \in \mathbf{F}_{2^m}$ and $b \neq 0$.

Theorem 1 ([LD99]). *Let* $P = (x, y), P_1 = (x_1, y_1), P_2 = (x_2, y_2)$ *be points on the elliptic curve. Assume that* $P_2 = P_1 + P$ *and* $x \neq 0$. *Then*

$$y_1 = (x_1 + x)\{(x_1 + x)(x_2 + x) + x^2 + y\}/x + y.$$

3.2 Recovering the y-Coordinate ($p \geq 3$)

Let p be a prime and $\mathbf{F}_{p^m}$ be a finite field with characteristic p. A Montgomery-form elliptic curve over $\mathbf{F}_{p^m}$ is defined as follow.

$$BY^2 = X^3 + AX^2 + X,$$

where $A, B \in \mathbf{F}_{p^m}$ and $B(A^2 - 4) \neq 0$.

First, we construct a method for recovering the y-coordinate on a Montgomery-form elliptic curve in a similar fashion to the method on the elliptic curve over $\mathbf{F}_{2^m}$. The proof of the propositions in this section is in the Appendix.

Theorem 2. *Let* $P = (x, y), P_1 = (x_1, y_1), P_2 = (x_2, y_2)$ *be points on a Montgomery-form elliptic curve. Assume that* $P_2 = P_1 + P$ *and* $y \neq 0$. *Then*

$$y_1 = \frac{(x_1 x + 1)(x_1 + x + 2A) - 2A - (x_1 - x)^2 x_2}{2By}.$$

Corollary 1. *Let* P, P_1 *and* P_2 *be as in Theorem 2. We express* $P_1 = (\frac{X_1}{Z_1}, \frac{Y_1}{Z_1})$, $P_2 = (\frac{X_2}{Z_2}, \frac{Y_2}{Z_2})$, *and define* $X_1^{rec}, Y_1^{rec}, Z_1^{rec}$ *which are given by the following:*

$$X_1^{rec} = 2ByZ_1Z_2X_1$$
$$Y_1^{rec} = Z_2\left[(X_1 + xZ_1 + 2AZ_1)(X_1x + Z_1) - 2AZ_1^2\right] - (X_1 - xZ_1)^2 X_2$$
$$Z_1^{rec} = 2ByZ_1Z_2Z_1$$

Then the relation $(X_1^{rec}, Y_1^{rec}, Z_1^{rec}) = (X_1, Y_1, Z_1)$ *holds in projective coordinates.*

This method for recovering the Y-coordinate needs to compute twelve multiplications and one squaring. An example of the algorithm using Corollary 1 is the next Algorithm 1.

> **Algorithm 1** : Algorithm for recovering the Y-coordinate
> **INPUT** x, y, X_1, Z_1, X_2, Z_2
> **OUTPUT** $X_1^{rec}, Y_1^{rec}, Z_1^{rec}$
>
> 1. $T_1 \leftarrow x \times Z_1$ 11. $T_1 \leftarrow T_1 \times Z_1$
> 2. $T_2 \leftarrow X_1 + T_1$ 12. $T_2 \leftarrow T_2 - T_1$
> 3. $T_3 \leftarrow X_1 - T_1$ 13. $T_2 \leftarrow T_2 \times Z_2$
> 4. $T_3 \leftarrow T_3 \times T_3$ 14. $Y_1^{rec} \leftarrow T_2 - T_3$
> 5. $T_3 \leftarrow T_3 \times X_2$ 15. $T_1 \leftarrow 2B \times y$
> 6. $T_1 \leftarrow 2A \times Z_1$ 16. $T_1 \leftarrow T_1 \times Z_1$
> 7. $T_2 \leftarrow T_2 + T_1$ 17. $T_1 \leftarrow T_1 \times Z_2$
> 8. $T_4 \leftarrow x \times X_1$ 18. $X_1^{rec} \leftarrow T_1 \times X_1$
> 9. $T_4 \leftarrow T_4 + Z_1$ 19. $Z_1^{rec} \leftarrow T_1 \times Z_1$
> 10. $T_2 \leftarrow T_2 \times T_4$

Next, we propose another method for recovering the y-coordinate on a Montgomery-form elliptic curve.

Theorem 3. *Let $P = (x, y), P_1 = (x_1, y_1), P_2 = (x_2, y_2), P_3 = (x_3, y_3)$ be points on a Montgomery-form elliptic curve. Assume that $P_2 = P_1 + P, P_3 = P_1 - P$ and $y \neq 0$. Then*

$$y_1 = \frac{(x_3 - x_2)(x_1 - x)^2}{4By}.$$

Corollary 2. *Let P, P_1, P_2 and P_3 be as in Theorem 3. We express $P_1 = (\frac{X_1}{Z_1}, \frac{Y_1}{Z_1})$, $P_2 = (\frac{X_2}{Z_2}, \frac{Y_2}{Z_2}), P_3 = (\frac{X_3}{Z_3}, \frac{Y_3}{Z_3})$, and define $X_1^{rec}, Y_1^{rec}, Z_1^{rec}$ which are given by the following:*

$$X_1^{rec} = 4ByZ_1Z_2Z_3X_1$$
$$Y_1^{rec} = (X_3Z_2 - Z_3X_2)(X_1 - Z_1x)^2$$
$$Z_1^{rec} = 4ByZ_1Z_2Z_3Z_1$$

Then $(X_1^{rec}, Y_1^{rec}, Z_1^{rec}) = (X_1, Y_1, Z_1)$ in projective coordinates.

This method for recovering the Y-coordinate in projective coordinates needs to compute ten multiplications and one squaring. Thus, this method is faster than that using Corollary 1. However, we have to compute the point P_3 before we use this method if P_3 is not given.

Proposition 1. *Let $P = (x, y)$ be a point on a Montgomery-form elliptic curve, and $kP = (x_k, y_k)$ for $k = 1, 2, \cdots$ be the scalar-multiplied point of the point P. For any $\frac{X_m}{Z_m} = x_m, \frac{X_n}{Z_n} = x_n$ and $\frac{X_{m+n}}{Z_{m+n}} = x_{m+n}$ $(m > n)$, we define X' and Z' which are given by the following:*

$$X' = Z_{m+n}[(X_m - Z_m)(X_n + Z_n) + (X_m + Z_m)(X_n - Z_n)]^2$$

$$Z' = X_{m+n}[(X_m - Z_m)(X_n + Z_n) - (X_m + Z_m)(X_n - Z_n)]^2$$

Then $\frac{X'}{Z'} = x_{m-n}$ is satisfied.

The calculation of X' and Z' needs to compute four multiplications and two squarings. Thus, recovering the Y-coordinate in projective coordinates without P_3 requires fourteen multiplications and three squarings.

We should notice that a combination of these formulae reduces the computation amount. Let us examine the computation amount of the later method in more detail. We have $x_d = \frac{X_d}{Z_d}, x_{d+1} = \frac{X_{d+1}}{Z_{d+1}}, x_{d-1} = \frac{X_{d-1}}{Z_{d-1}}$, and we transform the formula of y_1 on Theorem 3 to the formula in projective coordinates with the substitution of these values. Then we obtain the following equation:

$$y_d = \frac{(X_{d-1}Z_{d+1} - Z_{d-1}X_{d+1})(X_d - Z_dx)}{4ByZ_{d-1}Z_{d+1}Z_d^2}$$

Proposition 1 enables us to eliminate X_{d-1} and Z_{d-1} from the equation above. We obtain the following equation with the settings $X_1 = x$ and $Z_1 = 1$:

$$y_d = \frac{\{Z_{d+1}U + X_{d+1}V\}\{Z_{d+1}U - X_{d+1}V\}U^2}{ByZ_{d+1}X_{d+1}V^2Z_d^2},$$

where $U = X_d x - Z_d, V = X_d - xZ_d$. On the other hand, we have $x_d = \frac{X_d}{Z_d}$. We obtain

$$x_d = \frac{ByZ_{d+1}X_{d+1}Z_dV^2X_d}{ByZ_{d+1}X_{d+1}Z_dV^2Z_d}$$

with the reduction with the denominator of y_d for reducing the number of inversion.

M, S and I respectively denote $\mathbf{F}_{p^m}$-operations of multiplication, squaring, and inversion. The method for recovering the y-coordinate in affine coordinates needs the computation amount $15M + 2S + I$.

On the other hand, we set

$$X_d^{rec} = ByZ_{d+1}X_{d+1}Z_dV^2X_d$$
$$Y_d^{rec} = \{Z_{d+1}U + X_{d+1}V\}\{Z_{d+1}U - X_{d+1}V\}U^2$$
$$Z_d^{rec} = ByZ_{d+1}X_{d+1}Z_dV^2Z_d$$

Then the relation $(X_d^{rec}, Y_d^{rec}, Z_d^{rec}) = (X_d, Y_d, Z_d)$ holds in projective coordinates. The method for recovering the y-coordinate needs the computation amount $13M + 2S$. Therefore, the computation amount shrinks by one multiplication and one squaring. An example of the algorithm using this method is the following:

Algorithm 2 : Algorithm for recovering the Y-coordinate
INPUT $x, y, X_d, Z_d, X_{d+1}, Z_{d+1}$
OUTPUT $X_d^{rec}, Y_d^{rec}, Z_d^{rec}$

1. $T_1 \leftarrow X_d \times x$
2. $T_1 \leftarrow T_1 - Z_d$
3. $T_2 \leftarrow Z_d \times x$
4. $T_2 \leftarrow X_d - T_2$
5. $T_3 \leftarrow Z_{d+1} \times T_1$
6. $T_4 \leftarrow X_{d+1} \times T_2$
7. $T_1 \leftarrow T_1 \times T_1$
8. $T_2 \leftarrow T_2 \times T_2$
9. $T_2 \leftarrow T_2 \times Z_d$
10. $T_2 \leftarrow T_2 \times X_{d+1}$
11. $T_2 \leftarrow T_2 \times Z_{d+1}$
12. $T_2 \leftarrow T_2 \times y$
13. $T_2 \leftarrow T_2 \times B$
14. $X_d^{rec} \leftarrow T_2 \times X_d$
15. $Z_d^{rec} \leftarrow T_2 \times Z_d$
16. $T_2 \leftarrow T_3 + T_4$
17. $T_3 \leftarrow T_3 - T_4$
18. $T_1 \leftarrow T_1 \times T_2$
19. $Y_d^{rec} \leftarrow T_1 \times T_3$

In summary, Algorithm 1 needs the computation amount $12M + S$, and Algorithm 2 needs the computation amount $13M + 2S$. Therefore, Algorithm 1 is faster than Algorithm 2 by one multiplication and one squaring.

4   Montgomery Form versus Weierstrass Form

It was pointed out in the previous section that we are able to efficiently recover the y-coordinate of a scalar-multiplied point on a Montgomery-form elliptic curve. If we connect the traditional scalar multiplication algorithm with the algorithm for recovering the y-coordinate, we construct a fast scalar multiplication algorithm on a Montgomery-form elliptic curve which gives the whole coordinates of a scalar-multiplied point.

$T^{Mon}(l), T_x^{Mon}(l)$ and $T_y^{Mon}(l)$ denote the computation amount for the proposed scalar multiplication algorithm with l, the size of a scalar value,[2] that for the traditional scalar multiplication on a Montgomery-form elliptic curve, and that for recovery of the y-coordinate, respectively. Then we have the following:

$$T_x^{Mon}(l) = (6l - 3)M + (4l - 2)S$$
$$T_y^{Mon}(l) = 12M + S$$
$$T^{Mon}(l) = T_x^{Mon}(l) + T_y^{Mon}(l)$$
$$= (6l + 9)M + (4l - 1)S$$

We should recall that, on a scalar multiplication algorithm over a Weierstrass-form elliptic curve, the algorithm using the window method in the mixed modified Jacobian coordinates is one of the fastest [CMO98]. $T^{Wei}(w, l)$ denotes the computation amount with window width w and size l. According to [LH00] (and also see [CMO98]), $T^{Wei}(w, l)$ is estimated as follows.

$$T^{Wei}(w, l) = wI + \left(\frac{8l}{w+2} + 4l + 5 \cdot 2^{w-1} - 2w - 14 \right) M$$
$$+ \left(\frac{3l}{w+2} + 4l + 2^{w-1} - 2w - 2 \right) S$$

First, we compare the computation amount for the Montgomery-form elliptic curve to that for the Weierstrass-form elliptic curve with a window width of 4 in terms of size l. Assume that $T^{Mon}(l) > T^{Wei}(4, l)$, then we obtain

$$(I/M) < \left(\frac{1}{6}l - \frac{5}{2} \right) + \left(-\frac{1}{8}l + \frac{1}{4} \right) (S/M).$$

For simplicity, we denote s and t for (S/M) and (I/M), respectively. Then the inequality above is expressed by

$$l > \frac{24t - 6s + 54}{4 - 3s}.$$

For example, we set $s = 0.8$, and compute l for $t = 10, 20, 30, 40$ and 50. We obtain $l > 181, 331, 481, 631$ and 781, respectively. Thus, in the case that the size is smaller than the bits above, the scalar multiplication on a Montgomery-form elliptic curve is faster than that on a Weierstrass-form elliptic curve.

---

[2]   Actually, the size of a scalar value is approximately the size of the definition field.

Second, we compare the computation amount of a Montgomery-form elliptic curve to that of a Weierstrass-form elliptic curve with a window width of 5 in terms of size l. Assume that $T^{Mon}(l) > T^{Wei}(5, l)$, we obtain

$$l > \frac{35t + 35s + 329}{6 - 3s}.$$

Finally, we compare the computation amount for the Weierstrass-form elliptic curve with window width 4 to that with window width 5 in terms of size l. Assume that $T^{Wei}(4, l) > T^{Wei}(5, l)$, we obtain

$$l > \frac{42t + 252s + 1596}{8 + 3s}.$$

To sum up the comparison between the computation amount in terms of size l we have seen thus far, we obtain Table 1.

According to [LV00], elliptic curve cryptosystems over *prime* fields whose sizes are larger than 272 bits are believed to be secure until the year 2050, even if some cryptanalytic developments occur. Under a reasonable assumption that $(S/M) = 0.8$ and $(I/M) = 30$ for *prime* fields [LH00], we see from Table 1 that the scalar multiplication with $w = 5$ is faster than that with $w = 4$ if the size is larger than 295 bits. Thus, the scalar multiplication on a Montgomery-form elliptic curve is faster than that on a Weierstrass-form elliptic curve if the size is smaller than 391 bits. From this viewpoint, one may say that the scalar multiplication algorithm on a Montgomery-form elliptic curve is faster than that on a Weierstrass-form elliptic curve for cryptographic use.

5   Comparison of Our Proposed Method to Other Methods

In this section, we use computation amount to compare our proposed method, that is the scalar multiplication algorithm with recovery of the y-coordinate on a Montgomery-form elliptic curve, with other methods for several schemes (ECES, ECElGamal, ECDSA-V and ECSVDP-MQV) [ANSI,IEEEp1363,SEC-1]. On the comparison with methods to compute a scalar multiplication and ECDSA scheme for elliptic curves over $\mathbf{F}_{2^m}$, see [HHM00].

5.1   Elliptic Curve Encryption Scheme

An elliptic curve encryption scheme (ECES)[3] needs to compute the operation kP. We select Montgomery's method with/without recovering the y-coordinate and the window method with the width $w = 4, 5$ from the methods to compute kP, and compare the computation amounts for the size 160 bits.

To compute kP by Montgomery's method with (resp. without) recovery of the y-coordinate, the computation needs the computation amount $1480.2M$ (resp. $1467.4M$) with assuming $(S/M) = 0.8$.

---

[3] For further details about ECES, see [IEEEp1363] for example.

Table 1. Border key sizes between scalar multiplication methods

(S/M)	(I/M)	$w = 5/w = 4$	$w = 4/Mon$	$w = 5/Mon$
1.0	50	359	1249	705
	40	321	1009	589
	30	283	769	472
	20	245	529	355
	10	207	289	239
0.9	50	367	961	640
	40	328	776	534
	30	289	592	428
	20	249	407	322
	10	210	223	216
0.8	50	375	781	586
	40	335	631	489
	30	295	481	391
	20	254	331	294
	10	214	181	197
0.7	50	384	658	540
	40	342	532	450
	30	301	406	360
	20	259	279	271
	10	218	153	181
0.6	50	393	569	501
	40	350	460	417
	30	307	351	334
	20	265	242	251
	10	222	133	167
0.5	50	403	501	466
	40	359	405	389
	30	314	309	311
	20	270	213	233
	10	226	117	155

"$w = 4/Mon$" indicates the border key sizes between the scalar multiplication on a Weierstrass-form elliptic curve using the window method with a window width of 4 and that on a Montgomery-form elliptic curve. That is, the former is faster than the latter if the size is larger than the border size. "$w = 5/w = 4$" and "$w = 5/Mon$" are similar in meaning to "$w = 4/Mon$".

To compute kP by the window method with the width $w = 4$ (resp. $w = 5$), the computation amount $1446.4M + 4I$ (resp. $1449.4M + 5I$) is needed.

5.2   Elliptic Curve ElGamal Encryption Scheme

An elliptic curve ElGamal encryption scheme[4] needs to compute the operation $kP + Q$. We select Montgomery's method with recovery of the y-coordinate and

---

[4] For further details about the elliptic curve ElGamal encryption scheme, see [IEEEp1363] for example.

Table 2. Computation amounts for point multiplication kP

Method	Points stored	# of M	# of I
Montgomery (traditional)	0	1467.4	0
Montgomery (with recovery of y)	0	1480.2	0
Window Method ($w = 4$)	7	1446.4	4
Window Method ($w = 5$)	15	1449.4	5

the window method with the width $w = 4, 5$ from the methods to compute $kP + Q$, and compare the computation amounts for the size 160 bits.

To compute $kP+Q$ by Montgomery's method with recovery of the y-coordinate, the computation needs to compute the following operations:

(a) The scalar multiplication kP by Montgomery's method.
(b) The addition $kP + Q$.

(a) Since the size of k is 160 bits, the computation needs the computation amount $969M + 639S$ which includes the computation amount for recovering the y-coordinate.
(b) The computation needs the computation amount $11M + 2S$ for the addition in the projective coordinates on a Montgomery-form elliptic curve.

Thus, to compute $kP + Q$ by Montgomery's method with recovery of the y-coordinate needs the computation amount $1492.8M$, assuming $(S/M) = 0.8$.

To compute $kP + Q$ by the window method with the width $w = 4, 5$, the computation needs to compute the following operations:

(c) The scalar multiplication kP by window method.
(d) The addition $kP + Q$.

(c) The computation amount is $872M + 718S + 4I$ if $w = 4$, and it is $879M + 713S + 5I$ if $w = 5$.
(d) The computation amount is $8M + 3S$ by using the addition formulae of $J + A \rightarrow J$, where J is the Jacobian coordinates and A is the affine coordinates.

Thus, to compute $kP + Q$ by the window method, the computation needs the computation amount $1456.8M + 4I$ if $w = 4$, or $1459.8M + 5I$ if $w = 5$.

Table 3. Computation amount for point multiplication $kP + Q$

Method	Points stored	# of M	# of I	Remark
Montgomery (traditional)	-	-	-	impossible
Montgomery (with recovery of y)	0	1492.8	0	
Window Method ($w = 4$)	7	1456.8	4	
Window Method ($w = 5$)	15	1459.8	5	

5.3   ECDSA Scheme (Verification)

The signature verification of an elliptic curve digital signature algorithm (ECDSA)[5] needs to compute the operation $kP + lQ$ where P is a fixed point and Q is not known a priori. We select the fixed-base comb method [LL94] with the width $w = 4, 5$ + Montgomery's method, and a simultaneous method [ElG85,HHM00] with the width $w = 2$, and compare the computation amount for the size 160 bits.

To compute the fixed-base comb ($w = 4, 5$) + Montgomery method, the computation needs to compute the following operations:

(e) The scalar multiplication kP by the fixed-base comb method.
(f) The scalar multiplication lQ by Montgomery's method.
(g) The addition $kP + lQ$.

(e) In the case of the width $w = 4$, the computation needs the computation amount $445M + 338S$ by using the addition formulae of $J + A \rightarrow J^m$ for the additions, the doubling formulae of $J^m \rightarrow J$ for the doublings ahead of addition, and the doubling formulae of $J^m \rightarrow J^m$ for the doublings ahead of doubling, where J^m is the modified Jacobian coordinates. In the case of the width $w = 5$, the computation amount is $362M + 273S$.
(f) Since the point Q is on a Weierstrass-form elliptic curve, we transform this into a point on a Montgomery-form elliptic curve. The computation needs the computation amount $2M$. Then, we compute the scalar-multiplied point lQ by Montgomery's method with recovery of the y-coordinate. The computation amount is $969M + 639S$. Then, we transform the point into a point on the Weierstrass-form elliptic curve. The computation amount is $2M$.
(g) For the sake of fast computation of $kP + lQ$, we transform the point lQ in projective coordinates into a point in Chudnovsky Jacobian coordinates. The computation needs the computation amount $3M + S$. The computation amount $11M + 3S$ is needed for the addition $kP + lQ$.

Thus, to compute $kP + lQ$ by fixed-base comb ($w = 4$) + Montgomery method, the computation needs the computation amount $2216.8M$, assuming $(S/M) = 0.8$. The number of points stored is 14. In the case of the fixed-base comb ($w = 5$) + Montgomery method, the computation needs the computation amount $2081.8M$. The number of points stored is 30.

In the case of the simultaneous method with the width $w = 2$, the computation of points stored needs the computation amount $49M + 12S + 2I$ by using the Montgomery trick [Coh93]. The computation of multi scalar multiplication needs the computation amount $1223M + 1001S$ by using the addition formulae of $J + A \rightarrow J^m$ for the additions, the doubling formulae of $J^m \rightarrow J$ for the doublings ahead of addition and the doubling formulae of $J^m \rightarrow J^m$ for the doublings ahead of doubling. Thus, the computation amount $2084.4M + 3I$ is needed. The number of points stored is 13.

---

[5] For further details about ECDSA, see [ANSI] for example.

Memory Constrained As regards the situation in which memory is constrained, we examine methods in which the number of points stored is within 10.

In the case of fixed-base comb ($w = 3$) + Montgomery, the computation amount is $2420.0M$, and the number of points stored is 6. In the case of the width $w = 2$, the computation amount is $2762.0M$, and the number of points stored is 2. In the case of Montgomery + Montgomery, the computation amount is $2980.0M$, and no extra points are needed. In the case of simultaneous ($w = 1$), the computation amount is $2585.6M + I$, and the number of points stored is 1.

Table 4. Computation amount for point multiplication $kP + lQ$, P fixed

Method	Points stored	# of M	# of I
Fixed-base comb($w = 4$) + Montgomery	14	2216.8	0
Fixed-base comb($w = 5$) + Montgomery	30	2081.8	0
Simultaneous($w = 2$)	13	2082.4	2

Table 5. Computation amount for point multiplication $kP+lQ$, P fixed, when memory is constrained

Method	Points stored	# of M	# of I
Fixed-base comb($w = 2$) + Montgomery	2	2762.0	0
Fixed-base comb($w = 3$) + Montgomery	6	2420.0	0
Montgomery + Montgomery	0	2980.0	0
Simultaneous($w = 1$)	1	2585.6	1

5.4   ECSVDP-MQV

The elliptic curve secret value derivation primitive, Menezes-Qu-Vanstone version (ECSVDP-MQV)[6] needs to compute the operation $k(P + lQ)$, where l is half the size of k, and points P, Q are not known a priori.

To compute $k(P + lQ)$ by Montgomery's method (Montgomery $*$ Montgomery), the computation needs to compute the following operations:

(h) The scalar multiplication lQ by Montgomery's method.
(i) The addition $P + lQ$.
(j) The scalar multiplication $k(P + lQ)$ by Montgomery's method.

(h) Since l is half the size of k, the computation needs the computation amount $489M + 319S$, which includes the computation amount for recovering the y-coordinate.
(i) The computation needs the computation amount $14M + 2S$ for the addition on the Montgomery-form elliptic curve.

---
[6] For further details about ECSVDP-MQV, see [IEEEp1363] for example.

(j) The computation needs the computation amount $957M + 638S$.

Thus, to compute $k(P + lQ)$ by Montgomery's method, the computation needs the computation amount $2227.2M$.

In the case of the simultaneous method with the width $w = 2$, to compute the points stored needs $63M + 15S + 3I$, and to compute $kP + klQ$ by simultaneous method needs $1223M + 1001S$. Thus, the computation amount $2098.8 + 3I$ is needed.

Table 6. Computation amount for point multiplication $k(P + lQ)$, where l is half the size of k

Method	Points stored	# of M	# of I
Montgomery * Montgomery	0	2227.2	0
Simultaneous($w = 2$)	13	2098.8	3

References

[AMV93] Agnew,G.B., Mullin,R.C., Vanstone,S.A., *An Implementation of Elliptic Curve Cryptosystems Over $F_{2^{155}}$*, IEEE Journal on Selected Areas in Communications, vol.11,No.5,(1993),804-813.

[ANSI] ANSI X9.62, Public Key Cryptography for the Financial Services Industry, *The Elliptic Curve Digital Signature Algorithm(ECDSA)*,(1999).

[BP98] Bailey,D.V., Paar,C.,*Optimal Extension Fields for Fast Arithmetic in Public-Key Algorithms*, Advances in Cryptology - CRYPTO'98, LNCS1462, (1998), 472-485.

[BSS99] Blake,I.F.,Seroussi,G.,Smart,N.P., *Elliptic Curves in Cryptography*, Cambridge University Press,(1999).

[CMO98] Cohen,H., Miyaji,A., Ono,T., *Efficient Elliptic Curve Exponentiation Using Mixed Coordinates*, Advances in Cryptology - ASIACRYPT '98, LNCS1514, (1998), 51-65.

[Coh93] Cohen, H., *A course in computational algebraic number theory*, GTM138, Springer-Verlag, New York, (1993).

[ElG85] ElGamal, T., *A public key cryptosystem and a signature scheme based on discrete logarithms*, IEEE Transactions on Information Theory, 31 (1985), 469-472.

[Enge99] Enge, A., *Elliptic Curves and their applications to Cryptography*, Kluwer Academic publishers,(1999).

[HHM00] Hankerson, D., Hernandez, J.L., Menezes, A., *Software Implementation of Elliptic Curve Cryptography Over Binary Fields*, Pre-Proceedings of Workshop on Cryptographic Hardware and Embedded Systems (CHES2000), (2000), 1-24.

[IEEEp1363] IEEE P1363 Standard Specifications for Public-Key Cryptography (1999), Available at http://grouper.ieee.org/groups/1363/

[Kur98] Kurumatani, H. *A Japanese patent announcement P2000-187438A* (In Japanese) Submitted in 22nd of Dec. (1998), available from http://www.jpo-miti.go.jp/home.htm

[Kob87] Koblitz,N., *Elliptic curve cryptosystems*, Math. Comp.48, (1987),203-209.

[Koc]   Kocher,C., *Cryptanalysis of Diffie-Hellman,RSA,DSS, and Other Systems Using Timing Attacks*, Available at http://www.cryptography.com/

[Koc96] Kocher,C., *Timing Attacks on Implementations of Diffie-Hellman, RSA,DSS, and Other Systems*, Advances in Cryptology - CRYPTO '96, LNCS1109, (1996), 104-113.

[LD99] López,J., Dahab,R., *Fast Multiplication on Elliptic Curves over $GF(2^m)$ without Precomputation*, Cryptographic Hardware and Embedded Systems (CHES'99), LNCS1717, (1999), 316-327.

[LH00] Lim, C.H. and Hwang,H.S., *Fast implementation of Elliptic Curve Arithmetic in $GF(p^m)$*, Proc. PKC'00 LNCS1751, (2000), 405-421.

[LL94] Lim, C. and Lee, P., *More flexible exponentiation with precomputation*, Advances in Cryptology - CRYPTO '94, LNCS839, (1994), 95-107.

[LV00] Lenstra, A.K. and Verheul, E.R, *Selecting Cryptographic Key Sizes*, Proc. PKC'00 LNCS1751, (2000), 446-465.

[Mil86] Miller,V.S., *Use of elliptic curves in cryptography*, Advances in Cryptology - CRYPTO '85, LNCS218, (1986), 417-426.

[Mon87] Montgomery,P.L., *Speeding the Pollard and Elliptic Curve Methods of Factorizations*, Math. Comp. 48, (1987), 243-264

[OKS00] Okeya,K., Kurumatani,H., Sakurai,K., *Elliptic Curves with the Montgomery - Form and Their Cryptographic Applications*, Public Key Cryptography (PKC2000), LNCS1751, (2000), 238-257.

[OS00] Okeya,K., Sakurai,K., *Power Analysis Breaks Elliptic Curve Cryptosystems even Secure against the Timing Attack*, Progress in Cryptology - INDOCRYPT 2000, LNCS1977, (2000), 178-190.

[OSK99] Ohgishi,K., Sakai,R., Kasahara,M., *Elliptic Curve Signature Scheme with No y Coordinate*, Proc. SCIS'99,W4-1.3 (1999), 285-287.

[SEC-1] Standards for Efficient Cryptography, *Elliptic Curve Cryptography Ver.1.0*, (2000), Available at http://www.secg.org/secg_docs.htm

[Van97] Vanstone,S.A., *Accelerated finite field operations on an elliptic curve*, GB patent, Application number GB9713138.7 (Date Lodged, 20.06.1997).

A   Algorithms for Recovering y-Coordinate (Affine Version)

Algorithm 3 : algorithm for recovering y-coordinate
INPUT x, y, X_1, Z_1, X_2, Z_2
OUTPUT x_1, y_1

1. $T_1 \leftarrow x \times Z_1$ 11. $T_1 \leftarrow T_1 \times Z_1$
2. $T_2 \leftarrow X_1 + T_1$ 12. $T_2 \leftarrow T_2 - T_1$
3. $T_3 \leftarrow X_1 - T_1$ 13. $T_2 \leftarrow T_2 \times Z_2$
4. $T_3 \leftarrow X_3 \times T_3$ 14. $T_2 \leftarrow T_2 - T_3$
5. $T_3 \leftarrow T_3 \times X_2$ 15. $T_1 \leftarrow 2B \times y$
6. $T_1 \leftarrow 2A \times Z_1$ 16. $T_1 \leftarrow T_1 \times Z_1$
7. $T_2 \leftarrow T_2 + T_1$ 17. $T_1 \leftarrow T_1 \times Z_2$
8. $T_4 \leftarrow x \times X_1$ 18. $T_3 \leftarrow T_1 \times Z_1$
9. $T_4 \leftarrow T_4 + Z_1$ 19. $T_3 \leftarrow 1/T_3$
10. $T_2 \leftarrow T_2 \times T_4$ 20. $y_1 \leftarrow T_2 \times T_3$

21. $T_1 \leftarrow T_1 \times X_1$
22. $x_1 \leftarrow T_1 \times T_3$

The computation amount of Algorithm 3 is $14M + S + I$.

Algorithm 4 : algorithm for recovering y-coordinate
INPUT $x, y, X_d, Z_d, X_{d+1}, Z_{d+1}$
OUTPUT x_d, y_d

1. $T_1 \leftarrow X_d \times x$ 11. $T_2 \leftarrow T_2 \times Z_d$
2. $T_1 \leftarrow T_1 - Z_d$ 12. $T_4 \leftarrow T_2 \times X_d$
3. $T_2 \leftarrow Z_d \times x$ 13. $T_2 \leftarrow T_2 \times Z_d$
4. $T_2 \leftarrow X_d - T_2$ 14. $T_2 \leftarrow 1/T_2$
5. $T_3 \leftarrow X_{d+1} \times T_2$ 15. $x_d \leftarrow T_2 \times T_4$
6. $T_2 \leftarrow T_2 \times T_2$ 16. $T_4 \leftarrow T_1 \times Z_{d+1}$
7. $T_2 \leftarrow T_2 \times X_{d+1}$ 17. $T_1 \leftarrow T_1 \times T_1$
8. $T_2 \leftarrow T_2 \times Z_{d+1}$ 18. $T_2 \leftarrow T_1 \times T_2$
9. $T_2 \leftarrow T_2 \times y$ 19. $T_1 \leftarrow T_3 + T_4$
10. $T_2 \leftarrow T_2 \times B$ 20. $T_3 \leftarrow T_3 - T_4$

21. $T_1 \leftarrow T_1 \times T_3$
22. $y_d \leftarrow T_1 \times T_2$

The computation amount of Algorithm 4 is $15M + 2S + I$.

B   Proof of the Propositions

Proof (of Theorem 2). Since $P_2 = P_1 + P$, the x-coordinate x_2 is computed as follows.

$$x_2 = B \left(\frac{y_1 - y}{x_1 - x} \right)^2 - A - x_1 - x.$$

Since P_1 and P are on the Montgomery-form elliptic curve, it follows that $By_1^2 = x_1^3 + Ax_1^2 + x_1$ and $By^2 = x^3 + Ax^2 + x$. We find the following equation with an easy calculation from the equation above.

$$x_2 = \frac{x_1 + x - 2By_1y + 2Ax_1x + x_1x^2 + xx_1^2}{(x_1 - x)^2}.$$

The result follows from this equation.   □

Proof (of Theorem 3). Since $P_2 = P_1 + P$, $P_3 = P_1 - P$ and $-P = (x, -y)$, the x-coordinates x_2 and x_3 are computed as follows.

$$x_2 = B\left(\frac{y_1 - y}{x_1 - x}\right)^2 - A - x_1 - x \tag{1}$$

$$x_3 = B\left(\frac{y_1 + y}{x_1 - x}\right)^2 - A - x_1 - x \tag{2}$$

We obtain the following equations with multiplication by $(x_1 - x)^2$ at the equations (1) and (2).

$$B(y_1 - y)^2 = (x_2 + x_1 + x + A)(x_1 - x)^2 \tag{3}$$
$$B(y_1 + y)^2 = (x_3 + x_1 + x + A)(x_1 - x)^2 \tag{4}$$

We obtain the following equation with subtraction the equation (3) from the equation (4).

$$4By_1y = (x_3 - x_2)(x_1 - x)^2 \tag{5}$$

The result follows from this equation.   □

Proof (of Proposition 1). For simplicity, we set

$$\alpha = [(X_m - Z_m)(X_n + Z_n) + (X_m + Z_m)(X_n - Z_n)],$$

$$\beta = [(X_m - Z_m)(X_n + Z_n) - (X_m + Z_m)(X_n - Z_n)].$$

Then we have

$$\begin{aligned}
\frac{X'}{Z'} &= \frac{Z_{m+n}\alpha^2}{X_{m+n}\beta^2} \\
&= \frac{X_{m-n}\beta^2\alpha^2}{Z_{m-n}\alpha^2\beta^2} \qquad \text{(because of addition formulae)} \\
&= x_{m-n}.
\end{aligned}$$

□

Generating Elliptic Curves of Prime Order[*],[**]

Erkay Savaş[1], Thomas A. Schmidt[2], and Çetin K. Koç[1]

[1] Department of Electrical & Computer Engineering
Oregon State University, Corvallis, Oregon 97331, USA
{savas,koc}@ece.orst.edu
[2] Department of Mathematics
Oregon State University, Corvallis, Oregon 97331, USA
toms@math.orst.edu

Abstract. A variation of the Complex Multiplication (CM) method for generating elliptic curves of known order over finite fields is proposed. We give heuristics and timing statistics in the mildly restricted setting of prime curve order. These may be seen to corroborate earlier work of Koblitz in the class number one setting. Our heuristics are based upon a recent conjecture by R. Gross and J. Smith on numbers of twin primes in algebraic number fields.

Our variation precalculates class polynomials as a separate off-line process. Unlike the standard approach, which begins with a prime p and searches for an appropriate discriminant D, we choose a discriminant and then search for appropriate primes. Our on-line process is quick and can be compactly coded.

In practice, elliptic curves with near prime order are used. Thus, our timing estimates and data can be regarded as upper estimates for practical purposes.

1   Introduction

An important category of cryptographic algorithms is that of the elliptic curve cryptosystems defined over a finite field $\mathbb{F}_p$, see [9] for a recent overview. While there are many methods proposed for performing fast elliptic curve arithmetic, there is a paucity of efficient means for generating suitable elliptic curves. The methods proposed to date for curve generation mainly necessitate implementing complex and floating point arithmetic with high precision. However, this hinders the implementation of the proposed algorithms on simple processors with limited amounts of memory. In [13], Miyaji proposed a practical approach to construct "anomolous" elliptic curves; these elliptic curves, of order p over fields of characteristic p, have since been shown to be insecure, [14], [16], [19]. However, the idea of the construction can be applied to quickly find non-anomolous curves as well. We present such a variant of the method to construct elliptic curves of

---

[*] This research was supported by rTrust Technologies.

[**] The reader should note that Oregon State University has filed US and International patent applications for inventions described in this paper.

Ç.K. Koç, D. Naccache, and C. Paar (Eds.): CHES 2001, LNCS 2162, pp. 142–158, 2001.
© Springer-Verlag Berlin Heidelberg 2001

known prime orders. Our variant has less computational complexity in its online implementation than that proposed in the IEEE standards [7]. Heuristics and calculations show that our method is practical.

Timing estimates for the Complex Multiplication (CM) method of generating elliptic curves seem difficult to find in the public literature. The above mentioned survey article [9] mentions that in practice the method is fast, but cites a timing result for a single curve. Our timing statistics are averaged over 1000 curves per discriminant. As to previous theoretical bounds on running times, it seems that Koblitz's [8] conjectures and statistics for reduction of class number one CM curves defined over the rationals are taken to indicate that the CM method is in general speedy. We concur in our 6.3.

We thank the referees for helpful comments and for pointing us to important entries in the literature. The second-named author thanks Professor G. Frey and his team at the Institut für Experimentelle Mathematik for clarifying some of the basics of the theory of elliptic curves.

The paper is organized as follows. Section 2 summarizes the complex multiplication curve generation method. In section 3, we explain our variant which requires less data size and computation, while avoiding the weakness of Miyaji's method. Section 4 summarizes the method to construct the class polynomials, the most computationally intensive part of the CM method. In our approach, we pre-calculate a set of these and store the coefficients. Also in section 4, we give some experimental results which indicate the efficiency of our approach. In section 5, we provide more detailed implementation results. In section 6, we give heuristics for the number of trials necessary to find prime order elliptic curves. Section 7 is a brief conclusion.

2   Complex Multiplication Curve Generation Algorithm

For the ease of the reader, we summarize some basics of the theory of elliptic curves.

An elliptic curve $\mathcal{E}$ defined over a finite field $\mathbb{F}_p$, where $p > 3$, can be given as

$$\mathcal{E}(\mathbb{F}_p) : y^2 = x^3 + ax + b \qquad a, b \in F_p \tag{1}$$

Associated with $\mathcal{E}$, there are two important quantities:
the discriminant

$$\Delta = -16(4a^3 + 27b^2) \tag{2}$$

and the j-invariant

$$j = 1728(4a)^3/\Delta \tag{3}$$

where $\Delta \neq 0$.

Lemma 1. *Given $j_0 \in \mathbb{F}_p$ there is an elliptic curve, $\mathcal{E}$, defined over $\mathbb{F}_p$ such that $j(\mathcal{E}) = j_0$.*

An elliptic curve with a given j-invariant j_0 is constructed easily. We consider $j_0 \notin \{0, 1728\}$; these special cases are also easily handled. Let $k = j_0/(1728 - j_0)$, $j_0 \in \mathbb{F}_p$ then the equation

$$\mathcal{E}: y^2 = x^3 + 3kx + 2k \tag{4}$$

gives an elliptic curve with j-invariant $j(\mathcal{E}) = j_0$.

Theorem 1. *Isomorphic elliptic curves have the same j-invariant.*

Theorem 2. *(Hasse) Let $\#\mathcal{E}(\mathbb{F}_p)$ denote the number of points on the elliptic curve $\mathcal{E}(\mathbb{F}_p)$. If $\#\mathcal{E}(\mathbb{F}_p) = p + 1 - t$, then $|t| \leq 2\sqrt{p}$.*

Definition 1. *(Twist) Given $\mathcal{E}: y^2 = x^3 + ax + b$ with $a, b \in \mathbb{F}_p$ the twist of $\mathcal{E}$ by c is the elliptic curve given by*

$$\mathcal{E}_c : y^2 = x^3 + ac^2 x + bc^3 \tag{5}$$

where $c \in \mathbb{F}_p$.

Theorem 3. *Let $\mathcal{E}$ be defined over $\mathbb{F}_p$ and its order be $\#\mathcal{E}(\mathbb{F}_p) = p + 1 - t$. Then the order of its twist is given as*

$$\#\mathcal{E}_c(\mathbb{F}_p^*) = \begin{cases} p + 1 - t \text{ if } c \text{ is square in } \mathbb{F}_p \\ p + 1 + t \text{ if } c \text{ is non-square in } \mathbb{F}_p \end{cases} \tag{6}$$

For the above basics of elliptic curves, we refer to [18]. The following result is based upon work of M. Deuring in the 1940s. See [1] and [10].

Theorem 4. *(Atkin-Morain) Let p be an odd prime such that*

$$4p = t^2 + Ds^2 \tag{7}$$

for some $t, s \in \mathbb{Z}$. Then there is an elliptic curve $\mathcal{E}$ defined over $\mathbb{F}_p$ such that $\#\mathcal{E}(\mathbb{F}_p) = p + 1 - t$.

An integer D which satisfies (7) for a given p is called a *CM discriminant* of p. Indeed, the curve $\mathcal{E}$ has complex multiplication by the integers of $\mathbb{Q}(\sqrt{-D})$. Given such a D for a prime p, the j-invariant of the elliptic curve can be calculated due to class field theory. Once the j-invariant is known, the elliptic curve with $p+1-t$ points is easily constructed utilizing Lemma 1. Actually, the method gives an elliptic curve with either $p + 1 - t$ or $p + 1 + t$ points. If the constructed elliptic curve has $p + 1 + t$ points, then one must take the twist of this elliptic curve to obtain an elliptic curve with $p + 1 - t$ points. Fortunately, it is trivial to construct the desired curve when its twist is known, due to Theorem 3. This technique for constructing elliptic curves of known order is called the *Complex Multiplication* (CM) method.

A detailed explanation of the CM method is given in the P1363 standards. One can also profitably refer to [2]. We summarize the method in the following:

1. Given a prime number p, find the smallest D in (7) along with t (s is not needed in the computations).
2. The orders of the curves which can be constructed are $\#\mathcal{E}(\mathbb{F}_p) = p + 1 \pm t$. Check if one of the orders has an admissible factorization (by admissible factorization we mean a prime or nearly prime number as defined in the standards). If not, find another D and corresponding t. Repeat until an order with admissible factorization is found.
3. Construct the class polynomial $H_D(x)$ using the formulas given in the standards. (The class polynomial for a D is a fixed monic polynomial with integer coefficients. In particular, it is independent of p).
4. Find a root j_0 of $H_D(x) \pmod{p}$. This j_0 is the j-invariant of the curve to be constructed.
5. Set $k = j_0/(1728-j_0) \pmod{p}$ and the curve will be $\mathcal{E}$: $y^2 = x^3 + 3kx + 2k$.
6. Check the order of the curve. If it is not $p + 1 - t$, then construct the twist using a randomly selected nonsquare $c \in \mathbb{F}_p$.

With the CM method, one may first fix a prime number p, and thereafter construct an elliptic curve over $\mathbb{F}_p$. This has the possible advantage of allowing the use prime numbers of special forms, possibly permitting an improvement in efficiency of the underlying modular arithmetic for the curve operations. On the other hand, the method is efficient only when the degree of the class polynomial is small; in general, factoring a high degree polynomial is time consuming. Furthermore, the construction of the class polynomials requires multi-precision floating-point and complex number arithmetic.

3   A Variant of the CM Method

The variant is straightforward: Construct and store the corresponding class polynomials for D in $\mathcal{D}$ and search for primes whose CM discriminants are in this set. We thus avoid repeatedly calculating class polynomials; hence multi-precision floating and complex number arithmetic as well as the factorization of high degree class polynomials is avoided. Indeed, the original CM method as specified in the standards becomes inefficient if not impractical as the class polynomial degree becomes large.

Our algorithm is thus:

1. Off-line: Determine a set $\mathcal{D}$ of CM discriminants such that the corresponding class numbers are small.
2. Off-line: Calculate and store the class polynomials of CM discriminants in $\mathcal{D}$.
3. Select randomly a CM discriminant D in $\mathcal{D}$ and obtain the corresponding class polynomial $H_D(x)$.
4. Search for prime number p satisfying the equation $4p = t^2 + Ds^2$. (First, we select random t and s values of appropriate sizes and then determine if p is prime)

5. Compute $u_1 = p+1-t$ and $u_2 = p+1+t$, the orders of the candidate elliptic curves and determine if either of them has an admissible factorization (i.e. is a prime or nearly-prime number). If not, go to Step 4 and pick another random pair of t and s.
6. If u_1 has proper factorization set $u = q_1$, otherwise $u = q_2$.
7. Find a root j_0 of $H_D(x)$ mod p (this is the j-invariant of the curve).
8. Set $k = j_0/(1728 - j_0)$ mod p and the curve of order u_1 or u_2 will be

$$\mathcal{E}_c : y^2 = x^3 + ax + b \tag{8}$$

where $a = 3kc^2$, $b = kc^3$ and $c \in \mathbb{F}_p$ is randomly chosen.
9. Check the order of the curve. If it is u then stop. Otherwise, select a non-square number $e \in \mathbb{F}_p$ and calculate the twist by e, $\mathcal{E}_e(F_p) = x^3 + ae^2 + be^3$.

Our experiments and heuristics confirm that pairs p and u of the type sought can be found quickly.

As stated in the introduction, the above is a generalizing variation of Miyaji's simplification of the general CM method. Recently, A.K. Lenstra [11] has also suggested using restricted sets of discriminants. But, as Miyaji, Lenstra only considers the class number one candidate discriminants.

4   Constructing Class Polynomials

Although there are different methods to calculate class polynomials, we adopt that of [1], see also [4]. Let $D = b^2 - 4ac$ be the discriminant of a quadratic form

$$f(x,y) = ax^2 + bxy + cy^2$$

where a, b, c are integers. The quadratic form, $f(x,y)$ is commonly represented by the compact notation $[a, b, c]$. If the integers a, b, c have no common factor, then the quadratic form $[a, b, c]$ is called *primitive*. There are infinitely many quadratic forms of any possible discriminant. We reduce to a finite number by demanding that a root of $f(x, 1)$ lie in a certain region of the complex plane. Let the primitive quadratic form $[a, b, c]$ be of negative discriminant. Let τ be the root of $f(x, 1)$ which lies in the upper half-plane:

$$\tau = (-b + \sqrt{D})/2a$$

The $[a, b, c]$ is a *reduced form* if τ has complex norm greater than or equal to 1, and $\Re(\tau) \in [-1/2, 1/2]$. Given a discriminant $D < 0$, we can easily find all of the reduced quadratic forms of discriminant D. We then compute the class polynomial $H_D(x)$ which is the minimal polynomial of the $j(\tau)$. For each value of τ, the j-value (denoted j_i below) is computed as follows:

$$j(\sqrt{D}) = (256f(\tau) + 1)^3/f(\tau)$$

where

$$f(\tau) = \Delta(2\tau)/\Delta(\tau),$$

$$\Delta(\tau) = q \cdot [1 + \sum_{n \geq 1} (-1)^n (q^{3n(n+1/2)} + q^{3n(n-1/2)})]^{24},$$

and

$$q = e^{2\pi i \tau}.$$

Finally, the class polynomial can be constructed by using the following formula:

$$H_D(x) = \prod_{i=1}^{h} (x - j_i)$$

where h is the number of the reduced forms of D, commonly known as the *class number* of D. Since $H_D(x)$ has integer coefficients one must use sufficient accuracy during the computations.

Our approach, as stated earlier, is to construct class polynomials beforehand for given D values. We do this using some software tool specialized for mathematical calculations. In our implementation, we use Maple. Following [1], we set the precision for floating point arithmetic as follows:

$$\text{precision} = 10 + \binom{h}{\lfloor h/2 \rfloor} \cdot \pi \sqrt{D} \cdot \sum_{i=1}^{h} 1/a_i \,,$$

$$N = 10 + \binom{h}{\lfloor h/2 \rfloor} \cdot \sum_{i=1}^{h} 1/a_i \,.$$

Here N gives the number of terms to keep in the calculations involving the various $\Delta(\tau)$.

As stated earlier, other methods than the basic use of the j-function applied here can be employed to construct class polynomials. In each of these, one obtains some class-invariant polynomial for the CM discriminant D. One advantage of using different methods is to obtain class polynomials with relatively small integer coefficients. This is particularly important when the processor used to store the polynomial coefficients is of limited memory.

5   Implementation Results

We implemented the algorithm using the NTL number theory and algebra package [17] on a 450-MHz Pentium II based PC. We restricted to $t = 2v + 1$ and $s = 2w + 1$ where $v, w \in \mathbb{Z}$. Thus, the prime numbers found in this setting are of the form

$$p = v^2 + v + (w^2 + w)D + \frac{D+1}{4} \tag{9}$$

where D satisfies

$$D \equiv 3 \pmod 4.$$

Furthermore, D is chosen such that $(D+1)/4$ is odd, hence p is odd for any choice of v and w. Throughout, we avoid the imaginary quadratic field of exceptionally many units: We exclude $D = 3$. We obtained average times to find the prime p and prime u as well as to calculate the corresponding curve for the following values of D. Again, were u merely required to be nearly prime number, the search time for admissible pairs would decrease.

For

$$\mathcal{D} = \{ 163, 403, 883 \},$$

the corresponding class polynomials are given in the following:

$$H_{163}(x) = x + 640320;$$

$$H_{403}(x) = x^2 - 108844203402491055833088000000\, x$$

$$+ 2452811389229331391979520000;$$

$$H_{883}(x) = x^3 + 167990285381627318187575520800123387904000000000\, x^2$$

$$- 1519601111252452820338756195291244789760000000\, x$$

$$+ 3490393434101181903922429501193392896000.$$

We obtained efficiency results for these three cases. When the class number is one, the class polynomial is of degree one; hence the root is obtained without any computation. In the two other cases, we must determine a root for each p of the quadratic or cubic polynomial, respectively. The results are given in Table 1.

Table 1. Timings to build curves of known prime order.

D	class no	bitsize	Average time (s)	N_p	N_u
163	1	192	1.22	23	11
163	1	224	2.29	27	14
403	2	192	1.57	30	14
403	2	224	3.29	36	21
883	3	192	1.63	30	14
883	3	224	3.01	36	19

To find a root modulo p of a class polynomial takes approximately a constant time determined by the size of the modulus p and the degree of the polynomial. However, the time or the number of trials to find admissible pairs of p and u is of a more complicated nature. We have run our program repeatedly to build 1000 different curves with each value of D in Table 1. In the table, N_p indicates the approximate number of random pairs of v and w to be tried before a prime $p = v^2 + v + (w^2 + w)D + (D + 1)/4$ is found. Similarly, N_u is the average trial number of p of the form (9) to obtain a prime u.

The method remains efficient for larger class numbers, as shown in Table 2 and Figure 1.

Table 2. Timings to build curves of prime order for large class numbers.

bitsize	D	class no	Average time (s)	N_p	N_u
192	555	4	3.54	51	35
	1051	5	2.78	48	26
	451	6	5.70	86	57
	811	7	4.61	76	44
	1299	8	5.91	69	59
	1187	9	7.35	79	72
	611	10	12.53	126	128
	1283	11	9.42	99	92
	1235	12	10.62	107	104
	1451	13	11.08	106	108
	1211	14	14.22	124	142
	1259	15	15.61	132	154
	1379	16	13.54	135	131
	1091	17	17.46	159	168
	1691	18	15.35	136	146
	2099	19	14.64	128	139
	1739	20	17.45	150	166
	25259	72	23.20	140	160
	37571	95	24.90	152	157

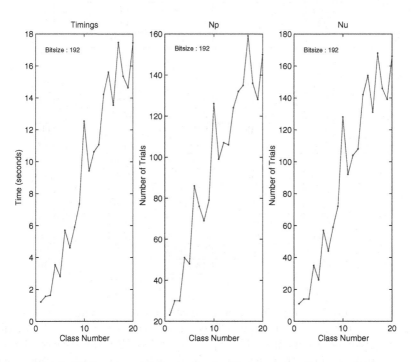

Fig. 1. Performance of the method with increasing class numbers.

Table 2 clearly indicates that the admissible pair search time increases with the class number. Although this increase is not monotone — the timing for class number 10 is much higher than those for class numbers 11, 12, and 13 — it is reasonable to claim that the time needed to find proper pairs is directly proportional to the class number. This result is consistent with the theoretical considerations in [12]; see the next section for specific comments. The dependence of the construction process on the particular value of D seems to account for the deviation from simple monoticity. Note also, just as the theoretical heuristics of the next section suggest, that the time to find an admissible pair (p, u) decreases with the size of D. This can be observed in Table 3. See also the Figures 2, 3, 4, 5, 6, 7.

Table 3. Timings for various class numbers.

field type		bitsize 192			bitsize 224		
class no	D	Average time (s)	N_p	N_u	Average time (s)	N_p	N_u
1	11	9.10	95	94	16.20	109	113
	19	3.86	68	39	7.15	81	49
	43	2.30	46	23	4.19	55	28
	67	1.87	37	18	3.55	44	23
	163	1.22	23	11	2.29	27	14
2	35	10.38	105	108	15.74	120	110
	123	3.49	57	35	5.93	64	40
	187	2.42	45	23	4.31	52	28
	235	2.09	40	20	3.98	48	26
	403	1.57	30	14	3.29	36	21
3	59	11.37	121	118	21.17	141	128
	83	10.01	102	104	16.93	118	117
	107	7.90	92	82	14.33	106	99
	379	2.63	47	25	4.85	56	32
	883	1.63	30	14	3.01	36	19
4	155	9.50	99	99	16.14	116	112
	195	6.46	88	66	11.90	105	82
	259	4.77	78	49	8.46	91	58
	355	3.76	64	37	6.87	77	46
	555	3.54	51	35	6.54	63	44
5	179	11.54	113	119	20.65	140	142
	227	9.33	103	97	17.42	122	120
	347	7.64	83	79	12.64	98	86
	443	6.65	73	68	11.81	86	81
	1051	2.78	48	26	5.52	55	36

Another important implementation aspect is code size. While one implementation [15] of the full CM method [7] requires 204KB on a PC with Windows NT, our implementation with NTL requires only 164KB code space on the same platform. In fact, the code space can be made much smaller when code is written expressly for curve generation. For sake of simplicity, we have written such

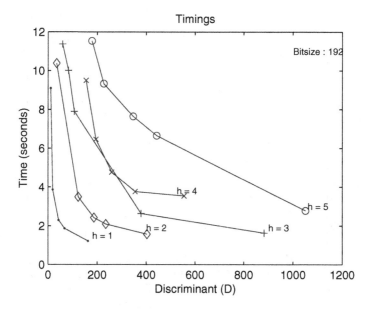

Fig. 2. Timings to build curves with increasing discriminants.

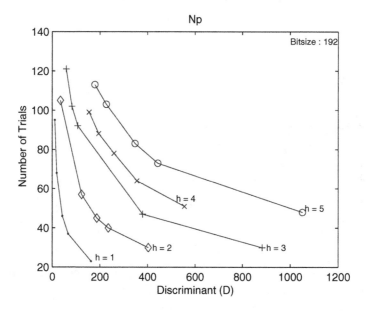

Fig. 3. Number of trials for p with increasing discriminants.

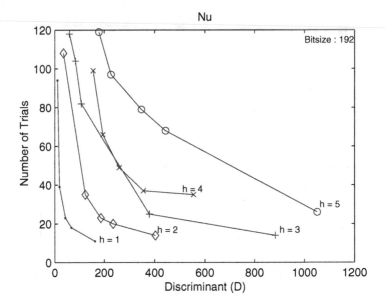

Fig. 4. Number of trials for u with increasing discriminants.

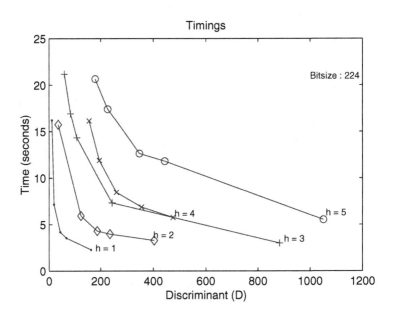

Fig. 5. Timings to build curves with increasing discriminants.

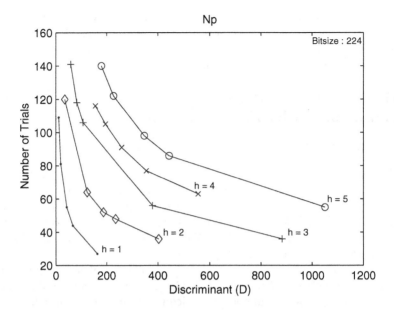

Fig. 6. Number of trials for p with increasing discriminants.

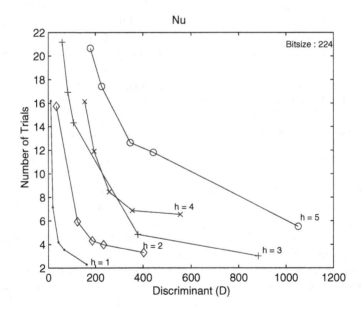

Fig. 7. Number of trials for u with increasing discriminants.

a program which treats only the class number one case. We found that only an extra 10 KB of object code space is needed for curve generation routines (assuming that the basic subroutines for arithmetic operations needed for elliptic curve arithmetic are already available).

6   Heuristics: Twin Primes and Prime Order Elliptic Curves

6.1   Finding Primes

The Prime Number Theorem states that for sufficiently large M, the number of primes in $[2, M]$ is approximately $M/\ln M$. But, with D as chosen, $4p = t^2 + s^2 D$ expresses that p is a norm of an element in the ring of integers $\mathbb{Q}(\sqrt{-D})$. The density of rational primes which are of this type is $1/(2h_D)$, where h_D is the class number of $\mathbb{Q}(\sqrt{-D})$. See [2,3,4]. We thus have that some $M/(2h_D \ln M)$ primes of size up to M are of our type.

With $p \leq M$, each pair $(s,t) \in \mathbb{Z}^2$ gives an integral lattice point inside the ellipse of equation $t^2 + s^2 D = M/4$. Gauss, see for example [3], found an asymptotic formula for the number of lattice points interior to an ellipse. Here, this gives that the the number of the lattice points (s,t) with s, t both positive is $L(M) = \pi(M)\sqrt{D} + O(\sqrt{M})$. Furthermore, our p are odd, we work with odd D and we desire the elliptic curve order $u = p + 1 \pm t$ to be prime, hence certainly odd. We thus only consider s and t odd. We thus search through a possible $L(M)/4$ distinct values of $t^2 + s^2 D$ for (s,t) interior to the ellipse.

We search for prime p in specific ranges of the form $[S, 2S]$, and hence expect to have find a prime p after a total number of trials of (v, w) of some $\bar{N}_p :=$ $c(\pi h_D \ln S)/\sqrt{D}$, for some constant c. Our experimental data confirms this, see Tables 1,2,3, where S is variously 2^{191} and 2^{223}.

6.2   Prime Order Elliptic Curves and Twin Primes

The order of the curve we seek is $u = p + 1 \pm t$, we ask for it to be prime. Now, p of our form is the norm of the element $\mathcal{P} = (t + s\sqrt{-D})/2$; note that t is the trace of $\mathcal{P}$. The norms of $\mathcal{P} \pm 1$ are easily seen to be the two possibilities for u. Thus, we are seeking twin pairs $(\mathcal{P}, \mathcal{P} \pm 1)$. Indeed, the theory of complex multiplication ensures that associated to each pair of this form is an elliptic curve defined over $\mathbb{F}_p$ where p is the norm of $\mathcal{P}$ and whose exact number of points over this field equals the norm of $\mathcal{P} \pm 1$.

Although it is not known if there are infinitely many twin prime (principal ideal) pairs in any quadratic field, there are conjectures as to their numbers within bounded regions. This is also the case for twin rational primes, for which Hardy and Littlewood [6] conjectured that there are some $C_2 \int_2^M 1/(\ln y)^2 \, dy$ twin primes of size less than M, with $C_2 = 2 \prod_{\text{odd prime } p} 1 - 1/(p-1)^2$. This constant is approximately 1.32032. The integral $\int_2^M 1/(\ln y)^2 \, dy$ is $M/(\ln M)^2 \times \gamma(M)$, where
$\gamma(M)$ is $(1 + 2!/\ln M + 3!/(\ln M)^2 + \cdots + n!/(\ln M)^{n-1}) + O((\ln M)^{n-1})$.

Recently, Gross and Smith [5] have stated general conjectures for the number of twin primes in algebraic number fields. For $\mathbb{Q}(\sqrt{-D})$ with D congruent to 3 modulo 8, their conjecture is that the number of twin primes of norm less than M should be

$$P(D, M) = 2\sqrt{D}/(\pi h_D^2) \times \beta(D) \times \int_2^M 1/(\ln y)^2 \, dy ,$$

with $\beta(D) = \prod_{\mathcal{Q}} (1 - 1/(N(\mathcal{Q}) - 1))^2$ where $\mathcal{Q}$ runs through the prime ideals of $\mathbb{Q}(\sqrt{-D})$ and $N(\mathcal{Q})$ denotes the norm to $\mathbb{Z}$. We thus see that the number of (v, w) which lead to elliptic curves of prime order over a prime field $\mathbb{F}_p$ with p of norm less than M should be $2\sqrt{D}/(\pi h_D^2) \times M/(\ln M)^2 \times \beta(D) \times \gamma(M)$.

We bound $\beta(D)$ for D congruent to 3 modulo 8 by considering (unachievably) extremal splitting behavior of rational prime ideals (p). Were every odd prime to split as the product of two distinct primes to such a field, then $\beta_{\text{split}} = 2/9 \times C_2^2 = 0.3874\ldots.$. If all odd primes were to remain inert, one finds $\beta_{\text{inert}} = 0.87299$.

We conclude that the number of trials of pairs (v, w) to find a prime pair (p, u) with p of norm in an interval $[S, 2S]$ should be $\bar{N}_p \times \bar{N}_u$ with $\bar{N}_u$ approximately a constant times $h_D \ln S/\beta(D)\sqrt{D}$. Again, our data confirm this. See in particular Figure 8.

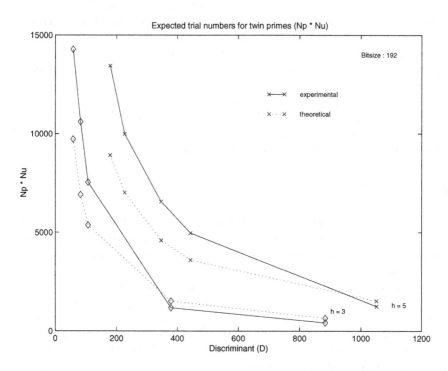

Fig. 8. A comparison of theoretic and experimental values for $N_p \times N_u$.

6.3   Special Case: Class Number One

The *reduction* of an equation over the integers $\mathbb{Z}$ with respect to a prime number p is given by reducing each coefficient of the equation modulo p. This can be extended to equations of the rational numbers; and indeed to equations over algebraic number fields, where one reduces by prime ideals.

Koblitz [8] used the Hardy-Littlewood heuristics to derive conjectures on the number of primes p for which the reduction of an elliptic curve defined over $\mathbb{Q}$ is an elliptic curve of prime order. In the class number one CM setting this number should be asymptotic to a constant times $M/(\ln M)^2$; the constant is explicit.

In deriving his conjecture, Koblitz does not directly use twin primes in $\mathbb{Q}(\sqrt{-D})$. It would be very interesting to relate his constant to the Gross-Smith $\beta(D)$ in this restricted case of class number one. We briefly review why there might well be such a relationship.

An elliptic curve of j-value $j_0 \pmod{p}$ found with the CM method is the reduction of an elliptic curve defined over the complex numbers having j-value the corresponding root of the class polynomial $H_D(x)$. The reduction is with respect to a prime lying above p in the algebraic number field in which the root lies. In the class number one case, the single root of $H_D(x)$ is in $\mathbb{Z}$. The corresponding elliptic curve is defined over $\mathbb{Q}$, and the CM method amounts to reducing the equation of this curve modulo primes which split to principal ideals in $\mathbb{Q}(\sqrt{-D})$. Thus, Conjecture B of [8] then predicts the number of primes up to M (up to choosing twists) that give prime order elliptic curves.

Table 4 gives a comparison between the Koblitz predicted value, the Gross-Smith twin primes value, and actual counts of twin primes and of anomolous primes. The anomolous values are primes naturally paired with themselves in our construction. (These are not counted as acceptable values of u in our timing and counts for the various N_u.) Whereas the Gross-Smith formula should give the number of twins, the Koblitz formula reasonably interpreted should give the number of twins plus half the number of the anomolous curves.

7   Conclusion

We present a variant of the complex multiplication (CM) elliptic curve generation algorithm for $\mathbb{F}_p$. We show that the new variant of the CM method allows off-line precalculation and therefore provides smaller, faster and more easily coded software on-line implementation. The theoretical analysis shows that there are numerous prime numbers in this subset and experimental results confirm that it is highly probable to construct a prime number belonging to this set with a fairly small number of searches. Our experiments also reveal the fact that the on-line performance of the modified CM method increases as the class number decreases. Another interesting result is that the new CM method performs better for larger discriminants of the same class.

Table 4. Twin primes: estimates and counts.

D	M	Koblitz	Gross-Smith	Twins	Anomolous
11	2000	10.9	12.1	12	4
	4000	17.9	19.2	20	4
	6000	24.1	25.5	23	5
	8000	30.1	31.3	26	5
	10000	35.7	36.7	33	5
19	2000	24.2	25.9	23	5
	4000	37.9	41.1	36	7
	6000	51.2	54.5	51	7
	8000	63.1	66.9	63	7
	10000	75.2	78.6	78	9
43	2000	41.7	46.1	45	4
	4000	67.1	73.2	72	5
	6000	89.2	97.0	88	5
	8000	111.1	119.0	105	6
	10000	131.5	139.9	122	7
67	2000	54.8	59.2	56	4
	4000	88.2	93.9	91	6
	6000	117.2	124.5	125	7
	8000	144.8	152.7	157	7
	10000	172.4	179.4	189	8
163	2000	76.6	94.3	72	4
	4000	128.9	149.6	127	5
	6000	180.0	198.3	183	6
	8000	225.4	243.3	234	6
	10000	265.4	285.8	272	6

References

1. A. O. L. Atkin and F. Morain. Elliptic curves and primality proving. *Mathematics of Computation*, 61(203):29–68, July 1993.
2. H. Cohen. *A Course in Computational Algebraic Number Theory*. Springer, Berlin, Germany, 1997.
3. H. Cohn. *Advanced Number Theory*. Dover Publications, New York, NY, 1980.
4. D. A. Cox. *Primes of the Form $x^2 + ny^2$: Fermat, Class Field Theory and Complex Multiplication*. John Wiley & Sons, New York, NY, 1989.
5. R. Gross and J. H. Smith. A generalization of a conjecture of hardy and littlewood to algebraic number fields. *Rocky Mountain J. Math*, 30(1):195–215, 2000.
6. G. H. Hardy and J. E. Littlewood. Some problems of 'partitio numerorum' iii: On the expression of a number as a sum of primes. *Acta. MAth*, 44:1–70, 1922.
7. IEEE. P1363: Standard specifications for public-key cryptography. Draft Version 13, November 12, 1999.
8. N. Koblitz. Primality of the number of points on an elliptic curve over a finite field. *Pacific J. Math.*, 131(1):157–165, 1988.

9. N. Koblitz, A. Menezes, and S. Vanstone. The state of elliptic curve cryptography. towards a quarter-century of public key cryptography. *Designs, Codes and Cryptography*, 19(2-3):173–193, 2000.
10. G.-H. Lay and H. G. Zimmer. Constructing elliptic curves with given group order over large finite fields. *Algorithmic number theory (Ithaca, NY, 1994)*, pages 157–165, 1994.
11. A. K. Lenstra. Efficient identity based parameter selection for elliptic curve cryptosystems. *Information Security and Privacy—ACISP '99 (Wollongong)*, pages 294–302, 1999.
12. H. W. Lenstra Jr. Factoring integers with elliptic curves. *Annals of Mathematics*, 126(3):649–673, 1987.
13. A. Miyaji. Elliptic curves over F_p suitable for cryptosystems. In J. Seberry and Y. Zheng, editors, *Advances in Cryptology – AUSCRYPT 92*, Lecture Notes in Computer Science, No. 718, pages 492–504. Springer, Berlin, Germany, 1992.
14. T. Satoh and K. Araki. Fermat quotients and the polynomial time discrete log algorithm for anomalous elliptic curves. *Commentarii Math. Univ. St. Pauli*, 47:81–92, 1998.
15. M. Scott. A C++ implementation of the complex cultiplication (CM) elliptic curve generation algorithm from Annex A. `http://grouper.ieee.org/groups/1363/P1363/implementations.html`, March 14, 2000.
16. I. A. Semaev. Evaluation of discrete logarithms in a group of p-torsion points of an elliptic curve in characteristic p. *Mathematics of Computation*, 67(221):353–356, January 1998.
17. V. Shoup. NTL: A Library for doing Number Theory (version 5.0c). http://shoup.net/ntl/, 2001.
18. J. H. Silverman. *The Arithmetic of Elliptic Curves*. Springer, Berlin, Germany, 1986.
19. N.P. Smart. The discrete logarithm problem on elliptic curves of trace one. *Journal of Cryptography*, 12:193–196, 1999.

New Directions in Croptography

Adi Shamir

Applied Math Department, The Weizmann Institute of Science
Rehovot 76100, Israel
shamir@wisdom.weizmann.ac.il

Abstract. Croptography is a relatively new area of research which uses optical techniques to solve cryptographic problems. Optical computations are characterized by extremely high speed and truly massive parallelism, but they can not be used as general purpose computers. In this talk I'll survey the field, and show that many natural problems in cryptography and cryptanalysis can be efficiently solved by simple optical techniques. In particular, I'll describe a new way to break LFSR-based stream ciphers by using commercially available optical devices.

Ç.K. Koç, D. Naccache, and C. Paar (Eds.): CHES 2001, LNCS 2162, p. 159, 2001.

A New Low Complexity Parallel Multiplier for a Class of Finite Fields

Manuel Leone

Telecom Italia Lab,
via G. Reiss Romoli 274, 10148 Torino, Italy
manuel.leone@tilab.com

Abstract. In this paper a new low complexity parallel multiplier for characteristic two finite fields $GF(2^m)$ is proposed. In particular our multiplier works with field elements represented through both Canonical Basis and Type I Optimal Normal Basis (ONB), provided that the irreducible polynomial generating the field is an All One Polynomial (AOP). The main advantage of the scheme is the resulting space complexity, significantly lower than the one provided by the other fast parallel multipliers currently available in the open literature and belonging to the same class.

1 Introduction

Finite fields have recently attracted a lot of attention due to the increasing number of cryptography and coding theory applications that require high performance finite field capabilities ([9]). Several new architectures have been proposed in order to fulfill the constraints imposed by specific purposes ([2,8,10]). Although different solutions can be compared from several points of view, *time complexity* and *space complexity* are, usually, the two most important parameters. The former is defined as the elapsed time between input and output of the circuit implementing the multiplier, and it is usually expressed as a function of the field degree m, the delay of an AND gate T_A and the delay of an XOR gate T_X. The latter, on the contrary, is defined as the pair of numbers Σ_A and Σ_X, of AND and XOR gates used respectively. Although a manifest improvement in space complexity over the best known algorithm is still possible, because of an achievable asymptotic space complexity given by $O(m \log_2 m \log_2 \log_2 m)$ ([1]), these two parameters are characterized by an evident trade off. In fact, reducing the number of gates causes, in general, a corresponding increase in the execution time. So, if performance is the most critical parameter, we can accept a greater space complexity, in exchange for a reduction of the corresponding time delay. Conversely, in other applications such as those based on smart cards, mobile phones, or other portable devices, a reduced space complexity is often the most important design aspect.

Because of these reasons we will focus on a special class of fast multipliers, characterized by a generator of type AOP, which can take advantage of the trade off between time and space complexity to achieve a space complexity significantly

Ç.K. Koç, D. Naccache, and C. Paar (Eds.): CHES 2001, LNCS 2162, pp. 160–170, 2001.

lower than those offered by the traditional bit-parallel multipliers of the same class ([3,4,5,6,7]), with a small increase in the corresponding time delay. In other words, a limited rise in the time complexity is accepted in order to obtain a more consistent reduction in the corresponding circuit area.

Therefore the paper is organized as follows: section two introduces some useful preliminaries; section three provides an architectural description of the multiplier when the field elements are represented through a Canonical Basis, while section four focuses on Type I ONB representations. The last section summarizes the results obtained and draws some conclusions.

2   Preliminaries

Characteristic two finite fields $GF(2^m)$ provide a plethora of methods to represent field elements according to their particular application. Specifically, the two most classical schemes reported in literature are *Canonical Basis* (also called Standard Basis) and *Optimal Normal Basis*, though other strategies have recently been proposed ([2]). The former represents the generic field element $a \in GF(2^m)$ through the m-bit vector $(a_0, a_1, \ldots, a_{m-1})$ with respect to the set $(1, \alpha, \alpha^2, \ldots, \alpha^{m-1})$, where α is the root of an irreducible polynomial of degree m over $GF(2)$, which corresponds to the expansion $a(\alpha) = \sum_{i=0}^{m-1} a_i \alpha^i$. On the contrary, the latter specializes the set as $(\gamma, \gamma^2, \ldots, \gamma^{2^{m-1}})$, where γ is now the root of an *N-polynomial* of degree m over $GF(2)$. In this case the expansion is therefore given by $a(\gamma) = \sum_{i=0}^{m-1} a_i \gamma^{2^i}$ (for more information see [9]).

In order to reduce the complexity of the field multiplication special classes of irreducible polynomials have been suggested ([7], [10]). Among them, the AOP generators have been shown to be particularly interesting. An AOP is a polynomial characterized by the form $p(x) = 1 + x + x^2 + \ldots + x^m$, which is irreducible if and only if $m + 1$ is prime and 2 is primitive modulo $m + 1$ ([9]). For instance, for $m \leq 100$ there are thirteen useful values: 2, 4, 10, 12, 18, 28, 36, 52, 58, 60, 66, 82, and 100. Moreover, each *N-polynomial* generating a Type I ONB is also an AOP ([9]). For this reason in the following we will focus on AOPs, discussing the advantages of this class in the context of both Canonical Basis and Type I ONB representations.

3   Canonical Basis

Let $p(x) = 1 + x + x^2 + \ldots + x^m$ an irreducible polynomial over $GF(2^m)$, and let $a(\alpha)$ and $b(\alpha)$ be two elements of $GF(2^m)$, represented through the m-tuples $(a_0, a_1, \ldots, a_{m-1})$ and $(b_0, b_1, \ldots, b_{m-1})$, with respect to the root α of $p(x)$. Our goal is the computation of the field element $(c_0, c_1, \ldots, c_{m-1})$ given by the product $c(\alpha) = a(\alpha) \cdot b(\alpha) \in GF(2^m)$. This product can be computed in two different phases:

1. computation of the ordinary product of two polynomials $\ell(x) = a(x) \cdot b(x)$ over $GF(2)$
2. computation of the field product $c(x) \in GF(2^m)$ as $c(x) = \ell(x) \mod p(x)$

3.1   Multiplication of Polynomials over GF(2)

First, we observe that the degrees of the polynomials $a(x)$ and $b(x)$ are both $\leq m-1$, therefore the degree of the polynomial $\ell(x)$ will be, in turn, $\leq 2m-2$. Formally we have:

$$\ell(x) = a(x) \cdot b(x) = \ell_0 + \ell_1 x + \ell_2 x^2 + \ldots + \ell_{2m-2} x^{2m-2} \qquad (1)$$

This polynomial can be computed by means of a divide-and-conquer approach originally proposed to increase the speed of integer multiplications ([11]). Actually this strategy, which we will slightly improve and extend respect to the results obtained in [8], in turn reminiscent of the Karatsuba-Ofman algorithm, has been also successfully applied in case of trinomial generators ([12]).

More precisely, let us to observe that in this context m is surely even, thanks to the sufficient conditions that make $p(x)$ irreducible. Therefore we can assume $m = 2N$. As a consequence the polynomials $a(x)$ and $b(x)$ can be rewritten as $a(x) = A(x) + x^N B(x)$ and $b(x) = C(x) + x^N D(x)$ respectively, where

$$A(x) = a_0 + a_1 x + a_2 x^2 + \ldots + a_{N-1} x^{N-1}$$
$$B(x) = a_N + a_{N+1} x + a_{N+2} x^2 + \ldots + a_{2N-1} x^{N-1}$$

and analogously

$$C(x) = b_0 + b_1 x + b_2 x^2 + \ldots + b_{N-1} x^{N-1}$$
$$D(x) = b_N + b_{N+1} x + b_{N+2} x^2 + \ldots + b_{2N-1} x^{N-1}$$

Therefore, the product $\ell(x)$ can be computed as

$$\ell(x) = a(x) \cdot b(x) = A(x)C(x) + x^N[B(x)C(x) + A(x)D(x)] + x^{2N}B(x)D(x) \quad (2)$$

which, introducing the following auxiliary polynomials

$$P_{AC}(x) = A(x) \cdot C(x)$$
$$P_{BD}(x) = B(x) \cdot D(x)$$
$$P_{A+B}(x) = A(x) + B(x)$$
$$P_{C+D}(x) = C(x) + D(x)$$

we can also express as

$$\ell(x) = P_{AC}(x) + x^N[P_{A+B}(x) \cdot P_{C+D}(x) + P_{AC}(x) + P_{BD}(x)] + x^{2N}P_{BD}(x) \quad (3)$$

Eq.(3) compute the product $a(x) \cdot b(x)$ by means of three multiplications of polynomials of degree $N-1$, together with shifts and "lettings-down" of α powers. Specifically, the architectural structure of the multiplier can be organized as follows:

- two circuits, composed of N XOR gates each, for the parallel computation of $A(x) + B(x)$ and $C(x) + D(x)$

- three circuits, composed by N^2 AND and $(N-1)^2$ XOR gates each, for the parallel computation of $A(x) \cdot C(x)$, $B(x) \cdot D(x)$, and $[A(x)+B(x)] \cdot [C(x)+D(x)]$; the XOR tree depth is $\lceil \log_2(N-1) \rceil$, provided that the polynomials involved have at most degree N
- one circuit, composed of $2N-1$ XOR gates, for the computation of $A(x)C(x) + B(x)D(x)$
- one circuit, composed of $2N-1$ XOR gates, for the computation of $[A(x)C(x) + B(x)D(x)] + [A(x)+B(x)][C(x)+D(x)]$
- one circuit, composed of $2N-2$ XOR gates, for the computation of $\ell(x)$ by means of the eq.(3), where each term, at this point, has been already pre-computed

As far as the time complexity is concerned, it should be noted that the overall circuit is able to produce the output $\ell(x)$ according to a time delay of $T_A + T_X(\lceil \log_2(N-1) \rceil + 3)$. In fact, after a period of time equal to T_X, the intermediate values $A(x)+B(x)$ and $C(x)+D(x)$ will be available; therefore, when other $T_A + T_X(\lceil \log_2(N-1) \rceil + 1)$ seconds have elapsed, the circuit will have also computed $[A(x)+B(x)] \cdot [C(x)+D(x)]$, $B(x)D(x)$, $A(x)C(x)$ and $A(x)C(x)+B(x)D(x)$, while waiting for other T_X seconds, also the computation of the term $A(x)C(x)+B(x)D(x)+[A(x)+B(x)] \cdot [C(x)+D(x)]$ will be completed. Therefore the result $\ell(x)$, which now needs other T_X seconds to be reached, just requires a time complexity equal to $T_A + T_X(\lceil \log_2(N-1) \rceil + 3)$.

The overall characteristics of the algorithm, whose details have been presented in Table 1, are respectively:

$$
\begin{aligned}
\Sigma'_A &= 3N^2 & &= \tfrac{3}{4}m^2 \\
\Sigma'_X &= 3N^2 + 2N - 1 & &= \tfrac{3}{4}m^2 + m - 1 \\
\Theta' &= T_A + T_X(\lceil \log_2(N-1) \rceil + 3) = T_A + T_X(\lceil \log_2(m-2) \rceil + 2)
\end{aligned} \tag{4}
$$

which can be compared with those provided by a direct parallel multiplication

$$
\begin{aligned}
\Sigma'_A &= m^2 \\
\Sigma'_X &= m^2 - 2m + 1 \\
\Theta' &= T_A + T_X(\lceil \log_2(m-1) \rceil)
\end{aligned} \tag{5}
$$

It is evident how the former strategy exchanges a part of its time complexity in order to gain a $\tfrac{3}{4}$ factor in the corresponding number of gates.

Anyway, the values in (4) can be also further manipulated and expressed as (see also Table 1)

$$
(\Sigma'_A)_m = 3(\Sigma'_A)_{m/2} \tag{6}
$$
$$
(\Sigma'_X)_m = 3(\Sigma'_X)_{m/2} + 4m - 4 \tag{7}
$$
$$
(\Theta')_m = (\Theta')_{m/2} + 3T_X \tag{8}
$$

where $(C)_d$ represents the complexity C of the multiplier, i.e. Σ'_A, Σ'_X and Θ', when the polynomials in input have degree at most $d-1$, that is d coefficients.

Eq.(6), (7), and (8) show that the product of two polynomials of degree $\leq m-1$ can be performed by means of three multiplications of two polynomials

Table 1. Time and space complexity to multiply polynomials over GF(2).

Operation	Σ_A	Σ_X	Θ	Register Size
$A(x) + B(x)$		N	T_X	N
$C(x) + D(x)$		N		N
$A(x)C(x)$	N^2	$(N-1)^2$	$T_A + T_X \lceil \log_2(N-1) \rceil$	$2N-1$
$B(x)D(x)$	N^2	$(N-1)^2$		$2N-1$
$(A(x) + B(x))(C(x) + D(x))$	N^2	$(N-1)^2$		$2N-1$
$A(x)C(x) + B(x)D(x)$		$2N-1$		$2N-1$
$A(x)C(x) + B(x)D(x)+$		$2N-1$	T_X	$2N-1$
$+(A(x) + B(x))(C(x) + D(x))$				$2N-1$
$\ell(x)$		$2N-2$	T_X	$4N-1$

of degree equal (at most) to about the half the original ones, plus a little overhead needed to combine the partial results and to obtain the final output. Moreover these three multiplications can be computed in a parallel way, and this is the reason why within the time complexity (8) does not appear the factor 3, present, in contrast, in (6) and (7). It should be also pointed out that this additional overhead is relatively small, being limited to $4m - 4$ XOR gates in (7) and characterized by an additional time delay equal to $3T_X$ in (8).

Moreover, provided that also $m/2$ is even, this strategy can be further applied, in order to gain a further reduction in the gate count. For instance, assuming that m is a power of 2, after k iterations we will obtain:

$$
\begin{aligned}
(\Sigma'_A)_m &= 3^k(\Sigma'_A)_{m/2^k} \\
(\Sigma'_X)_m &= 3^k(\Sigma'_X)_{m/2^k} + 8m[(3/2)^k - 1] - 2(3^k - 1) \\
(\Theta')_m &= (\Theta')_{m/2^k} + 3kT_X
\end{aligned}
\tag{9}
$$

These results show a clear trade off between time and space complexity. Therefore, to significantly reduce the number of gates we have to increase the corresponding number of iterations, although, as a side-effect, the time delay of the multiplier will also rise, just linearly in the same number of iterations. Of course, an interesting question is: how much can we iterate the algorithm, provided that we want to reduce the space complexity as much as possible? It is easy to see that the optimal stop condition for this recursion is $m/2^k = 4$, a value for which a parallel and direct multiplication is more advantageous over the recursive scheme. In fact, iterating the algorithm we obtain $(\Sigma'_A)_4 = 12$ and $(\Sigma'_X)_4 = 15$, from which $(\Sigma'_{TOT}) = (\Sigma'_A)_4 + (\Sigma'_X)_4 = 27$, while $(\Theta')_4 = T_A + 4T_X$. On the contrary, using a direct strategy we have $(\Sigma'_A)_4 = 16$ and $(\Sigma'_X)_4 = 9$, from which $(\Sigma'_{TOT}) = (\Sigma'_A)_4 + (\Sigma'_X)_4 = 25$, while $(\Theta')_4 = T_A + 2T_X$. Therefore, taking into account this stop condition, the corresponding complexities, in case of $m = 2^t$, will be:

$$
\begin{aligned}
(\Sigma'_A)_m &= 16 \cdot 3^{\log_2 m - 2} \\
(\Sigma'_X)_m &= 8m \cdot [(3/2)^{\log_2 m - 2} - 1] + 7 \cdot 3^{\log_2 m - 2} + 2 \\
(\Theta')_m &= T_A + T_X(3\log_2 m - 4)
\end{aligned}
\tag{10}
$$

Table 2. Comparing different polynomial multipliers over GF(2).

Scheme	Σ_A	Σ_X	Σ_{TOT}	Θ
Direct	m^2	$m^2 - 2m + 1$	$2m^2 - 2m + 1$	$T_A + T_X\lceil \log_2(m-1)\rceil$
$m = 256$	65,536	65,025	130,561	$T_A + 8T_X$
$m = 1024$	1,048,576	1,046,529	2,095,105	$T_A + 10T_X$
$m = 2048$	4,194,304	4,190,209	8,384,513	$T_A + 11T_X$
Paar ([8])	$m^{\log_2 3}$	$6m^{\log_2 3} - 8m + 2$	$7m^{\log_2 3} - 8m + 2$	$T_A + 3T_X\log_2 m$
$m = 256$	6,561	37,320	43,881	$T_A + 24T_X$
$m = 1024$	59,049	346,104	405,153	$T_A + 30T_X$
$m = 2048$	177,147	1,046,500	1,223,647	$T_A + 33T_X$
Proposed	$16 \cdot 3^{\log_2 m - 2}$	$8m[(\frac{3}{2})^{\log_2 m - 2} - 1]$ $+7 \cdot 3^{\log_2 m - 2} + 2$	$8m[(\frac{3}{2})^{\log_2 m - 2} - 1]$ $+23 \cdot 3^{\log_2 m - 2} + 2$	$T_A + T_X(3\log_2 m - 4)$
$m = 256$	11,664	26,385	38,049	$T_A + 20T_X$
$m = 1024$	104,976	247,689	352,665	$T_A + 26T_X$
$m = 2048$	314,928	751,255	1,066,183	$T_A + 29T_X$

which slightly improves the results reached in [8]. For a quantitative comparison see also Table 2, where it should be clear how our scheme pays a greater number of AND gates, if compared with [8], but in order to reduce both the overall number of gates Σ_{TOT} and the time complexity Θ.

Now we have to generalize the previous results, in order to make the scheme suitable for generating AOPs. In fact, it is possible to employ the same strategy also when m is not a power of 2. To make the design very modular, we do not optimize the structure of the multiplier distinguishing the two cases, m even and odd, as done in [12]. In contrast, we simply expand the circuit registers to handle, at each step, polynomials of odd degree, that is with an even number of coefficients. As a consequence the following generalization can be derived and used to multiply polynomials of any degree ($m \geq 4$):

$$
\begin{aligned}
(\Sigma_A')_m &= 16 \cdot 3^{\lceil \log_2 m \rceil - 2} \\
(\Sigma_X')_m &= 4 \cdot \sum_{i=0}^{\lceil \log_2 m \rceil - 3} 3^i \lceil \tfrac{m}{2^i} \rceil + 7 \cdot 3^{\lceil \log_2 m \rceil - 2} + 2 \\
(\Theta')_m &= T_A + T_X(3\lceil \log_2 m \rceil - 4)
\end{aligned}
\tag{11}
$$

At the end of this first phase, the circuit outputs the coefficients of the product polynomial $\ell(x)$, that is the bit vector $(\ell_0, \ell_1, \ldots, \ell_{2m-2})$. The subsequent step will be the computation of field element $c(x)$ as the remainder $c(x) = \ell(x) \mod p(x)$.

3.2   Reduction Phase

Let $\ell(x) = (\ell_0, \ell_1, \ldots, \ell_{2m-2})$ the polynomial given by the ordinary product of $a(x)$ and $b(x)$. The current phase prescribes the computation of field element $c(x) = a(x) \cdot b(x) \in GF(2^m)$ as the remainder of the polynomial division of $\ell(x)$ by the generator polynomial $p(x)$. To speed up this computation it is possible to take advantage of the structure of the generator $p(x)$. Thanks to the regular form of this polynomial it is easy to express the coefficients of the field element c_i in terms of coefficients ℓ_i. Specifically, it can be shown that the field element $c(x) \equiv (c_0, c_1, \ldots, c_{m-1})$ can be computed as

$$
c_i = \begin{cases} \ell_i + \ell_m + \ell_{m+i+1} & \text{if } i = 0, 1, \ldots, m-3 \\ \ell_{m-2} + \ell_m & \text{if } i = m-2 \\ \ell_{m-1} + \ell_m & \text{if } i = m-1 \end{cases}
$$

Of course this step can be accomplished according to a time complexity equal to $(\Theta'')_m = 2T_X$, while the relating space complexity is given by $(\Sigma''_X)_m = 2m - 2$.

As a consequence, the characteristics of the overall multiplier taking in input the two bit vectors $(a_0, a_1, \ldots, a_{m-1})$ and $(b_0, b_1, \ldots, b_{m-1})$ and producing, at the output of the circuit, the product element $(c_0, c_1, \ldots, c_{m-1})$, will be given by:

$$
\begin{aligned}
(\Sigma_A)_m &= (\Sigma'_A)_m + (\Sigma''_A)_m = 16 \cdot 3^{\lceil \log_2 m \rceil - 2} \\
(\Sigma_X)_m &= (\Sigma'_X)_m + (\Sigma''_X)_m = 4 \cdot \sum_{i=0}^{\lceil \log_2 m \rceil - 3} 3^i \lceil \tfrac{m}{2^i} \rceil + 7 \cdot 3^{\lceil \log_2 m \rceil - 2} + 2m \\
(\Theta)_m &= (\Theta')_m + (\Theta'')_m = T_A + T_X(3\lceil \log_2 m \rceil - 2)
\end{aligned}
\tag{12}
$$

It should be noted that the final space complexities are notably lower than those currently available in literature and belonging to the same class ([3,6,7]). For a direct comparison see also Table 3, where it is evident how our scheme does exchange time complexity in order to gain a more consistent reduction in both the number of AND and XOR gates. Moreover, this gain grows as m grows. For instance, if $m = 226$, our multiplier provides a factor reduction, in the overall gate count, equal to 2.7, with respect to the best method ([3]), paying a corresponding time expansion factor of 2. On the other hand, in case of $m = 2026$, the area reduction factor becomes 7.7, while the corresponding time expansion rises only up to 2.36.

As an example, in Figure 1 is reported the scheme of the overall multiplier, when the generating polynomial is $p(x) = 1 + x + x^2 + x^3 + x^4 + x^5 + x^6 + x^7 + x^8 + x^9 + x^{10}$. In this case the two inputs $a(x)$ and $b(x)$ have been rewritten as $a(x) = A(x) + x^5 B(x)$ and $b(x) = C(x) + x^5 D(x)$ respectively, where

$$
\begin{aligned}
A(x) &= a_0 + a_1 x + a_2 x^2 + a_3 x^3 + a_4 x^4 \\
B(x) &= a_5 + a_6 x + a_7 x^2 + a_8 x^3 + a_9 x^4
\end{aligned}
$$

and analogously

$$
\begin{aligned}
C(x) &= b_0 + b_1 x + b_2 x^2 + b_3 x^3 + b_4 x^4 \\
D(x) &= b_5 + b_6 x + b_7 x^2 + b_8 x^3 + b_9 x^4
\end{aligned}
$$

Therefore, the field element $c(x) = a(x) \cdot b(x) \in GF(2^{10})$ can be computed by means of three multiplication circuits for polynomials of degree 4, to obtain $(A+B) \cdot (C+D)$, $A \cdot C$ and $B \cdot D$, plus some XOR gates, needed to recombine partial results (block Recombination), and to perform the reduction phase (block

Table 3. Comparing different Canonical Basis multipliers with generating AOPs.

Scheme	Σ_A	Σ_X	Θ
Itoh-Tsujii [7]	$m^2 + 2m + 1$	$m^2 + 2m$	$T_A + T_X\lceil \log_2 m + \log_2(m+2)\rceil$
$m = 226$	51,529	51,528	$T_A + 16T_X$
$m = 1018$	1,038,361	1,038,360	$T_A + 20T_X$
$m = 2026$	4,108,729	4,108,728	$T_A + 22T_X$
Hasan et al. [5]	m^2	$m^2 + m - 2$	$T_A + T_X(\lceil \log_2(m-1)\rceil + m)$
$m = 226$	51,076	51,300	$T_A + 234T_X$
$m = 1018$	1,036,324	1,037,340	$T_A + 1028T_X$
$m = 2026$	4,104,676	4,106,700	$T_A + 2037T_X$
Koç-Sunar [3]	m^2	$m^2 - 1$	$T_A + T_X(\lceil \log_2(m-1)\rceil + 2)$
$m = 226$	51,076	51,075	$T_A + 10T_X$
$m = 1018$	1,036,324	1,036,323	$T_A + 12T_X$
$m = 2026$	4,104,676	4,104,675	$T_A + 13T_X$
Proposed	$16 \cdot 3^{\lceil \log_2 m\rceil - 2}$	$4 \cdot \sum_{i=0}^{\lceil \log_2 m\rceil - 3} 3^i \lceil \frac{m}{2^i}\rceil$ $+7 \cdot 3^{\lceil \log_2 m\rceil - 2} + 2m$	$T_A + T_X(3\lceil \log_2 m\rceil - 2)$
$m = 226$	11,664	25,635	$T_A + 22T_X$
$m = 1018$	104,976	249,627	$T_A + 28T_X$
$m = 2026$	314,928	754,365	$T_A + 31T_X$

Reduction Phase). To make fully modular the circuit design (which could be an advantage, especially if $m \gg 10$), we do not directly deal with these polynomials of degree 4. Instead we extend these polynomials by a single bit, in order to obtain polynomials of degree 5. This provides us with the possibility to further iterate the algorithm and to directly employ modules architecturally equivalent to the previous ones. In fact, each of these three products can be computed, in turn, by means of other three multiplication circuits for polynomials of degree 2, for the parallel computation of $(A' + B') \cdot (C' + D')$, $A' \cdot C'$ and $B' \cdot D'$, plus the XOR gates needed for the recombination. Conversely, the latter 9 polynomial multiplications are not further iterated, because of the lower time and space complexities provided by a direct multiplication.

4   Type I Optimal Normal Basis

The previous scheme can be also adopted in case of Type I ONB, following the smart strategy proposed in [3]. Specifically, let $p(x) = 1 + x + x^2 + \ldots + x^m$ an N-polynomial over $GF(2^m)$, and let $a(\gamma)$ and $b(\gamma)$ be two elements of $GF(2^m)$, represented through the m-bit vectors $(a_0, a_1, \ldots, a_{m-1})$ and $(b_0, b_1, \ldots, b_{m-1})$, with respect to the root γ of $p(x)$. Given that $p(x)$ is also an AOP, the root γ satisfies the property $\gamma^{m+1} = 1$, in fact

$$p(x) = 1 + x + x^2 + \ldots + x^m = \frac{x^{m+1} + 1}{x + 1} \tag{13}$$

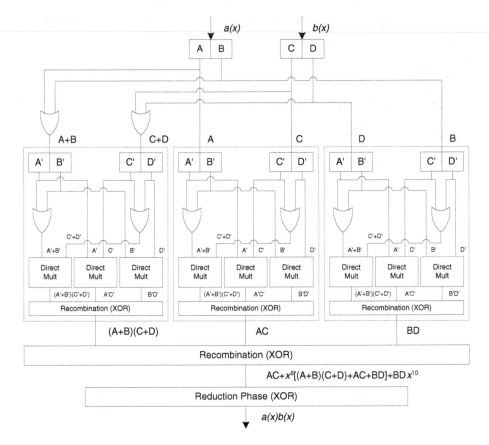

Fig. 1. Multiplier for Canonical Basis over $GF(2^{10})$ with generating polynomial AOP.

As a consequence, the set

$$\Psi = (\gamma, \gamma^2, \ldots, \gamma^m) \qquad (14)$$

can also be used as a basis for $GF(2^m)$. More precisely, (14) is nothing but a shifted version of the Canonical Basis, therefore the elements of $GF(2^m)$ represented in Type I ONB can be quickly converted in Canonical Basis, and vice-versa, by means of a simple permutation of the components. In fact, thanks to the relation $\gamma^{m+1} = 1$, we can write the conversion

$$a(\gamma) = \Sigma_{i=0}^{m-1} a_i \gamma^{2^i} = \Sigma_{i=1}^{m} a_i' \gamma^i \qquad (15)$$

by means of the permutation P defined as

$$a'_{2^i \bmod (m+1)} = a_i \qquad \text{for } i = 0, 1, \ldots, m-1 \qquad (16)$$

Therefore, the elements to be multiplied in Type I ONB will be simply converted in Canonical Basis, through the permutation P, before entering the multiplier. The output of the circuit, computed according to the complexities given

Table 4. Comparing different Type I ONB multipliers.

Scheme	Σ_A	Σ_X	Θ
Massey-Omura [4]	m^2	$2m^2 - 2m$	$T_A + T_X(\lceil \log_2(m-1)\rceil + 1)$
$m = 226$	51,076	101,700	$T_A + 9T_X$
$m = 1018$	1,036,324	2,070,612	$T_A + 11T_X$
$m = 2026$	4,104,676	8,205,300	$T_A + 12T_X$
Hasan et al. [6]	m^2	$m^2 - 1$	$T_A + T_X(\lceil \log_2(m-1)\rceil + 1)$
$m = 226$	51,076	51,075	$T_A + 9T_X$
$m = 1018$	1,036,324	1,036,323	$T_A + 11T_X$
$m = 2026$	4,104,676	4,104,675	$T_A + 12T_X$
Koç-Sunar [3]	m^2	$m^2 - 1$	$T_A + T_X(\lceil \log_2(m-1)\rceil + 2)$
$m = 226$	51,076	51,075	$T_A + 10T_X$
$m = 1018$	1,036,324	1,036,323	$T_A + 12T_X$
$m = 2026$	4,104,676	4,104,675	$T_A + 13T_X$
Proposed	$16 \cdot 3^{\lceil \log_2 m\rceil - 2}$	$4 \cdot \sum_{i=0}^{\lceil \log_2 m\rceil - 3} 3^i \lceil \frac{m}{2^i}\rceil$ $+7 \cdot 3^{\lceil \log_2 m\rceil - 2} + 2m$	$T_A + T_X(3\lceil \log_2 m\rceil - 2)$
$m = 226$	11,664	25,635	$T_A + 22T_X$
$m = 1018$	104,976	249,627	$T_A + 28T_X$
$m = 2026$	314,928	754,365	$T_A + 31T_X$

in (12) and still represented in Canonical Basis, will be restored in Normal Basis thanks to the inverse permutation P^{-1}. It should be noted that these two additional permutations do not increase the overall time and space complexity of the multiplier. In fact, P, and its inverse P^{-1}, can be directly implemented by wiring the fan-in and fan-out of the circuit, without modifying any complexity. Therefore, our scheme is able to maintain the previously discussed gate count reduction also in case of Type I ONB. This reduction is significant, especially if compared with the one provided by the other fast parallel schemes currently available in literature ([4,6,3]), as reported in Table 4. Finally, also in this case the gain factor becomes more consistent as soon as m grows, as previously seen for Canonical Basis.

5   Conclusions

In this paper we have proposed a new low space complexity scheme for fast parallel multiplication of field elements represented through both Canonical and Type I Optimal Normal Bases. Specifically, the discussed strategy shows how to avoid quadratic space complexity, paying only a limited increase in the corresponding time delay. As reported in Table 3 and 4, the proposed scheme offers a circuit complexity significantly lower compared to the other fast parallel schemes present in the open literature ([3,4,5,6,7]). This characteristic makes the employment of this multiplier particularly suitable for applications characterized by specific space constraints, such as those based on smart cards, token hardware, mobile phones or other portable devices.

References

1. Aho A.V., Hopcroft J.E., Ullman J.D., "The Design and Analysis of Computer Algorithms", Addison-Wesley, Reading, Mass., 1975.
2. Drolet G., "A New Representation of Elements of Finite Fields $GF(2^m)$ Yelding Small Complexity Arithmetic Circuit", IEEE Trans. on Computers, vol.47, pp.938-946, 1998.
3. Koç C.K., Sunar B., "Low Complexity Bit-Parallel Canonical and Normal Basis Mutipliers for a Class of Finite Fields", IEEE Trans. on Computers, vol.47, pp.353-356, March 1998.
4. Omura J., Massey J., "Computational method and apparatus for finite field arithmetic", U.S. Patent Number 4,587,627, May 1986.
5. Hasan M.H., Wang M.Z., Bhargava V.K., "Modular construction of low complexity parallel multipliers for a class of finite fields $GF(2^m)$", IEEE Trans. on Computers, vol.41, no. 8, pp.962-971, August 1992.
6. Hasan M.H., Wang M.Z., Bhargava V.K., "A modified Massey-Omura Multiplier for a class of finite fields", IEEE Trans. on Computers, vol.42, no. 10, pp.1278-1280, October 1993.
7. Itho T., Tsujii S., "Structure of parallel multipliers for a class of Finite Fields $GF(2^m)$", Information and Computation, vol.83, pp.21-40, 1989.
8. Paar C., "A new architecture for a parallel finite field multiplier with low complexity based on composite fields", IEEE Trans. on Computers, vol.45, no. 7, pp.846-861, July 1996.
9. Menezes A.J., Blake I., Gao X., Mullin R. Vanstone S. and Yaghoobian T., "Applications of Finite Fields", Boston, MA: Kluwer Academic Publisher, 1993.
10. Mastrovito E.D., "VLSI Architectures for multiplication over finite field $GF(2^m)$", In T. Mora, editor, Applied Algebra Algebraic Algorithms, and Error-Correcting Codes, 6-th International Conference, AAECC-6, pp. 297-309, Roma, Italy, July 1988. New York, NY: Springer-Verlag.
11. Knuth D.E., "The art of the computing programming", Vol.2: Seminumerical algorithms, Adison-Wilsey, Reading, MA., 1969.
12. Elia M., Leone M. and Visentin C., "Low Complexity bit-parallel multipliers for $GF(2^m)$ with generator polynomial $x^m + x^k + 1$", Electronics Letters, Vol.35, No.7, April 1999.

Efficient Rijndael Encryption Implementation with Composite Field Arithmetic

Atri Rudra[1], Pradeep K. Dubey[1], Charanjit S. Jutla[2], Vijay Kumar[*,1], Josyula R. Rao[2], and Pankaj Rohatgi[2]

[1] IBM India Research Lab, Block I, Indian Institue of Technology, Hauz Khas, New Delhi, 110016, India
{ratri,pkdubey,vijayk}@in.ibm.com
[2] IBM Thomas J. Watson Research Center, P.O.Box 704, Yorktown Heights, NY 10598, U.S.A.
{csjutla,jrrao,rohatgi}@watson.ibm.com

Abstract. We explore the use of subfield arithmetic for efficient implementations of Galois Field arithmetic especially in the context of the Rijndael block cipher. Our technique involves mapping field elements to a composite field representation. We describe how to select a representation which minimizes the computation cost of the relevant arithmetic, taking into account the cost of the mapping as well. Our method results in a very compact and fast gate circuit for Rijndael encryption.

In conjunction with bit-slicing techniques applied to newly proposed parallelizable modes of operation, our circuit leads to a high-performance software implementation for Rijndael encryption which offers significant speedup compared to previously reported implementations.

1 Introduction

In October 2000, the US National Institute of Standards and Technology (NIST) announced that it had selected the Rijndael Block Cipher [3] as the new Advanced Encryption Standard (AES). In addition to being the new standard, Rijndael is a cipher that offers a good "combination of security, performance, efficiency, implementability and flexibility" [20]. It has already attained considerable popularity and acceptance. Rijndael is a block cipher with a block size of 16 bytes, each of which represents an element in the Galois Field $GF(2^8)$. All operations in Rijndael are defined in terms of arithmetic in this field.

Apart from Rijndael, there are several other instances of the use of Galois Field arithmetic in cryptography and coding theory [10]. The efficiency and performance of such applications is dependent upon the representation of field elements and the implementation of field arithmetic. It is common practice to obtain efficiency by careful selection of the field representation [9,10,11]. In particular, it is well-known that the computational cost of certain Galois Field

---

[*] As of April 2001, the author can be reached at Amazon.com, 605 5th Ave South, Seattle, WA 98104, U.S.A.

Ç.K. Koç, D. Naccache, and C. Paar (Eds.): CHES 2001, LNCS 2162, pp. 171–184, 2001.

operations is lower when field elements are mapped to an isomorphic composite field, in which these operations are implemented using lower-cost subfield arithmetic operations as primitives [11]. Depending upon the computation involved and the choice of representation, there are costs associated with the mapping and conversion, and a trade-off has to be made between such costs and the savings obtained. The design task is to carefully evaluate these trade-offs to minimize the computational cost.

In addition to an efficient hardware implementation, a good circuit design is also useful in obtaining fast software implementations. Using the technique of bit-slicing [2] a circuit with a small number of gates can be simulated using a wide-word processor. Multiple instances of the underlying computation are thus performed in parallel to exploit the parallelism implicit in a wide-word computer. This technique has been used in [2] to obtain a fast DES implementation.

In this paper, we study the use of composite field techniques for Galois Field arithmetic in the context of the Rijndael cipher. We show that substantial gains in performance can be obtained through such an approach. We obtain a compact gate circuit for Rijndael and use its design to illustrate the trade-offs associated with design choices such as field polynomials and representations. We use our circuit design to obtain a simple and fast software implementation of Rijndael for wide-word architectures. The performances of both hardware as well as software implementations show large gains in comparison with previously reported performance figures.

The rest of this paper is organized as follows. In Section 2, we detail the mapping of Galois Field operations to composite field arithmetic. Section 3 outlines the data-slicing technique for realizing a highly parallel software implementation from a circuit design. In Section 4, we describe the mapping of Rijndael operations to a particular class of composite fields. The selection of field polynomials and representations and the associated optimizations are discussed in Sections 5 and 6 respectively. Finally, in Section 7 we present our results and a comparison with previously reported performance figures for Rijndael. Drawings of our Rijndael encryption circuit are included in the Appendix.

2   GF Arithmetic and Composite Fields

Composite fields are frequently used in implementations of Galois Field arithmetic [9,10,11]. In cases where arithmetic operations rely on table lookups, subfield arithmetic is used to reduce lookup-related costs. This technique has been used to obtain relatively efficient implementations for specific operations such as multiplication, inversion and exponentiation. Much of this work has been aimed at implementation of channel codes. The object has usually been to obtain better software implementations by using smaller tables through subfield arithmetic. Applications to hardware design (such as [10]) have been relatively infrequent.

Our techniques are directed at both hardware and software implementations. We take advantage of the efficiency obtained by the use of subfield arithmetic, not merely in the matter of smaller tables but the overall low-level (gate count) complexity of various arithmetic operations. The computation and comparison of such gains and cost is dependent upon several parameters – the overhead of mapping between the original and the composite field representations, the nature of the underlying computation and its composition in terms of the relative frequency of various arithmetic operations, and in case of software implementations, the constraints imposed by the target architecture and its instruction set. Based on these parameters we select the appropriate field and representation to optimize a hardware circuit design. As we shall see, there can be several objectives for this optimization, such as critical path lengths and gate counts, depending upon the overall design goals. The circuit design obtained can then be used to obtain parallelism in a software implementation by means of slicing techniques.

As described in [11], the two pairs $\{GF(2^n), Q(y)\}$ and $\{GF((2^n)^m), P(x)\}$ constitute a *composite field* if $GF(2^n)$ is constructed from $GF(2)$ by $Q(y)$ and $GF((2^n)^m)$ is constructed from $GF(2^n)$ by $P(x)$, where $Q(y)$ and $P(x)$ are polynomials of degree n and m respectively. The fields $GF((2^n)^m)$ and $GF(2^k)$, $k = nm$, are isomorphic to each other. Since the complexity of various arithmetic operations differs from one fieldto another, we can take advantage of the isomorphism to map a computation from one to the other in search of efficiency. For a given underlying field $GF(2^k)$, our gains depend on the choice of n and m as well as of the polynomials $Q(y)$ and $P(x)$.

While we restrict our description to composite fields of the type $GF((2^n)^m)$, it is easy to see that the underlying techniques are fully general and can be used for any composite field.

3   Slicing Techniques

Bit-slicing is a popular technique [2] that makes use of the inbuilt parallel-processing capability of a wide-word processor. Bit-slicing regards a W-bit processor as a SIMD parallel computer capable of performing W parallel 1-bit operations simultaneously. In this mode, an operand word contains W bits from W different instances of the computation. Initially, W different inputs are taken and arranged so that the first word of the re-arranged input contains the first bit from each of the W inputs, the second word contains the second bit from each input, and so on. The resulting bit-sliced computation can be regarded as simulating W instances of the hardware circuit for the original computation. Indeed, a bit-sliced computation is designed by first designing a hardware circuit and then simulating it using W-bit registers on the rearranged input described above.

A bit-sliced implementation corresponding to an N-gate circuit requires N instructions to carry out W instances of the underlying computation, or N/W instructions per instance. This can be particularly efficient for computations which are not efficiently supported by the target architecture. Consider for instance $GF(2^8)$ multiplication on AltiVec [4]. The straightforward implementation uses three table-lookups and one addition modulo 255. 16-parallel lookups in a 256-entry table can be performed on AltiVec in 20 instructions. Thus, a set of 128 multiplications would require 488 instructions. In comparison, our 137-gate multiplication circuit translates into a bit-sliced implementation that can perform 128 multiplications in 137 instructions!

The above computation ignores the cost of ordering the input in bit-sliced fashion and doing the reverse for the output. To evaluate the trade-off correctly, this cost has to be taken into account as well. In general, this cost will depend on the target instruction set.

However, it is possible to think of scenarios in which a particular operation may be efficiently supported in an architecture. For example, if the AltiVec architecture were to provide an instruction for 16 parallel $GF(2^8)$ multiplications which use the underlying field polynomial of interest to us (a hypothetical but nonetheless technically feasible scenario since the critical path of the multiplication circuit is only six gates deep), then a direct computation would require only eight instructions, compared to the 137 required by the bit-sliced version.

Now consider $GF(2^{16})$ multiplications on this hypothetical version of the AltiVec architecture. It is easy to see that the most efficient computation is neither a direct one, nor a bit-sliced version, but a *byte-sliced* computation, in which each $GF(2^{16})$ multiplication is mapped to a small number of $GF(2^8)$ operations, which are efficiently supported by the architecture in question. In general, the right "slice" to use would depend on the target architecture.

3.1   Encrypting without Chaining

Our Rijndael implementation processes 128 blocks of data in parallel. Traditionally, such a scheme would be regarded as more useful for decryption than for encryption, since encryption is usually performed in inherently sequential modes such as Cipher Block Chaining or CBC [17,18,19]. The well-known CBC [17,18,19] is used as a defense against replay attacks [12]. In the CBC mode of encryption, parallel blocks would not be available for encryption except where data from many streams is encrypted in parallel.

However, a new parallelizable variant of CBC [7] removes this limitation and makes it possible to use CBC encryption without the usual sequentiality. This makes it possible to utilize the high throughput rates of our implementation in conjunction with the popular CBC mode.

4   Rijndael in a Composite Field

Rijndael involves arithmetic on $GF(2^8)$ elements. In a straightforward implementation, inverse, multiplication and substitution are likely to be the operations that determine the overall complexity of the implementation. The most common approach is to use table lookups for these operations. By mapping the operations into a composite field, we are able to obtain both a small circuit in case of a hardware implementation as well as smaller instruction counts and table sizes in case of software implementations.

For our Rijndael implementation, we work in the composite field $GF((2^4)^2)$. We selected the field polynomial $Q(y) = y^4 + y + 1$ for $GF(2^4)$. For $P(x)$, we consider all primitive polynomials of the form $P(x) = x^2 + x + \lambda$ where λ is an element of $GF(2^4)$. There are four such polynomials, for each of which there are seven different transformation matrices to consider, one corresponding to each possible choice of basis. The criterion used by us to compare various choices is the gate count of the resulting Rijndael circuit implementation.

Rijndael operations translate to the composite field representation as follows. $\mathbf{H}$ denotes the mapping from $GF(2^8)$ to $GF((2^4)^2)$, and $\mathbf{T}$ the corresponding transformation matrix — that is, $\mathbf{H}(x) = \mathbf{T}x$. S is a 4×4 matrix (the *state*) on which all operations are performed.

- ByteSub transformation : This has essentially two sub-steps:
    1. $P_{ij} = (S_{ij})^{-1}$. In the composite field, $\mathbf{H}(P_{ij}) = (\mathbf{H}(S_{ij}))^{-1}$.
       The calculation of an inverse is as follows. Every $A \in GF((2^4)^2)$ can be represented as $A = a_0 + \beta a_1$ where $\beta^2 + \beta + \lambda = 0$, and $a_0, a_1 \in GF(2^4)$. The inverse is $B = A^{-1} = b_0 + \beta b_1$, $b_0, b_1 \in GF(2^4)$, such that $b_0 = (a_0 + a_1)\Delta^{-1}$ and $b_1 = a_1\Delta^{-1}$, where $\Delta = a_0(a_0 + a_1) + \lambda a_1^2$.
    2. $Q_{ij} = \mathbf{A}P_{ij} + \mathbf{c}$ where $\mathbf{A}$ is a fixed 8×8 matrix and $\mathbf{c} \in GF(2^8)$. In the composite field, $\mathbf{H}(Q_{ij}) = \mathbf{H}(\mathbf{A}P_{ij}) + \mathbf{H}(\mathbf{c}) = \mathbf{T}\mathbf{A}P_{ij} + \mathbf{H}(c) = \mathbf{T}\mathbf{A}\mathbf{T}^{-1}\mathbf{H}(P_{ij}) + \mathbf{H}(\mathbf{c})$.
- ShiftRow transformation : This step is independent of representation.
- MixColumn transformation : This involves essentially the computation $P_{ij} = a_1 S_{1j} + a_2 S_{2j} + a_3 S_{3j} + a_4 S_{4j}$, where (a_1, a_2, a_3, a_4) is a permutation of $(01, 01, 02, 03)$. In the composite field,
  $\mathbf{H}(P_{ij}) = \mathbf{H}(a_1)\mathbf{H}(S_{1j}) + \mathbf{H}(a_2)\mathbf{H}(S_{2j}) + \mathbf{H}(a_3)\mathbf{H}(S_{3j}) + \mathbf{H}(a_4)\mathbf{H}(S_{4j})$.
  The following observations are useful in the implementation -
    • If $x \in GF((2^4)^2)$ then $\mathbf{H}(01) \times x = x$ as the identity element is mapped to the identity element in a homomorphism.
    • $\mathbf{H}(03) = \mathbf{H}(02) + \mathbf{H}(01)$.
- Round Key addition : The operation is $P = S + K$ where K is the round key. In the composite field, $\mathbf{H}(P) = \mathbf{H}(S) + \mathbf{H}(K)$. Addition is simply an EXOR in either representation.

The mapping of the arithmetic to the composite field together with judicious choice of the field polynomial gives us a substantially smaller circuit, as we shall see in Section 7.

5   Optimizations

All operations in the Rijndael block cipher are in $GF(2^8)$. As outlined in section 4, some of these $GF(2^8)$ operations have relatively inefficient gate circuit implementations and can be implemented more efficiently in some isomorphic composite field. One overhead in using subfield arithmetic is the cost of the conversion from the original to the composite field and vice-versa. To illustrate, consider our Rijndael implementation, which uses subfield arithmetic. The cost of the transformations is dependent on the choice of the composite field. We describe below a method by which an *efficient*[1] transformation matrix from the set $\mathcal{T} = \{\mathbf{T}_0, \mathbf{T}_1, ...\}$ of valid transformation matrices can be chosen.

Let $\mathcal{C}(\theta)$ denote the cost of the operation θ, which in the present case is taken to be the gate count of the circuit implementation of θ. Depending upon design objectives and application, there can be alternative cost measures, such as the depth of the critical path, for instance. Let $\mathcal{W}(x)$ denote the *hamming weight* of x, i.e., the number of 1s in the polynomial representation of x.

The aim is to find $\mathbf{T}^*$, the most *efficient* transformation, and the corresponding choice of composite field. This is the composite field which minimizes the gate count of the Rijndael circuit implementation. Note that while comparing the cost for different transformations, we need to consider only those Rijndael operations whose costs are dependent upon the choice of composite field. The relevant operations are those which involve λ or the conversion matrices ($\mathbf{T}$ and $\mathbf{T}^{-1}$).

The costs of different operations are:

- Transform : This step involves computing $\mathbf{H}(S)$.
  Thus, $\mathcal{C}(\text{Transform}) = 16 \times \mathcal{C}(\mathbf{T}.x)$.
- ByteSub transformation : As noted earlier, this step consists of an inverse calculation and an affine transform –

  1. $P_{ij} = (S_{ij})^{-1}$. The only operation whose cost depends on the choice of field is the calculation of λa_1^2. So $\mathcal{C}(inverse) = 16 \times \mathcal{C}(\lambda.x)$.
  2. $Q_{ij} = \mathbf{A}P_{ij} + \mathbf{c}$, or, in the composite field, $\mathbf{H}(Q_{ij}) = \mathbf{H}(\mathbf{A}P_{ij}) + \mathbf{H}(\mathbf{c})$
     $= \mathbf{T}\mathbf{A}P_{ij} + \mathbf{H}(c)$
     $= \mathbf{T}\mathbf{A}\mathbf{T}^{-1}\mathbf{H}(P_{ij}) + \mathbf{H}(\mathbf{c})$.
     Thus $\mathcal{C}(affine) = 16 \times (\mathcal{C}(\mathbf{B}.x) + \mathcal{W}(\mathbf{H}(c)))$, where $\mathbf{B} = \mathbf{T}\mathbf{A}\mathbf{T}^{-1}$. [2].

- ShiftRow transformation : This step does not require any computation.
- MixColumn transformation :
  As note earlier, this step is the computation
  $\mathbf{H}(P_{ij}) = \mathbf{H}(a_1)\mathbf{H}(S_{1j}) + \mathbf{H}(a_2)\mathbf{H}(S_{2j}) + \mathbf{H}(a_3)\mathbf{H}(S_{3j}) + \mathbf{H}(a_4)\mathbf{H}(S_{4j})$.

  Since $\mathbf{H}(01).x = x$, $\mathcal{C}(mixClm) = 16 \times (\mathcal{C}(\mathbf{H}(02).x) + \mathcal{C}(\mathbf{H}(03).x))$.
- Round Key addition : The computation is $\mathbf{H}(P){=}\mathbf{H}(S){+}\mathbf{H}(K)$, so $\mathcal{C}(addKey)$
  $= 16 \times \mathcal{C}(\mathbf{T}.x)$.
- Inverse Transform : $\mathcal{C}(invTransform) = 16 \times \mathcal{C}(\mathbf{T}^{-1}.x)$.

$\mathbf{T}^*$ depends upon whether a pipelined (unrolled loop) or iterative (loop not unrolled) Rijndael circuit is to be obtained. The former offers superior performance compared to the latter at the cost of a larger gate count.

---

[1] In terms of the Rijndael gate-circuit implementation.
[2] Note that $\mathcal{W}(\mathbf{H}(c))$ is the number of *not* gates required to implement $\mathbf{H}(c){+}x$, where $x \in GF((2^4)^2)$.

The criterion for the best transformation can be represented as follows:

$$\mathbf{T}^* = \arg\min_{\mathbf{T}_i \in \mathcal{T}} (\qquad \mathcal{C}(transform) + n \times \mathcal{C}(inverse) + n \times \mathcal{C}(affine)$$

$$+m \times \mathcal{C}(mixClm) + (n+1) \times \mathcal{C}(addKey) + \mathcal{C}(invTransform)).$$

i.e.

$$\mathbf{T}^* = \arg\min_{\mathbf{T}_i \in \mathcal{T}} (\ (n+2) \times \mathcal{C}(\mathbf{T}.x) + n \times \mathcal{C}(\lambda.x) + n \times (\mathcal{C}(\mathbf{B}.x) + \mathcal{W}(\mathbf{H}(c))) \ )$$

$$+m \times (\ \mathcal{C}(\mathbf{H}(02).x) \ + \ \mathcal{C}(\mathbf{H}(03).x) \ ) + \mathcal{C}(\mathbf{T}^{-1}.x) \ )$$

where m and n are both 1 for an iterative circuit, and $\mathcal{R}$ and $\mathcal{R} - 1$ respectively for a pipelined circuit, where $\mathcal{R}$ is the number of *rounds* as specified in the Rijndael cipher.

Based on these considerations, we selected the polynomial $P(x) = x^2 + x + w^{14}$. That is, we chose λ to be w^{14} where w is the primitive element of $GF(2^4)$. The following transformation matrix maps an element from $GF(2^8)$ to the corresponding element in the chosen composite field:

$$\begin{pmatrix} 1 & 0 & 1 & 0 & 0 & 0 & 0 & 0 \\ 1 & 0 & 1 & 0 & 1 & 1 & 0 & 0 \\ 1 & 1 & 0 & 1 & 0 & 0 & 1 & 0 \\ 0 & 1 & 1 & 1 & 0 & 0 & 0 & 0 \\ 1 & 1 & 0 & 0 & 0 & 1 & 1 & 0 \\ 0 & 1 & 0 & 1 & 0 & 0 & 1 & 0 \\ 0 & 0 & 0 & 0 & 1 & 0 & 1 & 0 \\ 1 & 1 & 0 & 1 & 1 & 1 & 0 & 1 \end{pmatrix}$$

6   Finding a Transform

A method for generating a transformation matrix to map elements of $GF(2^k)$ to $GF((2^n)^m)$ can be found in literature [11] for the case where all the field polynomials involved are primitive polynomials. However, in the case of Rijndael the field polynomial is $R(z) = z^8 + z^4 + z^3 + z + 1$ is an irreducible polynomial but is not primitive. Since the fields involved are small, we use an exhaustive search method that can find the transformation in question in case $R(z)$ is irreducible but not primitive. The basic idea is to map α, the primitive element of $GF((2^n)^m)$ to γ, a primitive element of $GF(2^n)$, such that field homomorphism holds.

The algorithm is composed of the following three steps —

1. Get a primitive element γ of $GF(2^k)$ and map α^i to γ^i for $i \in [0..(2^k - 1)]$. Note that this step preserves the multiplicative group homomorphism — for any $i, j \in [0..(2^k - 1)]$, $\alpha^i \times \alpha^j = \alpha^{i+j}$ maps to $\gamma^i \times \gamma^j = \gamma^{i+j}$.
2. Perform the following check — $\forall i \in [0..(2^k - 1)]$, if $\alpha^r = \alpha^i + 1$ then $\gamma^r = \gamma^i + 1$. If so then we have the required mapping; else repeat this step for the next primitive element.

This is to verify additive group homomorphism, which requires that
$\forall i, j \in [0..(2^k - 1)] \; \alpha^t = \alpha^i + \alpha^j \Rightarrow \gamma^t = \gamma^i + \gamma^j$. That is,
$\alpha^t = \alpha^i \times (1 + \alpha^{j-i}) \Rightarrow \gamma^t = \gamma^i \times (1 + \gamma^{j-i})$.
Multiplicative group homomorphism implies that it is sufficient to verify whether
$\forall i, j \in [0..(2^k - 1)], \; \alpha^{t-i} = 1 + \alpha^{j-i} \Rightarrow \gamma^{t-i} = 1 + \gamma^{j-i}$.

3. The matrix, $\mathbf{T}^{-1}$ is obtained by placing in the ith column the element $\mathbf{H}(2^i)$ in the standard basis representation[3] for all i.

7   Performance

Our performance figures reported below are for Rijndael encryption circuit and software, which assume key size of 128 bits.

Our core circuit for Rijndael encryption contains less than four thousand gates. For the purpose of comparison, we report numbers based upon a circuit with 520 I/O pins that uses multiple cores in parallel.

Table 1. Circuit Performance Figures

	Transistor/Gate count	Cycles/block	Throughput
Ichikawa[4]et al.[6]	518K gates	?	1.95 Gbps
Weeks et al.[13]	642K transistors	?	606 Mbps
Elbirt et al.[5]	?	6	300Mbps@14MHz
(256-pin I/O)	?	2.1	1.938 Gbps@32 MHz
Our hardware circuit	256K gates	0.5	7.5 Gbps@32 MHz
	using 32 parallel cores (iterated) of 4k gates each and 252 gate levels		

Table 2 lists cycle counts and target architectures for various reported implementations. In our case, the numbers apply to any architecture that can support bitwise AND and EXOR in addition to LOAD and STORE operations. The three numbers we report correspond to architectures with effective datapath widths (number in parenthesis) of 256 bits, 384 bits and 512 bits respectively (this is perhaps the interesting range of architectures today). The cycle count goes down with increasing datapath width.

It may be mentioned that no minimization or synthesis tools were used for our circuit — the only minimization used is in the sense of section 5. The only gates in our circuit are XOR, AND and NOT gates.

---

[3] Here 2^i denotes the element whose bit representation contains all 0s except a 1 in the ith place. For example for $n = 4, m = 2$, 2^4 is the element 00010000, i.e., α.

[4] This circuit performs encryption as well as decryption.

Table 2. Cycle counts per block for software implementations

Worley et al[16]	284 (Pentium)	176 (PA-RISC)	124 (IA-64)
	Requires an 8KB table		
Weiss et al.[14]	210 (Alpha 21264)		
Wollinger et al.[15]	228 (TMS320C6x)		
Aoki et al.[1]	237 (Pentium II)		
Our bit-sliced software[5]	170 (256b)	119 (384b)	100 (512b)
	Requires only EXOR, AND, L/S, and 2KB table		

Acknowledgments

The authors would like to thank Christof Paar and Gaurav Aggarwal for helpful discussions.

References

1. Kazumaro Aoki and Helger Lipmaa, "Fast Implementations of AES candidates". In *Proc. Third AES Candidate Conference*, April 13-14, 2000. http://csrc.nist.gov/encryption/aes/round2/conf3/aes3papers.html
2. Eli Biham, "A Fast New DES Implementation in Software". In *Proc. Fast Software Encryption 4,1997*. http://www.cs.technion.ac.il/~biham/publications.html
3. Joan Daemen and Vincent Rijmen, "AES Proposal: Rijndael". http://www.esat.kuleuven.ac.be/~rijmen/rijndael.
4. Keith Diefendorff, Pradeep K. Dubey, Ron Hochsprung and Hunter Scales, "AltiVec Extension to PowerPC Accelerates Media Processing". In *IEEE Micro*, March-April 2000, pp85-95.
5. AJ Elbirt, W Yip, B Chetwynd and C Paar, "An FPGA Implementation and Performance Evaluation of the AES Block Cipher Candidate Algorithm Finalists". In *Proc. Third AES Candidate Conference*, April 13-14, 2000. http://csrc.nist.gov/encryption/aes/round2/conf3/aes3papers.html
6. Tetsuya Ichikawa, Tomomi Kasuya and Mitsuru Matsui, "Hardware Evaluation of the AES Finalists". In *Proc. Third AES Candidate Conference*, April 13-14, 2000. http://csrc.nist.gov/encryption/aes/round2/conf3/aes3papers.html
7. Charanjit S. Jutla, "Encryption Modes with Almost Free Message Integrity". Manuscript.
8. Rudolf Lidl and Harald Niederreiter, *Introduction to finite fields and their applications*. Cambridge University Press, Cambridge, Ma., 1986.
9. Edoardo D. Mastrovito, *VLSI Architectures for Computations in Galois Fields*. PhD Thesis, Dept. of EE, Linköping University, Linköping, Sweden 1991.
10. Christof Paar and Pedro Soria-Rodriguez, "Fast Arithmetic Architectures for Public-Key Algorithms over Galois Fields $GF((2^n)^m)$". In *Proc. EUROCRYPT '97*.

---

[5] The performance numbers include the cost of ordering the input in bit-sliced fashion and the reverse for the output.

11. Chirstof Paar, *Efficient VLSI Architectures for Bit-Parallel Computations in Galois Fields*. PhD Thesis, Institute for Experimental Mathematics, University of Essen, Germany, 1994.
    http://www.ece.wpi.edu/Research/crypt/theses/paar_thesispage.html.
12. Bruce Schneier, *Applied Cryptography*, John Wiley and Sons,1996.
13. Bryan Weeks, Mark Bean, Tom Rozylowicz and Chris Ficke, "Hardware Performance Simulations of Round 2 Advanced Encryption Standard Algorithm". In *Proc. Third AES Candidate Conference*, April 13-14, 2000.
    http://csrc.nist.gov/encryption/aes/round2/conf3/aes3papers.html
14. Richard Weiss and Nathan Binkert "A comparison of AES candidates on the Alpha 21264". In *Proc. Third AES Candidate Conference*, April 13-14, 2000.
    http://csrc.nist.gov/encryption/aes/round2/conf3/aes3papers.html
15. Thomas J. Wollinger, Min Wang, Jorge Guajardo and Christof Paar, "How Well Are High-End DSPs suited for AES Algorithms?" In *Proc. Third AES Candidate Conference*, April 13-14, 2000.
    http://csrc.nist.gov/encryption/aes/round2/conf3/aes3papers.html
16. John Worley, Bill Worley, Tom Christian and Christopher Worley, "AES Finalists on PA-RISC and IA-64: Implementations & Performance". In *Proc. Third AES Candidate Conference*, April 13-14, 2000.
    http://csrc.nist.gov/encryption/aes/round2/conf3/aes3papers.html
17. "American National Standard for Information Systems — Data Encryption Algorithm — Modes of Operation". ANSI X3.106, American National Standards Institute, 1983.
18. "Information processing — Modes of operation for a 64-bit block cipher algorithm". ISO 8372, International Organisation for Standardisation, Geneva, Switzerland, 1987.
19. "DES modes of operation". NBS FIPS PUB 81, National Bureau of Standards, U.S. Department of Commerce, 1980.
20. http://www.nist.gov/public_affairs/releases/g00-176.htm, US Commerce Department Press Release.

Appendix: Our Rijndael Ciruit

Presented below are drawings of our gate circuit for Rijndael encryption.The figures appear in the order of the level of detail in them – Figure 1 showing the high level view of our circuit.

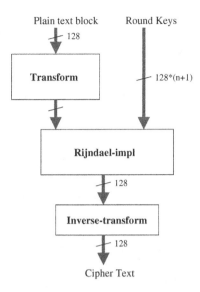

Fig. 1. This figure contains the high level view of the Rijndael encryption circuit. The *transform* function consists of 16 parallel ciruits for $\mathbf{T}^*.x$, where $x \in GF(2^8)$ and $\mathbf{T}^*$ is the matrix to convert elements from $GF(2^8)$ to elements of composite field as decided by section 5. Similarly, Inverse-transform consists of 16 parallel circuits for $(\mathbf{T}^*)^{-1}.x$. Circuits for the multiplication of a constant matrix with a vector are obtained from the method given in [11]

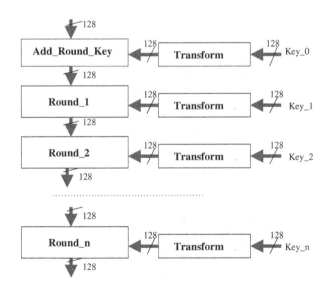

Fig. 2. This figure describes the *rijndael-impl* block in Figure 1

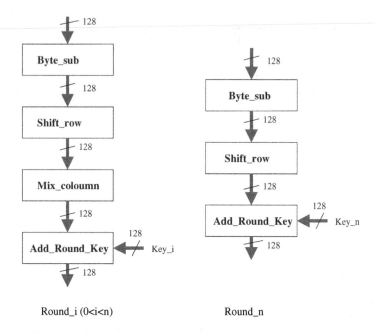

Fig. 3. This figure shows the composition of each round. Note that in our implementation, $n=10$. *Shift_row* does not require any gate. *Add_Round_Key* is simply the EXOR of the corresponding bits of the two inputs

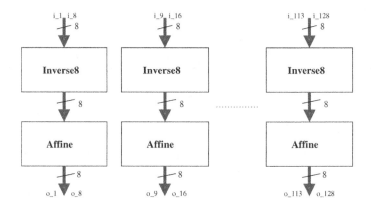

Fig. 4. This figure shows the implementation of the *Byte_sub* operation. *Affine* has 16 parallel circuits for calculating $\mathbf{T}^*A(\mathbf{T}^*)^{-1}.x + \mathbf{H(c)}$

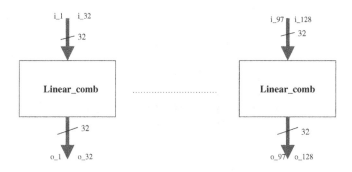

Fig. 5. *mix_column*

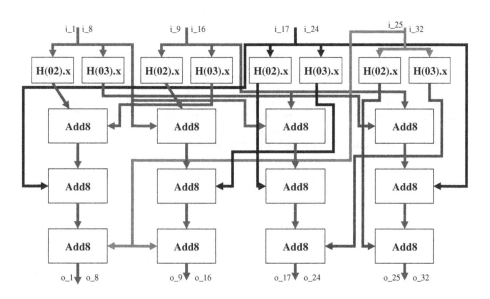

All datapaths are 8-bit wide

Fig. 6. This figure describes the *linear_comb* operation from Figure 5. *Add8* is simply the EXOR of the corresponding bits of the two inputs

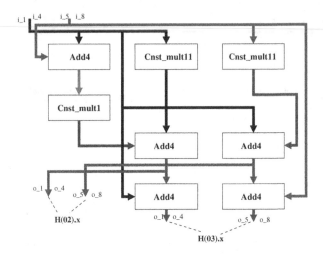

All datapaths are 4-bit wide

Fig. 7. This figure shows the circuits for calculating **H(02)**.*x* and **H(03)**.*x*; *Add4* is simply the EXOR of the corresponding bits of the two inputs. *Const_multi* evaluates the constant multiplication $\omega^i.x$, where ω is the primitive element of $GF(2^4)$ and $x \in GF(2^4)$. These circuits have been obtained from [11]

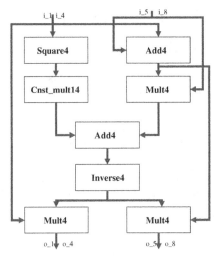

All datapaths are 4-bit wide

Fig. 8. This figure 8 shows the *Inverse8* operation in Figure 4. *Square4* is from [11]; *Mult4* and *Inverse4* are from [9]

High-Radix Design
of a Scalable Modular Multiplier⋆,⋆⋆

Alexandre F. Tenca, Georgi Todorov, and Çetin K. Koç

Department of Electrical & Computer Engineering
Oregon State University, Corvallis, Oregon 97331, USA
{tenca,todorov,koc}@ece.orst.edu

Abstract. This paper describes an algorithm and architecture based on an extension of a scalable radix-2 architecture proposed in a previous work. The algorithm is proven to be correct and the hardware design is discussed in detail. Experimental results are shown to compare a radix-8 implementation with a radix-2 design. The scalable Montgomery multiplier is adjustable to constrained areas yet being able to work on any given precision of the operands. Similar to some systolic implementations, this design avoid the high load on signals that broadcast to several components, making the delay independent of operand's precision.

Key Words: modular multiplier, montgomery multiplier, scalable architecture, high-radix.

1 Introduction

Several applications, such as RSA algorithm, [14] Diffie-Hellman key exchange algorithm [5], Digital Signature Standard [12], and Elliptic curve cryptography [6,9] use modular multiplication and modular exponentiation. The Montgomery Multiplication (MM) algorithm [10] provides certain advantages in the implementation of modular multiplication. Multiple software and hardware designs have been developed using the algorithm.

An aspect of cryptographic applications is that very large numbers are used. The precision varies from 128 and 256 bits for elliptic curve cryptography to 1024 and 2048 bits for applications based on exponentiation [15]. Most of the hardware designs for modular multiplication are fixed-precision solutions. That is, the operands cannot exceed a fixed bit-size. Designs that can take operands with an arbitrary precision are researched in the ASIC [18] and the FPGA [2] realms.

It is recognized that designing hardware requires making the area-time trade-off [21]. In the general case "faster means better". However, an application where this rule is not valid can always be found. Therefore, it is important that the designers have several options or choices that they can choose from.

⋆ This research was supported by rTrust Technologies.
⋆⋆ The reader should note that Oregon State University has filed US and International patent applications for inventions described in this paper.

Ç.K. Koç, D. Naccache, and C. Paar (Eds.): CHES 2001, LNCS 2162, pp. 185–201, 2001.

The basic idea of the scalable Montgomery multiplier has been presented in [18]. The main features of this multiplier are (1) the ability to work on any given operand precision at the kernel level,(2) be adjustable to any chip area, a (3) use a pipelined organization that reduces the impact on signal loads as a result of high precision of the operands.

The first feature is unique in comparison to other designs. The ability to handle long-precision numbers with small precision operations has been done using conventional multipliers, and a control algorithm that uses these multipliers [7]. The general approach is to reuse a hardware core with a fixed precision, usually at most 32 or 64 bits. The current publications show conventional multipliers that do not exceed a precision of 100 bits [16,1]. The control algorithm is usually complex in this case and the increase in parallelism involve multiple datapaths and high complexity at the system level. Other solutions that use systolic array implementation are designed for a fixed precision and the implementation must be modified if a precision larger than the one originally considered is required.

The second feature comes from the flexibility of the algorithm and hardware to be adjusted in both word size and number of processing elements. The more hardware is available, the better is the performance of the multiplier. Similar adjustment is also possible on algorithms based on conventional multipliers, at the cost already presented above. Beyond any doubt, cryptographic algorithms will be embedded in almost any application involving exchanging of information. Applications, such as smart cards [11] and hand-held devices require hardware designs restricted on area and power resources.

The high load on signals broadcast to several hardware components is an important factor to slow down high-precision Montgomery multiplier (MM) designs. For this reason, the use of systolic structures have been considered by other researchers. The organization presented in this paper is not purely systolic, and has a flavor of serial-parallel implementation of the multiplication algorithm.

In this work we present an evolution of the radix-2 algorithm proposed in previous papers, which lead us to a higher radix design of the system. This paper describes the issues involved in this design and the experimental results to compare with the former radix-2 design.

2   High-Radix Word-Based Montgomery Algorithm

The notation used throughout this text is shown in Table 1.

Figure 1 shows the Multiple-word High-Radix (2^k) Montgomery Multiplication algorithm (MWR2^kMM), a generalization of the MM algorithm presented in [18]. A full-precision High-Radix Montgomery algorithm has been presented and proven to be correct in [8]. To prove correctness of the algorithm in Figure 1 we show that it is equivalent to the one presented in [8].

The parameter k changes depending on how many bits of the multiplier X are scanned during each loop, or the *Radix* of the computation ($r = 2^k$). Each loop iteration (computational loop) scans k-bits of X (a radix-r digit X_i) and determines the value q_Y, according to Booth encoding [3]. Booth encoding is

Table 1. Notation

• M - modulus for modular multiplication;
• X - multiplier operand for modular multiplication;
• x_j - a single bit of X at position j;
• X_j - a single radix-r digit of X at position j;
• Y - multiplicand operand for modular multiplication;
• N - number of bits in the operands;
• r - Radix $(r = 2^k)$;
• S - partial product in the multiplication process;
• k - number of bits per digit in radix r;
• q_{Y_j} - coefficient that determines a multiple of Y which is added to the partial product S in the jth iteration of the computational loop;
• q_{M_j} - coefficient that determines a multiple of the modulus M which is added to the partial product S in the jth iteration of the computational loop;
• BPW - number of bits in a word of either Y, M or S;
• $NW = \lceil \frac{N+1}{BPW} \rceil$ - number of words in either Y, M or S;
• NS - number of stages;
• CS - carry-save;
• C_a, C_b - carry bits;
• $(Y^{(NW-1)}, ..., Y^{(1)}, Y^{(0)})$ - operand Y represented as multiple words;
• $S^{(i)}_{k-1..0}$ - bits $k-1$ to 0 of the ith word of S.

applied to a bit vector to reduce the complexity of multiple generation in the hardware. For radix-8 the Booth function for each digit is given as:

$$Booth(\underline{X_i}, x_{i-1}) = -4x_{i+2} + 2x_{i+1} + x_i + x_{i-1}$$

where $\underline{X_i} = (x_{i+2}, x_{i+1}, x_i)$ is a radix-8 digit ($i = km$ where m is an integer), $x_j \in \{0, 1\}$, and x_{i-1} is the most significant bit (MSbit) of the previous digit.

For Radix-2 computation $k = 1$ and $q_{Y_j} = x_j$ are used, making the algorithm equivalent to the one presented in [18]. C_a and C_b represent two carry bits that are propagated from the computation of one word to the computation of the next word. In order to make the least-significant k-bits of S all zeros, $q_{M_j}M$ is added to the partial product. This is required to avoid losing bits in the shift operation performed in Step 10. The value of q_{M_j} that satisfies this condition is determined by examining the least significant k-bits of S generated at Step 4.

In step 11 and 12 the most significant (MS) word of S is generated and sign extended. The use of Booth encoding may cause intermediate values of S to be negative. The final result in S, when Step 13 (*final reduction step*) is reached, is always positive and it can be a number greater than the modulus M. Its purpose is to reduce the result to a number less than the modulus. M is chosen as $2^{N-1} < M < 2^N$ and the result is bounded as $0 \leq S < 2M$. Therefore, a single subtraction of the modulus will assure that $S < M$, just in the case when the final result in S is greater than or equal to the modulus.

The MWR2^{k}MM is a multiple-word version of a full-precision algorithm presented in Figure 2, which is called in this work R2^{k}MM algorithm. To obtain the R2^{k}MM algorithm we transform the word-based sequence of operations into full-precision operations. It is shown in [8] that the requirement for q_M is given as:

$$q_M * M = -S \; (mod \; 2^k).$$

Step

1: $S := 0$

$x_{-1} := 0$

2: FOR $j := 0$ TO $N - 1$ STEP k

3: $q_{Y_j} = Booth(x_{j+k..j-1})$

4: $(C_a, S^{(0)}) := S^{(0)} + (q_{Y_j} * Y)^{(0)}$

5: $q_{M_j} := S^{(0)}_{k-1..0} * (2^k - M^{(0)^{-1}}_{k-1..0}) \bmod 2^k$

6: $(C_b, S^{(0)}) := S^{(0)} + (q_{M_j} * M)^{(0)}$

7: FOR $i := 1$ TO $NW - 1$

8: $(C_a, S^{(i)}) := C_a + S^{(i)} + (q_{Y_j} * Y)^{(i)}$

9: $(C_b, S^{(i)}) := C_b + S^{(i)} + (q_{M_j} * M)^{(i)}$

10: $S^{(i-1)} := (S^{(i)}_{k-1..0}, S^{(i-1)}_{BPW-1..k})$

END FOR;

11: $C_a := C_a$ or C_b

12: $S^{(NW-1)} := $ sign ext $(C_a, S^{(NW-1)}_{BPW-1..k})$

END FOR;

13: IF $S \geq M$ THEN $S := S - M$

END IF;

Fig. 1. Multiple-word   High-Radix   *(Radix-2^k)*   Montgomery   Multiplication (MWR2^{k}MM) Algorithm.

This requirement can be also rewritten as

$$S_{k-1..0} + q_M * M_{k-1..0} = 0 \bmod 2^k.$$

The latter equation is another representation of the requirement that the last k bits of S must be zeros. The Step 5 is equivalent to this requirement as shown below:

$$q_{M_j} = S_{k-1..0} * (2^k - M^{-1}_{k-1..0}) \bmod 2^k$$

$$q_{M_j} = S_{k-1..0} * (-M^{-1}_{k-1..0}) \bmod 2^k$$

$$S_{k-1..0} = S \bmod 2^k, M_{k-1..0} = M \bmod 2^k$$

Step

1: $S := 0$

$x_{-1} := 0$

2: FOR $j := 0$ TO $N - 1$ STEP k

3: $q_{Y_j} = Booth(x_{j+k..j-1})$

4: $S := S + q_{Y_j} * Y$

5: $q_{M_j} := S_{k-1..0} * (2^k - M^{-1}_{k-1..0}) \bmod 2^k$

6: $S := sign\ ext.\ (S + q_{M_j} * M)/2^k$

END FOR;

7: IF $S \geq M$ THEN $S := S - M$

END IF;

Fig. 2. High-Radix *(Radix-2^k)* Montgomery Multiplication (R2^{k}MM) Algorithm.

$$q_{M_j} = S * (-M^{-1}) \bmod 2^k$$

$$q_{M_j} * M = -S \bmod 2^k$$

It is also easy to show that

$$Y = \sum_{j=0}^{\lceil \frac{N-1}{k} \rceil} (2^k)^j * q_{Y_j},$$

from the Booth encoding properties.

The last two equations show that the coefficients q_{Y_j} and q_{M_j} are determined the same way as in [8], which makes both algorithms equivalent. In [8] there are requirements for X and Y that determine the boundaries for the result S. There are no such requirements in the R2^{k}MM algorithm. The R2^{k}MM algorithm inherits the boundaries for the result from the original MM algorithm.

3   High-Radix Montgomery Multiplier – System Level

For high-precision computation it is beneficial to divide the multiplicand Y, the modulus M and the result S into words [18]. The approach keeps the gates and the wire delays inside reasonable boundaries. With operands' precision of thousands of bits, a conventional design to multiply all the bits at once would have a high number of pins, increased fan-in for the gates, high gate loads, and gate outputs driving long wires.

The multiplications $(q_Y * Y)^{(*)}$ and $(q_M * M)^{(*)}$ shown in the MWR2^{k}MM algorithm can be implemented by multiplexers (MUXes) and adders. The shifting operation in Step 10 is simple in hardware. Additions can be done using Carry-Save Adders (CSA), and keeping S in redundant form. With this approach the carries generated during addition are not propagated but rather stored in a separate bit-vector along with a bit-vector for the sum bits. The most complex operations of finding the coefficients q_Y and q_M (steps 3 and 5) can be executed by table look-up. q_Y is pre-computed before the computational cycle begins since it depends only on the least significant k bits of X. This observation leaves the computation of q_M in the most critical part of the algorithm as it is also pointed out by other authors [13,20].

The architecture of a Montgomery multiplier implementing the MWR2^{k}MM algorithm is shown in Fig. 3. There are two main functional blocks: *Kernel* and *IO*. Only the data path is shown. The Kernel's datapath is where the computation takes place according to the algorithm. A control block (not shown) supplies the signals to synchronize the system.

The *final reduction* functional block computes the final result in a suitable form for the multiplier's output, implementing step 13 of the algorithm. More details are provided later.

The Kernel's datapath gets as inputs BPW-bit words of Y, M and S (represented in a Carry-Save form as SS and SC) and k bits of X. The outputs are BPW-bit words of the new partial product S. The superscript star (*) indicates

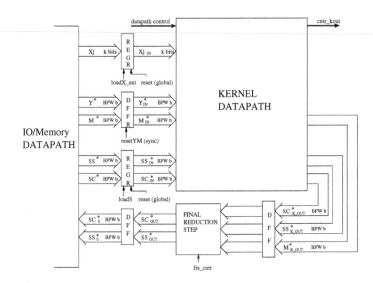

Fig. 3. System Level Diagram of Modular Multiplier.

that the signal is one word of the corresponding vector. For example, $Y^{(*)}$ represents one word of vector Y. These signals change every clock cycle. Depending on the kernel configuration (number of stages and word size) the operands must pass through the data path several times [18].

The signal X_j is a k-bit signal. It provides the bits of X needed for Step 3 of the MWR2^{k}MM algorithm.

The IO block provides the interface with the user and the memory elements for the operands, modulus, and partial result. This block can be implemented in different ways depending on the application where the multiplier will be used and/or the system's architecture in which the multiplier will be integrated. The solution for this block can be flexible and the only requirement for it is to meet the timing specifications for the kernel. Therefore, the architecture of this functional unit is out of the scope of this work. A detailed description of the signal's timing in the interface between I/O and kernel is presented in [19].

4   Kernel Datapath and Reduction

The kernel datapath is organized as a pipeline of cells (MMcell) separated by registers (Fig.4). A stage consists of a MMcell and a register. The MMcell implements one iteration of the FOR loop (steps 3 to 12) in the MWR2^{k}MM algorithm. Each stage gets as inputs one word of Y, M, SS and SC each clock cycle. Additionally, $(NS * k)$ bits of X are transferred to the kernel over $2 * NS$ clock periods, where NS corresponds to the number of stages. Depending on the computation's progress, k bits of X are loaded in a different stage every 2 clock cycles. Each stage needs these bits at different times. Thus, this signal is made common for all stages with internal control loading the signal in the right stage at the right time. The MS bit of X_i is used to Booth encode X_{i+1}, as explained in Section 2, thus, a cell must store these two pieces of information in order to properly encode a radix-r digit of X. The datapath outputs one word of each SS and SC every clock cycle. The pipeline outputs are $SS^{(*)}_{K\_OUT}$ and $SC^{(*)}_{K\_OUT}$.

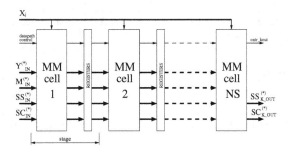

Fig. 4. Top Level Diagram of the Kernel datapath.

Each MMcell propagates the words of Y and M and the newly computed words of SS and SC to the next MMcell, which performs another computational loop of the Montgomery Multiplication algorithm and on its turn propagates the words of Y and M and the newly computed words of SS and SC, with a latency of 2 cycles.

The reduction block implements the final reduction step in the MWR2^{k}MM algorithm. The final reduction happens after the last iteration of the loop scanning the bits of X. During the intermediate iterations the *final reduction* block propagates the signals from the kernel datapath without operating on them. However, the design takes advantage of the word-serial output of the kernel datapath and implements the final reduction serially, on-the-fly, as the words of both vectors of the result are coming out of the kernel datapath. The condition $S \geq M$ will not be known before the last pair of words for S is computed in the datapath. The final reduction block implements the computation for both conditions, $S \geq M$, when $S - M$ is generated, and $S < M$, when the result is correct. In both cases the Carry-Save to non-redundant conversion is required. Both resulting vectors will be stored in the place for SS and SC (the two bit-vectors of the intermediate result) in the IO block. After the last pair of words of S is processed, a flag is set by the control circuitry indicating which condition is valid, $S \geq M$ or $S < M$. The result will be in either SS or SC. A detailed implementation of the final reduction block is presented in [19].

5   Kernel Implementation

The direct design of the kernel processing element leads to an organization shown in Figure 5(a). The figure shows the main blocks in the design: booth encoding,

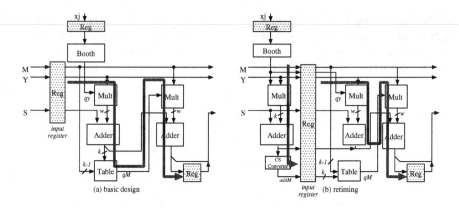

Fig. 5. Kernel cell organization: (a) first try, and (b) after re-timing.

multiple generation, adders, and registers (shaded boxes). Shifting and alignment is done by proper combination of signals.

The cell operates on $k+1$ bits of the multiplier X (one bit is obtained from the previous scan) and one word of each the multiplicand (Y), the modulus (M) and the partial product (S). Booth encoding is generated by a lookup table to find the coefficient q_{Y_j}. The negative multiples of Y are implemented by complementing their positive counter-pairs and adding a '1' (two's complement sign change). The coefficient q_{M_j} depends on the last k bits of the partial product S and the last $k-1$ bits of the modulus M (Step 5). Recall that M is odd. Before S is shifted to the right, the value $q_{M_j} M$ is added to S (Steps 6 and 9). The coefficient q_{M_j} is in the range $[0, 2^k - 1]$. For radix-8, the greatest value happens when $S_{2..0}^{(0)} = $ "001", and $M_{2..0}^{(0)} = $ "001" ($q_{M_j} = 7$). The lowest value happens when $S_{2..0}^{(0)} = $ "000", and $M_{2..0}^{(0)} = $ "001" ($q_{M_j} = 0$).

Multiple generation for high-radix designs is expensive because q_Y and q_M may assume values that are not powers of 2. As an example, the bit-vector $2Y$ can be produced from Y by left-shifting Y by one bit. However, the bit-vector $3Y$ is produced by adding Y and $2Y$.

The critical path in the basic design is very long and makes the design of such high-radix circuit less attractive. The high radix is going to increase the table delay and size, and the multiple generation delay and size. To increase the performance of this system, re-timing was applied, resulting in the design shown in Figure 5(b).

5.1   Improving the Performance Using Re-timing

Using re-timing, pieces of combinational logic are relocated to other other parts of a sequential system, modifying the critical path. One problem with the first direct implementation of the high-radix algorithm is the long critical path, passing through several modules, as shown in Figure 5(a). One can observe that the determination of q_{M_j} depends on k LSBits of the partial product from the previous computational cycle, $S^{(0)}_{k-1..0}$, the k LSBits of $Y^{(0)}$, and the coefficients q_{Y_j}. If the word size for S is more than $2k$ bits the k LSBits of S for the next pipeline stage will be available well before the whole word $S^{(0)}$ is available. The idea is to advance the information on the k least-significant bits (LSBits) of the shifted $S^{(0)}$. In the previous design, these bits were propagated between two registers with no logic operation done on them. Instead of simply propagating the bits, the logic determining q_M is performed on them, as shown in Figure 5(b).

The difference between these cell designs is that a portion of the first adder was moved to before the input registers, and this portion of the adder computes only the k LSBits of the not yet shifted partial product, which is required to compute q_M. The k-bit vector $addM$ in the Figure represents these bits in non-redundant form, and is applied to the Table that generates q_M in the next clock cycle, considering also $k - 1$ bits of the modulus M. As a result of this hardware organization, all possible path delays will not exceed the delay of two adders and two MUXes.

The computation done on the LSBits by the leftmost is also done for all the other remaining operand words. So, while the leftmost adder works on the LS bits of a word, the topmost adder (after the input register) should be working on the other bits of the same word. There is one clock cycle difference between the two circuits, and therefore, this situation must be considered carefully.

5.2 A Radix-8 Design

Without loss of generality, the details of this design will be explained based on a radix-8 implementation. The circuit in Fig. 6 shows the diagram for a Radix-8 MMcell.

One way of implementing the coefficients q_Y and q_M is to split them into some components that will generate simple multiples and add these multiples in the adder. For $r = 8$, two values could be used. For example, $q_Y = 3$ would be split into 2 and 1, and the $3 * Y$ multiple would be generated as $2 * Y + 1 * Y$ or $4 * Y - 1 * Y$ without actually performing the addition or subtraction but using two bit-vectors, $2 * Y$ and $1 * Y$ or $4 * Y$ and $-1 * Y$ in this example. It is efficient to choose only one of the components as a negative value. This is true because negative bit-vectors, like $-Y$, are implemented by inverting the positive bit-vector, Y in this case, and introducing a carry-in with a value of '1'. Since each four-to-two adder has only one carry-in input, only one of the components can be negative.

Two multiplexers generate the multiples $(q1_{Y_j} * Y)^{(*)}$ and $(q2_{Y_j} * Y)^{(*)}$. The Booth encoding is done according to Table 2 in DEC_XJ functional block. As an example, $(/2 * Y)$ means that the Y is multiplied by 2 and all the bits are complemented (or negated). Also, one can notice that the values 2 and -2 are formed in two different ways. This approach simplifies the decoding logic for X_j. The outputs of DEC_XJ are the control signals for the multiplexers as well as the carry-in bit for the first 4-to-2 adder (during the first computational cycle only).

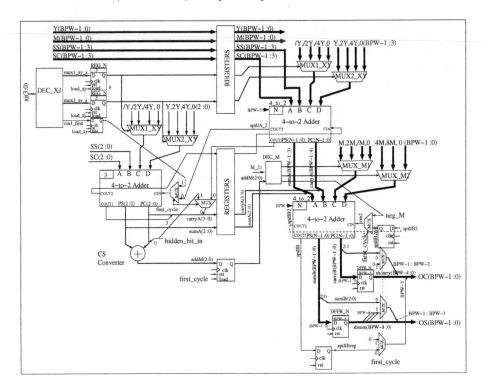

Fig. 6. Radix-8 MM Cell.

Because the coefficients q_Y and q_M are split into two each, the adders need to have an extra input. The two four-to-two adders have a total of two carry-out bits propagating between sequential words of the partial product S. One carry-out is inserted at the LSB position of vector $carryA$. The other carry-out is introduced back to the same adder as a carry-in bit for the next word of S.

The coefficient q_{M_j} depends on the 3 LSBits of the partial product S and the three LSBits of the modulus M. The product is represented by 2 vectors. There is one additional input bit, *hidden-bit*, which affects q_{M_j}. The hidden-bit is generated by carry propagation in the least significant bits of the least significant word computation, which are zeroed in the process. Knowing that the LSB of M is always '1' and the LSB of $carryA$ is always '0', q_{M_j} will depend only on eight bits: $sumA_{2..0}$, $carryA_{2..1}$, *hidden-bit* and $M_{2..1}^{(0)}$.

In Step 10 of the MWR8MM algorithm the partial product is right-shifted by three bits. Because carry-save representation (CS) is used for S, the LS words of the two bit-vectors $(sumB^{(0)}, carryB^{(0)})$ after Step 6 in the algorithm can be, for example: $sumB^{(0)} = \times.. \times 110$ and $carryB^{(0)} = \times.. \times 010$, where $\times$ represents any value of the bit in this position. The last three bits of S are equivalent to zeros when converted to a non-redundant form. However, data will be lost if these bits are shifted out without taking into account the carry propagation $(110 + 010 = \underline{1}000)$. The carry bit generated in this case is the *hidden-bit*.

Table 2. Booth encoding for q_Y, the backslash means bit-complement.

$X_j(3:0)$	q_{Y_j}	$q1_{Y_j}$	cin	$q2_{Y_j}$	$X_j(3:0)$	q_{Y_j}	$q1_{Y_j}$	cin	$q2_{Y_j}$
0000	0	0	0	0	1000	-4	/4	1	0
0001	1	0	0	1	1001	-3	/4	1	1
0010	1	0	0	1	1010	-3	/4	1	1
0011	2	0	0	2	1011	-2	/4	1	2
0100	2	/2	1	4	1100	-2	/2	1	0
0101	3	/1	1	4	1101	-1	/1	1	0
0110	3	/1	1	4	1110	-1	/1	1	0
0111	4	0	0	4	1111	0	0	0	0

Instead of using a carry propagate adder to obtain the hidden-bit, in radix 8 the following observation is made: the last bit of $carryB^{(0)}$ is always '0', therefore, to detect a hidden-bit it is enough to test if there is a 1 value in the second or third bits of either $carryB^{(0)}$ or $sumB^{(0)}$. The circuit for the hidden-bit detection is reduced to $sumB_2^{(0)} + sumB_1^{(0)}$. These two bits of $sumB^{(0)}$ are stored into flip-flops, thus, the hidden-bit logic does not stand in the critical path for the whole cell. Since the hidden bit is found after the operation on the LS word is done, it is transferred from one cell to another, as part of the LS word. It can be inserted in the free LSBit position in $carryA^{(0)}$ and also participates in determining q_M.

If all eight bits are used for a lookup table for q_M, the table will have 256 entries. The number of entries can be reduced by assimilating the carries for $sumA_{2..0}$, $carryA_{2..1}$, and *hidden-bit* by a three-bit adder. The resulting three-bit vector is named *addM*:

$$addM_{2..0} = (sumA_{2..0} + (carryA_{2..1}, 0) + (00, hiddenbit))\ mod\ 8.$$

which reduces the table for q_M to only 32 entries. It is represented by the *DEC_M* functional block according to Table 3. The decoder outputs are the control signals for the multiplexers implementing $(q1_{M_j} * M)^{(*)}$ and $(q2_{M_j} * M)^{(*)}$. The decoder also has an output which is asserted '1' whenever $q1_{M_j}$ is negative. This signal becomes a carry-in for the second four-to-two adder.

The multiples of Y and M, like $2Y, 4Y, 2M, 4M, 8M$, require that these operands be left-shifted. Caused by the word-serial scanning of this algorithm, this shifting requires some of the MSBits from the previous words of Y and M to be kept when the new words arrive. If it is the first word (*first_cycle*='1') then a number of zeros is shifted in to produce the needed multiple. Otherwise, the MSBits of the previous word are shifted in as the LSBits of the current word.

As described at the end of the previous section, the leftmost adder is operating on the LSbits of words j of S and $q_Y Y$ while the topmost adder is operating of the MSbits of word $j - 1$. This arrangement requires that the carry-out propagation among words of the partial sum A ($carryA$ and $sumA$) be considered carefully. The carry-out of the topmost adder, net *spillA2*, is introduced immediately as carry-in for the leftmost adder. The carry-out of the leftmost adder is delayed one clock cycle before it is introduced as carry-in to the topmost adder.

Table 3. Decoding for q_M.

$addM_{2..0}$	qM_j $M_{2..1}^{(0)}$				$q1_{M_j}$ $M_{2..1}^{(0)}$				$cin2$ $M_{2..1}^{(0)}$				$q2_{M_j}$ $M_{2..1}^{(0)}$			
	00	01	10	11	00	01	10	11	00	01	10	11	00	01	10	11
000	0	0	0	0	0	0	0	0	0	0	0	0	0	0	0	0
001	7	5	3	1	/1	1	/1	1	1	0	1	0	8	4	4	0
010	6	2	6	2	2	2	2	2	0	0	0	0	4	0	4	0
011	5	7	1	3	1	/1	1	/1	0	1	0	1	4	8	0	4
100	4	4	4	4	0	0	0	0	0	0	0	0	4	4	4	4
101	3	1	7	5	/1	1	/1	1	1	0	1	0	4	0	8	4
110	2	6	2	6	2	2	2	2	0	0	0	0	0	4	0	4
111	1	3	5	7	1	/1	1	/1	0	1	0	1	0	4	4	8

6   Experimental Results and Analysis

This section describes the experimental data obtained with the radix-8 Kernel designs and compares them with the radix-2 design. Although both radix-8 designs were implemented, only the results for the re-timed radix-8 design is presented in detail. The complete data is presented in [19].

6.1   Synthesis and Simulation Environment

The Mentor Graphics' package of applications was used to generate this data. The target technology was set to AMI05_slow ($0.5\mu m$) provided in the ASIC Design Kit (ADK) from the same company. A data-book for this technology is available at [4]. Before the designs were synthesized, they were simulated in ModelSim for functional correctness. The designs were described in VHDL, synthesized with Leonardo as flattened designs (no hierarchy), and laid-out using ICStation. This last tool provides RC parameter extraction. RC-extraction allows the determination of time delay values for each wire in the design, bringing further simulations closer to the real-silicon simulations. Using the information from ICStation and Leonardo, the designs were back annotated and verified with Velocity. The values presented in this section were obtained from several experiments.

The kernel area depends on the number of stages in the pipeline (NS) and the word size (BPW). The area for the radix-8 kernel was obtained as:

$$A_{kernel_{r8}} = 92 * BPW * NS + 269 * NS - 9.42 * BPW - 35.5.$$

The total computational time for the kernel is a product of the number of clock cycles (T_{CLKs}) and the clock period (t_p). The clock period is derived from the synthesis results, and will depend on the number of stages, the word size, and other parameters. The number of clock periods to complete a computation is obtained from the algorithm.

Table 4 shows the critical path delay (t_p) as a function of the number of stages for the re-timed radix-8 kernel as well as the number of bits per word in the operands. These two parameters also determine the design area. The bold-faced figures in the Table show tested configurations. The rest of the figures are produced by linear interpolation. An increase in area leads to an increase in the critical path delay. This is due to increased wire lengths (parasitic resistance and capacitance) and fan-outs for the gates. A setup time plus clock-to-Q propagation time of 1.2ns for flip-flops is given for AMI05-slow technology. The hold time requirement is insignificantly small. The setup and hold time requirements will scale with the technology giving the same proportional effect on the clock period.

Table 4. Critical path delay for radix-8 Kernel (nsec).

NS	Bits Per Word 8	16	32	64	128	NS	Bits Per Word 8	16	32	64	128
1	**10.7**	**10.3**	**13.1**	**18.9**	**20.2**	10	11.2	15.2			
2	10.8	**12.1**	14.4	**20.5**	**30.4**	11	11.2	15.3			
3	10.9	12.5	15.7	23.0		12	11.2	**15.4**			
4	11.0	**12.9**	**17.0**	**25.4**		13	**11.3**	15.4			
5	**11.1**	**12.7**	17.6			14	11.3	15.4			
6	11.1	13.5	18.2			15	11.3	**15.5**			
7	**11.2**	14.3	18.7			20	**11.4**				
8	11.2	**14.9**	**19.2**			26	**13.0**				
9	11.2	15.1									

Two cases should be considered: (1) when $NW \leq 2 * NS$, and (2) when $NW > 2 * NS$. The variable $NW = \lceil \frac{N+1}{BPW} \rceil$ represents the number of words in the N-bit operands with chosen word size of BPW bits [18]. Because of the extra register in the pipeline a word propagates through the pipeline for $(2 * NS + 1)$ clock cycles For Radix-8, since 3 bits of X are used in each stage, $\lceil \frac{N}{3*NS} \rceil$ pipeline cycles are required. Equation 1 represents the total number of clock cycles needed for the re-timed Radix-8 Montgomery multiplication design as:

$$T_{CLKs} = \begin{cases} \lceil \frac{N}{3*NS} \rceil * (2 * NS + 1) + NW + 1 \, , if \, NW \leq 2 * NS \\ \lceil \frac{N}{3*NS} \rceil * (NW + 1) + 2 * NS \quad \, , if \, NW > 2 * NS \end{cases} \tag{1}$$

It can be shown that when $NW < 2 * NS$ adding more stages to the pipeline has somewhat unpredictable effect on the total number of clock cycles. It happens because in this case the number of words NW has a small effect on the computational time, while the fraction $\lceil \frac{N}{3*NS} \rceil$ has minimums and maximums as the number of stages NS changes. Thus, it may be the case that a design with more stages will be slower than a design with less stages.

Figure 7 shows the total actual computational time ($T_{CLKs} \times t_p$) for $N = 256$ and $N = 1024$, using designs with different number of stages (NS) and word size (BPW). The first observable minimum computational time happens when the boundary $NW \leq 2*NS$ and $NW > 2*NS$ is crossed. With further increase in the number of pipeline stages the computational time goes through a series of minimal and maximal values. The boundary $NW > 2NS$ is crossed at a different number of stages for a different precision of the operands (a different number of words). Operands with precision 256 bits will require a smaller number of stages in the pipeline than operands with 1024 bits precision, in order to execute the operation in minimal time. The goal of choosing a design point is to have computational time for 256-bit precision close to its absolute minimal value and at the same time to have as small computational time for 1024-bit precision as possible.

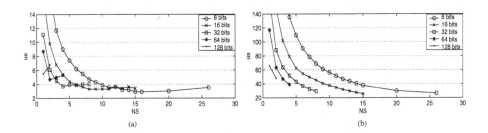

Fig. 7. Total time for 256-bit (a) and 1024-bit (b) operands for some values of NS and BPW.

It can be seen from the data obtained in the experiments that the fastest designs are achieved with a word size of 8 bits. For this word size and 256-bit precision, the first optimal design point is for $NS = 15$. The area is 14964 NOR gates. Each additional stage adds about 1005 to the gate count as can be obtained from the area equation. Other optimal points for this design, represented as NS/area pairs, are: 16/15969, 18/17979, 22/21999, 24/24009 and 26/26019.

For 1024-bits of precision, the time decreases asymptotically, with a faster decrease for a smaller number of stages.

Table 5. Some design points for radix-8 kernel, $BPW = 8$, $N = 256$ and $N = 1024$.

NS	15	16	18	22	24	26
Area, gates	14964	15969	17979	21999	24009	26019
$\frac{t_{NS=15}}{t}$ for 256-bit	1	1	1.05	1.04	0.92	0.83
$\frac{t_{NS=15}}{t}$ for 1024-bit	1	1.04	1.21	1.37	1.39	1.42

Table 5 compares several design points for the radix-8 kernel with $BPW = 8$. The Table presents the design area and the ratio of the computational time related to the point $NS = 15$. It can be seen that the design point with $NS = 22$ is very suitable since the computational time for 256-bit precision is very close to its minimal value. At the same time the computational time for 1024-bit precision is improved by 37% as compared to the point with $NS = 15$. With further increase of the number of stages the computational time for 256-bit precision worsens while the computational time for 1024-bit precision does not improve significantly (only 2% per stage).

A comparison of performance between the radix-2 design ([18]) and the radix-8 designs discussed in this paper is shown in Figure 8. The data shows the time to compute the modular multiplication for 256-bit operands as a function of the design area. For small areas, the radix-2 design (v1) performs as well as the radix-8 design with re-timing (v3). The basic design (v2) is worse than the radix-2 one. For areas of 10,000 gates or more, the radix-8 design with re-timing is better than the other two, which shows that the high-radix design has a better overall performance.

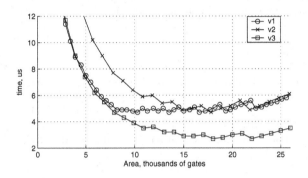

Fig. 8. Area×time comparison between radix-2 (v1), radix-8 basic (v2), and radix-8 with re-timing (v3) for 256-bit operands.

7   Conclusion

This paper presented the algorithm modifications and hardware implementation details of a high-radix implementation of the scalable modular multiplier presented in [18]. A radix-8 design was used to exemplify the design process, and to obtain experimental results that show the viability of using this approach. Experimental data shows that the radix-8 scalable multiplier is able to perform as well as the radix 2 design for small areas, and better than the radix-2 design for larger areas. The re-timing technique applied to the high-radix design was critical to obtain a competitive solution.

References

1. A. Bernal and A. Guyot. Design of a modular multiplier based on Montgomery's algorithm. In *13th Conference on Design of Circuits and Integrated Systems*, pages 680–685, Madrid, Spain, November 17–20 1998.

2. T. Blum and C. Paar. Montgomery modular exponentiation on reconfigurable hardware. In I. Koren and P. Kornerup, editors, *Proceedings, 14th Symposium on Computer Arithmetic*, pages 70–77, Bath, England, April 14–16 1999. IEEE Computer Society Press, Los Alamitos, CA.

3. A. D. Booth. A signed binary multiplication technique. *Q. J. Mech. Appl. Math.*, 4(2):236–240, 1951. (Also reprinted in [17], pp. 100–104).

4. Mentor Graphics Corporation. ASIC Design Kit. http://www.mentor.com/partners/hep/AsicDesignKit/ASICindex.html, 2001.

5. W. Diffie and M. E. Hellman. New directions in cryptography. *IEEE Transactions on Information Theory*, 22:644–654, November 1976.

6. N. Koblitz. Elliptic curve cryptosystems. *Mathematics of Computation*, 48(177):203–209, January 1987.

7. Ç. K. Koç, T. Acar, and B. S. Kaliski Jr. Analyzing and comparing Montgomery multiplication algorithms. *IEEE Micro*, 16(3):26–33, June 1996.

8. P. Kornerup. High-radix modular multiplication for cryptosystems. In E. Swartzlander, Jr., M. J. Irwin, and G. Jullien, editors, *Proceedings, 11th Symposium on Computer Arithmetic*, pages 277–283, Windsor, Ontario, June 29 – July 2 1993. IEEE Computer Society Press, Los Alamitos, CA.

9. A. J. Menezes, I. F. Blake, X. Gao, R. C. Mullen, S. A. Vanstone, and T. Yaghoobian. *Applications of Finite Fields*. Kluwer Academic Publishers, Boston, MA, 1993.

10. P. L. Montgomery. Modular multiplication without trial division. *Mathematics of Computation*, 44(170):519–521, April 1985.

11. D. Naccache and D. M'Raïhi. Cryptographic smart cards. *IEEE Micro*, 16(3):14–24, June 1996.

12. National Institute for Standards and Technology. Digital signature standard (DSS). *Federal Register*, 56:169, August 1991.

13. H. Orup. Simplifying quotient determination in high-radix modular multiplication. In S. Knowles and W. H. McAllister, editors, *Proceedings, 12th Symposium on Computer Arithmetic*, pages 193–199, Bath, England, July 19–21 1995. IEEE Computer Society Press, Los Alamitos, CA.

14. R. L. Rivest, A. Shamir, and L. Adleman. A method for obtaining digital signatures and public-key cryptosystems. *Communications of the ACM*, 21(2):120–126, February 1978.

15. E. Savaş, A. F. Tenca, and Ç. K. Koç. A scalable and unified multiplier architecture for finite fields $gf(p)$ and $gf(2^m)$. In Ç. K. Koç and C. Paar, editors, *Cryptographic Hardware and Embedded Systems - CHES 2000*, Lecture Notes in Computer Science No. 1965, pages 281–296. Springer, Berlin, Germany, 2000.

16. E. M. Schwarz, R. M. Averil III, and L. J. Sigal. A radix-8 CMOS S/390 multiplier. In T. Lang, J.-M. Muller, and N. Takagi, editors, *Proceedings, 13th Symposium on Computer Arithmetic*, pages 2–9, Bath, England, July 6–9 1997. IEEE Computer Society Press, Los Alamitos, CA.

17. E. E. Swartzlander, editor. *Computer Arithmetic*, volume I. IEEE Computer Society Press, Los Alamitos, CA, 1990.

18. A. F. Tenca and Ç. K. Koç. A scalable architecture for Montgomery multiplication. In Ç. K. Koç and C. Paar, editors, *Cryptographic Hardware and Embedded Systems*, Lecture Notes in Computer Science No. 1717, pages 94–108. Springer, Berlin, Germany, 1999.

19. G. Todorov. Asic design, implementation and analysis of a scalable high-radix montgomery multiplier. Master's thesis, Department of Electrical and Computer Engineering, Oregon State University, December 2000.

20. W. C. Tsai, C. B. Shung, and S. J. Wang. Two systolic architectures for Montgomery multiplication. *IEEE Transactions on VLSI Systems*, 8(1):103–107, February 2000.

21. C. D. Walter. Space/Time trade-offs for higher radix modular multiplication using repeated addition. *IEEE Transactions on Computers*, 46(2):139–141, February 1997.

A Bit-Serial Unified Multiplier Architecture for Finite Fields GF(p) and GF(2^m)

Johann Großschädl

Graz University of Technology
Institute for Applied Information Processing and Communications
Inffeldgasse 16a, A–8010 Graz, Austria
Johann.Groszschaedl@iaik.at

Abstract. The performance of elliptic curve cryptosystems is primarily determined by an efficient implementation of the arithmetic operations in the underlying finite field. This paper presents a hardware architecture for a unified multiplier which operates in two types of finite fields: GF(p) and GF(2^m). In both cases, the multiplication of field elements is performed by accumulation of partial-products to an intermediate result according to an MSB-first shift-and-add method. The reduction modulo the prime p (or the irreducible polynomial $p(t)$, respectively) is interleaved with the addition steps by repeated subtractions of $2p$ and/or p (or $p(t)$, respectively). A bit-serial multiplier executes a multiplication in GF(p) in approximately $1.5 \cdot \lceil \log_2(p) \rceil$ clock cycles, and the multiplication in GF(2^m) takes exactly m clock cycles. The unified multiplier requires only slightly more area than that of the multiplier for prime fields GF(p). Moreover, it is shown that the proposed architecture is highly regular and simple to design.

Keywords: Elliptic curve cryptography, finite field arithmetic, iterative modulo multiplication, polynomial basis representation, bit-serial multiplier architecture, smart card crypto-coprocessor.

1 Introduction

In the mid-eighties, N. Koblitz [9] and V. S. Miller [16] independently proposed using the group of points on an elliptic curve (EC) over a finite field in discrete logarithm cryptosystems. Elliptic curve cryptography can be used to provide digital signature schemes, encryption schemes, and key agreement schemes [10]. The primary advantage of elliptic curve systems over systems based on the multiplicative group of a finite field is the absence of a subexponential-time algorithm that could solve the discrete logarithm problem (DLP) in these groups [3]. Consequently, an elliptic curve group that is smaller in size can be used, while maintaining the same level of security [13]. The result is smaller key sizes, bandwidth savings, and faster implementations. These features make elliptic curve cryptosystems especially attractive for applications in environments where computational power is limited, such as smart cards or hand-held devices.

Ç.K. Koç, D. Naccache, and C. Paar (Eds.): CHES 2001, LNCS 2162, pp. 202–219, 2001.

The performance of an elliptic curve cryptosystem is primarily determined by the efficient realization of the arithmetic operations (addition, multiplication, and inversion) in the underlying finite field. Many practical implementations use *projective coordinates* [15] to represent points on the elliptic curve because they allow to perform a point addition/doubling without inversion. Therefore, coprocessors for elliptic curve cryptography are most frequently designed to accelerate the field multiplication.

1.1 Motivation for a Unified Multiplier Architecture

An elliptic curve can be defined over various mathematical structures such as a ring or field. In cryptography only finite fields are used because they allow to store and handle the field elements in a manageable way. Due to standardization activities, two special types of finite fields have become very important for the implementation of elliptic curve cryptosystems: The *prime field* GF(p) and the *binary extension field* GF(2^m). Various accredited standards bodies like the *National Institute of Standards and Technology* (NIST) recommended to use either GF(p) or GF(2^m) as the underlying finite field [19]. In order to promote interoperability between different implementations and to facilitate widespread use of well-accepted techniques, a crypto-coprocessor should operate in both types of finite fields. Therefore, it is an obvious idea to develop a unified multiplier architecture which can perform multiplications in GF(p) and GF(2^m). At a first glance, prime fields and binary extension fields seem to have dissimilar properties. However, the elements of either field can be represented using a bit-string. Furthermore, the arithmetic operations in both fields have structural similarities allowing a unified design. For example, a multiplication in GF(p) is performed modulo a prime p, and the multiplication in GF(2^m) is done modulo an irreducible polynomial $p(t)$ if polynomial basis representation is used.

1.2 Previous Work

In August 2000, E. Savaş *et al.* introduced a unified multiplier which operates in both types of finite fields, GF(p) and GF(2^m) [23]. From an algorithmic point of view, the multiplication in GF(p) is performed according to Montgomery's method [17]. The introduction of the Montgomery multiplication for the field GF(2^m) in [11] opened them up the possibility to develop a unified multiplier architecture by taking advantage of the fact that the Montgomery multiplication is in both fields essentially the same operation. Their implementation utilizes inherent concurrency in Montgomery multiplication and uses an array of word-size processing units organized in a pipeline. Savaş' architecture is highly scalable because a fixed-area multiplier can handle operands of any size. Moreover, the word-size of a processing unit as well as the number of pipeline stages can be selected according to the desired area/performance trade-off.

Another interesting VLSI implementation was reported by J. Goodman *et al.* [6]. Their so-called Domain Specific Reconfigurable Cryptographic Processor (DSRCP) provides a full suite of arithmetic operations (including inversion) over the integers modulo p, binary extension fields, and non-supersingular elliptic curves over $GF(2^m)$, with operands ranging in size from 8 to 1024 bits. These operations are implemented using a single computation unit whose datapath cells can be reconfigured on the fly. The modulo multiplication is realized according to an iterated radix-2 version of Montgomery multiplication. On the other hand, the multiplication in $GF(2^m)$ is based on an iterated MSB-first approach.

1.3 Our Contribution

We introduce a multiplier architecture for unified (dual-field) arithmetic. The modulo multiplication proceeds in a serial-parallel fashion according to an iterative approach, which means that the modulo reduction is performed during multiplication through concurrent reduction of the intermediate result.

The main contribution of this paper is a modification of the classical MSB-first version for iterative modulo multiplication that allows a very efficient hardware implementation. Additionally, we propose a bit-serial architecture using carry-save adders for the accumulation of partial-products to an intermediate result given in a redundant representation. The modulo reduction operation is interleaved with the partial-product additions by repeated subtractions of once or twice the modulus. The circuit to decide the multiple of the modulus to be subtracted is very simple and requires only the two highest order bits of the redundant intermediate result as inputs. Contrary to other designs, the subtrahend evaluation circuit of our multiplier does not cause a significant critical path.

We will show that the bit-serial multiplier can also perform multiplications in $GF(2^m)$ by simply setting all carry-bits of the intermediate result to 0. The area-cost of the unified multiplier is only slightly higher than that of the multiplier for the field $GF(p)$, providing significant area savings when both types of multiplier are needed. To the best of our knowledge, an MSB-first bit-serial architecture for multiplication in $GF(p)$ and $GF(2^m)$ has never been published before. Compared to the Montgomery multiplication used in Savaş' implementation, the MSB-first iterative algorithm requires neither a transformation of operands into Montgomery domain nor precomputed constants. The bit-serial architecture has a linear array structure with a bit-slice feature. A high degree of regularity and mainly local connections make the multiplier simple to design.

1.4 Paper Outline

The remainder of this paper is organized as follows: Section 2 provides some background information on MSB-first techniques for radix-2 multiplication with interleaved reduction. Section 3 presents a modified version of the classical "shift-and-add" algorithm for modulo multiplication. The modified algorithm uses a redundant representation of the intermediate result and profits from a novel quotient estimation technique which is detailed in subsection 3.1. Section 4 covers arithmetic in binary extension fields $GF(2^m)$ using a polynomial basis representation. The unified multiplier architecture for $GF(p)$ and $GF(2^m)$ is introduced in section 5. This section also describes the execution of a multiplication and presents an estimation of the computation time for both types of finite fields. The paper finishes with a summary of results and conclusions in section 6.

2 Preliminaries

The finite field GF(p), also denoted as *prime field* of order p, is the field of residue classes modulo p, where the field elements are the integers $0, 1, \ldots, p-1$. The field operations are modulo operations, i.e., addition and multiplication modulo the prime p. Beside the popular Montgomery multiplication [17] and the Barret modulo reduction method [1], also binary and higher-radix algorithms for MSB-first iterative modulo multiplication have been proposed.

2.1 MSB-First Iterative Modulo Multiplication

A usual way of multiplying two integers A and B is done by scanning the multiplier B one bit at a time, beginning with the most significant bit (MSB), and accumulating the partial-product $A \cdot B[i]$ to the intermediate result. The product P is a $2n$-bit integer if the operands are n bits long and can be written as

$$P = A \cdot B = A \cdot \left(\sum_{i=0}^{n-1} B[i]\, 2^i \right) = \sum_{i=0}^{n-1} (A \cdot B[i])\, 2^i \qquad (1)$$

The notation $X[i]$ indicates the i-th bit of an n-bit integer X; $X[0]$ is the LSB, and $X[n-1]$ is the MSB. After each addition of a partial-product, the intermediate result must be multiplied by 2 to align it to the next partial-product. Since a multiplication by 2 is a 1-bit left-shift in hardware, the described method is also known as *shift-and-add* multiplication. The shift-and-add multiplication typically results in a bit-serial architecture when implemented in hardware. Bit-serial multipliers offer a fair area/performance trade-off, which is an important aspect in the design of coprocessors for area-restricted devices like smart cards.

INPUT: An n-bit modulus M (i.e., $2^{n-1} \le M < 2^n$), a
        multiplicand $A < M$, and a multiplier $B < M$.
OUTPUT: Result $R = A \cdot B \bmod M$.

    1:   $R \leftarrow 0$
    2:   **for** i **from** $n - 1$ **downto** 0 **do**
    3:       $R \leftarrow 2 \cdot R + A \cdot B[i]$
    4:       $q \leftarrow \lfloor R/M \rfloor$
    5:       $R \leftarrow R - q \cdot M$
    6:   **endfor**

Fig. 1: MSB-first shift-and-add multiplication with interleaved modulo reduction.

Figure 1 shows that the simple shift-and-add multiplication can be easily extended to perform a modulo multiplication. The modulo reduction of the intermediate result R is interleaved with the addition steps and realized by subtraction of the product $q \cdot M$, whereby q is the quotient of R and the modulus M. The quotient q can be at most 2 since the term $2 \cdot R + A \cdot B[i]$ is always smaller than three times the modulus M (on condition that $A < M$):

$$q = \left\lfloor \frac{R}{M} \right\rfloor \quad \text{with} \quad q \in \{0, 1, 2\} \tag{2}$$

Therefore, the reduction of the intermediate result can be accomplished by subtraction of M or $2 \cdot M$ (i.e., addition of the two's complement of M or $2 \cdot M$). However, two serious problems arise when implementing this algorithm:

1. Addition of long integers can cause a significant delay due to carry propagation from LSB to MSB, which limits the clock frequency.
2. The exact comparison of the intermediate result R to the modulus M in order to decide whether the quotient q is 0, 1 or 2 is also difficult to perform for very long integers.

Various papers on the efficient implementation of MSB-first modulo multiplication can be found in literature. An algorithm published by G. R. Blakley realizes the reduction of the intermediate result by one or two subtractions of the modulus [4]. E. F. Brickell presented an architecture which performs a multiplication of two integers modulo p in $\lceil \log_2(p) \rceil + 7$ clock cycles [5]. This approach uses delayed carry adders to avoid the carry propagation delay, but has problems due to the difficulty of comparing long integers and conversion of the result from delayed carry representation to binary representation. C. D. Walter proposed another technique for speeding up modulo multiplication by scaling the modulus [26]. The modulus is scaled in such a way that a certain number of the most significant digits are fixed, resulting in a simplified reduction operation. However, the cost of this method is precalculation and storage of the scaled modulus. Y.-J. Jeong et al. presented an architecture for iterative modulo multiplication that performs the quotient estimation by table lookups [8]. Their design also requires storage of some precalculated complements of the modulus, resulting in an increase in needed resources. The partial-parallel multiplier introduced by H. Orup et al. contains a quotient estimation circuit that estimates the 12 highest order bits of the redundant partial sum, and then chooses an appropriate multiple of the modulus to be subtracted [20]. The most significant drawback of Orup's architecture is a long critical path introduced by the quotient estimation circuit, which limits the clock frequency. Higher-radix methods for MSB-first iterative modulo multiplication have been reported in [12,18,24,25].

2.2   Carry-Save Adders

The carry propagation in long integer addition is easily eliminated by the implementation of a *carry-save adder* (CSA). Carry-save adders are widely used in arithmetic circuits due to their performance in terms of speed and silicon area [21]. An n-bit CSA consists of n full-adders (FA), and solves the carry propagation problem by using a *redundant representation* for the result (i.e., the carries are saved). This means that the result is not a single binary number, but is represented by two n-bit numbers instead: R_S (the sum bits) and R_C (the carry bits). The delay of a carry-save adder is constant (i.e., independent of the length of the operands) and only determined by the delay of a single full-adder. In many applications, the sum output R_S and the carry output R_C are latched or registered, either for synchronization purposes or for pipelining.

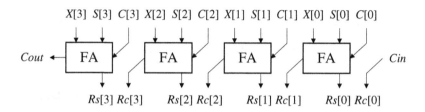

X[3] S[3] C[3] X[2] S[2] C[2] X[1] S[1] C[1] X[0] S[0] C[0]

Cout ← FA   FA   FA   FA   Cin

Rs[3] Rc[3]   Rs[2] Rc[2]   Rs[1] Rc[1]   Rs[0] Rc[0]

Fig. 2: Block diagram of a 4-bit carry-save adder.

Figure 2 illustrates a 4-bit carry-save adder. The basic principle of the carry-save addition is to reduce the sum of three binary numbers S, C, X to the sum of two binary numbers R_S, R_C without carry propagation according to the following equations:

$$R_S[i] = S[i] \otimes C[i] \otimes X[i] \tag{3}$$

$$R_C[i+1] = S[i] \cdot C[i] + S[i] \cdot X[i] + C[i] \cdot X[i] \quad \text{with} \quad R_C[0] = Cin = 0 \tag{4}$$

Note that the operators in the previous equations are logical operators and not arithmetic operators. When using carry-save adders, the intermediate result R is not a single binary number anymore, but is given in a redundant representation as a *sum and carry pair* (R_S, R_C) instead, whereby R_S denotes the sum part of the result, and R_C the carry part, respectively. Carry-save adders are advantageous if many subsequent additions have to be performed.

3   Optimized MSB-First Iterative Modulo Multiplication

The major hindrance of the bit-serial architectures for modulo multiplication described in subsection 2.1 is that they either require a costly quotient evaluation circuit or a circuit for performing comparisons of long integers. These circuits cause significant additional hardware and may limit the clock frequency due to a long critical path. Furthermore, some of the mentioned implementations need a large amount of storage for precomputed multiples of the modulus. If the modulus is to be dynamic, the stored modulus multiples must be updated whenever the modulus is changed.

INPUT: An n-bit modulus M (i.e., $2^{n-1} \leq M < 2^n$), a multiplicand A in the
       range of $0 \leq A < 2^n$, and a multiplier B in the range of $0 \leq B < 2^n$.
OUTPUT: The result R in the range of $0 \leq R < 2^n$. R is possibly not fully
       reduced, i.e., $R = A \cdot B \mod M + k \cdot M$ with $k \in \{0, 1\}$.

```
 1:   (R_S, R_C) ← 0
 2:   for i from n − 1 downto 0 do
 3:       (R_S, R_C) ← 2·(R_S, R_C) + A·B[i]
 4:       while (R_S, R_C) ≥ 2·2^n do (R_S, R_C) ← (R_S, R_C) − 2·M
 5:       while (R_S, R_C) ≥ 2^n do (R_S, R_C) ← (R_S, R_C) − M
 6:   endfor
 7:   R ← R_S + R_C    { red. to non-red. conversion }
 8:   if R ≥ 2^n then
 9:       (R_S, R_C) ← R − M
10:       R ← R_S + R_C    { red. to non-red. conversion }
11:   endif
```

Fig. 3: Optimized version of the MSB-first iterative modulo multiplication.

The most crucial operation of the classical MSB-first algorithm for iterative modulo multiplication is the calculation of the quotient q, which is the same as to decide whether the current intermediate result is smaller than M (and consequently $q = 0$), or bigger than M (and consequently $q = 1$), or bigger than $2 \cdot M$ (and consequently $q = 2$). This decision is difficult for long integers because an n-bit modulus M can vary between its minimum value M_{min} of 2^{n-1} and its maximum value M_{max} of $2^n - 1$:

$$2^{n-1} \leq M < 2^n \Rightarrow M_{min} = 2^{n-1} \text{ and } M_{max} = 2^n - 1 \tag{5}$$

Additionally, a redundant representation of the intermediate result does not make this task easier. An efficient solution for this problem is to compare the redundant intermediate result to 2^n and to $2 \cdot 2^n$ instead of the exact values of M and $2 \cdot M$, since these comparisons are simpler to implement in hardware, as will be demonstrated in subsection 3.1.

Figure 3 shows a modified version of the shift-and-add multiplication which is optimized for hardware implementation. The intermediate result is written in redundant representation (R_S, R_C) to indicate that the additions and subtractions should be performed by carry-save adders. Another interesting detail of the modified algorithm is the fact that the modulo reduction is not carried out "at once", but is split into continued subtractions of $2 \cdot M$ and/or M. The subtraction of M and $2 \cdot M$ can be realized by addition of the two's complement of M, and by addition of the 1-bit left-shifted two's complement of M, respectively. When using a carry-save adder for the two's complement addition, the subtraction is performed in constant time. During a modulo multiplication the intermediate result is always in redundant representation. After the last multiplier bit $B[0]$ has been processed, the result must be converted from redundant into non-redundant representation. This conversion can be performed by a pipelined *carry-lookahead*

Table 1: Redundant number estimations. R_S and R_C are both $(n+1)$-bit numbers, $R_S[n]$ is the MSB of R_S, and $R_C[n]$ is the MSB of R_C.

$R_S[n]$	$R_C[n]$	$R_S[n-1]$	$R_C[n-1]$	$R_S + R_C$	Estimation
0	0	0	0	$R_S+R_C < 2^{n-1}+2^{n-1}$	
0	0	0	1	$R_S+R_C < 2^{n-1}+2^n$	$(R_S, R_C) < 3 \cdot 2^{n-1}$
0	0	1	0	$R_S+R_C < 2^n+2^{n-1}$	
0	0	1	1	$R_S+R_C \geq 2^{n-1}+2^{n-1}$	
0	1	X	X	$R_S+R_C \geq 2^n$	$(R_S, R_C) \geq 2^n$
1	0	X	X	$R_S+R_C \geq 2^n$	
1	1	X	X	$R_S+R_C \geq 2^n+2^n$	$(R_S, R_C) \geq 2 \cdot 2^n$

adder (see section 5). If the non-redundant result R is bigger than 2^n, one final subtraction of M is necessary to bound the result within the range of $[0, 2^n)$. It must be emphasized, however, that the operands A and B do not need to be fully reduced, but they must be smaller than 2^n to ensure that the algorithm works correctly. A remaining problem is the comparison of the redundant intermediate result to $2 \cdot 2^n$ and 2^n, respectively. In the next subsection we present an efficient solution for this problem by applying a special estimation technique.

3.1   Redundant Number Estimation

The modified algorithm in figure 3 requires a comparison of the intermediate result to $2 \cdot 2^n$ and 2^n to decide whether or not a subtraction of $2 \cdot M$ or M has to be performed. For hardware implementation, this is a significant improvement over the first algorithm because it avoids the necessity for an exact comparison between the intermediate result and the modulus. Furthermore, the comparison to $2 \cdot 2^n$ and 2^n can be easily realized by a novel estimation technique, in the following denoted as *redundant number estimation*.

Table 1 shows a simplified logical truth-table to decide the two inequalities $(R_S, R_C) \geq 2^n$ and $(R_S, R_C) \geq 2 \cdot 2^n$. For decision of the first inequality, only the two most significant bits of R_S and R_C need to be scanned, and for the second inequality only the MSB of R_S and R_C, respectively. Note that R_S and R_C are both $(n+1)$-bit numbers, consequently the MSB of R_S is $R_S[n]$, and the MSB of R_C is $R_C[n]$. The hardware to decide the multiple of the modulus to be subtracted can be defined by the following two logical equations:

$$sub1 = R_S[n] + R_C[n] + (R_S[n-1] \cdot R_C[n-1]) \qquad (6)$$
$$sub2 = R_S[n] \cdot R_C[n] \qquad (7)$$

If $sub1 = 0$, then the intermediate result (R_S, R_C) is smaller than $3 \cdot 2^{n-1}$ and consequently also smaller than $3 \cdot M$. This estimation is correct for any value of M according to equation (5), even for $M = M_{min}$. On the other hand, if $sub1 = 1$, the intermediate result is bigger than 2^n, and consequently it can be estimated to be also bigger than M. Therefore, at least one subtraction of M is necessary, even if $M = M_{max}$.

For any n-bit modulus M satisfying $2^{n-1} \leq M < 2^n$, the redundant number estimations observed from table 1 can be summarized as follows:

$$sub1 = 0 \text{ and } sub2 = 0 \Rightarrow (R_S, R_C) < 3 \cdot M \qquad (8)$$

$$sub1 = 1 \text{ and } sub2 = 0 \Rightarrow (R_S, R_C) \geq M \qquad (9)$$

$$sub2 = 1 \Rightarrow (R_S, R_C) \geq 2 \cdot M \qquad (10)$$

The optimized MSB-first algorithm illustrated in figure 3 compares the intermediate result (R_S, R_C) to $2 \cdot 2^n$ and 2^n instead of the actual values $2 \cdot M$ and M. For this reason, it is possible that the intermediate result is not always fully reduced. But if the comparisons are performed according to the presented redundant number estimations, the algorithm guarantees that the intermediate result is always smaller than three times the modulus (i.e., smaller than $3 \cdot 2^{n-1}$) before the next multiplier bit $B[i]$ is processed. This is valid for any modulus M which satisfies equation (5), even for $M = M_{min}$.

After each addition of a partial-product, the modulo reduction is accomplished by continued subtractions of $2 \cdot M$ and M. Of course this raises the question how many subtractions of $2 \cdot M$ and/or M will be (at most) necessary. Because the redundant number estimation guarantees that the intermediate result (R_S, R_C) is smaller than $3 \cdot 2^{n-1}$ before the quantity $2 \cdot (R_S, R_C) + A \cdot B[i]$ is computed, the product $2 \cdot (R_S, R_C)$ is always smaller than $6 \cdot 2^{n-1}$. Since the partial-product $A \cdot B[i]$ is smaller than 2^n it is proven that the intermediate result is smaller than $8 \cdot 2^{n-1}$ before beginning the modulo reduction. Thus, for any modulus M satisfying equation (5), at most three subtractions of $2 \cdot M$ or M are necessary until (R_S, R_C) is smaller than $3 \cdot 2^{n-1}$. On the other hand, a more precise quotient evaluation would reduce the number of subtractions. However, the proposed method benefits from the fact that the redundant number estimation does not cause a significant critical path and that no multiples of M need to be precomputed and stored.

4   Arithmetic in Binary Extension Fields GF(2^m)

The elements of GF(2^m) are polynomials of degree less than m, with coefficients in GF(2). For example, if $a(t)$ is an element in GF(2^m), then one can have

$$a(t) = \sum_{i=0}^{m-1} a_i t^i = a_{m-1} t^{m-1} + \ldots + a_2 t^2 + a_1 t + a_0 \text{ with } a_i \in \{0, 1\} \quad (11)$$

This binary polynomial can also be written in bit-string form as $A[m-1..0]$, whereby $A[i]$ corresponds to the coefficient a_i. Finite fields of characteristic 2 are attractive for hardware implementation due to their "carry-free" arithmetic. The addition in GF(2^m) is implemented as component-wise exclusive OR (XOR), whilst the implementation of the multiplication depends on the *basis* chosen [14].

INPUT: An irreducible polynomial $p(t)$ of degree m, a multiplicand-polynomial $a(t)$, and a multiplier-polynomial $b(t)$.
OUTPUT: Result-polynomial $r(t) = a(t) \cdot b(t) \bmod p(t)$.

1:   $r(t) \leftarrow 0$
2:   **for** i **from** $m - 1$ **downto** 0 **do**
3:       $r(t) \leftarrow t \cdot r(t) + a(t) \cdot b_i$
4:       **if** $\mathrm{degree}(r(t)) = m$ **then** $r(t) \leftarrow r(t) - p(t)$
5:   **endfor**

Fig. 4: MSB-first iterative multiplication in GF(2^m).

The simplest representation is in polynomial basis, where the multiplication is performed modulo an *irreducible polynomial* of degree exactly m.

A bit-serial polynomial basis multiplier for GF(2^m) has an area complexity of $\mathcal{O}(m)$ and computes a multiplication in m clock cycles. They have been well known since the early 1970s due to their exploration in coding theory [22], and later they have also been proposed for use in cryptography [2]. A recent publication reports a bit-serial architecture which is able to perform additions and multiplications over a variety of binary fields up to an order of 2^m [7].

4.1   Addition

The addition in GF(2^m) is performed by adding the coefficients modulo 2, which is nothing else than bit-wise XOR-ing the coefficients of equal powers of t. Compared to the addition of integers, the addition in GF(2^m) is much easier as it does not cause carry propagation. It is well known that in the field GF(2^m) any element $a(t)$ is its own additive inverse since $a(t) + a(t) = 0$, the additive identity. Consequently, addition and subtraction are equivalent operations in GF(2^m).

4.2   Multiplication

Multiplication in GF(2^m) involves multiplying the two polynomials together (carry-free coefficient multiplication) and then finding the residue modulo a given irreducible polynomial $p(t)$. In general, the reduction modulo an irreducible polynomial $p(t)$ requires polynomial division. For an efficient implementation it is necessary to perform the field multiplication without polynomial division. One possibility is to interleave the reduction modulo $p(t)$ with the multiplication operation, instead of performing the reduction separately after the multiplication of the polynomials is finished. This leads to a characteristic 2 version of the shift-and-add method, where the multiplication is realized by addition of partial-products, and the reduction is performed by subtraction of the irreducible polynomial. The pseudocode illustrated in figure 4 describes this algorithm.

The multiplication of two polynomials $a(t), b(t) \in$ GF(2^m) modulo an irreducible polynomial $p(t)$ is done by scanning the coefficients of the multiplier-polynomial $b(t)$ from b_{m-1} to b_0 and adding the partial-product $a(t) \cdot b_i$ to the intermediate result $r(t)$. The partial-product $a(t) \cdot b_i$ is either 0 (if $b_i = 0$) or the multiplicand-polynomial $a(t)$ (if $b_i = 1$). After each partial-product addition, the intermediate result must be multiplied by t to align it for the next partial-product. The reduction modulo the irreducible polynomial $p(t)$ is interleaved with the partial-product additions by subtraction of $p(t)$ if the degree of the intermediate result is m, i.e., if the coefficient r_m is 1. It turns out that the computation of $r(t) = a(t) \cdot b(t) \bmod p(t)$ requires m steps, and at each step we perform the following operations:

– computation of $t \cdot r(t)$ (a 1-bit left-shift)
– generation of a partial-product (logical AND between b_i and $a(t)$)
– addition of the partial-product (an $(m+1)$-bit XOR operation)
– generation of the subtrahend (logical AND between r_m and $p(t)$)
– subtraction of the subtrahend (an $(m+1)$-bit XOR operation)

The required logical operations are AND, XOR, and 1-bit left-shifts, which makes a hardware implementation of this algorithm very straightforward.

5   Multiplier Architecture

When taking a closer look at the multiplication algorithms for $\mathrm{GF}(p)$ (figure 3) and for $\mathrm{GF}(2^m)$ (figure 4), it is easily observed that these algorithms have some similarities. In both algorithms, one operand (the multiplier) is scheduled bit by bit, beginning with the MSB, and the other operand (the multiplicand) is scheduled fully parallel. Both algorithms perform three basic operations: Addition of partial-products, 1-bit left-shifts of the intermediate result, and subtraction(s) of the modulus (or the irreducible polynomial, respectively). The main difference is the way how the addition or subtraction is performed. An addition in GF(p) involves addition of integers and can be performed by carry-save adders, using a redundant representation for the result. On the other hand, the addition in $\mathrm{GF}(2^m)$ is a simple logical XOR operation.

5.1   Implementation of the Field Arithmetic

Figure 5 illustrates an arithmetic unit for implementation of the field additions and subtractions, respectively. All carry-save additions have to be performed with $(n+1)$-bit precision. The sum output R_S and the carry output R_C of the adders are latched on each half-cycle for synchronization purposes. Note that the circuit for generation of the partial-product as well as the circuit for generation of the subtrahend are not shown in figure 5.

A subtraction is usually performed by adding the two's complement of the subtrahend S, which can be realized in our case by addition of the bitwise complement of S and setting the initial carry Cin to 1. Therefore, addition and subtraction are essentially the same operation. It must be emphasized that the MSB-first algorithm from figure 3 guarantees that the intermediate result will never become negative, i.e., the $Cout$ output of the carry-save adders can be

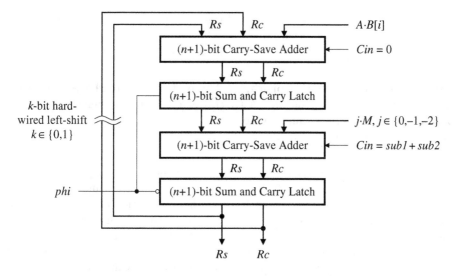

Fig. 5: Arithmetic unit of an n-bit unified multiplier.

ignored. In the following we describe how this arithmetic unit can be used to implement a modulo multiplication. Later in this section it will be shown that the arithmetic unit can also perform the addition/subtraction in GF(2^m).

According to the MSB-first iterative algorithm for modulo multiplication, the processing of a multiplier bit $B[i]$ takes place in the following way: The first carry-save adder at the top of figure 5 performs the addition of the partial-product $A \cdot B[i]$ to the current intermediate result. The sum output R_S and the carry output R_C of the first CSA are used to estimate the multiple of the modulus to become subtracted at the second CSA. This estimation is performed as described in section 3.1, and only the two highest order bits of R_S and R_C are needed to implement the logical functions of equation (6) and (7). Therefore, the hardware to decide whether to subtract $0 \cdot M$, $1 \cdot M$ or $2 \cdot M$ can be implemented very efficiently and will not cause a long critical path in the arithmetic unit.

The subtraction of M or $2 \cdot M$ is realized by addition of the two's complement of M or $2 \cdot M$ to the output of the first CSA, which takes place at the second CSA. But one subtraction of $2 \cdot M$ or M may not be enough to guarantee that the intermediate result is within the range of $[0, 3 \cdot 2^{n-1})$. Therefore, a control signal $xsub$ is generated according to equation (6) in order to decide whether or not an extra subtraction of M or $2 \cdot M$ is necessary. If an extra subtraction is required, the outputs R_S and R_C of the second CSA are fed back to the first (upper) CSA (without a left-shift). For an extra subtraction, the multiplier bit $B[i]$ must be masked off, so that no partial-product (i.e., zero) is added at the first CSA. After that, the extra subtraction of M or $2 \cdot M$ takes place again at the second CSA.

If no extra subtraction is required, the processing of the multiplier bit is finished. The outputs of the second CSA are fed back to the inputs of the first CSA with a 1-bit hardwired left-shift. R_S and R_C are now correctly aligned for addition of the next partial-product and the same procedure starts again. After the last multiplier bit has been processed, the sum and carry of the second CSA represent the redundant result (R_S, R_C) of the modulo multiplication.

Generation of the partial-product. The partial-product $A \cdot B[i]$ is either 0 (if $B[i]$ is 0), or the multiplicand A (if $B[i]$ is 1). Thus, the generation of the partial-product $A \cdot B[i]$ is simply done by a bit-wise AND operation between the multiplier bit $B[i]$ and all the bits of the multiplicand A.

Generation of the subtrahend. The subtrahend $S = j \cdot M, j \in \{0, -1, -2\}$ must be generated according to the requirements of the optimized MSB-first algorithm. In the presented arithmetic unit the subtraction of S is realized by addition of the bitwise complement of S and by setting the initial carry Cin of the CSA to 1. The control signals $sub1$ and $sub2$ introduced in section 3.1 indicate whether the subtrahend S has to be 0, M, or $2 \cdot M$, and they can be used for generating the subtrahend-bits $S[i]$ according to the following equations: [1]

$$S[i] = sub1 \cdot \overline{sub2} \cdot \overline{M[i]} + sub2 \cdot \overline{M[i-1]} \quad \text{for} \quad i = 1 \ldots n \tag{12}$$

$$S[0] = sub1 \cdot \overline{sub2} \cdot \overline{M[0]} + sub2 \tag{13}$$

Performing addition/subtraction in $GF(2^m)$. The sum bit $R_S[i]$ of a full-adder calculates the logical XOR of its three inputs (see equation (3)). By setting all carry bits of the adders to 0, the sum outputs $R_S[i]$ of the adders provide the functionality of a 2-input XOR gate. This is exactly the functionality required for addition/subtraction in $GF(2^m)$. Also the partial-products are generated in exactly the same way as described before, namely by a logical AND of the coefficient $B[i]$ and all the coefficients[2] of the multiplicand polynomial $a(t)$. A reduction of the intermediate result is necessary whenever the degree of the result-polynomial is m, i.e., if $R_S[m]$ is 1. The requirement for a subtraction of the irreducible polynomial $p(t)$ is indicated by the control signal $sub1$, since $sub1 = R_S[m]$ if the carry bits $R_C[i]$ are set to 0:

$$sub1 = R_S[m] + 0 + (R_S[m-1] \cdot 0) = R_S[m] \quad \text{and} \quad sub2 = R_S[m] \cdot 0 = 0$$

The control signal $sub2$ is always 0. As mentioned in subsection 4.2, the generation of the subtrahend S is a logical AND between the control signal $sub1$ and the bits of the irreducible polynomial, i.e., $S[i] = sub1 \cdot P[i] = R_S[m] \cdot P[i]$. The presented arithmetic unit provides exactly the functionality required for the multiplication in the binary extension field $GF(2^m)$ when the carry bits $R_C[i]$ are set to 0.

---

[1] The algorithm also works with the following control signals: $sub1 = R_S[n] \otimes R_C[n]$, $sub2 = R_S[n] \cdot R_C[n]$, and $xsub = R_S[n] + R_C[n] + (R_S[n-1] \cdot R_C[n-1])$. In this case the generation of the subtrahend bits $S[i]$ is simplified to the following equation: $S[i] = sub1 \cdot \overline{M[i]} + sub2 \cdot \overline{M[i-1]}$.

[2] According to the bit-string notation introduced in section 4.1, the coefficient x_i of a polynomial $x(t)$ is denoted as $X[i]$.

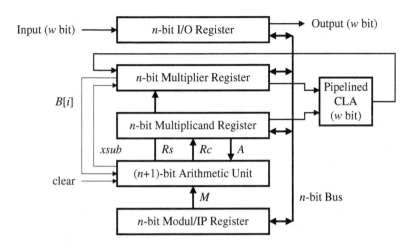

Fig. 6: Block diagram of the bit-serial multiplier architecture.

5.2 The Unified Multiplier Architecture

Figure 6 shows the bit-serial multiplier architecture, consisting of the $(n+1)$-bit arithmetic unit, four n-bit registers, and a pipelined w-bit carry-lookahead adder [21], whereby w denotes the wordsize of the registers (usually 8, 16, or 32 bits). The *I/O Register* performs data transfers from and to the world outside the multiplier. We prefer to provide a seperate register for I/O operations to ensure that the overall performance of the multiplier is not reduced by slow data transfers. The *Modulus/IP Register* is needed to store the bit-string representation of the modulus or the irreducible polynomial, respectively. *Multiplicand* and *Multiplier Register* are used for storing the current operands of the multiplication. Both registers can carry out w-bit shift operations in LSB direction, register *Multiplier* can additionally perform 1-bit shift operations in MSB direction (1-bit left-shifts). All four registers are connected through an n-bit bus.

After the operands have been loaded into the corresponding registers, a modulo multiplication takes place in the following way: The *Multiplier* register is shifted bit by bit in MSB direction to deliver the multiplier bits $B[n-1]$ to $B[0]$ to the arithmetic unit. The processing of the multiplier bits $B[i]$ is performed as described in subsection 5.1. The control signal *xsub* is generated from the two most significant bits of R_S and R_C of the second CSA according to equation (6). Whenever *xsub* is 1, the arithmetic unit has to perform an extra subtraction and register *Multiplier* must stop the left-shift until $xsub = 0$. After the least significant multiplier bit $B[0]$ has been processed, the redundant result (R_S, R_C) is loaded into registers *Multiplier* and *Multiplicand*, respectively. Note that the old values of the multiplier and multiplicand are not needed any more. Now the redundant result must be converted into non-redundant representation. This is done by the pipelined w-bit carry-lookahead adder (CLA) and requires $\lceil n/w \rceil$ clock cycles plus the delay of the CLA (usually $\log_2(w)$ clock cycles). The out-

Table 2: Typical subtraction sequences of $2 \cdot M$ and/or M depending on the range of (R_S, R_C) after addition of the partial-product.

Range of (R_S, R_C)	Typical sub-traction sequence	Clock cycles
$0 \leq (R_S, R_C) < 2^{n-1}$	—	1
$2^{n-1} \leq (R_S, R_C) < 2 \cdot 2^{n-1}$	—	1
$2 \cdot 2^{n-1} \leq (R_S, R_C) < 3 \cdot 2^{n-1}$	—	1
$3 \cdot 2^{n-1} \leq (R_S, R_C) < 4 \cdot 2^{n-1}$	M	1
$4 \cdot 2^{n-1} \leq (R_S, R_C) < 5 \cdot 2^{n-1}$	$2 \cdot M$	1
$5 \cdot 2^{n-1} \leq (R_S, R_C) < 6 \cdot 2^{n-1}$	$2 \cdot M, M$	2
$6 \cdot 2^{n-1} \leq (R_S, R_C) < 7 \cdot 2^{n-1}$	$2 \cdot M, 2 \cdot M$	2
$7 \cdot 2^{n-1} \leq (R_S, R_C) < 8 \cdot 2^{n-1}$	$2 \cdot M, 2 \cdot M, M$	3

put of the CLA is fed back to the *Multiplier* register. Since the non-redundant result may not be in the range of $[0, 2^n)$, an additional modulus subtraction and redundant to non-redundant conversion may be necessary. After the modulo multiplication has finished, the result resides within register *Multiplier*.

In $GF(2^m)$-mode, a multiplication is performed in a similar way, except that no extra subtractions and no redundant to non-redundant conversions of the result are necessary.

5.3   Performance Estimation

Since the carry-save adders are separated by latches, the addition of a partial-product and the first subtraction of M or $2 \cdot M$ are performed in one clock cycle. Any extra modulus subtraction requires an additional clock cycle. As stated in subsection 3.1, at most three subtractions of $2 \cdot M$ and/or M are necessary to guarantee that the intermediate result is smaller than $3 \cdot M$ (i.e., $3 \cdot 2^{n-1}$). Therefore, the processing of a single multiplier bit takes at most three clock cycles. The actual number of cycles depends on the size of the intermediate result *after* addition of the partial-product. Table 2 shows typical subtraction sequences depending on the range of the intermediate result (R_S, R_C). The values at the third column represent the number of clock cycles required for partial-product addition *and* the subtractions. For example, if $6 \cdot 2^{n-1} \leq (R_S, R_C) < 7 \cdot 2^{n-1}$ then typically two subtractions have to be performed. Consequently, two clock cycles are necessary for the processing of that multiplier bit.

According to the subtraction sequences shown in table 2, one can assume that any bit of the multiplier takes on average 1.5 clock cycles to be processed. When given arbitrary n-bit operands, the computation of $A \cdot B \bmod M$ requires approximately $1.5 \cdot n$ clock cycles. Moreover, one or two redundant to non-redundant conversions of the result are necessary, each needs $\lceil n/w \rceil + \log_2(w)$ clock cycles. For an $(n+1)$-bit arithmetic unit and a w-bit CLA, the number of clock cycles

Table 3: Principal operation characteristics of the unified multiplier.

Operation	Integer		GF(p)		GF(2^m)	
	add.	mult.	add.	mult.	add.	mult.
Cycles per bit	–	1	–	≈ 1.5	–	1
Max. op. length	$n-1$	$n/2$	n	n	n	n
Operand align	right	right	left	left	left	left

for a modulo multiplication can be estimated as follows:

$$c \approx 1.5 \cdot n + 1.5 \cdot \left(\left\lceil \frac{n}{w} \right\rceil + \log_2(w) \right) \approx 1.5 \cdot n \tag{14}$$

This means that a multiplication in the prime field GF(p) requires approximately $1.5 \cdot \lceil \log_2(p) \rceil$ clock cycles. On the other hand, a multiplication in GF(2^m) is finished after m cycles since any bit of the multiplier takes exactly one clock cycle to be processed.

6   Summary of Results and Conclusions

The subject of this paper was to present a novel bit-serial multiplier architecture which operates over finite fields GF(p) and GF(2^m). A multiplication in GF(p) is performed in a serial/parallel manner, which means that the multiplier is scheduled sequentially (bit by bit) and the multiplicand is scheduled fully parallel. The modulo reduction is interleaved with the multiplication by subtractions of once or twice the modulus. Thus, the arithmetic unit has to perform only three simple operations: Addition of partial-products, left-shift of the intermediate result, and subtraction of once or twice the modulus. Compared to other bit-serial multipliers, the proposed architecture profits from an efficient subtrahend estimation circuit which does not cause a significant critical path. The modulo multiplier described in this paper is also capable to perform multiplications in GF(2^m), i.e., it is a unified (dual-field) multiplier for GF(p) and GF(2^m). Contrary to architectures which use Montgomery multiplication, the introduced MSB-first algorithm requires neither operand transformation into Montgomery domain nor precomputed constants.

The presented design is scalable in size, and an n-bit multiplier operates over a wide range of finite fields. For example, a multiplier dimensioned for 200 bits can also be used for fields of smaller order, like 192 or 163 bits, by left-aligning all operands in the registers. Furthermore, the multiplier can also perform ordinary integer addition and multiplication, respectively. The operand size for ordinary integer multiplication is limited to about $n/2$ bits since the product can't exceed n-bit precision. Table 3 summarizes principal characteristics of addition and multiplication over integers, prime fields GF(p), and binary extension fields GF(2^m).

The unified multiplier can be implemented for an area-cost only slightly higher than that of the multiplier for the prime field GF(p), providing significant area savings when both types of multiplier are needed. To be more specific, the overhead introduced by the dual-field arithmetic is just a logic circuit for setting the carry bits of the CSA to 0, which means that this feature comes almost for free. Additionally, the architecture is neither restricted to use primes of a special form (e.g., generalized Mersenne primes), nor does it favor particular irreducible polynomials like trinomials or pentanomials. Another advantage of the bit-serial architecture is its high degree of regularity. The presented unified multiplier offers a fair area/performance trade-off, which makes it attractive for the implementation of a crypto-coprocessor for low-end 8-bit smart cards.

The correctness of the presented concepts was verified by a functional, cycle-based model of the multiplier architecture written is a hardware description language. Our future work will be a VLSI implementation of the multiplier.

References

1. P. Barrett. Implementing the Rivest, Shamir and Adleman public-key encryption algorithm on a standard digital signal processor. In A. M. Odlyzko (ed.), *Advances in Cryptology — CRYPTO '86*, vol. 263 of *Lecture Notes in Computer Science*, pp. 311–323. Springer-Verlag, Berlin, Germany, 1987.
2. T. Beth, B. M. Cook, and D. Gollmann. Architectures for exponentiation in $GF(2^n)$. In A. M. Odlyzko, (ed.), *Advances in Cryptology — CRYPTO '86*, vol. 263 of *Lecture Notes in Computer Science*, pp. 302–310. Springer-Verlag, Berlin, Germany, 1987.
3. I. F. Blake, G. Seroussi, and N. P. Smart. *Elliptic Curves in Cryptography*, vol. 265 of *London Mathematial Society Lecture Notes Series*. Cambridge University Press, Cambridge, UK, 1999.
4. G. R. Blakley. A computer algorithm for calculating the product AB modulo M. *IEEE Transactions on Computers*, 32(5):497–500, May 1983.
5. E. F. Brickell. A fast modular multiplication algorithm with application to two key cryptography. In D. Chaum, R. L. Rivest, and A. T. Sherman (eds.), *Advances in Cryptology: Proceedings of CRYPTO '82*, pp. 51–60. Plenum Press, New York, NY, USA, 1982.
6. J. Goodman and A. Chandrakasan. An energy efficient reconfigurable publik-key cryptography processor architecture. In Ç. K. Koç and C. Paar (eds.), *Cryptographic Hardware and Embedded Systems — CHES 2000*, vol. 1965 of *Lecture Notes in Computer Science*, pp. 174–191. Springer-Verlag, Berlin, Germany, 2000.
7. J. Großschädl. A low-power bit-serial multiplier for finite fields $GF(2^m)$. In *Proceedings of the 34th IEEE International Symposium on Circuits and Systems (ISCAS 2001)*, vol. IV, pp. 37–40, 2001.
8. Y.-J. Jeong and W. P. Burleson. VLSI array algorithms and architectures for RSA modular multiplication. *IEEE Transactions on Very Large Scale Integration (VLSI) Systems*, 5(2):211–217, June 1997.
9. N. Koblitz. Elliptic curve cryptosystems. *Mathematics of Computation*, vol. 48, no. 177, pp. 203–209, January 1987.
10. N. Koblitz, A. J. Menezes, and S. A. Vanstone. The state of elliptic curve cryptography. *Designs, Codes and Cryptography*, 19(2/3):173–193, March 2000.
11. Ç. K. Koç and T. Acar. Montgomery multiplication in $GF(2^k)$. *Designs, Codes and Cryptography*, 14(1):57–69, April 1998.

12. P. Kornerup. High-radix modular multiplication for cryptosystems. In G. Jullien, M. J. Irwin, and E. E. Swartzlander (eds.), *Proceedings of the 11th IEEE Symposium on Computer Arithmetic*, pp. 277–283. IEEE Computer Society Press, Los Alamitos, CA, USA, 1993.

13. A. K. Lenstra and E. R. Verheul. Selecting cryptographic key sizes. In H. Imai and Y. Zheng (eds.), *Public Key Cryptography — PKC 2000*, vol. 1751 of *Lecture Notes in Computer Science*, pp. 446–465. Springer-Verlag, Berlin, Germany, 2000.

14. R. Lidl and H. Niederreiter. *Introduction to Finite Fields and Their Applications.* Second edition. Cambridge University Press, Cambridge, UK, 1994.

15. A. J. Menezes. *Elliptic Curve Public Key Cryptosystems*, vol. 234 of *The Kluwer International Series in Engineering and Computer Science.* Kluwer Academic Publishers, Boston, MA, USA, 1993.

16. V. S. Miller. Use of elliptic curves in cryptography. In H. C. Williams (ed.), *Advances in Cryptology — CRYPTO '85*, vol. 218 of *Lecture Notes in Computer Science*, pp. 417–426. Springer-Verlag, Berlin, Germany, 1986.

17. P. L. Montgomery. Modular multiplication without trial division. *Mathematics of Computation*, 44(170):519–521, April 1985.

18. H. Morita. A fast modular-multiplication algorithm based on a higher radix. In G. Brassard (ed.), *Advances in Cryptology — CRYPTO '89*, vol. 435 of *Lecture Notes in Computer Science*, pp. 387–399. Springer-Verlag, Berlin, Germany, 1990.

19. National Institute of Standards and Technology (NIST). Digital Signature Standard (DSS). Federal Information Processing Standards (FIPS) Publication 186-2. Online available at `http://csrc.nist.gov/encryption`. February 2000.

20. H. Orup, E. Svendsen, and E. Andreasen. VICTOR an efficient RSA hardware implementation. In I. Damgård, (ed.), *Advances in Cryptology — EUROCRYPT '90*, vol. 473 of *Lecture Notes in Computer Science*, pp. 245–252. Springer-Verlag, Berlin, Germany, 1991.

21. B. Parhami. *Computer Arithmetic: Algorithms and Hardware Designs.* Oxford University Press, New York, NY, USA, 2000.

22. W. W. Peterson and E. J. Weldon. *Error-Correcting Codes.* Second edition. MIT Press, Cambridge, MA, USA, 1972.

23. E. Savaş, A. F. Tenca, and Ç. K. Koç. A scalable and unified multiplier architecture for finite fields GF(p) and GF(2^m). In Ç. K. Koç and C. Paar (eds.), *Cryptographic Hardware and Embedded Systems — CHES 2000*, vol. 1965 of *Lecture Notes in Computer Science*, pp. 277–292. Springer-Verlag, Berlin, Germany, 2000.

24. H. Sedlak. The RSA cryptography processor. In D. Chaum and W. L. Price (eds.), *Advances in Cryptology — EUROCRYPT '87*, vol. 304 of *Lecture Notes in Computer Science*, pp. 95–105. Springer Verlag, Berlin, Germany, 1988.

25. N. Takagi. A radix-4 modular multiplication hardware algorithm for modular exponentiation. *IEEE Transactions on Computers*, 41(8):949–956, August 1992.

26. C. D. Walter. Faster modular multiplication by operand scaling. In J. Feigenbaum (ed.), *Advances in Cryptology — CRYPTO '91*, vol. 576 of *Lecture Notes in Computer Science*, pp. 313–323. Springer-Verlag, Berlin, Germany, 1992.

Attacks on Cryptoprocessor Transaction Sets

Mike Bond

Computer Laboratory, University of Cambridge,
Pembroke Street, Cambridge, CB2 3QG, UK
Mike.Bond@cl.cam.ac.uk

Abstract. Attacks are presented on the IBM 4758 CCA and the Visa
Security Module. Two new attack principles are demonstrated. Related
key attacks use known or chosen differences between two cryptographic
keys. Data protected with one key can then be abused by manipulation
using the other key. Meet in the middle attacks work by generating a
large number of unknown keys of the same type, thus reducing the key
space that must be searched to discover the value of one of the keys in
the type. Design heuristics are presented to avoid these attacks and other
common errors.

1 Introduction

A cryptoprocessor is a tamper-resistant processor designed to manage cryptographic keys and data in high-risk situations. The concept of a cryptoprocessor
arose because conventional operating systems are too bug-ridden and computers
too physically insecure to be trusted with information of high value. A normal microprocessor is enclosed within a tamper-resistant environment, so that
sensitive information can only be altered or released through a tightly defined
software interface – a *transaction* set. In combination with *access control*, the
transaction set should prevent abuse of the sensitive information. However, as
the functionality and flexibility of transaction sets have been pushed up by manufacturers and clients, this extra complexity has made bugs in transaction sets
inevitable.

Sections 2 and 3 of this paper give an overview of cryptoprocessors in the
context of four important architectural principles, and then describe the new
vulnerabilities in a generalised way. Sections 4 and 5 introduce attacks on two
widely fielded cryptoprocessors – the IBM 4758, and the Visa Security Module.
Finally, some straightforward design heuristics are suggested that, whilst not
guaranteeing the security of a transaction set, will at least stop the same mistakes
being made over again.

2 Tour of a Cryptoprocessor

A cryptoprocessor's interface to the world is its *transaction set* – a group of
commands supported by the processor to manipulate and manage sensitive information, usually cryptographic keys. Users are limited to the subset of the

Ç.K. Koç, D. Naccache, and C. Paar (Eds.): CHES 2001, LNCS 2162, pp. 220–234, 2001.
© Springer-Verlag Berlin Heidelberg 2001

transaction set which reflects their needs using an *access control* system. The intended inputs and outputs of commands in a transaction set are described in terms of a *type system*, which describes the content of each type, and then assigns a type to each input and output of the commands. Keys tend to be stored in a *hierarchical structure* so that large amounts of information can be shared by securely sharing only a single piece of information at the base of a branch in the hierarchy.

2.1 Transaction Set Fundamentals

- *User commands* are the bulk of the cryptoprocessor's workload. The commands allow data to be processed (e.g. encrypted, decrypted, MACs generated/verified) using keys whose values are retained within the tamper-proof environment, remaining unknown to the user. The user is thus restricted to performing actions with these keys online, where procedural controls can be enforced. Application-specific commands may also exist, which manipulate encrypted inputs and return an encrypted output or maybe a simple return code (e.g. a yes/no answer to whether an entered PIN matched the correct value for an account number, without revealing either value).
- *Key Management commands* give users the ability to rearrange the key structure. Import and export commands will allow extraction of keys from the structure for sharing with other processors or environments, and commands to build up keys from multiple parts may be available to support dual control policies.
- *Administration commands* are highly dependent on implementation details, but would generally include commands for management of particularly sensitive high-level keys, modification of the access rights for other users, and output of clear PIN numbers in financial systems.

2.2 Access Control

Access control is necessary to ensure that only authorised users have access to powerful transactions which could be used to extract sensitive information. These can be used to enforce *procedural controls* such as *dual control*, or *m-of-n sharing schemes*, to prevent abuse of the more powerful transactions.

The simplest access control systems grant special authority to whoever has first use of the processor and then go into the default mode which affords no special privileges. An authorised person or group will load the sensitive information into the processor at power-up; afterwards the transaction set does not permit extraction of this information, only manipulation of other data using it. The next step up in access control is including a special *authorised* mode which can be enabled at any time with one or more passwords, physical key switches, or smartcards.

More versatile access control systems will maintain a record of which transactions each user can access, or a role-based approach to permit easier restructuring as the job of an individual real-world user changes, either in the long term or through the course of a working day. In circumstances where there are multiple levels of authorisation, the existence of a *'trusted path'* to users issuing special commands becomes important. Without using a secured session or physical access port separation, it would be easy for an unauthorised person to insert commands of their own into this session to extract sensitive information under the very nose of the authorised user.

2.3   Key Hierarchies

Storage of large numbers of keys becomes necessary when enforcing protection between multiple users, and serves to limit damage if one is compromised. The common storage method is a hierarchical structure, giving the fundamental advantage of efficient key sharing: access can be granted to an entire key set by granting access to the key at the next level up the hierarchy, under which the set is stored.

Confusion arises when the hierarchy serves more than one distinct role. Alternate roles include inferring the *type* of a key from its position in the hierarchy, or increasing the storage capacity of the cryptoprocessor by keeping only the top-level keys within the tamper-proofed environment, and storing the remainder externally, with each lower level encrypted using the appropriate key from the level above.

Figure 1 shows a common model with three layers of keys:

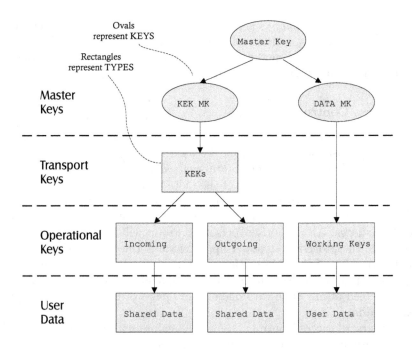

Fig. 1. An example key hierarchy

The top layer contains *'master keys'* which are never revealed outside the cryptoprocessor, the middle layer *'transport keys'* or *'key-encrypting-keys' (KEKs)* to allow sharing between processors, and the bottom layer working keys and session keys – together known as *'operational keys'*, The scope of some cryptoprocessors extends to an even lower layer, containing data encrypted with the operational keys.

2.4   Key Typing Systems

Assigning type information to keys is necessary for fine grain access control to the transaction set. This is because many transactions have the same core functionality, and without key typing an attacker could achieve the equivalent of execution of a transaction he doesn't have permission for by using an equivalent permitted transaction (e.g. calculating a MAC can be equivalent to CBC encryption, with all but the last block discarded). A well designed type system can prevent the abuse of the similarities between transactions.

An important example is the type distinction between communications data keys and PIN processing keys in financial systems. Customer PIN numbers are calculated by encrypting the account number with a PIN derivation key, thus commands using these keys are carefully controlled. However, if PIN keys and data keys were indistinguishable in type, any user with access to data manipulation transactions could calculate the PIN numbers from accounts: both employ the same DES or triple-DES (3DES) encryption algorithm to achieve their purpose.

IBM's financial products use the Common Cryptographic Architecture (CCA) – a standardised transaction set. The CCA name for the type information of a key is a control vector. Control vectors are bound to encrypted keys by XORing the control vector with the key used to encrypt, and including an unprotected copy for reference (1). The control vector is simply a bitpattern chosen to denote a particular type. If a naive attacker changes the clear copy of the control vector (i.e. the claimed key type), when the key is used, the cryptoprocessor's decryption operation should simply produce garbage (2). The implementation details are in 'Key Handling with Control Vectors' [2], and 'A Key Management Scheme Based on Control Vectors' [3].

$$
\begin{aligned}
&(1) \qquad E_{Km \oplus CV}(KEY) \ , \ \ CV \\
&(2) \qquad D_{Km \oplus CV_M OD}(E_{Km \oplus CV}(KEY)) \neq KEY
\end{aligned}
$$

3   The Attacker's Toolkit

The attacks in sections 4 and 5 are presented as combinations of attack *'building blocks'*. This section describes new building blocks, some intuitively dangerous in their own right, and others which only reap maximum damage in combination. The full set includes reapplications of existing techniques from other fields, and is augmented by the usual tools and methods available to an attacker (e.g. brute force search, cryptanalysis).

3.1   The Meet in the Middle Attack

Users can normally select which key is used to protect the output of a command, provided it is of the correct type. The flexibility gained from specification using the type system is at the price of risking catastrophic failure if the value of even just one key within a type is discovered – select the cracked key, and the command output will be decipherable. The meet in the middle attack is just common sense statistics: if you only need to crack a single key within a type to be successful, the more keys that you attack in parallel, the shorter the average time it takes to discover one of them using a brute force search.

The attacker first generates a large number of keys. 2^{16} (65,536) is a sensible target: somewhere between a minute and an hour's work for the cryptoprocessors examined. The same test vector must then be encrypted under each key, and the results recorded. Each encryption in the brute force search is then compared against all versions of the encrypted test pattern. Checking each key will now take slightly longer, but there will be many less to check. The observation at the heart of the attack is that it is much more efficient to perform a single encryption and compare the result against many different possibilities than it is to perform an encryption for each comparison.

The power of the attack is limited by the time the attacker can spend generating keys. It is reasonable to suppose that up to 20 bits of key space could be eliminated with this method. Single DES fails catastrophically, its 56 bit key space reduced to 40 bits or less. A 2^{40} search takes a few days on a home PC. Attacks on a 64 bit key space could be brought within range of funded organisations. The attack has been named a 'meet in the middle' attack because the brute force search machine and the cryptoprocessor attack the key space from opposite sides, and the effort expended by each meets somewhere in the middle.

3.2   Related Key Attacks

Allowing related keys to exist within a cryptoprocessor is dangerous, because it causes dependency between keys. Two keys can be considered *related* if the bitwise difference between them is known. Once the key set contains related keys, the security of one key is dependent upon the security of all keys related to it. It is impossible to audit for related keys without knowledge of what relationships might exist – and this would only be known by the attacker. Thus, the deliberate release of one key might inadvertently compromise another. *Partial relationships* between keys complicate the situation further. Suppose two keys become known to share certain bits in common. Compromise of one key could make a brute force attack feasible against the other. Related keys also endanger each other through increased susceptibility of the related group to a brute force search (see 3.1).

Keys with a *chosen* relationship can be even more dangerous because some architectures combine type information directly into the key bits. Ambiguity is inevitable: the combination of one key and one type might result in exactly the same final key as the combination of another key and type. Allowing a *chosen difference* between keys can lead to opportunities to subvert the type information, which is crucial to the security of the transaction set.

Although in most cryptoprocessors it is difficult to enter completely chosen keys (this usually leads straight to a severe security failure), obtaining a set of unknown keys with a chosen difference can be quite easy. Valuable keys (usually KEKs in the hierarchy diagram) are often transferred in multiple parts, combined using XOR to form the final key. At generation, the key parts would be given to separate couriers and data entry staff, so that a dual control policy could be implemented. Only collusion would reveal the value of the key. However, any key part holder could modify his part at will, so it is easy to choose a relationship between the actual value loaded, and the intended key value. The entry process could be repeated twice to obtain a pair of related keys. Some architectures allow a chosen value to be XORed with any key at any time.

3.3 Unauthorised Type-Casting

The commonality between transactions makes the integrity of the type system almost as important as the access controls over the transactions themselves. Once the type constraints of the transaction set are broken, abuse is easy (e.g. if some high security KEK could be retyped as a data key, keys protected with it could be exported in the clear using a standard data decipherment transaction).

Certain type casts are only 'unauthorised' in so far as that the designers never intended them to be possible. In some architectures it may even be difficult to tell whether or not an opportunity to type cast is a bug or a feature! Indeed, IBM describes a method in the manual for their 4758 CCA [1] to convert between key types during import to allow interoperability with earlier products which used a more primitive type system. The manual does not mention how easily this feature could be abused. If type casting is possible, it should also be possible to regulate it at all stages with the access control functions.

Cryptoprocessors which do not maintain internal state about their key structure have difficulties deleting keys. Once an encrypted version of a key has left the cryptoprocessor it cannot prevent an attacker storing his own copy for later re-introduction to the system. Thus, whenever this key undergoes an authorised type cast, it remains a member of the old type as well as adopting the new type. A key with membership of multiple types thus allows transplanting of parts of the old hierarchy between old and new types. Deletion can only be effected by changing the master keys at the top of the hierarchy, which is radical and costly.

3.4 Poor Key-Half Binding

Cryptographic keys get split into distinct parts, when the block length of the algorithm protecting them is shorter than the key length. 3DES is particularly common, and has a 112 bit key made up from two 56 bit single DES keys. When the association between the halves of keys is not kept, the security of the key is crippled. A number of cryptoprocessors allow the attacker to manipulate the actual keys simply by manipulating their encrypted versions in the desired manner. Known or chosen key halves could be substituted into unknown keys, immediately halving the keyspace. The same unknown half could be substituted into many different keys, creating a related key set, the dangers of which are described in section 3.2.

3DES has an interesting deliberate feature that makes absence of key-half binding even more dangerous. A 3DES encryption consists of a DES encryption using one key, a decryption using a second key, and another encryption with the first key. If both halves of the key are the same, the key behaves as a single length key. $(E_{K1}(D_{K2}(E_{K1}(data))) = E_K(data)$ when $K = K1 = K2)$. Pure manipulation of unknown key halves can yield a 3DES key which operates exactly as a single DES key. Some 3DES keys are thus within range of a brute force cracking effort.

3.5   Conjuring Keys from Nowhere

Cryptoprocessor designs which store encrypted keys outside the tamper-proof environment can be vulnerable to unauthorised key generation. For DES keys, the principle is simple: simply choose a random value and submit it as an encrypted key. The decrypted result will also be random, with a 1 in 2^8 chance of having the correct parity. Some early cryptoprocessors used this technique to generate keys (keys with bad parity were automatically corrected). Most now check parity but rarely enforce it, merely raising a warning. In the worst case, the attacker need only make trial encryptions with the keys, and observe whether key parity errors are raised. The odds of 1 in 2^{16} for 3DES keys are still quite feasible, and it is even easier if each half can be tested individually (see 3.4).

4   Attacks on the NSM (A Visa Security Module Clone)

The Visa Security Module (VSM) is a cryptoprocessor with a concise, focused transaction set, designed to protect PIN numbers transmitted over private bank ATM networks, and on the inter-bank link system supported by VISA. It was designed in the early eighties, and the NSM is a software compatible clone [5].

The VSM has two authorisation states (user and authorised) enabled using passwords. The NSM improves on this by splitting the authorised state in two – *supervisor* and *administrator*, selected by two key switches on the casing. The user state gives access to transactions to verify customers PINs in a number of ways, and to translate them between encryption keys to allow forwarding of requests to and from other banks in the network. The user state also contains transactions to permit key generation and update for session keys. The supervisor state is only enabled upon special procedural controls and enables transactions to allow extraction of PIN numbers to a printer connected to a dedicated port on the cryptoprocessor. Administrator authorisation allows generation of high-level master keys, and is rarely used. It recognises nine distinct types in total, shown by rectangles in figure 2. The ovals represent individual keys.

At the top of the key hierarchy are five 3DES master keys, stored in registers within the cryptoprocessor. These protect the five fundamental types, and all other types are likewise inferred implicitly from a key's position within the hierarchy. Apart from the 3DES master keys, all other keys are Single DES, and so must be changed regularly. The PIN derivation keys are an exception to the regular changes, but are afforded extra protection by measures to ensure that known plaintext/ciphertext pairs are not available to an attacker.

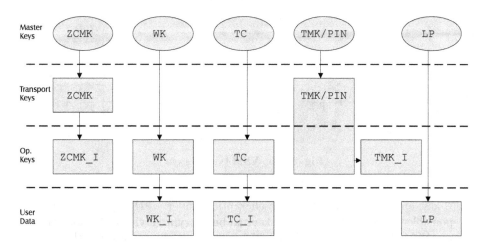

Fig. 2. The VSM key hierarchy

Terminal Master Keys (TMKs) are copies of those used in ATMs, available to the VSM so that it can prepare keysets allowing the ATMs to verify PINs themselves. PIN keys are used to convert account numbers into PIN numbers. The 4 digit PINs entered by customers are calculated from the result of encrypting the account number with the PIN key, using a publicly available algorithm. TMKs and PIN keys occupy the same type in the VSM, even though they are conceptually different. *Zone Control Master Keys* (ZCMKs) are keys to be shared with other banking networks, used to protect the exchange of working keys. *Working Keys* (WKs) are used to protect trial PINs that customers have entered, whilst they travel through the network on the way to the correct bank for verification, and are not used for intra-bank communications. *Terminal Communications keys* (TCs) are for protecting control information going to and from ATMs. Note that all *keys* sent to an ATM are protected with a TMK. Figure 3 shows the commands available to the normal user as lines between types. Two extra 'types' are shown: (RAND) and (CLEAR). The (RAND) type can be thought of as a source of unknown random numbers, so lines emanating from it represent key generation transactions. (CLEAR) is a source of user chosen values. The notation TYPE_I is used to stand for information encrypted with a key of type TYPE.

4.1   VSM Compatibles – A Poor Type System Attack

The amalgamation of the TMK and PIN types is responsible for a number of weaknesses in the VSM. One possible attack is to enter an account number as

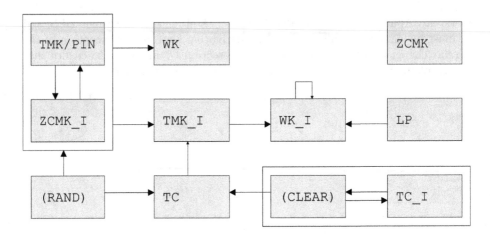

Fig. 3. The VSM type system

a `TC` key, and then translate this to encryption under a `PIN` key. The command responsible is designed to allow `TC` keys to be encrypted with a `TMK` for transfer to an ATM, but because `TMK`s and `PIN` keys share the same type, the `TC` can also be encrypted under a `PIN` key in the same way. This attack is very simple and effective, but is perhaps difficult to spot because the result of encryption with a `PIN` key is a sensitive value, and it is counterintuitive to imagine an encrypted value as sensitive when performing an analysis. Choosing a target account number `ACCNO`, the attack can be followed on the type transition diagram in figure 3, moving from (`CLEAR`) to `TC` (1), and finally to `TMK_I` (2).

$$(1) \qquad ACCNO \longrightarrow \{ACCNO\}TC \qquad (ACCNO \in CLEAR)$$
$$(2) \qquad \{ACCNO\}TC \longrightarrow \{ACCNO\}TMK\_I \qquad (TMK\_I = A\ PIN\ key)$$

Although the attack does not directly exploit any of the methods from section 3, it demonstrates the fragility of transaction sets, and is a good example of the characteristics of a broken transaction set when analysed in the context of *key hierarchies* and *type systems*.

4.2   VSM Compatibles – Meet in the Middle Attack

The meet in the middle attack can be used to compromise eight out of the nine types used by the VSM. The VSM does not impose limits or special authorisation requirements for key generation, so it is easy to populate all the types with large numbers of keys. Indeed, it *cannot* properly impose restrictions on key generation because of the 'key conjuring' attack (section 3.5) which works with many cryptoprocessors which store keys externally.

The target type should be populated with at least 2^{16} keys, and a test vector encrypted under each. The dedicated 'encrypt test vector' command narrowly escapes compromising all type because the default test vector does not have the correct parity to be accepted as a key. Instead, the facility to input a chosen terminal key (CLEAR ⟶ TC in figure 3) can be used to create the test vectors. The final step of the attack is to perform the 2^{40} brute force search offline.

The obvious types to attack are the PIN/TMK and WK types. Once a single PIN/TMK key has been discovered, all the rest can be translated to type TMK_I, encrypted under the compromised TMK. The attacker then decrypts these keys using a home PC. Compromise of a single Working Key (WK) allows all trial PINs entered by customers to be decrypted by translating them from encryption under their original WK to encryption under the compromised one (this command is shown by the looping arrow on WK_I in figure 3).

5   Attacks on the IBM 4758 CCA

The Common Cryptographic Architecture (CCA) is a standardised transaction set which is implemented by the majority of IBM's financial security products. The 4758 is a PC-compatible cryptographic coprocessor which implements the CCA. Control over the transaction set is quite flexible: role-based access control is available, and the users communicate via trusted paths protected with 3DES session keys. The transaction set itself is large and complex, with all the typical transactions described in section 2.1, as well as many specialised commands to support financial PIN processing. The CCA stores nearly all keys in encrypted form outside the cryptoprocessor, with a single 168-bit master key KM at the root of its key hierarchy:

The CCA holds type information on keys using *control vectors*. A control vector is synonymous with a type, and is bound to encrypted keys by XORing

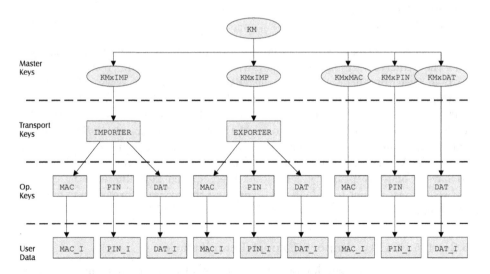

Fig. 4. The 4758 CCA key hierarchy

the control vector with the key used to encrypt, and including an unprotected copy for reference.

5.1   4758 CCA – Key Import Attack

One of the simplest attacks on the 4758 is to perform an unauthorised type cast using IBM's 'pre-exclusive-or' type casting method [1]. A typical case would be to import a PIN derivation key as a data key, so standard data ciphering commands could be used to calculate PIN numbers, or to import a KEK as a DATA key, to allow eavesdropping on future transmissions. The Key_Import command requires a KEK with permission to import (an IMPORTER), and the encrypted key to import. The attacker must have the necessary authorisation in his access control list to import to the destination type, but the original key can have any type. Nevertheless, with this attack, all information shared by another cryptoprocessor is open to abuse. More subtle type changes are worthy of mention, such as re-typing the right half of a 3DES key as a left half.

A related key set must first be generated (1). The 'Key_Part_Import' command acts to XOR together a chosen value with an encrypted key. If a dual control policy prevents the attacker from access to an initial key part, one can always be conjured (section 3.5). The chosen difference between keys is set to the difference between the existing and desired control vectors. Normal use of the 'Key_Import' command would import KEY as having the old_CV control vector. However, the identity (KEK1 $\oplus$ old_CV) = (KEK2$\oplus$new_CV) means that claiming that KEY was protected with KEK2, and having type new_CV will cause the cryptoprocessor to retrieve KEY correctly (3), but bind in the new type new_CV.

Related Key Set	(1)	$KEK1 = KORIG$
		$KEK2 = KORIG \oplus (old\_CV \oplus new\_CV)$
Received Key	(2)	$E_{KEK1 \oplus old\_CV}(KEY)$, old_CV
Import Process	(3)	$D_{KEK2 \oplus new\_CV}(E_{KEK1 \oplus old\_CV}(PKEY)) = PKEY$

A successful attack requires circumvention of the bank's procedural controls, and the attacker's ability to tamper with his own key part. IBM's advice is to take measures to prevent an attacker obtaining the necessary related keys. Optimal configuration of the access control system can indeed avoid the attack, but the onus is on banks to have tight procedural controls over key part assembly, with no detail in the manual as to what these controls should be. The manual will be fixed [4], but continuing to use XOR will make creating related key sets very easy. A long-term solution is to change the control vector binding method to have a one-way property, such that the required key difference to change between types cannot be calculated – keys and their type information cannot be unbound.

5.2   4758 CCA – Import/Export Loop Attack

The limitation of the key import attack described in 5.1 is that only keys sent from other cryptoprocessors are at risk from the attack, because these are the only ones that can be imported. The 'Import/Export Loop' attack builds upon the Key Import attack by demonstrating how to export keys from the crypto-processor, so their types can be converted as they are re-imported.

The simplest Import/Export loop would have the same key present as both an importer and an exporter. However, in order to achieve the type conversion, there must be a difference of (old_CV⊕new_CV) between the two keys. Generate a related key set (1), starting from a conjured key part if necessary. Now conjure a new key part KEKP, by repeated trial of key imports using IMPORTER1, and claiming type importer_CV, resulting in (2). Now import with IMPORTER2, claiming type exporter_CV, the type changes on import as before (3).

(1) $IMPORTER1 = RAND$
    $IMPORTER2 = RAND \oplus (importer\_CV \oplus exporter\_CV)$
(2) $E_{IMPORTER1 \oplus importer\_CV}(KEKP)$
(3) $D_{IMPORTER2 \oplus exporter\_CV}(E_{IMPORTER1 \oplus importer\_CV}(KEKP)) = KEKP$

(4) $EXPORT\_CONVERT = KEKP$
(5) $IMPORT\_CONVERT1 = KEKP \oplus (source1\_CV \oplus dest1\_CV)$
    $\cdots$
    $IMPORT\_CONVERTn = KEKP \oplus (source1\_CV \oplus destn\_CV)$

Now use Key_Part_Import to generate a related key set (5) which has chosen differences required for all type conversions you need to make. Any key with export permissions can now be exported with the exporter from the set (4), and re-imported as a new type using the appropriate importer key from the related key set (5). IBM recommends audit for same key used as both importer and exporter [1], but this attack employs a relationship between keys known only to the attacker, so conventional audit fails.

5.3   4758 CCA – 3DES Key Binding Attack

The 4758 CCA does not properly bind together the halves of its 3DES keys. Each half has a type associated, distinguishing between left halves, right halves, and single DES keys. However, for a given 3DES key, the type system does not specifically associate the left and right halves as members of that instance. The 'meet in the middle' technique can thus be successively applied to discover the halves of a 3DES key one at a time. This allows *all keys* to be extracted, including ones which do not have export permissions, so long as a known test vector can be encrypted.

4758 key generation gives the option to generate *replicate 3DES keys*. These are 3DES keys with both halves having the same value. The attacker generates a large number of replicate keys sharing the same type as the target key. A meet in the middle attack is then used to discover the value of two of the replicate keys (a 2^{41} search). The halves of the two replicate keys can then be exchanged to make two 3DES keys with differing halves. Strangely, the 4758 type system permits distinction between true 3DES keys and replicate 3DES keys, but the manual states that this feature is not implemented, and all share the generic 3DES key type. Now that a known 3DES key has been acquired, the conclusion of the attack is simple; let the key be an exporter key, and export all keys using it.

If the attacker does not have the permissions to make replicate keys, he must generate single length DES keys, and change their left half control vector to *'left half of a 3DES key'*. This type casting can be achieved using the *Key Import attack* (section 5.1). If the value of the imported key cannot be found beforehand, 2^{16} keys should be imported as *'single DES data keys'*, used to encrypt a test vector, and an offline 2^{41} search should find one. Re-import the unknown key as a *'left half of a 3DES key'*. Generate 2^{16} 3DES keys, and swap in the known left half with all of them. A 2^{40} search should yield one of them, thus giving you a known 3DES key.

If the attacker cannot easily encrypt a known test pattern under the target key type (as is usually the case for KEKs), he must bootstrap upwards by first discovering a 3DES key of a type under which he has permissions to encrypt a known test vector. This can then be used as the test vector for the higher level key, using a `Key_Export` to perform the encryption.

A given non-exportable key can also be extracted by making two new versions of it, one with the left half swapped for a known key, and likewise for the right half. A 2^{56} search would yield the key (looking for both versions in the same pass through the key space). A distributed effort or special hardware would be required to get results within a few days, but such a key would be a valuable long term key, justifying the expense. A brute force effort in software would be capable of searching for all non-exportable keys in the same pass, further justifying the expense.

6   Conclusions

The cryptoprocessors examined have disappointing dependency upon tight procedural controls in the operating environment – they have failed to realise the full potential of tamper-resistant enclosure. It is strange that the transaction sets of both simple, highly-specialised cryptoprocessors and flexible, complex cryptoprocessors have both been found vulnerable to an individual corrupt insider. Perhaps this is because in security the design rule 'keep it simple' collides with the need for explicitness. The complex systems fail to keep it simple, and the simple ones simplify too severely. The design heuristics presented below may go against the grain of the 'keep it simple' or 'be explicit' principles individually, but the best solution has to be a compromise. In the best case these heuristics go a long way to avoiding security pitfalls, and in the worst case, the heuristics at least reveal the areas in which compromises must be made.

6.1   Design Heuristics

– Known or chosen keys should not be allowed into the key hierarchy.

- Avoid related key sets. If you must have them, keep relationship secret to the cryptoprocessor, or generate them dynamically from a single key.
- Ensure there is a trusted path to the cryptoprocessor available for the issue of sensitive commands.
- Do not rely on key parity bits for integrity checking: the chance of accidental success is too high.
- Do not allow transactions to produce 'garbage': results with no clearly defined meaning when the inputs are invalid. This frustrates analysis.
- Keep access control as fine grain as possible: highly flexible transactions are dangerous without highly flexible access control for them.
- Avoid types whose roles cross hierarchical boundaries.
- If using encryption with short key lengths, limit membership levels of types to avoid the meet in the middle attack, or prevent test vector generation.
- Impose restrictions on key generation to limit the attackers options.
- Ensure that keys are 'atomic' : permitting manipulation of key parts is dangerous.
- Be explicit when generating your type system.
- Don't try to infer type information from a random number: ambiguity is inevitable.

6.2   Future Directions

The VSM and CCA architectures have been shown to be unsatisfactory, and a skeletal toolkit has been presented for analysing these shortcomings. Research awaiting publication includes the application of the new attack techniques to more transaction sets, and future research includes the enlargement of the analysis toolkit, and the long-term aim of designing a transaction set which is resistant to these modes of failure, and is well balanced between simplicity and explicitness.

Acknowledgements

The author wishes to thank (alphabetically) Ross Anderson, Richard Clayton, George Danezis and Larry Paulson for their assistance in verifying and understanding the consequences of these attacks. Work on the VSM was inspired by a talk given by Ross Anderson [7]. The research was conducted thanks to the generous funding of the UK Engineering and Physical Sciences Research Council (EPSRC).

References

1. IBM 4758 PCI Cryptographic Coprocessor, CCA Basic Services Reference And Guide, Release 1.31 for the IBM 4758-001
2. S.M. Matyas, 'Key Handling with Control Vectors', IBM Systems Journal v. 30 n. 2, 1991, p. 151-174

3. S.M. Matyas, A.V. Le, D.G. Abraham, 'A Key Management Scheme Based on Control Vectors', IBM Systems Journal v. 30 n. 2, 1991, pp. 175-191
4. IBM Comment on 'A Chosen Key Difference Attack on Control Vectors', Jan 2000
5. NSM Developers Manual, Computer Security Associates (Pty.) Ltd. , July 1990
6. 'Security Requirements for Cryptographic Modules' Federal Information Processing Standards 140-1
7. 'The Correctness of Crypto Transaction Sets' R. Anderson, April 2000

Bandwidth-Optimal Kleptographic Attacks

Adam Young[1] and Moti Yung[2]

[1] Dept. of Computer Science, Columbia University.
[2] CertCo New York, NY, USA.

Abstract. Cryptographic and physical leakage attacks on devices and systems which implement cryptosystems, is an area of much recent activities. One type of attacks are what is called kleptographic attacks which are mounted against black-box cryptosystems. They are issued by and serve solely the designer/manufacturer giving it unique advantage. Kleptographic attacks are capable of leaking the private keys of users securely and subliminally to the manufacturer of the black-box system (based on the availability of public values, such as keys (produced when the system is initiated) or signature/ciphertext values (produced by systems in operation). These attacks provide a very high level of security against reverse-engineering since even if the black-box is successfully reverse-engineered, no information can be obtained that compromises the secrets of the users (thus, the unique advantage of the attacker is retained).

Numerous open questions remain in the area. One issue is that the only key generation procedure with known attack is the RSA/ factoring based PKC, while for Discrete Logarithm based keys attacks are not known. Similarly open, is the existence of bandwidth-optimal leakage attacks, namely attacks on a "single signature" in Discrete Logarithm based signatures (both in the full group and prime order sub-group cases).

In this paper, we solve the above open questions. We develop new attack techniques, which unlike earlier attacks, require *only one value* in order to leak the secret. This gives an attack on modular exponentiation keys. We then show how to implement an attack on ElGamal signature which leaks the private key in each signature, and which requires only 160 bits of smoothness in $p - 1$, where p is the common ElGamal prime. The attack utilizes the Newton channel. This channel, however, does not extend to DSA, since DSA operates in a prime order subgroup of Z_p. In the second part of this work, we nevertheless show a subliminal channel attack on DSA that assumes the existence of a small amount of non-volatile memory in the device. This gives a kleptographic attack against DSA that leaks the private key in each signature as well. Non-volatility is only needed to assure the polynomial indistinguishability of the outputs of the devices under attack from that of a normal devices' outputs. We investigate our non-volatility assumption against hardware feasibility (in quite a popular EEPROM devices, used in manufacturing of smart-cards).

Key words: Leakage attacks, subliminal channels, the Newton channel, design methodologies for asymmetric ciphers, kleptographic attacks, attack bandwidth, discrete logarithm based systems, ElGamal, DSA,

Ç.K. Koç, D. Naccache, and C. Paar (Eds.): CHES 2001, LNCS 2162, pp. 235–250, 2001.
© Springer-Verlag Berlin Heidelberg 2001

tamper-proof hardware designs, trust, public scrutiny, non-volatile memory, hardware technologies: EEPROM, ferroelectric.

1   Introduction

This paper is concerned with attacks by the designer/manufacturer of black-box cryptographic systems. The goal is thus to expose non-trivial leakage attacks which are possible in black-box cipher designs (where the implementation design is not scrutinized, as in tamper-proof hardware devices) but which are not necessarily possible in public designs. Indeed, black box usage of cryptography has been encouraged by governments. The US government, for example, has proposed the use of Capstone, a general purpose crypto-processor which grew out of the Clipper Initiative. Furthermore, since the mid 80's the NSA's Commercial COMSEC Endorsement Program has been active in trying to base cryptography on government designed tamper-proof devices (see [Sch], page 598). In addition, DSA is often included in smart card tokens, which constitutes a black-box environment. DSA was proposed as the Digital Signature Standard in the US [DSS91]. The motivation of this paper is to investigate the possibility of (till now unknown) attacks. These attack involve the design of black-box discrete log based systems with sophisticated trapdoors that are bandwidth-optimal (i.e., leak based on availability of a single value), are hard to detect and immune to reverse-engineering, and at the same time are indistinguishable from the attack-free systems.

Note that it is easy to mount certain attacks on black-box devices, e.g., by fixing (or otherwise specifying) the randomness they use. However, when dealing with black box environments, the risks posed by the real possibility of successful reverse-engineering may out-weigh the benefits of this attack when viewed from the perspective of the malicious designer (being a malicious government, say). For example, if the "random" DSA exponent k is chosen pseudorandomly based on a secret seed rather than being chosen truly at random, then the reverse-engineer will gain as much knowledge as the designer if the seed is learned via reverse-engineering. Furthermore, even if the seed is chosen randomly for each chip, the company responsible for the programming of the chip learns the seeds. On the other hand for example, the attacks we present in this paper are carried out in such a way that even the programmer of the chip gains no knowledge that will help determine the private keys of users. The programmer of the crypto-chip will only learn that a suspicious looking variant of DSA is being implemented. A related, but different, attack on signature schemes which uses weak pseudorandomness has been presented in [BGM97] (in contrast, we use strong randomness/ pseudorandomness in all our attacks, but in combination with a public key and in a different operational setting).

There has been much interest in analyzing cryptosystems with respect to their subliminal leakage. Gus Simmons pioneered much of the work on subliminal channels where the leakage is universal (leaked to everyone) [Si85,Si93,Si94]. Recently, such leakages were suggested not only for leaking information subliminally, but securely (privately) even if the device is later reverse-engineered (increasing the awareness of the need of trust in the manufacturer of black-box devices that looks like they comply with the system's specifications). The basic notions underlying these attacks as well as tools that accomplish them were developed in [YY96,YY97a,YY97b]. Specifically, they introduced the notion of a SETUP attack where a secretly embedded trapdoor (public key) is used to securely leak the secret information out of the cryptosystem. Their attacks are geared specifically towards public key systems and exploit randomness and subliminal channels in key generation, message encryption, and signing. The number of leakages needed for recovery of the secret by the attacker was called the setup "bandwidth." For key generation stage which produces the key and nothing more, an optimal-bandwidth of one value is a must. All the earlier attacks on discrete log based systems like the ElGamal cryptosystem, the ElGamal Digital Signature algorithm and the DSA (Digital Signature Algorithm) leak the private signing key (say) over the course of two (or more) signatures and no bandwidth optimal attack was known. Therefore, key generation attacks on discrete log. systems were not known either (in contrast with RSA/factoring).

The entire issue of optimal bandwidth attacks was open in discrete log based system and we solve it in this work. We first utilize the elegant Newton subliminal channel to mount optimal-bandwidth attacks on discrete logarithm keys and ElGamal signatures. We then apply a new subliminal channel attack on DSA (the first technique does not apply to it). Our second attack requires a limited amount of non-volatile memory in the computing environment. We also investigate the feasibility and attack life time in the required environment in realistic hardware devices employing EEPROM and the emerging ferroelectric technologies.

Organization: Next we recall and present the basic definitions of the notions and systems we use. Section 3 presents the attack based on the Newton channel discrete log cryptosystems. Sections 4 and 5 then give and analyze the attack on the DSA scheme. The conclusion is in Section 6, and the Appendix presents detailed hardware background explaining available implementations of some of our conditions in existing hardware technologies.

2   Definitions

Our attacks utilize the notion of what is called a SETUP attack (Secretly Embedded Trapdoor with Universal Protection). The following is the definition of a (regular) setup [YY97a]:

Definition 1. *Assume that C is a black-box cryptosystem with a publicly known specification. A SETUP mechanism is an algorithmic modification made to C to get C' such that:*

1. *The input of C' agrees with the public specifications of the input of C.*
2. *C' computes efficiently using the attacker's public encryption function E (and possibly other functions as well), contained within C'.*

3. *The attacker's private decryption function D is not contained within C' and is known only by the attacker.*
4. *The output of C' agrees with the public specifications of the output of C. At the same time, it contains published bits (of the user's secret key) which are easily derivable by the attacker (the output can be generated during key-generation or during system operation like message sending).*
5. *Furthermore, the output of C and C' are polynomially indistinguishable to everyone except the attacker.*
6. *After the discovery of the specifics of the setup algorithm and after discovering its presence in the implementation (e.g., reverse-engineering of hardware tamper-proof device), users (except the attacker) cannot determine past (or future) keys.*

Observe that the above definition does not quantify the number of invocations of C' for which the SETUP attack is carried out. Hence, it is implicitly assumed that for all invocations of C', the output contains the published bits of the user's secret key. In this work we change this quantification from being unbounded to being polynomially bounded in some security parameter k (typically, the same security parameter as in the underlying cryptosystem). This small change of explicit bound is merely motivated by the reality of hardware devices, with finite ability to keep/ change a certain state (as a property of the underlying technology – we will see an example later). Informally the attack works as follows, the attacker chooses some polynomial $poly'$ (in k) and implements C'. For the first $poly'$ invocations of C', the SETUP attack will be in effect. The user then chooses his or her own polynomial $poly$, and runs C' that many times. Only if $poly > poly'$ are there invocations of C' for which the SETUP attack is not carried out (i.e., C' behaves honestly). In this case the last $poly - poly'$ invocations of C' are identical to C. In our attack on DSA, we show that if $poly'$ is large enough (which is achievable in practice), then C' will have to be invoked polynomially many times to reach the point at which it behaves identically to C (in the appendix we show how this can easily be 14 years under a reasonable pace assumption, by which time the technology is likely to become obsolete).

Below we give a definition of a SETUP attack to reflect this idea of boundedness.

Definition 2. *Assume that C is a black-box cryptosystem with a publicly known specification. A (poly)-bounded SETUP mechanism is an algorithmic modification made to C to get C' such that it has the six properties of SETUP and in addition it has the following property:*
7. The SETUP attack is carried out a polynomial number of times in k (where k is the security parameter of the underlying cryptosystem), after which C' behaves identically to C.

Signature Schemes:
The following is a review of the ElGamal digital signature algorithm [ElG85]. Let p be a large prime, and let $g \in Z_p$ be an element with order $p - 1$. The signing private key is $x \in_R Z_{p-1}$, and the public signature verification key is

$y = g^x \bmod p$. Let H be a one-way hash function. To sign an arbitrary message m, the following algorithm is performed:

1. $k \in_R Z_{p-1}$
2. $a = g^k \bmod p$
3. $b = k^{-1}(H(m) - xa) \bmod p - 1$
4. output the signature (a, b)

To verify (a, b) the verifier makes sure that $y^a a^b = g^{H(m)} \bmod p$.

We will review the Digital Signature Algorithm (DSA). Let p be a large prime number such that $q \mid p - 1$ where q concretely is chosen to be a 160 bit prime number and p is standardized to some concrete range (512-2048 bits length) as well. Let g be an element in Z_p with order q. The signing private key is x where $x \in_R Z_q$, and the public verification key is $y = g^x \bmod p$. Let SHA denote the Secure Hash Algorithm. To sign the message m, we compute:

1. $k \in_R Z_q$
2. $a = (g^k \bmod p) \bmod q$
3. $b = k^{-1}(SHA(m) + xa) \bmod q$
4. output the signature (a, b)

To verify (a, b) the verifier makes sure that $a = (g^{SHA(m)/b} y^{a/b} \bmod p) \bmod q$.

Finally, we will now introduce the underlying cryptographic assumption which is utilized in both attacks in this paper. This assumption is based on the Diffie-Hellman (DH) assumption [DH76], but adds additional hiding of the secret. Here g and the prime p are public, and v, v' which divide $p - 1$ are also public. We will refer to it as the Diffie-Hellman Plus Sum (DH-PS) assumption.

Diffie-Hellman Plus Sum Assumption: Let $A = g^a \bmod p$, $B = g^b \bmod p$, and $c = a + b \bmod v$, where $v \mid p - 1$. It is intractable to compute $(g^{ab} \bmod p) \bmod v'$ where $v' \mid p - 1$, and $|v'| \geq M$ (concretely M is 160), given A, B, and c.

Here $|v'|$ denotes the bit length of v'. Clearly, if we can solve DH, then we can solve the DH-PS assumption and the DH-PS is randomly self reducible (namely, we can randomize the input instance and if the randomized new instance is solvable, we can translate the result to the result of the original input instance).

3   SETUP Attacks Based on the Newton Channel

We start by showing optimal attacks on cryptosystems that operate in all of Z_p (ElGamal type), rather than in a prime order subgroup. Our SETUP attack utilizes the the Newton Channel and leaks the private key in each and every signature. The Newton Channel was given in [AVPN].

3.1   Review of the Newton Channel

Let $p = qm + 1$ be prime, and let q be prime. Furthermore, assume that m is smooth, and that g generates Z_p. For security it is assumed that computing discrete logs in the group generated by g^m is hard. Let c be the covert message that is to be displayed. To display c in an exponentiation mod p using base g, a value k' mod $(p - 1)/m$ is chosen randomly, and we solve for k in $k = c + k'm$ mod $p - 1$. Hence,

$$k \equiv c \; mod \; m$$

The user then publishes $r = g^k$ mod p, as in any discrete log based cryptosystem (such as the ElGamal digital signature scheme). The recipient, who can be anyone who decides to recover c, can recover c as follows. The recipient solves for z in the equation,

$$(g^q)^z \equiv r^q \; mod \; p$$

This can be done since the order of the subgroup of Z_p generated by g^q is smooth. Let B be the largest prime in m (i.e., its smoothness). Using Pohlig-Hellman [Poh78] and Polard's Rho [Pol78], this requires time $O(B^{1/2})$. It then follows that,

$$c \equiv z \; mod \; m$$

The clever Newton Channel was also modified to become narrowcast as opposed to the broadcast channel given above. This is done by replacing q with two different primes q_1 and q_2, and having the sender and receiver a priori secretly share the signing private key mod q_2 and having the sender keep the signing key mod q_1 private. This however, requires a more specialized form for the factorization of $p - 1$, and may result in reducing the security of the underlying system. In the SETUP we describe below, no such a priori secret exchange is required, and this specialized form for $p - 1$ is not needed. Thus, the SETUP attack can be utilized securely and subliminally under the observance of a warden, as in the case of Simmons original Prisoner's Problem, *without* requiring that the prisoners exchange a secret before going to prison.

3.2   Setting up a Discrete Log Based Key Generation

It is now not hard to add a setup attack to the Newton Channel to leak the private exponent x in $y = g^x$ mod p where g generates Z_p and $p = mm'q + 1$. Here m is smooth and q is a prime which is greater than or equal to 160 bits in length. m' can be any value. The attack is mounted by computing $c = E(seed)$, where E is a public key encryption algorithm. E can be an elliptic curve cryptosystem which outputs 310 bit ciphertexts. Hence, m must be 310 bits in this case. Provided $c < m$, the value for $seed$ is used in the attack. Rather than choosing k' randomly as in the Newton Channel, it can be chosen by applying a pseudorandom generator to the value $seed$. The range of the pseudorandom generator is $Z_{m'q}$. k is computed in the same way as in the Newton Channel. Therefore, anyone in possession of the private key corresponding to E can recover the value for $seed$ and reconstruct k' and hence k.

Theorem 1 *Assuming there is a smooth number within the factorization of $p-1$ which is large enough to be greater than the size of public key ciphertexts, there exists a SETUP attack against any public exponentiation modulo p under the Diffie-Hellman plus Sum assumption.*

3.3   Adding a SETUP Mechanism on Top of the Newton Channel

Let q be prime, and let $p = mm'q + 1$. We insist that m is smooth and even and 160 bits in length. We do not insist on any particular form for m'. We will make the simplifying assumption that q is 160 bits, though many different configurations on the sizes of m and q are possible. We only require that $q < m$. Let $x' \bmod q$ be the attacker's private key, and let $y' = g^{mm'x'} \bmod p$ be the attackers corresponding public key (which is not published). Let $x \in_R Z_{p-1}$ be the unwary user's private key, and let $y = g^x \bmod p$ be the corresponding public key. The attack aims to securely and subliminally leak x in the sense of a SETUP to the attacker via $r = g^k \bmod p$ (as in the Newton Channel), which is output by the device.

Assume that y' has been placed in the discrete log cryptosystem device that is to be SETUP. The attack is mounted as follows. The device chooses $R \in_R Z_q$. The device then solves for c in,

$$c = R + x \bmod q$$

Now, unlike in the Newton Channel, k' is *not* chosen randomly. Instead, the device computes k' pseudorandomly based on y' and c. To be more specific, the device solves for k' as follows.

$$k' = H(y'^R \bmod p)$$

where H is a public pseudorandom function [GGM86] which uses a secret seed that only the attacker and the device knows. We assume that the range of H is $Z_{m'q}$. The device then computes $k = c + k'm \bmod p - 1$. The device outputs $r = g^k \bmod p$ as in the Newton Channel. This value can, for instance be the first value in the pair of values which constitute and ElGamal digital signature.

The attacker can recover x from r as follows. The attacker recovers c in the same way as everyone can using the Newton Channel. The attacker then computes $t = g^c y^{-1} \bmod p$. Note that $t = g^R \bmod p$. The attacker then solves for k' as follows.

$$k' = H(t^{mm'x'} \bmod p)$$

k is then recovered by computing $k = c + k'm \bmod p - 1$. In most (if not all) digital signature algorithms, such as ElGamal, knowledge of k implies knowledge of x.

3.4   Security

Note that the overall security of x is inherently reduced for the users of the system overall, due to the existing smoothness in $p - 1$. If we suppose in the worst case that $(p - 1)/q$ is entirely smooth, then the users really only posses private keys of the form $x \bmod q$. So, it is this private key that we will show is intractable to recover without x'. Hence, to show security, we must show that it is intractable to recover $x \bmod q$ without x'. To show that it is a SETUP, we must show that the chosen r is polynomially indistinguishable from normally constructed (chosen) values r given $x \bmod q$ and not given the secret seed to H.

Claim 1 *It is intractable to recover $x \bmod q$ without x' given r, y', $x \bmod m'$, and the secret seed to H, assuming that the Diffie-Hellman plus Sum assumption holds.*

Proof. Since $p - 1$ has the requisite amount of smoothness, c can be computed efficiently from r by anyone. Thus, we know k iff we know k', because k is the Chinese Remainder of c and k'. Since k is the "randomly chosen" secret exponent used in the signature which is output (i.e., the secret exponent used to construct the ElGamal signature pair), k is known iff x is known. It follows that k' is known iff $x \bmod q$ is known, since we are given $x \bmod m'$. From c we then compute $t = g^R = g^c y^{-1} \bmod p$. Now, in the absence of the application of H in the attack, we know k' iff we can solve the DH-PS problem with $v = q$ and $v' = (p - 1)/q$, since we know $t = g^R \bmod p$, $y' = g^{x'} \bmod p$, and $c = R + x \bmod q$. Thus, adding the use of H in no way helps in recovering x without x'. Hence, for secrecy of $x \bmod q$, knowledge of the secret seed to H is thus superfluous. QED.

If $x \bmod m'$ is not given away, then the security of the system still holds. It follows that even if the device is reverse-engineered at a later time and y' is found, this does not help the reverse-engineer figure out x. Hence, property (6) in the definition of a SETUP holds. We note that we had originally tried to reduce the security of this system to that of DSA itself. The idea was to make c the DSA "signature equation", which has the same effect as above: it hides $x \bmod q$ using a randomly chosen value mod q. The problem is that all signature equations include a variable which is a commitment of the randomly chosen signature exponent, which in the case of our attack, hasn't even been computed yet (we *must* Chinese Remainder k' with c to get it).

Claim 2 *the random variables: k in the attack and k as computed normally are polynomially indistinguishable given x and y', but not given the secret seed to H.*

Proof. Everyone knows c for each signature. Since c and x are known, R can be found from the equation $c = R + x \bmod q$. Once R is obtained, the quantity $(y'^R \bmod p) \bmod (p - 1)/q$ can be computed. Recall that in a given signature which has been set up, this is the preimage under H of k'. However, without knowing the secret seed to the pseudorandom function H, it follows from the definition of a pseudorandom function that the output of H (in this case k') is indistinguishable from randomness (by standard arguments a distinguisher for the function can be constructed from a distinguisher for the random variables). Since c is truly random, and since k' is pseudorandom, when they are Chinese Remaindered, the resulting k is pseudorandom and the same argument follows. QED.

If the exponents used to compute the signatures in each case are indistinguishable (as random variables), then the presence of attacks in the device are also indistinguishable since from the perspective of a user who knows his own private key, k is the only information conveyed to the user by the device (it can be recovered using the user's own x). It follows that property (5) of a being a SETUP is satisfied. Note that if each device is given a unique secret seed, then reverse engineering one device does not help in determining whether another device is contaminated (in other words: under attack) or not. Also, whether or not this seed is known, forward security of x holds due to the use of DH-PS in the attack. Properties 1 through 4 of a SETUP hold for this system. So, we have therefore shown the following.

Theorem 2 *Assuming at least M ($M = 160$) bits of smoothness in $p - 1$, there exists a SETUP attack against ElGamal (and its variants) that leaks the private key in each digital signature, assuming the security of Diffie-Hellman plus Sum.*

4   Attack on Subgroup Based Signature Schemes

It was observed in [AVPN] that DSA does not support the Newton Channel. This is because all of the users of the system use a value g which generates a prime order subgroup of Z_p whereas the existence of the Newton Channel requires g whose order has some smoothness. The question therefore remains whether or not an optimal bandwidth SETUP attack exists against DSA and its variants (e.g., Nyberg Rueppel [NR94]). In this section we answer this question in the affirmative.

The attack below relies on two specific realistic conditions. First, we assume that each specific cryptographic black-box contains within it a unique private random identifier string. This requirement can be practically met using a keyed hash function during the programming of the crypto device (knowing the key for the hash function does not compromise the DSA private keys of users, however). Note that each Capstone chip has a unique device identifier[1].

The second requirement is that each black-box device has poly-sized nonvolatile memory which can be read and written to. This can be realized using

---

[1] which may differ from another identifier stored in Capstone's E^2PROM

Electrically Erasable Programmable Read-Only Memory (E^2PROM), for instance.

4.1   System Setup

To mount the attack, the designer generates a private key $x' \in_R Z_q$ and places the corresponding public key $y' = g^{x'} \mod p$ in the device. A portion of the non-volatile memory in the device will be used to store a counter cnt which is initially zero. This counter will be incremented by one for each signature that is output by the device. Let MAX denote the maximum value of cnt. Also, let ID denote the unique (cryptographically secure) identifier for the black-box. Hence, each device initially contains the triple (y', cnt, ID) where ID varies from device to device.

4.2   Signing and Verifying

To sign the message m, the device does not choose the DSA exponent k randomly, but rather chooses it pseudorandomly. Here x, y, g, p, q are as in DSA. The following is the SETUP version of the DSA signing algorithm:

1. read cnt from non-volatile memory
2. if $cnt \geq MAX$ then
3. $k \in_R Z_q$
4. else
5. $B = H(ID, cnt)$
6. $k' = B - x \mod q$
7. $k = (y'^{k'} \mod p) \mod q$
8.   write $cnt = cnt + 1$ to non-volatile memory
9. $a = (g^k \mod p) \mod q$
10. $b = k^{-1}(SHA(m) + xa) \mod q$
11. output (a, b) as the signature on m

     Here H is a publicly specified pseudorandom function, and ID is used as the secret seed to it. We assume that the range of H is Z_q. The signature is verified as in normal DSA. The intuition behind this attack is that B, which would typically be displayed through a subliminal channel, is in fact not displayed at all since it is already known to the malicious designer.

4.3   Recovering the Signing Private Key

Given x' and the list of device IDs, the signing private key x can be recovered from (y, m, a, b) as follows:

1. for each device identifier ID do:
2.   for $i = 0$ to MAX do:
3. $B = H(ID, i)$

4.　　　$k = ((g^B y^{-1})^{x'} \ mod \ p) \ mod \ q$
5.　　　if $a = (g^k \ mod \ p) \ mod \ q$ (i.e. the DSA signature check passes) then
6.　　　　　output $x = (bk - SHA(m))a^{-1} \ mod \ q$ and halt with TRUE
7. halt with FALSE

The private signing key is found iff the device halts with TRUE. Note that if MAX is really large, then an incremental search algorithm may be preferred over the above, depending upon the number of devices in existence and on how much is known about the particular device that was used to compute (a, b) (e.g., starting from an expected number of signatures at this point of time and searching up and down incrementally). Note that even the programmer of the signing algorithm cannot recover x, since the programmer does not know x', only the person who generates y' knows x' (which is presumably the person who gave the programmer the code to burn into the chip). Note that the user can re-key y anytime without affecting the attack. See the appendix for details on how the counter can be implemented using existing non-volatile semiconductor memory technologies.

5　Security

Claim 3 *It is intractable to recover x without x' given y', i, and the seed ID to H, assuming that the Diffie-Hellman plus Sum assumption holds.*

Proof. Given ID and i, the value for B is known. Thus, the value $g^{k'} \ mod \ p$ is known, since $g^B y^{-1} = g^{k'} \ mod \ p$. Now, due to the fact that k is used as the randomly chosen DSA signature exponent for the signature being constructed, k is known iff x is known (the signature which is output by the device is employed). It remains to show that k (and therefore x) can be found iff the Diffie-Hellman plus Sum assumption does not hold. Since B is pseudorandom, k' is pseudorandom, and hence finding k is exactly the Diffie-Hellman plus Sum problem with $v = v' = q$. QED.

Thus, even the reverse-engineer who obtains ID, y', and the secret seed to H cannot determine past or future private keys x. Hence, property (6) of a SETUP holds for this attack.

Claim 4 *The values for k which are used in the above attack are polynomially indistinguishable from the values k chosen in normal DSA signatures, given y', x, and i, but not given the secret seed ID to H.*

Proof. Since H is a privately seeded pseudorandom function using seed ID, for the first MAX invocations of the device B is chosen pseudorandomly and is indistinguishable from random choices. Since B is pseudorandom, it follows that k' is pseudorandom mod q. This means that k results from pseudorandomly chosen values from Z_p which are then reduced mod q, whereas the original k is generated similarly but with random elements in Z_p. If the spaces are polynomial-time distinguishable, by standard arguments one can contradict the pseudorandomness of H. It follows that the values for k in the first MAX invocations are indistinguishable from random choices. For the remaining invocations, k is chosen as in DSA itself. QED.

Therefore, the device's behavior is indistinguishable from an uncontaminated device, even for the user who knows x, and hence property (5) of a SETUP is therefore met. By placing unique ID's in each device, the reverse-engineer cannot distinguish contaminated devices from uncontaminated ones without individually reverse-engineering them all. Properties 1-4, and 7 hold for this attack. We have therefore shown the following.

Theorem 3 *There exists a poly-bounded SETUP attack against DSA which leaks the private key of the user in each signature based on the Diffie-Hellman plus Sum assumption in a prime order subgroup.*

We note that In the attack above, it would be possible to eliminate the need for writable non-volatile memory if a reliable source of time is available. If the time counter is never reset, and it has sufficient resolution that the same time value is never used for more than one signature, and the attacker can guess the time of signing well enough that it is practical to try all possibilities, then the counter can be eliminated and time can be used as the input to the pseudorandom function. Whether a counter or a timer is more practical depends on the application and the setting.

6   Conclusion

We showed how to use the Newton Channel to implement an optimal SETUP attack against ElGamal Signatures assuming 160 bits of smoothness in $p-1$, based on the Diffie-Hellman plus Sum problem. The notion of a poly-bounded SETUP attack was introduced and an optimal SETUP attack on DSA was presented which securely and subliminally leaks the DSA private key to the implementor in each signature. Hence, in the attack on DSA it was shown that explicit subliminal channels are not needed at all to effectively leak private DSA keys at an optimal bandwidth. These results imply that a single signature can leak a secret securely if a manufacturer attacks a black-box implementation. A cryptographic assumption of perhaps independent interest is utilized.

References

[AVPN]   R. Anderson, S. Vaudenay, B. Preneel, K. Nyberg. The Newton Channel. In *Workshop on Information Hiding*, Isaac Newton Institute, 1996. (also downloaded from Ross Anderson's homepage).

[BGM97]   M. Bellare, S. Goldwasser and D. Micciancio. Pseudo-Random Number Generation within Cryptographic Algorithms: the DSS Case. In *Advances in Cryptology—CRYPTO '97*, Springer-Verlag.

[DH76]   W. Diffie, M. Hellman. New Directions in Cryptography. In volume IT-22, n. 6 of *IEEE Transactions on Information Theory*, pages 644–654, Nov. 1976.

[DSS91]   Proposed Federal Information Processing Standard for Digital Signature Standard (DSS). In volume 56, n. 169 of *Federal Register*, pages 42980–42982, 1991.

[ElG85]   T. ElGamal. A Public-Key Cryptosystem and a Signature Scheme Based on Discrete Logarithms. In *Advances in Cryptology—CRYPTO '84*, pages 10–18, 1985. Springer-Verlag.

[GGM86]   O. Goldreich, S. Goldwasser, and S. Micali, How to Construct Random Functions. In *Journal of the ACM*, 33(4), pages 210–217, 1986.

[LMS]   J. Lacy, D. Mitchell, W. Schell. CryptoLib: Cryptography in Software. In *Proceedings of the IV UNIX Security Symposium*, USENIX Association.

[NR94]   K. Nyberg, R. Rueppel. Message Recovery for Signature Schemes Based on the Discrete Logarithm Problem. In *Advances in Cryptology—Eurocrypt '94*, pages 182–193, 1994. Springer-Verlag.

[Poh78]   S. C. Pohlig. An Improved Algorithm for Computing Logarithms over GF(p) and its Cryptographic Significance. In *IEEE Transactions on Information Theory*, v. 24, n. 1, pages 106–110, 1978.

[Pol78]   J. M. Pollard. Monte Carlo Methods for Index Computation (mod p). In *Mathematics of Computation*, v. 32, n. 143, pages 918–924, 1978.

[Sch]   B. Schneier. Applied Cryptography, 1994. John Wiley and Sons, Inc.

[Sc91]   C. Schnorr. Efficient Signature Generation by Smart Cards. In *Journal of Cryptology*, v. 4, pages 161–174, 1991.

[Si85]   G. J. Simmons. The subliminal Channel and Digital Signatures. In *Advances in Cryptology—Eurocrypt '84*, pages 51–57, 1985.

[Si93]   G. J. Simmons. Subliminal Communication is Easy Using the DSA. In *Advances in Cryptology—Eurocrypt '93*, 1993.

[Si94]   G. J. Simmons. Subliminal Channels: past and present. In *European Tra. on Telecommunications* V. 5, 1994, pages 459–473, 1994.

[YY96]   A. Young, M. Yung. The Dark Side of Black-Box Cryptography. In *Advances in Cryptology—CRYPTO '96*, pages 89–103, Springer-Verlag.

[YY97a]   A. Young, M. Yung. Kleptography: Using Cryptography against Cryptography. In *Advances in Cryptology—Eurocrypt '97*, pages 62–74. Springer-Verlag.

[YY97b]   A. Young, M. Yung. The Prevalence of Kleptographic Attacks on Discrete-Log Based Cryptosystems. In *Advances in Cryptology—CRYPTO '97*, Springer-Verlag.

A   Appendix: Implementing the Counter

We will now describe ways of implementing the non-volatile counter using existing technologies, taking care to observe the precise physical operating limitations of these technologies. In particular we describe how to implement the counter on the ST19SF64 chip from ST Microelectronics. We conclude with a description of how the counter can be greatly simplified using emerging (ferroelectric) technologies.

A.1 Background Information on EEPROMs

The predecessor of Electrically Erasable Programmable Read Only Memories (EEPROM) memories was Erasable PROM memories (EPROM) which require the use of UV light for erasure. Though EPROM memories can be rewritten a number of times, a quartz crystal window is needed in the chip to permit erasure, and erasing typically requires 20 minutes or so. The first available EEPROM chips also allowed multiple writes, but unlike EPROMs, the memory could be erased electrically using around 20 volts or so. This however required a separate pin on the chip for the high programming voltage, whereas only 5 volts (the standard operating voltage) was needed for the read operation. Eventually the technology advanced to where only 5 volts were needed for reads and writes. These chips contain voltage amplifiers internally to perform the erase operation.

It is a thesis of this paper that this 5 volt (and lower) EEPROM technology marked a major turning point in the level of trust that must be placed in the manufacturers of cryptographic processors, whether the processors contain non-volatile memory or not. The reason for this is that for the first time stateless tamper-proof microprocessors became indistinguishable from tamper-proof microprocessors containing EEPROM, since no crystal window is needed, and since the operating voltages are the same.

EEPROMs have two major operating characteristics: durability and data retention. Durability refers to the number of times in which a given byte can be erased and written to, and data retention refers to how long a byte can reliably store its value after it is written to. Modern EEPROM memories typically have an endurance of 10^5 and a data retention value of 10 years or so. Note that with these characteristics, in theory a byte can be used for more than 10 years, provided that it is not written to more than 100,000 times, and provided that no more than 10 years passes between each write (in many cases the retention has to do with the discharging of a capacitive layer in the memory cell). These operating characteristics imply that it is not possible to simply utilize 4 bytes of EEPROM as a 64 bit counter, since the lower order byte is not durable enough to handle that many writes.

The reasons for these limitations have to do with the device physics of modern EEPROMs. We will now briefly summarize why these limitations exist. Modern EEPROMs are based on a stored charge concept in which the presence or absence of a stored charge in a MOSFET transistor (typically in a "floating" gate which is isolated by SiO_2) affects the flow of electrons from the drain to the source leads. Another technology (SNOS) utilizes charge trapping material instead of a floating gate. The presence or absence of (a significant amount of current) between these leads indicates a binary 0 or 1, and this current is controlled by the electric field given off the stored charge if charge is present. A number of methods are used to inject and remove the stored electrons in the transistor, the most prominent being quantum mechanical tunneling, and hot electron injection.

The factors affecting endurance are tunnel oxide breakdown, gate oxide breakdown, and trap-up. The first two cause short circuits in the device, thus rendering it unable to store charge. Trap-up refers to electrons being trapped in the tunneling insulator, thus weakening the injection fields and therefore not allowing enough charge to get to the stored charge area during programming. For floating gate devices, there is no intrinsic retention problem (and is limited only by device defects). Clearly, full testing is not possible since the tests would be concluded long after the competitive lifetime of the chip. High temperature tests are thus performed, and most retention failures are actually endurance failures. The retention characteristics are different for charge trapping devices, though these are typically only used in military applications which require reliable operation in radioactive environments (e.g., to insure reliable missile guidance systems in fallout).

A.2   An Attack Using the ST19SF64

Below are the specifications for the ST19SF64 CMOS Smartcard MCU chip by ST Microelectronics, with 64k EEPROM, 32k user ROM, and 960 bytes RAM.

Byte write time = 1 milisecond
Data Retention = 10 years
Automatic write operation with internal control timer
V_{CC} = 5 Volts (or 3 volts)
Endurance = 100,000 erase/write cycles

Note that the read operation requires on the order of nanoseconds.

Typically, cryptoprocessors utilize a portion of E^2PROM for the cryptocode, so we will assume in our attack that 32k of E^2PROM is reserved for cryptographic operations and that 32k are available to implement the counter cnt. We assume that the secret cryptographic device identifier ID, and the attacker's public key y' are stored in the 32k of E^2PROM along with the cryptographic code.

A.3   Implementing the Non-volatile Counter

If we were to utilize, say 4 bytes of non-volatile memory for a counter cnt that is incremented from zero we will not get very far since only 100,000 writes can be made reliably. We thus need to design a counter that can exceed 100,000 utilizing the 32k available bytes. First observe that the counter value need not be incremented by one, since it is simply used as an argument to a random oracle H. Hence, all that is needed is a polynomial number of unique values for cnt. Using this observation, a counter permitting 2^{30} different values can be synthesized as follows.

The counter cnt is the entire 32k bytes. We divide the 32k byte memory space into 16k words, each of which is 2 bytes. Initially, every word is zero. To increment the counter, we read in the words from memory until the least significant word which is not all binary 1's is found (if any). We then add 1 to this value if found. Note that each word can only be incremented at most $2^{16} - 1$ times. It follows that each byte is only written to at most $2^{16} - 1$ times (which is less than 100,000 as required). The counter can no longer be incremented when all of the bits in the counter are 1. It follows that there are $2^{14} * 2^{16} = 2^{30}$ different possible values for cnt. This implementation of cnt requires that all 32k bytes of cnt be read in the computation of B using the random oracle H. Since reads require on the order of nanoseconds, this is still very fast in comparison to the time required to compute the signature.

A.4   Operating Statistics of the Attack

We were unable to find benchmarks for the time required to compute a DSA signature on a dedicated crypto-processor. So, we will cite the time required to compute a DSA signature in software on a SPARC II using CryptoLib. The time required in this case is 430 milliseconds where $|p| = 768$ bits [LMS]. Note that Cryptolib uses some of the best algorithms to do modular exponentiation, including Montgomery Reduction, Vector Addition Chains, and Karatsuba multiplication. Below we give some of the characteristics of our attack in this setting:

SPARC II CryptoLib DSA signing time = 430 ms
time to read cnt (i.e., time to read all 32k bytes) = 4.92 ms
time to update $cnt \leq 4.92 + 2 = 6.92$ ms
total non-volatile memory based overhead ≤ 11.84 ms
number of signatures which are SETUP = 2^{30}
time required to exhaust $cnt = 2^{30} * 430 \ ms > 14$ years

It follows from the above that the time required to mount the attack can be "absorbed" by the time required to compute the DSA signature. Measures should be taken to insure that the signing time is the same whether or not all values for cnt have been exhausted, to avoid detection of the attack.

Electromagnetic Analysis: Concrete Results

Karine Gandolfi, Christophe Mourtel, and Francis Olivier

Gemplus Card International, Card Security Group
Parc d'Activités de Gémenos, B.P. 100, 13881 Gémenos France
{Karine.Gandolfi, Christophe.Mourtel, Francis.Olivier}@gemplus.com
http://www.gemplus.com/smart

Abstract. Although the possibility of attacking smart-cards by analyzing their electromagnetic power radiation repeatedly appears in research papers, all accessible references evade the essence of reporting conclusive experiments where actual cryptographic algorithms such as DES or RSA were successfully attacked.

This work describes electromagnetic experiments conducted on three different CMOS chips, featuring different hardware protections and executing a DES, an alleged COMP128 and an RSA. In all cases the complete key material was successfully retrieved.

Keywords: smart cards, side channel leakage, electromagnetic analysis, SEMA, DEMA, DPA, SPA.

1 Introduction

In addition to its usual complexity postulates, cryptography silently assumes that secrets can be physically protected in tamper-proof locations.

All cryptographic operations are physical processes where data elements must be represented by physical quantities in physical structures. These physical quantities must be stored, sensed and combined by the elementary devices (*gates*) of any technology out of which we build tamper-resistant machinery. At any given point in the evolution of a technology, the smallest logic devices must have a definite *physical extent*, require a certain *minimum time* to perform their function and dissipate a minimal *switching energy* when transiting from one state to another.

This paper analyzes an area of recent interest – electromagnetic side-channel attacks – which exploits correlations between secret data and variations in power radiations emitted by tamper-resistant devices.

Since any electrical current flowing through a conductor induces electromagnetic (EM) emanations, it seems natural to look for the same phenomenon in the vicinity of a semiconductor. As the power consumption of a tamper-resistant device varies while data are being processed, so does the EM field and one may legitimately expect to extract secret information from a relevant EM analysis.

In some cases, power curves appear to convey no information: this happens when power does not vary or does vary but in a way seemingly uncorrelated to the

Ç.K. Koç, D. Naccache, and C. Paar (Eds.): CHES 2001, LNCS 2162, pp. 251–261, 2001.

secret data. Very much simplified, the chip's global current consumption can be looked upon as a big river concentrating the sum of the small tributaries flowing into it. If the subcomponents' contributions could be determined, then the small streams would be isolated. This is impossible by direct electrical measurement but should become possible by eavesdropping local EM radiations. By opposition to power analysis, this requires the design of special probes and the development of advanced measurement methods that focus very accurately selected points of the chip.

For the sake of scientific accuracy, we would like to precise that this paper does not claim the discovery of EM information leakage (which is attested by numerous accessible sources [1,2,3,8,9,10,12]); we rather report *complete* and conclusive experiments where secrets used by *specific* cryptographic algorithms running on eight-bit CMOS microcontrollers were *thoroughly* disclosed.

Intentionally, none of the tested programs featured software counter-measures against power or EM attacks and in each case the EM information leakage was compared to the result of power attacks performed under identical experimental conditions.

The rest of this work is organized as follows: in section 2 we describe the experimental conditions under which our results were obtained. The results themselves are presented, commented and compared to power leakage in section 3.

2   Electromagnetic Analysis

2.1   Probe Design

Chip-scale electromagnetic analysis requires very small probes, similar in dimension to the chip areas to be isolated. The standard layout of a smart card chip shows functional blocks of a few hundred microns (CPU, cryptoprocessor). This defines an upper bound for the probe size.

Although this experimental study was carried out by successively trying different kinds of sensors such as hard disk heads, integrated inductors and magnetic loops [5,7], the best EM signals were collected using simple hand-made probes. These are solenoids made of a coiled copper wire of outer diameters varying between 150 and 500 microns. An example is shown in Figure 1.

2.2   Electrical Behavior

An important advantage of such inductive sensors is their broadband. In other words, a resonance frequency which is much higher than the highest frequency that the analyzed chip is able to generate. The characterization of such sensors is a rather difficult task requiring the generation of a constant-magnitude magnetic-field over a very broad spectral band (several tens of MHz).

The main drawback of such probes is their very low output signal (typically 2 to 4 mV peak to peak). Sensitivity can be enhanced at the expense of bigger frequency selectivity, thereby resulting in some bandwidth loss. The trade-off

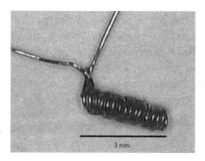

Fig. 1. Electromagnetic Probe.

was finally settled for the benefit of bandwidth as radiation spectra were unknown. The amplitude's weakness was compensated by the use of an advanced acquisition chain featuring a very efficient amplification stage.

Most chips are designed in CMOS technology. Figure 2 shows a CMOS logic inverter. The inverter can be looked upon as a push-pull switch: in grounded cuts off the top transistor, pulling out high. A high in does the inverse, pulling out to ground. CMOS inverters are the basic building-block of all digital CMOS logic, the logic family that has become dominant in very large scale integrated circuits (VLSI).

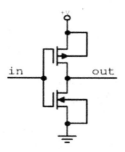

Fig. 2. Elementary CMOS gate.

During a transition from 0 to 1 or *vice-versa*, the device's n and p transistors are on for a short period of time. This results in a short current pulse from V_{dd} to V_{ss}. This (very partially) explains why information leaks when data flips and why the power curve is correlated to the transition's Hamming distance.

This sudden current pulse causes a sudden variation of the EM field surrounding the chip which can be monitored by inductive probes which are particularly sensitive to the related impulsion [5,7]. The electromotive force across the sensor (Lentz' law) relates to the variation of magnetic flux as follows:

$$V = -\frac{d\phi}{dt}$$

where V, ϕ and t denote the probe's output voltage, the magnetic flux sensed by probe and the time. In practice, parasitic resistors and inescapable measurement imprecisions require a slight correction of the probe's output.

Whenever a bit flips, the resulting time signal exhibits a high frequency damped oscillation. Acquisition was optimized to better reflect these variations and data dependencies. Frequency-tuned signal processing can be applied. This may require, approximately, a 1 GHz sampling frequency.

Figure 3 shows a power consumption example while Figure 4 shows the corresponding EM signal. The monitored signal is caused by the execution of a *transfer into accumulator* instruction (TIA) applied to 00h and FFh (the specific instruction name was deliberately changed to keep the chip's identity secret).

EM curves appear to be more noisy than power curves, but feature sharper data signatures. Moreover, EM signals can be phase-reversed given the minus sign in Lentz' law and the probe's spatial position: the magnetic flux is inverted by changing the side of the source where the sensor is present.

To reduce parasite signals, an attempt was made to host the chip and the probe in a Faraday cage. This had little effect and finally proved to be unnecessary. Isolating an experiment from external high frequency radiations proves to be a nontrivial engineering exercise for even if the probe can be hosted in a pollution-free cage, most elements in the acquisition chain remain sensitive to ambient EM noise and prone to mutual (cross-talk) perturbations.

2.3   Spatial Positioning

To increase the chances of capturing data-dependent signals, the probe was positioned in the neighborhood of a region that radiates while the program runs. Areas radiate with different intensities and various code dependencies but, experimentally, the most active points appear to be located near the CPU, data buses and power supply lines. Amongst these three, the CPU seemed to be the most data-dependent.

Each curve in Figure 5 is the difference between two traces: that of 00h $\oplus$ 00h and FFh $\oplus$ 00h. This simple experiment illustrates the information leakage of the exclusive-or instruction *via* the power consumption and EM radiation as measured at five different locations : ROM, EEPROM, RAM, the supply line and the CPU. Each area features a distinct signature either through the signal's shape or magnitude. The CPU clearly stands out by radiating the most informative signal.

Approximating the source as a long linear wire (or the probe as negligibly small), the field's magnitude B decreases (Biot and Savart's law) as the inverse of the distance r between the wire and the probe:

$$B = \frac{\mu_0}{2\pi} \frac{I}{r}$$

where I denotes the current flowing through the wire. It is thus important to perform measurements as closely as possible to the chip. Since the standard

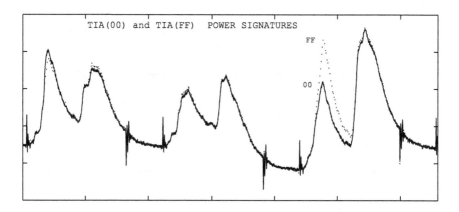

Fig. 3. Current consumption during TIA.

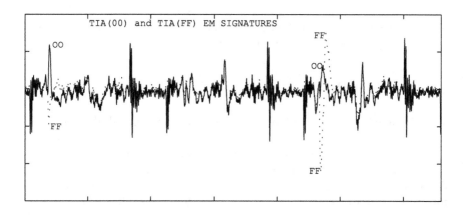

Fig. 4. EM radiation during TIA.

thickness of a card is 800 microns, landing the sensor on its back sets the observation point at 400 or 500 microns away from the target.

This distance may sometimes appear to be prohibitive given the weakness of the EM power radiant and its low signal to noise ratio. However, in some cases the chip's surface can be eroded by mechanical or chemical means [9,3]. This operation (called decapsulation) offers two important advantages: once the chip is bare (if still functional), the probe's coil can be lowered so as to touch the passivation layer and thereby capture the highest possible field. As a side effect, the chip becomes optically visible and its specific blocks can be pinpointed more accurately. Recapsulating the chip after the attack remains possible for industrially-equipped attackers.

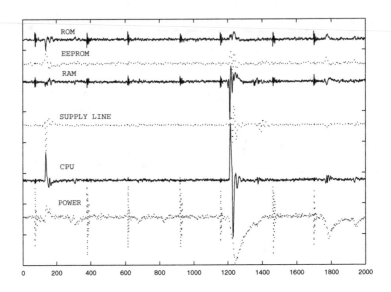

Fig. 5. Differentials between $B(\mathtt{00h} \oplus \mathtt{00h})$ and $B(\mathtt{FFh} \oplus \mathtt{00h})$: significative spikes are located near $t = 100$ and $t = 1200$; other regular spikes are just clock residues.

3   Practical Results

We conducted practical experiments on various devices and algorithms. In this section three of the most significant results are presented. Interestingly, the three were conducted on different chips made by different manufacturers.

One of these chips is protected by a shield and the other two feature randomly synthesized logic (RSL). This means that the CPU is scrambled with other functional and useless blocks to make specific functions difficult to identify. Such designs thwart physical intrusions using Focused Ion Beam test equipment (FIB).

The attacked algorithms were respectively the alleged COMP128 (described in [6] and hereafter denoted ACOMP128), DES and RSA. In all cases software counter-measures were deliberately turned off. For a comparative study, test cards were calibrated with known keys. Power and EM signals were systematically acquired simultaneously. Once conditioned, the EM signals were digitized and processed exactly the same way as classical power signals, using the same sampling frequency, digitizer and software tools. Only their physical nature differed.

J.-J. Quisquater and D. Samyde suggested [12] the following acronyms: DEMA for **D**ifferential **E**lectro**M**agnetic **A**nalysis, by analogy to P. Kocher's **D**ifferential **P**ower **A**nalysis (DPA) [8]. **S**imple **E**lectro**M**agnetic **A**nalysis (SEMA) relates in a similar way to **S**imple **P**ower **A**nalysis (SPA). DA and SA will be used for **D**ifferential and **S**imple **A**nalysis, when the leakage's physical nature happens to be irrelevant. D. Naccache coined the Greek term *cryptophthora* to generically address the phenomenon of side channel leakage.

3.1   Alleged COMP128

In this experiment, the smart card was not decapsulated and therefore the probe was positioned rather approximately. No software DPA/DEMA counter-measures were activated.

A DPA and a DEMA were performed simultaneously on the same batch of 256 chosen messages and related sets of curves. Results are shown in Figure 6: the two attacks generated differential spikes for the same right guess. Despite more noisy measurements, the DEMA provided better peaks than the DPA both in terms of contrast and signal to noise ratio. Equivalently, the DEMA required less acquisitions than the DPA. The sign opposition in the raw signatures remained visible throughout the whole differential analysis process. Moreover, since wrong guesses provided no peaks, the experimental evidence was brought that DEMA could work successfully.

3.2   DES

Having obtained these first results, a new DEMA was attempted on another component. Again, no decapsulation was performed thereby preventing a very accurate positioning. The attacked algorithm was a DES featuring no software counter-measures against DPA. For DPA and DEMA, 500 acquisitions and messages were necessary to infer the secret key.

While performing a DPA, it is expected that the right guess would yield the maximum peaks but, experimentally, strong differential peaks are often observed for wrong guesses. Such false alerts may even rise higher than the right spikes and confuse an attacker trying to make a final decision. This phenomenon stems from the consumption model that underlies classical DPA. Indeed, the signature is usually supposed to be correlated to the data's Hamming weight. In reality this may not match each and every VLSI behavior as other subparts of the chip may also consume power in a correlated manner.

In the present case, a DPA spotted the right guess successfully but with many difficulties. As shown in Figure 7, there were even examples of wrong guesses (39) whose peaks were higher than the right one (15) in absolute value. The corresponding DEMA yielded correctly ordered spikes, smearing the wrong guess peaks and enhancing the right one.

Compared to DPA and for a relevant pinpointed area, experiments generally showed that DEMA tended to reduce the dispersion of peaks to the benefit of the right guess. In other words, the number of wrong guesses was reduced and the final decision made easier. DEMA can therefore be potentially considered experimentally at least as efficient as DPA, in absence of specific software counter-measure.

3.3   Modular exponentiation

The third experiment concerned an RSA exponentiation performed in a decapsulated smart card. The chip's visibility allowed a very close positioning of the sensor and the monitoring of the most energetic part of the EM field.

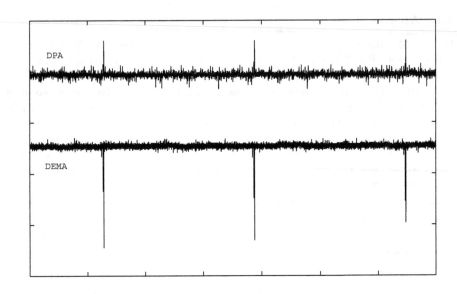

Fig. 6. DPA and DEMA right guess curves for ACOMP128.

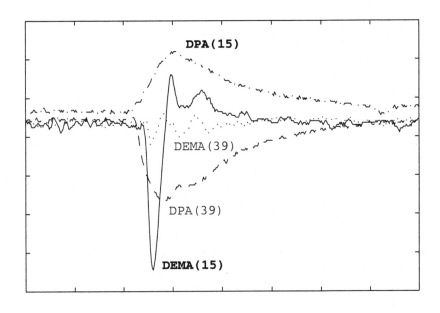

Fig. 7. DPA and DEMA DES curves for a right (15) and a wrong (39) guess.

No software EM/PA counter-measures were implemented to protect the exponentiation (except a constant time implementation). As shown in Figure 8 (lower traces) the power traces did not suggest any apparent pattern that could have exposed the chip to a potential SPA.

Having observed this, the target of our study became the isolation a data-correlated location which is why the chip's surface had to be scanned. The success of this tedious operation was not guaranteed but a suitable point was finally found after several manual positioning attempts.

Two EM signals monitored at this point are shown in Figure 8 (upper traces). They look less noisy than the power curves and happen to contain patterns that leak the key. This illustrates how complementary SEMA and SPA can be.

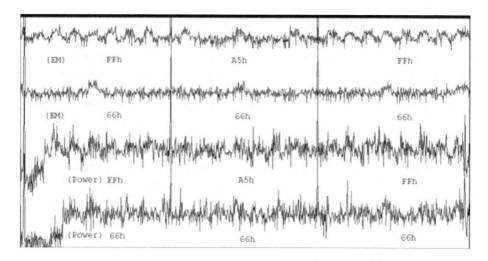

Fig. 8. EM and power traces for two different exponentiations involving three bytes of the private key : **FFA5FFh** and **666666h** (Same message and modulus). Artificial spikes delimitate the three-byte windows where patterns clearly appear.

4   Conclusion and Work in Progress

The purpose of this work was to find out if EM attacks can be implemented in practice; the answer is clearly positive.

Our experiments suggest that although more noisy, EM measurements finally yield better differentials than power signals. DEMA's SNR was higher than DPA's SNR and the correct guess identification was easier, as there were no false alerts due to erroneous peaks. The third experiment is particularly instructive as it shows that SEMA ≠> SPA. As is obvious, this shouldn't lead to the fallacious conclusion that SEMA is in some manner "more powerful" than SPA: we haven't encountered yet the opposite case (SEMA-proof, SPA-vulnerable) but nothing rules out a priori that it might exist. In other words, when PA or EMA does not suffice alone, both can be attempted simultaneously.

EMA's advantage is definitely its capability of exploiting local information. This geometrical degree of freedom is useful as it allows to pinpoint the problematic spots that leak information. PA's major advantage is undoubtedly the relative simplicity of electric measurements as opposed to EM ones.

The manual scanning of the chip's surface performed during this work are, of course, non-exhaustive. The next step in our investigation is the implementation of automatic cartography tools. Note that chip-spots characterized by intensive power radiations (e.g. clock lines) do not necessarily leak data-correlated EM signals. Procedures for evaluating the likelihood of data-correlated leakage are described in [4]. By running such tests on EM signals collected at various locations on a given chip, a cartography of leakage probabilities can be performed. This would give an immediate bird-eye view of the potentially problematic spots in each chip and allow cross-platform comparisons.

Natural EM hardware counter-measures typically include an upper metal layer (contain the radiation), variable random currents, flowing through an active grid and generating noisy fields (blur the radiation[1]) and successive technology shrinks that regularly reduce the elementary transistors' size and make the functional areas more compact (reduce the radiation). Particular synthesis of problematic functions (coding ones as $\{1, 0\}$ and zeros as $\{0, 1\}$) tries to partially cancel the radiation.

It is our opinion that the combination of such hardware counter-measures with particular software coding techniques that inherently prevent specific forms of leakage, provides an acceptable security-level for most commercial applications.

Acknowledgments

We are very grateful to David Naccache, Pascal Moitrel, Christophe Clavier and Marc Joye for their contribution and help which greatly improved the development of this study.

References

1. SEPI'88, Primo simposio nazionale su sicurezza elettromagnetica nella protezione dell'informazione, Rome (Italy), 1988.
2. SEPI'91, Symposium on electromagnetic security for information protection, Rome (Italy), 1991.
3. R. Anderson, M. Kuhn, Tamper Resistance - a Cautionary Note, Proc. of the Second USENIX Workshop on Electronic Commerce, USENIX Association, 1996.
4. J-S. Coron, P. Kocher, and D. Naccache, Statistics and Secret Leakage, Financial Cryptography 2000 (FC'00), Lecture Notes in Computer Science, Springer-Verlag, To appear.

---

[1] Such a counter-measure, called surface oscillators, is reportedly present in Clipper [3]

5. Y. Gao and I. Wolff, *A new miniature magnetic field probe for measuring three-dimensional fields in planar high frequency circuits*, IEEE Trans. on Microwave Theory and Techniques, vol. 44 no. 6, pp. 911–918, 1996.

6. H. Handschuh and P. Paillier, *Reducing the collision probability of alleged* COMP128, In J.-J. Quisquater and B. Schneier, editors, Smart Card Research and Applications (CARDIS'98), vol. 1820 of Lecture Notes in Computer Science, pp. 380–385, Springer-Verlag, 2000.

7. T. Harada, H. Sasaki and Y. Kami, *Investigation on radiated emission characteristics of multilayer printed circuits boards*, IEICE Trans. Commun, E80-B, no. 11, pp. 1645–1651, 1997.

8. P. Kocher, J. Jaffe and B. Jun, *Differential power analysis*, In M. Wiener, editor, Advances in Cryptology – CRYPTO'99, vol. 1666 of Lecture Notes in Computer Science, pp. 388–397, Springer-Verlag, 1999. Also available at: http://www.cryptography.com/dpa/Dpa.pdf.

9. O. Kömmerling and M. Kuhn, *Design principles for tamper-resistant smartcard processors*, In Proc. of the USENIX Workshop on Smartcard Technology (Smartcard'99), pp. 9–20. USENIX Association, 1999.

10. M. Kuhn and R. Anderson, *Soft tempest: Hidden data transmission using electromagnetic emanations*, In D. Aucsmith, editor, Information Hiding, vol. 1525 of Lecture Notes in Computer Science, pp. 124–142. Springer-Verlag, 1998.

11. T. Messerges and E. Dabbish, *Investigations of power analysis attacks on smartcards*, In Proc. of the USENIX Workshop on Smartcard Technology (Smartcard'99). USENIX Association, 1999.

12. J-J. Quisquater and D. Samyde, *A new tool for non-intrusive analysis of smart cards based on electro-magnetic emissions, the* SEMA *and* DEMA *methods*, Presented at the rump session of EUROCRYPT'2000.

NTRU in Constrained Devices

Daniel V. Bailey[1,2], Daniel Coffin[2], Adam Elbirt[2,4], Joseph H. Silverman[3,2], and Adam D. Woodbury[4,2]

[1] Computer Science Department, Brown University
[2] NTRU Cryptosystems, Inc.
[3] Mathematics Department, Brown University
[4] Electrical and Computer Engineering Department, Worcester Polytechnic Institute

Abstract. The growing connectivity offered by constrained computing devices signals a critical need for public-key cryptography in such environments. By their nature, however, public-key systems have been difficult to implement in systems with limited computational power. The NTRU public-key cryptosystem addresses this problem by offering better computational performance than previous practical systems. The efficiency of NTRU is applied to a wide variety of constrained devices in this paper, including the Palm Computing Platform, Advanced RISC Machines ARM7TDMI, the Research in Motion pager, and finally, the Xilinx Virtex 1000 family of FPGAs. On each of these platforms, NTRU offers exceptional performance, enabling a new range of applications to make use of the power of public-key cryptography.

1 Motivation

Since their introduction in the 1970s, the development of microprocessors and public-key cryptosystems has been intervolved. Ever faster, cheaper, better microprocessors have allowed the use of public-key cryptosystems in a dizzying array of applications.

One of the more popular of these is the use of desktop personal computers to mediate the purchase of goods and services on the Internet. For years now, desktop computers have offered adequate performance to make the arduous calculations involved in traditional public-key cryptosystems invisible to the casual user. This performance has resulted in the ubiquitous deployment of crypto-enabled web browsers such as Microsoft's Internet Explorer on desktop PCs.

Conversely, the need for public-key cryptography has led microprocessor vendors to add functionality to their products. Desktop eCommerce led Intel to add random-number generation and unique IDs to the Pentium/III processor. The need for secure authentication in GSM cellular telephone applications has resulted in 8-bit microcontrollers with custom hardware to accelerate modular exponentiation.

The number of embedded systems that require cryptography is about to explode. Just as the ubiquitous PC networking made possible by TCP/IP led to public-key crypto libraries in desktop web browsers, wireless networking is

Ç.K. Koç, D. Naccache, and C. Paar (Eds.): CHES 2001, LNCS 2162, pp. 262–272, 2001.

set to offer universal connectivity to a diverse array of computing devices. From washing machines to cell phones, televisions to automobiles, wireless networking standards such as Bluetooth and IEEE 802.11b will bring networking to devices that previously stood alone. As we've seen on the desktop, with communications comes the need for security, and so for public-key cryptosystems.

In contrast to their desktop-bound, powerful brethren, these embedded devices offer severely constrained computing capacity. Power, memory, and CPU cycles all must be judiciously conserved.

The computational efficiency of NTRU allows implementors to build efficient wirelessly-communicating embedded systems. Furthermore, algorithmic improvements introduced in [4] augment the original construction to allow for greater computational savings.

In this paper, we apply these results in the context of embedded systems. We report on fast NTRU implementations for the Palm Computing Platform, the Research in Motion pager, the Advanced RISC Machines ARM7TDMI, and finally field-programmable gate arrays (FPGAs).

2   The NTRU Public-Key Cryptosystem

NTRU is a public-key cryptosystem based on the Shortest Vector Problem in a lattice. Lattices find application in pure and applied mathematics, computer science, physics, and cryptography. In particular, the SVP has been intensively studied for more than one hundred years for its use in these and other areas of mathematics and science. Theory and experimentation [2] suggest the SVP is difficult in lattices of very high dimension. Such instances of the SVP form the basis of NTRU.

2.1   Basic Setup

NTRU is best described using the ring of polynomials

$$R = Z[X]/(X^N - 1).$$

These are polynomials with integer coefficients

$$a(X) = a_0 + a_1X + a_2X^2 + \cdots + a_{N-1}X^{N-1}$$

that are multiplied together using the extra rule $X^N \equiv 1$. So the product

$$c(X) = a(X) * b(X)$$

is given by

$$c_k = a_0b_k + a_1b_{k-1} + \cdots + a_{N-1}b_{k+1} = \Sigma_{i+j \equiv k \bmod N} \, a_ib_j.$$

In particular, if we write $a(X), b(X)$, and $c(X)$ as vectors

$$a = [a_0, a_1, \cdots, a_{N-1}], \quad b = [b_0, b_1, \cdots, b_{N-1}], \quad c = [c_0, c_1, \cdots, c_{N-1}],$$

then $c = a * b$ is the usual discrete convolution product of two vectors.

To quickly sum up the other relevant basic properties of NTRU:

1. NTRU uses three public parameters (N, p, q) with $\gcd(p, q) = 1$.
2. Typical parameter sets that yield security levels similar to 1024-bit RSA and 4096-bit RSA respectively are $(N, p, q) = (251, 3, 128)$ and $(N, p, q) = (503, 3, 256)$.
3. Coefficients of polynomials are reduced modulo p and/or modulo q.
4. The inverse of $a(X) \bmod q$ is the polynomial $A(X) \in R$ satisfying $a(X) * A(X) \equiv 1 \bmod q$.

The inverse (if it exists) is easily computed using the Extended Euclidean Algorithm. Inverses are only needed for key generation.

2.2   Key Generation

Choose random polynomials $F, g \in R$ with small coefficients and set $f = 1 + pF$. Compute the polynomial

$$h \equiv g * f^{-1} \bmod q.$$

The public key is h and the private key is f.

2.3   Encryption

The plaintext m is a polynomial with coefficients taken mod p. Choose a random polynomial r with small coefficients. The ciphertext is

$$e \equiv pr * h + m \bmod q.$$

2.4   Decryption

Compute

$$a \equiv e * f \bmod q,$$

choosing the coefficients of a to satisfy $A \leq a_i < A + q$. The value of A is fixed and is determined by a simple formula depending on the other parameters. Then $a \bmod p$ is equal to the plaintext m.

2.5   Why NTRU Works

The decryption process yields the polynomial

$$\begin{aligned}
a &\equiv e * f \bmod q \\
&\equiv (pr * h + m) * f \bmod q && \text{(since } e \equiv pr * h + m) \\
&\equiv pr * g + m * f \bmod q && \text{(since } h * f \equiv gf - 1 * f \equiv g)
\end{aligned}$$

The coefficients of r, g, m, and f are small, so the coefficients of

$$pr * g + m * f$$

will lie in an interval of length less than q. Choosing the appropriate interval, we recover

$$a = pr * g + m * f = pr * g + m * (1 + pF)$$

exactly, not merely modulo q. Then reduction modulo p yields $a \equiv m \bmod p$.

3 NTRU Algorithmic Optimizations

3.1 Choice of p

If the coefficients of the polynomial $pr*g+m*f$ do not lie in an interval of length at most q, then decryption will not work. Appropriate choices of parameters reduce this to a very low probability, which may be reduced even further by the following observation.

The discussion above assumes that p is an integer, where we recall that p and q must be relatively prime. However, as noted in [4], there is no particular reason that p must be an integer. It could instead be a polynomial, provided the ideals generated by p and q are relatively prime in the ring R. Our first choice for such a polynomial would naturally be a binomial $X^k \pm 1$. Unfortunately, the elements

$$X^k \pm 1 \text{ and } X^N - 1 \text{ and } 128$$

are not relatively prime in $Z[X]$.

The next natural candidate is $p = X + 2$. It is simple to verify the relative primality of p and q in this case:

$$X^N - 1 = X^N + 2^N - 2^N - 1 = (X^N + 2^N) - 128 \cdot 2^{N-7} - 1.$$

As noted in [1] and [4], operations modulo binomials are efficiently computed. Thus $p = X + 2$ and $q = 128$ form the basis for a very efficient implementation of NTRU.

3.2 Polynomials of Low Hamming Weight

The most time consuming part of NTRU encryption is computation of the product $r(X) * h(X) \bmod q$. Similarly, the most time consuming part of NTRU decryption is computation of the product $f(X) * e(X) \bmod q$. The polynomials $h(X)$ and $e(X)$ have coefficients that are more or less randomly distributed modulo q, while one normally takes $r(X)$ and $f(X)$ to have binary (i.e., 0 or 1) or ternary (i.e., -1, 0, or 1) coefficients.

Suppose that $r(X)$ is a binary polynomial with d ones. Then computation of the product $r(X) * h(X) \bmod q$ requires approximately dN operations, where one operation is an addition and a remainder modulo q.

A common trick (see [7] for instance) is to choose a polynomial of low Hamming weight. We extend this idea by taking a product of low Hamming weight polynomials as suggested in [5]. To this end, we write $r(X) = r_1(X)r_2(X)$, where r_1 and r_2 are binary polynomials with d_1 and d_2 ones respectively. Then $r(X)$ will have approximately d_1d_2 ones, a few twos, and rarely a three. Rather than computing $r(X) * h(X) \bmod q$ as $(r_1 * r_2) * h$, it is far more efficient to compute it as

$$r(X) * h(X) = r_1(X) * \big(r_2(X) * h(X)\big),$$

which requires only $(d_1 + d_2)N$ operations. Thus the computational complexity is proportional to the sum of d_1 and d_2.

On the other hand, the search space for the pair of polynomials (r_1, r_2) has size approximately $\binom{N-1}{d_1-1}\binom{N-1}{d_2-1}$, so is proportional to the product of the r_1 search space and the r_2 search space. In practice, there are meet-in-the-middle approaches that reduce the size of the search space, see [5] for details and security considerations. Further, the number of nonzero coefficients in $r_1(X)r_2(X)$ is essentially the product $d_1 d_2$. Thus one might say that using a product $r = r_1 r_2$ requires computation proportional to the sum $d_1 + d_2$ while giving security proportional to the product $d_1 d_2$. In rough terms, this explains why one obtains significant performance gains without changing the level of security. In the common case of $N = 251$ and $q = 128$, it is common to set $r = r_1 * r_2 + r_3$, where each of r_1, r_2, r_3 is binary with 8 nonzero coefficients.

Given the above, multiplication involving the private key $f(X)$ is aided by writing

$$f(X) = 1 + p * (f_1(X) * f_2(X) + f_3(X)).$$

3.3   A Fast Convolution Algorithm in Software

Under the assumption that the coefficients of f_1, f_2, f_3 are binary, we thus have an efficient algorithm for ring multiplication in software. The central idea is that rather than storing f or the individual f_i polynomials as N-element arrays in memory, it suffices to store those array offsets whose locations correspond to a nonzero entry. Thus, a polynomial $f_i(X) = X^{191} + X^{178} + \cdots + X^{14} + X^2$ would be stored in memory as the array $191, 178, \cdots, 14, 2$. For convenience, arrays representing the $f_i(X)$ polynomials are concatenated into a single array which we denote b.

Recall that the coefficients c_k of the product of $b(X)$ and some general polynomial $a(X)$ have the form

$$c_k = a_0 b_k + a_1 b_{k-1} + \cdots + a_{N-1} b_{k+1} = \sum_{i+j \equiv k \mod N} a_i b_j.$$

The sparse nature of $f_i(X)$ causes most of these inner product terms to be zero. So rather than employing a traditional polynomial multiplication algorithm that expends a great deal of effort computing zero terms, we take a different approach. Scanning the b array allows us to calculate only those inner product terms which may be non-zero. A particular non-zero coefficient will appear in N inner product terms.

The algorithm begins by zero-initializing an array of coefficients that will hold the result $c(X) = f_i(X)a(X)$. For each entry of the b array we calculate the N inner product terms corresponding to a non-zero coefficient in $f_i(X)$. Since $f_i(X)$ is binary, each non-zero inner product term is simply a coefficient of $a(X)$. These terms are individually accumulated in their corresponding location in the c array. Repeating this process for all non-zero coefficients calculates $f_i(X)a(X)$ at a cost of $d_i N$ additions of $\log_2(q)$-bit numbers.

With this procedure in hand, we may compute the overall $f(X)a(X)$ multiplication with the following steps:

1. $t(X) \leftarrow a(X)f_1(X)$
2. $c(X) \leftarrow t(X) * f_2(X) = a(X) * f_1(X) * f_2(X)$
3. $t(X) \leftarrow f_3(X) * a(X)$
4. $c(X) \leftarrow c_k + t_k \bmod N = f_3(X) * a(X) + f_1(X) * f_2(X) * a(X)$

Thus in the common practical case of $N = 251$ and $q = 128$ with each of f_1, f_2, f_3 having eight nonzero coefficients, the convolution is computed with $251 \times 8 \times 3 = 6024$ seven-bit additions and no multiplications. This algorithm is thus ideally suited for the low-power, low-clockrate, narrow arithmetic architectures found in constrained devices.

Pseudocode for this operation is found as Algorithm 1, where all array offsets are to be taken modulo N for clarity in exposition.

Algorithm 1. Fast Convolution Algorithm

Require: b an array of $d_1 + d_2 + d_3$ nonzero coefficient locations representing the polynomial $f(X) = 1 + p * (f_1(X) * f_2(X) + f_3(X))$, a the array $a(X) = \Sigma a_i$, N the number of coefficients in $f(X), a(X)$.

Ensure: c the array where $c(X) = f(X)a(X)$

  for $0 \leq j < d_1$ **do** {Compute $t(X) \leftarrow a(X) * f_1(X)$}
    for $0 \leq k \leq N - 1$ **do**
      $t_{k+b_j} \leftarrow t_{k+b_j} + a_k$
    end for
  end for
  for $d_1 \leq j < d_2$ **do** {Compute $c(X) \leftarrow t(X) * f_2(X)$}
    for $0 \leq k \leq N - 1$ **do**
      $c_{k+b_j} \leftarrow c_{k+b_j} + t_k$
    end for
  end for
  for $0 \leq k \leq N$ **do** {Zero out t}
    $t_k \leftarrow 0$
  end for
  for $d_2 \leq j < d_3$ **do** {Compute $t(X) \leftarrow f_3(X) * a(X)$}
    for $0 \leq k \leq N - 1$ **do**
      $t_{k+b_j} \leftarrow t_{k+b_j} + a_k$
    end for
  end for
  for $0 \leq k \leq N - 1$ **do** {$c(X) \leftarrow f_3(X) * a(X) + f_1(X) * f_2(X) * a(X)$}
    $c_k \leftarrow c_k + t_k \bmod q$
  end for

For sake of comparison, we implemented Karatsuba-Ofman polynomial multiplication and Algorithm 1 on a variety of embedded systems. These results are found in Table 1.

Table 1. Polynomial Multiplication Algorithm Comparison

Operation	MC68EX328 Dragonball (20 MHz Palm Vx)	Intel 80386 (20 MHz RIM 957)	37MHz ARM7
Karatsuba	25 msec	178 msec	12.75 msec
Algorithm 1	3.2 msec	28 msec	1.62 msec

4   NTRU Embedded Reference Implementation

The NTRU Embedded Reference Implementation package is designed for use in applications where both high performance and small footprint are important considerations. The package contains the NTRU algorithm [3], the NTRU Signature Scheme (NSS) [6], a random number generation utility, and public domain versions of the AES selected Rijndael symmetric cipher and the SHA-1 hash function.

The software library is implemented in ANSI C and is easily ported while maintaining high performance. Two important design choices include the use of an internal memory management scheme and support for 8/16/32/64-bit environments.

Internal Memory Management Scheme. Memory allocation on constrained devices is typically a source of inefficiency and portability problems. While some devices disallow the use of heap management functions (such as malloc, realloc, and free), others significantly restrict the use of stack space. Regardless of which operations are available, there is normally significant CPU overhead associated with native memory management functions. For efficiency and portability, the implementation establishes its own internal memory management scheme. When an application initializes the implementation, a block of memory is created from either the stack or the heap and used to satisfy the application's dynamic memory management needs. Thus, the implementation's memory management is abstracted from the application environment, improving portability, security and performance.

8/16/32/64-bit environments. One of the requirements of the software is to support many different devices. Popular microprocessors have word lengths ranging from 8–64 bits. To provide maximum flexibility, storage of public and private key information as well as intermediate results is generally in arrays of 8-bit types and all operations are 8 bits wide. While this provides a flexible approach supporting operation on different size devices, it may not be the most efficient approach on all devices. For example, on some devices a 16- or 32-bit operation has the same cycle cost as a corresponding 8-bit instruction. This fact can be exploited when tailoring NTRU for a specific platform.

4.1   NTRU C Performance Results

The NTRU design decisions lead to a generic software base that can be run on many different platforms. Outside of good software engineering practices, there are no platform specific C optimization tricks used in the reference implementation. Even without platform specific optimizations, the performance numbers, as shown in Table 2, are impressive on a variety of popular processors for constrained devices. In these tables, msec is taken to mean milliseconds. In addition, in this and all remaining sections of this paper, we report results for NTRU with parameters $(N, p, q) = (251, X + 2, 128)$.

Table 2. NTRU Performance Results

Operation	MC68EX328 Dragonball (20 MHz Palm Vx)	Intel 80386 (20 MHz RIM 957)	37MHz ARM7
Key Generation	1130 msec	858 msec	80.6 msec
Encryption	47 msec	39 msec	3.25 msec
Decryption	89 msec	72 msec	6.75 msec

4.2   NTRU Optimized for Palm Computing Platforms

The Motorola Dragonball microprocessor is widely used in Palm computing platforms. While the Dragonball supports 8-, 16-, and 32-bit data operations, memory is organized into 16-bit words. Although the NTRU fast convolution algorithm operates on 7-bit polynomial coefficients, each operand fetch actually retrieves a full 16-bit word. Assuming the coefficients are organized in memory along byte boundries, this leads to twice as many memory accesses as should be needed. While an easy choice would be to read the full word and use the two bytes separately, the task of extracting anything but the lowest byte in a register is more expensive than simply fetching the next byte from memory.

Since Algorithm 1 is nothing more than repeated coefficient addition, the arithmetic requirements on the Dragonball are minimal. The result is that most of the time is spent fetching coefficients and storing their sum. A great deal of optimization can be achieved simply by making these memory operations more efficient. Extensive use of the Dragonball's post-increment and pre-decrement pointer operations makes the code much faster than using pointer offsets, the approach taken by the C compiler.

Another performance-limiting factor is Algorithm 1's use of circular array indexing for fast modular reduction. Since the Dragonball has no native support for circular arrays, we can simply place two copies of a in adjacent memory locations and reduce the burden of pointer arithmetic. Figure 1 graphically displays the situation.

By taking the buffering idea one step further, we can exploit the 16-bit architecture of the Dragonball to perform two 7-bit coefficient additions in parallel. To this end, we simply pack two 7-bit coefficients into a word and add. Any overflow from the add operation can be removed by modular reduction via a logical and with $0x7F7F$. This effectively reduces each byte over $q = 128$. The main problem with this scheme is alignment of data on 16-bit boundaries. If the offset j is odd, then the above scheme with two copies of a will suffice to perform word additions instead of byte additions. If j is even however, none of the words would be aligned to perform the addition. If we make a third copy of a, again adjacent to the other two, we find that if j is odd, $a + (N - j)$ is unaligned, but $a + (2N - j)$ will be. This is shown in figure 2.

The current assembly improvements can be seen in Table 3.

$$a \quad a_0|a_1|a_2|a_3|a_4|a_5|a_6|a_0|a_1|a_2|a_3|a_4|a_5|a_6$$
$$\oplus \ \oplus \ \oplus \ \oplus \ \oplus \ \oplus \ \oplus$$
$$c \quad\qquad\qquad\qquad c_0|c_1|c_2|c_3|c_4|c_5|c_6$$
$$\downarrow \ \downarrow \ \downarrow \ \downarrow \ \downarrow \ \downarrow \ \downarrow$$
$$c' \quad\qquad\qquad\qquad c'_0|c'_1|c'_2|c'_3|c'_4|c'_5|c'_6$$

Fig. 1. Bytewise buffered convolution example; $b_j = 2, N = 7$

$$a \quad a_0 \ a_1|a_2 \ a_3|a_4 \ a_5|a_6 \ a_0|a_1 \ a_2|a_3 \ a_4|a_5 \ a_6|a_0 \ a_1|a_2 \ a_3|a_4 \ a_5|a_6$$
$$\oplus\qquad\ \oplus\qquad\ \oplus\qquad\ \oplus$$
$$c \quad\qquad\qquad\qquad\qquad\qquad c_0 \ c_1|c_2 \ c_3|c_4 \ c_5|c_6$$
$$\downarrow\qquad\quad \downarrow\qquad\quad \downarrow\qquad\quad \downarrow$$
$$c' \quad\qquad\qquad\qquad\qquad\qquad c'_0 \ c'_1|c'_2 \ c'_3|c'_4 \ c'_5|c'_6$$

Fig. 2. Wordwise buffered convolution example; $b_j = 2, N = 7$

Table 3. NTRU Palm Assembly Language Performance Improvements

Operation	Palm C code	Palm Assembly/C code
Key Generation	1130 msec	630 msec
Encryption	47 msec	33 msec
Decryption	89 msec	60 msec

5   NTRU in an FPGA

Due to its low complexity and parallel nature, the NTRU cryptosystem lends itself exremely well to hardware implementation. The primary function in the encryption algorithm is the convolution of the public key $h(X)$, by the random vector, $r(X)$, as described in Algorithm 1. The nature of the construction of r leads to the observation that with overwhelming probability, each coefficient of r is at most 15 (i.e., fits into at most 4 bits), with a limit on the number of non-zero coefficients. This allows the use of repeated coefficient addition as opposed to full coefficient multiplication to implement convolution.

The encryption engine operates in the following steps. First, the operands h, r, and m must be loaded serially, 251 bits at a time. Once the operands are loaded, the engine begins bit-scanning each r coefficient. For each non-zero coefficient, the engine adds h to the temporary result. This is repeated a number of times corresponding to the value of the current r coefficient. Once this is complete, or if the coefficient is zero, h is rotated left by one coeffcent (7 bits) to perform the modular reduction of the result over x^N. The next r coefficient is then scanned, repeating the above process until all r's have been processed. Finally, the engine adds the polynomial m to the result of the convolution and outputs this value as the encrypted message. Because of the expansive nature of encryption, the encrypted message is output serially. Note that h is retained in the encryption engine, and thus successive encryptions only require the loading of r and m, which takes 5 clock cycles.

For the provided implementation, the following tools were used:

- *Synthesis*: Synplicity's Synplify version 6.1.3.
- *Place and Route*: Xilinx's Design Manager version 2.1i_sp6.
- *Simulation*:Viewlogic's Powerview version 6.1 FusionHDL version 1.4 and Viewlogic's Workview Office version 7.53 Speedwave version 6.202.

For the provided implementation, the Xilinx Virtex 1000EFG860 FPGA was chosen as the target device. The package type chosen provides sufficient I/O (656 IOBs) and logic resources to satisfy the design requirements. Further information regarding the Virtex E family may be found in [8]. Note that the VHDL implementation is fully portable to ASIC technology, since no FPGA vendor-specific constructs were used in the provided implementation.

Table 4. FPGA Implementation Results

Encryption Cycles	259
Clock Period	19.975 ns
Clock Frequency	50.063 MHz
Encryption Time	5.174 μs
Encryption Throughput	48.52 Mbps
Slices Used	6373
Logic Resource Utilization	51%
Approximate Gate Count	60,000
Approximate Register Gate Count	40,000
I/O Used	506
I/O Utilization	77%

6   Conclusions

In this paper we have provided practical implementation results for NTRU running on a number of embedded systems including microcontrollers and FPGAs. In addition, we have provided a new fast convolution algorithm which eliminates the need for explicit multiplication in encryption and decryption.

References

1. D. V. Bailey and C. Paar. Efficient arithmetic in finite field extensions with application in elliptic curve cryptography. *Journal of Cryptology*, to appear.
2. D. Coppersmith and A. Shamir. Lattice attacks on NTRU. In *Advances in Cryptography — EUROCRYPT '97*, pages 52–61. Springer-Verlag, 1997. LNCS 1233.
3. J. Hoffstein, J. Pipher, and J. Silverman. NTRU: A new high speed public key cryptosystem. In J. Buhler, editor, *Lecture Notes in Computer Science 1423: Algorithmic Number Theory (ANTS III)*, pages 267–288. Springer-Verlag, Berlin, 1998.
4. J. Hoffstein and J. Silverman. Optimizations for NTRU. In *Proceedings of Public-Key Cryptography and Computational Number Theory*. de Gruyter, Warsaw, September 2000.
5. J. Hoffstein and J. Silverman. Small hamming weight products in cryptography. preprint, September 2000.
6. J. S. J. Hoffstein, J. Pipher. NSS: An NTRU lattice-based signature scheme. In *Advances in Cryptography — EUROCRYPT 2001*. Springer-Verlag, 2001. to appear.
7. A. J. Menezes. *Elliptic Curve Public Key Cryptosystems*. Kluwer Academic Publishers, Boston, 1993.
8. Xilinx Inc. *Virtex 2.5V Field Programmable Gate Arrays*, 1998.

Transparent Harddisk Encryption

Thomas Pornin

Département d'Informatique, École Normale Supérieure,
45 rue d'Ulm, 75005 Paris, France
thomas.pornin@ens.fr

Abstract. This paper introduces a new block cipher, and discusses its security. Its design is optimized for high-bandwidth applications that do not have high requirements on key-schedule latency. This paper also discusses several security issues about such an application: harddisk encryption.

Keywords: bitslice, encryption, harddisk, mobile computing

1 Introduction

Today's secret key cryptosystems are designed to be versatile enough to fit most usages in a wide variety of environments. The recently chosen new american standard of symetric encryption, the AES [1], is a perfect illustration of that fact: appart from its seemingly good security, it was chosen because it could run reasonably fast on a modern workstation, a low-end personal digital assistant, a smartcard or a specific ASIC. This speed and easiness of implementation are requirements for what the AES was designed to be: a standard; interoperability issues imply that all applications must use the same algorithm, so it must be good everywhere.

However, there are some applications where requirements are different: one of them is on-the-fly harddisk encryption. Such encryption is needed to prevent divulgation of important data if a harddisk is stolen, or scanned during an inactivity period (some sort of lunch-time passive attack). This is especially important for mobile systems, such as portable computers. Another class of attacks that could be worth to counter, is active attacks: an attacker modifies data on the disk. Even if the modification is essentially random, such tampering should be at least detected.

Let us detail what is needed, and what is not:

- We need a very fast cipher; security is not a goal in itself, but a necessary evil used to protect other jobs; and since modern operating systems implement multitasking, only a marginal proportion of the cpu power should be used to perform encryption.
- We do not care about key-schedule latency: the key-schedule is performed only once per session, at boot time, and the cost can be further reduced, so that it should doable in a user-compatible time (the user will not want to wait several minutes every morning).

Ç.K. Koç, D. Naccache, and C. Paar (Eds.): CHES 2001, LNCS 2162, pp. 273–285, 2001.

– We encrypt data-blocks of size multiple of 512 bytes: this is the standard size of an harddisk sector; all reads and writes from and to the disk are performed with this granularity at least (on some systems, it might be higher).
– We need to handle random accesses to the disk, with low overhead; we cannot afford, for instance, extra physical reads on the disk.
– We run on a modern computer, with many registers[1].

Classical block ciphers are ruled out for speed reasons; as a rule of thumb, the maximum allowed cpu overhead should be 15%, on a 1 GHz cpu, with a disk running at 20 Mbytes per second. This means that a bandwidth of at least 120 Mbytes per second (when full cpu is used) is needed. Algorithms such as the AES [1], Blowfish [2] or CS-Cipher [3], although considered as fast, will be limited to about 50 Mbytes per second.

Stream ciphers are also out of the question, due to random access; stream ciphers have a state, that needs to be maintained, in order to encipher and decipher. The initial state depends on the key, and its construction usually requires some time. For instance, although the bandwidth obtained with RC4 is high, the key schedule is rather slow with regards to the production of 512 bytes of stream. Besides, the ciphertext is often too malleable: if the attacker guesses the plaintext, he can easily change that plaintext to whatever he wants.

So we need some sort of very fast block cipher; we present such a cipher in this paper. We will first recall the so-called bitslice programming technique, as described by Eli Biham [4], then describe the algorithm itself, and discuss implementation and security issues. A final section will explicit some general problems related to harddisk encryption, and show how our cipher helps in solving them.

2   Bitslice

Bitslicing is an implementation trick, classical among electronicians, but never really published, and therefore rediscovered several times. Eli Biham was the first cryptographer to document it in [4]; the method basically boils down to an alternate representation of data that allows software implementations to work like hardware ones, with similar optimizations. Bitslice code is also called *orthogonal code*, to refer to this alternate representation.

2.1   Abilities of Modern Processors

Modern processors are more and more of the RISC trend; this means that they have many, wide registers, and are able to perform bitwise logic operations between these registers at high speed. They are however relatively bad at handling byte-formatted data, such as ASCII text.

---

[1] This extends to the PC, although the Intel instruction set does include only a limited number of addressable registers; see section 2.1.

An emblematic processor is the Alpha [5]: it has 32 64-bit registers, all of them being equivalent; there is no specialized register[2]. All calculating instructions take two registers as operands, and a third one as destination. This design is a good example of what processors will look like in the future; Intel chosed a similar design for its new, market-leading processor, the Itanium [6], which should replace the long-lived Pentium family. The Alpha and the Itanium are native 64-bit processors.

Actually, Pentium processors are already quite RISC: they sure still handle the old 8080-compatible CISC code, with few registers and many complex instructions; but most of those complex instructions are there for backward-compatibility only, and are slow, so the compilers do not use them. Besides, there are many internal registers, and the processor renames, aliases and duplicates the registers visible to the programmer. Memory accesses to the internal cache memory are also made very fast, so we can consider those processors as being on the RISC side. The Pentium is a 32-bit processor, but already owns some 64-bit registers, in the MMX unit.

2.2 Orthogonalization of Data

The natural reflex of the cryptosystem programmer, when a 32-bit data must be used, is to store it into a register. This approach has the following drawbacks:

- When the registers are wider than the data, some of the computing power of the processor is lost.
- Bit permutations cost much; those operations are current in cryptosystems since they help in creating a correct avalanche effect. But those permutations are a mere data routing, and do not perform any real calculation.

The orthogonal representation is the following: spread the data among many registers, one bit per register. You then calculate the algorithm as a circuit, with logic gates that map cleanly to the native bitwise operations of the processor. Since those operations are bitwise, they are performed on all bits of the registers at the same time; if you have n-bit registers, you perform n instances of the algorithm simultaneously. This is heavy parallelism, quite suited to situations where you have much data to encrypt, in ECB mode.

There remains the problem of getting input data to the appropriate storage ordering; this is equivalent to the transposition of a matrix. The figure 1 illustrates this transposition. See [7] for a $O(n \log n)$ method of transposition of a $n \times n$ matrix, when n-bitwise logical operations and shiftings are atomic.

2.3 Applicability

With bitslice, bit permutations are "free": the code just has to use the right register. This is solved at compilation time and does not induce runtime cost.

---

[2] There is actually one: the register 31 contains always 0; but since this value does not change, it can be safely "duplicated" inside the processor and therefore does not constitute a bottleneck.

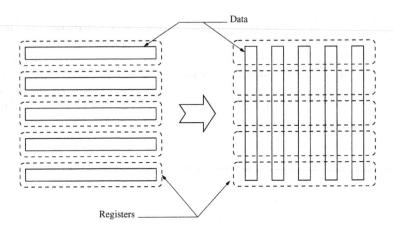

Fig. 1. othogonalization of data

Moreover, the ALU (Arithmetic and Logic Unit) is used at its full potential, since the whole width of registers is used. However, some operations become much more complex: table lookups must be replaced by equivalent circuitry, which means BDD (Binary Decision Diagrams); additions require manual carry propagation; multiplications are definitely out of the question.

Moreover, the algorithm must be representable as a circuit; this is anyway a desirable characteristic for block ciphers, since data-dependant branches lead to timing attacks [8].

To sum up, some cryptosystems are well-optimized for bitslice, others are not. DES can be implemented very efficiently this way; it was done for the DESchall [9] (a software-based DES cracking challenge by exhaustive search of the key space). Serpent [10], candidate to the AES, was also designed to be implemented using these technics. We present in this paper a new algorithm, called FBC (as "Fast Bitslice Cipher"), which is optimized for speed under a bitslice implementation.

3   The FBC Algorithm

3.1   General Structure

The FBC algorithm is a r-round Feistel cipher; it works on w-bit values (w is even). The confusion function is simple: each output bit is the bitwise combination of two different input bits. Four combinations are used: AND, OR, NAND and NOR. Which combinations are used on which bits, is key-dependant and round-dependant. The figure 2 illustrates this setup. Due to practical implementation issues, w must not exceed 512.

The three main ideas are:

– use a simple, fast round function with many rounds (for instance, $r = 64$);

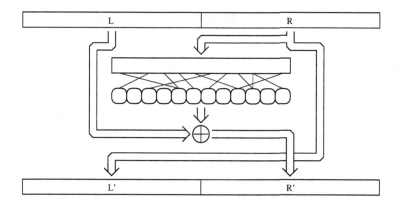

Fig. 2. one round of FBC

- derive each round subkey from the key using a cryptographically strong pseudo-random generator (so that attacks on subkeys cannot be proven to exist, neither can they compromise other subkeys);
- make code generation part of the key schedule; this is slow but allows for many key-dependant features.

In a more formal way: for each binary value, we count bits from left to right, leftmost bit is numbered 1. For the round i, the input is split into two equal parts of size $w/2$: the left part L_i and the right part R_i. There exist $w/2$ functions $\tau_i^j (1 \leq j \leq w/2)$ and two permutations ϕ_i and ψ_i of $w/2$ elements such that:

$$\forall j, \tau_i^j = \text{AND, OR, NAND or NOR}$$

$$\forall j, \phi_i(j) \neq \psi_i(j)$$

The result T_i of the confusion function is such that the bit j of T_i ($1 \leq j \leq w/2$) is equal to $\tau_i^j(\phi_i(j), \psi_i(j))$. The output of the round is the concatenation of L_i' and R_i', in that order, where:

$$L_i' = R_i$$
$$R_i' = L_i \oplus T_i$$

After the last round, the left and right part of the result are swapped; this is made so that the decryption algorithm is exactly the same than the encryption algorithm, but the definition of the ϕ_i, ψ_i and τ_i^j functions.

To complete this scheme, we must specify how those functions are chosen from the master key. We use the master key as a seed for a pseudo-random generator, that uses a cryptographically strong hash function.

3.2   The Pseudo-random Generator

The secret key is a k-bit value, where k ranges from 0 to 352. As usual, if k is lower than 80, the scheme is to be considered as vulnerable to exhaustive key search attacks. The AES defines key sizes of 128, 192 and 256 bits; FBC allows these, and other sizes as well, so any useful security level can be achieved with FBC.

We use the hash function SHA-1 as defined in [11]. This specification defines the application of SHA-1 on an arbitrary bit stream, and includes a padding method to extend the bit stream to a size multiple of 512. We do not use that padding, so "SHA" is to be considered in this paper as "application of the SHA-1 core function to an unpadded block of 512 bits".

The key K is extended to the 352-bit value K' by appending zeroes to its right. S is a 160-bit variable which will contain the "state" of the generator. The algorithm is the following:

- 1. $S \leftarrow 0$
- 2. $S \leftarrow \text{SHA}(K'||S)$
- 3. The 20 bytes of S are emitted (leftmost first)
- 4. Return in 2

($||$ denotes concatenation).

Therefore the generator emits bytes. These bytes will be used to choose random numbers between 0 and $w/2 - 1$, which is exactly why w must be at most 512; otherwise, the definition of the key schedule should be adapted.

We will have to choose integers ranging from 0 to some limit n, where n is a posivite number strictly smaller than $w/2$. We calculate m the greatest positive multiple of $n + 1$ that is smaller or equal to 256; for instance, if $n = 6$, we have $m = 252$.

To choose a random number from 0 to n, we get one byte b from the random generator; if this byte is greater or equal to m, we get another byte, until we have a value strictly smaller than m. It is easy to see that the average number of invocations of the random generator is at most 2, so this process is not especially slow. The random number is defined to be the euclidian rest of the division of b by $n + 1$. This process ensures that all integers between 0 and n have an equal probability to appear.

3.3   Choice of a Random Permutation

We must choose random permutations of $w/2$ elements; we will use the following algorithm:

- 1. Fill an array p of $w/2$ elements with the numbers from 1 to $w/2$ in ascending order ($\forall i, p[i] = i$); this array represents the identity permutation.
- 2. For i ranging from 2 to $w/2$
- 3. Choose a random integer a_i between 0 and $i - 1$
- 4. If $a_i + 1 \neq i$, swap the contents of $p[a_i + 1]$ and $p[i]$ (this is equivalent to the composition of p with the transposition $(i \ (a_i + 1))$)
- 5. End for

The chosen permutation is represented by the contents of p at the end of the execution of the algorithm ($p[5] = 8$ means that the permutation sends the fifth element of its input to the eigth emplacement of its output). This algorithm ensures that all permutations of $w/2$ elements have an identical probability to be chosen [12].

3.4   Choice of the Elements of Each Round

To choose the elements constituting the round i (the two permutations ϕ_i and ψ_i, and the $w/2$ boolean functions τ_i^j), we proceed this way:

- 1. Choose randomly ϕ_i.
- 2. Choose randomly ψ_i.
- 3. If there exists at least one j between 1 and $w/2$ such that $\phi_i(j) = \psi_i(j)$, go back to 2.
- 4. For each j from 1 to $w/2$, get one random byte; the euclidian rest of the division of that byte by 4 is a value between 0 and 3. The function τ_i^j will be a AND, OR, NAND and NOR for values of, respectively, 0, 1, 2 and 3.

The elements of each round are chosen from the first round to the last. On the average, for each ϕ_i, we will have to try $e \approx 2.7$ permutations ψ_i before finding one matching the criterion of point 3 (finding a matching ϕ_i is equivalent to finding $\psi_i \circ \phi_i^{-1}$, permutation with no fixed point; see [13] for the proportion of such permutations among all permutations of $w/2$ elements).

4   Implementation of FBC

4.1   Software Implementation

FBC is designed to be implemented in software, using bitslicing techniques. Such code is rather difficult to write, but we developed some sort of automatic tool to produce bitsliced C code from an *ad hoc* description of the algorithm, which can be generated from the key schedule algorithm. That tool is not very well developped but is available for free download and use (see [14]). The C code generated for a fully deployed 64-round FBC is a huge function with about 5000 local variables and 5000 statements; the C compiler fails utterly on such input, so the code must be sliced into small groups of four rounds or so, easier to understand by the compiler.

We ignore the cost of othogonalization of data before encrypting and after encryption; actually, not performing such orthogonalization is equivalent to performing a known, fixed permutation on input and output data blocks (the 512-bit blocks if we perform 64 parallel encryptions with a 64-bit block size). Such a permutation has no security implication, so we can add that permutation, which actually voids the cost of orthogonalization.

Encryption bandwidth achieved for the moment on an Alpha 21164 processor running at 500 MHz is about 32 Mbytes/s using FBC with 64-bit words and

64 rounds ($w = 64, r = 64$); the code is not yet fully optimized and we are still working on it. This speed is half the speed requested (we wanted 120 Mbytes/s on a 1 GHz processor) but is explanable by the relatively old design of the 21164 (that processor was first announced in August 1994, which is a very remote epoch in the rapidly moving chip industry). The 21164 can issue up to four instructions in each cycle, but only two load/store instructions and two logical instructions. Moreover, a load instruction cannot occur during the second next cycle of a store instruction. This restriction, bound to the aging design of the 21164, is responsible for the seemingly bad performance of FBC on that processor; the newer 21264 does not have that problem.

The number of logical τ functions to calculate for one encryption is $\frac{wr}{2}$. If n is the size of each register, the bitslice code will calculate n parallel instances of the algorithm, thus encrypting wn bits. The number of function evaluations needed for each data bit is then $\frac{wr}{2wn} = \frac{r}{2n}$. Since the wanted rate is about one bit per clock cycle, we must execute $\frac{r}{2n}$ τ functions per cycle (it is worth noticing that this value does not depend upon the block size used).

Bitslicing code uses many registers, much more than the really available registers in the processor; therefore, those are to be considered as a cache on the stack, where the values are stored. So data management still comes up as the most constricting issue. Each τ function will require two input operands and one output operand; since each input bit is used twiced in two different τ functions, the number of memory management operations needed can be reduced to one load and one store for each function. Due to the restrictions on such operations, an average of 3 cycles are needed per function. With the unavoidable additional cost of data transfering (this is administrative task outside the core of the cipher), this explains the "low" rate achieved on the 21164 (that rate is equal to the best rates achieved by ciphers such as the AES on the same machine).

However, the current market-leading Alpha processor is the 21264, which has much lower restrictions on memory accesses; from its specifications, it should achieve the correct performance (one cycle per bit enciphered), whereas classical cryptosystems, which use more complex structures of the processor, will not benefit as much of the generation shift (speed measurements [15] from the AES competition show that the fastest candidates would run at 2 clock cycles per bit enciphered on a 21264-equivalent processor). Optimization of the code on the 21264 architecture is still undergoing work.

To the very least, "64 rounds" is a conservative number, in a security point of view. That number could be lowered, and the speed of FBC would raise correspondingly.

4.2   Hardware Implementation

FBC is well-suited for FPGA ("Field Programmable Gate Arrays") implementations. FPGAs are programmable chips, which can host any circuit, and can be redesigned in little time (less than a second) with no loss.

For a FPGA implementation, the key schedule algorithm would produce a circuit design, to be loaded into the FPGA. Bitslicing (which is parallelization in space) becomes pipelining (parallelization in time), so a fully deployed FBC should run at one block per cycle; since each round is very simple (only one logic gate layer per round), a very fast clocking rate could be achieved. Since late Xilinx FPGA [16] chips may run at rates over 150 MHz, an instance of FBC with 64-bit words on such a chip would encipher over 10 Gbits of data per second; this is the fastest data rate achieved by the best production optic fibers.

If speed is at stake, specific hardware usable, and key schedule time unimportant, then FBC is the way to go.

5   Security of FBC

Security of FBC is based upon the following paradigms:

- many rounds,
- unpredictable random subkeys,
- key-dependant permutations and non-linear functions.

5.1   Many Rounds

It has been said for a long time that "take whatever round function you want, it will be secure if you put up enough rounds". This assertion used to be a joke, but it actually makes much sense.

Modern cryptanalytic attacks, such as differential and linear cryptanalysis, tend to have a complexity exponential in the number of rounds; especially, if the probabilistic advantage of the attacker is $1/2$ on one round, then 64 rounds will lower that advantage to 2^{-64}, a quite appropriate number for a FBC operating on 64-bit blocks.

5.2   Unpredictable Random Subkeys

Most cryptanalytic attacks use the fact that information on the key used in one round somehow shows up in a predictable way in some other rounds. Thus FBC produces all key-dependant round material with a cryptographically strong pseudo-random generator, seeded by the master key. If any information, learned or guessed, on the subkey of some rounds can be applied to another round by the attacker, then this would contradict the strength of the generator. Besides, even if all key-dependant material are guessed, thus giving some strong knowledge about the output of the generator, it would still be computationnaly infeasible to guess the master key; thus, a successful attack on a FBC-encrypted link with a simple daily key-updating policy would be limited to one day of decryption.

5.3   Key-Dependant Permutations and Non-linear Functions

In FBC, the permutations are made key-dependant as an attempt to make the avalanche effect unanalyzable by the attacker. One consequence is that permutations cannot be guaranteed to be "strong". We did some sample measures of the avalanche effect; here is the average number of data bit potentially modified by one bit after several rounds, for $w = 64$:

rounds	bits potentially modified
1	2.00
2	4.91
3	11.05
4	22.81
5	39.54
6	54.76
7	62.34
8	63.93
9	63.99
10	64.00

This means that the total avalanche effect is obtained in 10 rounds, to compare with the suggested value of 64 rounds.

The τ functions are dependant on the key, and chosen among the four functions AND, OR, NAND and NOR, which are the four symetric non-linear boolean functions. Given random inputs and random functions in this set, the output is well-balanced and statistically not correlated to the input.

5.4 Security Sum Up

The FBC design looks quite secure, with the rule of thumb $r = w$, which means "as many rounds as bits in the block size". This is a conservative estimation, based upon the assumption that if the block size if 64 bits, then the scheme should be secure against attacks using 2^{64} adaptively chosen plaintexts, which is far from being applicable in real life. Typically, if the enciphered text is a harddisk, the maximum amount of ciphertext provided is about 2^{32} blocks or so. Yet, security margins should not be too much fiddled with.

6 Harddisk Encryption

The problem of harddisk encryption is complex, and depends upon the type of attack considered. We will consider passive and active attacks, and detail the threat model and several corresponding solutions.

6.1 Passive Attacks

The model is the following: a computer stores confidential data on its harddisk; the computer or its disk might be stolen while it is not powered, therefore the data on the disk must be stored encrypted only. The attacker is supposed to be able to guess most of the encrypted plaintext, and must not learn anything about the remaining plaintexts.

Several products already address, or try to address this security issue. Some work on a file basis, masking the real names and internal contents of the files; this maps cleanly to network filesystems protocols such as NFS or Samba, which use file-oriented semantics. However, this leaks information, mainly the number of files created, their sizes and modification dates. Therefore the real security provided by those systems is only marginal.

Other products build up real enciphered blocks of data, upon which standard filesystems are applied. Those products use classical block ciphers and induce a performance hit which leads users into reserving encryption for really important data only. This may help the attacker know what computers hold his target inside a large company; good security can therefore be achieved only if all harddisks are completely enciphered, which is possible only if the performance hit is very small.

FBC is designed to encipher data in ECB mode, so that the parallelism given by the bitslice representation of data can be used. ECB mode has the following problem: input blocks are not randomized. Real life data is often very redundant, and equal blocks will be enciphered the same, and the attacker will be able to detect them. The countermeasure is to "add" a counter: each block, before encryption, is combined with its block number prior to encryption, with an addition or a bitwise XOR. The cost of such modification is neglectable with regards to the cost of encryption itself (on an Alpha, it will cost one cycle for 64 bits of data).

One FBC issue is that the key schedule implies the generation of code, a rather slow process (it can take up to several minutes) and which uses much code (a C compiler is not a small application, usually). This can be addressed the following way: the result of the key schedule, that is, the code that encrypts and decrypts, is stored encrypted on the disk, using some other block cipher, the AES for instance. The decryption is done only once at boot time, so there is no real performance issue here. The key used to decipher the FBC code needs not be the same key as the FBC one.

6.2   Active Modifying Attacks

We consider here the following model: the computer is stolen while being unpowered, its contents are modified, and the computer is put back in place before the theft is noticed. A random and destructive modification cannot be prevented, but we want to be sure that it would not go unnoticed. No existing product actually addresses this issue.

The classical solution is to store a MAC, which is easily built up with a hash function: the entire encrypted disk content, appended to some secret key, is processed through the function, and the result is written to some non-encrypted area of the disk (one such area must exist, to store the base decrypting software, that asks for the user key). The major drawbacks of this approach are:

- The speed of the process is limited to the speed of the disk, so it can take an impressive amount of time (one hour on today's typical disk); this has to be performed at boot time, and no work can take place during this check. This is not acceptable from the user's point of view.

- More critical, the MAC must be calculated again at shutdown time. This is even more impossible to force on the user, especially since some shutdowns are due to OS crash or low battery.
- Even if the disk is logically almost empty, its whole content must be processed. An alternative is to build the MAC only on the blocks that contains allocated data, but this still uses a gruesome amount of time (today's basic operating system installation uses several hundred megabytes of disk space, not including oversized applications).

Here is one solution addressing these problems: each block is double-encrypted in the following manner: if the block number N contains P, and E is the encryption function, then its encrypted counterpart is $C = E(E(P) \oplus N)$. For each file, the exclusive or of all its constituting blocks is stored inside a file-specific structure that is also encrypted (on some systems[3], such a structure exists and is called an *inode*). This encrypted XOR is the MAC.

Using this scheme, the verification of files can be made asynchronously, as a background task; only a locking procedure must be used so that an individual file may not be used prior to its verification. More important, the MAC of each file is maintained during normal operation; this means that a modification of a file requires the reading of either the overwritten data (so that its contribution to the file MAC can be taken away) or the remaining data (that is the recomputation of the MAC). This is not an important cost, because, most of the time, modifications of files are either appending data to the end of the file, or emptying the file and rewriting it from scratch. Anyway, when modifying a file, the size of the extra reads is limited to half the size of the file.

The XOR with the block number between the two encryptions ensures that the data blocks are not swappable by the attacker; this operation is isolated from the plaintext *and* from the ciphertext by the two encryptions. The assumption is that the block cipher is a random permutation, therefore any modification to the ciphertext leads to a random, uncontrollable modification of the plaintext.

The main drawback of this scheme is the double encryption, which halves performance. Therefore the use of a very fast cipher is critical for such a design.

7   Conclusion

We presented a new cipher, FBC, designed to achieve high encryption speed on a modern workstation, adapted to on-the-fly harddisk encryption. We presented some arguments with regards to its security, and discussed some implementation issues. We also discussed some issues related to the problem of harddisk encryption and presented a generic scheme to ensure data integrity at low cost.

We believe that such work will be more and more used in the future, as mobile computing is generalizing at a fast pace. As a side note, OpenBSD [17] (a Unix-like system specialized in security) already includes an encryption mechanism for

---

[3] Actually, all Unix-like systems, including MacOS and Windows NT/2000.

its swap space. An open question (which does not apply to swap space, since the contents of swap space are not used across reboots) is the possibility of building a secure integrity verification scheme, that does not imply a complex shutdown procedure, neither double encryption, nor too many extra reads when a file is modified.

References

1. The Advanced Encryption Standard, http://www.nist.gov/aes/
2. Bruce Schneier, *Description of a New Variable-Length Key, 64-Bit Block Cipher (Blowfish)*, Lecture Notes in Computer Science, Advances in Cryptology, proceedings of Fast Software Encryption 93, Springer-Verlag, 1994, pp. 191–204.
3. Jacques Stern and Serge Vaudenay, *CS-Cipher*, Lecture Notes in Computer Science, Advances in Cryptology, proceedings of Fast Software Encryption 98, Springer-Verlag, 1998, pp. 189–205.
4. Eli Biham, *A Fast New DES Implementation in Software*, Lecture Notes in Computer Science, Advances in Cryptology, proceedings of Fast Software Encryption 97, Springer-Verlag, 1997, pp. 260–272.
5. The Alpha OEM web site,
   http://www.digital.com/semiconductor/alpha/alpha.htm
6. The IA-64 web site,
   http://www.intel.com/eBusiness/products/ia64/index.htm
7. Donald E. Knuth, *The Art of Computer Programming*, Volume 3, Addison-Wesley, 1973, pp. 7 and 573.
8. Paul C. Kocher, *Timing Attacks on Implementations of Diffie-Hellman, RSA, DSS, and Other Systems*, Lecture Notes in Computer Science, Advances in Cryptology, proceedings of CRYPTO'96, Springer-Verlag, 1996, pp. 104–113.
9. The DES Challenge web site, http://www.distributed.net/des/
10. Ross Anderson, Eli Biham and Lars Knudsen, *Serpent: A New Block Cipher Proposal*, Lecture Notes in Computer Science, Advances in Cryptology, proceedings of Fast Software Encryption 98, Springer-Verlag, 1998, pp. 222–238.
11. The SHA-1 specification, FIPS 180-1,
    http://www.itl.nist.gov/fipspubs/fip180-1.htm
12. Donald E. Knuth, *The Art of Computer Programming*, Volume 2, Addison-Wesley, (2nd ed.), 1997, p. 139.
13. Donald E. Knuth, *The Art of Computer Programming*, Volume 1, Addison-Wesley, 1969, pp. 177–179.
14. Thomas Pornin, *Automatic Software Optimization of Block Ciphers using Bitslicing Techniques*, unpublished, http://www.di.ens.fr/~pornin/bitslice.ps
15. AES: best encryption timings for the submissions,
    http://www.di.ens.fr/~granboul/recherche/AES/timings.html
16. The Xilinx web site, http://www.xilinx.com/
17. The OpenBSD web site, http://www.openbsd.org/

Sliding Windows Succumbs to Big Mac Attack

C.D. Walter

Department of Computation, UMIST
PO Box 88, Manchester M60 1QD, UK
www.co.umist.ac.uk

Abstract. Sliding Windows is a general technique for obtaining an efficient exponentiation scheme. Big Mac is a specific form of attack on a cryptosystem in which bits of a secret key can be deduced independently, or almost so, of the others. Here such an attack on an implementation of the RSA cryptosystem is described. It assumes digit-by-digit computations are performed sequentially on a single k-bit multiplier and uses information which leaks through differential power analysis (DPA). With sufficiently powerful monitoring equipment, only a small number of exponentiations, independent of the key length, is enough to reveal the secret exponent from unknown plaintext inputs. Since the technique may work for a *single* exponentiation, many blinding techniques currently under consideration may be rendered useless. This is particularly relevant to implementations with single processors where a digit multiplication cannot be masked by other simultaneous processing. Moreover, the *longer* the key length, the *easier* the attacks becomes.

Key words: Cryptography, RSA, differential power analysis, blinding, DPA, smart card, exponentiation, sliding windows.

1 Introduction

Timing analysis and differential power analysis (DPA) techniques [8], [9], [2], [1] show that RSA cryptosystems [13] suffer from implementation weaknesses rather than lack of algorithmic strength. The secret signing or decryption exponent d often seems easy to recover from a smart card or other dedicated embedded system using DPA [8], [1], [3], [10], [4]. These attacks start by averaging a number of power traces in order to remove dependencies other than the quantity being sought and to reduce the effect of random noise. For the card described in [10] which uses the standard square and multiply algorithm for exponentiation, this immediately reveals the exponent because of the different shape of power traces for squarings and multiplications.

The power-related property on which the current attack is based depends on the fact that switching a gate consumes more power than not doing so. Generally, these tiny effects are submerged in too many other data dependent variations to be easily extracted. However, here we develop a novel way of combining sections of power traces which enhances the effect into a potentially very powerful

Ç.K. Koç, D. Naccache, and C. Paar (Eds.): CHES 2001, LNCS 2162, pp. 286–299, 2001.
© Springer-Verlag Berlin Heidelberg 2001

technique. We show that different multiplicands can be distinguished. As a result, the so-called m-ary and *sliding windows* methods of exponentiation [6], [7] become vulnerable as well as the square-and-multiply method.

A generally touted solution to this problem is to use different exponents with a randomly generated component on each decryption. In particular, Kocher, [8] §10, suggests using $d+r\phi(M)$ as the decryption key instead of d where M is the modulus and r is a random number generated anew for each decryption. This blinding certainly hides the exponent if averaging over a number of different decryptions has to be performed in order to reduce noise to levels at which the data dependencies are revealed. However, our simulations suggest that combining different sections of the power trace for just a *single* exponentiation may be sufficient to reveal the exponent, thereby negating the value of this type of blinding. Without such blinding, the technique certainly reduces the sample set that needs to be considered for DPA to be successful and implies that some sort of blinding should be a requirement in relevant cryptographic standards.

A *Big Mac Attack* on a secret key d is a method which enables d to be revealed bit by bit by nibbling at sections of d in any order. The implied independence of the derivation of different bits means that the total data and processing time required are only *linear* in the key length. This contrasts strongly with the *mathematical* strength of RSA, which is believed to be exponential in the key length. A well known brand product is so generously large as to be impossible to have a bite taken out of the whole at one go − like the method of attack, it must be nibbled at and consumed by tackling individual layers one by one in any order. Using DPA or other source of side-channel leakage, a similar arbitrary order of considering bits can eventually reveal the whole key, as we demonstrate. An example of another such attack, using timing information, was given in [16].

The context in which the attack may be mounted is a typical one for small embedded systems such as smart cards. We just require that a single k-bit multiplier be used to perform the RSA exponentiations in a digit sequential fashion, preferably with no other concurrent processing in progress.

2   Notation

An RSA cryptosystem (*resp.* signature scheme) over the integers [13] consists of a modulus $M = PQ$, which is the product of two large primes, and two keys d and e satisfying $A^{de} \equiv A \bmod M$. Message blocks A satisfying $0 \leq A < M$ are encrypted (*resp.* verified) with $C = A^e \bmod M$ and decrypted (*resp.* signed) using $A = C^d \bmod M$. The key e is generally chosen small with few non-zero bits (e.g. a Fermat prime, such as 3 or 17) so that encryption is relatively fast. The key d must be picked to satisfy $de \equiv 1 \bmod \phi(M)$ and therefore it usually has length comparable to M. The owner of the cryptosystem publishes M and e but keeps secret the factorization of M and the key d. Breaking the system means discovering d and is equivalent to factoring M, which is computationally infeasible for the size of primes used.

The computation of $A^d \bmod M$ is characterised by two main processes: modular multiplication and exponentiation. Our main assumption is that the implementation has a k-bit architecture and uses a single $k{\times}k$-bit multiplier to compute modular products $(A{\times}B) \bmod M$. So, except for the exponents d and e, each number X has a representation of the form $X = \sum_{i=0}^{n-1} x_i r^i$ where $r = 2^k$ is the *radix* or *base* of the representation, the coefficients x_i are its digits, and n is the number of digits required. The precise form or range of these digits is not important but we will see later that the larger n is, or the smaller k is, the more likely the attack is to succeed. The method is easily adapted to cases where the digit multiplier is not square.

2.1   Exponentiation

Exponentiation is often performed using the m-ary method [6] for which the exponent uses a representation with base m (here assumed to be a power of 2): $d = \sum_{i=0}^{t-1} d_i m^i$. The powers $C^i \bmod M$ $(i = 1,2,...,m-1)$ are pre-computed and allocated to table entries $C^{(i)}$. Then a partial product is repeatedly raised to the power m by squaring and the pre-computed power of C corresponding to the next digit of d multiplied in:

THE m-ARY (MODULAR) EXPONENTIATION ALGORITHM

```
{ Pre-condition: d = ∑_{i=0}^{t-1} d_i m^i }
C^(1)  := C ;
For i := 2 to m-1 do
       C^(i)  := C^(i-1)×C mod M ;
P := C^(d_{t-1}) ;
For i := t-2 downto 0 do
Begin
       P := P^m mod M ;
       If d_i ≠ 0 then P := P×C^(d_i) mod M ;
End ;
{ Post-condition: P = C^d mod M }
```

The *sliding window* technique [7] is a straightforward generalisation of this which makes more efficient use of the presence of zero bits in the exponent. It employs a mixed basis representation of the exponent, using powers of 2 and m. Only the odd powers $C^{(i)}$ need to be pre-computed and stored. The attack described here applies identically to this technique apart from the obvious modifications as a result of slightly different pre-computations, so it suffices to illustrate the ideas using the m-ary method.

Hardware power consumption depends critically on bus movement involved in low level operations such as fetching instructions, reading from and writing to memory, etc. Since the long integer multiplications take a large number of cycles to perform and a large number of consecutive multiplications are executed, attackers are usually able to establish correctly the boundaries in the power traces between the operations in the algorithm above.

2.2   Modular Multiplication

Each long integer multiplication or squaring consists of a large number of individual digit-by-digit multiplications. Normally the modular reductions are interleaved within the iterations of the multiplication:

CLASSICAL MODULAR MULTIPLICATION ALGORITHM:

{ Pre-condition: $A = \sum_{i=0}^{n-1} a_i r^i$ }
```
R := 0 ;
For i := n-1 downto 0 do
Begin
      R  := r×R + aᵢ×B ;
      qᵢ := R div M ;
      R  := R - qᵢ×M ;
End ;
```
{ Post-condition: $R \equiv (A \times B) \bmod M$ }

Montgomery's version of long integer modular multiplication [11] has a similar structure, just reversing the order of processing the digits a_i.

Both the classical algorithm above and Montgomery's version are usually implemented in a way which makes them behave identically as far as this attack is concerned. The main variation worth highlighting is that for each long integer multiplication of the exponentiation either input A or B may be chosen as the pre-computed power of the initial ciphertext C. For convenience, we assume this power of C is the first argument, namely A, in the above code. However, to avoid unnecessary movement of data, the hardware must usually choose the same order for every multiplication. Then it is easy for an attacker to try both possibilities and select the one which provides the expected correlations.

3   Selecting & Averaging the Power Traces for Big Mac

The attack requires side channel leakage which has a dependency on the data being processed by the multiplier. Apart from measuring power consumption of the whole chip [4], the methods of Gandolfi et al. [5] could be directed to measuring EMR from the multiplier itself.

Assume that discrete sampling of the cryptographic device provides a power (or EMR) trace function $tr : \mathbf{Z} \to \mathbf{R}$ for the pre-computations and exponentiation for a single decryption or signing. The definition of tr outside this computation interval is irrelevant here. Suppose further that the regular sampling provides a non-zero number of values for every digit multiplication. The more frequent the sampling, the better the results obtained for this attack, especially if a number of measurements can be made during each clock cycle. Typically, the standard smart card clock runs at 3.57 MHz and the current is sampled at 200 MHz, yielding a ratio of nearly 2^6 to 1. This current is recorded using one or two bytes per measurement. As far as possible, such sampling should be synchronised to take place at the same points of each clock cycle.

Sommer [12] noted that certain points in the clock cycle have much greater value for determining data dependencies than others. Initially, as gates are switched along paths in the multiplier, the current will be higher and be dependent on the activity. However, at the end of a clock cycle the combinational logic should have stabilised, and it will have a much lower data dependent contribution. We are only interested in points with data dependent power consumption. Assume that several such points have been identified in the clock cycle, and we are able to take a weighted average of them in the trace so that, as far as possible, the data dependent contribution to the power represents the number of gates being switched and any measurement errors are averaged out. All other points must be discarded from the trace, leaving only data dependent ones.

The main loop of the long integer modular multiplication algorithm contains a repetition of k-bit multiply-accumulate digit operations of the form

$$r_j + r \times carry \quad := \quad r_{j-1} + a_i \times b_j + carry \qquad (0 \le j < n)$$

which take place in a single cycle. It is only the sub-traces for these operations that are used in the attack. The sections of the trace corresponding to these can be identified easily because, by using the multiplier, they differ substantially from sections corresponding to other operations.

Suppose we have already distinguished squares from multiplies and wish to establish the value of the exponent digit, say d_s, associated with the sth long integer multiplication. Let tr_{sij} denote the function obtained by setting tr to 0 outside the sub-interval during which the attacker expects the digit product $a_i \times b_j$ to be computed within the sth multiplication, and then translating that subinterval to $[i\tau, (i+1)\tau-1]$ where τ is the common number of sample points for each such digit-by-digit multiply-accumulate. (After deleting irrelevant points and averaging as necessary, we may well have reduced τ to 1.)

Assuming, as stated, that A is the input which is a pre-computed power of C, define $tr_{si} = \frac{1}{n} \sum_{j=0}^{n-1} tr_{sij}$ to be the function given by averaging the tr_{sij} over all j. So tr_{si} depends on the single digit a_i of A but all the digits b_j and r_j of essentially random numbers B and R, and some carries. This averaging should produce a function tr_{si} for which the random variable associated with the value at any given point has contributions to the variance from its dependence on B and from random noise, both of which are only $\frac{1}{n}$ times those for a_i and for equivalent positions in tr. Because the multiply-accumulate operation uses k times as much hardware in a_i- and b_j-dependent computations than for accumulating the $carry$ and r_{j-1} digits, the contributions from r_{j-1} and the $carry$ are certainly lower, perhaps by k times, than that from B. Hence the clearest correlation that tr_{si} should exhibit will be with the value of a_i.

This averaging of the traces over the digits of B replaces the usual DPA averaging of traces over a number of different exponentiations. On the reasonable assumption that B is sufficiently random and has a number of digits, the resulting average trace will then have little dependence on B. (If the pre-computed power is the B input, we sum over i instead of j to obtain a result which again depends on a single digit of the pre-computed power of C.)

Lastly, define $tr_s : \mathbf{Z} \to \mathbf{R}$ by $tr_s = \sum_{i=0}^{n-1} tr_{si}$. As tr_s is the concatenation of the non-zero sections of the tr_{si}, it has a non-zero definition on $[0, n\tau-1]$ whose strongest data dependency is through the pre-computed argument A of the sth multiplication, i.e. the power of C corresponding to the exponent digit d_s. The obvious question to ask is whether this dependency is strong enough to identify d_s since then the secret exponent d can be discovered.

4   Simulation

In order to investigate the feasibility of the attack, a simple k-bit multiplier was simulated. It was built mostly from standard 3-to-2 full adders with a carry propagator and had a variable size k. This was used to count gate switching in the combinational logic only, with no account being taken of changes in registers which might contribute to power use.

Data-dependent power usage is immediately apparent when gate counts are partitioned into subsets according to the Hamming weight of the two inputs. There is a very clear increase in the number of gate switchings as the Hamming weight of either input is increased. Tables of these values displayed a difference of a little over k gate changes between adjacent cells in the centre of the table, where both Hamming weights are approximately $k/2$ and most input pairs are clustered. Except for extreme Hamming weights, the table entries were almost linear in each Hamming weight − sufficiently so to explain and justify the arguments below. Moreover, the results were essentially symmetrical, i.e. the same number of gates were switched on average when the two inputs were interchanged. This occurred under several configurations even though no attempt was made to balance the number of gates switched.

For a variety of values of k, modulus bit lengths and exponent bases m, a number of random sets of powers $\{C^{(1)}, C^{(2)}, ..., C^{(m-1)}\}$ were generated. These were used as input A of the modular multiplier and, to simulate the pre-comuptations, multiplied by a random long integer B to create a trace tr_i associated with each $C^{(i)}$. The trace consisted of a vector of gate switch counts for each digit of $C^{(i)}$. These individual counts were the sum of the gate switch counts for each product of the digit of $C^{(i)}$ by a digit of B. The traces then corresponded to the power traces tr_s. With the component from B averaged, the trace tr_i for each $C^{(i)}$ corresponded closely to the vector of true average gate switch counts for the digits of $C^{(i)}$. In particular, this meant the trace was reasonably characteristic of $C^{(i)}$ and its elements were closely related to the Hamming weights of the digits.

To simulate exponentiation multiplications, another random long integer B' was chosen, multiplied by a random member of $\{C^{(1)}, C^{(2)}, ..., C^{(m-1)}\}$, and the trace $tr_{B'}$ of gate switch counts created. Like tr_B, it was close to the true average gate switch counts for whichever $C^{(i)}$ had been selected. The trace was matched up with the traces tr_i of each $C^{(i)}$. Specifically, the Euclidean distance between it and every tr_i was computed, and the closest chosen to predict i.

The attack simply requires this prediction to be correct. For many typical values of k, n and m, the attack invariably succeeded. Table 1 gives the means

Table 1.   Gate Switch Statistics for 512-bit Modulus with $m = 4$.

Multiplier Size	$k = 64$	$k = 32$	$k = 24$	$k = 16$	$k = 8$
Av to nearest	4973	2709	2538	2428	2245
SD to nearest	2582	1482	1334	1183	1024
Av to others	17981	24312	19834	23475	19793
SD to others	1232	513	408	481	217

and standard deviations for i) the distances between $tr_{B'}$ and the correct tr_i and ii) $tr_{B'}$ and the incorrect tr_i. The difference between the two cases is startlingly large. Table 2 shows low error frequencies even in the worst cases, namely for the largest k and smallest n. If the number of bits in the modulus length is fixed, then the average distance to the nearest trace increases as k increases so that difference between nearest and non-nearest traces decreases. For fixed k, increasing the size of the modulus provides more digits over which to average and more elements in the vector, thereby improving the ability to determine the multiplier correctly. As one would expect, increasing m just makes the nearest trace closer and increases the variance in the distances to the rest.

Table 2.   Gate Switch Statistics for 32-bit multiplier with $m = 8$.

Modulus Length	256 bits	384 bits	512 bits	768 bits	1024 bits
Av to nearest	1529	2366	3750	4501	6246
SD to nearest	885	1403	2386	2535	3612
Av to others	5890	11753	17896	32594	53070
SD to others	1108	2412	2279	4646	4581
%age errors	0.9284	0.1155	0.2819	0.0000	0.0000

Squares and random products were distinguishable from multiplications by a $C^{(i)}$ because their traces were not close to any tr_i. Indeed, the statistics for each were similar to the non-nearest table entries. Thus, all long integer multiplicative operations, including squares, could normally be correctly distinguished in the simulation and hence the secret key recovered.

5   Distances between Power Traces

Suppose tr_{s1} and tr_{s2} are a pair of power traces constructed as above for the $s1$th and $s2$th multiplications of the exponentiation. As the traces are real-valued functions on the integer subinterval $[0, n\tau{-}1]$, they represent points in $\mathbf{R}^{n\tau}$. Define d to be the Euclidean metric on $\mathbf{R}^{n\tau}$ and let $d(s1, s2)$ be the distance between the points defined by tr_{s1} and tr_{s2}. One advantage of such a metric is that places where the traces differ most contribute much more highly to the distance between traces than places with the smallest differences. This should help to emphasise the contribution from parameter A, which is approximately n times the contribution from other parameters. It is important to omit from this metric the points without a noticable data-dependent contribution as they reduce the visibility of the data dependence which needs to be observed.

For equal exponent digits $d_{s1} = d_{s2}$ the corresponding multiplications share the same first argument. Since there are no other strong data dependencies, the value of $d(s1, s2)$ should be small, corresponding purely to noise and variation from the average of the digits appearing in the other arguments. For different exponent digits $d_{s1} \neq d_{s2}$ the value of $d(s1, s2)$ should be noticeably larger because of the greater dependence on the first arguments, which are different.

According to the simulation, the data dependent contribution to power consumption is roughly proportional to the Hamming weight of the arguments. So we can expect the distance between two traces to be approximately related to the distance between the vectors consisting of the Hamming weights of the digits of the multipliers A. Since the Hamming weights of digits are distributed binomially, it is easy to obtain statistics for the random variable associated with the distance between two such vectors and see that it has very similar behaviour to that observed in the simulation. Hence this gives an accurate guide to the effect of changing any parameters and enables accurate error predictions to be made. In particular, it justifies the observation that distances between pair of traces cluster around two points, one of which is 0.

6 Identifying Equal Exponent Digits

Next we present an algorithm for partitioning the set $T = \{0, 1, 2, ..., t-1\}$ of exponent digit indices into subsets for which the corresponding digits of d are the same. This partition, $\wp$, has to define m subsets, one for each (exponent) digit value in base m. The subset containing the zero exponent digits should already have been identified by using the ability to distinguish between (long integer) squares and multiplies to observe which exponent digits have no corresponding muliplication in the exponentiation algorithm. For the other digit subsets, the association of each subset with a particular non-zero base-m digit is performed in the next section.

The algorithm puts the indices either into a new subset of the partition, or into the subset of indices which is "nearest" in an obvious sense: the distance between a single point s and a non-empty set of points S is defined here as $d(s, \bar{S})$ where $\bar{S}$ is the centroid of S, i.e. $\bar{S} = |S|^{-1} \sum_{s' \in S} s'$.

For each pair of (non-zero) exponentiation digits with indices $s1$ and $s2$, arrange the distances $d(s1, s2)$ into descending order, and set up $m-1$ buckets to receive sets of indices, one for each exponent digit value. Then consider the pairs $(s1, s2)$ in order of decreasing distance between their two traces:

i) If both indices are in different buckets, then move to the next pair.
ii) If there is one unassociated index and an empty bucket then place that index in the empty bucket and again move on to the next pair.

iii) If neither index is associated with a bucket and there are (at least) two empty buckets, put the indices into separate empty buckets, and move to the next pair.
iv) If both indices are in the same bucket, compute the distances of $s1$ and $s2$ from the set of indices in each bucket. If both are already in the nearest bucket, move on to the next pair, but otherwise, move $s1$ and $s2$ into their nearest buckets, moving the nearer one first and recomputing distances before moving the second. Then move to the next pair.
v) If there is an unassociated index and no empty bucket, then put the new index in a temporary extra bucket, compute the distances between every pair of buckets and combine the pair of buckets which are the shortest distance apart to restore the original number of buckets. Move to the next pair.
vi) If neither index is associated but there is only one empty bucket, compute the distances from $s1$ and $s2$ to each non-empty bucket. If $s1$ is the nearer to its nearest bucket, then put $s1$ into that bucket and $s2$ into the remaining empty bucket. Otherwise, put $s2$ into its nearest bucket and $s1$ into the empty bucket. Then move on to the next pair.
vii) If neither index is associated and there are no empty buckets, then perform (v) for both $s1$ and $s2$ individually.

With perfect data, the algorithm should first treat all the pairs $(s1, s2)$ which correspond to different exponent digits and correctly put them into different buckets or find that they are already in different buckets. Then, from some point on, all pairs correspond to equal digits and so the indices should be found in the same bucket. The algorithm does not place indices in the same bucket until there are no empty buckets left. So it is likely for indices with the same exponent digit to be initially spread over several buckets. These buckets then need to be coalesced to provide empty buckets for unassociated indices. Process (v) does this. Once there are no empty buckets left, then action (iv) is used to ensure that the best assignments have been made previously.

With perfect information, each element of T can be assigned to one of the partition subsets by calculating at most $m-1$ distances. So fewer than mt distances are required to establish the partition correctly if all distances are clearly and correctly distinguished as small or not. Hence, with up to $t(t-1)/2$ pairs in total, there is considerable extra information to improve and confirm the construction of $\wp$ as it progresses. However, in case of error, all assignments can be ranked using distances to buckets, and the most likely tried first for correctness.

7   Associating Digit Values with Exponent Positions

The partition $\wp$ yields $(m-1)!$ possibilities for the key d, corresponding to the possible associations[1] of non-zero digits from 1 to $m-1$ with the $m-1$

---

[1]   We have not assumed any knowledge of the modulus M. However, as Adi Shamir pointed out during the presentation, if M and e are known, then in this section one can probably make the correct association by using the fact that the bits of the top half of the exponent coincide with those of a small multiple of M.

different non-zero equivalence classes for the induced equivalence relation on $T = \{0, 1, 2, ..., t-1\}$. However, the pre-computation of the powers $C^{(i)}$ for $i = 1, 2, ..., m-1$ means that we have a known multiplication involving $C^{(i)}$ for each exponent digit except 0 and $m-1$, namely $C^{(i+1)} = C^{(i)} \times C \mod M$ in the case of m-ary exponentiation and $C^{(i+2)} = C^{(i)} \times C^{(2)} \mod M$ in the case of sliding windows.

Following the algorithm of the previous section, each trace tr_i corresponding to the pre-computational multiplication with first argument $A = C^{(i)}$ is associated with its nearest bucket of exponent digit indices. This bucket is then labelled "i" and should correspond to exponent digit i. Ideally, this should not associate two labels with one bucket, and should leave one bucket unlabelled. This last bucket is labelled with the remaining exponent digit, namely $m-1$.

If inconsistencies arise from this labelling, then it is easy to rank each possible labelling using distances from each tr_i to each bucket. Each labelling can be tried in turn until overall consistency in achieved. As the m-ary method uses significant memory when used in an embedded cryptographic device, m is usually very small. So all $(m-1)!$ possibilities could be tested for correctness if necessary.

The trace-averaging process depends on the randomness of the B input and its independence from the A input in order to obtain a result which characterises the A input. During the pre-computations, both inputs are powers of the initial text C and therefore not independent of each other. However, since 3 is generally regarded as an acceptable encryption exponent, we can assume that the powers $C^{(i)}$ are sufficiently independent of C when i contains an odd divisor. Then the traces tr_i should be acceptable for every i which is not a power of 2. Assuming also that problems with powers of 2 decrease as the power increases, only traces for the exponent digits 1 and 2 might display dependency problems.

For digit 1, the power trace for $C^{(2)} = C \times C \mod M$ depends on both arguments. We present two solutions to this. First, one can expect to identify which subtraces corresponding to the digit products $a \times a$. They can be excluded from the averaged trace to obtain a new trace which at each point depends on a single digit of C and some other effectively independent, random digits. Such a revised trace behaves like the other averaged trace functions. Alternatively, we may assume $m > 2$ since if $m = 2$ there is nothing to decide: all the non-zero exponent digits must be 1. Each product $C^{(i+1)} = C^{(i)} \times C \mod M$ involves C as the *second* argument rather than the first. Thus, for any one of these multiplications, one can average the traces in a different way, this time summing over the different first digits while the second is kept fixed, rather than vice versa. Then for $m > 2$ the last such multiplication gives an alternative to the initial squaring used in the first method for providing a trace for C. If $m > 4$ then the remarks above about 3 as an encryption exponent establish that the two arguments are effectively independent when the last multiplication is used for a trace for C. However, if $m = 4$ then this multiplication is the product of C and $C^{(2)}$ and there may be cause for concern. We remark on this potential problem next, but otherwise it is reasonable to assume that a typical trace can be obtained for the class of the exponent digit 1 from the pre-computation multiplications.

The trace associated with digit 2 is derived from the product of $C^{(2)}$ and C. Using the second alternative above, this may also be the source of the trace associated with digit 1. However, the dependence between these arguments should be very weak since an essentially random multiple of M has been subtracted from C^2 to obtain $C^{(2)}$. So a usable trace should also be obtained for digit 2.

8   Big Mac

By omitting the cross-checking afforded by comparing multiplications of the exponentiation, we obtain the Big Mac attack in which exponent digits are determined independently, as in the simulation section. Each trace tr_s from a multiplication in the exponentiation is compared with each trace tr_i from the pre-computations and the nearest is selected to determine the exponent digit at position s. When no pre-computation trace is close to tr_s then digit $m-1$ (for which there is no pre-computation trace) is assigned. All t exponent digits can then be recovered in t times the time required for recovering one digit. Moreover, apart from pre-computations, only the power trace for a single multiplication is used to recover a single exponent digit. So t times the data, i.e. the whole exponentiation record, is required to recover all digits.

More precisely, suppose k and m are fixed and, as usual, $t \approx nk/\log_2 m$. We are interested in what happens when the bit length nk of the arguments is varied. For each long integer multiplication the number of k-bit multiplications is $O(t^2)$. But, for a common level of accuracy, all averaged traces could be compiled from a *fixed* number of these digit-by-digit multiplications which is independent of t. This would use only constant data per exponent digit and consequently $O(t)$ data for the whole attack. If the full quantity of data is used, the traces tr_s become more accurate as t (or nk) increases. Furthermore, if every pair $(s1, s2)$ is considered, then more cross-checking is possible as t increases. Hence, the attack becomes much more viable for larger keys!

9   Using a Set of Exponentiations

The method of attack described so far has been developed from the power trace associated with a single exponentiation. It depended on a reasonable separation between the powers of the initial input C when measured using the Euclidean metric on the associated vectors of digit Hamming weights. If any powers of C are too closely related the attack may fail to work. However, one could wait patiently for an input C where the Hamming weights of the pre-computed powers are sufficiently widely spread. For large n with small m, this should not take long.

To benefit from traces from a set of exponentiations, it is important *not* to average the traces. Instead, if the exponent is the same in each case, the sub-traces for each multiplication need to be *concatenated* to provide longer vectors for comparison. Alternatively, an observation matrix can be constructed with a row for each exponentiation and a column for each exponent digit index, and containing the best estimate for the exponent digit. Repeated use of the same digits at the same exponentiation points then leads to corresponding correlations between columns of this matrix. Standard statistical techniques should then reveal the exponent.

10   Some Final Details

10.1   Separating Squares and Multiplies

Finally, we consider some detail which, for the sake of simplicity, was left out of the above arguments. The first concerns differentiating squares from multiplies. The simulation section noted that squares behaved like multiplications by $C^{(m-1)}$, having no nearest multiplier. Therefore using distances from pre-multiplication traces to classify all long integer operations will place both these types in the same bucket. Since each multiplication must be preceded and followed by r squarings, the determination of which is which should be straightforward. Moreover, the multiplications by $C^{(m-1)}$ should all be close to each other, whilst the squarings should not. Indeed, this also enables the case $m = 2$ to be cracked. Thus, if the attack separates the different multipliers, it certainly also separates the squares.

10.2   Initial Exponent Digits

The next omission relates to the initial few multiplications of the exponentiation after any pre-computation has taken place. The first value assigned to P in the exponentiation algorithm of §2.1 corresponds to the first (non-zero) digit of d and involves no multiplication. Hence the method here appears to yield no information about it. Thus there may be $m-1$ times more possibilities for d than estimated above, one for each choice of the first non-zero digit of d. This is followed by r squarings. The first is of $C^{(d_1)}$. However, a trace for $C^{(d_1)}$ can be extracted in the same way as described in §7 for obtaining a trace of C from computing $C^{(2)}$. This should reveal d_1 using the usual nearest bucket method. Once the multiplications for P do start, the B argument of the modular multiplication is generally no longer sufficiently closely related to influence the power trace adversely. The attack will therefore work successfully from this point on. The only noticeable exception is the first multiplication (as opposed to a squaring) when $m = 2$ and the second digit of d is 1.

10.3   Zero Multiplier Digits

The last concern is if zero digits (base r) occur in the inputs to a modular multiplication and optimization causes the associated digit multiplications to be skipped. To avoid timing attacks, this should probably not occur. However, with typical values such as $r \approx 2^{32}$, $n \approx 2^5$, $m = 4$ and $t \approx 2^8$ for 1024-bit keys, we have about $mn = 2^7$ digits among the pre-computed powers, and about $nt(m-1)/m = 1.5 \times 2^{12}$ digits among the arguments B of the multiplications during an exponentiation. So the chances of encountering a digit 0 are small ($\approx nt/r$). In the unlikely event of a zero, the analysis should become much easier. If the zero digit lies in a pre-computed power, timing analysis immediately reveals which multiplications use that power. Otherwise the zero digit occurs in the B argument of a multiplication and one simply defines tr_{si} by averaging the traces over the non-zero digits of B. At worst, another decryption trace might be obtained to avoid the problem altogether.

10.4   Chinese Remainder Theorem

Implementations using the Chinese Remainder Theorem can be attacked in the same way because having a single digit multiplier forces the two exponentiations to be performed sequentially. The two exponents are then recovered one after the other in the way described above, yielding the secret key.

11   Conclusion

An unknown plaintext DPA attack on a single RSA exponentiation has been described where the implementation uses a single k-bit multiplier. This may well prove successful, particularly against a RISC processor where no other operations can be carried out to mask the multiplier's use of power. The attack becomes easier to perform accurately as the key length is increased because more useful data is available. For fixed k and using all available data, the running time is proportional to the key length cubed.

The attacker waits for a sufficiently helpful exponentiation, and then uses a careful and novel selection and combination of sections from a single power trace to recover secret decryption keys. If the same exponent is reused the attack becomes easier. Blinding keys is no defence if the attack succeeds on a single exponentiation. Then other methods are required. One solution might be to keep a processor/co-processor architecture where the two processes mask each other. Alternatively, a pipelined k-bit multiplier with several stages might be used, or CRT performed with the exponentiations using two separate multipliers in parallel. Yet another solution might be to use a systolic modular multiplier [15] where many unrelated digit multiplications are computed in parallel.

Certainly one concludes that performing a single, digit-level operation at one time, such as a multiplication, leads to a potentially unsafe implementation of the RSA cryptosystem.

References

1. D. Boneh, *Twenty Years of Attacks on the RSA Cryptosystem*, Notices of the AMS, **46**, no. 2, Feb 1999, pp 203-213.
2. D. Boneh, R. DeMillo & R. Lipton, *On the Importance of Checking Cryptographic Protocols for Faults*, Eurocrypt '97, Lecture Notes in Computer Science **1233**, Springer-Verlag, 1997, pp. 37-51.

3. D. Chaum, *Blind Signatures for Untraceable Payments*, Proc. Advances in Cryptology (Crypto '82), Plenum Press, 1983, pp. 199-203.
4. J.-S. Coron, *Resistance against Differential Power Analysis for Elliptic Curve Cryptosystems*, Cryptographic Hardware and Embedded Systems (Proc CHES 99), C. Paar & Ç. Koç editors, Lecture Notes in Computer Science **1717**, Springer-Verlag, 1999, pp. 292-302.
5. K. Gandolfi, C. Mourtel & F. Olivier, *Electromagnetic Analysis: Concrete Results*, Cryptographic Hardware and Embedded Systems (Proc CHES 2001), Ç. Koç, D. Naccache & C. Paar editors, Lecture Notes in Computer Science (*this volume*), Springer-Verlag, 2001.
6. D. E. Knuth, The Art of Computer Programming, vol. 2, *Seminumerical Algorithms*, 2nd Edition, Addison-Wesley, 1981, pp. 441-466.
7. Ç. K. Koç, *Analysis of Sliding Window Techniques for Exponentiation*, Computers and Mathematics with Applications, **30**, no. 10, 1995, pp.17-24.
8. P. Kocher, *Timing Attacks on Implementations of Diffie-Hellman, RSA, DSS, and Other Systems*, Advances in Cryptology, Proc Crypto 96, Lecture Notes in Computer Science **1109**, N. Koblitz editor, Springer-Verlag, 1996, pp 104-113.
9. P. Kocher, J. Jaffe & B. Jun, *Differential Power Analysis*, Advances in Cryptology − Crypto '99, Lecture Notes in Computer Science **1666**, M. Wiener (editor), Springer-Verlag, 1999, pp 388-397.
10. T. S. Messerges, E. A. Dabbish, R. H. Sloan, *Power Analysis Attacks of Modular Exponentiation in Smartcards*, Cryptographic Hardware and Embedded Systems (Proc CHES 99), C. Paar & Ç. Koç editors, Lecture Notes in Computer Science **1717**, Springer-Verlag, 1999, pp. 144-157.
11. P. L. Montgomery, *Modular Multiplication without Trial Division*, Math. Computation, **44**, 1985, pp. 519-521.
12. R. Mayer-Sommer, *Smartly Analyzing the Simplicity and the Power of Simple Power Analysis on Smartcards*, Cryptographic Hardware and Embedded Systems (Proc CHES 2000), C. Paar & Ç. Koç editors, Lecture Notes in Computer Science **1965**, Springer-Verlag, 2000, pp. 78-92.
13. R. L. Rivest, A. Shamir & L. Adleman, *A Method for obtaining Digital Signatures and Public-Key Cryptosystems*, Comm. ACM, **21**, 1978, pp. 120-126.
14. W. Schindler, *A Timing Attack against RSA with Chinese Remainder Theorem*, Cryptographic Hardware and Embedded Systems (Proc CHES 2000), C. Paar & Ç. Koç editors, Lecture Notes in Computer Science **1965**, Springer-Verlag, 2000, pp. 109-124.
15. C. D. Walter, *Systolic Modular Multiplication*, IEEE Transactions on Computers, **42**, no. 3, March 1993, pp. 376-378.
16. C. D. Walter & S. Thompson, *Distinguishing Exponent Digits by Observing Modular Subtractions*, Topics in Cryptology − CT-RSA 2001, D. Naccache (editor), Lecture Notes in Computer Science **2020**, Springer-Verlag, 2001, pp. 192-207.

Universal Exponentiation Algorithm

A First Step towards *Provable* SPA-Resistance

Christophe Clavier and Marc Joye

Gemplus Card International, Card Security Group
Parc d'Activités de Gémenos, B.P. 100, 13881 Gémenos, France
{christophe.clavier, marc.joye}@gemplus.com
http://www.geocities.com/MarcJoye/

Abstract. Very few countermeasures are known to protect an exponentiation against simple side-channel analyses. Moreover, all of them are heuristic.

This paper presents a universal exponentiation algorithm. By tying the exponent to a corresponding addition chain, our algorithm can virtually execute any exponentiation method.

Our aim is to transfer the security of the exponentiation method being implemented to the exponent itself. As a result, we hopefully tend to reconcile the provable security notions of modern cryptography with real-world implementations of exponentiation-based cryptosystems.

Keywords. Implementation, exponentiation, RSA cryptosystem, discrete logarithm, side-channel attacks, simple power analysis (SPA), addition chains, provable security, smart-cards.

1 Introduction

The security of a cryptosystem is evaluated as the latter's ability to resist attacks in a given adversarial model. It is very challenging to guess the strategy the adversary will follow in an attempt to break the system. So, the only assumptions made by modern cryptography refer to the *computational abilities* of the adversary [6]. Loosely speaking, a cryptosystem is then said *secure* if there is no polynomial-time adversary able to gain more "useful" information than a honest user by deviating from the "prescribed" behavior.

In [9,11], Kocher *et al.* launched a new class of attacks: the so-called *side-channel attacks*. In such a scenario, an adversary monitors some side-channel information (e.g., power consumption) during the execution of a crypto-algorithm and thereby may foil the security of the corresponding "provably secure" cryptosystem. So what does provable security mean? The security is usually proven by reduction: one shows that the only way to break the cryptosystem is to break the underlying cryptographic primitive (e.g., the RSA function). Since this is assumed to be computationally infeasible, the cryptosystem is declared secure. A side-channel attack does *not* violate this assumption, it just considers other directions to break the cryptographic primitive. Consequently, we stress that the

Ç.K. Koç, D. Naccache, and C. Paar (Eds.): CHES 2001, LNCS 2162, pp. 300–308, 2001.

notions of provable security, or more exactly *provable computational security*, are very useful and must be part of the analysis of any cryptosystem.

Unfortunately, there is no counterpart to side-channel attacks. Defining a security model for this class of attacks seems unrealistic since we do not see how to limit the power of the adversary. The best we can hope to prove is the security relative to one particular attack.

This paper focuses on modular exponentiation (e.g., the RSA function or the discrete logarithm function) as a cryptographic primitive. Using a representation with addition chains, we "transfer" the security of the exponentiation method actually implemented in the exponent itself (which is the secret data). The resulting algorithm, which we call *universal exponentiation algorithm*, works with virtually all exponentiation methods. It simply reads triplets of values $(\gamma(i) : \alpha(i), \beta(i))$, meaning that the content of register $R[\alpha(i)]$ must be multiplied by the content of register $R[\beta(i)]$ and that the result must be written into register $R[\gamma(i)]$. We provide in this way a kind of reduction. Instead of carefully analyzing a specific exponentiation method, the implementor simply verifies that the *atomic* operation $R[\gamma(i)] \leftarrow R[\alpha(i)] \cdot R[\beta(i)]$ does not leak any "useful" information through a given side-channel attack. This methodology is reminiscent of the traditional security proofs. In the traditional case, the security of a cryptographic primitive is conjectured (e.g., inverting the RSA function is infeasible) whereas in our case the security of an atomic operation is assessed through experiments (e.g., I cannot "break" a multiplication by SPA). The main difference is that the security assumption is scrutinized by fewer people and hence is more controversial.

The rest of this paper is organized as follows. The next section recalls the definition of an addition chain. Based on it, we then present our universal exponentiation algorithm. In Section 3, we discuss the merits of our approach from a security viewpoint. Section 4 suggests some modifications to our basic algorithm. Finally, we conclude in Section 5.

2   Universal Exponentiation Algorithm

2.1   Addition Chains

We start by a brief introduction to addition chains. For further details, we refer the reader to [8].

Definition 1. *An* addition chain *for a positive integer d is a sequence $\mathcal{C}(d) = \{d^{(0)}, d^{(1)}, \ldots, d^{(\ell)}\}$ satisfying*

1. *$d^{(0)} = 1$, $d^{(\ell)} = d$, and*
2. *for all $1 \leq i \leq \ell$, there exist $j(i), k(i) < i$ such that $d^{(i)} = d^{(j(i))} + d^{(k(i))}$.*

Integer ℓ defines the *length* of chain $\mathcal{C}$. An addition chain is called a *star-chain* if for all $1 \leq i \leq \ell$ there exists $k(i) < i$ such that $d^{(i)} = d^{(i-1)} + d^{(k(i))}$.

A slightly more general notion is that of addition-subtraction chains.

Definition 2. *An* addition-subtraction chain *for an integer d is a sequence $\mathcal{C}(d) = \{d^{(0)}, d^{(1)}, \ldots, d^{(\ell)}\}$ satisfying*

1. $d^{(0)} = 1$, $d^{(\ell)} = d$, and
2. for all $1 \leq i \leq \ell$ there exist $j(i), k(i) < i$ such that $d^{(i)} = \pm d^{(j(i))} \pm d^{(k(i))}$.

2.2   A Universal Algorithm

Let $\mathcal{C}(d) = \{d^{(0)}, d^{(1)}, \ldots, d^{(\ell)}\}$ be an addition chain for exponent d. So for all $1 \leq i \leq \ell$, we have $d^{(i)} = d^{(j(i))} + d^{(k(i))}$. This provides an easy means to evaluate $y = x^d$: For $i = 1$ to ℓ compute

$$x^{d^{(i)}} = x^{d^{(j(i))}} \cdot x^{d^{(k(i))}}$$

and then set $y = x^{d^{(\ell)}}$. So, from an addition chain of length ℓ, ℓ multiplications are required to compute y.

Example 1. An addition chain for 5 is $\mathcal{C}(5) = \{1, 2, 3, 5\}$ and so $x^1 = x$, $x^2 = x^1 \cdot x^1$, $x^3 = x^2 \cdot x^1$, and finally $x^5 = x^3 \cdot x^2$.

At step i, $x^{d^{(i)}}$ is evaluated as $x^{d^{(i)}} = x^{d^{(j(i))}} \cdot x^{d^{(k(i))}}$. Assuming that $x^{d^{(j(i))}}$ and $x^{d^{(k(i))}}$ respectively belong to registers $R[\alpha(i)]$ and $R[\beta(i)]$ and that the result, $x^{d^{(i)}}$, is written in register $R[\gamma(i)]$, exponent d can be represented by the *register sequence*

$$\Gamma(d) = \left\{ (\gamma(i) : \alpha(i), \beta(i)) \right\}_{1 \leq i \leq \ell}, \tag{1}$$

meaning that $R[\gamma(i)] = R[\alpha(i)] \cdot R[\beta(i)]$. (By convention, the value $d = 1$ is represented by $\Gamma(1) = \emptyset$.)

From this, we obtain the following exponentiation algorithm (for $d > 1$):

Input: $x, \Gamma(d)$
Output: $y = x^d$

$R[\alpha(1)] \leftarrow x$; $R[\beta(1)] \leftarrow x$
for $i = 1$ to ℓ do
  $R[\gamma(i)] \leftarrow R[\alpha(i)] \cdot R[\beta(i)]$
return $R[\gamma(\ell)]$

Algorithm 1. Universal exponentiation algorithm.

Note that $R[\alpha(1)]$ and $R[\beta(1)]$ are initialized to x because the second item of each addition chain is always $d^{(1)} = 2$. Note also that one may have $\alpha(1) = \beta(1)$.

For star chains, we have $d^{(i)} = d^{(i-1)} + d^{(k(i))}$. Therefore pairs are sufficient to represent d: $\alpha(i) = \gamma(i-1)$ for all $1 \leq i \leq \ell$ and can be omitted from the representation. Hence, we have the *star register sequence*

$$\Gamma^*(d) = \left\{ (\gamma(i) : \beta(i)) \right\}_{1 \leq i \leq \ell}. \tag{2}$$

The corresponding exponentiation algorithm is:

Input: $x, \Gamma^*(d)$
Output: $y = x^d$
$R[\gamma(0)] \leftarrow x;\ R[\beta(1)] \leftarrow x$
for $i = 1$ to ℓ do
$\quad R[\gamma(i)] \leftarrow R[\gamma(i-1)] \cdot R[\beta(i)]$
return $R[\gamma(\ell)]$

Algorithm2. Universal star exponentiation algorithm.

3 Towards Provable SPA-Resistance

The ultimate goal of smart-card manufacturers is a proof that their implementations are resistant to side-channel analysis. In this paper, we adopt the methodology of modern cryptography towards this goal.

Take for example the encryption scheme RSA-OAEP [3]. The minimal security requirement for an encryption scheme is *one-wayness* (OW). This captures the property that an adversary cannot recover the whole plaintext from a given ciphertext. In some cases, partial information about a plaintext may have disastrous consequences. This notion is captured by *semantic security* or the equivalent notion of *indistinguishability* [7]. Basically, indistinguishability means that the only strategy for an adversary to distinguish between the encryptions of any two plaintexts is to guess at random. The strongest attacks one can imagine (at the protocol level) are the so-called *adaptive chosen-ciphertext attacks* (CCA2). Those attacks consider an active adversary who can obtain the decryption of any ciphertext of her/his choice. From the pair of adversarial goal (IND) and adversarial model (CCA2), we derive the security notion of IND-CCA2. In an IND-CCA2 scenario, an adversary has access to a decryption oracle. S/he first outputs a pair of plaintexts m_0 and m_1. Then, given a challenge ciphertext c_b which is either the encryption of m_0 or m_1, the adversary has to guess with a probability nonnegligibly better than $1/2$ if c_b encrypts m_0 or m_1. The attack is called adaptive, if after receiving the challenge c_b, the adversary may still obtain decryptions of chosen ciphertexts, the only restriction being not to probe on c_b.

In [3], Bellare and Rogaway remarkably proved that if an adversary is able to break the IND-CCA2 security of RSA-OAEP then the same adversary is able to break the OW security of the RSA function, that is, to compute an eth root modulo a large composite number $N = pq$ (where typically p and q are 512-bit primes). Since the latter is assumed infeasible, RSA-OAEP is declared provably secure. We note that their proof only holds in the *random oracle model* [2], i.e., an ideal world where hash functions behave like random functions. To summarize, the security of RSA-OAEP is proven by

1. identifying the security goal and the adversarial model (i.e., IND-CCA2);
2. defining the working hypotheses (i.e., random oracle model);
3. exhibiting a reduction (i.e., breaking the IND-CCA2 of RSA-OAEP $\Rightarrow$ breaking the OW of the RSA function);

4. assuming that the reduced problem is intractable (i.e., inverting RSA is infeasible);
5. deducing the security notion (i.e., IND-CCA2 security of RSA-OAEP in the random oracle model).

The security of RSA-OAEP is at the protocol level. To break the IND-CCA2 security, the adversary has a black-box access to a decryption oracle: s/he knows the input and obtains the corresponding output. In the case of side-channel attacks, the adversary is more powerful: s/he gets access to some internal states of the computation.

So, by monitoring the power consumption of an RSA exponentiation, an attacker is even sometimes able to recover the secret decryption exponent d used in the computation of $y = x^d \bmod N$ and the OW assumption of the RSA function is no longer valid. Suppose for example that the RSA function is naively implemented with the square-and-multiply method. As shown in the next figure, the exponent can then be recovered very easily: a lower consumption level corresponds to a squaring and a higher consumption level corresponds to a multiplication.

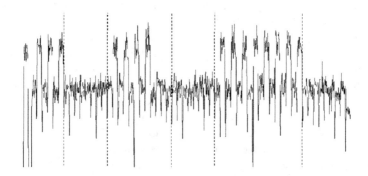

Fig. 1. Power trace of a square-and-multiply exponentiation.

In our simplified model, we consider the fundamental security goal of *unbreakability* (UB). A cryptosystem is said unbreakable if it is infeasible to recover the secret key. This kind of attack is usually referred to as a total breaking. We also consider an attacker who has access to some side-channel information. Depending on the side-channel information and the way it is treated, we define several adversarial models. In the *simple power analysis* (SPA) model, an attacker acquires the power trace of a single execution of the crypto-algorithm. From this, we derive the security notion of UB-SPA. Likewise, one can define the UB-DPA (DPA stands for *differential power analysis* [11]) and so on; one can also consider other security goals and derive security notions like OW-SPA or IND-SPA. It is worth noting here that, contrary to modern cryptography, the definition of an adversarial model is not *absolute*: in a CCA2 attack, an adversary obtains the plaintext corresponding to a chosen ciphertext whereas in an attack like a

SPA, the "quality" of the returned information depends on the acquisition tools among other things.

Concentrating on the exponentiation function and more particularly on the RSA function, one can show that if an adversary is able to break the UB-SPA security of the universal exponentiation algorithm, s/he is also able to invert the RSA function. (We note that the main threat for an RSA exponentiation is the SPA; for DPA, efficient counter-measures are known.) In order to break the UB-SPA, an adversary must be able to gain some secret information from the basic operation $R[\gamma(i)] \leftarrow R[\alpha(i)] \cdot R[\beta(i)]$ by SPA, that is, s/he must be able to, at least, differentiate among the triplets $(\gamma(i) : \alpha(i), \beta(i))$ and to recover *all* their values to break the UB property. Assuming that the latter is infeasible (this can be verified experimentally), one has strong evidence[1] that the universal exponentiation algorithm resists to SPA. As a conclusion, if RSA-OAEP is implemented with the universal exponentiation algorithm, we have strong evidence that it resists SPA attacks. Note here that the security is assessed at the implementation level.

From a security viewpoint, the advantage of our method is evident. It reduces the problem of scrutinizing *any* exponentiation algorithm to that of the simpler operation $R[\gamma(i)] \leftarrow R[\alpha(i)] \cdot R[\beta(i)]$. This makes the job of the implementor a lot easier since s/he has a better knowledge of the sensitive parts of her/his algorithm. Moreover, the security passes from a macroscopic level (a software exponentiation) to a microscopic level (a hardware multiplication). Finally, the analysis must be done once for all and remains valid whatever the exponentiation algorithm underlying a given Γ-representation.

Remark 1. In some ways, to relax the assumption the universal exponentiation algorithm is UB-SPA, one can always randomly add dummy operations at the expense of a longer running time (e.g., to add to a Γ representation, a triplet that does not affect the final result). One can also exploit the property that $R[\gamma(i)] \leftarrow R[\alpha(i)] \cdot R[\beta(i)]$ and $R[\gamma(i)] \leftarrow R[\beta(i)] \cdot R[\alpha(i)]$ both lead to the same result. Another solution consists to randomly permute the order of the registers and their values during the course of the exponentiation.

In addition to simplifying the security analysis, our universal exponentiation algorithm has the following features:

- it is *simple*: its implementation is straightforward and so programming errors are likely avoided;
- it is *flexible*: owing to the genericity of the Γ-representation, it can virtually execute all exponentiation algorithms;
- it is *fast*: contrary to the protected square-and-multiply method (a.k.a. square-and-multiply-always method) which requires $2 \log_2 d$ multiplications for computing $y = x^d$, our algorithm may require as few as $1.25 \log_2 d$ multiplications (cf. § 4.1);

---

[1] In contrast with modern cryptography, we cannot say that we have a proof of security because as aforementioned this depends on the quality of the experiments.

– it is *economic*: if the exponentiation algorithm underlying a Γ-representation happens to be flawed, it is enough to correct the Γ-representation: a complete re-programming is unnecessary.

The last property is especially interesting for a smart-card implementation. The program code is usually stored in ROM memory via an expensive process called masking and the secret key (e.g., the RSA decryption exponent d) is stored in EEPROM memory at the personalization stage. So in case of secret leakage or mis-programming, one has just to change or correct the Γ-representation of the secret exponent.

4   Practical Considerations

If we want to realize a smart-card implementation of the proposed algorithms (Algorithms 1 and 2), we face some constraints. A smart-card has a limited number of registers and so we need a way to produce Γ-representations with a predetermined number of registers. Moreover, a Γ-representation with fewer registers requires fewer memory for its storage. Another difficulty may occur when the secret exponent is generated outside the card by a third party because it is given in its binary representation.

In this section, we suggest two different approaches that alleviate the above limitations.

4.1   On-Line Generation

A straightforward solution is to produce a Γ-representation on-line, i.e., by the smart-card itself. Several good heuristics are known for producing relatively short addition chains. In [12], Walter suggests the following method to compute $y = x^d$ (see also [4]).

Define $d_0 = d$, $x_0 = x$, and $y_0 = 1$. Next, at each step, write $d_i = m_i d_{i+1} + r_i$ for appropriately chosen values for (m_i, r_i). Hence, letting $x_{i+1} = x_i{}^{m_i}$ and $y_{i+1} = x_i{}^{r_i} y_i$, we get

$$
\begin{aligned}
y = x_0{}^{d_0} y_0 &= (x_0{}^{m_0})^{d_1} (x_0{}^{r_0} y_0) \\
&= x_1{}^{d_1} y_1 = (x_1{}^{m_1})^{d_2} (x_1{}^{r_1} y_1) \\
&= x_2{}^{d_2} y_2 = (x_2{}^{m_2})^{d_3} (x_2{}^{r_2} y_2) \\
&= x_3{}^{d_3} y_3 = \cdots
\end{aligned}
$$

The idea behind Walter's method is to find pairs (m_i, r_i) so that the evaluations of both $x_i{}^{m_i}$ and $x_i{}^{r_i}$ are inexpensive. This is the case when r_i lies in the addition chain used to evaluate $x_i{}^{m_i}$.

Such a method is very well suited to a smart-card implementation. It is easy to implement and the corresponding register sequence, $\Gamma(d)$, requires only one more register than the standard square-and-multiply method. Furthermore, the average length of $\Gamma(d)$ is only $1.25 \log_2 d$, with a very small deviation. See [12] for details.

Note that the computation of $\Gamma(d)$ must be performed in a secured environment since its disclosure reveals the value of secret exponent d. For example, this can performed at the personalization of the card.

4.2   Exponent Splitting

The second solution we propose relies on the simple observation that

$$x^d = x^a \cdot x^{d-a} \tag{3}$$

for some a. The idea of splitting the data was already abstracted in [5] as a general countermeasure against differential power analysis attacks. We note that the values of *both* a and $(d-a)$ are required to recover the value of d. In other words, only one exponentiation, x^a or x^{d-a}, needs to be secured.

Given a register sequence for a, $\Gamma(a)$ or $\Gamma^*(a)$, we can compute $y' = x^a$ and $d' = d - a$, and so $x^d = y' \cdot x^{d'}$. There are two possible alternatives. The first one is, for a given a, to store a *chosen* (and thus fixed) register sequence, $\Gamma(a)$, during the personalization of the card. (In this case a star representation, $\Gamma^*(a)$, may be preferred since it requires fewer memory.) The advantage of this approach is that this imposes the underlying methods for computing $y' = x^a$ and $d' = d - a$.

Another alternative consists in *randomly* computing a register sequence, $\Gamma(a)$ or $\Gamma^*(a)$, for a "on the fly". The advantages of this second approach are twofold. First, no register sequence needs to be stored in non-volatile memory and so this results in some memory savings. Second, the methods for evaluating $y' = x^a$ and $d' = d - a$ differ at each execution. Independently, this randomization also helps to prevent differential attacks like the DPA.

5   Conclusion

In this paper, we presented an universal exponentiation algorithm. Through the notion of register sequence, $\Gamma(d) = \{(\gamma(i) : \alpha(i), \beta(i))\}_{1 \le i \le \ell}$, built from addition chains, we explained how this helps to protect an exponentiation-based cryptosystem against simple side-channel attacks like SPA. Assuming that a more atomic operation (i.e., the multiplication of registers $R[\gamma(i)] \leftarrow R[\alpha(i)] \cdot R[\beta(i)]$) does not leak secret information, we "proved" the security of our implementation. There is no secret at all involved in our universal exponentiation algorithm: the secret exponent d is intimately tied to $\Gamma(d)$ and recovering the value of d supposes the recovery of the whole sequence $\Gamma(d)$, which is a contradiction. Furthermore, our algorithm can be trivially implemented and it greatly simplifies the security analysis since the critical (i.e., sensitive) parts are better understood.

As a final conclusion, we hope that this first step towards provable security of real-world implementations will be a motivating starting-point for further research in this very important subject.

Acknowledgements

The authors are grateful to Jacques Fournier, Karine Gandolfi and Florence Quès for some comments.

References

1. Mihir Bellare, Anand Desai, David Pointcheval, and Phillip Rogaway. Relations among notions of security for public-key encryption schemes. Full paper (30 pages), February 1999. An extended abstract appears in H. Krawczyk, ed., Advances in Cryptology – CRYPTO '98, volume 1462 of Lecture Notes in Computer Science, pages 26–45, Springer-Verlag, 1998.
2. Mihir Bellare and Phillip Rogaway. Random oracles are practical: A paradigm for designing efficient protocols. In First ACM Conference on Computer and Communications Security, pages 62–73. ACM Press, 1993.
3. Mihir Bellare and Phillip Rogaway. Optimal asymmetric encryption. In A. De Santis, editor, Advances in Cryptology – EUROCRYPT '94, volume 950 of Lecture Notes in Computer Science, pages 92–111. Springer-Verlag, 1995.
4. F. Bergeron, J. Berstel, S. Brlek, and C. Duboc. Addition chains using continued fractions. Journal of Algorithms, 10(3):403–412, September 1989.
5. Suresh Chari, Charanjit S. Jutla, Josyula R. Rao, and Pankaj Rohatgi. Towards sound approaches to counteract power-analysis attacks. In M. Wiener, editor, Advances in Cryptology – CRYPTO '99, volume 1666 of Lecture Notes in Computer Science, pages 398–412. Springer-Verlag, 1999.
6. Oded Goldreich. On the foundations of modern cryptography. In B. Kaliski, editor, Advances in Cryptology – CRYPTO '97, volume 1294 of Lecture Notes in Computer Science, pages 46–74. Springer-Verlag, 1997.
7. Shafi Goldwasser and Silvio Micali. Probabilistic encryption. Journal of Computer and System Sciences, 28:270–299, 1984.
8. Donald E. Knuth. The art of computer programming/Seminumerical algorithms, volume 2. Addison-Wesley, 2nd edition, 1981.
9. Paul Kocher. Timing attacks on implementations of Diffie-Hellman, RSA, DSS, and other systems. In N. Koblitz, editor, Advances in Cryptology – CRYPTO '96, volume 1109 of Lecture Notes in Computer Science, pages 104–113. Springer-Verlag, 1996.
10. Paul Kocher. Secure modular exponentiation with leak minimization for smart cards and other cryptosystems. International patent WO 99/67909, March 1998.
11. Paul Kocher, Joshua Jaffe, and Benjamin Jun. Differential power analysis. In M. Wiener, editor, Advances in Cryptology – CRYPTO '99, volume 1666 of Lecture Notes in Computer Science, pages 388–397. Springer-Verlag, 1999.
12. Colin D. Walter. Exponentiation using division chains. IEEE Transactions on Computers, 47(7):757–765, July 1998.
13. Yacov Yacobi. Exponentiating faster with addition chains. In Advances in Cryptology – EUROCRYPT '90, volume 473 of Lecture Notes in Computer Science, pages 222–229. Springer-Verlag, 1991.

An Implementation of DES and AES, Secure against Some Attacks

Mehdi-Laurent Akkar[1] and Christophe Giraud[2]

[1] Schlumberger CP8,
68 route de Versailles, 78431 Louveciennes, France.
ml.akkar@free.fr
[2] Oberthur Card Systems,
25, rue Auguste Blanche, 92800 Puteaux, France.
c.giraud@oberthurcs.com

Abstract. Since Power Analysis on smart cards was introduced by Paul Kocher [7], many countermeasures have been proposed to protect implementations of cryptographic algorithms. In this paper we propose a new protection principle: the transformed masking method. We apply this method to protect two of the most popular block ciphers: DES and the AES Rijndael. To this end we introduce some transformed S-boxes for DES and a new masking method and its applications to the non-linear part of Rijndael.

Keywords: AES, Rijndael, DES, Transformed mask, Multiplicative mask, Power analysis, DPA, SPA, Smart Cards.

1 Introduction

Since Kocher, Jaffe and Jun introduced Differential Power Analysis, many countermeasures have been proposed to protect the card against power analysis type attacks (SPA, DPA, HODPA):

- insertion of dummy instructions;
- randomization of operations;
- transformation of the data (i.e. Duplication Method [6]);
- masking of the data [2,3]: boolean, arithmetic...

In this paper we present a practical implementation of DES ([10]) and AES ([5]) using some of these countermeasures combined with new methods. We will essentially use a new idea -an adapted masking method- combined with a bit-per-bit randomization of many operations during the computation.

2 Transformed Masking Method

2.1 Principle

The idea is the following: the message is masked at the beginning of the algorithm and after this, everything (or nearly) is as usual. Most of the previous proposed methods must respect a masking condition at each step of the

Ç.K. Koç, D. Naccache, and C. Paar (Eds.): CHES 2001, LNCS 2162, pp. 309–318, 2001.
© Springer-Verlag Berlin Heidelberg 2001

algorithm, but here we only need to know the value of the mask at a fixed step (for example at the end of a round or at the end of a non-linear part) and we reestablish the expected value at the end of the algorithm.

It is easy to see that the problem of implementing a masking countermeasure comes from the non-linear parts of the algorithm. Furthermore the security of a symmetric cryptographic algorithm is essentially based in these parts.

2.2   DES

In the case of the DES, the most appropriate mask is a boolean mask X which is applied before the Initial Permutation IP (we XOR the 64-bit message M with a 64-bit value X). The only non-linear part of the DES is the S-Box, so when using a masking countermeasure, we use a modified S-Box. This also enables us to reestablish the mask value. It is only after the Final Permutation FP that the mask will be removed to obtain the right result.

2.3   AES

For this algorithm, the method is slightly different. We still use a XOR operation as a masking countermeasure, but now the mask is arithmetic on $GF(2^8)$. This operation is compatible with the AES structure except for the inversion in $GF(2^8)$. For this, we use a new technique to transform the boolean mask into a multiplicative mask. This allows us to keep the same level of security throughout the algorithm. As for the DES, the mask will be reestablished at the end of each round and the value will be unmasked at the end of the algorithm.

3   Applications

3.1   Securing the DES

DES Structure We want to cipher a 64-bit message M with the DES. We choose a 64-bit mask X which will be XOR-ed with the message M at the beginning of the DES. Then we start with the value $M \oplus X$.

Just before the S-box, it is easy to see (fig.1) that we have an intermediary value masked with $X2 = EP(X1_{32-63})$ where:

- $X1$ represents the 64-bit value $IP(X)$;
- IP represents the initial permutation;
- $X1_{0-31}$ (respectively $X1_{32-63}$) represents the 32-bit low-weight (respectively high-weight) part of the 64-bit mask X;
- $X2$ represents the 48-bit value $EP(X1_{32-63})$;
- EP represents the expansive permutation of a DES round.

The method chosen in the case of the DES is to reestablish the mask $X1$ at each round. To obtain this result, we will use a modified S-box, denoted SM-Box. The output of the SM-Box, after the permutation P and after being XOR-ed

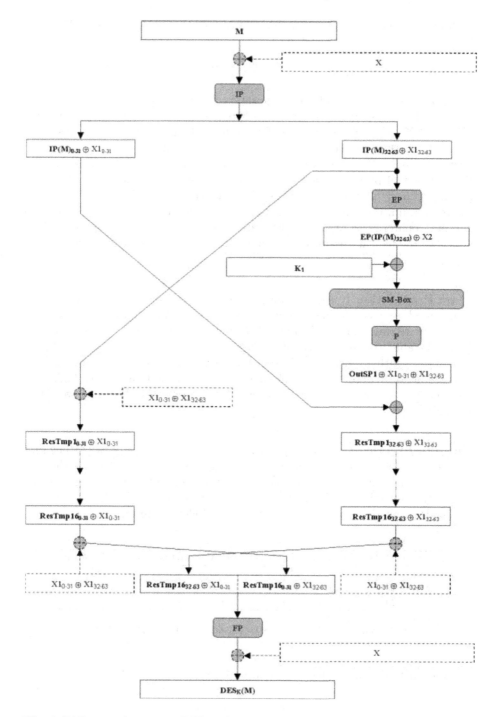

Fig. 1. Differences between a DES without countermeasure and a DES with masking countermeasure.

with the left part of the message, must have a mask corresponding to $X1_{32-63}$. So, the SM-box is now defined by:

$$SM\text{-}Box(A) = S\text{-}Box(A \oplus X2) \oplus P^{-1}(X1_{0-31} \oplus X1_{32-63}) \qquad (1)$$

where P^{-1} is the inverse of the permutation P applied after the S-Box.

It is also necessary to modify the left part of the message, we XOR it with $X1_{0-31} \oplus X1_{32-63}$. So, at the end of the round, the mask $X1$ will be preserved.

After the last round, the two 32-bit parts are interchanged, so it will be necessary to XOR these two parts with the 32-bit value $X1_{0-31} \oplus X1_{32-63}$ before the final permutation FP. The correct cipher is obtained after the final permutation by unmasking the value with the 64-bit mask X.

To sum up, the following scheme represents the differences between a DES without countermeasure and a DES with masking countermeasure. Operations added to implement the masking countermeasure are represented with dotted lines.

Mask Preparation It is important to note that the preparation of the different values used as mask during the cipher (X, $X1$ and $X2$) must be computed in a very secure way. Indeed, if an attacker succeeds in finding X, $X1$ or $X2$ then he will be able to break our countermeasure. So the method used is to compute these values with a randomized bit-per-bit calculation. This computation is slow but is done only once at the beginning of each DES and guarantees high-level security. In the worst case, the attacker will learn only the Hamming weight of the mask.

Put into Practice We have implemented this countermeasure twice. The first implementation was done entirely in C using a 32-bit risc CPU and the second was done in assembly code using another 32-bit risc CPU with specialized assembly instructions to facilitate a DES implementation.

For the first implementation we obtain the following results:

Type of DES	Timing at 5 Mhz	Space of ROM in bytes	Space of RAM in bytes
Normal DES	9.4 ms	1540	42
DES with CM1	18.6 ms	2660	187
DES with CM2	21.2 ms	2656	452

Fig. 2. Timings and memory space used for non-optimized C code.

And for the second implementation we obtain:

Type of DES	Timing at 5 Mhz	Space of ROM in bytes	Space of RAM in bytes
Normal DES	46.2 μs	596	16
DES with CM2	237.6 μs	2017	272

Fig. 3. Timings and memory space used for assembly code.

Where:

- Normal DES : a non-optimized implementation without countermeasure. This DES served as a basis for the construction of the "secure" implementations,
- CM1 : classical countermeasure (cf. [1]) where the message or its complement is ciphered,
- CM2 : DES with the masking countermeasure on the message and with randomization.

3.2   AES

For the AES algorithm, the method is close to the one used for the DES when we want to secure the affine and linear parts of the algorithm: we simply keep the same mask at each round. Next, we show how to deal with the non-linear parts.

The first part of an AES round is the *ByteSub* transformation which is the only non-linear part of the AES. It is an S-Box which is the composition of two transformations (a multiplicative inversion in GF(2^8) and an affine transformation f) applied on each byte $A_{i,j}$ of the input A:

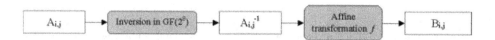

Fig. 4. The ByteSub transformation.

With the masking countermeasure, we want to obtain the following scheme where $X_{i,j}$ is the 8-bit value which masks $A_{i,j}$ and $X1_{i,j} = f(X_{i,j}) \oplus 0x63$ (this comes from the affine property of f):

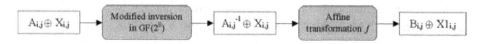

Fig. 5. The ByteSub transformation with masking countermeasure.

We must resolve the following problem: how to obtain $A_{i,j}^{-1} \oplus X_{i,j}$ when we have $A_{i,j} \oplus X_{i,j}$ without compromising the 8-bit value $A_{i,j}$.

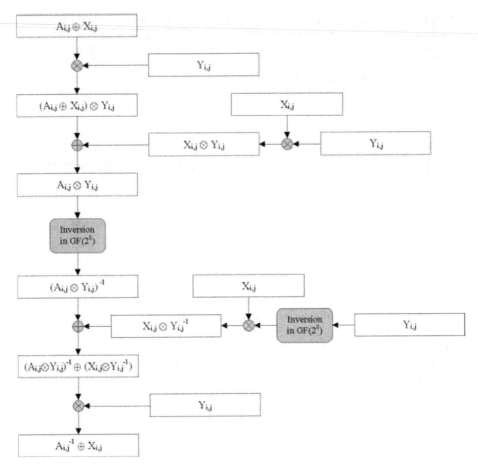

Fig. 6. Modified inversion in $GF(2^8)$ with masking countermeasure.

The first idea is, like in the DES algorithm, to use a modified S-Box computed each time we start an AES. However, in the AES case, the size of the table goes from 256 bytes to $(256 * 16)$ bytes, equal to 4 Ko when we choose a 128-bit message. This solution is not possible when working in a smart card environment (this table is dynamic and must be located in RAM).

The approach selected is the following: an operation compatible with inversion is multiplication, so we obtain the trivial formula: $(X.Y)^{-1} = X^{-1}.Y^{-1}$. The problem lies in transforming a boolean mask into a multiplicative mask. If we denote by $Y_{i,j}$ an 8-bit random different from zero and by $\otimes$ the multiplication in $GF(2^8)$ using the irreducible polynomial $m(x) = x^8 + x^4 + x^3 + x + 1$ as modulus, the mask transformation is obtained as follows:

During all stages of the transformation boolean mask / multiplicative mask, intermediary values are independent of $A_{i,j}$:

1. we multiply with a non-zero 8-bit random $Y_{i,j}$,
2. and we XOR with $X_{i,j} \otimes Y_{i,j}$.

After the inversion in $\mathrm{GF}(2^8)$ we have a multiplicative mask and to reestablish the boolean mask we use values independent of $A_{i,j}$:

1. we XOR with $X_{i,j} \otimes Y_{i,j}^{-1}$,
2. and we multiply with $Y_{i,j}$.

Now, let us see the difference between a round of the AES without counter-measure and a round with masking countermeasure (fig.7).

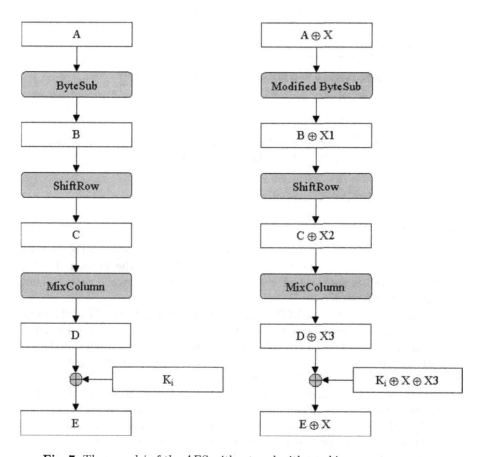

Fig. 7. The round i of the AES without and with masking countermeasure.

Where:

- X represents the mask applied;
- $X1 = f1(X)$ where $f1$ is the linear part of the affine transformation f of ByteSub;
- $X2 = ShiftRow(X1)$;
- $X3 = MixColumn(X2)$;
- K_i represents the round key i.

With this, it is possible to compute an AES and to keep the same random mask at each round.

Put into practice. The following timings come from the encryption of a 128-bit message using a 128-bit key. The implementation was done in assembly code using a 8-bit CPU.

Type of AES	Timing at 5 Mhz	Space of ROM in bytes	Space of RAM in bytes
Normal AES	18.1 ms	730	41
AES with CM2	58.7 ms	1752	121

Fig. 8. Timings and memory space used for assembly code.

Where:

- Normal AES : a non-optimized implementation without countermeasure,
- AES with CM2 : AES with masking countermeasure.

4   Some Security Considerations

4.1   Against SPA

All the permutations have been randomized so (presumably) the only thing the attacker can read is the Hamming weight (HW) of the permuted value. Moreover the values are masked meaning that an attacker would need to know the value of the mask too.

During the key scheduling of DES, the attacker could get the HW of the round keys K_i, construct linear equations on the 16 rounds and acquire information about the key. To avoid such problems the bits of the entire key (56 bits or even 64) are processed at each round. Therefore the only information that the attacker could obtain is the HW of the key.

During the other operations (XOR, load, store), we think that the 32-bit operations prevent an attacker from being able to get the precise 32-bit value that is loaded in one operation. But due to high-order DPA (HODPA) it would be better to randomly load, store and XOR these values bit-per-bit.

Of course, at the beginning of the DES while computing $X1$ and $X2$, one should be careful and use randomization too. It is still true for the AES; moreover the operations involved in the AES are well adapted to usual processors and the problem of the bit-permutation does not exist here.

4.2   Against DPA

We will not present the general DPA attack but simply consider the following fact: an ordinary DPA attack is based on the prediction of one intermediate value of the computation during the algorithm. Based on this fact, it seems that our implementation is fully protected against such a -simple- attack. Indeed, from the beginning of the DES (input message) to the end of it (cipher text) none of the "real" intermediate values appear.

Due to the general random mask, we are not vulnerable to the kind of attacks described in either [4] or [1]. Indeed, at each computation, unless one knows the mask used, the output of the non-linear part (S-Box for DES / *ByteSub* transformation for the AES) is random and not just masked by 0x00 or 0xFF.

Fundamentally we are subject to second-order DPA (see [8,9]) due to the method of masking. But if we consider a real high-order DPA, some other aspects appear: due to the randomization of all operations, the place, (i, j) for example, showing correlation in a HODPA attack, changes a lot. Indeed, in the general case the value i and j will both have 32 possibilities (if we consider that the bit in question is in a 32-bit value). Therefore this gives 1024 positions for the DPA peak and considerably increases a "normal" HODPA.

5   Conclusion

We have described some new ideas for a practical implementation of DES and AES: adapted mask, modified S-Box, transformation boolean mask / multiplicative mask. As is seen from the timings of our implementations, these countermeasures against SPA and DPA can be implemented in a smart-card environment where the memory space is restricted and the processor speed is slow.

References

1. M.-L. Akkar, R. Bévan, P. Dischamp, and D. Moyart. Power analysis, what is now possible. *Asiacrypt*, 2000.
2. S. Chari, C. Jutla, J.R. Rao, and P. Rohatgi. A cautionary note regarding evaluation of aes candidates on smart-cards. *The Second AES Candidate Conference*, 1999.
3. S. Chari, C. Jutla, J.R. Rao, and P. Rohatgi. Towards sound approaches to counteract power-analysis attacks. *Crypto*, 1999.
4. J.-S. Coron and L. Goubin. On boolean and arithmetic masking against differential power analysis. *CHES*, 2000.
5. Joan Daemen and Vincent Rijmen. The block cipher rijndael. *Web Page: http://www.esat.kuleuven.ac.be/~rijmen/rijndael/*, 2000.
6. L. Goubin and J. Patarin. Des and differential power analysis, the duplication method. *CHES*, 1999.
7. P. Kocher, J. Jaffe, and B. Jun. Differential power analysis. *Web Site: www.cryptography.com/dpa*, 1998.
8. P. Kocher, J. Jaffe, and B. Jun. Differential power analysis. *Crypto*, 1999.

318   M.-L. Akkar and C. Giraud

9. T.S. Messerges. Using second-order power analysis to attack dpa resistant software. *CHES*, 2000.
10. National Bureau of Standards. The data encryption standard. *FIPS PUB 46*, 1977.

Efficient Implementation
of "Large" Stream Cipher Systems

Palash Sarkar[1] and Subhamoy Maitra[2]

[1] Centre for Applied Cryptographic Research
Department of Combinatorics and Optimization, University of Waterloo,
200 University Avenue West, Waterloo, Ontario, Canada N2L 3G1
psarkar@cacr.math.uwaterloo.ca
[2] Computer & Statistical Service Centre, Indian Statistical Institute
203, B.T. Road, Calcutta 700 035, India
subho@isical.ac.in

Abstract. A standard model of stream cipher combines the outputs of several independent Linear Feedback Shift Register (LFSR) sequences using a nonlinear Boolean function to produce the key stream. Here we present a low cost hardware architecture for such secret-key cryptosystems using a relatively large number of LFSRs. We propose implementation of the LFSRs using Cellular Automata in VLSI. This provides a regular and uniform two dimensional array of flip flops with only local interconnections. The main bottleneck in the implementation of stream ciphers using a relatively large number of LFSRs is the implementation of the combining Boolean function. We show that this bottleneck can be removed and it is feasible to implement "large" cryptographically secure Boolean functions using a reconfigurable pipelined architecture.
Keywords : Stream Ciphers, Boolean functions, Linear Feedback Shift Registers, Cellular Automata, Reconfigurable Hardware, Pipelined Architecture.

1 Introduction

In the most common model of stream ciphers, the outputs of several independent Linear Feedback Shift Registers (LFSRs) are combined using a nonlinear Boolean function (see Figure 1a). The initial conditions of the LFSRs constitute the secret key of the system. In Figure 1b we provide an example of an LFSR. Here the recurrence relation is $b_n = b_{n-2} \oplus b_{n-5} \oplus b_{n-6}$. The initial condition in the LFSR is $b_5 b_4 b_3 b_2 b_1 b_0$. After the first step, the output of the system is the bit b_0 and the new bit $b_6 = b_4 \oplus b_1 \oplus b_0$. See [3] for more details about LFSR. In such a system, n bits from the n different LFSR's are generated at each clock. These n bits are provided as n input values to the combining function. That is, the LFSRs provide the input bit streams $X_1, X_2, \ldots, X_n$ to the combining Boolean function f. The output of the combining function is the key stream (K) which is XORed with the message stream (M) to obtain the cipher stream (C).

The combining Boolean functions must possess certain cryptographic properties for the overall system to be secure. Design of proper Boolean function have

Ç.K. Koç, D. Naccache, and C. Paar (Eds.): CHES 2001, LNCS 2162, pp. 319–332, 2001.

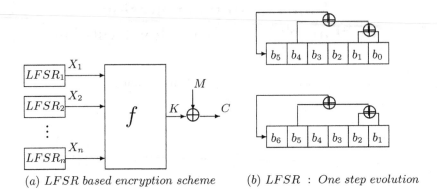

(a) *LFSR based encryption scheme*   (b) *LFSR : One step evolution*

Fig. 1. Stream Cipher System

received a lot of attention in recent times as evidenced by the papers [4,8,10,12]. This has answered many theoretical questions on the design of Boolean functions for stream cipher applications. It is now time to turn to the implementation issues of such Boolean functions and their actual use in stream cipher cryptography.

LFSR based stream cipher systems are usually implemented using a Boolean function on a small number of variables, typically 8 to 10. The main reason being the difficulty in efficiently implementing a Boolean function on a large number of variables (say 20 or more variables). However, if one were to use such a function with properly selected parameters, then none of the currently known attacks would have even a remote chance of success.

The VLSI area used in implementing stream cipher systems have two components.

1. The area used to implement the LFSRs.
2. The area used to implement the Boolean function.

Suppose the system uses an n-input Boolean function and (for simplicity) assume the length of all the LFSRs are same (say L). Then the area used to implement the LFSRs is proportional to $L \times n$ while the area used to implement the Boolean function can be proportional to 2^n. Consequently, while the area required by the LFSRs increase linearly with n, the area required by the Boolean function can be exponential in n. Thus, by increasing the number of inputs to the Boolean function, the main hurdle would be in implementing the Boolean function and not the LFSRs.

Let us compute some real parameters to get a feel of the problem. Suppose a 32-variable combining function is used where the length of the LFSRs is 64 bits long on average (shortly we will discuss why we will not use equal length LFSRs). Then the number of flip-flops required to implement the LFSRs is only 2048, while a direct implementation of the Boolean function can require area proportional to 2^{32}. The key size of such an LFSR system is estimated as follows. The secret key of the system are the initial states of the LFSRs and hence account for $32 \times 64 = 2048$ key bits. While this is a large key, it should be noted that currently RSA systems are also being advocated with 2048 bit keys.

In this paper we tackle the implementation issue of Boolean functions on a large number of variables. (Here we consider a Boolean function on 24 or more variables to be a "large" one.) There is no general purpose implementation method and implementation is dependent on the specific design of the Boolean function. We present an algorithm and hardware description of the recursive construction method presented in [4]. The functions in [4] are built recursively. Thus a function F of n variables is built up from a function h of k variables. It is important to note that, if we use a function h which is optimum with respect to the parameters algebraic degree, order of resiliency and nonlinearity, then the function F is also optimum with respect to these parameters [9]. We describe an algorithm which uses the function h as a black box (an oracle) and computes the output of F on an n-bit input in time linear in $n - k$. The space required by the algorithm is $O(1)$ plus the space required to implement h.

In an LFSR based stream cipher system, an n-bit input is provided to the function at each clock cycle. Thus our algorithm cannot be directly translated into a hardware circuit. Instead we use a regular pipelined architecture to map the algorithm to hardware. The pipeline takes $n - k$ cycles to fill up and after that, it can handle an n-bit input at each clock cycle. There are $n - k$ stages to the pipeline which are all similar to each other providing a uniform design. Implementation of each stage can be done by a circuit or look up table of constant size. The total space required to implement F is the space required to implement h plus an additional $O(n - k)$ size circuit. Usually the number of variables k of the function h will be significantly less than the number of variables n of the function F, and in our system space required to implement F is of the same order as the space required to implement h. This makes it feasible to implement functions of 24 or more variables with nominal cost.

An important parameter is the linear complexity of the generated key sequence. To obtain the maximum possible linear complexity of the key sequence, we need to use LFSRs whose lengths are coprime to each other [1]. Thus the LFSRs are going to be of different lengths. A direct implementation of such different length LFSRs is going to produce a very irregular VLSI structure. To obtain a more regular structure, we suggest the use of a uniform two dimensional array of flip flops connected in a suitable fashion. Some of the flip flops in the two dimensional array will not functional. This is the price to pay for obtaining uniformity in the design.

Now consider implementing the different length LFSRs on this two dimensional structure. Each LFSR must have a large number of tap cells to resist cryptanalytic attacks [15]. Further, each of the LFSRs are going to have a long feedback connection. Thus the overall connection pattern on the two dimensional array is going to be highly irregular. This is also considered to be a disadvantage in VLSI implementation.

Here we suggest the use of cellular automata (CA) to replace the LFSRs. The class of CA we suggest are algebraically equivalent to LFSRs. Hence the

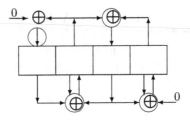

Fig. 2. A $\langle 90, 150, 90, 150 \rangle$ CA

security of the system is not affected by this change. The advantage would be that a CA based design would provide a uniform and regular structure with only local interconnections, which is very attractive from VLSI point of view. CA based architectures have been proposed for many traditional LFSR applications (see [2]).

In Section 2, we briefly outline the necessary details of CA required to replace LFSRs in stream cipher cryptography. The cryptographically useful Boolean functions from [4,9,6] are described in Section 3. We summarize the main points and gloss over the cryptographic properties since our purpose here is to discuss the implementation of these functions. The actual algorithm and hardware description is presented in Section 4. Finally we conclude with some remarks on future work in Section 5.

2   Cellular Automata

A cellular automaton is a finite array of cells, where each cell can store a bit of information. The collection of values of the cells constitute the global state of the CA, whereas the state of a cell is called its local state. The CA evolves globally in discrete time steps, with the state of each cell changing at each time step. The change is affected by the values of the two neighbouring cells and also optionally itself. This is pictorially depicted in Figure 2. The cell at the left end does not have a left neighbour and one at the right end does not have a right neighbour. If the next state of a cell depends on its two neighbours and itself, then the cell is said to follow rule 150. If the next state of the cell depends only on its two neighbours and not on itself then it is said to follow rule 90. (See [16] for an explanation and nomenclature of CA rules). A CA having cells which use only rules 90 and 150 is called a 90/150 CA. In the rest of the discussion we will be interested in only 90/150 CA. The next state evolution of a CA can be totally described by a tridiagonal matrix as follows. Consider a 4-cell CA with rules $\langle 90, 150, 90, 150 \rangle$ (see Figure 2). If the current state is (x_0, x_1, x_2, x_3), then the next state (y_0, y_1, y_2, y_3) is given by

$$(x_0, x_1, x_2, x_3) \begin{bmatrix} 0\,1\,0\,0 \\ 1\,1\,1\,0 \\ 0\,1\,0\,1 \\ 0\,0\,1\,1 \end{bmatrix} = (y_0, y_1, y_2, y_3).$$

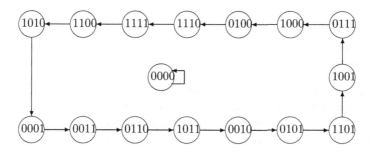

Fig. 3. STD for the CA in Figure 2.

Thus starting from an initial configuration, the CA evolves in discrete time state under the action of the state transition matrix. See Figure 3 for the next state behaviour of the $\langle 90, 150, 90, 150 \rangle$ CA. The initial configuration is loaded in parallel into the CA cells. In our setup this initial configuration is the secret key for the CA being used. The output of the CA can be taken as the output of any particular cell of the CA. The sequence generated by any cell is same as any other cell except for a circular shift in the sequence. Note that unlike the LFSRs the amount of shift between two consecutive cells may be more than 1.

The tridiagonal matrix which governs the behaviour of the CA is called the state transition matrix. It is known [2] that *if the characteristic polynomial of this matrix is primitive over $GF(2)$ then an n-cell CA will cycle through all the possible $2^n - 1$ non null states*. The characteristic polynomial of the $\langle 90, 150, 90, 150 \rangle$ CA is $x^4 + x + 1$, which is primitive over $GF(2)$ and hence the CA cycles through all the non zero states as shown in Figure 3. The output sequence of the CA is completely determined by the characteristic polynomial of the state transition matrix. This is the basis for replacing LFSRs by CA.

Given a primitive polynomial it is easy to design an LFSR which has this polynomial as its connection polynomial. On the other hand the design method for CA is not straightforward. One approach is to form the companion matrix and then use the Lanczos tridiagonalization over $GF(2)$. This approach has been carried out in [11]. However, a simpler and a more elegant algorithm has been presented by Tezuka and Fushimi [13]. The matter that interests us here is the fact that *given any primitive polynomial it is possible to design a CA whose state transition matrix has this primitive polynomial as its characteristic polynomial*.

Following the above discussion it is clear that the use of CA does not alter the stream cipher system in any essential way and hence the security of the system remains unaltered. The only advantage to be gained is the simplicity in VLSI implementation. The use of CA over LFSR has been suggested for several advantages in VLSI design. The local connection structure of CA makes it a regular and cascadable architecture. On the other hand, the long feedback connection of LFSRs introduce delays and is also undesirable from a VLSI layout point of view (see [2]). Also see [7] for a survey on CA.

2.1   CA Based Implementation

As mentioned in the Section 1, the main difficulties in the implementation of the LFSRs are the following.

1. To have the maximum linear complexity, the LFSR lengths need to be pairwise relatively prime. A direct implementation would have to use registers of different lengths resulting in a non uniform structure.
2. The connection pattern for an LFSR is highly irregular. The tap points of an LFSR are in general not regularly placed. In addition, the number of taps in the LFSR must be high to resist against certain types of attacks [15]. Further, an LFSR has a long feedback connection and the length of this feedback connection can be equal to the length of the LFSR.

Thus a direct implementation of the LFSRs leads to an irregular and non uniform design. This is considered to be a distinct disadvantage in VLSI implementation. We discuss how the above problems can be tackled.

To tackle the first problem, we suggest the use of a two dimensional array $n \times L$ of flip flops, where n is the number of inputs to the Boolean function and L is the maximum degree of a connection polynomial (say 128). In each row of this structure, the connection pattern for a single polynomial is implemented. Thus in each row, some of the flip flops will not be functional. The cost incurred due to this would be offset by the design advantage in using a uniform two dimensional array.

The solution to the second problem is to use 90/150 CA to implement the LFSRs. Corresponding to a primitive polynomial we will be able to get the corresponding 90/150 CA using the algorithm provided in [13]. Each cell in such a CA will be connected to its left and right neighbours. Further if the rule for the cell is 150, then it will also be connected to itself. Thus all connections are local and regular. Also the long feedback connection of the LFSR is eliminated.

In the two dimensional array of flip flops, for each row, the number of flip flops used is equal to the length of the corresponding CA. The outputs of all the CA are taken in a bit slice manner from one end (say the right end) of the two dimensional array. In this case the non functional flip flops will be towards the left end. Thus the overall design is a two dimensional array of flip flops with only local connections and the output is provided in a bit slice manner by the rightmost column of the two dimensional array. Such a structure will be simple to implement in VLSI and will also provide easy reconfigurability using standard structures like FPGA.

3   Cryptographically Useful Boolean Functions

We present a brief overview of the various cryptographic properties that a Boolean function must satisfy in order to be used for stream cipher systems. Since our purpose in this paper is implementation, we briefly mention the properties. For more detailed definitions we refer to [4,8].

An n-variable function is said to be *balanced* if the output column of its truth table has equal number of zeros as ones. It is said to be *m-resilient*, if the probability of the output being one is half even if atmost m of the inputs are fixed to constant values. The algebraic normal form of a Boolean function is its canonical sum of products representation as a multivariate polynomial over $GF(2)$. The degree of the polynomial is called the *algebraic degree* or simply degree of the function. Functions of degree atmost one are called affine functions. Given a Boolean function, its *nonlinearity* is its Hamming distance to the set of affine function, i.e., its Hamming distance to its best affine approximation.

A method of designing cryptographically useful Boolean functions is to start from an initial good function and recursively build up the desired function. Several such recursive methods have been proposed [4,12]. The method proposed in [4] is simple, though it does not always result in the best function. The reason being the use of an unbalanced, highly nonlinear initial function which was not optimized with respect to nonlinearity, algebraic degree and order of resiliency. However, for a suitable initial function, the method of [4] produces optimized functions. These initial functions have to belong to one of the *saturated sequences* discussed in [9]. For example, if we use a 7-variable, 2-resilient, degree 4, nonlinearity 56 function [6], then the resulting sequence of functions constructed using the method of [4] are the best possible with respect to nonlinearity, algebraic degree and order of resiliency. Thus we restrict ourselves to implementation of the recursive method of [4], noting that the initial function h must be an optimized function with respect to nonlinearity, algebraic degree and order of resiliency.

Suppose an n-variable function $F(X_n, \ldots, X_1)$ is to be used in the stream cipher system. Following the method of [4], this F is represented by a sequence $(h, S_1, \ldots, S_t)$, where h is the initial function of k variables $X_k, \ldots, X_1$ and S_i's are the recursive operators used to build up the function F. Each $S_i \in \{Q, R\} \times \{r, c, rc\}$, where the action of S_i is described as follows. Let $F_0 = h\}$ and F_i be the function produced after application of S_i. Suppose $S_i = (\Psi_i, \tau_i)$, where $\Psi_i \in \{Q, R\}$ and $\tau_i \in \{r, c, rc\}$.
If $\Psi_i = Q$ then,
$$F_i(X_{i+k}, X_{i+k-1}, \ldots, X_{k+1}, X_k, \ldots, X_1)$$

$$= (1 \oplus X_{i+k})F_{i-1}(X_{i+k-1}, \ldots, X_{k+1}, X_k, \ldots, X_1)$$
$$\oplus X_{i+k}(a \oplus F_{i-1}(b \oplus X_{i+k-1}, \ldots, b \oplus X_{k+1}, b \oplus X_k, \ldots, b \oplus X_1)).$$

If $\Psi_i = R$, then
$$F_i(X_{i+k}, X_{i+k-1}, \ldots, X_{k+1}, X_k, \ldots, X_1)$$

$$= (1 \oplus X_{i+k-1})F_{i-1}(X_{i+k}, X_{i+k-2} \ldots, X_{k+1}, X_k, \ldots, X_1)$$
$$\oplus X_{i+k-1}(a \oplus F_{i-1}(b \oplus X_{i+k}, b \oplus X_{i+k-2} \ldots, b \oplus X_{k+1}, b \oplus X_k, \ldots, b \oplus X_1)).$$

The value of τ_i determine the values of a and b in the following manner. If $\tau_i = r$, then $a = 0, b = 1$. If $\tau_i = c$, then $a = 1, b = 0$ and if $\tau_i = rc$, then $a = b = 1$.

It is important to note that at each step either $\tau_i \in \{r, c\}$ or $\tau_i \in \{rc, c\}$. This is required to increase the order of resiliency by 1 at each step (see [4]).

The actual set of possible values for τ_i is determined recursively as follows. If the order of resiliency of h is even then $\tau_1 \in \{r, c\}$, else $\tau_1 \in \{rc, c\}$. In general, if the order of resiliency of F_{i-1} is even then $\tau_i \in \{r, c\}$, else $\tau_i \in \{c, rc\}$.

In this paper, we will solely be concerned with the implementation of F as represented by the sequence $(h, S_1, \ldots, S_t)$. For cryptographic properties we refer the reader to [4,9]. Note that $n = k + t$, and $F = F_t$. If h has the order of resiliency m_1, then F has the order of resiliency $m = m_1 + t$. The algebraic degree of F and h are same and the nonlinearity of F is 2^t times the nonlinearity of h.

4   Boolean Function Implementation

In this section we provide algorithms and hardware for resilient functions on large number of input variables. The algorithm we present needs one step for initialization and then t steps in loop to generate the output. For LFSR based stream ciphers, the LFSRs output one bit at each clock and hence an n-bit input is presented to the non linear combining function at each clock. Thus an algorithm which takes more that one clock cycle to compute the output of the Boolean function will introduce delays into the system leading to a degradation of performance. We solve this problem by using a pipelined architecture to map the algorithm to hardware. The pipeline takes t clock cycles to fill up and from then on provides a bit of output at each clock cycle. The total delay for obtaining all the key bits is t clock cycles instead of a delay of t clock cycles for each key bit. Thus the pipeline ensures that there is no effective degradation in the performance of the system.

4.1   Algorithm

We present an algorithm to compute the output of a function F on an n-bit input $(X_n, \ldots, X_{k+1}, X_k, \ldots, X_1)$. The function F is represented by $(h(X_k, \ldots, X_1), S_1, \ldots, S_{n-k})$, where h is presented as a black box and can be implemented either by a combinational circuit or by a look up table. The algorithm requires both time and space linear in m.

Let F be represented by $(h, S_1, \ldots, S_{n-k})$, where h is a function of k variables. Define $F_0 = h$ and F_i to be a function represented by $(h, S_1, \ldots, S_i)$. Then $F_{n-k} = F$. We will refer to the recursive definition of F_i provided in Section 3. First we present an inefficient but obvious algorithm to compute $F_t = F_{n-k} = F(X_n, \ldots, X_1)$ based on the recursive definition in Section 4.

$recCompute(F_i(X_{i+k}, \ldots, X_1))$

1. if $(i = 0)$ return $h(X_k, \ldots, X_1)$;
2. if $(\Psi_i = Q)$ $\{X = X_{i+k};\}$
3. else $\{X = X_{i+k-1}; X_{i+k-1} = X_{i+k};\}$
4. if $(X = 0)$ return $recCompute(F_{i-1}(X_{i+k-1}, \ldots, X_1))$;
5. else
6.   if $(\tau_i = c)$ return $1 \oplus recCompute(F_{i-1}(X_{i+k-1}, \ldots, X_1))$;

7.   if $(\tau_i = c)$ return $recCompute(F_{i-1}(1 \oplus X_{i+k-1}, \ldots, 1 \oplus X_1));$
8.   if $(\tau_i = rc)$ return $1 \oplus recCompute(1 \oplus F_{i-1}(X_{i+k-1}, \ldots, 1 \oplus X_1));$
9. end if
end

Steps 2 and 3 of the above algorithm interchanges the variables X_{i+k} and X_{i+k-1} if $\Psi_i = R$. The rest of the algorithm works according to the recursive definition of F_i. Note that the recursive approach is top down, i.e., it starts processing the variable X_n first and then descends to lower numbered variables. It is easy to see that the algorithm takes time $O(t)$. However, the stack depth of the algorithm is also $O(t)$, which is undesirable. Hence we map it to an iterative algorithm. There are a few key observations to do this.

1. There is no need to carry the variables $X_{k-1}, \ldots, X_1$ through the algorithm. If $\Psi_1 = Q$, then let $Y = X_k$ else $Y = X_{k+1}$. Set $v_0 = h(Y, X_{k-1}, \ldots, X_1)$ and $v_1 = h(1 \oplus Y, 1 \oplus X_{k-1}, \ldots, 1 \oplus X_1)$. Then we will ultimately have to output v_i or $1 \oplus v_i$, depending on the variables $X_n, \ldots, X_k$.
2. At each recursive call, depending on the value of τ_i we either complement the input or the output or both. Thus at each stage it is sufficient to record whether the input/output of the next evaluation has to be complemented. This is managed by two bit variables a and b. The variable a records whether the output needs to be complemented and the variable b records whether the input needs to be complemented.

Based on these observations, we next present the algorithm $computeTD(.)$, which converts the recursive algorithm $recCompute()$ to an iterative algorithm.
$computeTD(X_n, \ldots, X_1)$ {
    if $(\Psi_1 = Q)$ then $Y = X_k$;
    if $(\Psi_1 = R)$ then $Y = X_{k+1}$;
    $v_0 = h(Y, X_{k-1}, \ldots, X_1)$; $v_1 = h(1 \oplus Y, 1 \oplus X_{k-1}, \ldots, 1 \oplus X_1)$;
    $a = 0$; $b = 0$;
    for $i = t$ downto 1 do {
        (1*) if $(\Psi_i = Q)$ then $X = X_{i+k}$;
        (2*) if $(\Psi_i = R)$ then { $X = X_{i+k-1}$; $X_{i+k-1} = X_{i+k}$; }
        if $(b \oplus X = 1)$ then {
            if $(\tau_i = c)$ then $a = a \oplus 1$;
            if $(\tau_i = r)$ then $b = b \oplus 1$;
            if $(\tau_i = rc)$ then $\{a = a \oplus 1; b = b \oplus 1; \}$
        }
    }
    return $a \oplus v_b$;
}

Based on the previous discussion, we get the following result.

Theorem 1. *The algorithm $computeTD(X_n, \ldots, X_1)$ correctly computes $F(X_n, \ldots, X_1)$ in $O(t)$ time.*

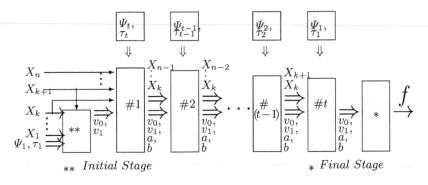

Fig. 4. Pipelined Implementation of $computeTD(.)$

4.2   Hardware Implementation of $computeTD(.)$

Here we show how very low cost pipelined hardware can be developed where the output of F on successive tuples of n-bit input is available at each clock pulse after initial t clocks, i.e., starting from $(t + 1)$-th clock.

In the hardware description, we will be manipulating Ψ, τ_i as binary values. To do this we need to describe how they will be encoded as bits. If $\Psi_i = Q$, then this is encoded by putting $\Psi_i = 0$. If $\Psi_i = R$, then this is encoded by putting $\Psi_i = 1$. If $\tau_i = c$, then this is always coded by putting $\tau_i = 1$. On the other hand $\tau_i = 0$ codes $\tau_i = r$ or $\tau_i = rc$ according as $i \not\equiv m_1 \bmod 2$ or $i \equiv m_1 \bmod 2$, where m_1 is the order of resiliency of the initial function h (see Section 3).

The pipeline has t stages numbered #1 to #t (see Figure 4). Stage #i stores the current values of $X_k, \ldots, X_{n-i+1}$. The two bits v_0 and v_1 are present at each stage along with the two other work bits a and b.

The initial stage (Figure 5a) of the algorithm performs the computation required to get the values v_0, v_1. For this the function h needs to be evaluated twice. We are assuming that each evaluation of the function h takes one clock cycle and hence h is implemented either as a look up table or by a small depth computational circuit.

The intermediate stages of the pipeline perform the task of variable interchange and updation of the bits a and b (see Figure 5b). The bits v_0, v_1 are carried forward unchanged. If $\Psi_i = R$ the value of X_{i+k} and X_{i+k-1} should be properly interchanged for the next stage as in lines (1*) and (2*) of the algorithm. The 2×1 multiplexer ensures that the output is X as required by the algorithm. If X and b are unequal, then the two & gates are activated, otherwise a and b are carried forward unchanged to the next stage. If $\tau_i = 0$, then τ_i represents r or rc and the input has to be complemented. The & of $(X \oplus b)$ and $\overline{\tau}_i$ ensures this. If $\tau_i = 1$, then τ_i is c and the output certainly needs to be complemented. Also if $\tau_i = 0$ but represents rc, then also the output needs to be complemented. But τ_i can represent rc only if $i - m_1 \equiv 0 \bmod 2$. The value of the function $const(i)$ is $(i - m_1 + 1) \bmod 2$, and the combination of the or and & gate ensures that a is updated as required.

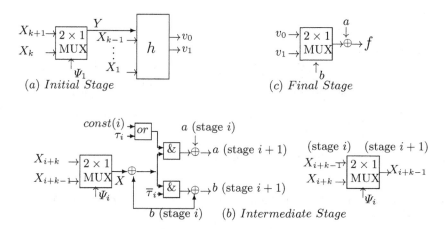

Fig. 5. Components of Top Down Architecture

The final stage (Figure 5c) is simple. Depending on the value of b, it outputs either v_0 or v_1 and a is simply EXORed with the output of the 2×1 multiplexer.

The whole circuit operates as follows. At each clock, stage $\#i$ forwards the values of the variables to the next stage and updates the values of work bits a, b for the next stage. The values v_0 and v_1 are forwarded unchanged. It is important to understand the need for generation of v_0, v_1 at the first stage and carrying them through all the t stages. We need these two bits only at the end for the final circuit (Figure 5c). However, the values of v_0, v_1 are generated from the variables X_1 to X_{k+1}. It is more efficient to carry two bits v_0, v_1 through the t stages instead of carrying the $k+1$ bits $X_1, \ldots, X_{k+1}$. Since there are t stages, the whole pipeline takes t clock cycles to be completely filled up. Hence the first output appears at $(t+1)$-th clock and consequently a bit of output appears at each clock.

We use both the rising and falling edge of the clock. Each stage stores two buffers, one input and another output (see Figure 6). At the leading edge the values of the input buffer registers of stage $\#i$ are latched to the output buffer registers of the same stage. The signals $X_k, \ldots, X_{i+k-2}$ and v_0, v_1 go directly from input buffer to output buffer. The other three signals X_{i+k-1}, a, b are generated through the inbuilt combinational circuit (Figure 5b) from X_{i+k}, X_{i+k-1}, a, b and Ψ_i, τ_i. That is, the stage C in Figure 6 contains the circuit of Figure 5c. At the falling edge of the clock, the output buffer registers of stage $\#i$ are latched to the input buffer registers of the stage $\#(i+1)$. The inbuilt combinational circuit being small enough, it is justified to consider that the delay of the circuit is much less than the clock width and hence there is no problem in using both the leading and falling edge of the clock in the hardware. The inbuilt combinational circuit blocks in this architecture can also be implemented using small lookup table.

Note that the Boolean function is reconfigurable. If we can load a new set of values for $(\Psi_t, \tau_t), \ldots, (\Psi_1, \tau_1)$, then the function F will change, keeping the cryptographic parameters same. This will help in accessing the elements of a large

Stage i Stage $i+1$

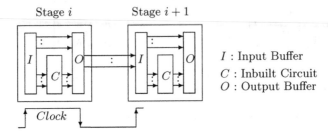

I : Input Buffer
C : Inbuilt Circuit
O : Output Buffer

Fig. 6. Input Output Latching for Intermediate Stages

set of Boolean functions with minimum possible change, changing the pattern of $2t$ bit values.

We also address the issue of synchronization at this point. The same kind of system will be available to both the sender and receiver. Once both sides start with a specific key, the first output comes after a delay of t clock cycles, i.e., starting from the $(t+1)$-th clock. Now consider the case when the key of the system is going to be changed. In that case, when the new key is loaded, then the pipeline will contain some data generated from the earlier key. The data coming from the next key will be operational after t clock cycles after it is loaded in the LFSRs. This is the same case in both the sender and receiver end. Hence, there is no additional requirement for synchronization in this setup.

4.3   A Specific Example

Consider the implementation of a function F on 24 variables. We take the initial function h to be a 16-variable function, with order of resiliency 8, algebraic degree 7 and nonlinearity $2^{15} - 2^9$ [6]. The function h is optimized with respect to the parameters considered here. Now we use a pipeline of 8 levels to get the 24-variable function F with order of resiliency 16, algebraic degree 7, and nonlinearity $2^{23} - 2^{17}$. These are also a set of best possible parameters. The user has an option of selecting $2 \times 8 = 16$ bits for $(\Psi_8, \tau_8), \ldots, (\Psi_1, \tau_1)$, to get a fairly wide range (2^{16}) of choices for F. Further, it is possible to design a suitable architecture so that the values of these 16 bits can be programmable and the design can be implemented using an FPGA structure. Thus it is possible to design a reconfigurable structure which can be programmed to implement any one of the 2^{16} possible 24-variable Boolean functions F. The VLSI area required to implement the reconfigurable structure is rougly equal to the VLSI area required to implement the 16-variable initial function h. An overall delay of only 8 clock cycles is introduced in the system due to the pipeline. Note that the delay is a constant 8 clock cycles and is independent of the length of the key stream.

In this system, we will have 24 different LFSRs. We implement the LFSRs by CA. Depending on the requirement of the total key size, we need to choose the length of the CAs, where the lengths of any two CAs are coprime. Let us consider the maximum length of an CA will be less than 128. As a specific

example, consider that the lengths will be the following values :
$41, 43, 47, 53, 57, 59, 61, 67, 71, 73, 74 = 2 \times 37, 77 = 7 \times 11, 79, 83, 89, 93 = 3 \times 31, 97, 101, 103, 107, 109, 113, 115 = 5 \times 23, 119$. The total summation of these lengths, i.e., the key size of the system is 1931. Since the resiliency of F is 16, the first affine function to which F will have non zero correlation must be non degenerate on 17 variables. Hence, the best possible correlation attack will need estimating an equivalent polynomial of length x from the cipher text or the key sequence. Let x be the sum of the first 17 values in the above sequence. Here $x = 1164$, and hence any known attack is infeasible. It is also important to note that the connection polynomial of the equivalent LFSR is the product of the connection polynomials of the individual LFSRs.

The two dimesional array of flip flops required to implement the CAs is going to be an 24×128 array. Thus the total number of flip flops is going to be 3072. Out of these only 1931 are going to be used. This is a small trade off to obtain a uniform design. Also note that this number of flip flops are going to be non functional irrespective of whether CA or LFSR is used. The use of CA ensures that the connection structure of the array is going to be uniform.

5   Conclusion

In this paper we have proposed LFSR systems employing large Boolean functions. We have described hardware implementation of large Boolean functions constructed using the recursive method of [4], with optimized function as an initial one [9]. The main point we have tried to make is that LFSR systems employing large Boolean functions are feasible to implement in hardware. We provide a reconfigurable pipelined architecture for the large Boolean function and propose the use of cellular automata for a regular VLSI structure of different length LFSRs. Given the known attacks (see [14] and the references in this paper) and the current advancement of the computer systems, it is improbable that this kind of system will be vulnerable in near future. To the best of our knowledge this is the first effort to consider this problem. Several questions remain as to the best possible implementation and the implementation of Boolean functions constructed using other recursive methods. We feel these can be possible future research topics.

References

1. C. Ding, G. Xiao, and W. Shan. *The Stability Theory of Stream Ciphers*. Number 561 in Lecture Notes in Computer Science. Springer-Verlag, 1991.
2. P. P. Chaudhuri. Additive cellular automata: theory and applications, volume 1. IEEE Press, NJ, 1997.
3. S. W. Golomb. Shift Register Sequences. Aegean Park Press, 1982.
4. S. Maitra and P. Sarkar. Highly nonlinear resilient functions optimizing Siegenthaler's inequality. In *Advances in Cryptology - CRYPTO'99*, number 1666 in Lecture Notes in Computer Science, pages 198–215. Springer Verlag, August 1999.

5. A. J. Menezes, P. C. van Oorschot, and S. A. Vanstone. *Handbook of Applied Cryptography*. CRC Press, 1997.
6. E. Pasalic, S. Maitra, T. Johansson and P. Sarkar. New constructions of resilent and correlation immune boolean functions achieving upper bounds on nonlinearity. In *Proceedings of the Workshop on Cryptography and Coding Theory*, Paris, 2001.
7. P. Sarkar. A brief history of cellular automata. *ACM Computing Surveys* Volume 32, Issue 1 (2000), Pages 80-107.
8. P. Sarkar and S. Maitra. Construction of nonlinear Boolean functions with important cryptographic properties. In *Advances in Cryptology - EUROCRYPT 2000*, number 1807 in Lecture Notes in Computer Science, pages 491–512. Springer Verlag, 2000.
9. P. Sarkar and S. Maitra. Nonlinearity bounds and constructions of resilient boolean functions. In *Advances in Cryptology - CRYPTO 2000*, number 1880 in Lecture Notes in Computer Science, pages 515–532. Springer Verlag, 2000.
10. J. Seberry, X. M. Zhang, and Y. Zheng. On constructions and nonlinearity of correlation immune Boolean functions. In *Advances in Cryptology - EUROCRYPT'93*, pages 181–199. Springer-Verlag, 1994.
11. M. Serra and T. Slater. A Lanczos algorithm in a finite field and its applications. *Journal of Combinatorial Mathematics and Combinatorial Computing*, 1990.
12. Y. V. Tarannikov. On resilient Boolean functions with maximum possible nonlinearity. *Proceedings of INDOCRYPT 2000*, volume 1977 of LNCS, pages 19-30.
13. S. Tezuka and M. Fushimi. A method of designing cellular automata as pseudorandom number generators for built-in self-test for VLSI. In *Finite Fields: Theory, Applications and Algorithms*, Contemporary Mathematics, AMS, pages 363–367, 1994.
14. T. Johansson and F. Jonsson. Fast Correlation Attacks through Reconstruction of Linear Polynomials. *Proceedings of CRYPTO 2000*, volume 1880 of LNCS, pages 300-315.
15. W. Meier and O. Stafflebach. Fast correlation attacks on certain stream ciphers. *Journal of Cryptology*, 1:159–176, 1989.
16. S. Wolfram. Theory and applications of cellular automata: including selected papers 1983-1986. World Scientific, NJ, 1986.

Tradeoffs in Parallel and Serial Implementations of the International Data Encryption Algorithm IDEA

O.Y.H. Cheung[1], K.H. Tsoi[1], P.H.W. Leong[1], and M.P. Leong[1]

Department of Computer Science and Engineering,
The Chinese University of Hong Kong, Shatin, N.T., Hong Kong
{yhcheung,khtsoi,phwl,mpleong}@cse.cuhk.edu.hk
http://www.cse.cuhk.edu.hk

Abstract. A high-performance implementation of the International Data Encryption Algorithm (IDEA) is presented in this paper. The design was implemented in both bit-parallel and bit-serial architectures and a comparison of design tradeoffs using various measures is presented. On an Xilinx Virtex XCV300-6 FPGA, the bit-parallel implementation delivers an encryption rate of 1166 Mb/sec at a 82 MHz system clock rate, whereas the bit-serial implementation offers a 600 Mb/sec throughput at 150 MHz. Both designs are suitable for real-time applications, such as on-line high-speed networks. The implementation is runtime reconfigurable such that key-scheduling is done by directly modifying the bitstream downloaded to the FPGA, hence enabling an implementation without the logic required for key-scheduling. Both implementations are scalable such that higher throughput is obtained with increased resource requirements. The estimated performances of the bit-parallel and bit-serial implementations on an XCV1000-6 device are 5.25 Gb/sec and 2.40 Gb/sec respectively.

Keywords: Cryptographic hardware, digital-design, reconfigurable-computing, performance-tradeoffs.

1 Introduction

Cryptography is concerned with the transfer of information between parties so that only the intended parties can read the data. Despite an assumption that an adversary may have full knowledge of the algorithms used, and has access to the media where data is transmitted, the aim of cryptography is to make it intractable to retrieve the data without knowledge of a secret piece of information called a key. Cryptography is an ideal application for custom computing machines since they offer the following advantages over VLSI technologies

– it is possible to use the same Field-Programmable Custom Computing Machine (FCCM) hardware for many different cryptographic protocols

Ç.K. Koç, D. Naccache, and C. Paar (Eds.): CHES 2001, LNCS 2162, pp. 333–347, 2001.

- Moore's law continues to offer improved silicon technology at exponential rates which is available to FCCM designers without the costly manufacturing process required in VLSI
- it is possible to specialize the hardware to an extent not possible in VLSI devices to improve performance
- the reconfigurable nature makes it feasible to attempt designs employing more sophisticated algorithms which leads to an improvement in performance.

The Data Encryption Standard (DES) algorithm has been a popular secret key encryption algorithm and is used in many commercial and financial applications. Although introduced in 1976, it has proved resistant to all forms of cryptanalysis. However, its key size is too small by current standards and its entire 56-bit key space can be searched in approximately 22 hours [9].

In 1990, Lai and Massay introduced an iterated block cipher known as Proposed Encryption Standard (PES) [16]. The same authors, joined by Murphy, proposed a modification of PES called Improved PES (IPES) [17], which improves the security of the original algorithm against differential analysis and truncated differentials [13,15,5]. In 1992, IPES was commercialized and was renamed the International Data Encryption Algorithm (IDEA). Some believe that, to date, the algorithm is the best and the most secure block algorithm available to the public [26].

Although IDEA involves only simple 16-bit operations, software implementations of this algorithm still cannot offer the encryption rate required for on-line encryption in high-speed networks. Ascom's implementation of IDEA (Ascom are the holders of the patent on the IDEA algorithm) achieves 0.37×10^6 encryptions per seconds, or an equivalent encryption rate of 23.53 Mb/sec, on an Intel Pentium II 450 MHz machine. Implementation of IDEA using the Intel MMX multimedia instructions was proposed by Helger [20] and achieves 0.51×10^6 encryption per seconds or a equivalent encryption rate 32.9 Mb/sec, on an Intel Pentium II 233 MHz machine. Our optimized software implementation running on a Sun Enterprise E4500 machine with twelve 400 MHz Ultra-IIi processor, performs 2.30×10^6 encryptions per second or a equivalent encryption rate of 147.13 Mb/sec, still cannot be applied to applications such as encryption for 155 Mb/sec Asynchronous Transfer Mode (ATM) networks.

Hardware implementations offer significant speed improvements over software implementations by exploiting parallelism among operators. In addition, they are likely to be cheaper, having lower power consumption and smaller footprint than a high speed software implementation. A paper design of an IDEA processor which achieves 528 Mb/sec on four XC4020XL devices was proposed by Mencer et. al. [23]. The first VLSI implementation of IDEA was developed and verified by Bonnenberg et. al. in 1992 using a 1.5 μm CMOS technology [4]. This implementation had an encryption rate of 44 Mb/sec. In 1994, VINCI, a 177 Mb/sec VLSI implementation of the IDEA algorithm in 1.2 μm CMOS technology, was reported by Curiger et. al. [7,31]. A 355 Mb/sec implementation in 0.8 μm technology of IDEA was reported in 1995 by Wolter et. al. [27], followed by a 424 Mb/sec single chip implementation of 0.7 μm technology by Salomao et. al. [25] was reported. In 2000, Leong et. al. proposed a 500 Mb/sec bit-serial implementation of IDEA on an Xilinx Virtex XCV300-6 FPGA which is scalable on larger devices [18]. Later, Goldstein et. al reported an implementation on the PipeRench FPGA which achieves 1013 Mb/sec [11]. A commercial implementation of IDEA called the IDEACrypt Kernel developed by Ascom achieves 720 Mb/sec [3] at 0.25 μm technology. The implementation dervied from the IDEACrypt Kernel, called the IDEACrypt Coprocessor, has a throughput of 300 Mb/sec [2].

In this paper, two Xilinx Virtex Field Programmable Gate Array (FPGA) based implementations of the IDEA algorithm are described. On an XCV300-6 device, the bit-parallel implementation offers a 1166 Mb/sec encryption rate, while the bit-serial implementation has a throughput of 600 Mb/sec. The implementation is scalable so that throughput and area tradeoffs can be addressed. Applications of these designs include virtual private networks (VPNs) and embedded encryption/decryption devices. To illustrate various design tradeoffs, an analysis on both of the designs in terms of area, latency, throughput and other design measures was carried out.

Key-scheduling in both implementations is achieved by modifying the bit-stream downloading to the FPGA, in a manner similar to that described by Patterson in an implementation of DES [24]. Instead of doing this using the JBits Applications Programming Interface (API), a technique for the direct modification of the binary bitstream was used. The approach is advantageous because dedicated logic for key-scheduling is not required in the designs hence leaving more logic resources for performing computation.

This paper is organized as follows. In Section 2 the IDEA algorithm as well as algorithms for multiplication modulo $2^n + 1$ are described. The bit-parallel and bit-serial implementations of IDEA are presented in Section 3 and 4 respectively. In Section 5 the methodology to achieve runtime reconfigurability is described. In Section 6 results are given. Conclusions are drawn in Section 7.

2   The IDEA Algorithm

IDEA belongs to a class of cryptosystems called secret-key cryptosystems which is characterized by the symmetry of encryption and decryption processes, and the possibility of implying the decryption key from the encryption key and vice versa. IDEA takes 64-bit plaintext inputs and produces 64-bit ciphertext outputs using a 128-bit key.

The design philosophy behind IDEA is to mix operations from different algebraic groups including XOR, addition modulo 2^{16}, and multiplication modulo the Fermat prime $2^{16} + 1$. All these operations work on 16-bit sub-blocks.

The IDEA block cipher [26] (depicted in Figure 1) consists of a cascade of eight identical blocks known as rounds, followed by a half-round or output transformation. In each round, XOR, addition and modular multiplication operations are applied. IDEA is believed to possess strong cryptographic strength because

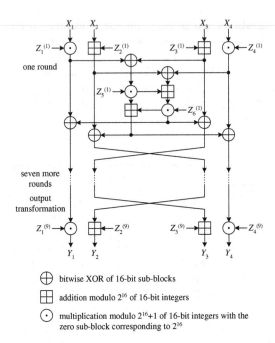

Fig. 1. Block diagram of the IDEA algorithm.

- its primitive operations are of three distinct algebraic groups of 2^{16} elements
- multiplication modulo $2^{16} + 1$ provides desirable statistical independence between plaintext and ciphertext
- its property of having iterative rounds made differential attacks difficult.

The encryption process is as follows. The 64-bit plaintext is divided into four 16-bit plaintext sub-blocks, X_1 to X_4. The algorithm converts the plaintext blocks into ciphertext blocks of the same bit-length, similarly divided into four 16-bit sub-blocks, Y_1 to Y_4. 52 16-bit subkeys, $Z_i^{(r)}$, where i and r are the subkey number and round number respectively, are computed from the 128-bit secret key. Each round uses six subkeys and the remaining four subkeys are used in the output transformation. The decryption process is essentially the same as the encryption process except that the subkeys are derived using a different algorithm [26].

The algorithm for computing the encryption subkeys (called the key-schedule) involves only logical rotations. Order the 52 subkeys as $Z_1^{(1)}, \ldots, Z_6^{(1)}, Z_1^{(2)}, \ldots,$ $Z_6^{(2)}, \ldots, Z_1^{(8)}, \ldots, Z_6^{(8)}, Z_1^{(9)}, \ldots, Z_4^{(9)}$. The procedure begins by partitioning the 128-key secret key Z into eight 16-bit blocks and assigning them directly to the first eight subkeys. Z is then rotated left by 25 bits, partitioned into eight 16-bit blocks and again assigned to the next eight subkeys. The process continues until all 52 subkeys are assigned. The decryption subkeys $Z'^{(r)}_i$ can be computed from the encryption subkeys with reference to Table 1.

Table 1. IDEA decryption subkeys $Z'^{(i)}_r$ derived from encryption subkeys $Z^{(i)}_r$. $-Z_i$ and Z_i^{-1} denote additive inverse modulo 2^{16} and multiplicative inverse $2^{16} + 1$ of Z_i respectively.

	$r = 1$	$2 \leq r \leq 8$	$r = 9$
$Z'^{(r)}_1$	$(Z_1^{(10-r)})^{-1}$	$(Z_1^{(10-r)})^{-1}$	$(Z_1^{(10-r)})^{-1}$
$Z'^{(r)}_2$	$-Z_2^{(10-r)}$	$-Z_3^{(10-r)}$	$-Z_2^{(10-r)}$
$Z'^{(r)}_3$	$-Z_3^{(10-r)}$	$-Z_2^{(10-r)}$	$-Z_3^{(10-r)}$
$Z'^{(r)}_4$	$(Z_4^{(10-r)})^{-1}$	$(Z_4^{(10-r)})^{-1}$	$(Z_4^{(10-r)})^{-1}$
$Z'^{(r)}_5$	$Z_5^{(9-r)}$	$Z_5^{(9-r)}$	N/A
$Z'^{(r)}_6$	$Z_6^{(9-r)}$	$Z_6^{(9-r)}$	N/A

In Electronic Codebook (ECB) mode [26], the data dependencies of the IDEA algorithm have no feedback paths. Additionally, in practice, latencies of order of microseconds are acceptable. These features make deeply pipelined implementations possible.

2.1 Multiplication modulo $2^n + 1$

Of the basic operations used in the IDEA algorithm, multiplication modulo $2^{16} + 1$ is the most complicated and occupies most of the hardware. Curiger et. al. [8] described and compared several VLSI architectures for multiplication modulo $2^n + 1$ and found that an architecture proposed by Meier and Zimmerman [22], using modulo 2^n adders with bit-pair recoding offers the best performance.

The C code for the multiplication modulo $2^{16} + 1$ operation by modulo 2^{16} adders using bit-pair recoding is as follows.

```
1    uint16 mulmod(uint16 x, uint16 y)
2    {
3        uint16 xd, yd, th, tl;
4        uint32 t;
5        xd = (x - 1) & 0xFFFF;
6        yd = (y - 1) & 0xFFFF;
7        t = (uint32) xd * yd + xd + yd + 1;
8        tl = t & 0xFFFF;
9        th = t >> 16;
10       return (tl - th) + (tl <= th);
11   }
```

This algorithm requires a total of six additions and subtractions, one 16-bit multiplication and one comparison. However, in IDEA one of the operands of a modular multiplication operation is always a subkey, so the second subtraction can be eliminated if the associated subkeys are pre-decremented.

3 Bit-Parallel Implementation

3.1 Multiplication modulo $2^{16} + 1$

Modulo multiplication is the bottleneck in the IDEA algorithm. In a single round of the algorithm there are four modular multiplications so a well-designed multiplication modulo $2^{16} + 1$ operator is crucial since it directly affects the system performance both in terms of area and throughput.

The modular multiplication algorithm described in Section 2.1 was used in our design, but instead of taking x and y as inputs, the operator takes x and y_d as inputs. As one of the operands is a subkey which is regarded as a constant, the modification eliminates one subtraction operator by taking the advantage of pre-decremented subkeys (Section 2.1, pseudocode line 6).

In order to implement a well-designed multiplication modulo $2^{16} + 1$ operator, the throughput of the operator is maximized by introducing more pipeline stages. In our design, 16-bit mulitplier used in Section 2.1 (pseudocode line 7) is constructed by Xilinx CORE Generator [30] which has a latency of 4 cycles. And the multiplication modulo $2^{16} + 1$ operator pipeline has a latency of 7 cycles.

3.2 Bit-Parallel IDEA Core

The IDEA algorithm is a cascade of eight identical rounds of operations, followed by a output transformation. By instantiating building blocks, that is, additions, XORs and modular multiplications, and inserting appropriate stage latches for time-alignment, a module for one round of computation is formed. For the best area-efficiency, stage latches are constructed by Virtex SRL16E primitives [29,10].

Due to limited hardware resources, each round of the algorithm shares the same physical resource, but with different key-schedules. Output transformation also reuses the resource. In our implementation the key-schedules are stored inside ROM primitives. The architecture of the bit-parallel IDEA core is shown in Figure 2.

As mentioned earlier, for ECB mode operations, data dependencies of the IDEA algorithm have no feedback paths. This property enabled the round architecture to take input values until the pipelined is filled, and output values are redirected to the input of the pipeline subsequently. In an IDEA round, the data passes through three multiplication modulo $2^{16} + 1$ operators, each of which has a latency of 7 cycles. Thus the full round pipeline has a latency of 21 cycles For an output transformation, the data must pass through a single multiplication modulo $2^{16} + 1$ operator with pipeline latency of 7 cycles. Therefore the core has a total latency of $21 \times 8 + 7 = 175$ cycles. The core takes 21 64-bit plaintexts per $21 \times 9 = 189$ cycles, equivalently performing encryption at

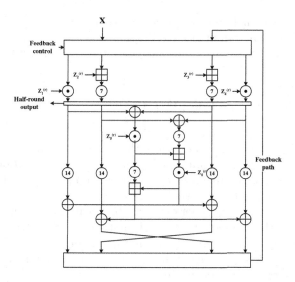

Fig. 2. Architecture of the bit-parallel IDEA core.

$(21 \div 189) \times 64 \times f$ Mb/sec with a system clock rate of f MHz. For instance, at a 82 MHz clock rate, the core delivers an encryption rate of 583 Mb/sec with a latency of 2.134 μs.

4   Bit-Serial Implementation

The bit-serial implementation mentioned below is an improved implementation of [18]. By register reordering and register duplication, the improved implementation offers an encryption throughput of 600 Mb/sec, 20% faster than the original implementation.

Bit-serial architectures are characterized by the property that operators perform their computations in a bitwise fashion and communications between operators are multiplexed in time over a single wire. Dataflow begins with either the least significant bit or the most significant bit, but the former is more commonly used due to its compatibility with two's complement arithmetic. In a typical bit-serial implementation, each variable is associated with a control signal which is set high only when the first bit is transferred along associated data bus. To reduce area, control signals can be shared among the variables. Since bit-serial operators usually require the first bits of their operands to enter the operators on the same clock cycle, appropriate stage latches must be inserted for time-alignment [12].

Two of the primitive operators used in IDEA, namely XOR and addition modulo 2^{16}, can be easily implemented bit-serially. These two operators have latencies of one clock cycle and are capable of taking consecutive bit-serial operands. The multiplication modulo $2^{16} + 1$ operator has a latency of 35 clock cycles. As in the parallel implementation, stage latches and constants are implemented using SRL16E primitives. Additionally, constants are also implemented as SRL16E primitives, with its output connected to its input to form a cyclic shift register.

4.1   Multiplication modulo $2^{16} + 1$

The modular multiplication algorithm described in Section 2.1 was directly applied in the bit-serial implementation of the algorithm. The operator optimization used in the bit-parallel implementation, described in Section 3.1, was not applied in the bit-serial implementation because comparisons in bit-serial architectures are not efficient in terms of latency.

An $N \times N$-bit multiplier generates a $2N$-bit result, and requires $2N$ cycles to complete. Thus, throughput of bit-serial multipliers are restricted because the minimum interval between consecutive multiplications must be at least $2N$ cycles. In the IDEA algorithm one of the operands of every modular multiplication is a subkey and treated as a constant.

Recall in the modular multiplication algorithm that the intermediate result t is divided into two portions (Section 2.1, pseudocode line 7-9). The two portions, t_h and t_l, are respectively the upper and lower 16-bits of the double-word, which are operands to subsequent operations. A design that computes the upper and lower words of t independently is desirable, allowing all the inputs, outputs and intermediate variables of the operator to be 16-bit long. Using this scheme and duplicating hardware, the throughput of a modular multiplication operation can be doubled.

A modified version of Lyon's parallel-serial multiplier [21] was developed which addresses this problem. To generate two 16-bit results in 16 cycles, the throughput of the multiplier must be doubled. We achieved this by duplicating the hardware for multiplication, as illustrated in Figure 3. Registers storing the constant are shared among the two multiplication pipelines. The outputs p and q correspond to the results of two consecutive multiplications, where the two 32-bit long variables have a time-difference of 16 cycles. The control signal, which is high one clock cycle before the least significant bit enters the module, toggles the control register. The vector of input variables $a_{n-1} \ldots a_1 a_0$ is consequently redirected into the two multiplication pipelines alternately. While the vector is being redirected to one pipeline, logic zero enters the other pipeline carrying out zero-padding.

To obtain the time-aligned upper and lower words of t, a 16 stage shift register is required. The input and output of the shift register are the upper and lower words of t respectively, 16 cycles after t is valid. In the implementation the shift register is implemented as a SRL16E [29] primitive. The complete architecture for the modular multiplication operation is shown in Figure 4. Upon initialization, the subkey associated with the operator is passed into the operator bit-serially. The pre-decremented subkey is shifted into the registers of the multiplier, and at the same time stored into the SRL16E primitive responsible for key storage.

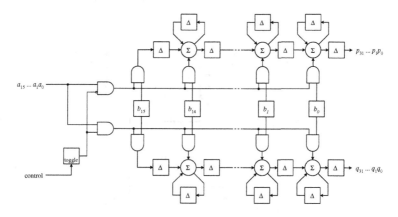

Fig. 3. Parallel-serial multiplier modified for increased throughput.

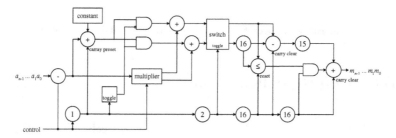

Fig. 4. Bit-serial architecture for multiplication modulo $2^{16} + 1$ operations.

Utilizing the idea of multiple pipelines, the modular multiplication operation offers a throughput of 16 cycles, even though a 32-bit intermediate result is computed. This scheme doubles the throughput but since sharing of the b registers can occur, the hardware cost is less than double.

4.2 Bit-Serial IDEA Core

The core implementation of IDEA is obtained by cascading eight identical rounds of operations shown in Figure 5, followed by a output transformation. The core takes one 64-bit plaintext once every 16 cycles, yielding an effective encryption rate of $f \times 64 \div 16$ Mb/sec at a system clock rate of f MHz. At 150 MHz, for example, the performance of the core is 600 Mb/sec.

Each round has a latency of 109 cycles. The output transformation has a latency of 35 cycles. Each serial-to-parallel converter at the outputs has a latency of 16 cycles. Therefore, the IDEA core has an overall latency of $109 \times 8 + 35 + 16 = 923$ cycles. At a 150 MHz system clock rate, the equivalent latency is 6.153 μs.

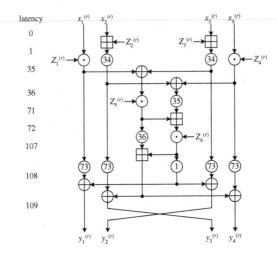

Fig. 5. Bit-serial architecture for one round of IDEA algorithm.

5   Bitstream Reconfiguration

The basic building block of the Virtex FPGA is the logic cell (LC). A LC includes a 4-input function generator, carry logic and a storage element. Each Virtex Configurable Logic Blocks (CLB) contains four LCs, organized in two slices. The 4-input function generator are implemented as 4-input LUTs. Each of them can provide the functions of one 4-input LUT or a 16×1-bit synchronous RAM (called "distributed RAM"). Furthermore, two LUTs in a slice can be combined to create a 16×2-bit or 32×1-bit synchronous RAM, or a 16×1-bit dual-port synchronous RAM.

The contents of the LUTs upon initialization are encoded in the bitstream. Xilinx disclosed the format of bitstream for Virtex series FPGA [14,6], hence it is possible to edit the bitstream and alter the contents of LUTs. Our approach to achieve runtime reconfigurability is to build all configurable blocks from LUTs and later modify the bitstream.

More specifically, the key-schedule is stored only inside ROM or SRL16E primitives which are implemented as LUTs. After technology-mapping, placement and routing, a circuit description (with a *.ncd* extension) is generated. Using the *ncdread* tool provided by Xilinx, the contents of the circuit description can be converted into a human-readable format. It is possible to extract the physical location of individual LUTs from the output of *ncdread*.

We have developed software to customize bitstreams for different key-schedules. In the first step (which need only be performed once for a given design), information concerning the physical location of individual LUTs which are used in the key schedule is extracted from the *.ncd* file and written to a location file (`locfile`). To modify a bitstream, the LUTs are directly modified by a program to use a given key-schedule. The pseudocode below describes the technique that was used.

```
1    changekeys(locfile, bitstream)
2    {
3        locdb = read(locfile);
4        foreach bit in the key
5        {
6            Find location of the LUT using locdb;
7            Modify the value of the bit in the LUT;
8        }
9        Recompute CRC for the bitstream;
10       Write bitstream;
11   }
```

On an Intel Pentium III 866 MHz machine, the reconfiguration process requires the modification of 6×16 LUTs and changing a key takes approximately 0.12 seconds.

In some applications, runtime reconfiguration may not be desirable e.g. if the bitstream is placed in a ROM or in an Application-Specific Integrated Circuit (ASIC) implementation. For these cases, shift registers can be employed for the key-schedule. The shift registers are linked to form a large shift register when key-schedules are being fetched. This long shift register breaks down into the original shift registers after initialization. This method requires minimal logic and routing resources.

6   Results

Both the bit-parallel and bit-serial IDEA processor was verified with Synopsys VHDL Simulator, and was synthesized using Synopsys FPGA Express 3.5 and Xilinx Foundation Series 3.1i, with Xilinx Virtex XCV300-6 as target device.

Our serial and parallel implementations of IDEA were successfully implemented on Annapolis Micro Systems Wildcard Reconfigurable Computing Engine [1]. The device is a Type II PCMCIA Card with a 33 MHz 32-bit CardBus interface, consisting of an Xilinx Virtex XCV300–6 FPGA as Processing Element (PE) and two $64k \times 32$-bit SDRAMs. A single core parallel implementation was also tested using a Pilchard card [19] which uses a memory slot interface instead of a CardBus interface.

6.1   Performance of IDEA Core

For the bit-parallel implementation, a single core/round of the algorithm requires 1178 Virtex slices. An XCV300 device can accommodate two rounds of the algorithm, accounting for 2444 slices (including extra logic required for scaling), or 79.56% of the total 3072 slices.

For the bit-serial implementation, the fully-pipelined implementation (8 rounds plus output transformation), with parallel-to-serial converters at inputs and serial-to-parallel converters at outputs, requires 2878 Virtex slices which occupies 93.68% of CLB resources.

It was observed that the building blocks offer faster computations in the stand-alone configuration, but performance degrades when they are being used as components in the hierarchical design. Hence, core performance improvement may be obtained by floorplanning, such that inter-component routing is minimized. The performance of the cores (assuming a high-bandwidth interface to the data sources and sinks) is summarized in Table 2.

Table 2. Summary of performance for the two implementations on an Virtex XCV300-6 device.

	Bit-parallel	Bit-serial
Number of Cores	2	1
Clock rate (MHz)	82.0	150.0
Encryptions per second ($\times 10^6$)	18.220	9.375
Encryption rate (Mb/sec)	1166.08	600.0
Latency (μs)	2.134	6.153

In an attempt to explore tradeoffs between performance and area, the core was generated for FPGAs of different capacities. Since there are no data dependencies, the implementations can be easily scalable by instantiation of multiple cores. The designs were maximally scaled within the resource limitation of each device to produce the results summarized in Table 3.

6.2 Performance

On the Wildcard implementation, the time taken to complete a transaction between the FPGA and host is dominated by the setup time of CardBus interface. When designing the interface between the IDEA core and the host, it is crucial that the number of discrete transactions is minimized and the amount of data transfered per transaction is maximized.

Data from host is written directly to the core using a burst mode transfer of 1024 64-bit plaintext blocks. After the latency period, the ciphertext is written to consecutive locations in the BlockRAM. For XCV300 devices, there are eight 256×32-bits BlockRAM [28] on the chip and they are all used in the host/IDEA interface. The results are read by the host from the IDEA processor by doing a

Table 3. Tradeoffs between performance and area of the IDEA cores on different devices.

Device (speed grade -6)	Bit-parallel			Bit-serial		
	XCV300	XCV600	XCV1000	XCV300	XCV600	XCV1000
Scaling	2×	5×	9×	1×	2×	4×
Number of slices	2444	6368	11602	2878	5756	11512
Device utilization	79.56%	92.13%	94.42%	93.68%	83.28%	93.68%
Encryptions per second ($\times 10^6$)	18.220	45.551	81.991	9.375	18.750	37.500
Encryption rate (Mb/sec)	1166.1	2915.3	5247.4	600.0	1200.0	2400.0

burst mode transfer of the contents of the BlockRAM. The decryption process is similar except the ciphertext is written to the IDEA core and the plaintext appears in the BlockRAM.

The interface between host and IDEA core on Wildcard requires approximately an additional 160 slices, resulting in a total of 2606 slices (84.83%) and 3039 slices (98.93%) utilization of the XCV300 for the bit-parallel and bit-serial implementations respectively.

The burst transfer rate of CardBus is $33 \times 32 = 1056$ Mb/sec. However, due to large overheads in the CardBus transactions, both the implementations achieve a measured performance of 0.61×10^6 encryptions per second (39 Mb/sec) on a 300 MHz Intel Pentium II laptop computer. The situation could be improved by using Direct Memory Access (DMA) channels. In addition, utilizing the two 64k × 32-bits SDRAMs on Wildcard could provide a larger buffer for ciphertext storage hence reducing the number of transactions.

6.3   Pilchard

In an attempt to improve the PC to FPGA data transfer rate, the bit-parallel implementation was ported to a Pilchard card [19] which utilizes a memory slot interface for improved performance over a CardBus interface. The Pilchard card used the same XCV300–6 device as in the Wildcard. The implementation uses only a single IDEA core/round and requires a total of 1319 slices (42.93% utilization). Pilchard offers a higher bandwidth between the PC and FPGA and the implementation achieved a measured encryption performance of 146 Mb/sec on an Intel Pentium IIII 866 MHz desktop PC.

7   Conclusion

Two high-performance runtime reconfigurable implementations of the IDEA algorithm were presented in this paper. In both designs, the bitstream is customize for a particular key and this procedure saved hardware resources in our design. In implementations on the same XCV300-6 part, the bit-parallel version achieved an encryption rate of 1166 Mb/sec using an 82 MHz clock, whereas the bit-serial implementation achieved a 600 Mb/sec throughput at a clock rate of 150 MHz. The bit-parallel implementation achieved a higher throughput with lower latency than the bit-serial implementation, while the bit-serial implementation permits a minimal area fully-pipelined design.

References

1. Annapolis Micro Systems, Inc. *Wildcard Reference Manual*, 1999. Revision 1.1.
2. Ascom. *IDEACrypt Coprocessor Data Sheet*, 1999. (http:// www.ascom.ch/ infosec/ downloads/ IDEACrypt_Coprocessor.pdf).
3. Ascom. *IDEACrypt Kernel Data Sheet*, 1999. (http:// www.ascom.ch/ infosec/ downloads/ IDEACrypt_Kernel.pdf).
4. H. Bonnenberg, A. Curiger, N. Felber, H. Kaeslin, and X. Lai. VLSI implementation of a new block cipher. In *Proceedings of the IEEE International Conference on Computer Design: VLSI in Computer and Processors*, pages 501–513, 1991.
5. J. Borst. Differential-linear cryptanalysis of IDEA. ESAT–COSIC Technical Report 96–2, Department of Electrical Engineering, Katholieke Universiteit Leuven, February 1997.
6. C. Carmichael. *Virtex FPGA Series Configuration and Readback*. Xilinx, Inc., September 1999. Application Note XAPP152, Version 1.2.
7. A. Curiger, H. Bonnenberg, R. Zimmerman, N. Felber, H. Kaeslin, and W. Fichtner. VINCI: VLSI implementation of the new secret-key block cipher IDEA. In *Proceedings of the IEEE Custom Integrated Circuits Conference*, pages 15.5.1–15.5.4, 1993.
8. A. V. Curiger, H. Bonnenberg, and H. Kaeslin. Regular VLSI architectures for multiplication modulo $2^n + 1$. *IEEE Journal of Solid-State Circuits*, 26(7):990–994, July 1991.
9. Electronic Frontier Foundation. DES challenge III broken in record 22 hours, January 1999. (http:// www.eff.org/ pub/ Privacy/ Crypto_misc/ DESCracker/ HTML/ 19990119_deschallenge3.html).
10. M. George and P. Alfke. *Linear Feedback Shift Registers in Virtex Devices*. Xilinx, Inc., August 1999. Application Note XAPP210, Version 1.0.
11. S. C. Goldstein, H. Schmit, M. Budiu, M. Moe, and R. R. Taylor. PipeRench: A reconfigurable architecture and compiler. *Computer*, 33(4):70–77, April 2000.
12. R. Hartley and K. K. Parhi. *Digit-Serial Computation*. Kluwer Academic Publishers, 1995.
13. M. Hellman and S. Langford. Differential-linear cryptanalysis. In *Advances in Cryptology, Proceedings of Eurocrypt 1994*, pages 26–36, 1994.
14. S. Kelem. *Virtex Configuration Architecture Advanced Users' Guide*. Xilinx, Inc., September 1999. Application Note XAPP151, Version 1.2.
15. L. R. Knudsen. Truncated and higher order differentials. In *Proceedings of the Second International Workshop on Fast Software Encryption*, pages 196–211, 1995.
16. X. Lai and J. Massay. A proposal for a new block encryption standard. In *Advances in Cryptology, Proceedings of Eurocrypt 1990*, pages 389–404, 1990.
17. X. Lai, J. Massay, and S. Murphy. Markov ciphers and differential cryptanalysis. In *Advances in Cryptology, Proceedings of Eurocrypt 1991*, pages 17–38, 1991.

18. M. P. Leong, O. Y. H. Cheung, K. H. Tsoi, and P. H. W. Leong. A bit-serial implementation of the international data encryption algorithm (IDEA). In *Proceedings of the IEEE Symposium on Field-Programmable Custom Computing Machines*, pages 122–131, April 2000.

19. P. H. W. Leong, M. P. Leong, O. Y. H. Cheung, T. Tung, C. M. Kwok, M. Y. Wong, and K. H. Lee. Pilchard - a reconfigurable computing platform with memory slot interface. In *Proceedings of the IEEE Symposium on Field-Programmable Custom Computing Machines (to appear)*, April 2001.

20. Helger Lipmaa. Idea: A cipher for multimedia architectures? In *Selected Areas in Cryptography '98*, pages 253–268, August 1998.

21. R. F. Lyon. Two's complement pipeline multipliers. *IEEE Transactions on Communications*, 12:418–425, April 1976.

22. C. Meier and R. Zimmerman. A multiplier modulo ($2^n + 1$). Diploma thesis, Institut für Integrierte Systeme, ETH, Zürich, Switzerland, February 1991.

23. O. Mencer, M. Morf, and M. J. Flynn. Hardware software tri-design of encryption for mobile communication units. In *Proceedings of the IEEE International Conference on Acoustics, Speech and Signal Processing*, volume 5, pages 3045–3048, May 1998.

24. C. Patterson. High performance DES encryption in Virtex FPGAs using JBits. In *Proceedings of the IEEE Symposium on Field-Programmable Custom Computing Machines*, pages 113–121, April 2000.

25. S. L. C. Salomao, V. C. Alves, and E. M. C. Filho. HiPCrypto: A high-performance VLSI cryptographic chip. In *Proceedings of the Eleventh Annual IEEE ASIC Conference*, pages 7–11, 1998.

26. B. Schneider. *Applied Cryptography*. John Wiley & Sons, second edition, 1996.

27. S. Wolter, H. Matz, A. Schubert, and R. Laur. On the VLSI implementation of the international data encryption algorithm IDEA. In *Proceedings of the IEEE International Symposium on Circuits and Systems*, volume 1, pages 397–400, 1995.

28. Xilinx. *The Programmable Logic Data Book*, 2000.

29. Xilinx, Inc. *Xilinx Libraries Guide*, 1999.

30. Xilinx, Inc. *Xilinx Coregen Reference Guide*, 2000. Version 3.1i.

31. R. Zimmermann, A. Curiger, H. Bonnenberg, H. Kaeslin, N. Felber, and W. Fichtner. A 177Mb/sec VLSI implementation of the international data encryption algorithm. *IEEE Journal of Solid-State Circuits*, 29(3):303–307, March 1994.

A Scalable $GF(p)$ Elliptic Curve Processor Architecture for Programmable Hardware

Gerardo Orlando[1] and Christof Paar[2]

[1] General Dynamics Communication Systems
77 A St., Needham MA 02494-2892, USA
gerardo.orlando@gd-cs.com
[2] ECE Department, Worcester Polytechnic Institute
100 Institute Road, Worcester, MA 01609, USA
christof@ece.wpi.edu

Abstract. This work proposes a new elliptic curve processor architecture for the computation of point multiplication for curves defined over fields $GF(p)$. This is a scalable architecture in terms of area and speed specially suited for memory-rich hardware platforms such a field programmable gate arrays (FPGAs). This processor uses a new type of high-radix Montgomery multiplier that relies on the precomputation of frequently used values and on the use of multiple processing engines.

1 Introduction

This work introduces, to the authors' knowledge, the first documented processor architecture for the computation of elliptic curves point multiplications for curves defined over fields $GF(p)$. Hardware implementations have been documented for the computation of point multiplications for curves defined over $GF(2^m)$. The most notable implementations include [1,2,3,4,5,6].

The architecture presented here is based on the standalone elliptic curve processor architecture introduced in [6]. This architecture is modular, programmable, and suitable for algorithms that rely on precomputations.

Multiplication is typically the most critical operation in the computation of elliptic curves point multiplications. The architecture introduced here uses a Montgomery multiplier. This type of multiplier has been the subject of extensive research, see for example [7,8,9,10,11].

For the elliptic curve processor (ECP) introduced here, this work develops a new multiplier architecture that draws from [9,12] an approach for high radix multiplication, from [8,9] the ability to delay quotient resolution, and from [10] the use of precomputation. In particular, this work extends the concept of precomputation. The resulting multiplier architecture is a high-radix, precomputation-based modular multiplier.

2 Mathematical Background

This section provides a brief introduction to elliptic curve point multiplication. Additional information can be found in [13,14].

Ç.K. Koç, D. Naccache, and C. Paar (Eds.): CHES 2001, LNCS 2162, pp. 348–363, 2001.
© Springer-Verlag Berlin Heidelberg 2001

The ECP computes elliptic curve point multiplications for arbitrary curves defined over $GF(p)$. Point multiplication is defined as the product $kP = \underbrace{P + P + \ldots P}_{k \text{ times}}$, where k is an integer and P is a point on the elliptic curve. For fields $GF(p)$, the curves of interest are defined by $y^2 = x^3 + ax + b$, where $4a^3 + 27b^2 \not\equiv 0 \bmod M$ and $M > 3$.

One can visualize the computation of point multiplications as a hierarchy of processing functions. At the top of the hierarchy are the point multiplication functions. These functions compute point multiplications with repeated point additions and point doubles. At the next level of the hierarchy are the point addition and point double functions, which are intimately related to the co-ordinates used to represent the points. At the bottom of the hierarchy are the finite field functions required to perform the point addition and the point double functions. Figure 1 shows how this hierarchy maps into the ECP architecture.

The ECP is best suited for the computation of point multiplications using projective coordinates. When compared against algorithms for affine coordinates, algorithms for projective coordinates trade inversions in the point addition and in the point double operations for a larger number of multiplications and a single inversion at the end of the algorithm. This inversion can be computed with repetitive multiplications: $a^{-1} \bmod M \equiv a^{M-2} \bmod M$, for prime modulus M.

The ECP uses a Montgomery multiplier. The main advantage of this type of multiplier is that it facilitates quotient estimation and facilitates carry propagation in hardware adders. Their main disadvantage is that they compute weighted products: $\text{mult}(A,B) = ABR^{-1} \bmod M$, where R is a constant.

For Montgomery multiplication to be effective, the input operands to the point multiplication algorithm must be transformed into weighted residues of the form $AR \bmod M$. The algorithm is then executed using these residues. At the end of the algorithm, the results are then transformed back to not weighted residues. Note that as described in [15] the addition and subtraction of these residues can be performed using traditional modular addition and subtraction operations. For most cryptographic algorithms, the cost of these transformations is amortized over a large number of operations.

3   Processor Architecture

The elliptic curve processor (ECP), shown in Figure 1, consists of three main components. These components are the main controller (MC), the arithmetic unit controller (AUC), and the arithmetic unit (AU). The MC is the ECP's main controller. It orchestrates the computation of kP and interacts with the host system. The AUC controls the AU. It orchestrates the computation of point additions/subtractions, point doubles, and coordinate conversions. It also guides the AU in the computation of field inversions. The AU is the hardware that computes field additions/subtractions and multiplications, and performs comparisons.

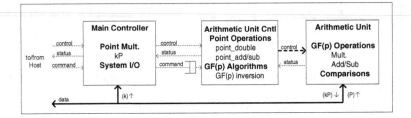

Fig. 1. Elliptic curve processor architecture

The following is a typical sequence of steps for the computation of kP in the ECP using the double-and-add algorithm and the projective coordinates algorithms shown in the appendix.

First, the host loads k into the MC, loads the coordinates of P into the AU, and commands the MC to start processing. The MC does its initialization and then commands the AUC to do its initialization. The AUC initialization includes the conversion of P from affine to projective coordinates and the conversion of these coordinates into weighted residues ($\tilde{X} = XR \bmod M$, $\tilde{Y} = YR \bmod M$, $\tilde{Z} = R \bmod M$). During the computation of kP, the MC scans one bit of k at time starting with the second most significant coefficient and ending with the least significant one. In each of these iterations, the MC commands the AU/AUC to do a point double. If the scanned bit is a 1, it also commands the AU/AUC to do a point addition. For each of these point operations, the AUC generates the control sequence that guides the AU through the computation of the required field and comparison operations. After the least significant bit of k is processed, the MC commands the AU/AUC to convert the result back to affine coordinates. The AU/AUC first converts the result to affine coordinates and then converts the coordinates to not weighted residues (x, y). Then, the MC signals to the host the completion of the kP operation. Finally, the host reads the coordinates of kP from the AU.

The ECP uses two loosely coupled controllers, the MC and the AUC, that execute their respective operations concurrently. These are programmable processors that execute one instruction per clock cycle.

The AU incorporates a multiplier, an adder (or adders), and a register file, all of which can operate in parallel on different data. The AU's large register set supports algorithms that rely on precomputations. An example of a precomutation-based algorithm is an adaptation of a fixed base exponentiation method introduced in [16] for operations involving a known point. This algorithm requires on average $\lfloor m/w \rfloor + 2^w$ point additions, the storage of $\lceil m/w \rceil$ points, and no point doubles. In the previous expressions, w is the window size, which is a measure of the number of bits processed in parallel. To illustrate the benefits of precomputation, consider a fixed point multiplication for an arbitrary curve defined over $GF(2^{192} - 2^{64} - 1)$, which is one of the fields recommended in [17]. Compared to the traditional double-and-add algorithm, the fixed point algorithm is over four times faster (assuming the use of the projective coordinates in [18] with $Z = 1$ and $w = 4$).

4   Arithmetic Unit

The Arithmetic Unit (AU) is the ECP's main processing unit. As Figure 2 shows, it consists of a register file, an adder (or adders), and a multiplier. The multiplier is the AU's most critical component, and, consequently, it is the component that drives the AU's architecture. The AU's architecture is defined at a high level by the multiplication algorithm it implements and at a low level by the number representation it uses.

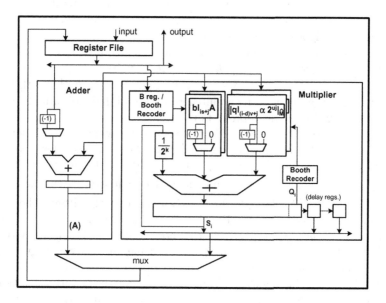

Fig. 2. Arithmetic Unit

The most popular cryptographic algorithms in use today require arithmetic with large operands ($160 \ldots 1024^+$ bits). To achieve a high rate of computation, most hardware implementations resort to iterated multiplication methods that approximate the desired result rather than computing exact ones. The approximated results are then refined to exact results in post-processing operations. The tradeoff is accuracy for speed. The ECP's multiplier is an example. It implements an iterated multiplication algorithm that approximates the multiplication of $AR \bmod M$ and $BR \bmod M$ as $ABR \bmod M + \epsilon M$, where ϵM is a measure of the accuracy of the multiplication. Note that for the basic forms of Montgomery multiplication $\epsilon = 1$.

Number representation is an important element of an arithmetic architecture. It defines how the numbers are represented and consequently how arithmetic is conducted. The selection of a number representation is influenced by the design methodology, the target architecture, and the area-time (or cost-speed) goals. The ECP architecture is independent of number representations. To validate the

ECP architecture a prototype that uses redundant number representation was developed. The implementation results are discussed in section 8.

5   Modular Multiplication Algorithm

Algorithm 1 shows the ECP's main multiplication algorithm. This algorithm is a generalized version of the Montgomery multiplication algorithm with quotient pipelining introduced in [9]. This generalized version supports positive and negative operands and incorporates Booth recoding and precomputation. Positive and negative numbers arise naturally in Booth recoding and they are often used in elliptic curve algorithms.

Booth recoding is a technique that allows the representation of a two's complement number $B = \sum_{i=0}^{s-1} B_i 2^{ui}$, where $s = n/u$, $B_{i<s-1} \in [0, 2^u)$ and $B_{s-1} \in [-2^{u-1}, 2^{u-1})$, as $B = \sum_{i=0}^{s-1} B_i' 2^{ui}$ where $B_i' \in [-2^{u-1}, 2^{u-1}]$. Here we assume that B is represented by an integer number of digits of radix 2^u and also that its most significant bit represents the sign.

This work uses the Modified Booth Algorithm, which is a window based method [19,20]. This method uses s windows, where each window$_i$ groups the set of bits $(b_{iu+(u-1)} b_{iu+(u-2)}..b_{iu-1})_2$ for $i = 0..s - 1$, and where $b_{-1} = 0$ ($B_i = \sum_{j=0}^{u-1} b_{iu+j} 2^j$). The set of bits enclosed by window$_i$, is encoded as $B_i' = -b_{iu+(u-1)} 2^{u-1} + (\sum_{j=0}^{u-2} b_{iu+j} 2^j) + b_{iu-1}$. Note that in Algorithm 1 the recoding is done on a digit-by-digit basis. For this algorithm r, s, u, and v divide k. The variables qh_i and bh_i are respectively the most significant bits of Q_i and B_i.

The validity of Algorithm 1 can be proven using an induction argument similar to the one used in [9] to prove the validity of the Montgomery multiplication algorithm in which this algorithm is based. One can verify with induction on i that Equation (1) defines an invariant of the loop. For this verification note that $\lfloor Si/2^k \rfloor$ defines a truncated division equivalent to $(S_i - Q_i)/2^k$.

Notation: The symbol $|x|_{\hat{M}}$ is used to express an approximate modulo reduction that satisfies the following relation: $|x|_{\hat{M}} = x \bmod M + \epsilon M \equiv x \bmod M$. $|x|_M$ is used to express least residue; that is, $|\,|x|_M\,| < M$, where the symbol $|y|$ represents the absolute value of y.

Using the loop invariant in Equation (1), one can verify that when $i = n+d+1$ the output of the algorithm satisfies Equation (2). This equation establishes that the multiplication output is $S_{n+d+2} \equiv |ABR^{-1}|_{\hat{M}}$ (note that $QM \equiv 0 \bmod M$). This equation also defines the range, or accuracy, of the multiplication result in terms of the maximum values of A and B (note $B_{i \geq n} = 0$); the maximum value for the reduction terms, QM, which is defined in Equations (4-5)(note $Q_0 = 0$); the value of the multiplication constant $R = 2^{kn}$; and the quotient resolution delay, d.

Algorithm 1: Modular Multiplication with Precomputation

Inputs:

$A \in (-\mathcal{A}, \mathcal{A}), \mathcal{A} > 0$

$B = \sum_{i=0}^{n+d} B_i 2^{ki} \in (-\mathcal{B}, \mathcal{B}), \mathcal{B} > 0, B_{i<t-1} \in [0, 2^k), B_{i=t-1} \in [-2^{k-1}, 2^{k-1}),$
     $B_{i \geq t} = 0, t \leq n$

$\alpha \equiv \left| 2^{-k(d+1)} \right|_M, \; gcd(M, 2) = 1, \; R = 2^{kn}, \; d -$ quotient resolution delay

Output:

$S_{n+d+2} \equiv |AB/R|_{\hat{M}} \in (-(\mathcal{AB} + \mathcal{QM})/R, (\mathcal{AB} + \mathcal{QM})/R)$

/* Pre-processing */

1. $S_0 = 0, Q_{i<0} = 0$
2.   for $i = 0$ to 2^{r-1} do
2.1. $A[i] = iA$
       end for
3.   for $i = 0$ to 2^{u-1} do
3.1.   for $j = 0$ to $v - 1$ do
3.1.1. $\alpha[i, j] = \left| i\alpha 2^{uj} \right|_{\hat{M}}$
         end for
       end for

/* Processing */

4.   for $i = 0$ to $n + d$ do
       /* Quotient Determination */
4.1. $Q_i = |S_i|_{2^k}$
       /* Recoding: $ql_j \in [-2^{u-1}, 2^{u-1}]$; $bl_j \in [-2^{r-1}, 2^{r-1}]$; $qh_j, bh_j \in [0, 1]$ */
4.2. $qh_i 2^k + \sum_{j=0}^{v-1} ql_{iv+j} 2^{uj} = Q_i + qh_{i-1}$ /* $k = uv$ */
4.3.   if $i < n$ then
             $bh_i 2^k + \sum_{j=0}^{s-1} bl_{is+j} 2^{rj} = B_i + bh_{i-1}$ /* $k = rs$ */
         else
             $\sum_{j=0}^{s-1} bl_{is+j} 2^{rj} = 0$ /* $B_{i \geq n} = 0$ */
         end if
       /* Reduction */
4.4. $\widetilde{Q\alpha}_i = \sum_{j=0}^{v-1} \alpha[\ |ql_{iv+j}|\ , j\ ](sign(ql_{iv+j}))$
4.5. $\widetilde{AB}_i = \sum_{j=0}^{s-1} A[\ |bl_{is+j}|\ ](sign(bl_{is+j}))2^{rj}$
4.6. $S_{i+1} = \lfloor S_i/2^k \rfloor + \widetilde{Q\alpha}_{i-d} + \widetilde{AB}_i$
       end for

/* Post-processing */

5. $S_{n+d+2} = 2^{kd} S_{n+d+1} + \sum_{i=0}^{d-1} Q_{n+1+i} 2^{ki} + qh_n$
     Loop Invariant:

$$2^{ki} S_i + 2^{k(i-d)} \sum_{j=0}^{d-1} Q_{i+j-d} 2^{kj} + qh_{i-d-1} 2^{k(i-d)} = \tag{1}$$

$$2^k A\left(\left(\sum_{j=0}^{i-1} B_j 2^{kj} \right) - bh_{i-1} 2^{ki} \right) + 2^k \sum_{j=0}^{i-d-2} \left(\widetilde{Q\alpha}_{j+1} 2^{k(d+1)} - \widetilde{Q}_{j+1} \right) 2^{kj}$$

Result after n+d+1 loop iterations:

$$2^{kd}S_{n+d+1} + \sum_{j=0}^{d-1} Q_{n+1+j}2^{kj} + qh_n = \frac{AB + \sum_{j=0}^{n-1}(\widetilde{Q\alpha}_{j+1}2^{k(d+1)} - \widetilde{Q}_{j+1})2^{kj}}{R}$$

$$(2)$$

$$= (AB + QM)/R$$
$$\in (-(\mathcal{AB} + \mathcal{QM})/R, (\mathcal{AB} + \mathcal{QM})/R))$$

QM:

$$\widetilde{Q}_i = \sum_{j=0}^{v-1} ql_{iv+j}2^{uj} \tag{3}$$

$$QM = \sum_{j=0}^{n-1}(\widetilde{Q\alpha}_{j+1}2^{k(d+1)} - \widetilde{Q}_{j+1})2^{kj} \tag{4}$$

$$\in (-\mathcal{QM}, \mathcal{QM})$$
$$\mathcal{QM} > max(\ |QM|\ ) \tag{5}$$

Note that implementations can take advantage of the parallelism defined in steps 4.2-4.6 of Algorithm 1 without using Booth recoding. These implementations can set $qh_i = bh_i = 0$ for all i, and use digits $ql_{iv+j} \in [0, 2^u)$ and $bl_{is+j} \in [0, 2^r)$.

6   Analysis of Modular Multiplication Algorithm

In order to realize an area efficient multiplier, the ECP implements Algorithm 1 using precomputation. Precomputation reduces the complexity of the multiple input adder needed to add all the terms in step 4.6 of Algorithm 1 at the expense of a set of additions at the beginning of the algorithm (steps 2 and 3) and storage. The issues associated with the implementation of Algorithm 1 using precomputations are studied in the next sections.

6.1   Accuracy

The accuracy of the modular multiplication result is influenced by the range of the input operands, the method employed to compute reduction terms, the multiplication constant R, and the quotient resolution delay d.

In [12] two methods are defined for the computation of the reduction terms $|x\alpha|_{\hat{M}}$. These methods are referred to as multiplication-based and lookup-based reduction methods. The multiplication-based approach computes $|x\alpha|_{\hat{M}} = x|\alpha|_M$. The lookup-based method computes $|x\alpha|_{\hat{M}} = |x\alpha|_M$. The accuracy of one multiplication-based and two lookup-based reduction methods are summarized in Table 1. (Note that the reduction method affects the value of $\widetilde{Q\alpha}_i$.)

R is a design parameter that influences the reduction accuracy of the multiplier. As Table 1 shows, the accuracy of the result is bounded by the magnitude of $\mathcal{QM}$, which grows proportionally with R. For applications requiring iterated multiplications, such as modular exponentiations, R is often chosen so that the accuracy of a multiplication result falls in the range $(-2\mathcal{QM}/R, 2\mathcal{QM}/R)$, or $[0, 2\mathcal{QM}/R)$ when handling only positive numbers. Examples for this last application can be found in [9], for which $A, B \in [0, 2(2^{k(d+1)}M))$, $R > 4(2^{k(d+1)}M)$ and $\mathcal{QM} \in [0, 2^{k(d+1)}MR)$.

The results in Table 1 correspond to the worse case values for $\mathcal{QM}$, where the value of a modulo reductions is approximated as M. Parameter selection can greatly improve the accuracy and speed of a multiplication; for example, [17] specifies modulus of the form $M = \sum_{i=t}^{m-1} m_i 2^i {}^+/_- 1$, for which $\left| 2^{-kx} \right|_M = (M\,{}^-/_+\,1)/2^{kx}$ for $t \geq kx$. For $t \geq k(d+1)$, $\mathcal{QM} < MR$ for all the reduction methods listed in Table 1.

Table 1. Accuracy of multiplication- and lookup-based reduction methods

Red. method	$Q\alpha_i$		$\mathcal{QM}$ (worst case)	
Multiplication	$\left\| \sum_{j=0}^{v-1} ql_{iv+j} \right\|\, 2^{-k(d+1)} \Big\|_M$	2^{uj}	$2^{k(d+1)} M \left(\frac{2^{kn}-1}{2^u-1} \right) \left(\frac{2^u}{2} \right)$	$< 2^{k(d+1)} MR$
Lookup 1	$\left\| \sum_{j=0}^{v-1} \left| ql_{iv+j} \right| 2^{-k(d+1)} \right\|_M$	2^{uj}	$2^{k(d+1)} M \left(\frac{2^{kn}-1}{2^u-1} \right)$	$< 2^{k(d+1)} MR \left(\frac{2}{2^u} \right)$
Lookup 2	$\left\| \sum_{j=0}^{v-1} \left| ql_{iv+j} \right| 2^{-k(d+1)} 2^{uj} \right\|_M$		$2^{k(d+1)} M \left(\frac{2^{kn}-1}{2^k-1} \right) v$	$< 2^{kd} MR(2v)$

6.2   Processing Time

Equation (6) provides a processing time approximation for Algorithm 1. This equation assumes that a single precomputation engine performs all the precomputations and transmits them to the respective processing units. In this equation Tb and Tq represent the processing time for the computation of $\widetilde{AB_i}$ and $\widetilde{Q\alpha_i}$ for $i = 0..n+d$. The processing time is the sum of the precomputation time, which is identified with the p subscript, and the processing time, which is identified with the m subscript. (Note that the processing time Tb_m include n processing operations because $B_{i \geq n} = 0$. This condition does not apply to Tq_m.)

The expression in Equation (6) is normalized with respect to a reference unit of time. The processing cost of a precomputation operation is weighted by a factor a and the processing cost of a processing operation is weighted by the factor b. The factor c defines the number of multiplications over which the precomputation cost is amortized. (Note that it is common in many cryptographic algorithms to perform a large number of consecutive operations using the same modulus.)

The factor e represents the number of precomputation sets to be computed. As written, Algorithm 1 requires one set for the scalar products $\widetilde{AB_i}$ and up to v sets for the scalar products $\widetilde{Q\alpha_i}$. Note that for the Lookup 2 reduction method v sets need to be computed in step 3.1. For the multiplication and the

Lookup 1 reduction methods, the precomputation engine can broadcast a single precomputation set to the relevant processing engines. For the precomputation of a single set, eliminate the loop in step 3.1, compute $\alpha[i] = |i\alpha|_{\hat{M}}$ in step 3.1.1, and compute $\widetilde{Q\alpha_i} = \sum_{j=0}^{v-1} \alpha[\ |ql_{iv+j}|\ ](sign(ql_{iv+j}))2^{uj}$ in step 4.4.

$$T_{MM} = Tb + Tq = (Tb_p + Tb_m) + (Tq_p + Tq_m) \tag{6}$$
$$= \left(\frac{a_b e_b}{c_b}2^{r-1} + b_b n)\right) + \left(\frac{a_q e_q}{c_q}2^{u-1} + b_q(n+d)\right)$$

To determine the optimum number of precomputations it is best to express Equation (6) in terms of $m = \lceil log_2 M \rceil$. Equation (7) provides an approximation, where $n = \lceil m/k \rceil + d + f$, f is a constant and $R = 2^{m+k(d+f)}$. According to Equation (2) and the possible cases in Table 1, $f \in [0, 2]$ when $\mathcal{A} = \mathcal{B} = 2^{k/2}Q\mathcal{M}/R$ and the target multiplication accuracy is $S_{n+d+2} \in (-2(Q\mathcal{M}/R), 2Q\mathcal{M}/R)$. These parameters are of interest here because they define a small number of iterations for Algorithm 1 that generate results suitable for repeated multiplications and they also allow a number of additions to be performed between multiplications without the need for reduction. Unless otherwise specified, this document will assume the use of the aforementioned parameters for general multiplications.

$$T_{MM} = \left(\frac{a_b e_b}{c_b}2^{r-1} + b_b\lceil m/rs \rceil + b_b(d+f)\right) \tag{7}$$
$$+ \left(\frac{a_q e_q}{c_q}2^{u-1} + b_q\lceil m/uv \rceil + b_q(2d+f)\right)$$

6.3   Operations of Interest for Scalar Point Multiplication

Table 2 list some of the operations of interest in the computation of point multiplications. This table assumes that $\mathcal{A} = \mathcal{B} = 2^{k/2}Q\mathcal{M}/R$. Entries 1 and 2 in this table are used in the projective coordinate algorithms defined in [18]. Entry 1 corresponds to the classical multiplication operation. Entry 2 defines a division by 2 requiring just $d + 2$ iterations of the loop in Algorithm 1. Entry 3 defines a multiplication of a special form which is used here to reduce the magnitude of a value presumed to be $|0|_M$ before comparing it to zero. Note that for Entry 3, $Q\mathcal{M}$ is defined with respect to x ($n = x$) as shown in Table 1, and this value may be different from the value of $Q\mathcal{M}$ used to define $\mathcal{A}$.

Some of the elliptic curve algorithms defined in the open literature, such as the ones in [18], use comparisons in time critical functions, such as point addition and point double. Comparisons are used, among others, to identify the point at infinity during point add and point double operations. These comparisons involve field elements, therefore numbers A and B are considered equal if $A - B \equiv |0|_M$, which implies that their difference is a multiple of M.

The accuracy of Algorithm 1 is of the order $Q\mathcal{M}/R$, where $Q\mathcal{M}$ is defined in Table 1. Rather than adding specialized circuitry to perform this function, here we recommend an approach that multiplies a value presumed to be zero by a constant. The idea is to perform this multiplication with high accuracy in a short amount of time. To achieve high accuracy, we recommend the use of Algorithm 1 with low quotient resolution delay ($d \approx 0$) and possibly by using a more exact version of Algorithm 1 (see Table 1). To achieve a short processing time, we recommend multiplication by $\left|2^{-kx}\right|_{\hat{M}}$ according to Table 2, where the parameter x is adjusted so that the value of the multiplication result is close to the value of M.

The recommended algorithm for the comparison of two field elements A and B works as follows. First compute $A - B$. The result of this operation is a multiple of M if $A \equiv |B|_M$, and, if that is the case, $\left|(A - B)/2^{kx}\right|_{\hat{M}}$ will also be a multiple of M. Then, compute $\left|(A - B)/2^{kx}\right|_{\hat{M}}$ according to Table 2. Finally, refine the result to a value in the range $(-M, M)$ and compare it against 0.

For the comparison of A with zero, assume that $\mathcal{A} = 2^{k/2+k(d_a+1)}M$, which could correspond to the Multiplication-based reduction method shown in Table 1, and that the operation $\left|A/2^{kx}\right|_{\hat{M}}$ is done using the Lookup 2 reduction method with $d = 0$ and $x = d_a + 2$, where d_a corresponds to the quotient resolution delay associated with A. For this example, the result of $\left|A/2^{k(d_a+2)}\right|_{\hat{M}}$ falls in the range $(-(2v+1)M, (2v+1)M)$. This result can be computed with d_a+3 iterations of the loop in Algorithm 1, but because these iterations are computed without quotient resolution delay ($d = 0$) each one can take up to d_a clock cycles. In other words, a multiplier can compute multiplications with and without quotient resolution delay, but when performing operations involving no quotient resolution delay, the multiplier must wait for the quotient resolution. The quotient resolution is assumed to take up to d_a clock cycles.

Note that the algorithm just described is useful for a large set of applications. If additional accuracy is needed for the reduction operations, one can implement in the ECP a more accurate version of the multiplication algorithm, one such algorithm is presented in [9].

Table 2. Multiplications of interest

#	Mult.	B	$\mathcal{AB}$	R	n	$\left|S_{n+d+2}\right|$
1	$\left|ABR^{-1}\right|_{\hat{M}}$	B	$< 2^k(\mathcal{QM}/R)^2$	$> (2^k\mathcal{QM})^{1/2}$	$log_{2^k} R$	$< 2\mathcal{QM}/R$
2	$\left|A/2\right|_{\hat{M}}$	2^{k-1}	$2^{k-1}\mathcal{A}$	2^k	1	$< \mathcal{A}$
3	$\left|A/2^{kx}\right|_{\hat{M}}$	1	$\mathcal{A}$	2^{kx}	x	$< (\mathcal{A} + \mathcal{QM})/2^{kx}$

6.4   Area and Storage

The most complex operation of Algorithm 1 is the computation of the two scalar multiplications $\widetilde{AB}_i$ and $\widetilde{Q}\alpha_i$ – the multiplication in step 5 is just a shift operation. These scalar multiplications can be computed using scalar multipliers. For the computation of a scalar multiplication, a scalar multiplier would add up to $k/2$ numbers per clock cycle when employing Booth recoding and k copies when using no recoding. Assuming that all the operands in Algorithm 1 are of the same size, the concurrent computation of step 4.6 would require the addition of $k + 1$ operands when using recoding or $2k + 1$ when using no recoding. On the other hand, when using precomputation the concurrent computation of step 4.6 requires the addition of $s + v + 1$ operands.

A limiting factor in the practical implementation of multiplication with pre-computation is the size of the memory required to store the precomputed values. The use of Booth recoding in Algorithm 1, reduces the memory requirements by half when no storage is provided for values known to have zero value (e.g., $0 * A$). Assuming that each precomputed product used in the computation of $\widehat{AB}_i$ requires $m + k(d + 1) + r$-bits of storage, that each precomputed scalar product used in the computation of $\widetilde{Q\alpha}_i$ requires $m + u$-bits of storage, and that each processing unit stores its own set of precomputed values, Algorithm 1 requires $s2^{r-1}(m + k(d + 1) + r) + v2^{u-1}(m + u)$ -bits of storage. Note that if multiple reduction methods are used concurrently, such as the use of a reduction method with $d \neq 0$ and one with $d = 0$, more than one copy of reduction coefficients needs to be stored.

Note that the relationships between r and s, and, between u and v, allow designers to control the memory size; for example, to achieve a given k, a designer could fix r and then derive s, which defines the required number of processing elements. This approach is particularly attractive for architectures that employ fixed size memory elements, such as field programmable gate arrays (FPGAs).

6.5   Effect of Quotient Pipelining

Quotient pipelining is the technique that allows fast rate of computations by allowing the use of delayed reduction terms ($d \neq 0$). The delay is reflected in steps 4.4 and 4.6 of Algorithm 1. The computation in step 4.4 occurs in the background and takes d iterations to complete. To avoid stalling, the results from step 4.4 are consumed as they become available in step 4.6.

The cost of this technique is reduced accuracy, increased processing time and increased area. The impact of this technique can be reduced by eliminating processing functions associated with the quotients, such as recoding, and by hiding quotient operations behind other functions. For example, the scalar products in step 4.6 of Algorithm 1 could be computed serially with all the processing engines dedicated to the computation of a scalar multiplication, instead of having two sets, each working on a different scalar product.

6.6   Number Representation

The previous discussion considered the upper layers of the ECP architecture, which are independent of the number representation. This section considers the specific example of stored-carry representation.

Stored-carry representation is attractive for the implementation of an ECP, among others, because of its support for fast addition using carry-save addition, natural interaction with non-redundant number representation, and its ability to support two's complement arithmetic.

The main drawbacks of stored-carry representation stem from its representation of a number with two numbers; for example, $A = C + S$, where A, B, and C are numbers of almost equal size. This representation doubles the storage requirements for an operand with respect to non-redundant representation and makes comparisons difficult. A comparison can be carried out by performing a subtraction, converting the result to non-redundant representation and then comparing the result against zero.

The use of Booth recoding in Algorithm 1 alleviates the storage requirements imposed by stored-carry representation. In addition, the ability to amortize pre-computations over a large number of operations can be used to reduce memory requirements by storing precomputed values in non-redundant representation. The ECP's multiplier architecture, shown in Figure 2, also makes provisions for the conversion of numbers to non-redundant representation; for example, the conversion of B can be done in a digit-by-digit basis before recoding. In addition, the system could employ a carry propagate adder for the conversion of numbers to non-redundant representation before storing them in the register file.

7   Multiplier Architecture

The AU's architecture is shown in Figure 2. The multiplier and adder together implement Algorithm 1. The adder, which is optimized for accumulation ($A = A + B$), feeds precomputation values to the multiplier. Both the adder and the multiplier receive one of their inputs from the register file. They also output results to the register file.

To accomplish a high rate of computation, the architecture shown in Figure 2 can be implemented using stored-carry representation. To balance storage and processing speed requirements one can choose to represent some numbers in stored-carry representation and others in non-redundant representation.

The reduction terms $\left|i\alpha 2^{uj}\right|_{\hat{M}}$ and some of the temporary results can be converted to non-redundant representation before storage. Operand B of the multiplication can be loaded to the multiplier in stored-carry form and then converted to non-redundant representation one digit at a time as the loop in Algorithm 1 progresses. The reduction terms Q_i can also be converted to non-redundant representation before applying Booth recoding.

To support stored-carry representation, the architecture in Figure 2 must be enhanced with a carry propagate adder and with an efficient way to store numbers represented in stored-carry representation. For the ECP prototype described in the next section, we implemented a carry propagate adder with a digit-serial adder placed at point **(A)** in Figure 2. For the storage of numbers represented in stored-carry representation, we recommend that the output multiplexer in Figure 2 be able to independently forward to the register file each of the numbers used to represent a number in stored-carry representation; that is, for $A = C + S$, this multiplexer can send either C or S to the register file.

Note that the two numbers used to represent a number in stored-carry representation can be treated as two numbers represented in non-redundant representation. Therefore, for the terms represented in stored-carry representation, such as $A[\ |bl_{is+j}|\ ](sign(bl_{is+j}))$, one can use two processing units per term. Where each processing unit handles numbers represented in non-redundant representation. This design approach allows the use of a common processing unit architecture for stored-carry and non-redundant number representations.

8   Prototype Implementation

The validity of the ECP architecture was verified with a prototype that implemented the double-and-add algorithm using the projective coordinates algorithms defined in [18] for point addition and point double operations (the algorithms are shown in the appendix). This prototype was programmed to support the field $GF(2^{192} - 2^{64} - 1)$, which is one of the fields specified in [17].

To verify the ECP's architectural scalability to larger fields, a modular multiplier for fields as large as $GF(2^{521} - 1)$ was also prototyped. This field is the biggest one recommended in [17] for elliptic curves defined over $GF(p)$. This prototype exhibits the same area scalability and frequency of operation as does the multiplier of the ECP prototype. The following discussion focuses exclusively on the ECP prototype.

The ECP prototype used a 16-bit MC processor with 256 words of program memory, a 32-bit AUC processor with 2048 words of program memory, and a dual set of 128 registers, each of which is $m + k(d + 2)$ bits wide. The dual set of registers permits the storage of numbers in stored-carry representation. (Note that a single register set capable of storing stored-carry numbers could have been used instead.) The prototype provided a 32-bit I/O interface to the host system. The ECP multiplier exhibits the following attributes: $s = v = 2$, $r = u = 4$, $k = 8$, $m = 192$, and $d = 4$.

The ECP prototype for $GF(2^{192}-2^{64}-1)$ uses 11,416 LUTs, 5,735 Flip-Flops, and 35 BlockRAMS. LUTs are lookup-tables that are used in the prototype as 16x1-bit RAMs or as 4-input gates. The BlockRAMs are dual-ported 4k-bit blocks of RAM, which are used in the register file, in the MC and AUC as program memory, and in the multiplier as Booth recoders. The frequency of operation of the prototype was 40 MHz. (The frequency of operation of the 521-bit multiplier was 37.3 MHz.)

The validity of the prototype was verified with non-optimized code. Assuming that the ECP is coded in a form that extracts 100% throughput from its multiplier, it will compute a point multiplication for an arbitrary point on a curve defined over $GF(2^{192} - 2^{64} - 1)$ in approximately 3 msecs ($n = 192/8 + 1$, $d = 4$, $k = rs = uv = 8$) using the algorithms shown in the appendix. This estimate ignores the processing cost of additions and overhead operations and it assumes the computation of $17m$ multiplications per point multiplication: $15.5m$ for the point double and the point add operations and $1.5m$ for the inverse required in the conversion to affine coordinates. For the modular multiplications, this estimate assumes negligible precomputation cost for the reduction terms, $\widetilde{Q}\alpha_i$, and assumes the precomputation of $2^3 - 2$ values for the terms $\widehat{AB_i}$ (no computation required for $0A$ or $1A$).

The prototypes were implemented using the Xilinix's XCV1000E-8-BG680 (Virtex E) FPGA. The prototypes were coded in VHDL. They were synthesized with Synopsis' FPGA Compiler 3.5.0 and Xilinx's Design Manager M3.1i.

8.1   Comparisons with Other Implementations

Table 3 summarizes the features of the multiplier used in the ECP prototype and the features of one of the multiplier architectures introduced in [10] which also relies on precomputation. Both of these multipliers exhibit comparable area requirements (#LUTs), when one assumes $s = v = 1$ and $r = u = 4$. Note that the multiplier in [10] uses a fixed value of k, where this value is highly dependent on the underlying FPGA architecture.

It should be pointed out that the multiplier architecture introduced in [10] can be enhanced with some of the techniques introduced here. For example, to overcome the radix limitation, currently fixed at 2^4, this multiplier could employ multiple processing engines per cell $(s, v \neq 1)$, and to reduce memory requirements it could use Booth recoding.

Table 3. ECP multiplier vs. Design 2 multiplier [10]

Characteristic	ECP	Design 2 $(k = 4)$[10]
Type	semi-systolic	systolic
Main Application	Elliptic Curves	Exponentiation
Basic Operation	$\lvert ABR^{-1} \rvert_{\hat{M}}$	$\lvert ABR^{-1} \rvert_{\hat{M}}$ & $\lvert ACR^{-1} \rvert_{\hat{M}}$
Throughput(mult./#clks)	$1/(\lceil m/k \rceil + 2d)$	$2/(2\lceil m/k \rceil)$
Latency (#clks)	$< \lceil m/k \rceil + 2d$	$2\lceil m/k \rceil$
Accuracy	$\leq 2(2^{k(d+1)}M)$	$2(2^k)M$
Max. Radix	2^{rs}	2^k
#LUT	$(2 + 4(2s + v))(m + k(d + 1))$	$12m$
# Flip-Flops	$(2 + 2s + v)(m + k(d + 1))$	$12m$
Frequency (MHz)	40	48
FPGA	XCV1000E-8-BG680	XC4000

9   Conclusions

This work proposed a new elliptic curve processor architecture for the computation of point multiplication for curves defined over fields $GF(p)$. This processor uses a new type of high-radix Montgomery multiplier that relies on the precomputation of frequently used values and on the use of multiple processing engines.

The ECP's architectural scalability was verified with prototype implementations suitable for the implementation of secure elliptic curve cryptosystems

(192- and 521-bits). Our estimates reflect that if were possible to extract 100% throughput from our multiplier, the computation of a point multiplication in a curve defined over $GF(2^{192} - 2^{64} - 1)$ could be computed in about 3 msecs using the double-and-add algorithm and the projective coordinates algorithms defined in [18].

References

1. G. Agnew, R. Mullin, and S. Vanstone, "An implementation of elliptic curve cryptosystems over $F_{2^{155}}$," *IEEE Journal on Selected areas in Communications*, vol. 11, pp. 804–813, June 1993.
2. M. Rosner, "Elliptic curve cryptosystems on reconfigurable hardware," Master's thesis, ECE Dept., Worcester Polytechnic Institute, Worcester, USA, May 1998.
3. L. Gao, S. Shrivastava, and G. Sobelman, "Elliptic curve scalar multiplier design using FPGAs," in *Workshop on Cryptographic Hardware and Embedded Systems (CHES '99)* (C. Koc and C. Paar, eds.), vol. LNCS 1717, Springer-Verlag, August 1999.
4. S. Sutikno, R. Effendi, and A. Surya, "Design and implementation of arithmetic processor $F_{2^{155}}$ for elliptic curve cryptosystems," in *The 1998 IEEE Asia-Pacific Conference on Circuits and Systems*, pp. 647–650, November 1998.
5. K. Leung, K. Ma, W. Wong, and P. Leong, "FPGA implementation of a microcoded elliptic curve cryptographic processor," in *Eight Annual IEEE Symposuium on Field-Programmable Custom Computing Machines, FCCM '00*, (Napa Valley, California, USA), 2000.
6. G. Orlando and C. Paar, "A high performance elliptic curve processor for $GF(2^m)$," in *Workshop on Cryptographic Hardware and Embedded Systems - CHES 2000*, vol. LNCS 1965, (Worcester, Massachusetts, USA), Springer-Verlag, August 2000.
7. P. Kornerup, "A systolic, linear-array multiplier for a class of right-shift algorithms," *IEEE Transactions on Computers*, vol. 43, pp. 892–898, August 1994.
8. M. Shand and J. Vuillemin, "Fast implementations of RSA cryptography," in *Proceedings 11th Symposium on Computer Arithmetic*, pp. 252–259, 1993.
9. H. Orup, "Simplifying quotient determination in high-radix modular multiplication," in *Proceedings 12th Symposium on Computer Arithmetic*, pp. 193–199, 1995.
10. T. Blum, "Modular exponentiation on reconfigurable hardware," Master's thesis, Dept. of ECE, Worcester Polytechnic Institute, Worcester, U.S.A., May 1999.
11. S. E. Eldridge and C. D. Walter, "Hardware implementation of Montgomery's modular multiplication algorithm," *IEEE Transactions on Computers*, vol. 42, pp. 693–699, July 1993.
12. W. Freking and K. Parhi, "A unified method for iterative computation of modular multiplications and reduction operations," in *International Conference on Computer Design (ICCD '99)*, pp. 80–87, 1999.
13. A. J. Menezes, P. C. van Oorschot, and S. A. Vanstone, *Handbook of Applied Cryptography*. CRC Press, 1997.
14. I. Blake, G. Seroussi, and N. Smart, *Elliptic Curves in Cryptography*. Cambridge, UK: Cambridge University Press, first ed., 1999.
15. P. Montgomery, "Modular multiplication without trial division," *Mathematics of Computation*, vol. 44, pp. 519–521, April 1985.
16. E. Brickell, D. Gordon, K. McCurley, and D. Wilson, "Fast exponentiation with precomputation," in *Lecture Notes in Computer Science 658: Advances in Cryptology — EUROCRYPT '92*, pp. 200 – 207, Springer-Verlag, Berlin, 1993.

17. F. I. P. S. Publication, "FIPS 186-2: Digital Signature Standard (DSS)," January 2000.

18. P1363, *Standard Specifications for Public-key Cryptography (Draft Version 8)*. IEEE, October 1998.

19. B. Parhami, *Computer Arithmetic Algorithms and Hardware Designs*. New York: Oxford University Press, Inc., 1999.

20. I. Koren, *Computer Arithmetic Architectures*. Prentice-Hall, 1993.

A   Elliptic Curve Point Multiplication

Algorithm 2: Double-and-add point multiplication using the projective coordinates algorithms defined in [18]

$\text{double\_and\_add}(x, y, k)$	$\text{add}(X_0, Y_0, Z_0, X_1, Y_1, Z_1)$
$\quad (X, Y, Z) = \text{conv\_projective}(x, y)$	$\quad /^* \text{ if } P_1 = \mathcal{O} \text{ then return } P_0 ^*/$
$\quad (X_0, Y_0, Z_0) = (X, Y, Z) \; /^* \; P_0 = P \; ^*/$	$\quad \text{if } (X_1, Y_1, Z_1) = \mathcal{O} \text{ then}$
$\quad \text{for } i = l - 2 \text{ down to } 0 \text{ do}$	$\quad\quad \text{return}(X_0, Y_0, Z_0)$
$\quad\quad (X, Y, Z) = \text{double}(X, Y, Z) \; /^* \; P = 2P \; ^*/$	$\quad /^* \text{ else if } P_0 = -P_1 \text{ then return } \mathcal{O} ^*/$
$\quad\quad \text{if } k_i = 1 \text{ then } /^* \; P = P + P_0 \; ^*/$	$\quad \text{else if } (X_0, Y_0, Z_0) = -(X_1, Y_1, Z_1) \text{ then}$
$\quad\quad\quad (X, Y, Z) = \text{add}(X_0, Y_0, Z_0, X, Y, Z)$	$\quad\quad \text{return}(\mathcal{O})$
$\quad\quad \text{end if}$	$\quad /^* \text{ else if } P_0 = P_1 \text{ then return } 2P_0 ^*/$
$\quad \text{end for}$	$\quad \text{else if } (X_0, Y_0, Z_0) = (X_1, Y_1, Z_1) \text{ then}$
$\quad (x, y) = \text{conv\_affine}(X, Y, Z)$	$\quad\quad (X_2, Y_2, Z_2) = \text{double}(X_0, Y_0, Z_0)$
$\text{return } (x, y)$	$\quad \text{else } /^* \text{ return } P_2 = P_0 + P_1 \; ^*/$
$\text{double}(X_1, Y_1, Z_1)$	$\quad\quad U_0 = X_0 Z_1^2$
$\quad /^* \text{ if } P = \mathcal{O} \text{ then return } \mathcal{O} ^*/$	$\quad\quad S_0 = Y_0 Z_1^3$
$\quad \text{if } (X_1, Y_1, Z_1) = \mathcal{O} \text{ then return}(\mathcal{O})$	$\quad\quad U_1 = X_1 Z_0^2$
$\quad \text{else } /^* \; P \neq \mathcal{O} \text{ return } 2P \; ^*/$	$\quad\quad S_1 = Y_1 Z_0^3$
$\quad\quad M = 3X_1^2 + a Z_1^4$	$\quad\quad W = U_0 - U_1$
$\quad\quad Z_2 = 2Y_1 Z_1$	$\quad\quad R = S_0 - S_1$
$\quad\quad S = 4X_1 Y_1^2$	$\quad\quad T = U_0 + U_1$
$\quad\quad X_2 = M^2 - 2S$	$\quad\quad M = S_0 + S_1$
$\quad\quad T = 8Y_1^4$	$\quad\quad Z_2 = Z_0 Z_1 W$
$\quad\quad Y_2 = M(S - X_2) - T$	$\quad\quad X_2 = R^2 - TW^2$
$\quad \text{endif}$	$\quad\quad V = TW^2 - 2X_2$
$\text{return}(X_2, Y_2, Z_2)$	$\quad\quad 2Y_2 = VR - MW^3$
$\text{conv\_projective}(x, y)$	$\quad \text{endif}$
$\text{return } (X = x, Y = y, Z = 1)$	$\text{return}(X_2, Y_2, Z_2)$
$\text{conv\_affine}(X, Y, Z)$	
$\text{return}(x = X/Z^2, y = Y/Z^3)$	

Implementation of RSA Algorithm
Based on RNS Montgomery Multiplication

Hanae Nozaki, Masahiko Motoyama, Atsushi Shimbo, and Shinichi Kawamura

Corporate Research and Development Center, Toshiba Corporation
1, Komukai Toshiba-cho, Saiwai-ku, Kawasaki 212-8582, Japan
{hanae.nozaki, masahiko.motoyama, atsushi.shimbo,
shinichi2.kawamura}@toshiba.co.jp

Abstract. We proposed a fast parallel algorithm of Montgomery multiplication based on Residue Number Systems (RNS). An implementation
of RSA cryptosystem using the RNS Montgomery multiplication is described in this paper. We discuss how to choose the base size of RNS
and the number of parallel processing units. An implementation method
using the Chinese Remainder Theorem (CRT) is also presented. An LSI
prototype adopting the proposed Cox-Rower Architecture achieves 1024-
bit RSA transactions in 4.2 msec without CRT and 2.4 msec with CRT,
when the operating frequency is 80 MHz and the total number of logic
gates is 333 KG for 11 parallel processing units.

Keywords: RSA cryptography, residue number systems, Montgomery
multiplication, modular exponentiation

1 Introduction

Computational performance of large integers is important in the implementation of public key cryptography and digital signature. We proposed a fast parallel Montgomery multiplication algorithm based on Residue Number Systems
(RNS) [1]. In RNS, an integer is represented by a set of its residues in terms
of base elements of RNS, and thus addition, subtraction, and multiplication
can be independently carried out for every base element. On the other hand,
Montgomery multiplication is a method for performing modular multiplication
by substituting addition and multiplication for division. Therefore, the combination of RNS and Montgomery multiplication is expected to be well suited to
parallel processing of modular exponentiation, and several studies concerning it
have been reported [2], [3], [4].

The main purpose of our previous paper [1] was to improve the base transformation algorithm which consumes most of the processing time in the RNS
Montgomery multiplication. We also proposed a hardware "Cox-Rower Architecture" suitable for the RNS Montgomery multiplication. The base transformation operation is efficiently realized by the Cox-Rower Architecture where Rower
units perform parallel processing in cooperation with one Cox unit. Based on

Ç.K. Koç, D. Naccache, and C. Paar (Eds.): CHES 2001, LNCS 2162, pp. 364–376, 2001.

this architecture, the performance of 1 Mbps has been estimated for 1024-bit RSA cryptosystem at the operating frequency of 100 MHz.

In this paper, we investigate an implementation of RSA cryptosystem using the proposed RNS Montgomery multiplication algorithm, and design an RSA LSI to confirm the performance and feasibility of the proposed algorithm. As implementation methods, RSA decryption procedures without and with the Chinese Remainder Theorem (CRT) are presented. The Cox-Rower Architecture is characterized by the scalability for operating time and chip size depending on the number of Rower units. In implementation, the relation between the number of Rower units and the base size in RNS representation becomes important for the performance, because operations for each base element are performed in parallel at Rower units. For an LSI prototype using 0.25 μm CMOS, we obtain 4.2 msec for 1024-bit RSA cryptosystem without CRT and 2.4 msec with CRT. This result is comparable with the present best performance of commercial chips.

The organization of the paper is as follows: In the next section, the RNS Montgomery multiplication algorithm proposed in Ref. [1] is surveyed. In Sec. 3, we present RSA decryption procedures without and with CRT, and discuss the base size of RNS and the number of parallel processing units from the viewpoint of implementation. In Sec. 4, for the designed LSI, a hardware structure and its specifications are described. Finally, a short summary is given in Sec. 5.

2 Algorithm

2.1 Residue Number Systems

In RNS, an integer x is represented by

$$\langle x \rangle_a = (x[a_1], x[a_2], \ldots, x[a_n]), \tag{1}$$

where $x[a_i] = x \bmod a_i$. The set $a = \{a_1, a_2, \ldots, a_n\}$ is called a base and the number of elements n is its base size. The elements are required to satisfy $\gcd(a_i, a_j) = 1$ for $i \neq j$. CRT assures that the integer x which satisfies $0 \leq x < A$ ($A = \prod_{i=1}^{n} a_i$) is uniquely represented by $\langle x \rangle_a$.

The RNS representation has an advantage in which addition, subtraction, and multiplication can be realized by modular addition, subtraction, and multiplication for each RNS element as follows:

$$\langle x \pm y \rangle_a = ((x[a_1] \pm y[a_1])[a_1], \ldots, (x[a_n] \pm y[a_n])[a_n]), \tag{2}$$

$$\langle x \cdot y \rangle_a = ((x[a_1] \cdot y[a_1])[a_1], \ldots, (x[a_n] \cdot y[a_n])[a_n]), \tag{3}$$

which enables parallel computation using n processing units. However, we have not known how to perform comparison and division efficiently based on the RNS representation. To overcome this disadvantage, combination with Montgomery multiplication has been proposed [1], [2], [3], [4].

2.2   Montgomery Multiplication

Montgomery multiplication is known to be an efficient method for implementing modular exponentiation used in public key cryptographies. In the algorithm shown below, the inputs are x, y, and N $(x, y < N)$ and the output is $w \equiv xyR^{-1}$ (mod N) $(w < 2N)$, where $\gcd(R, N) = 1$ and $N < R$.

$$
\begin{aligned}
&1\text{:} \quad s \leftarrow x \cdot y \\
&2\text{:} \quad t \leftarrow s \cdot (-N^{-1}) \bmod R \\
&3\text{:} \quad u \leftarrow t \cdot N \\
&4\text{:} \quad v \leftarrow s + u \\
&5\text{:} \quad w \leftarrow v/R
\end{aligned}
$$

The Montgomery constant R is chosen so as to make division in steps 2 and 5 simple. For example, R is generally set to 2's power in a radix 2 representation.

It is characteristic of Montgomery multiplication to perform modular multiplication by substituting addition and multiplication for division. Since the advantage of RNS is that addition, subtraction, and multiplication can be independently performed for each RNS element, the combination of RNS and Montgomery multiplication is expected to realize fast parallel processing effectively.

2.3   RNS Montgomery Multiplication

The RNS Montgomery multiplication algorithm proposed in Ref. [1] is briefly described in this subsection. The above-mentioned Montgomery multiplication procedure is rewritten by using RNS as shown in Fig. 1. Two bases a and b are introduced, and $B\ (= \prod_{i=1}^{n} b_i)$ is used as the Montgomery constant. We assume here both a and b have the base size n, and denote the RNS representation of x based on a and b by $\langle x \rangle_{a \cup b}$ or simply by $\langle x \rangle$. The bases a and b satisfy $A, B > 8N$, $\gcd(A, B) = 1$, and $\gcd(B, N) = 1$.

Function: $\langle w \rangle_{a \cup b} = \mathrm{MM}(\langle x \rangle_{a \cup b}, \langle y \rangle_{a \cup b}, N)$	
Input: $\langle x \rangle_{a \cup b}, \langle y \rangle_{a \cup b}$ $(x, y < 2N)$	
Output: $\langle w \rangle_{a \cup b}$ $(w \equiv xyB^{-1}$ (mod N), $w < 2N)$	
Base a operation	Base b operation
1: $\langle s \rangle_a \leftarrow \langle xy \rangle_a$	$\langle s \rangle_b \leftarrow \langle xy \rangle_b$
2:	$\langle t \rangle_b \leftarrow \langle s(-N^{-1}) \rangle_b$
3: $\langle t \rangle_a \leftarrow \mathrm{BT}(\langle t \rangle_b, 0)$	
4: $\langle u \rangle_a \leftarrow \langle tN \rangle_a$	
5: $\langle v \rangle_a \leftarrow \langle s + u \rangle_a$	
6: $\langle w \rangle_a \leftarrow \langle vB^{-1} \rangle_a$	
7: $\langle w \rangle_b \leftarrow \mathrm{BT}(\langle w \rangle_a, 0.5)$	

Fig. 1. RNS Montgomery multiplication algorithm.

Steps 3 and 7 in Fig. 1 are base transformation (BT) between a and b (see Fig. 2). According to CRT, x in radix representation is calculated from $\langle x \rangle_a$ by

$$x = \sum_{i=1}^{n} \xi_i A_i \bmod A, \tag{4}$$

where $\xi_i = x[a_i] A_i^{-1}[a_i] \bmod a_i$ and $A_i = A/a_i$. Equation (4) is rewritten by

$$x = \left(\sum_{i=1}^{n} \xi_i A_i \right) - kA, \tag{5}$$

with an unknown parameter k. Dividing both sides of Eq. (5) by A, we obtain

$$k = \left\lfloor \sum_{i=1}^{n} \frac{\xi_i}{a_i} \right\rfloor, \tag{6}$$

from $0 \le x/A < 1$ and $k \le \sum_{i=1}^{n} \xi_i/a_i < k+1$. Figure 2 shows a procedure of the base transformation from a to b. In this procedure, k is approximated by

$$\hat{k} = \left\lfloor \sum_{i=1}^{n} \frac{\mathrm{trunc}(\xi_i)}{2^r} + \alpha \right\rfloor, \tag{7}$$

where $\mathrm{trunc}(\xi_i)$ is a function to approximate ξ_i by its most significant $g\ (<r)$ bits: i.e. $\mathrm{trunc}(\xi_i) = \xi_i \bigwedge (\overbrace{1\ldots1}^{g}\overbrace{0\ldots0}^{(r-g)})_{(2)}$, $\bigwedge$ means a bitwise AND operation, and r is the bit length of processing units. An offset value α is required as a correction caused by the approximation, and is set to 0 at step 3 and 0.5 at step 7 in Fig. 1. The parameter $\hat{k}$ is computed recursively by k_i as shown at steps 4-6 in Fig. 2, where k_i satisfies $\hat{k} = \sum_{i=1}^{n} k_i$ and $k_i \in \{0, 1\}$.

Function: $\langle x \rangle_b = \mathrm{BT}(\langle x \rangle_a, \alpha)$

Input: $\langle x \rangle_a$, $\alpha = 0$ or 0.5

Output: $\langle x \rangle_b$

Precomputation: $\langle A_i^{-1} \rangle_a$, $\langle A_i \rangle_b$, $\langle -A \rangle_b$

1:   $\xi_i = x[a_i] A_i^{-1}[a_i] \bmod a_i$

2:   $\sigma_0 = \alpha,\ y_{i0} = 0$

3:   For $j = 1, \ldots, n$

4:       $\sigma_j = \sigma_{j-1} + \mathrm{trunc}(\xi_{(i+1-j)})/2^r$

5:       $k_{(i+1-j)} = \lfloor \sigma_j \rfloor$

6:       $\sigma_j = \sigma_j - k_{(i+1-j)}$

7:       $y_{ij} = y_{i(j-1)} + \xi_{(i+1-j)} \cdot A_{(i+1-j)}[b_i] + k_{(i+1-j)} \cdot (-A)[b_i]$

8:   Next j

9:   $x[b_i] = y_{in} \bmod b_i$

Fig. 2. Base transformation algorithm.

Function: $\langle y \rangle_{a \cup b} = \mathrm{MEXP}(\langle x \rangle_{a \cup b}, d, N)$

Input: $\langle x \rangle_{a \cup b}$, $d = (d_\kappa, \ldots, d_1)_{(2^4)}$

Output: $\langle y \rangle_{a \cup b}$, s.t. $y = x^d B^{-(d-1)} \bmod N$

Precomputation: $\langle B_N \rangle_{a \cup b}$, s.t. $B_N = B \bmod N$

1: $\langle x_N^0 \rangle \leftarrow \langle B_N \rangle$

2: $\langle x_N^1 \rangle \leftarrow \langle x \rangle$

3: $\langle x_N^{i+1} \rangle \leftarrow \mathrm{MM}(\langle x_N^i \rangle, \langle x \rangle, N)$ (for $i = 1, \ldots, 14$)

4: $\langle y \rangle \leftarrow \langle x_N^{d_\kappa} \rangle$

5: For $i = \kappa - 1, \ldots, 1$

6:      For $j = 1, \ldots, 4$

7:          $\langle y \rangle \leftarrow \mathrm{MM}(\langle y \rangle, \langle y \rangle, N)$

8:      Next j

9:          $\langle y \rangle \leftarrow \mathrm{MM}(\langle y \rangle, \langle x_N^{d_i} \rangle, N)$

10: Next i

Fig. 3. RNS modular exponentiation algorithm.

As compared with the previous RNS Montgomery multiplication algorithm [2], the above-mentioned algorithm has an advantage in that the base transformation at step 7 in Fig. 1 is error-free and does not need extra steps for error correction. Moreover, the correction factor k_i is computed only by an adder as will be described in Sec. 4.1, which can make the hardware structure simpler than that in Ref. [2].

An exponentiation algorithm based on a 4-bit window method is realized by the RNS Montgomery multiplication as shown in Fig. 3. It is assumed that an input variable has been transformed previously into $x' = xB \bmod N$, because of the essential feature of the Montgomery multiplication in which the Montgomery constant B is introduced. From this assumption, we obtain $y = x^d B \bmod N$ as an output.

The clocks to perform the RNS Montgomery multiplication are $O(n^2/u)$, where u is the number of parallel processing units. The RNS modular exponentiation (MEXP) is realized as the iteration operation of the RNS Montgomery multiplication (MM), and the number of iterations is proportionate to the key length $|N|$. From $n \propto |N|$, the performance of the RNS modular exponentiation is consequently estimated by $O(n^3/u)$. This relation means that there is the scalability for performance and chip size depending on the number of parallel processing units u, since the chip size is determined by u.

3   Implementation

Figure 4 shows an RSA decryption procedure using the RNS modular exponentiation algorithm. In steps 1 and 2, modular arithmetic based on the radix 2 representation is required. We assume that this modular arithmetic is performed at a dedicated divider unit. In step 3, $\langle -N^{-1} \rangle_b$ which is used in MM() is calculated from $b_i - (N^{\lambda_i - 1} \bmod b_i)$, where λ_i, the Carmichael function [5] of

Input: C, d, N

Output: $m = C^d \bmod N$

1: $B_N \leftarrow B \bmod N$
2: $B_N^2 \leftarrow B^2 \bmod N$
3: Compute $\langle -N^{-1} \rangle_b$
4: Radix-RNS conversion: N, B_N, B_N^2, C
5: $\langle C' \rangle \leftarrow \mathrm{MM}(\langle C \rangle, \langle B_N^2 \rangle, N)$
6: $\langle m' \rangle \leftarrow \mathrm{MEXP}(\langle C' \rangle, d, N)$
7: $\langle m \rangle \leftarrow \mathrm{MM}(\langle m' \rangle, \langle 1 \rangle, N)$
8: RNS-Radix conversion: $\langle m \rangle_a$
9: $m \leftarrow m - cN \quad (c = 0 \text{ or } 1)$

Fig. 4. RSA decryption algorithm.

b_i, is precomputed and stored in ROMs. Since steps 1–4 (except for C at step 4) depend only on the key N, it is effective to precompute these steps, if N is not changed frequently. As mentioned above, it is assumed in MEXP() that the input and the output are variables multiplied by the Montgomery constant B. From this condition, steps 5 and 7 are required as a transformation to get $C' = CB \bmod N$ and as its inverse transformation, respectively. Finally, step 9 is a correction to assure $m < N$, because m obtained in step 7 is less than $2N$.

Radix-RNS and RNS-Radix conversions are defined by

$$x[a_i] = \left(\sum_{j=0}^{n-1} x(j) \cdot 2^{r \cdot j}[a_i] \right) \bmod a_i, \tag{8}$$

$$x = (2^{r \cdot (n-1)}, \ldots, 2^r, 1) \sum_{i=1}^{n} \left[\xi_i \begin{pmatrix} A_i(n-1) \\ \vdots \\ A_i(1) \\ A_i(0) \end{pmatrix} - k_i \begin{pmatrix} A(n-1) \\ \vdots \\ A(1) \\ A(0) \end{pmatrix} \right], \tag{9}$$

where the notation $x(i)$ means the radix-2^r representation of x: i.e. $x = \sum_{i=0}^{n-1} x(i) \cdot 2^{r \cdot i}$. In the RNS-Radix conversion, carry propagation is needed after the summation has been finished.

3.1   Base Size and Number of Parallel Units

The operation shown in Fig. 4, except for steps 1 and 2 performed at the additional divider unit and the carry propagation in the RNS-Radix conversion, is independently carried out for every base element a_i and b_i at parallel processing units. Here, the base size n has the relation $n \geq \lceil (|N| + r)/r \rceil$ with the bit length $|N|$ of the modulus N. The number of parallel processing units u can be chosen in the range of $1 \leq u \leq n$. If $u < n$, time-sharing processing for some base elements is performed in each unit. When the base size n is fixed, RSA transaction performance improves in proportion to u. Obviously, it is efficient to set u as a divisor of n in order to control all processing units by the same procedure. By choosing u appropriately, a variety of chips can be realized in terms of performance and size.

In the implementation, it is realistic that all parameters which depend only on the base sets a and b are precomputed and stored in ROMs. A chip loaded with base sets for an RSA key length L can deal with key lengths which are shorter than L. However, processing time of a key length l ($< L$) is reduced only to l/L as compared with that of the key length L, although $(l/L)^3$ is achieved ideally. The overhead time is caused by the fact that the performance of RNS Montgomery multiplication is determined from the base size, and thus the amount of operations does not decrease.

In order to perform an efficient computation for shorter key lengths, it is necessary to prepare some base sets for typical key lengths: e.g. 512, 1024, and 2048 bits. For these key lengths, minimum base sizes become 17, 33, and 65 in the case of $r = 32$. There are several implementation methods to deal with different-sized base sets. Among them, it is advantageous to set a base size to a multiple of u from the viewpoint of the simplicity of a control circuit. Therefore, if $u = 11$, appropriate base sizes are 22, 33, and 66 for key lengths 512, 1024, and 2048 bits, respectively. In this case, it is expected that 1024-bit and 2048-bit RSA processing has good performance, whereas 512-bit processing has overhead time.

3.2   CRT Mode

An RSA decryption procedure with CRT is given by

$$
\begin{aligned}
m &= (C^{d_p} \bmod p)(q^{-1} \bmod p)\, q + (C^{d_q} \bmod q)(p^{-1} \bmod q)\, p \pmod{N} \\
&= [(C^{d_p} \bmod p)(q^{-1} \bmod p) \bmod p]\, q \\
&\quad + [(C^{d_q} \bmod q)(p^{-1} \bmod q) \bmod q]\, p \pmod{N},
\end{aligned} \tag{10}
$$

where $N = pq$, $d_p = d \bmod (p-1)$, and $d_q = d \bmod (q-1)$. A procedure to perform Eq. (10) is shown in Fig. 5. The operations for p and q are carried out sequentially. Precomputations of steps 1, 2, 4, and 5 (except for C_p and C_q) are effective, if the secret keys p and q are not changed frequently. Here, it should be noted that we need the RNS representation of m by means of the base $a \cup b$ in the RNS-Radix conversion at step 11, because the modulus N in RSA processing with CRT is represented uniquely not by a single base a or b but by the base $a \cup b$. In contrast, only $\langle m \rangle_a$ (or $\langle m \rangle_b$) is sufficient for the RNS-Radix conversion in Fig. 4. Step 12 is a correction to assure $m < N$ the same as step 9 in Fig. 4. In this case, m obtained in step 10 is less than $4N$, because u_p and u_q ($< 2N$) are added to each other without mod N operation.

The processing time of Fig. 5 is dominated by MEXP() at step 7. Since the base size n can be reduced to $n/2$ by adopting CRT, the processing time of MEXP() becomes $1/8$ of that in Fig. 4. As a result, reduction of about $1/4$ is achieved in total processing time, because the operations for p and q are

Input: C, d_p, d_q, N, p, q, $q_{\mathrm{inv}}(= q^{-1} \bmod p)$, $p_{\mathrm{inv}}(= p^{-1} \bmod q)$
Output: $m = C^d \bmod N$

	Operation for p	Operation for q
1:	$B_p \leftarrow B \bmod p$	$B_q \leftarrow B \bmod q$
2:	$B_p^2 \leftarrow B^2 \bmod p$	$B_q^2 \leftarrow B^2 \bmod q$
3:	$C_p \leftarrow C \bmod p$	$C_q \leftarrow C \bmod q$
4:	Compute $\langle -p^{-1} \rangle_b$	Compute $\langle -q^{-1} \rangle_b$
5:	Radix-RNS: p, q_{inv}, B_p, B_p^2, C_p	Radix-RNS: q, p_{inv}, B_q, B_q^2, C_q
6:	$\langle C_p' \rangle \leftarrow \mathrm{MM}(\langle C_p \rangle, \langle B_p^2 \rangle, p)$	$\langle C_q' \rangle \leftarrow \mathrm{MM}(\langle C_q \rangle, \langle B_q^2 \rangle, q)$
7:	$\langle m_p' \rangle \leftarrow \mathrm{MEXP}(\langle C_p' \rangle, d_p, p)$	$\langle m_q' \rangle \leftarrow \mathrm{MEXP}(\langle C_q' \rangle, d_q, q)$
8:	$\langle t_p \rangle \leftarrow \mathrm{MM}(\langle m_p' \rangle, \langle q_{\mathrm{inv}} \rangle, p)$	$\langle t_q \rangle \leftarrow \mathrm{MM}(\langle m_q' \rangle, \langle p_{\mathrm{inv}} \rangle, q)$
9:	$\langle u_p \rangle \leftarrow \mathrm{MUL}(\langle t_p \rangle, \langle q \rangle)$	$\langle u_q \rangle \leftarrow \mathrm{MUL}(\langle t_q \rangle, \langle p \rangle)$
10:	$\langle m \rangle \leftarrow \mathrm{ADD}(\langle u_p \rangle, \langle u_q \rangle)$	
11:	RNS-Radix conversion: $\langle m \rangle_{a \cup b}$	
12:	$m \leftarrow m - cN \quad (c = 0, 1, 2, \text{ or } 3)$	

Fig. 5. RSA decryption algorithm with CRT.

performed sequentially. The same reduction ratio is obtained in a general case based on the radix 2 representation.

4 Prototype

We prototyped an LSI adopting the Cox-Rower Architecture. In this section, an outline of the LSI is described.

4.1 Architecture

The Cox-Rower Architecture was proposed as a hardware suitable for the RNS Montgomery multiplication [1]. The name is derived from its original structure where plural "Rower" units perform parallel processing in cooperation with one "Cox" unit which computes a correction factor in the base transformation.

A hardware structure of the Cox-Rower Architecture in this work is shown in Fig. 6. It consists of u sets of Rower units which individually have a multiplier-and-accumulator with modular reduction unit by base element a_i and b_i. Figure 6 is different from the original structure proposed in Ref. [1] in regard to the following two points:

(i) Rower units are connected by ring connection instead of by bus connection.
(ii) A Cox unit is embedded in every Rower unit.

In the base transformation, ξ_i $(i = 1, \ldots, n)$ which has been computed in each Rower unit needs to be transferred to the other Rower units. The original architecture uses bus connection for this transfer. We have found that ring connection can also realize the transfer of ξ_i's by sending them to an adjoining Rower unit in turn. In addition, since the original architecture has only one Cox unit, it also

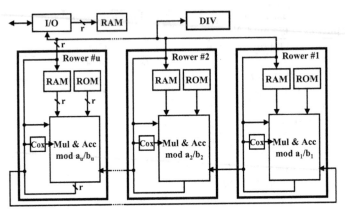

Fig. 6. Cox-Rower Architecture.

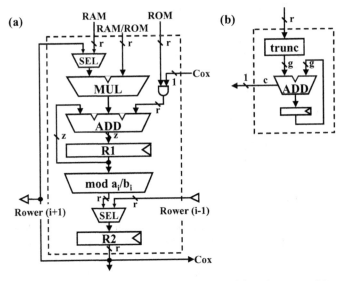

Fig. 7. Multiplier-and-accumulator (a) and Cox unit (b), where $r = 32$, $z = 72$, and $g = 9$.

needs bus connection to broadcast the correction factor k_i, which is computed in the Cox unit, to all Rower units. This broadcast is, however, avoidable by embedding a Cox unit in each Rower unit as shown in Fig. 6, which further enables us to control all Rower units by the same procedure. Consequently, we have adopted the ring connection in this work to lower data driving load and improve the modularity of Rower units.

Structures of the multiplier-and-accumulator and the Cox unit are shown in Fig. 7. The multiplier-and-accumulator has two stages: one is to accumulate a result of multiplication-and-addition and the other is to perform modular reduction by the base elements. The Cox unit consists of a truncation unit, a g-bit

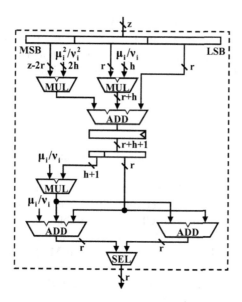

Fig. 8. Modular reduction unit, where $h = 10$.

adder, and a register in order to compute k_i in the base transformation according to steps 4–6 in Fig. 2. One of the advantages of the proposed RNS Montgomery multiplication algorithm is in this simple structure of the Cox unit.

Here, let us consider the base transformation procedure at Rower unit i. First, at step 1 in Fig. 2, ξ_i is calculated from $x[a_i]$ and $A_i^{-1}[a_i]$ and is stored in the register R2. Next, in the loop for $j = 1$, k_i is computed from ξ_i at the Cox unit, and then y_{i1} is obtained and stored in the register R1. Before the next loop for $j = 2$, ξ_{i-1} which has been computed at Rower unit $i - 1$ is transferred by ring connection and is stored in R2. Then, the loop for $j = 2$ is carried out based on ξ_{i-1}, and y_{i2} is obtained. After all loop processes for $j = 1, \ldots, n$ have been finished, $x[b_i]$ is computed from y_{in} at step 9 and is stored in R2.

Figure 8 shows a structure of the modular reduction unit in Fig. 7(a). The base elements a_i and b_i can be given as $2^r - \mu_i$ and $2^r - \nu_i$. Small integers μ_i and ν_i ($\ll 2^r$) are chosen so as to make the base elements coprime. In this case, modular computation for a_i and b_i can be realized by multipliers and adders, where the multipliers perform multiplication by μ_i and ν_i as shown in Fig. 8. The maximum bit length h of μ_i and ν_i is 10 bits for the base size $n = 66$. With respect to the output y of the operation $x \bmod a_i$, the modular reduction unit has the condition $y < 2^r$ instead of $y < a_i$, i.e. if $x \bmod a_i < \mu_i$, $y = x \bmod a_i + a_i$. We have ascertained that this condition does not affect the RNS Montgomery multiplication algorithm.

The Cox-Rower Architecture additionally has a divider which performs division based on the radix 2 representation. This divider is required for steps 1 and 2 in Fig. 4 and steps 1–3 in Fig. 5.

As described above, the Cox-Rower Architecture is designed to be suitable for the RNS Montgomery multiplication algorithm, particularly for the base transformation algorithm. The other operations such as the Radix-RNS and the RNS-Radix conversions can also be implemented efficiently in this architecture.

4.2   Specifications

The specifications of the LSI prototype are summarized in Table 1. In the LSI, the standard length of 32 bits is adopted as the bit length of processing units r. The number of Rower units u is set to 11 from the consideration for chip size. We can use the base sizes of 22, 33, and 66, which realize maximum key lengths of 672, 1024, and 2080 bits, respectively. Therefore, key lengths up to 2048 bits without CRT and 4096 bits with CRT are available.

SHA-1 which is required as a Hash function in digital signature is additionally implemented in the LSI. The SHA-1 core has an MGF1 function used in RSA standard spec PKCS#1 Ver.2.0 [6].

In Rower unit i $(i = 1, \ldots, 11)$, operations for the base elements a_j and b_j are performed, where $j = i + 11\ell$ $(\ell = 0, \ldots, 5)$. Thus, parameters in terms of a_j and b_j are stored in ROM of Rower unit i. Table 2 lists the parameters. These parameters for the three base sizes $n = 22, 33$, and 66 are prepared in the LSI, which needs the memory size shown in Table 3. In this table, memory sizes in the case of shorter maximum key lengths are also estimated. Since the LSI has been designed to provide long key lengths such as 2048 and 4096 bits, the increase in memory size causes a big core size. It is possible to reduce the memory size depending on maximum key lengths as shown in Table 3.

Figure 9 shows the details of the processing time. The transactions of I/O and precomputation for keys are negligible in the total processing time and

Table 1. Specifications.

Process	0.25 μm CMOS
Operating frequency	80 MHz
Operating voltage	2.5 V
Functions	RSA without and with CRT
	SHA-1 Hash code generation
	MGF1 (PKCS#1 Ver.2.0)
Performance	1024-bit RSA: 4.2 ms / 2.4 ms
(without/with CRT)	2048-bit RSA: 29.2 ms / 8.9 ms
	4096-bit RSA: — / 60.4 ms
Core size	6.9 mm × 6.9 mm
No. of Rower units	11
No. of logic gates	333 KG (Total)
	221 KG (RSA core)
	36 KG (Divider)
	57 KG (SHA-1)
	19 KG (I/O etc.)

Table 2. Parameters stored in ROM.

Base transformation	
$\langle x \rangle_a \Longrightarrow \langle x \rangle_b$	$A_j^{-1}[a_j], A_1[b_j], \ldots, A_n[b_j], -A[b_j]$
$\langle x \rangle_b \Longrightarrow \langle x \rangle_a$	$B_j^{-1}[b_j], B_1[a_j], \ldots, B_n[a_j], -B[a_j]$
Radix-RNS conversion	
$x \Longrightarrow \langle x \rangle_a$	$2^r[a_j], 2^{r \cdot 2}[a_j], \ldots, 2^{r \cdot (n-1)}[a_j]$
$x \Longrightarrow \langle x \rangle_b$	$2^r[b_j], 2^{r \cdot 2}[b_j], \ldots, 2^{r \cdot (n-1)}[b_j]$
RNS-Radix conversion	
$\langle x \rangle_a \Longrightarrow x$	$A_1(j-1), \ldots, A_n(j-1), -A(j-1)$
$\langle x \rangle_{a \cup b} \Longrightarrow x$ (CRT mode)	$(AB/a_j)^{-1}[a_j], (AB/b_j)^{-1}[b_j],$
	$(AB/a_1)(j-1), \ldots, (AB/a_n)(j-1),$
	$(AB/b_1)(j-1), \ldots, (AB/b_n)(j-1), -AB(j-1)$

Table 3. Memory size.

Maximum RSA key length	ROM (KByte)	RAM (KByte)
2048 & 4096 (CRT) *	209	24
2048 & 2048 (CRT)	138	20
1024 & 2048 (CRT)	57	12

* Designed LSI

are not exhibited in this figure. It is found that the contribution from division based on the radix 2 representation becomes large in the processing of shorter key lengths and in CRT mode. The latter condition means that the number of parameters which are computed in the divider increases in CRT mode. In a comparison between the performance without and with CRT, reduction ratio of 0.3 is obtained in 2048-bit RSA processing, which is close to an ideal ratio of 1/4. However, reduction ratio becomes 0.5 in 1024-bit processing. This increase in reduction ratio is due to the use of a redundant base size in CRT mode. In non-CRT mode of 1024-bit processing, we use the base size $n = 33$ which is optimum for this key length. In contrast, the base size $n = 22$ used in CRT mode is too long for the key length of 512 bits. These results indicate that base

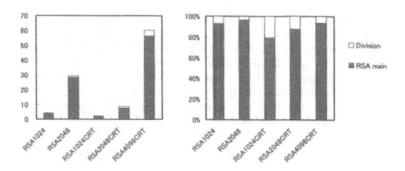

Fig. 9. Performance.

sizes strongly affect the performance of the Cox-Rower Architecture as discussed in Sec. 3.1.

At present, the best performance of 1024-bit RSA processing in commercial chips is, as far as we know, reported for Rainbow's chip (5 msec with CRT) [7] and Pijnenburg's chip (3 msec and 1.5 msec with CRT) [8], which is comparable with the performance in this work. The Cox-Rower Architecture can equip up to 33 Rower units for 1024-bit RSA processing. In that case, three-times speedup can be realized and the processing time which is less than 1 msec becomes feasible.

5 Conclusions

This paper presented the implementation of RSA algorithm based on the RNS Montgomery multiplication. We showed RSA decryption procedures and discussed the relation between the base size of RNS and the number of parallel processing units. The designed LSI adopting the Cox-Rower Architecture can deal with key lengths up to 4096 bits in CRT mode. Using 11 Rower units, we obtained 1024-bit RSA transactions in 4.2 msec without CRT and 2.4 msec with CRT, at the operating frequency of 80 MHz. This result gives us a prospect of realizing a high performance. Downsizing of chips and speedup by using more Rower units are subjects to be tackled in the next phase of this work.

Acknowledgment

The authors would like to thank Hidekazu Shimizu of Toshiba Information Systems Corporation for his collaboration in LSI design.

References

1. S. Kawamura, M. Koike, F. Sano, and A. Shimbo, "Cox-Rower Architecture for Fast Montgomery Multiplication," EUROCRYPT 2000, pp. 523–538 (2000).
2. K. C. Posch and R. Posch, "Modulo Reduction in Residue Number Systems," IEEE Tr. Parallel and Distributed Systems, Vol. 6, No. 5, pp. 449–454 (1995).
3. J.-C. Bajard, L.-S. Didier, and P. Kornerup, "An RNS Montgomery Multiplication Algorithm," Proceedings of ARITH13, IEEE Computer Society, pp. 234-239 (1997).
4. P. Paillier, "Low-Cost Double-Size Modular Exponentiation or How to Stretch Your Cryptoprocessor," PKC99, pp. 223–234 (1999).
5. E. Kranakis, "Primality and Cryptography," Wiley-Teubner Series in Computer Science, John Willy & Sons (1986).
6. RSA Laboratories, "PKCS#1 Ver.2.0: RSA Cryptography Standard," Oct. 1 (1998).
7. http://www.rainbow.com/cryptoswift.
8. http://www.pcc.pijnenburg.nl/pcc-ises.htm.

Protections against Differential Analysis for Elliptic Curve Cryptography
– An Algebraic Approach –

Marc Joye[1] and Christophe Tymen[2]

[1] Gemplus Card International, Card Security Group
Parc d'Activités de Gémenos, B.P. 100, 13881 Gémenos, France
marc.joye@gemplus.com – http://www.geocities.com/MarcJoye/
[2] École Normale Supérieure
45 rue d'Ulm, 75230 Paris, France
christophe.tymen@gemplus.com

Abstract. We propose several new methods to protect the scalar multi-plication on an elliptic curve against Differential Analysis. The basic idea consists in transforming the curve through various random morphisms to provide a non-deterministic execution of the algorithm.
The solutions we suggest complement and improve the state-of-the-art, but also provide a practical toolbox of efficient countermeasures. These should suit most of the needs for protecting implementations of crypto-algorithms based on elliptic curves.

Keywords. Public-key cryptography, Side-channel attacks, Differential power analysis (DPA), Timing attacks, Elliptic curves, Smart-cards.

1   Introduction

Since the introduction of the timing attacks [10] by Paul Kocher in 1996 and subsequently of the Differential Power Analysis (DPA) [9], the so-called side-channel attacks have become a major threat against tamper-resistant devices like smart-cards, to the point where the immediate relevance of classical security notions is somewhat questionable. Furthermore, numerous experiments show that most of the time, perfunctory countermeasures do not suffice to thwart those attacks.

In the case of public-key cryptosystems based on the discrete logarithm on elliptic curves, the running time does not really represent a bottleneck for smart-card applications, which are equipped with additional devices for fast computa-tion in finite fields. Therefore, investigating the security of these applications, less constrained by performance criteria, against side-channel attacks is very relevant.

Compared to the previous works of [5] and [7], this paper systematically develops the same idea: assuming that an elliptic curve cryptosystem executes some operations in the group of a curve E, the whole algorithm is transposed

Ç.K. Koç, D. Naccache, and C. Paar (Eds.): CHES 2001, LNCS 2162, pp. 377–390, 2001.

to a curve $\phi(E)$, where ϕ is a random morphism. The rich algebraic structure of elliptic curves enables numerous possible choices for such morphisms.

The rest of this paper is organized as follows. In the next section, we provide a brief description of elliptic curves. We refer the reader to Appendix A for further mathematical details. The general principles of differential analysis and how this can reveal the secret keys of an elliptic curve cryptosystem are explained in Section 3. Next, we provide two main classes of possible morphisms to randomize the basepoint. Finally, we present in Section 5 a new randomization of the encoding of the multiplier in the case of Anomalous Binary Curves (ABC).

2   Elliptic Curves

Let $\mathbb{K}$ be a field. An *elliptic curve over* $\mathbb{K}$ is a pair $(E, \boldsymbol{O})$ where E is a non-singular curve of genus one over $\mathbb{K}$ with a point $\boldsymbol{O} \in E$. It is well known that the set of points $(x, y) \in \mathbb{K} \times \mathbb{K}$ verifying the (non-singular) Weierstraß equation

$$E_{/\mathbb{K}} : y^2 + a_1 xy + a_3 y = x^3 + a_2 x^2 + a_4 x + a_6 \qquad (a_i \in \mathbb{K}) \qquad (1)$$

together with $\boldsymbol{O}$ form an elliptic curve and that an elliptic curve can always be expressed in such a form. The point $\boldsymbol{O}$ is called the *point at infinity*.

The set of points (x, y) satisfying Eq. (1) and $\boldsymbol{O}$ form an Abelian group where $\boldsymbol{O}$ is the neutral element. This group is denoted by $E(\mathbb{K})$ and the group operation is denoted by $+$. The operation consisting in computing the multiple of a point, $\boldsymbol{Q} = k\boldsymbol{P} := \boldsymbol{P} + \cdots + \boldsymbol{P}$ (k times), is called *(elliptic curve) scalar multiplication*. We refer the unfamiliar reader to Appendix A for the required background on this particular topic.

3   Differential Analysis

In his CRYPTO '96 paper [10] and thereafter in [9] with Jaffe and Jun, Kocher launched a new class of attacks, the so-called *side-channel attacks*.

The basic idea of the side-channel attacks is that some side-channel information (e.g., timing, power consumption, electromagnetic radiation) of a device depends on the operations it performs. For instance, it is well known that the modification of a memory state yields a different power consumption according to the memory goes from one to zero, or the opposite.

By capturing this information, it may be possible to recover some secret keys involved during the execution of a crypto-algorithm, at least in a careless implementation. When a single input is used in eliciting information, the process is referred to as a *Simple Analysis* and when there are several inputs used together with statistical tools, it is referred to as a *Differential Analysis*. In this paper, we are concerned with the second type of attack, and in particular in the context of elliptic curve cryptography.

For elliptic curve cryptosystems, this type of attack applies to the scalar multiplication. Following [5], a simple countermeasure to defeat simple analysis attacks resides in replacing the standard double-and-add algorithm by a double-and-add-*always* algorithm for computing $Q = kP$ on an elliptic curve (see also [7] for further countermeasures dedicated to ABC curves). However, such an algorithm is still susceptible to a differential analysis attack. Let $k = (k_{m-1}, \ldots, k_0)_2$ be the binary expansion of multiplier k. Suppose that an attacker already knows the highest bits, $k_{m-1}, \ldots, k_{j+1}$, of k. Then, he *guesses* that the next bit k_j is equal to one. He randomly chooses several points $P_1, \ldots, P_t$ and computes $Q_r = (\sum_{i=j}^{m-1} k_i) P_r$ for $1 \le r \le t$. Using a boolean selection function g, he prepares two sets: the first set, $\mathcal{S}_{\text{true}}$, contains the points P_r such that $g(Q_r) = \text{true}$ and the second set, $\mathcal{S}_{\text{false}}$, contains those such that $g(Q_r) = \text{false}$. Depending on the side-channel information monitored by the attacker and the actual implementation, a selection function may, for example, be the value of a given bit in the representation of Q_r.

Let $C(r)$ denote the side-channel information associated to the computation of kP_r by the cryptographic device (e.g., the power consumption). If the guess $k_j = 1$ is incorrect then the difference

$$\langle C(r) \rangle_{\substack{1 \le r \le t \\ P_r \in \mathcal{S}_{\text{true}}}} - \langle C(r) \rangle_{\substack{1 \le r \le t \\ P_r \in \mathcal{S}_{\text{false}}}}$$

will be ≈ 0 as the two sets appear as two random (i.e. uncorrelated) sets; otherwise the guess is correct. Once k_j is known, the remaining bits, $k_{j-1}, \ldots, k_0$, are recovered recursively, in the same way. We note that such attacks are not restricted to binary methods and can be adapted to work with other scalar multiplication methods, as well.

To thwart differential attacks, it is recommended to randomize the basepoint P and the multiplier k in the computation of $Q = kP$. Several countermeasures are already known. See [5] for general curves and [7] for ABC curves. The next section proposes two techniques for randomizing the basepoint and Section 5 shows how to randomize the multiplier for an ABC curve.

4   Randomizing the Basepoint

4.1   Elliptic Curve Isomorphisms

We first recall some results on isomorphisms between elliptic curves. We say that two elliptic curves over a field $\mathbb{K}$ defined by their Weierstraß equations E and E' are *isomorphic over* $\mathbb{K}$ (or $\mathbb{K}$-*isomorphic*) if they are isomorphic as projective varieties. It turns out that curve isomorphisms induce group morphisms. The determination of isomorphisms between two given elliptic curves is solved in the next two corollaries.

Corollary 1. *Let $\mathbb{K}$ be a field with* $\text{Char } \mathbb{K} \ne 2, 3$. *The elliptic curves given by* $E_{/\mathbb{K}} : y^2 = x^3 + ax + b$ *and* $E'_{/\mathbb{K}} : y^2 = x^3 + a'x + b'$ *are $\mathbb{K}$-isomorphic if and only if there exists $u \in \mathbb{K}^*$ such that $u^4 a' = a$ and $u^6 b' = b$. Furthermore, we have*

$$\varphi : E(\mathbb{K}) \tilde{\rightarrow} E'(\mathbb{K}), \begin{cases} O \mapsto O \\ (x, y) \mapsto (u^{-2} x, u^{-3} y) \end{cases} \tag{2}$$

and

$$\varphi^{-1} : E'(\mathbb{K}) \xrightarrow{\sim} E(\mathbb{K}), \begin{cases} O \mapsto O \\ (x, y) \mapsto (u^2 x, u^3 y) \end{cases} \quad . \tag{3}$$

Proof. With the notations of Proposition 2 (in appendix), we obtain $r = s = t = 0$ and so $u^4 a'_4 = a_4$ and $u^6 a'_6 = a_6 \iff u^4 a' = a$ and $u^6 b' = b$ for some $u \in \mathbb{K}^*$. $\quad\square$

Corollary 2. *Let $\mathbb{K}$ be a field with* $\mathrm{Char}\,\mathbb{K} = 2$. *The (non-supersingular) elliptic curves given by $E_{/\mathbb{K}} : y^2 + xy = x^3 + ax^2 + b$ and $E'_{/\mathbb{K}} : y^2 + xy = x^3 + a'x^2 + b'$ are $\mathbb{K}$-isomorphic if and only if there exists $s \in \mathbb{K}$ such that $a' = a + s + s^2$ and $b' = b$. Furthermore, we have*

$$\varphi : E(\mathbb{K}) \xrightarrow{\sim} E'(\mathbb{K}), \begin{cases} O \mapsto O \\ (x, y) \mapsto (x, y + sx) \end{cases} \tag{4}$$

and

$$\varphi^{-1} : E'(\mathbb{K}) \xrightarrow{\sim} E(\mathbb{K}), \begin{cases} O \mapsto O \\ (x, y) \mapsto (x, y + sx) \end{cases} \quad . \tag{5}$$

Proof. From Proposition 2, the relation $ua'_1 = a_1 + 2s$ gives $u = 1$. The third and fourth relations give $r = 0$ and $t = 0$, respectively. Hence, from the second relation we have $a'_2 = a_2 - s - s^2$ whereas the last one yields $a'_6 = a_6 \iff a' = a + s + s^2$ and $b' = b$. $\quad\square$

We can thus randomize the scalar multiplication algorithm as follows. We perform the scalar multiplication on a random isomorphic elliptic curve and then we come back to the original elliptic curve. More formally, if φ is a random isomorphism from $E_{/\mathbb{K}}$ to $E'_{/\mathbb{K}}$, we propose to compute $Q = kP$ in $E(\mathbb{K})$ according to

$$Q = \varphi^{-1}\big(k\big(\varphi(P)\big)\big), \tag{6}$$

or schematically,

$$
\begin{array}{ccc}
P \in E(\mathbb{K}) & \xrightarrow{\text{mult. by } k \text{ map}} & Q = kP \in E(\mathbb{K}) \\
\varphi \downarrow & & \uparrow \varphi^{-1} \\
P' \in E'(\mathbb{K}) & \xrightarrow{\text{mult. by } k \text{ map}} & Q' = kP' \in E'(\mathbb{K})
\end{array}
$$

Corollaries 1 and 2 indicate that computing the image of a point through an elliptic curve isomorphism can be done using only a few elementary field operations. This yields a very efficient means to randomize the computation of $Q = kP$.

Algorithm 1 (Scalar Multiplication via Random Isomorphic Elliptic Curves for Char $\mathbb{K} \neq 2, 3$).

Input:	A point $P = (x_1, y_1) \in E(\mathbb{K})$ with $E_{/\mathbb{K}} : y^2 = x^3 + ax + b$.
	An integer k.
Output:	The point $Q = kP$.

1. Randomly choose an element $u \in \mathbb{K}^*$;
2. Form the point $P' \leftarrow (u^{-2}x_1, u^{-3}y_1)$;
3. Evaluate $a' \leftarrow u^{-4}a$;
4. Compute $Q' \leftarrow kP'$ in $E'(\mathbb{K})$ with $E'_{/\mathbb{K}} : y^2 = x^3 + a'x + b'$;[1]
5. If $(Q' = O)$ then return $Q = O$ and stop. Otherwise set $Q' \leftarrow (x'_3, y'_3)$;
6. Return $Q = (u^2 x'_3, u^3 y'_3)$.

In [5, § 5.3], Coron suggests the randomization of projective coordinates in order to blind the basepoint P: $P = (x_1, y_1)$ is randomized into $(t^2 x_1 : t^3 y_1 : t)$ in Jacobian coordinates (or into $(tx_1 : ty_1 : t)$ in homogeneous coordinates) for some $t \in \mathbb{K}^*$. The advantage of the proposed countermeasure is that, in Step 2 of Algorithm 1, we can represent P' as the projective point $P' = (u^{-2}x_1 : u^{-3}y_1 : 1)$, that is, a point with its Z-coordinate equal to 1. This results in a faster scalar multiplication algorithm. Using the values of Table 2, we precisely quantify the number of (field) multiplications needed to compute $Q = kP$, considering in each case the faster coordinate system. This is summarized in the next table.[2]

Table 1. Average number of (field) multiplications to compute $Q = kP$.

	Random. proj. coord. ([5])		Algorithm 1	
	$a \neq -3$	$a = -3$		
Double-and-add	$17\frac{1}{2} \cdot \lvert k \rvert_2$ $(\mathcal{J}^m)$	$16 \cdot \lvert k \rvert_2$ $(\mathcal{J})$	$15 \cdot \lvert k \rvert_2$ $(\mathcal{J}^m)$	
Double-and-add-or-sub.	$15\frac{1}{3} \cdot \lvert k \rvert_2$ $(\mathcal{J}^m)$	$13\frac{1}{3} \cdot \lvert k \rvert_2$ $(\mathcal{J})$	$12\frac{2}{3} \cdot \lvert k \rvert_2$ $(\mathcal{J}^m)$	
Double-and-add-always	$25 \cdot \lvert k \rvert_2$ $(\mathcal{J}^c)$	$23 \cdot \lvert k \rvert_2$ $(\mathcal{J}^c)$	$21 \cdot \lvert k \rvert_2$ $(\mathcal{J})$	

For fields of characteristic 2, random isomorphisms of elliptic curves cannot be considered *alone* as a means to protect against differential analysis. The x-coordinate of basepoint P remains invariant through isomorphism φ (cf. Eq. (4)) and so the resulting implementation may still be subject to a differential analysis attack. However, it can be combined with other countermeasures to offer an additional security level.

The next section presents a countermeasure that randomizes both the x- and the y-coordinates of point P, whatever the characteristic of the field we are working with.

---

[1] Note that parameter b' is not required by the scalar multiplication algorithm.

[2] $\mathcal{J}, \mathcal{J}^c$ and $\mathcal{J}^m$ respectively refer to the Jacobian coordinates, Chudnovsky Jacobian coordinates (see Appendix A.1).

4.2   Field Isomorphisms

Up to isomorphism, there is one and only one finite field L of characteristic p with p^n elements. Every such field may be viewed as the field generated (over $\mathbb{F}_p$) by a root of an irreducible monic polynomial Π of degree n. Given $\Pi(X)$, any element of L can be represented as a polynomial in $\mathbb{F}_p[X]/(\Pi)$. If $e \in L$, we note $\vartheta_\Pi(e)$ its corresponding representation in $\mathbb{F}_p[X]/(\Pi)$. From another irreducible monic polynomial $\Pi'(Y)$ of degree n, we obtain another representation for the elements $e \in L$, $\vartheta_{\Pi'}(e) \in \mathbb{F}_p[Y]/(\Pi')$. The fields $\mathbb{K} := \mathbb{F}_p[X]/(\Pi)$ and $\mathbb{K}' := \mathbb{F}_p[Y]/(\Pi')$ being isomorphic, we let ϕ denote such an isomorphism from $\mathbb{K}$ to $\mathbb{K}'$. The map ϕ extends to $\mathbb{K} \times \mathbb{K}$ with $\phi(x,y) = (\phi(x), \phi(y))$. In particular, ϕ transforms the equation of an elliptic curve over $\mathbb{K}$ into the equation of an elliptic curve over $\mathbb{K}'$, i.e.,

$$E_{/\mathbb{K}} : y^2 + a_1 xy + a_3 y = x^3 + a_2 x^2 + a_4 x + a_6$$

is transformed into

$$E'_{/\mathbb{K}'} : y^2 + \phi(a_1)xy + \phi(a_3)y = x^3 + \phi(a_2)x^2 + \phi(a_4)x + \phi(a_6) \ .$$

Consequently, isomorphisms between fields can be used to randomize the representation of the basepoint $\boldsymbol{P}$. To compute $\boldsymbol{Q} = k\boldsymbol{P}$, we first choose randomly a field $\mathbb{K}'$ isomorphic to $\mathbb{K}$ through isomorphism ϕ. Then, we compute $\boldsymbol{Q}$ as

$$\boldsymbol{Q} = \phi^{-1}\big(k(\phi(\boldsymbol{P}))\big) \ . \tag{7}$$

In other words, we represent $\boldsymbol{P} \in E(\mathbb{K})$ as a point $\boldsymbol{P}' \in E'(\mathbb{K}')$, next we compute $\boldsymbol{Q}' := k\boldsymbol{P}'$ in $E'(\mathbb{K}')$, and finally we go back to the original representation by representing $\boldsymbol{Q}'$ as a point $\boldsymbol{Q} \in E(\mathbb{K})$.

At first glance, it is unclear that this could lead to an countermeasure efficient in a constrained environment. Indeed, to build a field $\mathbb{K}'$ isomorphic to $\mathbb{K}$, a natural way consists in determining an irreducible monic polynomial of degree n, $\Pi' \in \mathbb{F}_p[Y]$. An isomorphism ϕ is then obtained by computing a root α of Π in $\mathbb{K}'$:

$$\phi : \mathbb{K} \overset{\sim}{\to} \mathbb{K}' : x \mapsto \sum_{i=0}^{n-1} x_i \, \alpha^i \ , \tag{8}$$

where $x = \sum_{i=0}^{n-1} x_i X^i \in \mathbb{K} = \mathbb{F}_p[X]/(\Pi)$. Likewise, the inverse map, from $\mathbb{K}'$ to $\mathbb{K}$, requires to find a root β of Π' in $\mathbb{K}$.

However, we can do much better when some permanent writable memory is at disposal (e.g., the EEPROM in a smart-card implementation). The general idea is, given an isomorphism $\phi : \mathbb{K} \overset{\sim}{\to} \mathbb{K}'$ stored in EEPROM, to determine from ϕ and $\mathbb{K}'$ a new field $\mathbb{K}''$ and a new isomorphism $\phi' : \mathbb{K} \overset{\sim}{\to} \mathbb{K}''$, and so on. This can be done thanks to Proposition 1, which yields a recursive method for constructing irreducible polynomials of same degree.

Proposition 1. *Let T be a polynomial permutation[3] of $\mathbb{F}_{p^n}$ and let Π be an irreducible polynomial in $\mathbb{F}_p[X]$ of degree n. Then polynomial $\Pi \circ T$ has at least one irreducible factor of degree n, say Π', in $\mathbb{F}_p[X]$.*

---

[3] A polynomial T with coefficients in $\mathbb{F}_p$ is a *polynomial permutation of* $\mathbb{F}_{p^n}$ if the map $x \mapsto T(x)$ permutes $\mathbb{F}_{p^n}$.

Proof. Let α be a root of Π. As Π is irreducible, the orbit of α under the action of the Frobenius is of cardinality n. T being a permutation, the image of this orbit through T^{-1} is still of cardinality n. Since T is a polynomial with coefficients in $\mathbb{F}_p$, it commutes with the Frobenius, and thus the image of the orbit of α through T^{-1} appears as the orbit of $T^{-1}(\alpha)$. Consequently, the polynomial $\prod_i (X - (T^{-1}(\alpha))^{p^i})$ is irreducible of degree n, and divides $\Pi \circ T$. $\square$

Hence, if we choose a polynomial permutation T of small degree (e.g., 2 or 3), we compute $\Pi \circ T$ and factor it with a *specific* algorithm to find Π'. A further generalization consists in storing a family of polynomial permutations $\mathfrak{S} = \{T_i\}$ in EEPROM and to randomly choose $T \in \mathfrak{S}$ when constructing Π'.

We note Π the publicly known polynomial which defines the field $\mathbb{K} = \mathbb{F}_p[X]/(\Pi)$ used as the reference field. We assume that another polynomial $\Pi^{(1)}$ defines the field $\mathbb{K}^{(1)}$ isomorphic to $\mathbb{K}$. We also assume that two polynomials $\alpha^{(1)}, \beta^{(1)} \in \mathbb{F}_p[X]$ of degree at most n verifying Eqs. (9) have initially been stored in EEPROM. These additional data must of course be kept secret. At the jth execution of the scalar multiplication algorithm, the EEPROM contains an irreducible monic polynomial $\Pi^{(j)} \in \mathbb{F}_p[X]$ of degree n, and two polynomials $\alpha^{(j)}, \beta^{(j)} \in \mathbb{F}_p[X]$ such that

$$\begin{cases} \Pi(\beta^{(j)}) & \equiv 0 \quad (\Pi^{(j)}) \\ \Pi^{(j)}(\alpha^{(j)}) \equiv 0 \quad (\Pi) \end{cases} \quad . \tag{9}$$

These relations simply say that $\alpha^{(j)}$ and $\beta^{(j)}$ respectively define an isomorphism $\phi^{(j)}$ and its inverse from the field $\mathbb{K}$ to the field $\mathbb{F}_p[X]/(\Pi^{(j)})$ denoted by $\mathbb{K}^{(j)}$.

We are now ready to give the algorithm. We choose randomly $T \in \mathfrak{S}$ and determine an irreducible monic polynomial $\Pi^{(j+1)}$ of degree n in $\mathbb{F}_p[X]$ that divides $\Pi^{(j)} \circ T$ with a method that will be explained later. Then we set $\beta^{(j+1)} = \beta^{(j)} \circ T \bmod \Pi^{(j+1)}$, $\alpha^{(j+1)} = T^{-1}(\alpha^{(j)}) \bmod \Pi$, and we store $\alpha^{(j+1)}, \beta^{(j+1)}$ and $\Pi^{(j+1)}$ in EEPROM. Here, T^{-1} denotes the permutation inverse of T. It is easy to check that $\alpha^{(j+1)}, \beta^{(j+1)}$ and $\Pi^{(j+1)}$ still verify Eqs. (9), and thus define an isomorphism $\phi^{(j+1)}$ and its inverse from $\mathbb{K}$ to $\mathbb{F}_p[X]/(\Pi^{(j)})$. It remains to compute $\boldsymbol{P'} = \phi^{(j+1)}(\boldsymbol{P})$ and the coefficients of E'. Finally, we compute $k\boldsymbol{P'}$ in E' and convert the resulting point by the inverse isomorphism to obtain $\boldsymbol{Q} = k\boldsymbol{P}$. From the viewpoint of the running time, one of the advantages of this method is to skip the root finding step.

We still have to show how to solve Step 2 in the above algorithm. We illustrate the technique in the case $\mathbb{K} = \mathbb{F}_2[X]/(\Pi)$ with Π of degree n and $\gcd(2^n-1, 3) = 1$ (this case includes the popular choice $n = 163$ for elliptic curve cryptosystems), but we stress that the proposed technique is fully general and can be adapted to the other cases, as well.

First, note that:

Lemma 1. *If* $\gcd(2^n - 1, 3) = 1$ *then the elements of*

$$\mathfrak{S} = \left\{ X^3, 1 + X^3, X + X^2 + X^3, 1 + X + X^2 + X^3 \right\} \subset \mathbb{F}_2[X]$$

permute $\mathbb{F}_{2^n}$.

Algorithm 2 (Scalar Multiplication via Random Isomorphic Fields).

Input: A point $P = (x_1, y_1) \in E(\mathbb{K})$
           with $\begin{cases} E_{/\mathbb{K}} : y^2 + xy = x^3 + ax^2 + b & \text{if Char}\,\mathbb{K} = 2 \\ E_{/\mathbb{K}} : y^2 = x^3 + ax + b & \text{if Char}\,\mathbb{K} > 3 \end{cases}$.
           An integer k.
           [EEPROM: Polynomials $\alpha^{(j)}$, $\beta^{(j)}$ and $\Pi^{(j)}$.]
Output: The point $Q = kP$.

1. Randomly choose $T \in \mathfrak{S}$;
2. Determine, in $\mathbb{F}_p[X]$, an irreducible monic polynomial $\Pi^{(j+1)}$ s.t.

$$\Pi^{(j+1)} \text{ divides } \Pi^{(j)} \circ T;$$

3. Set $\beta^{(j+1)} \leftarrow \beta^{(j)} \circ T \bmod \Pi^{(j+1)}$;
4. Set $\alpha^{(j+1)} \leftarrow T^{-1}(\alpha^{(j)}) \bmod \Pi$;
5. Update the EEPROM with $\alpha^{(j+1)}$, $\beta^{(j+1)}$ and $\Pi^{(j+1)}$;
6. Form $P' \leftarrow P \circ \beta^{(j+1)} \bmod \Pi^{(j+1)}$;
7. Evaluate $a' \leftarrow a \circ \beta^{(j+1)} \bmod \Pi^{(j+1)}$;
8. Compute $Q' \leftarrow kP'$ in $E'\left(\mathbb{F}_p[X]/(\Pi^{(j+1)})\right)$;
9. If ($Q' = O$) then return $Q = O$ and stop. Otherwise set $Q' \leftarrow (x'_3, y'_3)$;
10. Return $Q = (x'_3, y'_3) \circ \alpha^{(j+1)} \bmod \Pi$.

Proof. Let α be a primitive element of $\mathbb{F}_{2^n}^*$ (remember that $\mathbb{F}_{2^n} = \mathbb{F}_{2^n}^* \cup \{0\}$). Then $\langle \alpha^3 \rangle$ generates a subgroup of order $(2^n - 1)/\gcd(2^n - 1, 3) = 2^n - 1$ and so α^3 is a primitive element or equivalently X^3 permutes $\mathbb{F}_{2^n}$. Suppose that there exist $\alpha, \beta \in \mathbb{F}_{2^n}$ s.t. $\alpha^3 + 1 = \beta^3 + 1 \iff \alpha^3 = \beta^3$. This implies $\alpha = \beta$ since X^3 is a permutation polynomial. The remaining cases are proved similarly by noting that $\alpha^2 - \beta^2 = (\alpha - \beta)^2$. $\square$

Given a set $\mathfrak{S}$ of permutation polynomials, write $Q := \Pi^{(j)} \circ T$ for some $T \in \mathfrak{S}$ and Π irreducible of degree n. The fact that Q has degree $3n$ enables us to specialize the classical factorization algorithms (see, e.g., [3, p. 125]):

1. Compute $R = X^{2^n} - X \bmod Q$;
2. Then, using Proposition 1, $\Pi' = \gcd(Q, R)$ is irreducible of degree n in $\mathbb{F}_2[X]$.

5   Randomizing the Multiplier on ABC Curves

The other side of countermeasures for elliptic curve cryptography is the introduction of a random to blind the multiplier during the scalar multiplication. This technique is useful to prevent Differential Analysis, but may also contribute to an additional security level against Simple Analysis, as the multiplier is in general secret.

The proposed method is specific to ABC curves (see Appendix A.2 for the definitions) where the multiplier first goes through several encoding functions before being used in the scalar multiplication loop itself. We take advantage of the properties of this encoding to randomize the multiplier.

Building on previous works by Koblitz [8] and Meier-Staffelbach [11], Solinas presents in [14] a very efficient algorithm to compute $Q = kP$ on an ABC curve. Letting $\tau : (x, y) \mapsto (x^2, y^2)$ the Frobenius endomorphism, his algorithm proceeds as follows.

1. Compute, in $\mathbb{Z}[\tau]$, $\kappa \leftarrow k \bmod (\tau^n - 1)$;
2. Using [14, Algorithm 4], evaluate the τ-NAF of κ, $\kappa = \sum_i k_i \tau^i$;
3. Compute $Q \leftarrow kP$ as $Q = \sum_i k_i \tau^i(P)$;
4. Return Q.

Our randomization method exploits the structure of $\mathbb{Z}[\tau] \subseteq \text{End}(E)$. Let $\rho \in \mathbb{Z}[\tau]$. If $x \equiv y \pmod{\rho(\tau^n - 1)}$ then x and y still act identically on the curve. Consequently, instead of reducing the multiplier modulo $\tau^n - 1$ (cf. Step 1 in the previous algorithm), we can reduce it modulo $\rho(\tau^n - 1)$ where ρ is a random element of $\mathbb{Z}[\tau]$. The length of the τ-NAF produced is approximately equal to $n + \log_2 N(\rho)$, which penalizes the scalar multiplication by $\log_2 N(\rho)$ additional steps. This enables to control very easily the trade-off between the running time and the expected security. Typically, for $n = 163$, we might impose that $N(\rho) \approx 2^{40}$, which roughly produces τ-NAF of 200 digits (in $\{-1, 0, 1\}$) instead of 160 with the deterministic method. The detailed algorithm is presented below.

Algorithm 3 (Scalar Multiplication via Random Exponent Recoding for ABC Curves).

Input:	A point $P = (x_1, y_1) \in E(\mathbb{F}_{2^n})$, an ABC curve.
	An integer k.
	A trade-off parameter l (typically, $l = 40$).
Output:	The point $Q = kP$.

1. Randomly choose an element $\rho \in \mathbb{Z}[\tau]$ with $N(\rho) < 2^l$;
2. Compute, in $\mathbb{Z}[\tau]$, $\kappa' \leftarrow k \bmod \rho(\tau^n - 1)$;
3. Evaluate the τ-NAF of κ', $\kappa' = \sum_i \kappa'_i \tau^i$;
4. Compute $Q \leftarrow \sum_i \kappa'_i \tau^i(P)$;
5. Return Q.

An interesting feature of this algorithm is that no additional routine needs to be implemented. It only requires a slight modification of the deterministic version. Furthermore, the random component ρ is spread over the full length of the multiplier. This may be better than simply adding to the multiplier a multiple of the order of the curve, as was suggested in [5, §. 5.1].

6 Conclusion

We proposed two new methods to blind the basepoint for an elliptic curve cryptosystem. These methods come from the idea of transposing the computation in another curve through a random morphism. In addition, we presented a new technique to randomize the encoding of the multiplier in the case of anomalous binary curves.

References

1. IEEE Std 1363-2000. *IEEE Standard Specifications for Public-Key Cryptography*. IEEE Computer Society, August 29, 2000.
2. D.V. Chudnovsky and G.V. Chudnovsky. Sequences of numbers generated by addition in formal groups and new primality and factorization tests. *Advances in Applied Math.*, 7:385–434, 1986/7.
3. Henri Cohen. *A Course in Computational Algebraic Number Theory*. Number 138 in Graduate Texts in Mathematics. Springer-Verlag, 1993.
4. Henri Cohen, Atsuko Miyaji, and Takatoshi Ono. Efficient elliptic curve exponentiation using mixed coordinates. In K. Ohta and D. Pei, editors, *Advances in Cryptology – ASIACRYPT '98*, volume 1514 of *Lecture Notes in Computer Science*, pages 51–65. Springer-Verlag, 1998.
5. Jean-Sébastien Coron. Resistance against differential power analysis for elliptic curve cryptosystems. In Ç.K. Koç and C. Paar, editors, *Cryptographic Hardware and Embedded Systems (CHES '99)*, volume 1717 of *Lecture Notes in Computer Science*, pages 292–302. Springer-Verlag, 1999.
6. Daniel M. Gordon. A survey on fast exponentiation methods. *Journal of Algorithms*, 27:129–146, 1998.
7. M. Anwar Hasan. Power analysis attacks and algorithmic approaches to their countermeasures for Koblitz curve cryptosystems. In Ç.K. Koç and C. Paar, editors, *Cryptographic Hardware and Embedded Systems – CHES 2000*, volume 1965 of *Lecture Notes in Computer Science*, pages 93–108. Springer-Verlag, 2000.
8. Neal Koblitz. CM-curves with good cryptographic protocols. In J. Feigenbaum, editor, *Advances in Cryptology – CRYPTO '91*, volume 576 of *Lecture Notes in Computer Science*, pages 279–287. Springer-Verlag, 1992.
9. Paul Kocher, Joshua Jaffe, and Benjamin Jun. Differential power analysis. In M. Wiener, editor, *Advances in Cryptology – CRYPTO '99*, volume 1666 of *Lecture Notes in Computer Science*, pages 388–397. Springer-Verlag, 1999.
10. Paul C. Kocher. Timing attacks on implementations of Diffie-Hellman, RSA, DSS, and other systems. In N. Koblitz, editor, *Advances in Cryptology – CRYPTO '96*, volume 1109 of *Lecture Notes in Computer Science*, pages 104–113. Springer-Verlag, 1996.
11. W. Meier and O. Staffelbach. Efficient multiplication on certain non-supersingular elliptic curves. In E.F. Brickell, editor, *Advances in Cryptology – CRYPTO '92*, volume 740 of *Lecture Notes in Computer Science*, pages 333–344. Springer-Verlag, 1993.
12. Alfred J. Menezes. *Elliptic Curve Public Key Cryptosystems*. Kluwer Academic Publishers, 1993.
13. Atsuko Miyaji, Takatoshi Ono, and Henri Cohen. Efficient elliptic curve exponentiation. In Y. Han, T. Okamoto, and S. Qing, editors, *Information and Communications Security (ICICS '97)*, volume 1334 of *Lecture Notes in Computer Science*, pages 282–290. Springer-Verlag, 1997.
14. Jerome A. Solinas. An improved algorithm for arithmetic on a family of elliptic curves. In B. Kaliski, editor, *Advances in Cryptology – CRYPTO '97*, volume 1294 of *Lecture Notes in Computer Science*, pages 357–371. Springer-Verlag, 1997.

A   Mathematical Background

This appendix details the elliptic curve addition formulæ. It also reviews some well-known techniques for computing $Q = kP$ in an elliptic curve $E(\mathbb{K})$. An excellent survey by Gordon, including the most recent developments, can be found in [6].

In the sequel, we only consider the cases of a field $\mathbb{K}$ with $\operatorname{Char} \mathbb{K} \neq 2, 3$ and $\operatorname{Char} \mathbb{K} = 2$. In these cases, the general Weierstraß equation (cf. Eq. (1)) can be simplified considerably through an appropriate *admissible change of variables*. This is explicited in the next proposition.

Proposition 2 ([12, Theorem 2.2]). *The elliptic curves given by the Weierstraß equations*

$$E_{/\mathbb{K}} : y^2 + a_1 xy + a_3 y = x^3 + a_2 x^2 + a_4 x + a_6 \text{ and}$$
$$E'_{/\mathbb{K}} : y^2 + a'_1 xy + a'_3 y = x^3 + a'_2 x^2 + a'_4 x + a'_6$$

are isomorphic over $\mathbb{K}$ if and only if there exists $u \in \mathbb{K}^*$ and $r, s, t \in \mathbb{K}$ such that the change of variables

$$(x, y) \leftarrow (u^2 x + r, u^3 y + u^2 sx + t)$$

transforms equation E into equation E'. Such a transformation is referred to as an admissible change of variables. Furthermore,

$$\begin{cases} ua'_1 = a_1 + 2s, \\ u^2 a'_2 = a_2 - sa_1 + 3r - s^2, \\ u^3 a'_3 = a_3 + ra_1 + 2t, \\ u^4 a'_4 = a_4 - sa_3 + 2ra_2 - (t + rs)a_1 + 3r^2 - 2st, \\ u^6 a'_6 = a_6 + ra_4 - ta_3 + r^2 a_2 - rta_1 + r^3 - t^2. \end{cases}$$

A.1   Elliptic Curves over a Field $\mathbb{K}$ with $\operatorname{Char} \mathbb{K} \neq 2, 3$

When the characteristic of field $\mathbb{K}$ is different from $2, 3$, the Weierstraß equation of an elliptic curve can be simplified to:

$$E_{/\mathbb{K}} : y^2 = x^3 + ax + b \qquad (4a^3 + 27b^2 \neq 0) . \tag{10}$$

For any $P \in E(\mathbb{K})$, we have $P + O = O + P = P$. Let $P = (x_1, y_1)$ and $Q = (x_2, y_2) \in E(\mathbb{K})$. The inverse of P is $-P = (x_1, -y_1)$. If $Q = -P$ then $P + Q = O$; otherwise the sum $P + Q = (x_3, y_3)$ is given by

$$x_3 = \lambda^2 - x_1 - x_2, \quad y_3 = \lambda(x_1 - x_3) - y_1 \tag{11}$$

with $\lambda = \begin{cases} \dfrac{y_2 - y_1}{x_2 - x_1}, & \text{if } P \neq Q, \\ \dfrac{3x_1^2 + a}{2y_1}, & \text{if } P = Q. \end{cases}$

To avoid the division in the computation of λ, one usually works in projective coordinates. There are basically two ways to project Eq. (10): (i) set $x = X/Z$ and $y = Y/Z$, that is, $(X : Y : Z)$ are the *homogeneous coordinates*; or (ii) set $x = X/Z^2$ and $y = Y/Z^3$, $(X : Y : Z)$ are then referred to as the *Jacobian coordinates*. Hence, to compute $Q = kP$ on an elliptic curve, one first represents point $P = (x_1, y_1)$ as $(X_1 : Y_1 : Z_1)$, computes $(X_2 : Y_2 : Z_2) = k(X_1 : Y_1 : Z_1)$, and recovers $Q = (x_2, y_2)$ from its projective form.

Homogeneous coordinates. In homogeneous coordinates, $(X : Y : Z)$ and $(tX : tY : tZ)$ (with $t \in \mathbb{K}^*$) are two equivalent representations of a same point. The point at infinity $\boldsymbol{O}$ is represented by $(0 : 1 : 0)$; it is the only point with its Z-coordinate equal to 0. Putting $x = X/Z$ and $y = Y/Z$ in Eq. (12), the Weierstraß equation of an elliptic curve becomes

$$E_{/\mathbb{K}} : Y^2 Z = X^3 + aXZ^2 + bZ^3 \ . \tag{12}$$

The formula to double a point $\boldsymbol{P} = (X_1 : Y_1 : Z_1)$ is $2\boldsymbol{P} = (X_3 : Y_3 : Z_3)$, where

$$X_3 = SH, \quad Y_3 = W(T - H) - 2M^2 \quad \text{and} \quad Z_3 = S^3 \tag{13}$$

with $W = 3X_1^2 + aZ_1^2$, $S = 2Y_1Z_1$, $M = Y_1S$, $T = 2X_1M$ and $H = W^2 - 2T$. This requires 12 multiplications. Notice that if $a = -3$ then $W = 3(X_1 - Z_1)(X_1 + Z_1)$; in that case, the number of multiplications decreases to 10. The sum $\boldsymbol{R} = (X_3 : Y_3 : Z_3)$ of two points $\boldsymbol{P} = (X_1 : Y_1 : Z_1)$ and $\boldsymbol{Q} = (X_2 : Y_2 : Z_2)$ (with $\boldsymbol{P} \neq \pm\boldsymbol{Q}$) is given by

$$X_3 = WX_3', \quad 2Y_3 = RV - MW^3 \quad \text{and} \quad Z_3 = Z'W^3 \tag{14}$$

with $U_1 = X_1Z_2$, $U_2 = X_2Z_1$, $S_1 = Y_1Z_2$, $S_2 = Y_2Z_1$, $T = U_1 + U_2$, $W = U_1 - U_2$, $M = S_1 + S_2$, $R = S_1 - S_2$, $Z' = Z_1Z_2$, $H = TW^2$, $X_3' = -H + Z'R^2$ and $V = H - 2X_3'$. The addition of two points can thus be done with only 14 multiplications. If one of the two points has its Z-coordinate equal to 1 then the number of multiplications decreases to 11.

Jacobian coordinates. The use of Jacobian coordinates is suggested in the P1363 IEEE Standard [1] because it allows faster arithmetic [2]. In Jacobian coordinates, also, the representation of points is not unique, $(X : Y : Z)$ and $(t^2X : t^3Y : tZ)$ (with $t \in \mathbb{K}^*$) are equivalent representations. The Weierstraß equation is given by

$$E_{/\mathbb{K}} : Y^2 = X^3 + aXZ^4 + bZ^6 \tag{15}$$

and the point at infinity is represented by $(1 : 1 : 0)$.

The double of point $\boldsymbol{P} = (X_1 : Y_1 : Z_1)$ is equal to $2\boldsymbol{P} = (X_3 : Y_3 : Z_3)$ where

$$X_3 = M^2 - 2S, \quad Y_3 = M(S - X_3) - T \quad \text{and} \quad Z_3 = 2Y_1Z_1 \tag{16}$$

with $M = 3X_1^2 + aZ_1^4$, $S = 4X_1Y_1^2$ and $T = 8Y_1^4$. So doubling a point requires 10 multiplications. Here too, we see that the value $a = -3$ enables to reduce the number of multiplications; in this case, it decreases to 8.

The sum $\boldsymbol{R} = (X_3 : Y_3 : Z_3)$ of points $\boldsymbol{P} = (X_1 : Y_1 : Z_1)$ and $\boldsymbol{Q} = (X_2 : Y_2 : Z_2)$ (with $\boldsymbol{P} \neq \pm\boldsymbol{Q}$) is given by

$$X_3 = R^2 - TW^2, \quad 2Y_3 = RV - MW^3 \quad \text{and} \quad Z_3 = Z_1Z_2W \tag{17}$$

Table 2. Number of multiplications in addition formulæ.

	Addition		Doubling	
	$Z_2 \neq 1$	$Z_2 = 1$	$a \neq -3$	$a = -3$
Homogeneous coord.	14	11	12	10
Jacobian coord.	16	11	10	8
Chudnovsky Jacobian coord.	14	11	11	9
Modified Jacobian coord.	19	14	8	8

with $U_1 = X_1 Z_2^2$, $U_2 = X_2 Z_1^2$, $S_1 = Y_1 Z_2^3$, $S_2 = Y_2 Z_1^3$, $T = U_1 + U_2$, $W = U_1 - U_2$, $M = S_1 + S_2$, $R = S_1 - S_2$ and $V = TW^2 - 2X_3$. An addition requires 16 multiplications. When one of the two points has its Z-coordinate equal to 1 then an addition requires only 11 multiplications. A slightly different (but equally efficient) formula for addition can be found in [13]. Using the same notations as above, the sum $\boldsymbol{R} = (X_3 : Y_3 : Z_3)$ is then given by

$$X_3 = R^2 - TW^2, \quad Y_3 = -RX_3 + (RU_1 - S_1)W^2 \quad \text{and} \quad Z_3 = Z_1 Z_2 W \ . \quad (17')$$

Mixed coordinates. In the general case, we have seen that Jacobian coordinates offer a faster doubling but a slower addition than homogeneous coordinates (see Table 2). Chudnovsky and Chudnovsky [2] proposed to internally represent a point $(X : Y : Z)$ in Jacobian coordinates as a 5-tuple (X, Y, Z, Z^2, Z^3). In *Chudnovsky Jacobian coordinates*, the addition formula for $\boldsymbol{P} = (X_1 : Y_1 : Z_1)$ and $\boldsymbol{Q} = (X_2 : Y_2 : Z_2)$, respectively represented as $(X_1, Y_1, Z_1, Z_1^2, Z_1^3)$ and $(X_2, Y_2, Z_2, Z_2^2, Z_2^3)$, remains the same as given by Eq. (17). The advantage is that the values of Z_1^2, Z_1^3, Z_2^2 and Z_2^3 being available, they do not have to be computed; only Z_3^2 and Z_3^3 have to be be computed to represent the result $\boldsymbol{R} = \boldsymbol{P} + \boldsymbol{Q} = (X_3 : Y_3 : Z_3)$ as the 5-tuple $(X_3, Y_3, Z_3, Z_3^2, Z_3^3)$. Therefore, Chudnovsky Jacobian coordinates require $(4 - 2) = 2$ multiplications less than ordinary Jacobian coordinates to add two points. On the other hand, the doubling is more expensive: it requires $(2 - 1) = 1$ multiplication more for computing $\boldsymbol{R} = 2\boldsymbol{P} = (X_3 : Y_3 : Z_3)$ since Z_1^2 has not to be computed (see Eq. (16)) but Z_3^2 and Z_3^3 have to.

The above strategy was optimized by Cohen, Miyaji and Ono [4] in order to provide the fastest known doubling algorithm on a general elliptic curve. With their coordinates, called *modified Jacobian coordinates*, a point $(X : Y : Z)$ is internally represented as a 4-tuple (X, Y, Z, aZ^4). A point is doubled with only 8 multiplications *whatever* the value of parameter a. However, this fast doubling is done at the expense of a slower addition: 19 multiplications are required to add two points in the general case and 14 multiplications when one of the two points has its Z-coordinate equal to 1.

A.2   Elliptic Curves over a Field $\mathbb{K}$ with Char $\mathbb{K} = 2$

For fields of characteristic 2, the simplified Weierstraß equation depends on whether the curve is supersingular or not. For cryptographic applications, we are only interested in non-supersingular curves. In that case, it can be shown that an admissible change of variables yields the simplified Weierstraß equation

$$E_{/\mathbb{K}} : y^2 + xy = x^3 + ax^2 + b \qquad (b \neq 0) \ . \tag{18}$$

O being the neutral element, we have $P + O = O + P = P$ for any $P \in E(\mathbb{K})$. Let $P = (x_1, y_1)$ and $Q = (x_2, y_2) \in E(\mathbb{K})$. The inverse of P is $-P = (x_1, x_1 + y_1)$. If $Q = -P$ then $P + Q = O$; otherwise the sum $P + Q = (x_3, y_3)$ is calculated as follows.
 – If $P \neq Q$ then

$$x_3 = \lambda^2 + \lambda + x_1 + x_2 + a \ , \quad y_3 = \lambda(x_1 + x_3) + x_3 + y_1 \tag{19}$$

with $\lambda = \dfrac{y_1 + y_2}{x_1 + x_2}$.
 – If $P = Q$ then

$$x_3 = \lambda^2 + \lambda + a \ , \quad y_3 = x_1^2 + (\lambda + 1)x_3 \tag{20}$$

with $\lambda = x_1 + \dfrac{y_1}{x_1}$.

An important subclass of elliptic curves has been introduced by Koblitz in [8]: the *Anomalous Binary Curves* (or ABC curves in short), sometimes also referred to as *Koblitz curves*. These are elliptic curves given by Eq. (18) with $b = 1$ and $a \in \{0, 1\}$. For such curves, the Frobenius endomorphism, $\tau : (x, y) \mapsto (x^2, y^2)$, satisfies the characteristic equation

$$u^2 - (-1)^{1-a} u + 2 = 0 \ .$$

Koblitz suggests to speed the computation of $Q = kP$ by noticing that $2P = (-1)^{1-a}\tau(P) - \tau^2(P)$. He also suggests to write k as a Frobenius expansion since scalar multiplication by k is an endomorphism and $\mathbb{Z} \subseteq \mathbb{Z}[\tau] \subseteq \mathrm{End}(E)$. The ring $\mathbb{Z}[\tau]$ is an Euclidean domain with respect to the norm $\mathrm{N}(r + s\tau) = r^2 + (-1)^{1-a} rs + 2s^2$. Furthermore, as $\mathrm{N}(\tau) = 2$, every element $r + s\tau$ in $\mathbb{Z}[\tau]$ can be written as a τ-*adic non-adjacent form* (τ-NAF, in short), that is,

$$r + s\tau = \sum_i k_i \tau^i \quad \text{with} \begin{cases} k_i \in \{-1, 0, 1\} \\ k_i \cdot k_{i+1} = 0 \end{cases} . \tag{21}$$

As already remarked in [8], the drawback in this method is that the Frobenius expansion (21) is roughly twice longer than the usual balanced binary expansion and so, even if the evaluation of τ is very fast, it is not clear that the resulting method is faster. The drawback was loopholed in [11,14] with the following observation. We obviously have $\tau^n = 1$ and thus $Q = k'P$ with $k' = k \bmod (\tau^n - 1)$. As $\mathrm{N}(\tau^n - 1) = \#E_a(\mathbb{F}_{2^n}) \approx 2^n$ by Hasse's Theorem, the τ-NAF expression of k', $k' = \sum_i k_i' \tau^i$, would have a length approximatively equal to that of the (usual) NAF expression of k. The non-adjacency property (i.e., $k_i' \cdot k_{i+1}' = 0$) implies that, on average, only one third of the digits are nonzero [6]. Together with the property that the evaluation of τP is very fast, this yields a very efficient algorithm for computing $Q = kP$.

Preventing SPA/DPA in ECC Systems Using the Jacobi Form

P.-Y. Liardet[1] and N.P. Smart[2]

[1] STMicroelectronics, Dept. System Engineering,
Z.I. Rousset, 13 106 Rousset Cedex, France
`Pierre-Yvan.Liardet@st.com`
[2] Dept. Computer Science, University of Bristol,
Merchant Venturers Building, Woodland Road,
Bristol, BS8 1UB, United Kingdom
`nigel@cs.bris.ac.uk`

Abstract. In this paper we show how using a representation of an elliptic curve as the intersection of two quadrics in $\mathbb{P}^3$ can provide a defence against Simple and Differential Power Analysis (SPA/DPA) style attacks. We combine this with a 'random window' method of point multiplication and point blinding. The proposed method offers considerable advantages over standard algorithmic techniques of preventing SPA and DPA which usually require a significant increased computational cost, usually more than double. Our method requires roughly a seventy percent increase in computational cost of the basic cryptographic operation, although we give some indication as to how this can be reduced. In addition we show that the Jacobi form is also more efficient than the standard Weierstrass form for elliptic curves in the situation where SPA and DPA are not a concern.

1 Introduction

Elliptic curve based cryptosystems are particularly suited for cost-effective implementations of public key primitives on low powered computational devices such as Smart Cards, Mobile Phones and PDAs. Nevertheless, the use of side channel information, such as that provided by Simple and Differential Power Analysis (SPA/DPA) [7] on naive implementations can lead to the revelation of the secrets that the algorithm is working on.

Elliptic curve systems have the advantage of almost always using a new random ephemeral secret integer in the *double and add* algorithm for each run of a protocol, unlike RSA. Hence, a DPA attack on ECC is harder to mount for this reason than one against RSA. On the other hand smart card vendors require any implementation to be as immune as possible from SPA and DPA.

One problem with elliptic curve systems is that the doubling operation is significantly more efficient than the general addition operation. This needs to be compared to the RSA case, where squaring is only slightly more efficient than general multiplication. Hence, it may be possible to use SPA to recover some bits

Ç.K. Koç, D. Naccache, and C. Paar (Eds.): CHES 2001, LNCS 2162, pp. 391–401, 2001.
© Springer-Verlag Berlin Heidelberg 2001

of each ephemeral exponent, since one may be able to distinguish an addition from a doubling. Recall [6] that for EC-DSA only a few bits of each ephemeral exponent need to be leaked in this way per message, for the underlying secret key to be revealed.

Hence, various proposals have been made to completely secure elliptic curve systems against SPA and DPA. To protect against DPA it has been proposed to use a randomised projective coordinate system. Here the base point on the curve $P = (x, y)$ on each protocol run is first randomised by replacing P with the (Jacobian) projective point

$$P' = (xz^2, yz^3, z),$$

or the (homogeneous) projective point

$$P'' = (xz, yz, z),$$

for some random non-zero field element z. This still allows some of the efficient techniques for point multiplication to be used, such as those described in [1] and [5]. The use of mixed coordinate (i.e. affine and projective coordinates used together) multiplication algorithms are, however, not used which causes some efficiency loss.

Moreover, the above defence will not protect against SPA, hence for SPA protection one of two defences are usually proposed. The first is as follows, instead of computing $[k]P$ one computes $[k + rq]P$, where q is the order of P and r is some random integer. This defence significantly increases the cost of a point multiplication. This does not provide any defence against SPA since if one can recover $k' = k + rq$ from a single run then one can recover $k = k'$ (mod q) for this run since q is known. A second technique is to take a random integer r and compute $k' = rk$ (mod q) and $r' = 1/r$ (mod q). One then computes $Q = [k']P$ and then $[r']Q = [k]P$, again a task which significantly increases computational cost.

Neither of these defences against SPA address the underlying cause, which is the disparity between the addition and doubling algorithms. A model for the elliptic curve in which addition and doubling are given by the same formulae will not suffer from such side channel analysis on the code dependent nature of the operation. In this paper we proposed such a model, based on the Jacobi form of an elliptic curve. Our model, for certain elliptic curves, will provide a defence against SPA and will only give a 70 percent increase in computational cost.

To understand our defence against SPA we first explain roughly how an SPA attack on a standard elliptic curve binary point multiplication method would proceed. Recall the binary method for point multiplication proceeds as in the following algorithm.

Binary Multiplication Method

```
INPUT:  A point P and an integer k
OUTPUT: The point Q = [k]P .
```

```
1.  Q ← O.
2.  For i from t down to 0 do:
3.      Q ← [2]Q.
4.      If (k_i = 1) then
5.          Q ← Q + P.
6.  Return Q.
```

With a standard representation an attacker can attempt to determine the bits of k by seeing how the program behaves at the *if*-statement. The test is always carried out but the subroutine for point addition will only be called when the ith bit of k is set. The attacker can attempt to spot this jump to a subroutine, which will have a different power trace to point doubling, and hence determine k.

The most common idea to make point addition and doubling indistinguishable, is to unify the common code part for both operations, and add dummy code to balance the difference between point addition and point doubling. Ideally one needs to execute the same code at the same addresses but with different results, but this is unfortunatelly not possible if point addition and point doubling are not unified.

Now suppose exactly the same code was called for point addition and point doubling with the same power trace profile for both operations. The attacker would now need to determine whether one or two calls to this procedure were performed on each iteration. This is a much harder problem for SPA to solve, but if this is still a worry one can unroll the loop to make this task harder for the attacker. But for standard elliptic curve Weierstrass models one cannot use the point addition code in the case where the two points are equal, since the addition formulae contain a singularity when the inputs are the same.

Notice that the defence of simply adding spurious multiplication operations into the doubling code, as mentioned above, would not be a suitable defence since the point doubling and point addition code would still have seperate execution profiles, and would reside in different areas of memory or hardware.

Nevertheless, with the basic double and add algorithm a little bit of information can leak from the bit test, even if the same code is used for point addition and doubling. A carefull implementation can make this information not usable in practice from the point of view of an attacker. Moreover, we present in the last section a multiplication algorithm that reduce significantly the amount of information that can leak from point multiplication.

One is still left open to a DPA style attack whereby internal data bits are guessed (depending on whether the *if* statement produces a branch) and these are correlated over a number of runs. However, for ECC systems these are easily prevented by point blinding (essentially using the redundancy of a projective coordinate representation) or by the protocol using ephemeral point multiples on each run.

2   Intersection of Two Quadrics

Let K denote our ground field, which in applications will be a finite field $\mathbb{F}_p$ of characteristic greater than three. It is well known that an intersection of two quadric surfaces in $\mathbb{P}^3$

$$\mathcal{Q} : \{Q_1(x_0, x_1, x_2, x_3) = 0\} \cap \{Q_2(x_0, x_1, x_2, x_3) = 0\}$$

generically defines a curve of genus one. Hence, assuming $\mathcal{Q}$ has a point defined over K, the curve $\mathcal{Q}$ is birationally equivalent to an elliptic curve, also defined over K.

Just as the chord-tangent law defines a geometric group law on the elliptic curve we can also define a group law on $\mathcal{Q}$ in geometric terms, see [8]. We first let P_0 denote our given K-rational point on $\mathcal{Q}$, which we shall treat as the identity. Three points $P_1, P_2, P_3 \in \mathcal{Q}(K)$ will sum to zero if and only if the four points P_0, P_1, P_2 and P_3 are coplanar. The negation of a point $-P_1$ is given as the residual intersection of the plane through P_1 containing the tangent line to $\mathcal{Q}$ at P_0.

An algorithm to pass from a general intersection of two quadric surfaces with a K-rational point to an elliptic curve is given in [2, p 36]. In [3, pp 63–64] a method is given to pass in the other direction, from a general elliptic curve over K

$$E : Y^2 = X^3 + AX + B,$$

to the intersection of two quadrics given by

$$\mathcal{Q} : \begin{cases} z_1^2 - Bz_3^2 - Az_2z_3 - z_0z_2 = 0, \\ z_2^2 - z_0z_3 = 0. \end{cases}$$

The map from a point $(X, Y) \in E(K)$ to a point $(z_0, z_1, z_2, z_3) \in \mathcal{Q}(K)$ is given by $z_0 = X^2$, $z_1 = Y$, $z_2 = X$ and $z_3 = 1$.

Also in [3] formulae are given to add points on $\mathcal{Q}(K)$. If we let $\mathbf{a} = (a_0, a_1, a_2, a_3)$ and $\mathbf{b} = (b_0, b_1, b_2, b_3)$ denote two points on $\mathcal{Q}(K)$ then their sum is given by $\mathbf{c} = \mathbf{a} + \mathbf{b}$ with

$$\begin{aligned}
c_0 &= R(\mathbf{a}, \mathbf{b})^2, \\
c_1 &= b_1 S(\mathbf{a}, \mathbf{b}) + a_1 S(\mathbf{b}, \mathbf{a}), \\
c_2 &= R(\mathbf{a}, \mathbf{b}) \cdot T(\mathbf{a}, \mathbf{b}), \\
c_3 &= T(\mathbf{a}, \mathbf{b})^2,
\end{aligned}$$

where

$$\begin{aligned}
R(\mathbf{a}, \mathbf{b}) &= a_0b_0 - 2Aa_2b_2 - 4Ba_3b_2 - 4Ba_2b_3 + A^2a_3b_3, \\
S(\mathbf{a}, \mathbf{b}) &= a_0^2b_0 + 2Aa_2a_0b_2 + 4Ba_2a_0b_3 + 3Aa_3a_0b_0 \\
&\quad + 12Ba_3a_0b_2 - 3A^2a_3a_0b_3 + 4Ba_3a_2b_0 - 2A^2a_3a_2b_2 \\
&\quad - 4ABa_3a_2b_3 - A^3a_3^2b_3 - 8B^2a_3^2b_3, \\
T(\mathbf{a}, \mathbf{b}) &= 2a_1b_1 + a_2b_0 + a_0b_2 + Aa_3b_2 + 2Ba_3b_3.
\end{aligned}$$

What is remarkable about these equations is that they also hold when $\mathbf{a} = \mathbf{b}$, i.e. when a doubling operation is performed. Hence, the use of such a representation will remove the distinction between doubling and adding, and hence help to defeat SPA as argued above. However, the above formulae are overly complicated and therefore not particularly suited to a real life implementation, so in the next section we reduce to a special class of elliptic curves over K for which the above formulae can be made particularly simple leading to efficient implementation.

3   Jacobi Form

To make the formulae from the above section more amenable to machine calculation we require that our quadrics Q be simultaneously diagonalisable over K. This is equivalent to saying that our initial elliptic curve has three points of order two defined over K, or equivalently that the polynomial $X^3 + AX + B$ has all three roots defined over K.

Hence, from now on we shall assume we have chosen an elliptic curve

$$E : Y^2 = X^3 + AX + B$$

which has three points of order two defined over K. This means that the group order $N = \#E(F_p)$ is divisible by 4, hence we should choose such a curve with $N = 4q$ with q a prime.

By applying a standard Möbius transformation we can move the three points of order two to the positions $(0,0), (-1,0)$ and $(-\lambda, 0)$ where $\lambda \in K$. Our elliptic curve has then become

$$E' : y^2 = x(x+1)(x+\lambda).$$

To obtain this transformation, first write the factorisation of $X^3 + AX + B$ over K as

$$X^3 + AX + B = (X - \theta_1)(X - \theta_2)(X - \theta_3).$$

Then we define the following Möbius transformation, where $\{i, j, k\} = \{1, 2, 3\}$,

$$x = \frac{X - \theta_i Z}{(\theta_i - \theta_j)^2},$$

$$z = \frac{Z}{\theta_i - \theta_j},$$

$$y = Y(\theta_i - \theta_j)^{5/2},$$

where (X, Y, Z) is a homogeneous projective point on $E(K)$ and (x, y, z) is a homogeneous projective point on $E'(K)$. Then setting

$$\lambda = \frac{\theta_i - \theta_k}{\theta_i - \theta_j}$$

we see that the curve E is mapped to the curve E' since

$$x(x+z)(x+z\lambda) = \frac{1}{(\theta_i - \theta_j)^6}(X - \theta_1 Z)(X - \theta_2 Z)(X - \theta_3 Z)$$

$$= \frac{Y^2}{(\theta_i - \theta_j)^6} = y^2 z.$$

This change of variable requires that for some $1 \leq i, j \leq 3$ with $i \neq j$ we have that $\theta_i - \theta_j$ is a square modulo p. If $p \equiv 3 \pmod{4}$ then -1 will not be a square modulo p and so either

$$\theta_i - \theta_j \text{ or } \theta_j - \theta_i$$

will be a square modulo p, for all possible i and j. When $p \equiv 1 \pmod{4}$ then there is a $1/8$ chance for given $\theta_1, \theta_2, \theta_3$ that we cannot find a pair of indices such that $\theta_i - \theta_j$ is a square modulo p.

In [4] Chudnovsky and Chudnovsky consider the following intersection of two quadrics

$$\mathcal{Q} : \begin{cases} x_0^2 + x_1^2 - x_3^2 = 0, \\ k^2 x_0^2 + x_2^2 - x_3^2 = 0. \end{cases}$$

From two points (a_0, a_1, a_2, a_3) and (b_0, b_1, b_2, b_3) on $\mathcal{Q}$ we can compute their sum (c_0, c_1, c_2, c_3) via the formulae

$$c_0 = a_3 b_1 \cdot a_0 b_2 + a_2 b_0 \cdot a_1 b_3,$$
$$c_1 = a_3 b_1 \cdot a_1 b_3 - a_2 b_0 \cdot a_0 b_2,$$
$$c_2 = a_3 a_2 b_3 b_2 - k^2 a_0 a_1 b_0 b_1,$$
$$c_3 = (a_3 b_1)^2 + (a_2 b_0)^2.$$

The zero of this group law is given by the point $(0, 1, 1, 1)$. The above formulae for the group law on $\mathcal{Q}$ are also valid when $(a_0, a_1, a_2, a_3) = (b_0, b_1, b_2, b_3)$, and so the same formulae can be used both for doubling and general addition. Each addition or doubling can be efficiently implemented so that it requires a total of 16 field multiplications.

For use in signed window methods of point multiplication we require the formulae for point negation in the Jacobi model. Given the addition formulae above it is easy to see that

$$-(a_0, a_1, a_2, a_3) = (-a_0, a_1, a_2, a_3).$$

We now, for a moment, leave our main application of defences against SPA and DPA and turn to the use of Jacobi form as a way of speeding up algorithms for elliptic curve point multiplication in environments where SPA and DPA are not a concern.

By using the doubling formulae given in [4]

$$c_0 = 2 a_1 a_3 \cdot a_2 a_0,$$
$$c_1 = (a_1 a_3)^2 - (a_2 a_3)^2 + (a_1 a_2)^2,$$
$$c_2 = (a_2 a_3)^2 - (a_1 a_3)^2 + (a_1 a_2)^2,$$
$$c_3 = (a_2 a_3)^2 + (a_1 a_3)^2 - (a_1 a_2)^2,$$

where $(c_0, c_1, c_2, c_3) = [2](a_0, a_1, a_2, a_3)$, we obtain doubling formulae which only requires eight field multiplications.

However, with a little care one can even achieve doubling in seven field multiplications, which is more efficient than doubling in projective coordinates on a standard Weierstrass equation in odd characteristic.

Lemma 1. *A point can be doubled in the Jacobi model using seven field multiplications.*

Proof. We first take the doubling formulae obtained from specialising the general point addition method to obtain

$$c_0 = 2a_3a_1 \cdot a_2a_0,$$
$$c_1 = (a_3a_1)^2 - (a_2a_0)^2,$$
$$c_2 = (a_3a_2)^2 - k^2(a_0a_1)^2,$$
$$c_3 = (a_3a_1)^2 + (a_2a_0)^2,$$

which requires ten field multiplications to evaluate. Using the equations of the curve,

$$k^2a_0^2 = a_3^2 - a_2^2 \text{ and } a_0^2 = a_3^2 - a_1^2,$$

we see that we can, assuming $a_2 \neq 0$, rewrite c_2 as

$$c_2 = (a_0a_2)^2 - (a_1a_3)^2 + 2(a_1a_2)^2.$$

Then we can perform a doubling by evaluating

$$\ell_1 = a_3a_1,$$
$$\ell_2 = a_0a_2,$$
$$\ell_3 = 2(a_1a_2)^2,$$
$$c_0 = 2\ell_1\ell_2,$$
$$c_3 = (\ell_1 + \ell_2)^2 - c_0,$$
$$c_1 = c_3 - 2\ell_2^2,$$
$$c_2 = -c_1 + \ell_3.$$

It is easy to verify that the same equations hold when $a_2 = 0$.

It is interesting to note that this means we can triple a point in $16 + 7 = 23$ field multiplications. Note, in [4] triplication formulae for points in the Jacobi model are also given, which also require only 23 field multiplications.

To use these formulae all that remains is to produce the link between $\mathcal{Q}$ and E'. The two parameters k and λ defining $\mathcal{Q}$ and E' are linked by the equation

$$\lambda = 1 - k^2.$$

To describe the map from E' to $\mathcal{Q}$, let (x, y, z) denote a projective point on E', i.e.

$$y^2z = x(x + z)(x + z\lambda),$$

such a point is obtained from (X, Y) by generating a random $z \in K^*$ and putting $(x, y, z) = (Xz, Yz, z)$, note this homogeneous projective representation, as remarked on both above and below, is needed to prevent DPA attacks. The equivalent point on $\mathcal{Q}$ is then given by the equations

$$
\begin{aligned}
x_0 &= -2(x + z)y, \\
x_1 &= -z^2 + z^2k^2 + 2z\,k^2x + k^2x^2 + y^2 - x^2 - 2z\,x, \\
&= \lambda(-x^2 - z^2 - 2xz) + y^2, \\
x_2 &= -2z\,k^2x - k^2x^2 - z^2k^2 + z^2 + 2z\,x + y^2 + x^2, \\
&= \lambda(x^2 + z^2 + 2xz) + y^2, \\
x_3 &= -z^2k^2 + k^2x^2 + z^2 + 2z\,x + y^2 + x^2, \\
&= \lambda z^2 + y^2 + 2xz + (2 - \lambda)x^2.
\end{aligned}
$$

The reverse operation is obtained by computing

$$
\begin{aligned}
x &= (x_2 - x_3)\lambda, \\
y &= x_0\lambda k^2, \\
z &= x_1k^2 - x_2 + x_3\lambda.
\end{aligned}
$$

Suppose we implemented a standard point multiplication algorithm using a signed window method with $r = 5$, see [1, Algorithm IV.7], on the elliptic curve E over $\mathbb{F}_p$, where p is a 192-bit prime number. This would, on average, require 191 point doublings and 38 general point additions. The standard projective coordinate methods on the curve E require 16 field multiplications to perform a general addition and 8 field multiplications to perform a doubling. Hence, the average number of field operations required would be 2136.

Using our Jacobi representation and the same multiplication algorithm we would require on average 3664 field multiplications since both doubling and general addition requires 16 field operations. Hence, we obtain about 70 percent performance penalty as compared to the standard method. However, since doubling and addition is performed by the same code we hopefully obtain a better defence against SPA attacks.

If we were not concerned with a defence against SPA/DPA then using the Jacobi model we can perform a point multiplication in, on average, 1945 field multiplications. This is because we can perform a double in seven field multiplications. Therefore, the Jacobi model gives roughly a ten percent performance improvement over the standard Weierstrass model.

Returning to our main interest of defending against SPA/DPA we can obtain a better performance in the following way. We can flip a coin before doubling to decide whether we use the 7 or the 16 field operations formulae for doubling. The average number of field multiplications then becomes 2040, which is more efficient than the standard algorithm using a Weierstrass model. Hence, we obtain greater efficiency and a defence against SPA/DPA at the same time.

Chudnovsky and Chudnovsky [4] give a number of possible other improvements to multiplication algorithms in Jacobi models. However, they address this problem from the point of view of efficiency and not from the point of view of minimising the effect of DPA. We leave it as an open research problem to reconcile these two approaches for elliptic curves in Jacobi form.

To protect even further against DPA type attacks we stress we need to perform a method of point blinding, whilst transforming from the standard form to the Jacobi form, as above. Assume the affine point $P = (X, Y) \in E(K)$ is given, on every protocol run one then randomises the representation of P by taking a homogeneous representation. This is achieved by generating a random element $Z' \in K^*$ and replacing P by the equivalent point $P' = (X', Y', Z')$ where $X' = XZ'$ and $Y' = YZ'$.

3.1   Example Curve

The prime field $\mathbb{F}_p$ defined by

$$p = 2^{192} - 2^{64} - 1$$

is a popular choice for elliptic curve systems, since it offers a number of efficiency advantages. For this field one could choose the curve defined by

$$\lambda = 421$$

which has group order

627710173538668076383578942332099749700157383631391 0896964

which is four times a 190 bit prime.

4   Randomised Signed Windows Method

To add even further defence against side channel analysis we propose the use of a signed window multiplication algorithm, which uses a random window width. This defence can also be used for standard elliptic curve systems, and not just those in the Jacobi model considered above.

We keep the main signed window algorithm as standard, see for example [1, Algorithm IV.7]. However, we alter the preprocessing of the 'exponent', as in [1, Algorithm IV.6], so as to produce a random window width. We assume that the system will multiply a fixed point P by a random number k, using a lookup table of the point multiples

$$P_i = [2i + 1]P,$$

for $0 \le i \le 2^{R-2} - 1$. The preprocessing in the signed window algorithm is used to express k as

$$k = \sum_{i=0}^{d-1} b_i 2^{e_i}$$

where $e_i \in \mathbb{Z}_{\geq 0}$ and

$$b_i \in \{-2^{R-1} + 1, -2^{R-1} + 3, \ldots, 2^{R-1} - 3, 2^{R-1} - 1\}.$$

Usually one uses fixed window lengths so that $e_{i+1} - e_i \geq R$ for $0 \leq i \leq d - 2$. The following algorithm produces a randomised signed window representation of k which will provide a more difficult target for side channel analysis.

Signed m-ary Window Decomposition

INPUT: An integer $k = \sum_{j=0}^{\ell} k_j 2^j$, $k_j \in \{0, 1\}$, $k_\ell = 0$.
OUTPUT: A sequence of pairs $\{(b_i, e_i)\}_{i=0}^{d-1}$.

1. $d \leftarrow 0$, $j \leftarrow 0$.
2.   While $j \leq \ell$ do:
3.   If $k_j = 0$ then $j \leftarrow j + 1$.
4.   Else do:
5. $r \leftarrow_{\mathcal{R}} \{1, \ldots, R\}$.
6. $t \leftarrow \min\{\ell, j + r - 1\}$, $h_d \leftarrow (k_t k_{t-1} \cdots k_j)_2$.
7.   If $h_d > 2^{r-1}$ then do:
8. $b_d \leftarrow h_d - 2^r$,
9.   increment the number $(k_\ell k_{\ell-1} \cdots k_{t+1})_2$ by 1.
10.   Else $b_d \leftarrow h_d$.
11. $e_d \leftarrow j$, $d \leftarrow d + 1$, $j \leftarrow t + 1$.
12. Return the sequence $(b_0, e_0), (b_1, e_1), \ldots, (b_{d-1}, e_{d-1})$.

The only change from the standard algorithm is the addition of line 5, where $\leftarrow_{\mathcal{R}}$ denotes a random assignment to the variable on the left from the set on the right.

5   Conclusion

In this paper we have proposed two new defences against side channel analysis for elliptic curve based cryptosystems. Firstly, the use of the Jacobi form for an elliptic curve means that the time/power required to perform a point addition will be almost identical to that of a point doubling. Such a balanced approach is a well known design technique for defeating side channel analysis, and this is the first time a truly balanced technique has been proposed for use in elliptic curve systems. Secondly, the use of a randomised window method creates another level of defence.

In addition our Jacobi form representation can be made more efficient than the standard Weierstrass representation for implementations where SPA and DPA are not a concern.

References

1. I.F. Blake, G. Seroussi and N.P. Smart. *Elliptic curves in cryptography*. Cambridge University Press, 1999.
2. J.W.S. Cassels. *Lectures on Elliptic Curves*. LMS Student Texts, Cambridge University Press, 1991.
3. J.W.S. Cassels and E.V. Flynn. *Prolegomena to a Middlebrow Arithmetic of Curves of Genus 2*. Cambridge University Press, 1996.
4. D.V. Chudnovsky and G.V. Chudnovsky. Sequences of numbers generated by addition in formal groups and new primality and factorisation tests. *Adv. in Appl. Math.*, **7**, 385–434, 1987.
5. H. Cohen, A. Miyaji and T. Ono. Efficient elliptic curve exponentiation using mixed coordinates. In *Advances in Cryptology, ASIACRYPT 98*. Springer-Verlag, LNCS 1514, 51–65, 1998.
6. N.A. Howgrave-Graham and N.P. Smart. Lattice attacks on digital signature schemes. To appear *Designs, Codes and Cryptography*.
7. P. Kocher, J. Jaffe and B. Bun. Differential power analysis. In *Advances in Cryptology, CRYPTO '99*, Springer LNCS 1666, pp 388–397, 1999.
8. J.R. Merriman, S. Siksek, and N.P. Smart. Explicit 4–descents on an elliptic curve. *Acta. Arith.*, **77**, 385–404, 1996.

Hessian Elliptic Curves
and Side-Channel Attacks

Marc Joye[1] and Jean-Jacques Quisquater[2]

[1] Gemplus Card International, Card Security Group
Parc d'Activités de Gémenos, B.P. 100, 13881 Gémenos, France
marc.joye@gemplus.com
http://www.geocities.com/MarcJoye/
[2] UCL Crypto Group, Université catholique de Louvain
Place du Levant 3, 1348 Louvain-la-Neuve, Belgium
jjq@dice.ucl.ac.be

Abstract. Side-channel attacks are a recent class of attacks that have been revealed to be very powerful in practice. By measuring some side-channel information (running time, power consumption, . . .), an attacker is able to recover some secret data from a carelessly implemented crypto-algorithm. This paper investigates the Hessian parameterization of an elliptic curve as a step towards resistance against such attacks in the context of elliptic curve cryptography. The idea is to use the same procedure to compute the addition, the doubling or the subtraction of points. As a result, this gives a 33% performance improvement as compared to the best reported methods and requires much less memory.

Keywords. Elliptic curves, Cryptography, Side-channel attacks, Implementation, Smart-cards.

1   Introduction

Side-channel attacks are a recent class of attacks that have been revealed to be very powerful in practice. By measuring some side-channel information (running time, power consumption, . . .), an attacker is able to recover some secret data from a carelessly implemented crypto-algorithm. This paper investigates the Hessian parameterization of an elliptic curve as a step towards resistance against such attacks in the context of elliptic curve cryptography. The idea is to use the same procedure to compute the addition, the doubling or the subtraction of points. As a result, this gives a 33% performance improvement as compared to the best reported methods and requires much less memory.

The rest of this paper is organized as follows. The next section introduces the theory of elliptic curves and reviews the related work for computing the multiple of a point on an elliptic curve. Section 3 presents the Hessian parameterization of an elliptic curve. It also proves some useful results on this special parameterization. The side-channel attacks are defined in Section 4 and some

Ç.K. Koç, D. Naccache, and C. Paar (Eds.): CHES 2001, LNCS 2162, pp. 402–410, 2001.

countermeasures are discussed. Finally, Section 5 shows how the Hessian parameterization helps to efficiently foil such attacks in the context of elliptic curve cryptography.

2   Elliptic Curve Multiplication

To ease the exposition we assume throughout this paper that $\mathbb{K}$ is a field of characteristic $p > 3$.

2.1   Basic Facts

We start with a short introduction to elliptic curves.

Definition 1. *Up to a birational equivalence, an* elliptic curve *over a field $\mathbb{K}$ is a plane nonsingular cubic curve with a $\mathbb{K}$-rational point.*

Elliptic curves are often expressed in terms of Weierstraß equations:

$$E_{/\mathbb{K}} : y^2 = x^3 + ax + b \quad \text{(with } 4a^3 + 27b^2 \neq 0 \text{)} \tag{1}$$

where a and $b \in \mathbb{K}$. The condition $4a^3 + 27b^2 \neq 0$ ensures that the *discriminant*

$$\Delta = -16(4a^3 + 27b^2) \tag{2}$$

is nonzero, or equivalently that the points (x, y) on the curve are nonsingular.

More importantly, together with the *point at infinity O*, the points of an elliptic curve form an Abelian group (with identity element O) under the *chord-and-tangent rule* defined as follows. If $P = (x_1, y_1)$, then its inverse is given by $-P = (x_1, -y_1)$. The sum of two points $P = (x_1, y_1)$ and $Q = (x_2, y_2)$ (with $Q \neq -P$) is equal to $R = (x_3, y_3)$ where

$$x_3 = \lambda^2 - x_1 - x_2 \quad \text{and} \quad y_3 = \lambda(x_1 - x_3) - y_1$$

with $\lambda = \begin{cases} \dfrac{3x_1^2 + a}{2y_1} & \text{if } x_1 = x_2, \\ \dfrac{y_1 - y_2}{x_1 - x_2} & \text{otherwise} . \end{cases}$

The previous formulæ require 2 or 3 multiplications and 1 inversion to add two points. Since this latter operation is costly (an inversion roughly takes the same amount of time as 23 multiplications [8]), *projective* representations of Weierstraß equations may be preferred.

3   Hessian Curves

In this section, we formally define the Hessian elliptic curves [10] (see also [2, p. 36] and [15]) and give some results on this special parameterization.

Definition 2. *An Hessian elliptic curve over* $\mathbb{K}$ *is a plane cubic curve given by an equation of the form*

$$E_{/\mathbb{K}} : u^3 + v^3 + 1 = 3Duv , \qquad (3)$$

or in projective coordinates,

$$E_{/\mathbb{K}} : U^3 + V^3 + W^3 = 3DUVW \qquad (4)$$

where $D \in \mathbb{K}$ *and* $D^3 \neq 1$.

As shown in the next lemma, the condition $D^3 \neq 1$ imposes that the curve is nonsingular, that is, elliptic.

Lemma 1. *An Hessian cubic curve* $E_D(\mathbb{K})$ *is singular if and only if* $D^3 = 1$.

Proof. Let $\boldsymbol{P} = (U_1 : V_1 : W_1)$ be a singular point. Then $U_1^2 - DV_1W_1 = V_1^2 - DU_1W_1 = W_1^2 - DV_1W_1 = 0$, hence $U_1^3 = V_1^3 = W_1^3 \, (\neq 0)$. Therefore there exist $k \in \mathbb{K}^*$ and $r, s, t \in \mathbb{Z}_3$ such that $U_1 = k\omega^r$, $V_1 = k\omega^s$ and $W_1 = k\omega^t$ where ω is a non-trivial cubic root of unity. Together with Eq. (4), this yields $3k^3 = 3Dk^3\omega^{r+s+t}$, or equivalently, $D^3 = 1$. $\qquad\square$

Proposition 1. *The Hessian curve given by Eq. (3) is birationnally equivalent to the Weierstraß equation*

$$y^2 = x^3 - 27D(D^3 + 8)x + 54(D^6 - 20D^3 - 8) , \qquad (5)$$

under the transformations

$$(u, v) = \big(\eta(x + 9D^2), -1 + \eta(3D^3 - Dx - 12)\big) \qquad (6)$$

and

$$(x, y) = \big(-9D^2 + \xi u, 3\xi(v - 1)\big) \qquad (7)$$

where $\eta = \frac{6(D^3-1)(y+9D^3-3Dx-36)}{(x+9D^2)^3+(3D^3-Dx-12)^3}$ *and* $\xi = \frac{12(D^3-1)}{Du+v+1}$.

Proof. Sending the point $\boldsymbol{P_0} = (0, -1)$ to the origin via the map $v \mapsto v - 1$, Eq. (3) becomes

$$\sum_{i=1}^{3} c_i(u, v) = 0 \qquad (*)$$

where $c_3(u, v) = u^3 + v^3$, $c_2(u, v) = -3v(Du + v)$ and $c_1(u, v) = 3(Du + v)$. The slope λ of the tangent at $\boldsymbol{P_0}$ is equal to $-D$. Letting $d(u, v) = c_2(u, v)^2 - 4c_1(u, v)c_3(u, v)$, we have $d(u, \lambda u + 1) = 12(D^3-1)u^3 - 27D^2u^2 + 18Du - 3$. Hence, by Nagell reduction (see Theorem 7.4.9 in [5, p. 393]) and letting $B = 12(D^3-1)$, Eq. (*) is birationnally equivalent to $y^2 = x^3 - 27D^2x^2 + 18DBx - 3B^2$ under the transformations

$$(u, v) = \Big(\frac{x(By - c_2(x, \lambda x + B))}{2c_3(x, \lambda x + B)}, \frac{(\lambda x + B)(By - c_2(x, \lambda x + B))}{2c_3(x, \lambda x + B)}\Big)$$

$$= \Big(\frac{Bx(y + 3B - 3Dx)}{2(x^3 + (B - Dx)^3)}, \frac{B(B - Dx)(y + 3B - 3Dx)}{2(x^3 + (B - Dx)^3)}\Big)$$

and, noting from Eq. (*) that $2c_3(u, v) + c_2(u, v) = -2c_1(u, v) - c_2(u, v)$,

$$(x, y) = \left(\frac{Bu}{v - \lambda u}, \frac{B(2c_3(u,v) + c_2(u,v))}{(v - \lambda u)^2}\right) = \left(\frac{12(D^3 - 1)u}{Du + v}, \frac{36(D^3 - 1)(v - 2)}{Du + v}\right) .$$

Replacing now x by $x + 9D^2$, we finally obtain the required equation and the corresponding transformations.   □

A 'straight-forward' application of the chord-and-tangent rule yields rather cumbersome formulæ for the doubling and the addition on an Hessian curve. The correct way is to use the Cauchy-Desboves' s formulæ (see Appendix A), which exploit the symmetry of Eq. (4). Plugging $W = 0$ into Eq. (4), we get the point at infinity $\boldsymbol{O} = (1 : -1 : 0)$. The inverse of $\boldsymbol{O}$ is $\boldsymbol{O}$. For $\boldsymbol{P} \neq \boldsymbol{O}$ we can work in affine coordinates. Let $\boldsymbol{P} = (u_1, v_1)$ be a point on the curve. The line $v = -u + (u_1 + v_1)$ contains the point $\boldsymbol{P}$ and, considering its projective version $V = -U + (u_1 + v_1)Z$, it also contains the point at infinity $\boldsymbol{O}$. Therefore, $-\boldsymbol{P}$ is the third point of intersection of this line connecting $\boldsymbol{P}$ and $\boldsymbol{O}$ with the curve. Substituting $v = -u + (u_1 + v_1)$ into Eq. (3), we obtain

$$u^3 + (-u + (u_1 + v_1))^3 + 1 = 3Du(-u + (u_1 + v_1))$$
$$\Longleftrightarrow 3(u_1 + v_1 + D)u^2 - 3(u_1 + v_1)(u_1 + v_1 + D)u + (u_1 + v_1)^3 + 1 = 0$$
$$\Longleftrightarrow u^2 - (u_1 + v_1)u + u_1 v_1 = 0 .$$

(Note that $u_1 + v_1 + D \neq 0$ because $D^3 \neq 1$.) So, the u-coordinate of $-\boldsymbol{P}$ is v_1, and hence its v-coordinate is u_1, i.e., $-\boldsymbol{P} = (v_1, u_1)$ or, in projective coordinates,

$$-\boldsymbol{P} = (V_1 : U_1 : W_1) . \tag{8}$$

We use the same notations as in Appendix A. The tangent at $\boldsymbol{P} = (U_1 : V_1 : W_1)$ intersects the curve at the third point $-2\boldsymbol{P}$ whose coordinates are given by Eq. (15), with $F(U, V, W) = U^3 + V^3 + W^3 - 3DUVW$. We have $\varphi = 3(U_1^2 - DV_1W_1)$, $\chi = 3(V_1^2 - DU_1W_1)$ and $\psi = 3(W_1^2 - DU_1V_1)$ and so, $-2\boldsymbol{P} = ((\psi^3 - \chi^3)/U_1^2 : (-\psi^3 + \varphi^3)/V_1^2 : (\chi^3 - \varphi^3)/W_1^2)$. A short calculation gives

$$\psi^3 - \chi^3 = 27(W_1^2 - DU_1V_1)^3 - 27(V_1^2 - DU_1W_1)^3$$
$$= 27[(W_1^6 - V_1^6) + D^3U_1^3(W_1^3 - V_1^3) - 3DU_1V_1W_1(W_1^3 - V_1^3)]$$
$$= 27(W_1^3 - V_1^3)(D^3 - 1)U_1^3 ,$$

and, by symmetry, $-\psi^3 + \varphi^3 = 27(U_1^3 - W_1^3)(D^3 - 1)V_1^3$ and $\chi^3 - \varphi^3 = 27(V_1^3 - U_1^3)(D^3 - 1)W_1^3$. Hence, with Eq. (8), we finally obtain

$$2\boldsymbol{P} = (V_1(U_1^3 - W_1^3) : U_1(W_1^3 - V_1^3) : W_1(V_1^3 - U_1^3)) . \tag{9}$$

From Eq. (16) (in Appendix A), the line connecting the points $\boldsymbol{P} = (U_1 : V_1 : W_1)$ and $\boldsymbol{Q} = (U_2 : V_2 : W_2)$ intersects the curve at the third point $-(\boldsymbol{P} + \boldsymbol{Q}) = (U_1\Theta - U_2\Upsilon : V_1\Theta - V_2\Upsilon : W_1\Theta - W_2\Upsilon)$, where $\Theta = 3U_1(U_2^2 - DV_2W_2) +$

$3V_1(V_2{}^2 - DU_2W_2) + 3W_1(W_2{}^2 - DU_2V_2)$ and $\Upsilon = 3U_2(U_1{}^2 - DV_1W_1) + 3V_2(V_1{}^2 - DU_1W_1) + 3W_2(W_1{}^2 - DU_1V_1)$. We have

$$
\begin{aligned}
U_1\Theta - U_2\Upsilon &= 3V_1V_2(U_1V_2 - U_2V_1) \\
&\quad + 3W_1W_2(U_1W_2 - U_2W_1) - 3D(U_1{}^2V_2W_2 - U_2{}^2V_1W_1), \\
V_1\Theta - V_2\Upsilon &= 3U_1U_2(U_2V_1 - U_1V_2) \\
&\quad + 3W_1W_2(V_1W_2 - V_2W_1) - 3D(V_1{}^2U_2W_2 - V_2{}^2U_1W_1), \\
W_1\Theta - W_2\Upsilon &= 3U_1U_2(U_2W_1 - U_1W_2) \\
&\quad + 3V_1V_2(V_2W_1 - V_1W_2) - 3D(W_1{}^2U_2V_2 - W_2{}^2U_1V_1),
\end{aligned}
$$

and thus, exploiting the fact that P and Q belong to the curve [9, no. 12], we obtain

$$
\frac{U_1\Theta - U_2\Upsilon}{W_1\Theta - W_2\Upsilon} = \frac{U_1{}^2V_2W_2 - U_2{}^2V_1W_1}{W_1{}^2U_2V_2 - W_2{}^2U_1V_1},
$$

$$
\frac{V_1\Theta - V_2\Upsilon}{W_1\Theta - W_2\Upsilon} = \frac{V_1{}^2U_2W_2 - V_2{}^2U_1W_1}{W_1{}^2U_2V_2 - W_2{}^2U_1V_1}.
$$

Therefore, with Eq. (8), the sum $R = P + Q$ is given by

$$
R = \left(V_1{}^2U_2W_2 - V_2{}^2U_1W_1 : U_1{}^2V_2W_2 - U_2{}^2V_1W_1 : W_1{}^2U_2V_2 - W_2{}^2U_1V_1\right). \quad (10)
$$

We now study the points of order 2 and 3. We work in affine coordinates since we are looking at points $P \neq O$ such that $2P = O$ or $3P = O$. Let $P = (u_1, v_1)$. The condition $2P = O$ is equivalent to $P = -P$. Therefore, since $-P = (v_1, u_1)$, the points $P = (u_1, v_1)$ of order 2 are those for which $u_1 = v_1$.

Suppose $P = (u_1, v_1)$ with $u_1 \neq v_1$, that is, $P, 2P \neq O$. To find the points P of order 3, we use the doubling formula: $3P = O \iff 2P = -P$. So, a few algebra shows that the points of order 3 are exactly those with $u_1 = 0$ or $v_1 = 0$. In particular, the points $(0, -1)$ and $(-1, 0)$ have order 3.

Finally, it is interesting to note that a generic point $P = (U : V : W)$ on the Hessian curve (4) satisfies

$$
(D^2 + D + 1)(U + V + W)^3 = 3(DU + V + W)(U + DV + W)(U + V + DW), \quad (11)
$$

since $(D^2 + D + 1)(U + V + W)^3 - 3(DU + V + W)(U + DV + W)(U + V + DW) = (D - 1)^2(U^3 + V^3 + W^3 - 3DUVW) = 0$. Moreover, since $(DU + V + W) + (U + DV + W) + (U + V + DW) = (D + 2)(U + V + W)$, it follows that

$$
(\tilde{U} + \tilde{V} + \tilde{W})^3 = 3\tilde{D}\tilde{U}\tilde{V}\tilde{W}, \quad (12)
$$

where $\begin{cases} \tilde{U} = DU + V + W \\ \tilde{V} = U + DV + W \\ \tilde{W} = U + V + DW \end{cases}$ and $\tilde{D} = \dfrac{(D+2)^3}{D^2 + D + 1}$.

4   Side-Channel Attacks

At CRYPTO '96 and subsequently at CRYPTO '99, Kocher *et al.* introduced a new class of attacks, the so-called *side-channel attacks*. By measuring some side-channel information (e.g., timing [11], power consumption [12]), they were able to find the secret keys from tamper-resistant devices.

When only a single measurement is performed the attack is referred to as *simple side-channel attack*, and when there are several correlated measurements sometimes it is referred to as a *differential side-channel attack*. The main concern at the moment for public-key cryptography are the simple side-channel attacks [12]. Efficient countermeasures are known for exponentiation-based cryptosystems (e.g., [4]), but they require the atomic operations to be indistinguishable. For elliptic curve cryptography, the atomic operations are addition, subtraction and doubling of points. Within the Weierstraß model, as suggested in [1], these operations appear to be different and some secret information may therefore leak through side-channel analysis.

The next section shows that the Hessian parameterization allows one to implement the same algorithm for the addition (or subtraction) of two points or for the doubling of a point.

5   Implementing the Hessian Curves

Figure 1 gives a detailed implementation to add two (different) points on an Hessian curve. The algorithm requires 12 multiplications (or 10 multiplications if one point has its last coordinate equal to 1) and 7 temporary variables.

Input: $P = (U_1 : V_1 : W_1)$ and $Q = (U_2 : V_2 : W_2)$ with $P \neq Q$
Output: $P + Q = (U_3 : V_3 : W_3)$

$T_1 \leftarrow U_1;\ T_2 \leftarrow V_1;\ T_3 \leftarrow W_1\ T_4 \leftarrow U_2;\ T_5 \leftarrow V_2;\ T_6 \leftarrow W_2$
$T_7 \leftarrow T_1 \cdot T_6\ (= U_1 W_2)$
$T_1 \leftarrow T_1 \cdot T_5\ (= U_1 V_2)$
$T_5 \leftarrow T_3 \cdot T_5\ (= W_1 V_2)$
$T_3 \leftarrow T_3 \cdot T_4\ (= W_1 U_2)$
$T_4 \leftarrow T_2 \cdot T_4\ (= V_1 U_2)$
$T_2 \leftarrow T_2 \cdot T_6\ (= V_1 W_2)$
$T_6 \leftarrow T_2 \cdot T_7\ (= U_1 V_1 W_2^2)$
$T_2 \leftarrow T_2 \cdot T_4\ (= V_1^2 U_2 W_2)$
$T_4 \leftarrow T_3 \cdot T_4\ (= V_1 W_1 U_2^2)$
$T_3 \leftarrow T_3 \cdot T_5\ (= W_1^2 U_2 V_2)$
$T_5 \leftarrow T_1 \cdot T_5\ (= U_1 W_1 V_2^2)$
$T_1 \leftarrow T_1 \cdot T_7\ (= U_1^2 V_2 W_2)$
$T_1 \leftarrow T_1 - T_4;\ T_2 \leftarrow T_2 - T_5;\ T_3 \leftarrow T_3 - T_6$
$U_3 \leftarrow T_2;\ V_3 \leftarrow T_1;\ W_3 \leftarrow T_3$

Fig. 1. AddHesse(P, Q): Addition algorithm on an Hessian curve.

We note that there are variants for this implementation. For instance, we are able to describe similar implementations with only 4 auxiliary variables and 18 multiplications, 5 auxiliary variables and 16 multiplications, and 6 auxiliary variables and 14 multiplications.

More remarkably, owing to the high symmetry of the Hessian parameterization, the *same* algorithm can be used for doubling a point. We have:

Proposition 2. *Let* $\boldsymbol{P} = (U_1 : V_1 : W_1)$ *be a point on an Hessian elliptic curve* $E_D(\mathbb{K})$. *Then*

$$2(U_1 : V_1 : W_1) = (W_1 : U_1 : V_1) + (V_1 : W_1 : U_1) . \tag{13}$$

Furthermore, we have $(W_1 : U_1 : V_1) \neq (V_1 : W_1 : U_1)$.

Proof. Addition formula (10) yields $(W_1 : U_1 : V_1) + (V_1 : W_1 : U_1) = (U_1{}^2 V_1 U_1 - W_1{}^2 W_1 V_1 : W_1{}^2 W_1 U_1 - V_1{}^2 U_1 V_1 : V_1{}^2 V_1 W_1 - U_1{}^2 W_1 U_1) = (V_1(U_1{}^3 - W_1{}^3) : U_1(W_1{}^3 - V_1{}^3) : W_1(V_1{}^3 - U_1{}^3)) = 2(U_1 : V_1 : W_1)$ by Eq. (9).

The second part of the proposition follows by contradiction. Suppose that $(W_1 : U_1 : V_1) = (V_1 : W_1 : U_1)$, i.e., that there exists some $t \in \mathbb{K}^*$ s.t. $W_1 = tV_1$, $U_1 = tW_1$ and $V_1 = tU_1$. This implies $W_1 \neq 0$ and $t^3 = 1$. Moreover, since $(U_1 : V_1 : W_1) \in E_D(\mathbb{K})$, $U_1{}^3 + V_1{}^3 + W_1{}^3 = 3DU_1V_1W_1$, which in turn implies $(t^3 + t^6 + 1)W_1{}^3 = 3Dt^3W_1{}^3$ and thus $D = 1$, a contradiction by Lemma 1.   □

In [13], Liardet and Smart suggest to represent elliptic curves as the intersection of two quadrics in $\mathbb{P}^3$ as a means to protect against side-channel attacks. Considering the special case of an elliptic curve whose order is divisible by 4 (i.e., the Jacobi form), they observe that the same algorithm can be used for adding and doubling points with **16 multiplications** (see also [3] for the formulæ). Using the proposed Hessian parameterization, only **12 multiplications** are necessary for adding or doubling points. The Hessian parameterization gives thus a **33% improvement** over the Jacobi parameterization. Another advantage of the Hessian parameterization is that points are represented with fewer coordinates, which results in substantial memory savings.

Finally, contrary to other parameterizations, there is no (field) subtraction to compute the inverse of a point (see Eq. (8)). Hence, our addition algorithm can be used *as is* for subtracting two points $\boldsymbol{P} = (U_1 : V_1 : W_1)$ and $\boldsymbol{Q} = (U_2 : V_2 : W_2)$ on an Hessian elliptic curve:

$$(U_1 : V_1 : W_1) - (U_2 : V_2 : W_2) = (U_1 : V_1 : W_1) + (V_2 : U_2 : W_2) . \tag{14}$$

To sum up, by adapting the order of the inputs accordingly to Eq. (13) or (14), the addition algorithm presented in Fig. 1 can be used *indifferently* for

- adding two (different) points;
- doubling a point;
- subtracting two points;

with only 12 multiplications and 7 auxiliary variables including the 3 result variables. This results in the *fastest* known method for implementing the elliptic curve scalar multiplication towards resistance against side-channel attacks.

Acknowledgements

The first author would like to acknowledge Prof. Laih and the members of his lab for their generous hospitality while part of this work was performed. Thanks also to the anonymous referees.

References

1. IEEE Std 1363-2000, *IEEE standard specifications for public-key cryptography*, IEEE Computer Society, August 29, 2000.
2. J. W. S. Cassels, *Lectures on elliptic curves*, London Mathematical Society Student Texts, vol. 24, Cambridge University Press, 1991.
3. D. V. Chudnovsky and G. V. Chudnovsky, *Sequences of numbers generated by addition in formal groups and new primality and factorization tests*, Advances in Applied Math. **7** (1986/7), 385–434.
4. Christophe Clavier and Marc Joye, *Universal exponentiation algorithm: A first step towards provable SPA-resistance*, these proceedings.
5. Henri Cohen, *A course in computational algebraic number theory*, Graduate Texts in Mathematics, vol. 138, Springer-Verlag, 1993.
6. Henri Cohen, Atsuko Miyaji, and Takatoshi Ono, *Efficient elliptic curve exponentiation using mixed coordinates*, Advances in Cryptology – ASIACRYPT '98 (K. Ohta and D. Pei, eds.), Lecture Notes in Computer Science, vol. 1514, Springer-Verlag, 1998, pp. 51–65.
7. Jean-Sébastien Coron, *Resistance against differential power analysis for elliptic curve cryptosystems*, Cryptographic Hardware and Embedded Systems (CHES '99) (Ç.K. Koç and C. Paar, eds.), Lecture Notes in Computer Science, vol. 1717, Springer-Verlag, 1999, pp. 292–302.
8. Erik De Win, Serge Mister, Bart Preneel, and Michael Wiener, *On the performance of signature schemes based on elliptic curves*, Algorithmic Number Theory Symposium (J.-P. Buhler, ed.), Lecture Notes in Computer Science, vol. 1423, Springer-Verlag, 1998, pp. 252–266.
9. M. Desboves, *Résolution, en nombres entiers et sous sa forme la plus générale, de l'équation cubique, homogène, à trois inconnues*, Ann. de Mathémat. **45** (1886), 545–579.
10. Otto Hesse, *Über die Elimination der Variabeln aus drei algebraischen Gleichungen vom zweiten Grade mit zwei Variabeln*, Journal für die reine und angewandte Mathematik **10** (1844), 68–96.
11. Paul C. Kocher, *Timing attacks on implementations of Diffie-Hellman, RSA, DSS, and other systems*, Advances in Cryptology – CRYPTO '96 (N. Koblitz, ed.), Lecture Notes in Computer Science, vol. 1109, Springer-Verlag, 1996, pp. 104–113.
12. Paul Kocher, Joshua Jaffe, and Benjamin Jun, *Differential power analysis*, Advances in Cryptology – CRYPTO '99 (M. Wiener, ed.), Lecture Notes in Computer Science, vol. 1666, Springer-Verlag, 1999, pp. 388–397.
13. Pierre-Yvan Liardet and Nigel P. Smart, *Preventing SPA/DPA in ECC systems using the Jacobi form*, these proceedings.
14. Thomas S. Messerges, Ezzy A. Dabbish, and Robert H. Sloan, *Power analysis attacks of modular exponentiation in smartcards*, Cryptographic Hardware and Embedded Systems (CHES '99) (Ç.K. Koç and C. Paar, eds.), Lecture Notes in Computer Science, vol. 1717, Springer-Verlag, 1999, pp. 144–157.
15. Nigel P. Smart, *The Hessian form of an elliptic curve*, these proceedings.

A   Cauchy-Desboves' s Formulæ

Let $F(U, V, W) = 0$ be the (homogeneous) equation of a general cubic curve and let $\boldsymbol{P_1} = (U_1 : V_1 : W_1)$ and $\boldsymbol{P_2} = (U_2 : V_2 : W_2)$ be two points on the curve.

We let denote $\varphi = \frac{\partial F(\boldsymbol{P_1})}{\partial U}$, $\chi = \frac{\partial F(\boldsymbol{P_1})}{\partial V}$ and $\psi = \frac{\partial F(\boldsymbol{P_1})}{\partial W}$. Then the tangent at $\boldsymbol{P_1}$ intersects the curve at the third point [9, Eq. (16)] given by

$$\left(\frac{F(0, \psi, -\chi)}{U_1{}^2} : \frac{F(-\psi, 0, \varphi)}{V_1{}^2} : \frac{F(\chi, -\varphi, 0)}{W_1{}^2} \right) . \tag{15}$$

Moreover, the secant joining $\boldsymbol{P_1}$ and $\boldsymbol{P_2}$ intersects the curve at the third point [9, Eq. (16)] given by

$$(U_1 \Theta - U_2 \Upsilon : V_1 \Theta - V_2 \Upsilon : W_1 \Theta - W_2 \Upsilon) , \tag{16}$$

where $\Theta = U_1 \frac{\partial F(\boldsymbol{P_2})}{\partial U} + V_1 \frac{\partial F(\boldsymbol{P_2})}{\partial V} + W_1 \frac{\partial F(\boldsymbol{P_2})}{\partial W}$ and $\Upsilon = U_2 \frac{\partial F(\boldsymbol{P_1})}{\partial U} + V_2 \frac{\partial F(\boldsymbol{P_1})}{\partial V} + W_2 \frac{\partial F(\boldsymbol{P_1})}{\partial W}$.

B   Samples

Here are two examples of cryptographic Hessian elliptic curves $E_D(\mathbb{F}_p)$ defined over the prime field $\mathbb{F}_p$ with $p = 2^{160} - 2933$ and $p = 2^{224} - 2^{10} - 1$, respectively. Both curves are adapted from [6] using Proposition 1. Note that since $(0, -1)$ is on the curve whatever the values of D and p and that this point has order 3, the order of an Hessian curve, $\#E_D(\mathbb{F}_p)$, is always a multiple of 3. Note also that this specialized representation does not impact the security of the resulting cryptographic applications.

B.1   160-Bit Prime

$p = 2^{160} - 2933$
$D = 945639186043697550302587435415597619883075636292$
$\#E_D(\mathbb{F}_p) = 3 \cdot 5 \cdot 157 \cdot 620595175087432237029165529381611169224913337$

B.2   224-Bit Prime

$p = 2^{224} - 2^{10} - 1$
$D = 25840187014857916932759133078916563544400020237401312879815735566345$
$\#E_D(\mathbb{F}_p) = 3 \cdot 23 \cdot 390723864741313620212565436043762777771282351667\backslash$
$\qquad\qquad\qquad\qquad\qquad\qquad\qquad\qquad 3432244734573782061$

Author Index

Lecture Notes in Computer Science

For information about Vols. 1–2065
please contact your bookseller or Springer-Verlag

Vol. 2101: S. Quaglini, P. Barahona, S. Andreassen (Eds.), Artificial Intelligence in Medicine. Proceedings, 2001. XIV, 469 pages. 2001. (Subseries LNAI).

Vol. 2102: G. Berry, H. Comon, A. Finkel (Eds.), Computer-Aided Verification. Proceedings, 2001. XIII, 520 pages. 2001.

Vol. 2103: M. Hannebauer, J. Wendler, E. Pagello (Eds.), Balancing Reactivity and Social Deliberation in Multi-Agent Systems. VIII, 237 pages. 2001. (Subseries LNAI).

Vol. 2104: R. Eigenmann, M.J. Voss (Eds.), OpenMP Shared Memory Parallel Programming. Proceedings, 2001. X, 185 pages. 2001.

Vol. 2105: W. Kim, T.-W. Ling, Y-J. Lee, S.-S. Park (Eds.), The Human Society and the Internet. Proceedings, 2001. XVI, 470 pages. 2001.

Vol. 2106: M. Kerckhove (Ed.), Scale-Space and Morphology in Computer Vision. Proceedings, 2001. XI, 435 pages. 2001.

Vol. 2107: F.T. Chong, C. Kozyrakis, M. Oskin (Eds.), Intelligent Memory Systems. Proceedings, 2000. VIII, 193 pages. 2001.

Vol. 2108: J. Wang (Ed.), Computing and Combinatorics. Proceedings, 2001. XIII, 602 pages. 2001.

Vol. 2109: M. Bauer, P.J. Gymtrasiewicz, J. Vassileva (Eds.), User Modelind 2001. Proceedings, 2001. XIII, 318 pages. 2001. (Subseries LNAI).

Vol. 2110: B. Hertzberger, A. Hoekstra, R. Williams (Eds.), High-Performance Computing and Networking. Proceedings, 2001. XVII, 733 pages. 2001.

Vol. 2111: D. Helmbold, B. Williamson (Eds.), Computational Learning Theory. Proceedings, 2001. IX, 631 pages. 2001. (Subseries LNAI).

Vol. 2116: V. Akman, P. Bouquet, R. Thomason, R.A. Young (Eds.), Modeling and Using Context. Proceedings, 2001. XII, 472 pages. 2001. (Subseries LNAI).

Vol. 2117: M. Beynon, C.L. Nehaniv, K. Dautenhahn (Eds.), Cognitive Technology: Instruments of Mind. Proceedings, 2001. XV, 522 pages. 2001. (Subseries LNAI).

Vol. 2118: X.S. Wang, G. Yu, H. Lu (Eds.), Advances in Web-Age Information Management. Proceedings, 2001. XV, 418 pages. 2001.

Vol. 2119: V. Varadharajan, Y. Mu (Eds.), Information Security and Privacy. Proceedings, 2001. XI, 522 pages. 2001.

Vol. 2120: H.S. Delugach, G. Stumme (Eds.), Conceptual Structures: Broadening the Base. Proceedings, 2001. X, 377 pages. 2001. (Subseries LNAI).

Vol. 2121: C.S. Jensen, M. Schneider, B. Seeger, V.J. Tsotras (Eds.), Advances in Spatial and Temporal Databases. Proceedings, 2001. XI, 543 pages. 2001.

Vol. 2123: P. Perner (Ed.), Machine Learning and Data Mining in Pattern Recognition. Proceedings, 2001. XI, 363 pages. 2001. (Subseries LNAI).

Vol. 2124: W. Skarbek (Ed.), Computer Analysis of Images and Patterns. Proceedings, 2001. XV, 743 pages. 2001.

Vol. 2125: F. Dehne, J.-R. Sack, R. Tamassia (Eds.), Algorithms and Data Structures. Proceedings, 2001. XII, 484 pages. 2001.

Vol. 2126: P. Cousot (Ed.), Static Analysis. Proceedings, 2001. XI, 439 pages. 2001.

Vol. 2129: M. Goemans, K. Jansen, J.D.P. Rolim, L. Trevisan (Eds.), Approximation, Randomization, and Combinatorial Optimization. Proceedings, 2001. IX, 297 pages. 2001.

Vol. 2130: G. Dorffner, H. Bischof, K. Hornik (Eds.), Artificial Neural Networks – ICANN 2001. Proceedings, 2001. XXII, 1259 pages. 2001.

Vol. 2132: S.-T. Yuan, M. Yokoo (Eds.), Intelligent Agents. Specification. Modeling. and Application. Proceedings, 2001. X, 237 pages. 2001. (Subseries LNAI).

Vol. 2136: J. Sgall, A. Pultr, P. Kolman (Eds.), Mathematical Foundations of Computer Science 2001. Proceedings, 2001. XII, 716 pages. 2001.

Vol. 2138: R. Freivalds (Ed.), Fundamentals of Computation Theory. Proceedings, 2001. XIII, 542 pages. 2001.

Vol. 2139: J. Kilian (Ed.), Advances in Cryptology – CRYPTO 2001. Proceedings, 2001. XI, 599 pages. 2001.

Vol. 2141: G.S. Brodal, D. Frigioni, A. Marchetti-Spaccamela (Eds.), Algorithm Engineering. Proceedings, 2001. X, 199 pages. 2001.

Vol. 2142: L. Fribourg (Ed.), Computer Science Logic. Proceedings, 2001. XII, 615 pages. 2001.

Vol. 2143: S. Benferhat, P. Besnard (Eds.), Symbolic and Quantitative Approaches to Reasoning with Uncertainty. Proceedings, 2001. XIV, 818 pages. 2001. (Subseries LNAI).

Vol. 2146: J.H. Silverman (Eds.), Cryptography and Lattices. Proceedings, 2001. VII, 219 pages. 2001.

Vol. 2147: G. Brebner, R. Woods (Eds.), Field-Programmable Logic and Applications. Proceedings, 2001. XV, 665 pages. 2001.

Vol. 2149: O. Gascuel, B.M.E. Moret (Eds.), Algorithms in Bioinformatics. Proceedings, 2001. X, 307 pages. 2001.

Vol. 2150: R. Sakellariou, J. Keane, J. Gurd, L. Freeman (Eds.), Euro-Par 2001 Parallel Processing. Proceedings, 2001. XXX, 943 pages. 2001.

Vol. 2152: R.J. Boulton, P.B. Jackson (Eds.), Theorem Proving in Higher Order Logics. Proceedings, 2001. X, 395 pages. 2001.

Vol. 2154: K.G. Larsen, M. Nielsen (Eds.), CONCUR 2001 – Concurrency Theory. Proceedings, 2001. XI, 583 pages. 2001.

Vol. 2157: C. Rouveirol, M. Sebag (Eds.), Inductive Logic Programming. Proceedings, 2001. X, 261 pages. 2001. (Subseries LNAI).

Vol. 2161: F. Meyer auf der Heide (Ed.), Algorithms – ESA 2001. Proceedings, 2001. XII, 538 pages. 2001.

Vol. 2162: Ç. K. Koç, D. Naccache, C. Paar (Eds.), Cryptographic Hardware and Embedded Systems – CHES 2001. Proceedings, 2001. XIV, 411 pages. 2001.

Vol. 2164: S. Pierre, R. Glitho (Eds.), Mobile Agents for Telecommunication Applications. Proceedings, 2001. XI, 292 pages. 2001.

Vol. 2166: V. Matoušek, P. Mautner, R. Mouček, K. Taušer (Eds.), Text, Speech and Dialogue. Proceedings, 2001. XIII, 452 pages. 2001. (Subseries LNAI).